PRAGUE, VIENNA & BUDAPEST

JENNIFER D. WALKER & AUBURN SCALLON

GERMANY

Děčín

Liberec

13

Teplice

Ústí nad
Labem

Česká
Lípa

Turnov

Most

Litoměřice

Český
ráj

Náchod

37

D7

Mladá
Boleslav

Hradec
Králové

16

D10

11

Karlovy
Vary

Kladno

Elbe River

Pardubice

Sokolov

VÁCLAV HAVEL
AIRPORT PRAGUE

D11

Kolín

PRAGUE

Kutná
Hora

Chrudim

Šumperk

21

D5

Plzeň

D5

Příbram

18

CZECH

REPUBLIC

14

D35

Olomouc

Prostějov

Havlíčkův
Brod

Žďár
nad Sázavou

19

Klatovy

20

Vltava River

19

Písek

Tábor

Jihlava

Třebíč

Brno

D1

Strakonice

D3

23

Jindřichův
Hradec

38

D52

D2

Hodonín

4

České
Budějovice

Znojmo

Mikulov

39

Český
Krumlov

Břeclav

A5

GERMANY

D2

Krems an
der Donau

Linz

A3

Mauthausen

Dürnstein

S5

Melk

VIENNA

VIENNA
INTERNATIONAL
AIRPORT

Wels

B1

St. Pölten

Danube River

Mödling

BRATISLAVA

Steyr

A21

A3

M1

Baden

Wiener
Neustadt

Sopron

A8

Salzburg

S4

Hallein

56

S31

84

B320

AUSTRIA

B7

The Austrian Alps

S536

A9

535

Szombathely

A10

Graz

86

Wolfsberg

Zalaegerszeg

© MOON.COM

Villach

Klagenfurt

Contents

Although every effort was made to make sure the information in this book was accurate when going to press, research was impacted by the COVID-19 pandemic and things may have changed since the time of writing. Be sure to confirm specific details, like opening hours, closures, and travel guidelines and restrictions, when making your travel plans. For more detailed information, see page 496.

DISCOVER

Prague, Vienna
& Budapest

Prague, Vienna, and Budapest offer travelers a rich tapestry of history and culture.

Before World War I, all three cities resided within the Austro-Hungarian Empire, and traces of the crumbled Habsburg dynasty still linger in the decadent palaces and wide boulevards lined with extravagant buildings. Central Europe echoes the "World of Yesterday," with its gilded opera houses, grand hotels, and the wood-paneled cafés perfumed with percolating coffee and freshly baked cakes. Against this historic backdrop, modern (futuristic, even) innovations, from cryptocurrency-friendly cafés to eye-catching public art installations, are a delightful contrast.

Life is slow, even reflective, and flows with the seasons. Locals flock to the beer gardens perched up in Letná Park in Prague to escape the summer heat. When the leaves rust as fall arrives, the Viennese drink "this year's wine" in the Heurige near the city's vineyards overlooking the Vienna Woods. And when the temperature drops in December, the scent of spiced hot wine winds around the cities' Christmas markets. Music, art, and literature lovers can follow in the footsteps of giants, whether it's visiting Dvořák's grave in Prague, Freud's favorite café in Vienna, or Liszt's apartment in Budapest.

Clockwise from top left: Gellért Baths in Budapest; a narrow alley in old town Vienna; Sachertorte in Café Sacher in Vienna; Český Krumlov; Riesenrad in the Prater, Vienna; Prague's Old Town Square.

10 TOP EXPERIENCES

1 Admiring **spectacular architecture,** from Prague's dramatic Gothic monuments to colorful art nouveau in Budapest to Habsburg grandeur in Vienna (page 29).

∨ ∨ ∨
∨ ∨

2 Soaking in Budapest's **thermal baths** (page 380).

3 Sipping foam-topped pivo (beer) in **Prague's beer gardens** (page 99).

4 Listening to **classical music in Vienna,** the city where Mozart, Beethoven, Strauss, and Schubert composed and conducted (page 261).

5 Following in the Habsburgs' footsteps at **Schönbrunn,** their summer palace in Vienna (page 239).

>>>

6 Boating or cycling through the **Wachau Valley,** where crumbling castles, vineyards, and rolling hills line the banks of the Danube (page 310).

>>>

7 Getting to know **Prague's outer neighborhoods,** where you can still get a taste of the untouched-by-tourists vibe the city was once known for (page 85).

8 Exploring the vast complex of Prague's **Vyšehrad,** which is no less impressive (and much less crowded) than the Prague Castle (page 83).

<<<

9 Sipping a Melange in a cozy booth within a classic **Viennese coffeehouse** (page 270).

>>>

10 Browsing the stalls and enjoying a warm drink al fresco at a **Christmas market** in the Czech Republic. For a local atmosphere and fewer crowds, head to a market outside Prague (page 180).

<<<

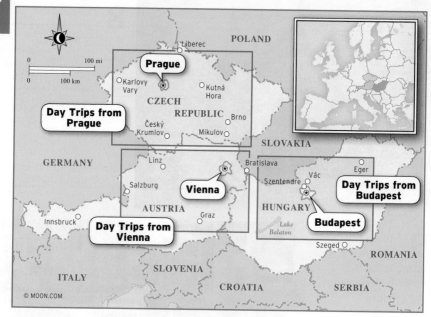

Planning Your Trip

Where to Go

Prague

Since regaining independence in the Velvet Revolution of 1989, Prague's **architectural beauty, fairy-tale atmosphere,** and **delicious beverages** have secured the Central European capital a prominent place on travelers' lists. Postcard-worthy sights like the **Charles Bridge, St. Vitus Cathedral** at the **Prague Castle,** or the church spires and **Astronomical Clock** of **Old Town Square** draw significant crowds to admire (and photograph) their beauty. Prague's **surrounding neighborhoods** still hold plenty of **undiscovered character** to contrast the typical tourist experience of the historical city center. Head to hilltop **Vyšehrad Complex** for peaceful sightseeing, enjoy a night of culture inside the old-world glamour of

Prague's **theaters and concert halls,** and pair any activity, any time of day, with a nice cold pivo (beer).

Day Trips from Prague

For a quick trip, head north to **Liberec** to visit the mountaintop Ještěd Tower and embrace the summertime vibe at the reservoir, or reconnect with nature on a hike through the forests and sandstone rocks of **Bohemian Paradise.** The eastern town of **Kutná Hora** holds an impressive collection of churches (including one decorated in bones) and contemporary art. Free-flowing fountains of mineral springs draw a quieter crowd to the western spa town of **Karlovy Vary.** Combine a river rafting adventure with a visit to the picturesque castle of South Bohemia's beloved

Stephansplatz in Vienna

Český Krumlov. Venture farther east into South Moravia to discover the diverse architecture and lively nightlife scene in **Brno** or pair local wines with stately chateaux in **Mikulov, Lendnice, and Valtice.**

Vienna

Once the heart of the Austro-Hungarian Empire, Vienna still bears the grandeur of the Habsburgs with its **grand palaces,** the **Spanish Riding School,** and extravagant parkland. Trace the footsteps of **Gustav Klimt,** then while away the hours in Vienna's **world-class art museums** and galleries. Music aficionados should make pilgrimages to **Mozart, Beethoven,** and **Strauss's** former homes before taking in an **opera** at the world famous **Staatsoper.** Visit Freud's former home, ride a **100-year-old Ferris wheel** in the Prater, and round up the day people-watching in one of Vienna's **classic cafés.**

Day Trips from Vienna

Nestled in the Alps, **Salzburg**—home to both Mozart and *The Sound of Music*—is just two hours from Vienna. Closer to the capital, you can **sail up the Danube** as it winds through the **Wachau Valley** where castles and monasteries dot the landscape, or hop on a train to **Bratislava, Slovakia,** to add another country to your itinerary. **Mauthausen Concentration Camp** is a poignant reminder of the horrors of the Holocaust. Right outside Vienna are the **Vienna Woods,** where you can visit the fairy-tale Liechtenstein Castle just outside Mödling, or relax in the spa town of Baden bei Wien.

Budapest

A tale of two cities, Budapest is divided by the **Danube River** with spectacular vistas wherever you look. See sights like **Buda Castle** on Castle Hill, then spend some time soaking in one of the many **thermal baths.** By night crowds flock to the famous **ruin pubs** in the Jewish Quarter. Ride back into history on the **Children's Railway,** the retro train operated by children, as it chugs up into the Buda Hills, or head over to **Memento Park,** where communist statues go to die. Once

If You Want...

- **Art museums:** You could spend weeks exploring Vienna's iconic art museums. Try Prague's Holešovice neighborhood or Kutná Hora's GASK Gallery for the Czech contemporary art scene.

- **Grand palaces:** Vienna's Hofburg and Schönbrunn Palace; Lednice and Valtice chateaux.

- **Classical music:** Concerts and opera in elegant settings in Vienna and Prague.

- **Hiking:** Vienna Woods (very accessible from the city); Bohemian Paradise outside Prague.

- **Other outdoor activities:** Caving in Budapest; boating or cycling down the Danube in the Wachau Valley; cycling from Budapest to Szentendre or along the Danube Bend; rafting the Vltava River outside Český Krumlov.

- **Beer:** Prague's beer gardens and craft beer pubs.

- **Wine:** Vienna's Heurige; Eger and the Valley of the Beautiful Woman; Lake Balaton; Prague's Karlín neighborhood; the National Wine Cellar at the Valtice Chateau.

- **Jewish history:** Prague's medieval Jewish Quarter; Mikulov's Jewish Cemetery; Budapest's Dohány Street Synagogue; Vienna's Jewish museums.

- **Communist history:** Budapest's Memento Park; Prague's John Lennon Wall and spy tower in the St. Nicholas Bell Tower.

cycle path near the Danube River in Wachau Valley

- **Street food:** Try lángos (deep fried savory dough topped with cheese and sour cream) in Budapest or sausages from the Würstelstand in Vienna.

- **Markets:** Vienna's Naschmarkt; Budapest's Central Market Hall; Prague's Manifesto Smíchov.

- **Cheap thrills:** Prague and Budapest are affordable cities; Vienna not so much.

you've seen the sites and eaten your fill of goulash, delve deeper by visiting one of the city's hundreds of **caves** or ride a boat up the Danube to one of the **Danube beaches.**

Day Trips from Budapest

It's easy to escape Budapest for the day. Take the train down to **Lake Balaton,** Central Europe's largest lake, where you can explore the magical peninsula of Tihany, stroll the promenade in Balatonfüred, or sunbathe and party down in Siófok. Alternatively, you can **sail down the Danube Bend,** hike up to the citadel at Visegrád for stunning views over the Danube, or explore the former Serbian community-turned-artists-colony in picturesque **Szentendre.** Get on the bus for a couple of hours to the city of **Eger** in north eastern Hungary, famous for resisting an Ottoman siege at its historic castle and also famous for its **spicy red wines** served down in the evocatively named **Valley of the Beautiful Woman.**

When to Go

There is no right or wrong time to embark on a journey through Central Europe. Prague, Vienna, and Budapest are beautiful year-round, with plenty to offer throughout the seasons.

High Season (Jun-Aug and Dec)

Summers can be scorching (sometimes rising above 40°C/104°F) and often come punctuated with flash storms. But this is when you can sail along the Vltava River, sunbathe on a beach beside the Danube, or grab a picnic in a leafy park. Skip July and August if you want to avoid the crowds, especially in Prague or Budapest, when the Sziget Festival is usually in full swing in the latter.

December, when the Christmas markets set up shop, is also a busy time in each city.

Shoulder Season (Apr-May and Sep-Nov)

If you're outdoorsy, spring and fall may be your best bet. You get to escape intense temperatures of the summer months and the dreary cold weather of the winter. In the spring, cherry and apricot blossoms burst into bloom, and in the fall, the trees paint the landscape with a palette of rusty colors. Culinary and wine festivals take over the public spaces of the towns and cities—like the wine festival in Buda Castle—so if you're a foodie it's a good time to visit, with fewer crowds than you'll experience in summer or December.

Low Season (Jan-Mar)

Winters can dip down to subzero temperatures (as low as -15°C/5°F), yet Central Europe is at its most beautiful in the snow. When the temperatures plunge, you can escape the chill in a museum or a cozy café with its own curious cast of local characters. Going during the off-season can be easier on the wallet, as hotels often have rooms available at lower prices, but many outdoor attractions close down or operate with limited opening hours.

winter in Prague

Day Trips at a Glance

If You Like...	Destination	Access Points
	Czech Republic	
Bone churches	Marvel at a famous ossuary adorned with more than 40,000 human skeletons in **Kutná Hora** (page 147).	Prague (1 hour by train)
Local life	Survey **Liberec** and the countryside from a mountaintop tower, and then join the locals at a reservoir (page 154).	Prague (1 hour by bus)
Hiking	Trek past castle ruins and sandstone formations in **Bohemian Paradise** (page 157).	Prague (2 hours by train)
Spas and thermal springs	Fill your cup at the free-flowing thermal springs, and then make a spa appointment to be pampered, Czech-style, in **Karlovy Vary** (page 162).	Prague (2 hours by bus)
Castles	Explore the medieval town and 13th-century castle in **Český Krumlov** (page 167).	Prague (3 hours by train or bus)
Cities	Admire a bone church, and then relax at a lively pub or craft cocktail bar in **Brno,** the Czech Republic's second-largest city (page 175).	Prague (2.5 hours by train); Vienna (1.5 hours)
Wine and chateaux	Explore a chateau that once housed the aristocracy of the Austro-Hungarian Empire, and then taste wine from the surrounding vineyards in the **Lednice and Valtice** area (page 183).	Prague (4 hours by train); Vienna (3 hours by train)
	Austria	
Hiking	Visit a historic castle and hike amid oak and beech forests in the **Vienna Woods** (page 299).	Vienna (20 minutes by train)

If You Like...	Destination	Access Points
Boat rides	Vineyards and castles—best viewed by boat—line the Danube banks in the **Wachau Valley** (page 310).	Vienna (1.5 hours by boat; 1 hour by train)
World War II history	The former concentration camp of **Mauthausen** is moving and poignant (page 318).	Vienna (1 hour by train, followed by 40 minutes on a bus)
Sound of Music **lore**	Mozart's hometown of **Salzburg** spreads out below the snowcapped Alps and was the setting for a famous musical (page 320).	Vienna (2.5 hours by train)
Slovakia		
Cities	**Bratislava,** Slovakia's capital, has a characteristic old town and vibrant cafés (page 325).	Vienna (1 hour by train); Budapest (2.5 hours by train)
Hungary		
Local artwork	Explore Hungarian village life and then shop for handicrafts in **Szentendre** (page 436).	Budapest (40 minutes by train; 1.5 hours by boat)
Scenery	Visit historic small towns, a medieval citadel, and a looming basilica with international views on the **Danube Bend** (page 443).	Budapest (25 minutes-1 hour by train; 1.5 hours by bus; 40 minutes-1.5 hours by boat)
Beaches	Join the locals at golden lakeside beaches and energetic pubs in Siófok, **Lake Balaton** (page 452).	Budapest (1.5 hours by train)
Wine tasting	Explore a fortress-like castle in **Eger,** and then duck into wine cellars housed in natural caves in the Valley of the Beautiful Woman (page 466).	Budapest (2 hours by train or bus)

Before You Go

Passports and Visas

Travelers from the **United States, Canada, Australia,** or **New Zealand** do not need a visa to enter the EU for visits lasting under 90 days. To enter Europe, all you need is a passport that's valid at least three months after your departure from the EU. (A visa is required for travelers from **South Africa**.) UK travelers should check for new regulations post-Brexit. At the time of writing, citizens from the UK were able to enter visa-free for a period lasting under 90 days. However, at the time of writing, there are proposed changes coming in 2022 that will affect **non-EU travelers.** Non-EU travelers who used to enter the Schengen Area freely on visa-waiver agreements, including US and UK travelers, will eventually be required to apply for **ETIAS authorization** (www.etiasvisa.com) before traveling.

Once you arrive in Central Europe, you can usually cross the borders without having your passport or ID checked. However, in some instances, like the Budapest to Vienna train, you may need to show your passport to the border control.

Advance Reservations

In general, it's a good idea to purchase tickets for museums in advance, as you can save a lot of time skipping the lines when you arrive. Usually, you can do this before you set out in the morning—just ask your hotel to print out the ticket before you go.

However, there are some reservations that are worth making before you even get on the plane:

PRAGUE

Special events in the Czech Republic, such as the **Prague Spring** classical music festival (www.festival.cz) or **Karlovy Vary International Film Festival** (www.kviff.com) can sell out months in advance. Most sights and experiences do not require reservations, but it can help to book English-language tours for the **Prague Castle, Český Krumlov's Baroque Theater,** or **Valtice Chateau** in advance.

VIENNA

It's a good idea to book tours for the **Third Man Tour of the Vienna Sewers,** which run one English language tour a day, or the **Spanish Riding School** in advance.

BUDAPEST

Book your ticket for the **Hungarian Parliament** before going. Spots are limited and fill up quickly in high season.

Transportation

GETTING TO CENTRAL EUROPE

You can get to Central Europe by flying into Prague, Vienna, or Budapest directly, although there are more frequent international flights to nearby destinations like Frankfurt, Munich, or

What's New

- In Prague, the **riverside boardwalks** (called "náplavka") along Smíchov and New Town underwent a huge makeover in 2020. Underground vaults built into the retaining walls became cafés and gallery spaces with giant, swiveling, glass lenses as entrances.

- The **Marian Column** is a new—and controversial—add to Prague's Old Town Square.

- In Vienna, the **Sigmund Freud Museum** reopened in fall 2020 after an extensive renovation that opened even more of the psychoanalyst's former home to the public.

- Regiojet (www.regiojet.com) has introduced a **direct train route** between Prague, Vienna, and Budapest, making it easier than ever to zip between the three cities.

Berlin. **Vienna International Airport** (VIE; Wien-Flughafen, Schwechat; tel. 01/7007-22233; www.viennaairport.com) has the most long-haul connections out of the three cities, including many cities in the US and Canada. **Václav Havel Airport Prague** (PRG; Aviatická; tel. 02/20-111-888; www.prg.aero) has a few seasonal connections to the US and Canada. **Budapest Ferenc Liszt International Airport** (BUD; Budapest; tel. 01/296-9696; www.bud.hu) has a couple of transcontinental flights to Toronto, New York, Chicago, and Philadelphia (temporarily suspended at the time of writing due to COVID). If you're coming from Australia, New Zealand, or South Africa, you will have to change at a larger airport like Dubai or Istanbul before flying on to Central Europe. You can also get direct flights to the main airports in all three cities from London—and you also have the option of flying into Bratislava as well.

TRAVELING BETWEEN PRAGUE, VIENNA, AND BUDAPEST

Once you reach Central Europe, traveling between the three cities is pretty straightforward. Europe has excellent rail connections, and you can go between Prague, Vienna, and Budapest directly with RegioJet's **Prague-Vienna-Budapest line** (www.regiojet.com), which was launched in 2020 and connects the three cities directly by rail. This service runs twice a day and takes 2 hours 40 minutes to go from Budapest to Vienna, and 4 hours 30 minutes from Vienna to Prague.

Since Budapest and Vienna, and Vienna and Prague are fairly close to each other, it's not worth flying between the cities, which is expensive and may take just as much time as the train if you factor in check-in and security checks. This is especially true with the new direct route between Prague-Vienna-Budapest with RegioJet (www.regiojet.com). If you really have to take a plane, **Austrian Airlines** (www.austrian.com) does connect Vienna with both cities. **Czech Airlines** (www.csa.cz) runs regular flights between Budapest and Prague.

Dohány Street Synagogue in Budapest

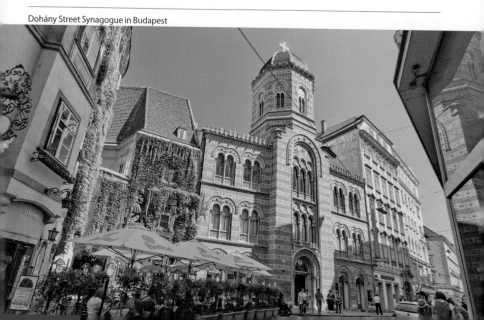

The Best of Prague, Vienna & Budapest

These three cities—and the appealing day trips beyond them—each offer a unique slice of Central Europe.

Some international travelers will need to go back to Prague at the end of their trip for their flight home. However, if you can book two one-way tickets, it would make more sense to fly back home from Budapest.

Prague

DAY 1: PRAGUE

Spend the day in the historical city center, with art nouveau paintings in the morning at the **Alfons Mucha Museum** and views over Old Town and New Town from Prague's **town hall towers.** Round out the day with a walk along the **Náplavka Boardwalk** and a drink at the **Letná Beer Garden.**

DAY 2: PRAGUE

Get an early start at the **Prague Castle** complex to avoid the crowds. Then wander through peaceful **Petřín Park** and check out the views from the **St. Nicholas Bell Tower.** Give your feet a break and treat your stomach to a decadent dinner of **Czech cuisine** before crossing the **Charles Bridge** under the stars.

DAY 3: DAY TRIP TO LIBEREC

After a one-hour bus from the Černy Most station to Liberec, hop on Tram 3 at **Fugnerova** to Horní Hanychov and follow signs to catch a cable car to **Ještěd Hotel and TV Tower.** Have lunch at the retro-futuristic restaurant and take in the mountaintop view.

Cable car down again and jump on Tram 3 to **Mikyna** for quality coffee. Then, head southeast to the **Liberec Reservoir** where you can

Take a walk along the Náplavka riverbank.

What to Eat in Prague, Vienna, and Budapest

Your tastebuds are on vacation, too, and you'd be remiss if you didn't treat them to the unique flavors of these three cities. Don't miss:

- **Svíčková:** Thinly sliced sirloin beef in vegetable cream sauce with cranberries, cream, and bread dumplings. A Czech specialty that's beloved by children and adults alike.

- **Schnitzel:** A thin slice of pork or veal coated with breadcrumbs and fried, and usually drizzled with lemon. Austria's specialty.

- **Gulyásleves (Hungarian goulash):** Rich beef soup accented with paprika. Hungary's signature.

- **Sachertorte:** Chocolate sponge cake layered with apricot jam and covered in chocolate icing. Vienna's iconic dessert.

For complete lists of local specialties in Prague, Vienna, and Budapest, see pages 120, 275, and 410.

traditional Hungarian goulash

sip Svijany beer on the lawn or circle the two-kilometer (about one-mile) path around this semi-secluded body of water.

Around 5pm, walk about 15 minutes to the center to admire the exterior of the **Liberec Town Hall** and David Černý's sculptural bus stop. **Radniční Sklípek** serves traditional Czech meals underneath the town hall. Catch the last bus back to Prague at 8pm.

DAY 4: PRAGUE LIKE A LOCAL

For a taste of life outside the city center, start with the **Vyšehrad Complex** for skyline views, a Gothic church, and an ornate cemetery. Stop for a drink and a snack at the **Hospůdka Na Hradbách** beer garden before digging into local history at the **National Monument to the Heroes of the Heydrich Terror.** Hop on the metro to the Karlín neighborhood for dinner and drinks at a local **wine bar.**

DAY 5: PRAGUE TO VIENNA

Spend a last morning soaking up the atmosphere in Prague before boarding a 4-hour train to Vienna and settling into your hotel.

Vienna

DAY 6: VIENNA

Explore the **Hofburg** and **St. Stephen's Cathedral,** taking time for a quick **schnitzel** before seeing Klimt's iconic *The Kiss* at the Belvedere Palace. End your day with sunset views from the **Riesenrad,** the historic Ferris wheel in the Prater.

DAY 7: VIENNA

View avant-garde art at the **Secession,** followed by a bite and browsing at the stalls of the **Naschmarkt.** After lunch, explore the former Habsburg residence of **Schönbrunn Palace.**

DAY 8: VIENNA LIKE A LOCAL

See some of architect **Friedensreich Hundertwasser**'s most spectacular buildings, along with the stunning art nouveau **St. Leopold Church** by Otto Wagner. Grab a Käsekrainer, a sausage filled with cheese, at one of Vienna's iconic sausage stands, drink coffee with the locals, and finish out your day with nightlife at a local hidden bar, like **Tür 7**.

DAY 9: DAY TRIP TO THE WACHAU VALLEY

Hop on a train heading to **Melk** from the Westbahnhof. After an hour's journey, you will already see the striking orange **Melk Abbey** on the hill in front of you as you exit the station. Follow the signs up the hill to the abbey and spend a couple of hours exploring, then head down to town for lunch.

Take the Wachau Cruise ferry departing at 1:45pm from Melk down the Danube through the Wachau Valley. Get off at Dürnstein and hike up to the famous ruins of **Dürnstein Castle** and then take the bus on to **Krems an der Donau.**

Get the train back to Vienna to Wien Franz-Josefs-Bahnhof (1 hour).

Back in Vienna, cross the Danube Canal over to the **Augarten** for some late afternoon sun.

DAY 10: VIENNA TO BUDAPEST

Have one last Melange in one of Vienna's famous cafés before heading to Wien Hauptbahnhof to take the **train to Budapest Keleti.** The journey will take just under three hours and will bring you right into the heart of Budapest. Take the metro to the city center—line 2 will take you to downtown Pest and over to Buda just north of Castle Hill, whereas line 4 will take you to the southern part of Buda around the trendy Bartók Béla Avenue. If you arrive in Budapest Déli you can take metro line 2, or if you arrive in Budapest Kelenföld, you can take metro 4. Get settled in and take a **walk along the Danube** before grabbing dinner downtown.

Budapest
DAY 11: BUDAPEST
Spend your first day in Budapest exploring

Ještěd Tower in Liberec

Melk Abbey in Wachau Valley

Wine Tasting in Central Europe

Wine tasting in Central Europe can be about the experience and atmosphere as much as the wine itself. Sip and savor outdoors in the fresh air in Vienna and Hungary's Valley of the Beautiful Woman, or head to a grand chateau in the Czech Republic to sample the best wine the country has to offer.

VIENNA'S HEURIGE (WINE TAVERNS)

Vienna is one of the only European capitals with its own significant wine region, and the best place to sample the local wine is at a famous Heuriger (wine tavern; page 256). Most of Vienna's Heurige back onto the vineyards in the Vienna Woods outside the city center, and also serve hearty Austrian food. They're popular in summer but really come to life in the fall. If you can't make it to a Heuriger, visit a **Stadtheuriger,** which is the in-city version.

Mayer am Nussberg winery by Vienna

HUNGARY'S VALLEY OF THE BEAUTIFUL WOMAN

Take a day trip from Budapest to this crescent-shaped valley, where cellars carved into hillsides serve the red cuvee known as Bull's Blood. Some cellars have terraces so you can sip out in the sunshine (page 470).

THE CZECH REPUBLIC'S NATIONAL WINE CENTER

Tour the grand Valtice Chateau, then head down to the basement to taste wine. Only the 100 best Czech wines, selected by experts each year, are served here (page 189).

---

the Castle District. Take in the views from **Fisherman's Bastion,** making time for quirky Hospital in the Rock in the afternoon, followed by a sweet at Budapest's oldest cukrászda (confectionary). Visit the **Hungarian National Gallery** in the late afternoon.

DAY 12: BUDAPEST

Take in the views from the top of **St. Stephen's Basilica,** explore the **Postal Savings Bank** and **Hungarian Parliament,** then kick back on

a **Danube cruise.** Spend the end of your day in some of Budapest's most famous bars.

DAY 13: BUDAPEST LIKE A LOCAL

Head out of the city center and into the Buda Hills, taking a ride on the **Children's Railway,** a small railway run by children as a relic left over from Communist times. Take in the views from the **Elizabeth Lookout Tower,** then spend the day soaking and swimming in **Lukács Thermal Bath,** the local favorite of all of Budapest's baths.

pathway to Lake Balaton in Balatonfüred

DAY 14: DAY TRIP TO LAKE BALATON
Grab the train from Budapest Déli Pályaudvar train station to **Balatonfüred** (2 hours). Once you reach Balatonfüred, hop on a bus to **Tihany** (you will find the buses go from the train station), which will take another 30 minutes. The bus will put you down in the center of the town, so head up to the **Benedictine Abbey of Tihany** for amazing views over the lake. Stop in at **Rege Cukrászda** for a coffee and a cake—try the lavender-infused custard cream cake—or grab some lunch in the village. Make sure you pick up some lavender-based gifts before heading back to Balatonfüred. Back in Balatonfüred, drink from the **Kossuth Lajos spring** before strolling down the **Tagore Promenade** along the lake side. Grab something to eat at one of the restaurants before taking the train back to Budapest.

DAY 15: GOODBYE, CENTRAL EUROPE
If your flight home leaves from Prague, you can take the train from Budapest Nyugati Pályaudvar or Déli (or the night train from Budapest Keleti Pályaudvar) back to the Czech capital and head on to the airport from there. Otherwise, head to the Budapest airport for your flight home.

Spectacular Architecture

The Golden Triangle of Central Europe is famed for its stunning architecture. Head to Prague for dramatic Gothic architecture, art nouveau, and cubism; Budapest for Baroque grandeur, intricate art nouveau, or social realism; and Vienna for Habsburg grandeur and Otto Wagner's stunning art nouveau buildings. You could lose yourself in the details of each building as you wander through the streets of these cities, and remember: Always look up!

Prague

World War II did comparably little damage to the Czech capital compared to its Central European neighbors. This has left centuries of diverse architectural styles, from dark Gothic structures to ornate exteriors and modern masterpieces, standing shoulder to shoulder along Prague's cobblestoned streets.

- **Náměstí Republiky:** Simply turn your head while standing on the corner of Na Příkopě street in New Town to survey the architectural mix of the Powder Tower (Gothic), Municipal House (art nouveau), Hybernia Theater (Empire-style), and Czech National Bank (International).

- **Basilica of Sts. Peter and Paul:** The dark, neo-Gothic silhouette of this Vyšehrad cathedral houses gorgeous art nouveau décor inside its doors.

- **Dancing House:** This 1990s collaboration between Canadian-American Frank Gehry and Croatian-Czech Vlado Milunić was inspired by and named after Fred Astaire and Ginger Rogers. The intertwined glass and stone towers beside the Vltava River symbolize Prague's delicate balance between its proud historical past and developing modern identity.

- **Žižkov TV Tower:** Love it or hate it, Prague's tallest building gets people talking. Built in the

Prague's Astronomical Clock ("Orloj" in Czech)

Dancing House in Prague (known as Tančící dům)

late 1980s, the gray, rocket-like tower dominates the skyline outside of the Old Town.

- **Cubist architecture:** Cubism as an architectural trend never really took off, but it did make its mark in Prague. Old Town's **Grand Café Orient** incorporates right angles into every detail from the coat hooks to the coffee cups, and the world's only cubist lamppost stands outside the pub **U Pinkasu** just off Wenceslas Square.

Outside Prague

- **Ještěd Hotel and TV Tower:** The curved walls of this unique building in Liberec slope skyward into an upside-down funnel shape, earning an International Perret Architecture Award for blending seamlessly into the mountain range it sits atop.
- Two ornate ossuaries (often called "bone churches") in **Kutná Hora** and **Brno** manage to create a serene, artistic atmosphere with spaces decorated entirely by human bones.

Vienna

Vienna is overwhelmed with Baroque and Historicist grandeur, punctuated with Secessionist avant-garde buildings offering a breath of fresh air.

- **St. Leopold Church:** This gold-domed church is Otto Wagner's most spectacular masterpiece. It's out of the way but worth the architectural pilgrimage.
- **Hundertwasserhaus:** A contrast to the Biedermeier and Habsburg buildings dotted around Vienna, Friedensreich Hundertwasser's multicolored house of uneven proportions and playful angles is an architectural breath of fresh air.
- **Secession:** The Secession caused a scandal when it opened in 1897, with its "Golden Cabbage" crowning the austere white cube-like structure. Today it's a symbol of Vienna's modernism, and still used as a hub of contemporary art.
- **MuseumsQuartier:** The former imperial stables are now the cutting edge of the avant-garde, not only when it comes to art, but architecture too. Check out the simple lines of

the lounge of Hundertwasser Village

Vajdahunyad Castle

the mumok and Leopold museums—both of which are a stark contrast against the grander, more elaborate buildings in downtown Vienna.

- **Schönbrunn Palace:** The shade of yellow of this imperial summer palace is so iconic it has a color named after it. Schönbrunn Palace is the most opulent and spectacular out of the Habsburg Palaces around Vienna, and worth the day just to revel around its splendorous wings both inside and out.

Outside Vienna

- **Blue Church in Bratislava:** This church in various hues of blue by Hungarian architect Ödön Lechner is a must visit in Bratislava if you love art nouveau architecture.

Budapest

Budapest has a lot in common architecturally with its sister cities, but there are a few nuances that set it apart. The iconic buildings found in the Hungarian capital dating from the golden age around the year 1900 have architect Miklós Ybl to thank, who built the Hungarian State Opera House and the finishing touches on St. Stephen's Basilica. And of course, there's also the work of Ödön Lechner, the architect who pioneered Hungary's own brand of art nouveau, blending orientalism with Hungarian folk art in his style with brightly colored glazed architectural ceramics.

- **Hungarian Parliament:** This piece of neo-Gothic grandeur on the Danube is one of the city's most iconic architectural legacies and impressive whether viewed from afar in Buda or up close in Pest.

- **Geological Institute of Hungary:** One of Ödön Lechner's most spectacular buildings is an exquisite piece of Hungarian art nouveau. From afar, admire its blue tiled roof topped with globes held up by Atlas statues, and from close up see how many geological references you can spot.

- **Gellért Thermal Baths:** Unimpressive on the outside, the interior of these thermal baths are a temple to the golden age of Hungary's spa culture. The baths are lined with mosaics and

Best Views

PRAGUE

- **Petřín Lookout Tower:** Climb 299 steps (or take an elevator) to the observation deck of this tower, which is one of the highest viewpoints in the city (page 76).

- **Vyšehrad:** This hilltop castle complex affords views over the Vltava River and Prague's iconic red rooftops (page 83).

- **Vitkov Hill:** The courtyard platform outside the National Memorial is an incredible spot to watch the sun set over the Prague Castle (page 80).

VIENNA

- **St. Stephen's Cathedral:** Take the elevator up to the top of the north tower or climb the 343 steps in the south tower for views of Vienna's old inner city beyond the cathedral's colorful mosaic rooftop (page 204).

- **Danube Tower:** Shoot up in the elevator to the top of the highest human-made point in the city for views over the Danube, the old town, and the Vienna Woods beyond (page 242).

- **Riesenrad:** Hop on this iconic 100-year-old Ferris wheel for changing views over Vienna and the Prater (page 233).

- **Schönbrunn Palace Park's Gloriette:** Hike up to this triumphal hilltop arch in Schönbrunn Palace Park for sweeping vistas over brilliant yellow Schönbrunn Palace and the park's manicured hedges, with the Vienna Woods and the city rising in the backdrop (page 240).

BUDAPEST

- **Fisherman's Bastion:** Although any view from Pest's Castle Hill won't disappoint, this turreted neo-Gothic lookout platform is Budapest's most romantic spot (page 348).

- **Gellért Hill:** Hike up Gellért Hill for vistas of Budapest's most iconic sites. Just before you reach the Citadella, there is a small lookout point where you can see the Royal Palace, the Danube, and the Hungarian Parliament all from the same spot (page 370).

- **St. Stephen's Basilica:** A platform circling this basilica's iconic domed roof offers views of the inner city and famous landmarks, with some of the basilica towers cutting into the stunning backdrop (page 356).

- **Elizabeth Lookout:** Take the chairlift, the Children's Railway, or hike to the Elizabeth Lookout, the highest point in Budapest. If the weather conditions are right, you may see a hint of the mountains in Slovakia (page 379).

DANUBE BEND

- **Visegrád Citadel:** It's worth the hike (or taxi ride) up to the Visegrád Citadel just to see the Danube Bend from above. This is perhaps one of the most spectacular viewing points in the whole of Hungary (page 446).

glazed ceramics in 50 shades of subterranean blue and turquoise.

- **Vajdahunyad Castle:** Built to celebrate architecture from Hungary and its former territories, Vajdahunyad Castle is a blend of different castles, churches, and palaces from different eras, and worth the visit for an interactive introduction to Hungarian architecture.

- **Dohány Street Synagogue:** Europe's largest synagogue (and one of Budapest's most beautiful buildings) blends neo-orientalism with elements of a Christian church. Inside, a vast rose window rises above the pews, while parts of the exterior synagogue resemble a mosque, with Moorish style design.

Prague

So much of Prague's beauty is reflected in the
coexistence of its past and present. The castles and royal gardens of powerful monarchies in Malá Strana and Vyšehrad complement the World War II museums and monuments commemorating struggles for independence in New Town. Medieval church spires and synagogues on the cobblestones of Old Town symbolize the depth of Czech history, while neighborhoods like Smíchov and Holešovice are repurposing industrial spaces into modern artistic venues and international restaurants. The popularity of sites like the Náplavka Boardwalk and Letná Park speak to a deep Czech love of enjoying life outdoors.

Along with Prague's often-described fairy-tale atmosphere, Czech culture includes an affinity for whimsy and ideals of freedom and

Highlights

Look for ★ to find recommended sights, activities, dining, and lodging.

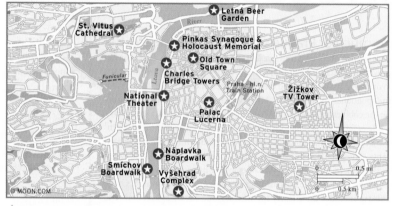

© MOON.COM

★ **Old Town Square:** Soak in Prague's history and architectural beauty amid Gothic towers, religious monuments, colorful rooftops, and a 15th-century astronomical clock (page 48).

★ **Pinkas Synagogue and Holocaust Memorial:** Located in Prague's Josefov neighborhood—one of the most intact Jewish quarters in Central Europe—this powerful Holocaust memorial, which includes walls lined with family names and an exhibit of children's drawings, ensures that history is never forgotten (page 55).

★ **Palac Lucerna:** This arcade-style passageway is a time capsule of life on Wenceslas Square. Snap a picture of the upside-down horse sculpture on your way to the 1900s-era café Kavárna Lucerna or the modern rooftop bar Střecha Lucerny (page 59).

★ **Náplavka and Smíchov Boardwalks:** Stroll below street level along these cobble-stoned riverside boardwalks, where renovated vaults hold underground cafés and gallery spaces (page 63 and 77).

★ **Charles Bridge Towers:** These towers flanking 650-year-old Charles Bridge offer prime perspectives over the Vltava River—especially beautiful around sunset (page 65).

★ **St. Vitus Cathedral:** Prepare to be awed while taking in the Gothic towers, intricate rose window, and stained glass of this cathedral within the Prague Castle complex (page 72).

★ **Žižkov TV Tower:** Sculptures of babies by Czech artist David Černý crawl the walls of Prague's tallest structure—often compared to a rocket ship in the skyline (page 78).

★ **Vyšehrad Complex:** Prague's "other castle" offers a more peaceful vibe than the Prague Castle. The cemetery provides the resting place of some local legends, while today's locals enjoy the beer garden in the summer (page 83).

★ **Letná Beer Garden:** Located in massive Letná park, one of the city's largest beer gardens affords hillside views of red rooftops and the Vltava River (page 100).

★ **National Theater:** With plush red seats, golden opera boxes, and a chandelier hanging from the muraled ceiling, this glamorous theater is the perfect backdrop for artistic performances (page 107).

beauty. This can be seen in the John Lennon graffiti wall, David Černý's often controversial public art pieces, or adults unironically wearing hoodies with animal ears—although, to be fair, the dark humor and cautiously pessimistic local character resembles a Brothers Grimm story more closely than a lighthearted cartoon. Replace "… they all lived happily ever after" with the national motto of "truth prevails," and you'll start to get the picture.

This multi-dimensional culture can please an entire spectrum of interests: architecture, fine arts and culture, culinary curiosities, niche museums, and a local beverage to fit every mood. There is a laid-back, live-and-let-live attitude and a strong sense of enjoying your free time with as much enthusiasm as you spend striving for professional success.

HISTORY

The Prague fairy tale begins around the year 870, when the Přemyslid dynasty (Prague's earliest line of ruling families) founded the Prague Castle. This remained the seat of power until the 11th century, when Vratislav II, King of Bohemia, chose to rule from Vyšehrad instead. These two hillside fortified complexes on opposite sides of the Vltava River helped to ensure the safety and prominence of Prague's early aristocracy.

Wenceslas I (known as Václav in Czech), now the patron saint of the Czech Republic and inspiration for the Christmas carol "Good King Wenceslas," ruled as the Duke of Bohemia from 922-935. He was known for being a devout Christian in an era when paganism was still quite popular. Wenceslas died a martyr's death on September 28, 935, killed by his own brother, Boleslav the Cruel. You can pay your respects to the good king at his chapel inside St. Vitus Cathedral, or at the enormous statue of the saint on horseback at the top of Wenceslas Square.

Another hero of Czech history arrives centuries later. After the Přemyslid dynasty failed to produce an heir in the early 1300s, the title was passed to John of Luxembourg and then to his son Charles IV, who ruled over Prague's Golden Age during the 14th century. Charles (Karel in Czech) was named both King of Bohemia and Holy Roman Emperor, giving his seat in Prague even more importance. Charles's legacy includes the establishment of the New Town and the founding of Charles University in 1348, plus the construction of the Charles Bridge in 1357.

The early 14th century was a time of religious conflict led by Jan Hus, the religious leader behind the Hussite movement. Hus stood up to the Catholic Church by giving sermons on reformation directly to the people in their local language. This didn't go over well and he was burned at the stake in 1415. A statue of Jan Hus and his followers now dominates the center of Old Town Square, and July 6 is a public holiday in his honor.

Defenestration (the act of throwing authority figures out of high windows) is notorious in Prague. The First Defenestration of 1419 was carried out by a group of Hus's followers who stormed the New Town Hall and demanded the release of prisoners. When their demands were refused, they took it out on the officials in the tower that now stands on Charles Square (Karlovo náměstí). This act began the Hussite Wars that lasted until 1434.

The Habsburg dynasty took over in 1526, moving the seat of power to Vienna and solidifying Prague's connection with the surrounding regions of Austria and Hungary for the next few centuries. Prague enjoyed a brief resurgence in the late 16th century.

The Second Defenestration took place in 1618 at the Prague Castle, and is marked with a plaque both inside and outside of the tower. Tossing two officials out this window was a Protestant response to Emperor Ferdinand II attempting to impose Catholicism as the law of the land. This act led to the Thirty Years' War that raged across Europe from 1618-1648.

Previous: Prague skyline; the 14th-century Charles Bridge; city streets in Prague are a sight all on their own.

Prague

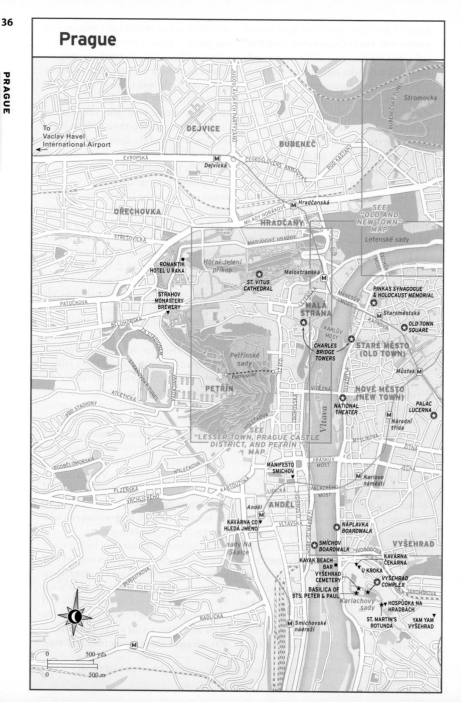

To Vaclav Havel International Airport

DEJVICE

BUBENEČ

Stromovka

EVROPSKÁ

🅜 Dejvická

ČESKOSLOVENS. ARMÁDY

POD KAŠTANY

🅜 Hradčanská

OŘECHOVKA

MILADY HORÁKOVÉ

HRADČANY

SEE "OLD AND NEW TOWN" MAP

STŘEŠOVICKÁ

MARIÁNSKÉ HRADBY

Letenské sady

ROMANTIK HOTEL U RAKA

Horní Jelení příkop

Malostranská 🅜

PATOČKOVA

ST. VITUS CATHEDRAL

PINKAS SYNAGOGUE & HOLOCAUST MEMORIAL

STRAHOV MONASTERY BREWERY

MANESŮV MOST

Staroměstská 🅜

OLD TOWN SQUARE

BĚLOHORSKÁ

MALÁ STRANA

KARLŮV MOST

STARÉ MĚSTO (OLD TOWN)

Petřínské sady

CHARLES BRIDGE TOWERS

Můstek 🅜

ATLETICKÁ

PETŘÍN

Funicular

VÍTĚZNÁ

NOVÉ MĚSTO (NEW TOWN)

POD STADIONY

NATIONAL THEATER

PALAC LUCERNA

Národní třída 🅜

PODBĚLOHORSKÁ

SEE "LESSER TOWN, PRAGUE CASTLE DISTRICT, AND PETŘÍN" MAP

MYSLÍKOVA

Vltava

ŽITNÁ

HOLEČKOVA

JIRÁSKŮV MOST

JEČNÁ

PLZEŇSKÁ

MANIFESTO SMÍCHOV

Karlovo náměstí 🅜

VRCHLICKÉHO

LIDICKÁ

PALACKÉHO MOST

Andĕl

ANDĔL

KAVÁRNA CO HLEDÁ JMÉNO

VLTAVSKÁ

NÁPLAVKA BOARDWALK

VYŠEHRAD

sady Na Skalce

SMÍCHOV BOARDWALK

SVOBODOVA

KAVÁRNA ČEKÁRNA

PŘÍJŮTKOVA

KAYAK BEACH BAR

U KROKA

VYŠEHRAD CEMETERY

VYŠEHRAD COMPLEX

JAROMÍROVA

BASILICA OF STS. PETER & PAUL

Karlachovy sady

HOSPŮDKA NA HRADBÁCH

RADLICKÁ

Smíchovské nádraží 🅜

ST. MARTIN'S ROTUNDA

YAM YAM VYŠEHRAD

JUGOSLÁVSKÝCH PARTYZÁNŮ

BUBENEČSKÝ TUNEL

LETENSKÁ

LETENSKÝ TUNEL

0 ___ 500 yds

0 ___ 500 m

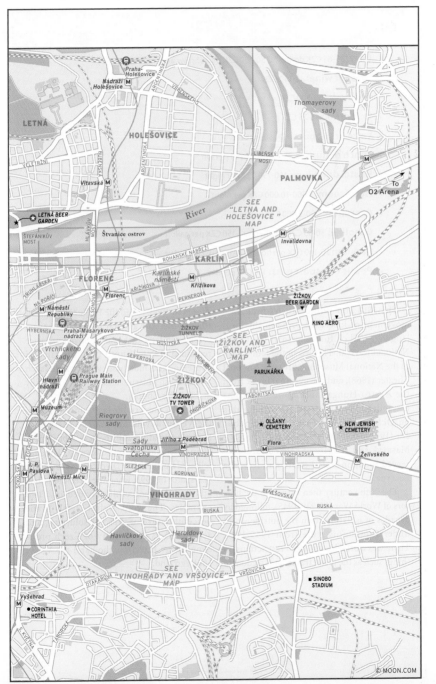

LETNÁ

Praha-
Holešovice
Nádraží
Holešovice

HOLEŠOVICE

Thomayerovy
sady

LIBEŇSKÝ
MOST

PALMOVKA

To
O2 Arena

Vltavská

VELETRŽNÍ

LETNÁ BEER
GARDEN

ŠTEFÁNIKŮV
MOST

Štvanice ostrov

River

SEE
"LETNÁ AND
HOLEŠOVICE"
MAP

Invalidovna

ROHANSKÉ NÁBŘEŽÍ

KARLÍN

Karlínské
náměstí

FLORENC

Florenc

Křižíkova

ŽIŽKOV
BEER GARDEN

PERNEROVA

KINO AERO

Náměstí
Republiky

Praha-Masarykovo
nádraží

HYBERNSKÁ

ŽIŽKOV
TUNNELS

HUSITSKÁ

SEE
"ŽIŽKOV AND
KARLÍN" MAP

Vrchlického
sady

SEIFERTOVA

PARUKÁŘKA

Hlavní
nádraží

Prague Main
Railway Station

ŽIŽKOV

ŽIŽKOV
TV TOWER

TÁBORITSKÁ

Muzeum

ONDŘÍČKOVA

OLŠANY
CEMETERY

NEW JEWISH
CEMETERY

Riegrovy
sady

Sády
Svatopluka
Čecha

Jiřího z Poděbrad

VINOHRADSKÁ

Flora

Želivského

VINOHRADSKÁ

I. P.
Pavlova

Náměstí Míru

SLEZSKÁ

KORUNNÍ

VINOHRADY

BENEŠOVSKÁ

RUSKÁ

RUSKÁ

FRANCOUZSKÁ

Havlíčkovy
sady

Heroldovy
sady

VRŠOVICKÁ

SEE
"VINOHRADY AND VRŠOVICE"
MAP

SINOBO
STADIUM

OTAKAROVA

Vyšehrad

CORINTHIA
HOTEL

© MOON.COM

Budgeting

- **Beer:** 35-65 CZK domestic, 50-100 CZK microbrews and imported
- **Glass of wine:** 35-150 CZK
- **Cocktail:** 100-300 CZK
- **Soft drink:** 45-75 CZK
- **Latte or cappuccino:** 50-85 CZK
- **Lunch or dinner:** 150-500 CZK per person
- **Hostel dorm bed:** 150-750 CZK per night
- **Hotel room:** 1,500-10,000 CZK per night
- **Car rental:** 900-5,000 CZK per day
- **Gasoline:** 30-35 CZK per liter, 100-150 CZK per gallon
- **Parking:** 25-100 CZK per hour, 200-1,000 CZK per day
- **Public transport pass:** 110 CZK per day

The 18th and 19th centuries brought a movement of increased pride in the local language and culture known as the Czech National Revival. This led to the foundation of the National Museum (1818), the National Theater (1868), and the eventual break from the Austro-Hungarian Empire to become the independent state of Czechoslovakia on October 28, 1918. The First Republic era (1918-1938) under President Tomas G. Masaryk saw the rise of café culture, preserved today in Café Louvre and Kavárna Lucerna.

The 20th century then turned to the horrors of World War II (1939-1945), followed by decades of isolation from the outside world under Communist rule from 1945-1989. There was a brief loosening of restrictions on things such as the press, travel, and freedom of speech in 1968, called the Prague Spring, but this was met with a brutal Soviet invasion and crackdown later that year. A Soviet presence remained in Prague until 1989. You can find deeper insights into these events at sights such as the Jewish Museum and the Town Belfry by St. Nicholas Church.

Prague's modern life began in 1989, when the Velvet Revolution marked the end of Soviet occupation and the re-establishment of an independent Czechoslovakia. This was followed by the Velvet Divorce just a few short years later in 1993, when the Czech Republic and Slovakia peacefully divided into two countries. The word "Velvet" refers to the peaceful nature of these dissolutions, and acknowledges the affinity of Czech president Václav Havel for the band the Velvet Underground.

Orientation and Planning

ORIENTATION

The historic center of Prague is packed with history and interesting sights, but it can also be packed with people vying for the best photographs. For a deeper sense of the city, split your time between visiting monuments and getting to know the surrounding neighborhoods of Holešovice, Letná, Smíchov, Karlín, Vinohrady, or Žižkov.

Old Town (Staré Město)

The **cobblestoned streets** and **century-spanning architecture** of this neighborhood inspired the UNESCO World Heritage Center to crown the entire Historic Center of Prague a protected site in 1992. The well-preserved buildings have become more of a monument to the past than an example of local life. Many residents have been priced out of living in the area while touristy shops and restaurants replaced local amenities. This twisted maze of streets around **Old Town Square** can get a bit crowded. Early mornings and off-seasons are a great time to enjoy this area with a little more breathing room.

The Jewish quarter known as **Josefov** sits in the northwest corner of Old Town, surrounded by the curve of the Vltava River.

New Town (Nové Město)

The name New Town applies to a large semi-circle that wraps from one edge of the Vltava River, around the Old Town, to the other side of the river bend. Charles IV founded this neighborhood along with Charles University in 1348 (not exactly "new" by today's standards) in order to expand the size and influence of the city toward his grand dreams. Walking from the **Municipal House** and **Powder Tower** on one edge to the **National Theater** and **Dancing House** on the other could take half an hour (without stopping to sightsee). Three micro-neighborhoods are centered around New Town's main squares: **Náměstí Republiky, Václavské náměstí,** and **Karlovo náměstí.**

Lesser Town (Malá Strana)

Malá Strana, the Czech name for the neighborhood sprawled around the base of the

Swans on the Vltava River add to the fairy-tale atmosphere.

Prague Castle, loosely translates to "Lesser Town" or "Little Quarter," but it deserves far more credit than this nickname implies. Long before joining Hradčany, Old Town, and New Town to form a unified Prague in 1784, this eighth-century market area was **Prague's oldest settlement.** Situated between two of the city's most popular tourist attractions (**Charles Bridge** and the Prague Castle), these cobblestoned streets were an essential part of the Royal Route during the processions of newly ordained kings. These days, the area's **historic charm** is tempered with a fairly heavy presence of touristy souvenir shops and camera-wielding tourists. However, the history and beauty surrounding these cobblestoned streets are worth taking a few side steps around the crowds to discover semi-hidden sights, such as the **Vrtba Garden** and **Kampa Island.** As you head south along the base of Petřín Park, historic Malá Strana blends into the more modern dining and drinking district of Smíchov.

Prague Castle District (Hradčany)

The hillside castle district of Hradčany, across the Vltava River from Old Town and above

Malá Strana, is dominated by the **Prague Castle** grounds and surrounding gardens, with a few **luxury hotels** and **cafés** dotting the residential area around it. Beware that a deceptively easy walk plotted on a map may actually take double the time you anticipate; you may have to climb stairs or find one of a few hard-to-spot entrances among the fortified castle walls. This area is more of a destination than a place to get lost among the streets, so choose your entry point, note your tram stops, and enjoy the view from the geographical vantage point that drew the royal residence in the first place.

Petřín

The **massive green hillside** on the western side of the Vltava River separates the historic castle district of Hradčany to the north from the bustling cosmopolitan life around the Anděl business district in the **Smíchov** neighborhood. Largely dominated by **Petřín Park,** this quiet side of Prague is an ideal place for an outdoor picnic, a romantic (if a bit strenuous) walk through the park, a chance to sprawl out on the grass and admire the city skyline, or visit the swans along the Smíchov Boardwalk.

Old Town Prague

Vinohrady and Vršovice

This popular home for **international residents** is filled with **restaurants** that reflect that diversity, and **bars** that cater to the wide-ranging clientele. The surrounding **parks** such as **Havlíčkovy sady** and **Riegrovy sady** often host food and wine festivals during warmer months, and the Christmas market at **Náměstí Miru** is a local favorite. Just southeast of Wenceslas Square, Karlovo náměstí, and the edges of New Town, these are easy baby steps off the traditional tourist path. The southeastern edge of Vinohrady blends into neighboring **Vršovice**, best known for the nightlife destination of **Krymská Street.**

Žižkov

This formerly **working-class neighborhood,** stretching from Prague's main train station (Hlavní Nádraží) in New Town along the northern edge of Vinohrady, may be rapidly changing, but it hasn't completely lost its gritty, take-it-or-leave-it spirit. Case in point: you shouldn't necessarily expect an English menu or a smiling server in every establishment. You can pinpoint Žižkov from almost anywhere in Prague thanks to the rocket-shaped **TV Tower** dominating the city skyline. The **pub-heavy neighborhood** was named for Hussite hero Jan Žižka, whose statue sits atop neighboring Vítkov Hill.

Karlín

After massive flooding in 2002, Karlín experienced an extensive revitalization effort. Today this sophisticated neighborhood is better known for its **culinary scene, wine bars,** and prime location for househunting young families. The **artsy vibe** is less dance party and more conversations over Cabernet, with **repurposed spaces** such as **Přístav 18600** and **Kasarna Karlín** adding more life to the changing landscape. Karlín stretches east from the edge of New Town and Florenc bus station along the banks of the Vltava River

Letná and Holešovice

Letná, located across the river to the north of Old Town and west of Hradčany, is best known for the massive **Letná Park** that lines its southern edge. The **Letná Beer Garden** inside the park is a major summertime hot spot, and the surrounding **trendy residential streets** are lined with cafés, international restaurants, and the **National Gallery's Trade Fair Palace.**

There are no ideas too weird for the **industrial** neighborhood of Holešovice to the east of Letná. Theatrical space in a former slaughterhouse? Check. Dance club covered in pipes and gears? Sure. Cryptoanarchist coffee shop that only accepts virtual currencies? Why not? From **street art** to a **contemporary arts center** focused on socially conscious exhibitions, this neighborhood is full of surprises.

Vyšehrad

The area around Vyšehrad (meaning "high castle") south of New Town walks a fine line—it's not quite the center of town, but not quite the suburbs—and includes **the Vyšehrad Complex,** a major tourist attraction that doubles as a locally loved destination for relaxation. The beauty and importance of the Vyšehrad Complex rivals the Prague Castle, but draws a fraction of the crowds, and the surrounding streets and restaurants showcase more **local life** than souvenir stands.

PLANNING YOUR TIME

You could do a whirlwind tour of Prague in a fast-paced **two days** by picking and choosing the sights most important to you. A **long weekend** will give you the extra time needed to explore the lesser-known sights and neighborhoods for the less-crowded corners of character and culture. Add a day trip to one of the surrounding towns, such as Kutná Hora or Liberec. **One week** in the Czech Republic is a great way to compare the cosmopolitan life of Prague with a second destination, such as the spa town of Karlovy Vary or the wine region surrounding the town of Mikulov.

Summer, Easter, and **Christmas** holidays are peak times, and around Christmas, in particular, you will receive an incredibly festive atmosphere in exchange for longer lines at most major sights. It's best to arrange hotel reservations, tickets to performances, and even restaurant reservations as far in advance as possible for the best selection and rates.

Daily Reminders

The importance of work-life balance in Czech means that many cafés, restaurants, and independent shops have limited hours on weekends, especially Sundays. There are still plenty of restaurants focused on an international clientele where you can find a good meal. Cafés also open later in the day as opposed to early mornings, so save your coffee breaks for the afternoons. At the time of writing, some sights had reduced their hours in response to COVID-19 conditions, so double check hours for your visit.

SATURDAY

- The sights of the Jewish quarter are closed.
- Weekly farmers market is held at Náplavka.

SUNDAY

- St. Vitus Cathedral has limited hours (noon-4pm).
- Many shops have limited hours.

MONDAY

- Old Town Hall Tower opens later (11am).

The following sights are closed:

- Convent of St. Agnes
- Lobkowicz Palace (temporarily)
- National Monument to the Heroes of the Heydrich Terror
- National Gallery
- DOX Center for Contemporary Art

TUESDAY

The following sights are closed:

- Lobkowicz Palace (temporarily)
- DOX Center for Contemporary Art

WEDNESDAY

- Lobkowicz Palace is closed (temporarily).
- National Gallery—Trade Fair Palace is open late (until 8pm).
- DOX Center for Contemporary Art is open late (until 9pm).

Public Holidays

There are a number of Czech public holidays that visitors may not expect: **Good Friday** and **Easter Monday** may have limited shopping hours, but the long weekend also brings Easter markets to many town squares. **May 1** and **May 8** are national holidays marking Labor Day and Victory in Europe (VE) Day. Both **July 5** and **July 6** are public holidays likely to limit access to some museums and shops. **September 28** (St. Wenceslas Day), **October 28** (the foundation of Czechoslovakia), and **November 17** (commemorating the Struggle for Freedom and Democracy) are often marked with performances, events, or protests in Wenceslas Square. Christmas is celebrated on **December 24** in the Czech Republic, with additional public holidays on **December 25** and **26,** but you'll also find Christmas markets popping up around the beginning of December.

Advance Booking and Time-Saving Tips
SIGHTS

Many of Prague's sights require buying tickets or arranging tours onsite. However, one important activity that you can book in advance is a guided tour of the **Prague Castle** (via email at info@hrad.cz).

RESTAURANTS AND NIGHTLIFE

One quirk of Prague's restaurant and café scene is a near obsession with reservations.

Yes, people often book seats to meet their friends for an afternoon coffee or a drink at a pub or cocktail bar. The growing demand for high-quality dining and the response of constant restaurant openings mean that everyone (including the locals) wants to try the latest places. Some restaurants offer online reservation systems, while others require a phone call, which hotel concierges can often help with. The English-friendly website and mobile app **Restu.cz** (scroll to the bottom to choose your language) is also a good option for a middleman to arrange your reservation without any miscommunications of the time and number of guests.

Many pubs and restaurants are often booked with company holiday parties throughout the month of December, so double check availability with any place you plan to visit before arriving.

Sightseeing Passes

A **Prague Card** (www.praguecard.com) offers free admission or discounts on many of the city's attractions, including certain areas of the Prague Castle, Petřín Tower, the Jewish Museum, the Charles Bridge Towers, St. Nicholas' Town Belfry, and the Mucha Museum. It can be purchased for two days (about 1,500 CZK), three days (about 1,700 CZK), or four days (about 2,000 CZK). The card also works as a valid ticket for all public transport in Prague (e.g. buses, trams, and the metro), but must be presented along with an ID if inspected. The card can be purchased in-person or ordered online and collected at Tourist Information Centers at the Prague Airport (8am-8pm) or at the two Centers in their Old Town locations (9am-7pm).

The Prague card is definitely useful, but not an essential tool for exploring the city. It provides many valuable discounts, but usually doesn't offer priority entry or exclusive access. A basic three-day public transport pass costs 310 CZK and the average entrance to Prague's sights ranges from free to around 250 CZK. However, if you combine the Jewish Museum with access to multiple tower views where you only spend half an hour, these admissions can add up. Getting value for your purchase depends on how many of the included sights are on your preferred itinerary, so peruse the list before purchasing.

Entrance to the Astronomical Clock Tower, the Powder Tower, both Charles Bridge Towers, and the St. Nicholas Bell Tower are all discounted by 50 percent during the first hour after opening.

Art fans with a longer stay could benefit from a 10-day pass (500 CZK) to all of the permanent collections from the National Gallery of Prague, including the Convent of St. Agnes (220 CZK) and the National Gallery-Trade Fair Palace (220 CZK). The National Gallery pass is only available in person at any cash desk.

Itinerary Ideas

DAY 1

Before you set out for the day, put on comfortable shoes and a top with covered shoulders for the Pinkas Synagogue, and check seasonal opening hours of the Old Town Hall Tower. Make early afternoon lunch reservations at U Dvou Koček and dinner reservations around 6:30-7pm at Martin's Bistro.

1 Start the day with breakfast at **Grand Café Orient,** a cubist coffee shop just off Náměstí Republiky.

2 Walk five minutes along Celetná street to reach the postcard views of **Old Town**

Square. Proceed straight to the Old Town Hall Tower for 360-degree views from above the Astronomical Clock.

3 Exit Old Town Square onto Pařížská Street next to the domed St. Nicholas Church and turn left onto Široká street to reach the **Pinkas Synagogue.** Spend 90 minutes at this touching Holocaust memorial. Exit through the Old Jewish Cemetery, included in the ticket.

4 Follow Maiselova street south for about 10 minutes, eventually turning into Jilská street, then turn left on Skořepka street to reach **U Dvou Koček.** Choose from the daily lunch menu of soups and specials at this classic Czech pub.

5 Turn right twice out of the pub and walk 3-5 minutes along Perlová street, passing through the busy intersection of Jungmannova Square. Look behind the statue of Josef Jungmann on your left to find the entrance to the **Franciscan Gardens.** Take a quiet walk through the small, peaceful park or grab coffee from Café Truhlárna, near the garden entrance, and relax on a bench under flowered trellises.

6 Exit the Franciscan Gardens in the opposite corner, through Pasáž Světozor, then cross the street and turn right on Vodičkova street to enter **Palac Lucerna.** Stand underneath the horseback statue of St. Wenceslas, have a drink at Kavárna Lucerna for a glimpse of old-world glamour, or take the paternoster elevator to the Střecha Lucerny rooftop bar (open Sat-Mon) in good weather. As you survey Wenceslas Square below, imagine thousands of citizens in 1989 shaking their keys in the air as then-Czechoslovakia regained its independence.

7 From Palac Lucerna, turn left onto Štěpánská street. Pause to look up and down Wenceslas Square, then take a five-minute walk heading down the square, turning right onto Jindřišská street and left on Panská street to reach the **Alfons Mucha Museum.** Spend around 90 minutes exploring the swirling style of an art nouveau master before browsing the gift shop.

8 Head back to Wenceslas Square to find the Můstek metro stop at the bottom of the square. Take the green Metro line A three stops to Jiřího z Poděbrad square in Vinohrady and have a Czech microbrew at **Beer Geek Bar** on the south side of the square. (If you prefer wine or coffee, grab an outdoor table at Le Caveau on the north side of the square instead.)

9 After your beverage break, cross Jiřího z Poděbrad square behind the church to find Přemyslovská street. Continue one street up to **Martin's Bistro** for dinner, then call it an early night after a long day of being on your feet.

DAY 2

The Malá Strana neighborhood is home to a few lesser-known sights scattered among the most popular tourist attractions. You'll want comfortable shoes again, and before you leave for the day, make reservations for dinner at U modré kachničky. Note that the Prague Castle's Royal Summer Gardens and South Gardens are open April-October.

1 Start with coffee and a fluffy Benedict soufflé for breakfast at **Kavárna Co Hledá Jméno,** a local favorite hidden inside a parking lot in the Anděl neighborhood.

2 After brunch, turn left twice and head toward the river for five minutes to reach the **Smíchov Boardwalk.** Walk north along the embankment to see swans against the city skyline.

3 Exit the boardwalk near the docked Admiral Botel, turning left onto J. Plachty street, then right onto Nádražní street to find the Anděl tram stop. Take the #12 or #20 north five stops to Malostranské náměstí. Look to your left to find the **St. Nicholas Bell Tower.** Buy a ticket and climb the stairs through six platforms of Prague history.

4 From the tower, turn left down Mostecká street. Instead of crossing the Charles Bridge (don't worry, you will later), spend half an hour climbing the **Lesser Town Bridge Tower** for a bird's-eye view of the afternoon crowds.

5 Head a few steps back into Malá Strana to grab a coffee or beer and a bite to eat at **Roesel—Beer & Food,** a friendly local café tucked just off this touristy street.

6 After your light lunch, walk back toward the Lesser Town Bridge Tower. Turn left before the bridge and follow Míšeňská to U Lužického semináře street for five minutes, looking for the entrance to the **Vojan Gardens** on your left. Spend half an hour in this peaceful oasis of park benches and free-roaming peacocks.

7 Leaving the gardens, turn left and around the corner to Malostranská to catch tram 22 for a quick visit to the Prague Castle. Jump off at tram stop Královský letohrádek to enter through the Royal Summer Gardens and find **St. Vitus Cathedral.** You'll want to spend at least half an hour admiring both the interior and exterior of this iconic monument and surrounding buildings.

8 Exit the Prague Castle by heading west through the South Gardens, stopping for a few panoramic photos. Follow the stairs downhill and head east on Thunovská street, then south into Malá Strana to arrive at **U modré kachničky** for a multi-course dinner (book in advance).

9 After dinner, take a moonlit walk across the **Charles Bridge** with a little more breathing room than you'll find during any daylight hours.

PRAGUE LIKE A LOCAL

After two busy days, give yourself a late start and a hotel breakfast before finding the nearest metro station to the Vyšehrad stop on the red Metro line. Before setting out for the day, book reservations for dinner at Eska and wine at Veltlin. Note that the National Monument to the Heroes of the Heydrich Terror is closed on Mondays.

1 From the metro, follow the brown tourist signs (or small crowds) about 10 minutes to the Vyšehrad grounds. Walk through the parks, pay your respects to the famous names inside the cemetery, and admire the art nouveau interior of the **Basilica of Sts. Peter and Paul.**

2 There is no need to be bashful about day drinking in this beer-loving capital. Grab a cold beverage and a snack at the laid-back **Hospůdka Na Hradbách** beer garden inside the Vyšehrad Complex, five minutes east of the basilica.

3 After your beer break, head west through the park toward the river to find the stairs in front of the cemetery and basilica entrance. Continue downhill and walk about 15 minutes toward the railway bridge to reach the **Náplavka Boardwalk.** Wander the length of the embankment along the New Town side, and add an extra hour here if you hit the Saturday farmers market.

4 A 15-minute walk along Náplavka will take you to the **Dancing House.** Take the elevator to the top-floor Glass Bar and order any beverage for access to the 360-degree viewing platform. Then cross the street to snap a photo of this unusual architectural wonder.

5 Add a touch of local history to your afternoon at the free **National Monument to the Heroes of the Heydrich Terror,** just a three-minute walk up Resslova street. You

Itinerary Ideas

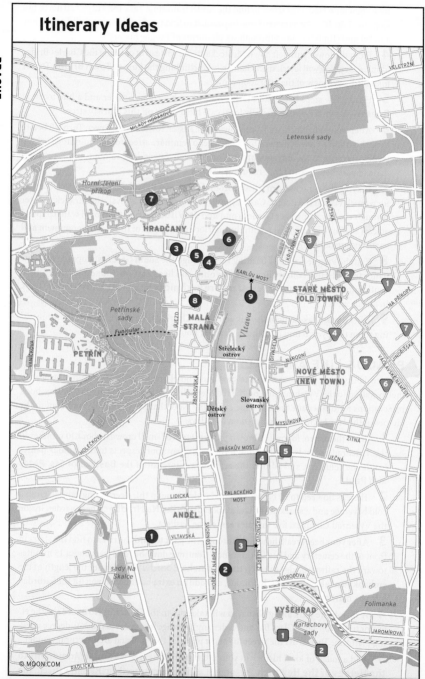

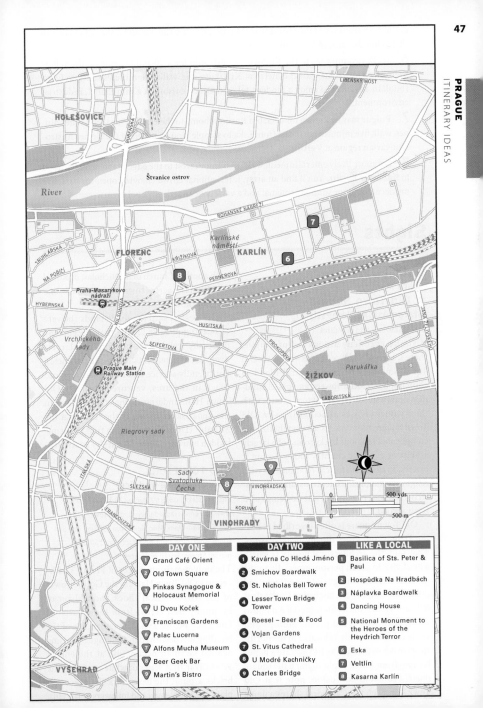

DAY ONE

1. Grand Café Orient
2. Old Town Square
3. Pinkas Synagogue & Holocaust Memorial
4. U Dvou Koček
5. Franciscan Gardens
6. Palac Lucerna
7. Alfons Mucha Museum
8. Beer Geek Bar
9. Martin's Bistro

DAY TWO

1. Kavárna Co Hledá Jméno
2. Smíchov Boardwalk
3. St. Nicholas Bell Tower
4. Lesser Town Bridge Tower
5. Roesel – Beer & Food
6. Vojan Gardens
7. St. Vitus Cathedral
8. U Modré Kachničky
9. Charles Bridge

LIKE A LOCAL

1. Basilica of Sts. Peter & Paul
2. Hospůdka Na Hradbách
3. Náplavka Boardwalk
4. Dancing House
5. National Monument to the Heroes of the Heydrich Terror
6. Eska
7. Veltlin
8. Kasarna Karlín

can absorb the story of the World War II heroes, who are the reason for the bullet holes in these church walls, in less than an hour.

6 Walk two minutes to the Karlovo náměstí stop for a 20-minute ride on the yellow Metro line to Karlín. Exit the metro at Křižíkova and walk five minutes south to **Eska** (book in advance) to enjoy a modern take on Czech cuisine in a minimalist, industrial environment.

7 Prague may be known for beer, but Karlín is home to the Czech wine scene. After dinner, walk five minutes northeast from Eska to sample víno from across the former Austro-Hungarian region at **Veltlin**.

8 For more lively entertainment, walk 15 minutes west to the edge of the neighborhood to **Kasarna Karlín.** You'll find an artsy, international crowd enjoying open-air bars, live music, an outdoor summer cinema, and a variety of effortlessly cool events.

Sights

OLD TOWN
(Staré Město)
★ Old Town Square
(Staroměstské Náměstí)
metro: Staroměstská or Můstek

If you've ever seen a postcard of Prague, there's a good chance it was taken in Old Town Square. The architectural blend of church spires, Gothic towers, and pastel buildings draw a steady stream of tour groups with their camera lenses aimed at the sky. Old Town Square monuments also symbolize the complicated religious background of a largely atheist or agnostic country today. To put it briefly, Prague's historical relationship with religion is complex, contentious, and often intertwined with resentment toward being ruled from abroad.

Old Town Square is often described as having Disneyland vibes during peak seasons. That said, the architectural beauty is worth a brief visit to see in person, especially in the quieter early mornings, late evenings, and off-season months. **St. Nicholas Cathedral** (Chrám sv. Mikuláše; Staroměstské náměstí 1101), with its curved green rooftops and white columned walls, is located in the northwest corner of the square. Its steps are a popular spot from which to photograph the square itself. (To avoid confusion, note that Old Town's St. Nicholas Cathedral shares a name

with another Church of St. Nicholas, or Kostel sv. Mikuláše, across town in the Malá Strana neighborhood.)

It's best to skip the food stands (beware of heaping piles of Prague ham deceptively priced by weight, not portion) and largely overpriced restaurants lining the perimeter. For friendly service and a reasonably priced snack in the area, venture left of the Old Town Hall, underneath the etched scenes in the Renaissance façade of the "House at the Minute" (Dum U Minuty), to find the semi-hidden entrance to the **Skautsky Institut.**

OLD TOWN HALL
(Staroměstská Radnice)
Staroměstské náměstí 1; tel. +420 775 400 052; www.staromestskaradnicepraha.cz; tower open Tue-Sun 9am-9pm, Mon 11am-9pm Jul-Sep, Tue-Sun 10am-8pm, Mon 11am-8pm Oct-Jun; 250 CZK; metro: Staroměstská or Můstek

The only remaining pieces of Prague's 14th-century Old Town Hall are the Gothic Tower of the Astronomical Clock and a sliver of burgundy wall across from the Church of Our Lady Before Týn. The remainder of the building was destroyed in the Prague Uprising against German occupation at the end of World War II. A series of white crosses in the bricks around the base mark the execution place of 27 noblemen and followers of Jan Hus.

Old and New Town

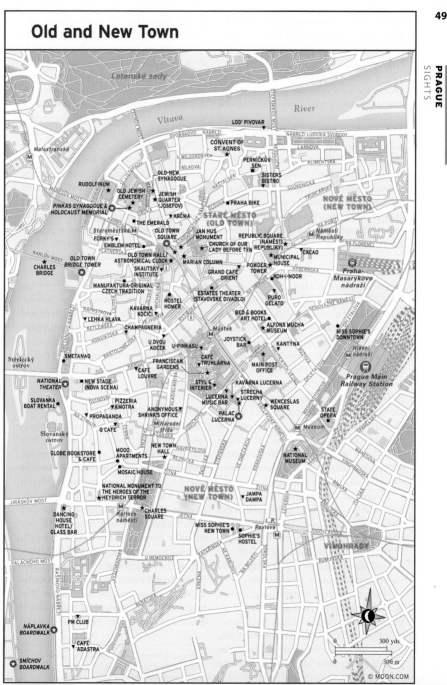

Latenské sady

Vltava

River

STEFÁNIKŮV MOST

LOĎ PIVOVAR

Malostranská Ⓜ

DVOŘÁKOVO NÁBŘEŽÍ

NÁBŘEŽÍ LUDVÍKA SVOBODY

CONVENT OF
ST. AGNES

U MILOSRDNÝCH

LANNOVA

BÍLKOVA

PERNÍČKŮV
SEN

KLIMENTSKÁ

OLD-NEW
SYNAGOGUE

SISTERS
BISTRO

HAŠTALSKÁ

SOUKENICKÁ

TRUHLÁŘSKÁ

RUDOLFINUM

OLD JEWISH
CEMETERY

JEWISH
QUARTER
(JOSEFOV)

BLOUH

PRAHA BIKE

NOVÉ MĚSTO
(NEW TOWN)

MÁNESŮV MOST

PINKAS SYNAGOGUE &
HOLOCAUST MEMORIAL

THE EMERALD

KRČMA

ŠIROKÁ

STARÉ MĚSTO
(OLD TOWN)

Náměstí
Republiky Ⓜ

NA FLORENCI

Staroměstská Ⓜ

FORKY'S

OLD TOWN
SQUARE

JAN HUS
MONUMENT

REPUBLIC SQUARE
(NÁMĚSTÍ
REPUBLIKY)

CACAO

KAPROVA

EMBLEM HOTEL

PLATNÉŘSKÁ

OLD TOWN HALL/
ASTRONOMICAL CLOCK

CHURCH OF OUR
LADY BEFORE TÝN

MUNICIPAL
HOUSE

KARLŮV MOST

OLD TOWN
BRIDGE TOWER

SKAUTSKÝ
INSTITUTE

MARIAN COLUMN

POWDER
TOWER

HYBERNSKÁ

Praha-
Masarykovo
nádraží

CHARLES
BRIDGE

MANUFAKTURA-ORIGINAL
CZECH TRADITION

GRAND CAFÉ
ORIENT

KOH-I-NOOR

NÁPRSTKOVA

KAVÁRNA
KOČIČÍ

ESTATES THEATER
(STAVOVSKÉ DIVADLO)

PURO
GELATO

SENOVÁŽNÉ NÁMĚSTÍ

MICHALSKÁ

LEHKÁ HLAVA

HOSTEL
HOMER

BED & BOOKS
ART HOTEL

MISS SOPHIE'S
DOWNTOWN

BETLÉMSKÁ

CHAMPAGNERIA

RYTÍŘSKÁ

ALFONS MUCHA
MUSEUM

Hlavní
nádraží Ⓜ

KONVIKTSKÁ

U DVOU
KOČEK

Můstek Ⓜ

JOYSTICK
BAR

KANTÝNA

Prague Main
Railway Station

SMETANA Q

U-PINKASU

FRANCISCAN
GARDENS

CAFÉ
TRUHLÁRNA

MAIN POST
OFFICE

Strelecký
ostrov

BARTOLOMĚJSKÁ

CAFÉ
LOUVRE

NATIONAL
THEATER

NEW STAGE
(NOVÁ SCÉNA)

STYL &
INTERIÉR

KAVÁRNA LUCERNA

STATE
OPERA

SLOVANKA
BOAT RENTAL

OSTROVNÍ

PIZZERIA
KMOTRA

LUCERNA
MUSIC BAR

STŘECHA
LUCERNY

WENCESLAS
SQUARE

Muzeum Ⓜ

PROPAGANDA

ANONYMOUS
SHRINK'S OFFICE

PALAC
LUCERNA

Slovanský
ostrov

Q CAFÉ

Národní
třída Ⓜ

GLOBE BOOKSTORE
& CAFÉ

MOOO
APARTMENTS

NEW TOWN
HALL

NAVRÁTILOVA

ŘEZNICKÁ

NATIONAL
MUSEUM

MOSAIC HOUSE

ŽITNÁ

NOVÉ MĚSTO
(NEW TOWN)

NATIONAL MONUMENT TO
THE HEROES OF THE
HEYDRICH TERROR

JAMPA
DAMPA

JIRÁSKŮV MOST

DANCING
HOUSE
HOTEL/
GLASS BAR

Karlovo
náměstí Ⓜ

CHARLES
SQUARE

JEČNÁ

MISS SOPHIE'S
NEW TOWN

I. P.
Pavlova Ⓜ

VINOHRADY

SOPHIE'S
HOSTEL

PALACKÉHO MOST

U NEMOCNICE

RAŠÍNOVO NÁBŘEŽÍ

NÁPLAVKA
BOARDWALK

PM CLUB

CAFÉ
ADASTRA

SMÍCHOV
BOARDWALK

0   300 yds

0   300 m

© MOON.COM

These men led a Protestant revolt in the early 1600s with Prague's Second Defenestration (throwing someone out a window) at the Prague Castle.

Admission to the Old Town Hall includes a bird's eye view from the top of the **clock tower**—accessible via elevator—coupled with access to a few historical interior halls and the Chapel of the Virgin Mary. Note that the Old Town Hall interiors are not wheelchair accessible and may close earlier (7pm Oct-Jun, 8pm Jul-Sep) than the clock tower.

Entrance to the Astronomical Clock Tower is discounted by 50 percent for the first hour after opening. Two-hour English-language tours (250 CZK) are also available on select scheduled evenings, often on Fridays.

ASTRONOMICAL CLOCK

Prague's Astronomical Clock (known as "Orloj" in Czech) is more than 600 years old. You might overhear walking tour guides claiming that clock master Hanuš was blinded so that he couldn't replicate its beauty for any other city, but this often-repeated tale has actually been debunked. Documentation from 1410 gives credit to clockmaker Mikuláš of Kadaň and an astronomy and math professor Jan Šindel (who each kept their eyes). The façade and machinery got a careful restorative makeover to repair some residual damage from World War II for the 2018 celebrations of Czechoslovakia's 100th anniversary, brightening the colors of the clock face.

The amount of information held on the colorful faces is as impressive as the fact that this 15th-century timepiece is still ticking today. The golden swirls of the upper circle track a 12-hour and 24-hour clock, the time of sunrise and sunset, the current zodiac sign, and a variety of other historic time systems.

When the hour is approaching, crowds gather on the street in front of the clock in anticipation. When the bells chime hourly from 9am-11pm, the four characters on either side come to life, with vanity staring in a mirror, greed holding a purse full of money, a skeleton (death) ringing his bell, and a musical Turk shaking his head in denial. A parade of the 12 apostles rotates through the doors above the clock face. Full disclaimer: despite its fame, many find the just-under-a-minute animation underwhelming, so feel free to skip the show and arrive between the hours. Then wait for the masses to disperse to admire the impressive external beauty of the clock faces up close.

The stationary statues flanking the lower face are known as the Philosopher, the Archangel Michael, the Astronomer, and the Chronicler. Inside the ring, a 365-day calendar fans out around the paintings of zodiac signs. If you look closely, you'll see a name or two written beside each number, representing a Czech name day (or "svátek"). That's right—most Czechs have one of these traditional names, and parents who want to deviate have to register for official government permission. As a result, Czechs get two yearly excuses to celebrate: the day they were born, and the day that their name falls on the calendar. You'll find Adam and Eva on December 24 (in connection with Christmas), and Czechs take their name for New Year's Eve, "Silvestr," from December 31.

JAN HUS MONUMENT

The large, hooded, stone figure in the center of Old Town Square represents an early 14th-century figure of rebellion against the Catholic Church. Jan Hus may not have the international name recognition of Martin Luther, but he was fighting for religious reform roughly a century before the Protestant Reformation gained momentum. Sadly, like so many enemies of the Catholic church, Hus was burned at the stake on July 6, 1415. This statue was unveiled in 1915, exactly 500 years after his execution, and July 6 remains a Czech national holiday in his honor. The base of the statue is engraved with multiple quotes, including one from Hus himself:

1: Prague's Astronomical Clock 2: the crooked headstones of the Old Jewish Cemetery 3: religious monuments in Old Town Square

"Love each other, and wish the truth to everyone" ("Milujte se, pravdy každému přejte").

MARIAN COLUMN
(Mariánský sloup)

In June 2020, a new religious monument added some spiritual tension in Old Town Square. Marian columns, topped with depictions of the Virgin Mary, were erected in Catholic countries around the 16th-17th centuries as a symbol of gratitude for surviving a plague or tragic event. Prague's Marian column first stood in this square in 1650, after the end of the Thirty Years' War.

However, not all Czechs supported a symbol of Catholicism, seen by some as forcefully imposed by the Hapsburg dynasty, in the center of their city. The column stood through another 250 years of Austro-Hungarian rule, but as soon as an independent Czechoslovakia was established in 1918, a mob of Prague residents took to the streets and tore the column down, leaving the Jan Hus monument (erected in 1915) to stand alone.

In 1989, when Czechoslovakia once again gained independence, a group called the Association for the Renewal of the Marian Column began planning to reinstall the historical monument. It took another three decades of petitions, protests, and arguments to return a replica of the Virgin Mary, wearing a halo of golden stars atop a 15-meter (50-ft) column, to stand beside pre-Protestant Jan Hus and just a few streets away from Prague's Jewish Quarter.

CHURCH OF OUR LADY BEFORE TÝN
(Chrám Matky Boží před Týnem)

Staroměstské náměstí 604; tel. +420 222 318 186 or +420 602 204 213; www.tyn.cz; Tue-Sat 10am-1pm and 3pm-5pm, Sun 10am-noon; donation recommended; metro: Staroměstská or Můstek

One of Old Town's most prominent religious symbols, The Church of Our Lady Before Týn stands on the east side of Old Town Square. If you look closely, you'll see that the church's pair of Gothic columns

(called "Adam and Eve") are not actually symmetrical. Long construction delays and wars beginning in the mid-14th century contributed to the uneven appearance. Take a look between the towers as well. The church was first adorned with a statue of the Virgin Mary, which was replaced during the 1400s by a golden chalice and statue of the first Hussite King George of Poděbrad. When Catholics regained control under the Hapsburg Empire in the 16th century, the chalice was melted down and Mary retook her place of power.

The interior of the church is visible only through a gate just inside the entryway, which serves as a small viewing area for visitors, and photography is prohibited. Architecture fans might enjoy a quick peek at the Baroque design, golden touches, and the oldest organ in all of Prague. The entrance is hidden beneath the arches below, tucked between art galleries and restaurants. Otherwise, this church is best admired from across the square, particularly when overlooking seasonal Christmas and Easter markets.

Convent of St. Agnes
(Klášter Sv. Anežky České)

U Milosrdných 17; tel. +420 778 725 086; www.ngprague.cz; Tue-Sun 10am-6pm, Wed 10am-8pm; 220 CZK; tram: Dlouhá třída

One of the National Gallery's most peaceful properties houses a vast collection of religious art and a relaxing sculpture garden that wraps around the building. This is one of Old Town's less frequented sights, providing a mellow experience compared to the nearby sights in Old Town Square.

The convent's namesake, St. Agnes of Bohemia, was canonized in 1989, the same year then-Czechoslovakia gained independence from Communist rule. She helped to found this convent, now a museum, in the early 13th century. The lower level includes her grave, with signage explaining the legend of her missing remains, along with a children's room and 12 sculpture fragments that visitors are able to touch (intended to

Learning at least some of the local names for monuments, metro stations, and neighborhoods will help visitors immensely when trying to navigate Prague more easily. Some names, including Old Town Square and Wenceslas Square, have become relatively common translations in English conversation; others not so much. A couple tips:

- Most names that include "Náměstí" (meaning "square" and pronounced "NAHM-yes-tee") sound odd in any form other than Czech, even to the resident English speakers. So although Náměstí Republiky translates to Republic Square, stick to Czech names when asking for directions.

- English signage, particularly around public transportation, is extremely limited. For example, you won't find signs for "Old Town Square" around the metro stations or street signs, but looking for "Staroměstská" will get you to Old Town.

Street signs are usually written in Czech.

- On public transit, tram and metro stops are only announced in Czech. Keep your ears tuned to make sure you don't miss your stop. (Staying quiet is polite anyway, as tram and metro rides are a place for either silence or very quiet conversation.)

provide a tactile experience for visually impaired visitors).

The upper levels of the museum contain a vast collection of medieval religious art from 1200-1550, including more than 30 representations of the Madonna (in a wide range of skin tones) ranging from nursing mothers to a fierce protectress standing on top of a lion. Descriptions in Czech and English offer explanations of symbolism. It would take at least 90 minutes to appreciate every installation in the 15 rooms. Choose your pace based on interest and stamina, skip ahead when desired, and take breaks on cushioned benches spread throughout the exhibit as needed.

St. Agnes's **outdoor sculpture gardens** (daily 10am-4pm Nov-Feb, 10am-6pm Mar-May and Sep-Oct, 10am-10pm Jun-Aug; free), renovated in 2016, are a hidden gem—go now, before they're discovered en masse. Enter from a gate along the riverbank, just west of Loď Pivovar (a restaurant and brewery on a boat), or near the main entrance of the

convent. The benches and grass near the convent entrance are a popular place to relax after visiting the convent, but don't miss a walk all the way around the building to find hidden sculptures from Czech artists tucked under trees and into corners. To refuel after a visit, stop by nearby **Sisters Bistro** for open-faced sandwiches called chlebíčky or **Perníčkův sen** for a gingerbread pick-me-up.

Rudolfinum

Alšovo nábřeží 12; tel. +420 227 059 227;
www.rudolfinum.cz; tram or metro: Staroměstská

This concert hall has played host to more than just incredible symphonies. After hosting classical concerts and gallery exhibitions from 1885-1918, the Rudolfinum became the home of the new Czechoslovakian parliament. Concert halls were renovated into meeting rooms and didn't return to a home of culture until the midst of World War II, when it housed the German Philharmonic from 1942-1945 and served as a meeting place for Nazi officials.

This period of German occupation spawned a legend around the statues lining the rooftop. In the novel *Mendelssohn Is on the Roof*, Reinhard Heydrich (one of Hitler's high-ranking deputies) orders the statue of Jewish composer Felix Mendelssohn-Bartholdy to be removed. The fictional plot sends two workers to the roof who don't know which one Mendelssohn is, and they almost demolish Richard Wagner, one of Hitler's favorite German composers, because of his large nose. While this story is often repeated as factual by walking-tour guides, none of them are able to point out the statue of Wagner on the rooftop. Wagner was never actually part of the crowd, but you can find Bach, Beethoven, Mendelssohn, and Mozart.

Today this building is home to the Czech Philharmonic Orchestra and serves as one of the premiere venues of the Prague Spring Festival. The lower floors of the building hold a free gallery space (www.galerierudolfinum.cz) and children's interactive exhibitions, as well as a column-lined café (www.rudolfinumcafe.cz), accessible on the lower left side of the building while facing the entrance.

Jewish Quarter
(Josefov)

Prague's Jewish Quarter, tucked into the river bend around Old Town, has roots as early as the 10th century. This former ghetto was officially walled in after a 13th-century decree requiring the separation of Jewish and Christian communities. Restrictions lightened in the 16th century under Rudolf II, who worked with many Jewish families involved in banking, then tightened again under Maria-Theresa in the 17th century. An Edict of Tolerance was finally granted in 1781 by Emperor Josef II, namesake of the neighborhood.

One of the darker reasons that Prague's Jewish Quarter is more intact than its Central European neighbors was Hitler's affinity for Prague. The Nazi dictator's plans to establish a "monument to an extinguished race" kept the bombs of World War II from demolishing

the area. This horrific intention resulted in the preservation of centuries-old streets and synagogues from an inhumane era of occupation, so that today's visitors can focus on the rich, vast history of the Jewish community in Prague.

The majority of sights, including the Old Jewish Cemetery and Pinkas Synagogue, are managed by the **Jewish Museum** (www.jewishmuseum.cz), which includes packaged admission (350 CZK) to a collection of seven buildings and sites. A combination ticket to the Jewish Town of Prague (420 CZK) also includes admission to the Old-New Synagogue, which is the only sight available to purchase individually (100 CZK). Tickets may be purchased at the Pinkas Synagogue, the Klausen Synagogue, the Information and Reservations Center located at Maiselova 15, or online.

Interested parties could easily spend multiple days exploring Josefov. There is a quiet air of reverence and remembrance around the individual sights and synagogues, but the surrounding streets are full of modern life, hotels, and some of the city's most high-end shopping on Pařížská Street. Most religious sites around the neighborhood are closed on Saturdays, but the restaurants, cafés, and designer shops remain open. The seclusion of previous centuries has faded away, with the area now existing as a part of tourist trails and daily life in the city center.

When visiting the sights below, note that shoulders should be covered, and men will be required to wear a head covering in some locations.

Old-New Synagogue
(Staronová Synagoga)

Červená; tel. +420 224 800 812 or +420 224 800 813; www.synagogue.cz; Sun-Thu 9am-5pm Nov-Mar, Sun-Thu 9am-6pm Apr-Oct, Fridays until one hour before Shabbat; 100 CZK; metro and tram: Staroměstská

The Old-New Synagogue holds the title of oldest working synagogue in all of Europe. Originally known as "New" or "Great" when it was built in the 13th century, the ironic name developed when younger buildings popped up in the 16th century. The simplicity of the high ceilings, arched Gothic windows, and dark ironwork inside provide a contrast to the more ornate embellishments of its neighbors.

Legend surrounds the attic, which is said to house a giant clay creature created by Rabbi Löw sometime around 1590. The Rabbi supposedly created the mythical Golem to protect the Jewish community from harm, and then put him to bed every Friday night to rest for the Sabbath. When the Golem's temper began to turn more Frankenstein than friend, the Rabbi put him into long-term hibernation in the attic, where he waits to be awakened if needed again. The attic remains off limits to visitors today, so consider yourself safe. The building is also rumored to have survived for so long, through fires and wars, under the protective cover of angel wings transformed into doves.

Guided tours (80 CZK) held in English around 10:30am or 2pm (other times available upon request) can help to add context and legend to the experience. Visit the Information and Reservations Center, located at Maiselova 15, in person to confirm that day's availability.

The Old-New Synagogue is not part of the Jewish museum, but entrance can be combined with entrance to all Jewish Museum sights under the Jewish Town of Prague ticket (420 CZK). You can purchase an advanced ticket (90 CZK) to just the Old-New Synagogue online at www.synagogue.cz.

Old Jewish Cemetery
(Starý Židovský Hřbitov)

Široká 3; tel. +420 222 749 211; www.jewishmuseum. cz; daily 9am-4:30pm Nov-Mar, 9am-6pm Apr-Oct; entry covered by Jewish Museum ticket (350 CZK); metro and tram: Staroměstská

Roughly 12,000 crooked headstones are crowded into the Old Jewish Cemetery, likely representing thousands more buried below. Many of the gravestones, ranging from the early 15th century to 1787, are marked with symbols connected to their occupations or family names. You're likely to find a crowd

around Rabbi Löw in connection with the tale of the Golem at the Old-New Synagogue. Wandering the narrow paths through the graves is both a peaceful and powerful experience, illustrating the confinement that this community endured along with a warm reverence of maintaining the tradition of honoring these lives. Instead of flowers, you may spot evidence of the Jewish tradition of leaving small rocks on top of individual headstones. This historic resting place is tucked just off the Vltava riverbank near the Rudolfinum Concert Hall. Wheelchair access to the cemetery is available from the exit at U Starého Hřbitova street.

★ Pinkas Synagogue and Holocaust Memorial
(Pinkasova Synagoga)

Široká 3; tel. +420 222 749 211; www.jewishmuseum.cz; daily 9am-4:30pm Nov-Mar, 9am-6pm Apr-Oct; entry covered by Jewish Museum ticket (350 CZK); metro and tram: Staroměstská

The second-oldest synagogue in Prague, built in 1535, now functions as a somber memorial to nearly 80,000 victims of the Shoah (a Hebrew word meaning calamity or destruction, and now used as a preferred term by many in the Jewish community for the Holocaust). Names, grouped both by family name and the victims' Bohemian and Moravian hometowns, were handwritten on the synagogue's interior walls between 1992-1996 to create this moving site of remembrance.

Continue through a hall of drawings made by children who were held at the Jewish ghetto of Terezín while en route to the concentration camps at Treblinka or Auschwitz. The pictures were saved by Friedl Dicker-Brandeis, who taught art classes while also held at Terezín (1942-1944) to help the youngest residents process their emotions. She hid the drawings in two suitcases when she was transported from the premises, resulting in their preservation. The drawings are a heart-wrenching (and, for many, tear-inducing) combination of happy memories and expressions of despair.

A visit to the Pinkas Synagogue may be emotional, but it is important. It embodies the notion from philosopher George Santayana that "Those who cannot remember the past are condemned to repeat it." The Pinkas Synagogue is not accessible to travelers who use a wheelchair.

NEW TOWN
(Nové Město)
Republic Square
(Náměstí Republiky)

This northeastern side of New Town holds an incredible collection of original architectural styles. From the curve of Na Příkopě street you are surrounded by the dark Gothic stone of the Powder Tower, the swirling art nouveau elegance of the Municipal House, the columned entrance of the Empire-style **Hybernia Theater,** the sturdy International façade of the **Czech National Bank,** and the stark gray cement of the KB banking building.

Powder Tower
(Prašná Brána)

Náměstí Republiky 5; tel. +420 725 847 875; www.prague.eu/en/object/places/102/powder-gate-tower-prasna-brana; 10am-6pm Oct-Jun, 9am-9pm Jul-Aug, 10am-7pm Sep; 150 CZK; tram or metro: Náměstí Republiky

The Powder Tower is named for one of its many previous uses: storing gunpowder in the 18th century. Centuries before, this 1475 Gothic tower marked the historical entrance to Old Town and the beginning of the royal coronation route to the Prague Castle. Admission gains you access to a spiral staircase of 186 stone steps and an overview of the Old Town that is often less crowded, and shared less often on social media, than the iconic bird's eye view from Charles Bridge Towers. Otherwise, and if there are no cars coming, take a quick detour off the sidewalk and strut underneath the arch connecting

New Town to Old Town with your best royal posture. Entrance to the Powder Tower is discounted by 50 percent for the first hour after opening. No elevator or wheelchair access available.

Municipal House
(Obecní Dům)

Náměstí Republiky 5; tel. +420 222 002 101; www.obecnidum.cz; daily 10am-8pm; tours 200 CZK; tram or metro: Náměstí Republiky

This modern-day concert hall has been instrumental in the country's political history. On October 28, 1918, the independent state of Czechoslovakia was announced from its balcony, and later Václav Havel, first president of the Czech Republic, held his early meetings with Communist-era Prime Minister Ladislav Adamec inside these halls.

The Municipal House was built on the site of the King's Court in the 14th-15th centuries, which served as the residence of Bohemian kings during that period. The art nouveau exterior reflects the decadence of the early 20th century and symbolizes part of the Czech National Revival leading up to the First Republic of Czechoslovakia. The swirling exterior includes a mosaic entitled an "Homage to Prague" framed by a quote from Svatopluk Čech, proclaiming, "Hail to you Prague! Defy time and malice as you have weathered all storms throughout the ages!"

The interior holds a number of concert spaces, most notably **Smetana Hall,** which serves as home to the Prague Symphony Orchestra (FOK) and where the Prague Spring Music Festival kicks off each year. Access to the upstairs halls require concert tickets or guided tours (200-600 CZK) that you can book online (www.obecnidum.cz) or at the Municipal House box office on the left side of the ground floor between 10am-8pm. Feel free to wander the bottom floors to admire the art nouveau details in the pricey, ornately decorated restaurant and café (beers around 100 CZK).

1: Prague's art nouveau Municipal House and Gothic Powder Tower 2: the (actually rectangular) Wenceslas Square 3: passageway inside Palac Lucerna 4: peaceful Franciscan Gardens

Alfons Mucha Museum

Panská 7; tel. +420 224 216 415; www.mucha.cz; daily 10am-6pm; 300 CZK; tram: Jindřišska, metro: Můstek

While the art nouveau movement is generally associated with Paris, one of its original innovators is an undeniably local hero, Alfons Mucha. This three-room museum offers an easy introduction to one of the most revered Czech artists, whose work contributed to the beauty of the Municipal House and St. Vitus Cathedral.

After growing up in the South Moravian region of the Czech Republic, Mucha made his name doing interior decoration for the aristocracy of the Austro-Hungarian Empire and designing theatrical posters in Paris that ultimately established his signature swirling designs. Later in life, he returned to his homeland to focus on more political works that captured the essence of the Czech character.

Admire the theatrical posters in the front of the museum, and don't miss the 30-minute video about his life tucked into the rear of the building. Before you leave, stop by the adjoining gift shop for a wide range of sophisticated souvenirs to delight the art fan in your life.

Wenceslas Square
(Václavské Náměstí)

This center of economic activity and political change may not look like much more than a business district at first glance, but the streets around this long rectangular "square" have witnessed some world-changing history. The only hints of its early 14th-century days as Koňský trh (Horse Market) are the massive statue of St. Wenceslas, the patron saint of the Czech Republic, on horseback at the top of the square. The highway dividing the square from the National Museum was renamed Wilsonova in 1989, a symbolic departure from its previous name, Vítězného února (Victorious February) that marked the Communist takeover in 1948.

Today the busy square holds pieces of past and present influences. **The National Museum** (Václavské náměstí 68; www.

nm.cz), with its domed rooftop and arched windows sits at the top of the square, behind the statue of St. Wenceslas (known as Vaclav in Czech). The museum reopened in 2019 after a decade of renovations and small fires, but is generally regarded as more impressive from the outside than for its interior exhibits. It was built alongside the National Theater and Municipal House as part of the Czech National Revival, a late-19th century effort to reclaim a sense of national pride and cultural identity. The revival movement eventually led to the establishment of an independent Czechoslovakia in 1918 and the glamorous First Republic era.

Today, international shopping outlets, tourist-focused restaurants, hotels, and fast-food chains occupy many of the historic buildings surrounding Wenceslas Square. The city has long-term plans to revitalize this pedestrian space and bring local life back to the center. For now, take a walk through the benches engraved with inspirational quotes that line the center islands and absorb the years of political protests that marked this space over the years. As recently as 2020, Czech citizens packed these streets to express their discontent with the local government.

Main Post Office
(Hlavní Pošta)

Jindřišská 14; tel. +420 221 131 111; 2am-midnight; free; tram: Václavské náměstí, metro: Muzeum or Můstek

Even if you have nothing to mail, the Main Post Office is worth a peek inside. Look up: Swirling frescoed designs line the walls around arched windows beneath a vaulted glass ceiling. A shop in the corner sells stationery, stickers, and packing materials, but whether or not the employees working at the counters speak English is hit-or-miss. Stop in almost any time—the building only closes between midnight and 2am—but stick to mental pictures to avoid a reprimand from the security staff. Photography is not allowed inside this government building.

★ Palac Lucerna

Štěpánská 61; tel. +420 224 224 537; www.lucerna.cz; free; passage open 24 hours; tram: Václavské náměstí

Prague's city center is filled with covered passageways, known as "pasáž" in Czech, that connect the cafés, shops, and venues housed in the buildings that surround them. In the early 1900s, Palac Lucerna (Lantern Palace) was the first of these shopping and culture centers built in the Czech Republic. The design and construction were carried out by Vácslav Havel, grandfather of future president Václav Havel. Today, one of the biggest draws for visitors is the highly photographable David Černý sculpture hanging from its domed ceiling. In contrast to the proud statue of St. Wenceslas on the square outside, Černý's rider sits astride an upside-down horse, with rumors that the saint's face resembles various modern politicians.

The hallways surrounding the sculpture lead to the historic 1909 **Kino Lucerna** cinema, a glamorous First Republic-style café in **Kavárna Lucerna,** and one of Prague's longest-running dance clubs, **Lucerna Music Bar.** In the summer, a new rooftop bar called **Střecha Lucerny** (www.strechalucerny.cz; 100 CZK entry) draws laid-back, all-ages crowds to enjoy the views from this central vantage point between 2pm-sunset from May-October.

Franciscan Gardens
(Františkánská Zahrada)

Jungmannovo náměstí; tel. +420 221 097 231; daily 7am-10pm mid-Apr to mid-Sept, 7am-8pm mid-Sept to mid-Oct, 8am-7pm mid-Oct to mid-Apr; free; tram: Václavské náměstí

This peaceful, relaxing outdoor garden hidden in an inner courtyard provides an escape from busy Wenceslas Square. The pace of life is slow in this little oasis, with families enjoying ice cream on benches surrounded by latticed fences covered in rose vines. The tall, arched windows and red rooftops of the massive Church of Our Lady of the Snows watches over the children's playground near its base. Take a

moment to imagine the Prague landscape if this house of worship extended all the way to the Vltava River's edge, as originally planned. Lighthearted sculptures and a bubbling fountain round out the overall sense of calm.

The Franciscan Gardens are accessible from the Svetozor Passage on Vodičkova Street or an unmarked gate tucked into the back corner of Jungmannovo náměstí. Stop by **Café Truhlárna,** on the west side of the garden near Jungmannovo náměstí, for coffee and pastries.

Charles Square
(Karlovo Náměstí)

The most residential part of New Town stretches from Prague's National Theater along the Vltava riverbank and around the larger rectangular park of Karlovo náměstí, yet another site named for the beloved King Charles IV. The square, established in 1348, was also known as the Cattle Market (Dobytčí trh) or the New Town Square, for its proximity to the New Town Hall (Novoměstská radnice).

These days, the square is more likely to serve as a site of relaxation than radical protest. The two rectangular halves of green space are divided by busy streets of tram tracks and traffic, but inside the border of trees and flowered gardens a Baroque fountain, curving pathways, and benches to rest your feet cultivate a peaceful vibe.

NEW TOWN HALL
(Novoměstská Radnice)

Karlovo náměstí 1; tel. +420 224 948 225; www. novomestskaradnice.cz; Tue-Sun 10am-6pm spring-autumn (dependent on weather); 60 CZK; tram: Novoměstská radnice, metro: Karlovo náměstí

The Gothic Tower of the New Town Hall in the corner of Karlovo náměstí was the site of Prague's First Defenestration (the act of throwing someone, usually an authority figure, out a window). In 1419, an angry crowd of Jan Hus's followers demanded the release of Protestant prisoners before tossing seven council members from the tower, an early

Student Protests and Occupations

Political demonstrations and celebrations have often centered around Wenceslas Square and the surrounding streets of New Town.

memorial commemorating the protest of 1989

- **Celebration of Czechoslovakia's independence (Oct 28, 1918):** Crowds gathered on Wenceslas Square to celebrate the newfound independence of Czechoslovakia from the Austro-Hungarian Empire. This day remains a national holiday, and 2018 marked joyful celebrations of the 100th anniversary, even though Czechoslovakia doesn't technically exist today.

- **Student protests against German invasion (Oct 28, 1939):** Student protesters marked the anniversary of Czech independence by taking to the streets, including Old Town Square and Wenceslas Square, to express outrage against the growing German occupation of Czechoslovakia. When German soldiers tried to get the crowds under control, a young medical student, Jan Opletal, was shot in the stomach and died in the hospital.

- **Anti-Nazi protests (Nov 15, 1939):** A funeral for Jan Opletal, the man who was killed in protests just weeks earlier, turned into another spontaneous anti-Nazi protest. In response, German soldiers raided the dormitories and executed nine of the student organizers behind the events on November 17, 1939. Nazi occupation continued until the end of World War II. Opletalova Street, running from Wenceslas Square to Prague's main train station (Hlavní nádraží), is named after the man who sacrificed his life, and November 17 became known as International Students' Day.

- **Student protests against the Soviet occupation (1969):** To protest the restrictive Soviet occupation under the Communist government, young philosophy student Jan Palach lit himself on fire in Wenceslas Square on January 16, 1969. A second act of self-immolation, by student Jan Zajíc, occurred on February 25, 1969. Despite their extreme efforts, Soviet occupation continued for another 20 years. A cross in bricks in front of the National Museum marks the spot where Palach lit himself on fire, and a sculptural memorial near Rudolfinum commemorates both Palach and his mother's grief.

- **International Students' Day anniversary (Nov 1989):** By November 17, 1989, the Berlin Wall had crumbled and Communist regimes were falling around Europe. Students gathered at Vyšehrad for a demonstration to mark the 50th anniversary of their outspoken predecessors and to express their desire for independence. Thousands of citizens joined the march along the Vltava River toward Wenceslas Square, but were stopped and brutally attacked by riot police. A memorial of hands reaching out from Národní třída street pays tribute to this massacre.

- **Celebrations of independence from Communism (Dec 1989):** The November demonstrations led to the formation of the Civic Forum and its elected leader Václav Havel. Demonstrations continued for weeks in Wenceslas Square, with protesters jingling their keys in the air to symbolize time for the Communist government to go home. Top officials resigned within weeks, and Havel was officially elected president on December 29, 1989. Chants of "Havel na hrad" (Havel to the castle) marked the end of the Velvet Revolution, named for its casualty-free (if not entirely peaceful) transition of power.

act of the religious conflict that led to the Hussite Wars.

Visitors can get an up-close look at the site of the historic action, plus views of the surrounding area, by climbing the tower's 221 wooden steps. Entrance also includes an exhibit on the history of the area in a former guard's apartment and a small art gallery.

National Monument to the Heroes of the Heydrich Terror
(Národní Památník Hrdinů Heydrichiády)

Resslova 9a; tel. +420 222 540 718 or +420 720 988 421; www.vhu.cz; Tue-Sun 9am-5pm; free; tram or metro: Karlovo náměstí

The National Monument to the Heroes of the Heydrich Terror is a moving tribute to one brave act of World War II resistance efforts. The memorial is in the basement of the Baroque Church of Sts. Cyril and Methodius, which played an important role in the story. After successfully assassinating Reinhard Heydrich, one of Hitler's top deputies, the small group of men who carried out the plan took refuge inside this church, where they hid for weeks from a city-wide manhunt. This eventually led to a standoff with the Nazi army that ended in their deaths. You'll find a plaque that describes the events (in Czech) flanked by small statues of a paratrooper and a priest outside the church above original bullet holes on the church wall. The year 1942 is also embedded in the sidewalk below the plaque.

Inside the free memorial is a small exhibition of letters and photos in glass cases that tell the stories of the soldiers in both Czech and English. Visitors may also enter the crypt where most of the men ultimately lost their lives. The Church of Sts. Cyril and Methodius itself is only open during Orthodox masses on Sundays. The separate entrance to the memorial is located at street level beside steps to the church.

Dancing House
(Tančící Dům)

Jiraskovo Namesti 6; observation deck 9am-midnight; tram: Jiráskovo náměstí

The twisted glass-and-stone walls of the Dancing House look like a hand reached out of the clouds and squeezed one corner of the skyline, yet somehow it blends seamlessly into the city landscape. The architectural landmark stands on a site accidentally bombed by the American army in 1945, which stood empty until after the Velvet Revolution.

the Dancing House

Heroes of the Resistance: The Anthropoid Mission

Prague is known for its history of foreign rulers and occupations, but the local character is also defined by acts of resistance from brave, everyday citizens standing up to injustice in the face of impossible odds. The Anthropoid mission of 1942 is one of these stories, recently catching Hollywood's attention with two English-language films (the painstakingly researched *Anthropoid* in 2016 and Heydrich-focused *The Man with the Iron Heart* in 2017). Spoilers ahead, in case you want to watch them first.

A pair of paratroopers living in exile during World War II were sent back to Czechoslovakia in late 1941 with a daunting task—to assassinate Reinhard Heydrich, one of Hitler's cruelest deputies who was nicknamed "The Butcher of Prague." Josef Gabčík and Jan Kubiš teamed up with a small group of fellow dissidents, who often risked their lives to house or meet with the men. The group observed the Nazi leader's movements and concocted a plan.

bullet holes in a church remain from the Anthropoid mission

On May 27, 1942, they stopped Heydrich's car in the outskirts of the city, en route to the Prague Castle. Josef Gabčík jumped in front of the car and attempted to shoot Heydrich, but his gun failed. Jan Kubiš turned to Plan B and tossed a grenade toward the car. Its blast lodged a piece of metal into Heydrich's body. The Anthropoid team retreated and Heydrich was taken to the hospital, where he died from infection roughly one week later.

A seven-man team went into hiding, eventually given sanctuary inside the Church of Sts. Cyril and Methodius. Their location was given up by a fellow paratrooper, Karel Čurda, resulting in a standoff at the church on June 18, 1942. The men opened fire on the Nazi army when they entered, and took refuge in the basement, where they were attacked with tear gas and rising water. Five men saved their last bullets to take their own lives and avoid capture. Many of the families who housed them turned to cyanide capsules to avoid interrogation. Nazi retaliation for the assassination wiped out the village of Lidice and killed hundreds more.

The modern collaboration between two 20th-century architects, Canadian-American Frank Gehry and Croatian-Czech Vlado Milunić, was inspired by the shape of famous dancing couple Fred Astaire and Ginger Rogers, after whom the top-floor restaurant is named. Its tension and intertwined embrace between the materials also represents the mid-1990s state of the Czech Republic, blending respect for the past while charging optimistically into the future, navigating cultural influences of East and West. Visitors often stop by purely to pose for silly photographs, staged as pinching or kicking its exterior from across the street (similar to Italy's Leaning Tower of Pisa), but there are reasons to venture inside as well.

The ground floor houses a small gallery (www.galerietancicidum.cz), with the lovely boutique Dancing House Hotel (www.dancinghousehotel.com) and office space occupying the middle floors. The overpriced Fred and Ginger restaurant shares the top floor with the more worthwhile Glass Bar (www.galerietancicidum.cz/glass-bar-en), whose observation deck wraps around the twisted metal orb on top of the building and offers 360-degree views of the Vltava River, the Prague Castle, and city skylines. The small observation platform, with binoculars on the edges and limited bench seating in the center, can get crowded on summer afternoons but is often peaceful in the morning, after dark, and during off-seasons.

★ Náplavka Boardwalk
(Rašínovo nábřeží)

Náplavka, stretching from Slovansky Island to the Výtoň tram and ferry stops; tel. +420 222 013 618; www.prazskenaplavky.cz; free; tram: Palackého náměstí, metro: Karlovo náměstí

Náplavka Boardwalk (also called the Náplavka Embankment, Rašín Embankment, or simply Náplavka) is a roughly 1.2-km (0.75-mi) cobblestone walkway below street level along the Vltava River. Year-round, it's the staging place for Saturday farmers markets, food festivals, or just midweek evening strolls. Visitors are welcome to bring their own food and drink as well, drawing crowds of swans to beg for crumbs from anyone dangling their legs over the edge.

An extensive renovation project completed in 2020 added enormous glass lenses as doorways that swivel to open underground vaults lining the retaining walls. A series of cafés with minimalist décor inside these vaults (called "kobky" in Czech) also serve café tables outdoors. At the time of writing, many of the cafés had delayed openings or fluctuating hours under COVID-19 restrictions, but most have plans to operate in heated spaces year-round. A series of boat bars also dock in this area, including Lod' Tajemstvi's **Ship Of Secrets** (http://lodtajemstvi.cz), which hosts live music, and the floating beer garden on **Lod' Pavla.**

You can access the Náplavka Embankment via ramps and stairs at various points from around the Dancing House all the way to the railway bridge just below Vyšehrad. You can also catch a five-minute ride on one of the small summer ferry boats here, included in the Prague public transport system, to the opposite riverbank of Smíchovská náplavka. Ferries run every 10-15 minutes from 8am-8pm, April-October.

LESSER TOWN
(Malá Strana)
Charles Bridge
(Karlův Most)

Karlův most; free; tram: Malostranské náměstí or Staroměstská

Construction of the Charles Bridge famously began in 1357 on July 9 at 5:31am, based on Charles IV's belief (from numerology and astrology) that 1-3-5-7-9-7-5-3-1 would bring good luck. Whether he was right, or whether the rumored combination of eggs, wine, or milk mixed into the foundations kept the oldest of Prague's bridges safe for centuries, is one of the structure's many secrets. Thirty Baroque statues along the edges of the bridge were installed between the late 17th century and 1928, upping the landmark's visual appeal.

CROSSING CHARLES BRIDGE

Crossing the bridge begins by passing through glorious Gothic splendor under the arches of the **Old Town Bridge Tower** (Staroměstská mostecká věž) on one side and the **Lesser Town Bridge Towers** (Malostranské mostecké věže) of Malá Strana on the other. These famous figures include **St. Wenceslas in prayer** on your right as you enter from Malá Strana, and **Sts. Cyril and Methodius,** credited for bringing Christianity to the area, baptizing the Czechs and Slovaks. They're the fifth statue on your right entering from Old Town.

By far the most popular statue is **St. John of Napomuk,** crowned with a golden halo of five stars near the center of the bridge. St. John was famously martyred by King Wenceslas IV for either jealousy or politics—protecting the confessional secrets of Queen Sofia, or disrespecting Wenceslas by confirming a monastery without his permission—depending on who you ask. Although it's a custom with little cultural or historical credibility, many tourists stop to rub the image of Sofia at the base of his statue, as well as an unrelated dog engraved on the left side, based on an urban tour guide

Lesser Town, Prague Castle District, and Petřín

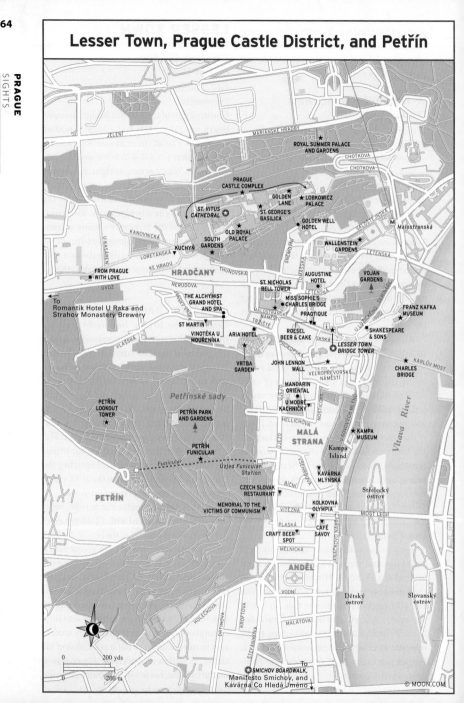

MARIANSKÉ HRADBY

JELENÍ

CHOTKOVA

★ ROYAL SUMMER PALACE
AND GARDENS

CHOTKOVA

PRAGUE
CASTLE COMPLEX ★

GOLDEN
LANE ★

★ LOBKOWICZ
PALACE

ST. VITUS ★
CATHEDRAL ✚

ST. GEORGE'S
BASILICA

● GOLDEN WELL
HOTEL

M Malostranská

KANOVNICKÁ

U KASÁREN

OLD ROYAL
PALACE

VALDŠTEJNSKÁ

SOUTH
GARDENS ★

★ WALLENSTEIN ★
GARDENS

LETENSKÁ

KUCHYŇ ▼

LORETÁNSKÁ

KE HRADU

HRADČANY

THUNOVSKÁ

SNĚMOVNÍ

● FROM PRAGUE
WITH LOVE

AUGUSTINE
HOTEL ●

VOJAN ★
GARDENS

ÚVOZ

NERUDOVA

ST. NICHOLAS ★
BELL TOWER

LETENSKÁ

To
Romantik Hotel U Raka and
Strahov Monastery Brewery

THE ALCHYMIST
GRAND HOTEL
AND SPA ●

MISS SOPHIE'S ●
CHARLES BRIDGE

U LUŽICKÉHO SEMINÁŘE

FRANZ KAFKA ★
MUSEUM

MALOSTRANSKÉ
NÁMĚSTÍ

PRAGTIQUE ●

ŠAŠKA

ST MARTIN ▼

● i

SHAKESPEARE ★
& SONS

VINOTÉKA U
MOUŘENÍNA ●

ARIA HOTEL ●

ROESEL ●
BEER & CAKE

LESSER TOWN ★
BRIDGE TOWER

VLAŠSKÁ

PROKOPSKÁ

KARLŮV MOST

VRTBA ●
GARDEN

JOHN LENNON ●
WALL

VELKOPŘEVORSKÉ
NÁMĚSTÍ

CHARLES ★
BRIDGE

Petřínské sady

ÚJEZD

MANDARIN ●
ORIENTAL

NOSTICOVA

Vltava River

PETŘÍN
LOOKOUT
TOWER ★

PETŘÍN PARK
AND GARDENS ♣

U MODRÉ ●
KACHNIČKY

HELLICHOVA

MALÁ
STRANA

★ KAMPA
MUSEUM

PETŘÍN
FUNICULAR ★

Funicular

Újezd Funicular
Station

Kampa
Island

ŘÍČNÍ

KAVÁRNA
MLÝNSKÁ ▼

Střelecký
ostrov

PETŘÍN

VŠEHRDOVA

CZECH SLOVAK
RESTAURANT ▼

KOLKOVNA
OLYMPIA ▼

MOST LEGIÍ

MEMORIAL TO THE
VICTIMS OF COMMUNISM ★

VÍTĚZNÁ

PLASKÁ

CAFÉ ▼
SAVOY

CRAFT BEER ●
SPOT

MĚLNICKÁ

ANDĚL

VODNÍ

Dětský
ostrov

Slovanský
ostrov

HOLEČKOVA

DŘÍTÍNOVA

KROFTOVA

MALÁTOVA

ŠTEFÁNIKOVA

0   200 yds

0   200 m

To
● SMÍCHOV BOARDWALK,
Manifesto Smíchov, and
Kavárna Co Hledá Uměno

© MOON.COM

myth that this brings either good luck or a return visit to Prague.

An ornate plaque of swirling iron a few steps to the right of St. John of Napomuk's statue marks the site where his body was thrown into the Vltava River on Wenceslas's orders. Please don't attach any "love locks" to this essential grave marker—or really on any historical bridge in the city. A local preservation group removes them monthly to maintain structural integrity, and a photo is a much better way to commemorate a romantic moment.

Crossing the bridge can take anywhere from 7-20 minutes, depending on your ability to dodge selfie sticks.

During peak seasons, this popular pedestrian bridge is generally packed with people. You'll need to be up at dawn with the photographers, stumbling home in the early morning hours, or visiting on an off-peak weekday in questionable weather to catch a quiet moment. To avoid pedestrian traffic jams, be mindful of the people around you while you pause to admire the details of statues and monuments.

★ CHARLES BRIDGE TOWERS

www.prague.eu; daily 10am-6pm Oct-June, 9am-9pm July-Aug, 10am-7pm Sept; 150 CZK each or 225 CZK combined ticket

Visitors can climb two towers that flank the bridge: the Old Town Bridge Tower (Staroměstská mostecká věž, www.prague.eu/en/object/places/197/old-town-bridge-tower-staromestska-mostecka-vez) on one side, and the taller of the two Lesser Town Bridge Towers (Malostranské mostecké věže, www.prague.eu/en/object/places/204/lesser-town-bridge-towers-malostranske-mostecke-veze) on the Malá Strana side. Entrance to either viewing tower is accessible from 9am or 10am to roughly sunset, depending on the time of year, offering a coveted bird's-eye view over the hordes of tourists below. In both towers, landings along the stairwells that lead to the viewing platform also hold very small exhibits on the history and construction of the bridge, which are included in the ticket price.

It requires patience (and maybe a little luck) to get a prime spot in either tower around sunset, but the views are worth the wait. The most popular view from the Old Town Bridge Tower looks out at the Prague Castle over the Vltava River. The Lesser Town Bridge Tower is usually a slightly less crowded experience, with 360-degree views overlooking the Malá Strana neighborhood and the river toward Old Town. Splurge on both perspectives to document the city with photographs of every direction.

Admission to either tower is discounted 50 percent during the first hour of opening. Note there is no wheelchair access available or much space to social distance.

John Lennon Wall
(Zeď Johna Lennona)

Velkopřevorské náměstí; free; tram: Malostranské náměstí or Hellichova

John Lennon never visited Czechoslovakia, but his messages of peace and rebellious spirit still managed to reach the hearts of its residents. The John Lennon Wall was born shortly after Lennon's assassination in 1980, when an unknown artist covered the wall surrounding a courtyard with Beatles lyrics alongside the singer's likeness. Under Communist rule, which prohibited Western music and influences, this was a criminal act. The wall was painted over multiple times, but never stayed blank for very long.

In November of 2014, 25 years after the Velvet Revolution, the wall was completely whitewashed by a group of local art students who left only the words "Wall Is Over." The group later released a statement saying that they were opening "free space for new messages of the current generation." Prague's art community responded to the challenge, and within days of the event, the interactive monument was covered again with its latest incarnation of peaceful words and political grievances. The Beatles imagery was refreshed again by local artists in March of 2019 to mark the anniversary of the Velvet Revolution, covered with messages about climate change

Prague's Musical History

Music has long been intertwined with Czech culture, from classical composers such as Antonín Dvořák and Bedřich Smetana to the music festivals that fill the countryside each summer. The influence of music has also made its mark on modern-day politics and tourism. Here are a few of my favorite pieces of Czech musical trivia:

- Austria may be able to claim Mozart's birthplace, but the **statue outside the Estates Theater,** where he premiered the opera *Don Giovanni,* is a testament to his notorious love (and, some would argue, preference) for Prague audiences.

- The arrest of the psychedelic band **Plastic People of the Universe** for disturbing the peace under Communist Czechoslovakia helped to inspire the Charter 77 petition of 1976. These signatures became a who's who of political dissidents, many of whom received government retaliation for speaking up for personal freedoms (and for the right to rock and roll).

- Two charismatic political leaders took the stage at **Reduta Jazz Club** for an impromptu saxophone jam session in 1994. A plaque marks the site where Czech President Václav Havel joined US President Bill Clinton onstage for the joy of making music in a democratic society.

- You can thank the **Rolling Stones** for keeping the Prague Castle visible throughout the night. As one of the first rock bands to play in Prague after the fall of Communism, and as friends of President Havel, the band designed and financed the lighting design in 1995.

- Prague has even made its mark on contemporary pop music. The dance club at **Radost FX** (Bělehradská 12; tel. +420 224 254 776; www.radostfx.cz) was featured in Rihanna's music video for the song "Please Don't Stop the Music" in 2007.

- **Metallica** won local praise in 2018 when they performed a cover of 1970s Czech folk classic "Jožin z bažin" ("Jožin of the Swamp") for a packed house. A quick online search for the video, with English subtitles and iconic dance moves, will introduce you to one of the greatest quirky fairy tales ever told in song, and also give you a taste of Czech humor.

by environmental activists in April 2019, and refreshed again in November 2019 for International Students' Day and the Struggle for Freedom and Democracy.

The Knights of Malta (who own this private property) and the city officials have grown increasingly frustrated that the original character of the wall, with portraits of its namesake musician alongside Beatles lyrics and messages of hope, had been overtaken by random graffiti, Instagram handles, and vulgar phrases. A plaque was added to the wall, describing the space as a memorial, and two security cameras now monitor for illegal spray painting throughout the night. If you choose to interact with the wall, please consider the

history, significance, and context of what it symbolizes.

St. Nicholas Bell Tower
(Svatomikulášská Městská Zvonice)

Malostranské náměstí 556/29; tel. +420 725 847 927; www.prague.eu/en/object/places/175/st-nicholas-bell-tower-svatomikulasska-mestska-zvonice; daily 10am-6pm Oct-Jun, 9am-9pm Jul-Aug, 10am-7pm Sep; 150 CZK; tram: Malostranské náměstí

The six floors or platforms of this belfry (which is not actually part of the domed house of worship next door), spread across 215 steps, take you through a decade-by-decade tour of Czech history. Climb the stairs from the bedrooms of 18th-century watchmen, through a shadowy bell tower, all the way up to recreated holographic conversations of the top floor, which was used as a Communist spy center in the 1980s. A multimedia presentation just

---

1: Náplavka Boardwalk 2: memorial to the martyred St. John of Nepomuk on Charles Bridge

below the spy center tells the story of Lesser Town (Malá Strana's) role in resistance efforts from May 5-9, 1945 that led to the end of World War II. Take advantage of 360-degree views of the Charles Bridge and the Prague Castle on both the outdoor gallery level and covered windows of the top floor. Note that the narrow stone staircases and small exhibition spaces provide little room for social distancing, and there are no elevators or wheelchair access available.

Vrtba Garden
(Vrtbovská Zahrada)

Letenská 4; tel. +420 272 088 350 or +420 603 233 912; www.vrtbovska.cz; daily 10am-6pm Apr-Oct; 100 CZK; tram or metro: Malostranské náměstí

Fans of landscape architecture should visit the Italian-style terraces of the Vrtba Garden, with the added bonus of a raised viewpoint over panoramic city skylines and an almost eye-level perspective of the Prague Castle. This quiet, 18th-century oasis decorated with swirling grass, expressive statues of Roman gods, and a curved staircase leading to a hillside pavilion is a popular site for weddings and engagement photos. The entrance, down an unassuming driveway on your right while walking away from St. Nicholas Church on Karmelitská street, can be easy to miss, so keep your eyes peeled for the small sign.

Kampa Museum

U Sovových mlýnů 2; tel. +420 257 286 147; www.museumkampa.cz; noon-6pm Mon-Fri, 10am-6pm Sat-Sun; 190-300 CZK; tram: Hellichova

You can spot Kampa Museum, housed in a former mill inside Park Kampa, from the opposite side of the Vltava River thanks to its line of glowing yellow penguins. The collection of modern art, curated by Jan and Meda Mládek, focuses on Central European artists expressing the struggles of working under oppression in the second half of the 20th century, as well as temporary exhibitions on modern themes. You could spend as little as one hour or an entire afternoon in this space. As you leave, don't miss a photo op with three

of David Černý's creepy-but-cute bronze babies with bar codes for faces, crawling in the grass beside the museum. Discounted tickets offering limited access to specific exhibitions are available.

Franz Kafka Museum

Cihelná 2b; tel. +420 257 535 507; www.kafkamuseum.cz; daily 10am-6pm; 260 CZK; tram or metro: Malostranská

Inside this museum, fans of this complicated literary legend will find letters, diaries, photographs, music, and installations that explore the connection between his most famous works and their underlying connections to the city of his birth. Kafka was raised by German-speaking Jewish parents and was educated in both German and Czech schools in the Czech Republic. Many of his novels were written in German, but he was able to speak and write both languages. A thorough read of extracts from the letters and manuscripts that have been translated into English could take a couple of hours if you want to fully immerse yourself.

Even if you don't step foot inside the museum, it's worth visiting the courtyard, which holds one of David Černý's many controversial sculptures—two men pissing into a pool in the shape of the Czech Republic. To get here, take a riverside walk just north of the Charles Bridge.

PRAGUE CASTLE DISTRICT
(Hradčany)
Prague Castle
(Pražský Hrad)

Pražský hrad; tel. +420 224 372 423 or +420 224 371 111; www.hrad.cz; upper tram: Královský letohrádek, Pražský hrad, or Pohořelec, lower metro: Malostranská or Malostranské náměstí

The name Prague Castle can be a bit misleading. The "castle" is not one building of turrets

---

1: the John Lennon Wall, a living breathing monument **2:** St. Nicholas Bell Tower and Church **3:** Penguins created by the Cracking Art Group line the river behind Kampa Museum.

and royal residences, but actually refers to a massive fortified area of government buildings, churches, museums, and manicured gardens. This roughly 70,000-square-meter area (more than 17 ac) holds the Guinness World Record for the largest castle complex in the world.

The castle's history covers roughly a century of royal families and architectural styles. Duke of Bohemia Bořivoj I and his wife Ludmila founded the castle around the year 880. Future residents included their grandson Wenceslas I (later known as St. Wenceslas), members of the Habsburg royal family, and Thomas Garrigue Masaryk, the first president of Czechoslovakia in 1918. The Prague Castle remains the seat of the Czech president today, with the flag flying on days he (or she) is in town. The stone-faced, unmovable castle guards outside the main Matthias Gates put on a "Changing of the Guards" ceremony at noon, with a smaller version happening every hour from 7am.

The mixed-and-matched architectural style—from the Gothic-Renaissance-Baroque blend of the St. Vitus Cathedral to the Baroque exterior and Romanesque interior of St. George's Basilica—chronicles an ongoing "home improvement" project that stretched from 880 to the early 1900s. You can spot the more modern elements of Slovenian architect Josip Plečnik's 20th-century touches around the grounds.

VISITING THE PRAGUE CASTLE

The Prague Castle can easily be a multi-hour excursion, and visiting every corner would take multiple days. That said, you can pick and choose the areas that interest you most to customize your exploration, and a combination of 2-4 buildings and gardens can be enough to give you a taste of the castle experience. Those in a hurry or on a budget can take a peek inside St. Vitus Cathedral followed by a walk along the South Garden's panoramic city views, both for free. Add on an hour-long visit to the Lobkowicz Palace for a single-admission entrance to explore aristocratic

interiors and an enviable balcony view, plus the optional add-on of an afternoon classical-music concert.

The castle grounds themselves are open from 6am-10pm, while the buildings and museums have shorter hours. Be prepared for a steady stream of tour groups from open to close in high seasons, with slightly more breathing room during off seasons and weekdays.

Ticket options are valid for 2 days and include **Prague Castle—Circuit A** (350 CZK), which comprises St. Vitus Cathedral, the Old Royal Palace, "The Story of Prague Castle" exhibition, St. George's Basilica, Golden Lane with the Daliborka Tower, and Rosenberg Palace. **Prague Castle—Circuit B** (250 CZK), includes St. Vitus Cathedral, the Old Royal Palace, St. George's Basilica, and Golden Lane with the Daliborka Tower. Many areas were closed during the coronavirus pandemic, so confirm availability before purchasing. A pass to photograph the interiors of the Prague Castle requires an additional 50 CZK ticket.

An official **tour guide** in English (100 CZK pp per hour) adds much more color and personalized explanations than an **audio guide** (350 CZK per device for 3 hours, 450 CZK per device per day). To book a guide, visit the information center in the Third Courtyard near the entrance to St. Vitus Cathedral or email info@hrad.cz.

Increased security measures were implemented after protest art group Ztohoven snuck onto the grounds in 2015 and replaced the Czech flag with a giant pair of red boxer shorts. Entrances now require a security checkpoint, no large bags are allowed inside, and drones are prohibited from flying overhead.

ROYAL SUMMER PALACE AND GARDENS
(Letohrádek Královny Anny)

Mariánské hradby 1; tel. +420 224 372 434 or +420 224 372 415; www.hrad.cz; daily 10am-6pm Apr-Oct; free; tram: Královský letohrádek

Sunset Over Prague

sunset beside the river at Náplavka

Thanks to a spire-filled skyline, a hilly landscape, and a local affinity for nature and being out-doors, watching the sunset on a summer evening in Prague is a spectacular experience. Sunsets in Prague happen around 9pm in June and July and roughly 4pm in December or January. Grab a picnic and a partner (or go solo and peaceful) and try any of these prime viewing spots.

- **Náplavka:** Dangle your legs over the edge of this riverside boardwalk between the southern edge of New Town and Vyšehrad and admire the swans on the Vltava River as the evening turns to night (page 63).

- **Riegrovy Park:** The great sloping lawn of this Vinohrady park offers a tree-framed sunset view of the Prague Castle over a sea of red roofs. In the early evening, open space becomes scarce in between couples and families on picnic blankets, dogs curled beside their people, and the occasional Frisbee player or acoustic guitarist setting a soft soundtrack (page 89).

- **Parukářka:** For a quieter contrast to crowd-favorite Riegrovy sady, head farther east to Žižkov's lesser-known park. The steep hills in a slightly grittier setting, with dirt paths and playground structures scattered across the landscape, provide more open space to watch the sun set behind the silhouette of the Žižkov TV Tower.

- **Vítkov Hill:** My personal favorite sunset spot requires a 20-minute gentle climb from the edge of Žižkov up to the courtyard outside the National Memorial on Vítkov Hill (U Památníku; www.nm.cz). Find a seat on the stairs or stand underneath the massive equestrian statue of Jan Žižka and survey the lands of Old Town, New Town, Karlín, and Malá Strana. This lesser-known vantage point in the outskirts of Prague provides a quieter experience to end the day (page 80).

For a peaceful start to your castle tour during the warmer months, use the smaller entrance one tram stop before the main entrance at **Queen Anne's Summer Palace and Royal Gardens.** The 16th-century Italian Renaissance villa is etched with scenes of love above its columned terrace arches. Sadly, the story behind that romance is tragic—King Ferdinand I of the Habsburg empire family started construction for his beloved Queen Anne, but she passed away before it was completed after giving birth to her 15th (!) child.

To understand the name of the "singing fountain" in the courtyard, you have to actually crouch underneath and put your ear to the cement basin to hear the vibrations. Then peek between the trees in the corner for a first glimpse of the hilltop views over Malá Strana before a leisurely stroll through the gardens toward the castle gates.

★ ST. VITUS CATHEDRAL
(Katedrála Sv. Víta)

Pražský hrad-III. nádvoří; tel. +420 224 372 423; www.katedralasvatehovita.cz; Mon-Sat 10am-6pm, Sun noon-6pm Apr-Oct, Mon-Sat 9am-4pm, Sun noon-4pm Nov-Mar; limited free access, full access with Circuit A (350 CZK) or B (250 CZK); tram: Pohořelec

St. Vitus Cathedral is the dominant figure of the Prague skyline. It's what most people associate with the historic castle grounds, although it wasn't entirely completed until the 20th century. Wenceslas I first built a Romanesque rotunda on this spot in the 10th century. Charles IV began construction of the Gothic beauty, whose official full name is the Cathedral of St. Vitus, Václav, and Vojtěch, in 1344. The long name recognizes the man who founded it (Václav or Wenceslas). An arm bone of the Sicilian St. Vitus—the patron

saint of dancers and performing artists, who also protects against dog bites, lightning, and oversleeping—is buried in St. Wenceslas's tomb. The third name, Vojtěch, represents a Bohemian bishop killed during missionary work and also buried on this site, although with far less name recognition and fanfare than his famous counterparts.

Construction began in the 14th century but wasn't finished for 600 years. Work on the cathedral was interrupted or damaged throughout the centuries by events like the 15th-century Hussite wars, 16th-century fires, the Thirty Years' War in the 17th century, multiple conflicts under Maria Theresa's 18th-century rule, and neglect by the Habsburgs in the 19th century. It took the spirit of the Czech National Revival and the creation of the Association for the Completion of the St. Vitus Temple in 1859 to see the project through to consecration in 1929.

Exterior: The intricate façade over the western entrance to St. Vitus has a historical look, but this area was actually part of the building's finishing touches. For example, both the rose window and the decorative doors covered with images from the cathedral's storied history weren't completed until the mid-1900s. The four proud architects of

Queen Anne's Summer Palace at the Prague Castle

this final construction era also weren't shy about adding statues of themselves just below the rose window.

Around the corner to the right of the church exterior lies the truly historical 14th-century **Golden Gate,** on the southern side of the building. The tall pointed doorways of this former entrance, no longer in use, sit underneath mosaics of the Last Judgement, made with around one million individual pieces of glass and marble around 1370.

Interior: The entrance to the cathedral is on the left-hand side of the Western façade, with lines often wrapped around the corner of the building. Both ticketed and non-ticketed visitors stand in the same line. The rear of the church just inside the entryway is as far as non-ticketed visitors are allowed to go, so waves of tour groups come inside to get one shot of the church layout bathed in the light of stained glass. Photos without ticketed permission are not technically allowed, but the prohibition has usually been loosely enforced in this area.

The first perk for ticketed visitors, just past the turnstiles on your left, is an unobstructed view of Alfons Mucha's window scene depicting Christianity coming to the Czech lands. It's painted, not stained glass, which sets it apart from the remaining windows, all done by different Czech artists.

Continuing down the left aisle, the center of the cathedral marks the border between old and new construction, with this expansion shifting the organ to this unusual position on a side wall. The wooden relief on the right side of the aisle depicts four areas (Malá Strana, Hradčany, Old Town, and New Town) that were united in 1784 to form the city of Prague—this feature is often overlooked, but it can be fun to pick out city sights or where you're staying. Crowds generally form a bottleneck at the rear curve of the cathedral and shuffle slowly around the two-ton silver sculpture that tops St. John of Napomuk's coffin.

St. Wenceslas Chapel lies on this opposite side of the building. It's worth craning your neck to see, through the doorways, the rectangular area that's restricted to all visitors. This chapel also serves as the entrance to the crown jewel storage area, but they're on strict lockdown and only displayed to the public on rare special occasions and anniversaries. Opening the door requires seven keys that are split between public figures, including the Czech president, the Prime Minister, and the Archbishop.

Tickets and tours: The quick, budget-friendly way to see St. Vitus Cathedral is a free peek from just inside the neo-Gothic entryway (which requires waiting in line with ticketed visitors). Any of the sights beyond the entryway of the church require a packaged castle ticket, either Circuit A (350 CZK) or Circuit B (250 CZK). If you decide on an all-access castle ticket, splurge on a tour guide (100 CZK pp, per hour) for detailed stories that add color to the historic figures represented inside all of the buildings. You can book a guide in person at the information center in the Third Courtyard near the entrance to St. Vitus Cathedral or via email to info@hrad.cz.

Old Royal Palace
(Starý Královský Palác)
Třetí nádvoří Pražského hradu 2; tel. +420 224 372 434; www.hrad.cz; daily 10am-6pm Apr-Oct, 9am-4pm Nov-Mar; admission only with Circuit A (350 CZK) or B (250 CZK); tram: Pohořelec or Pražský hrad

The Old Royal Palace, one of the castle's earliest buildings (from the 12th century), is a fun stop for history buffs. The former royal residence and receiving area only retains a few small glimpses of its former glamour, but is best known as the site of war-causing conflict. The intricately webbed ceiling of Vradislav Hall covers a long central corridor that was historically used for jousting matches, and can be seen in the wide "Rider's Staircase" used to exit the room. The palace tower also marks the site of the Second (more famous) Defenestration of Prague in 1618. Another religious rebellion, this time in response to the closure of Protestant chapels in Bohemia by Catholic Emperor Ferdinand II of the Habsburgs, saw two government officials and their secretary tossed out the window. The fall was not fatal—as legend has it, they landed in a pile of excrement before being taken in by Polyxena Lobkowicz at her nearby palace—but that doesn't mean it didn't have consequences. The act is credited for starting the Thirty Years' War that wreaked havoc on Central Europe. The window is marked inside and also marked by a ground-level plaque, and is visible free of charge from the Southern Gardens.

St. George's Basilica
(Bazilika Sv. Jiří)

Náměstí U Svatého Jiří; tel. +420 224 372 434; www.hrad.cz; daily 10am-6pm Apr-Oct, 9am-4pm Nov-Mar; admission only with Circuit A (350 CZK) or B (250 CZK); tram: Pohořelec or Pražský hrad

Entrance to St. George's Basilica gives architecture buffs a chance to compare the orange-red Baroque exterior with the minimalist Romanesque arched ceilings inside (and also offers tired tourists a seat in the pews to rest their feet). The large stone coffin in the center of the chapel holds Boleslav I, also known as Boleslav the Cruel, the younger brother of Wenceslas who was responsible for his murder. It also holds the chapel of St. Ludmila, grandmother of Boleslav and Wenceslas, on the right side of the central staircases. Ludmila's figure is usually depicted with a scarf or veil around her neck to symbolize her death by strangulation, rumored to have been ordered by her daughter-in-law Drahomira. Ludmila raised Wenceslas as a Christian, while Drahomira was loyal to the pagans of Bohemia: yet another instance of Czech resentment over the imposition of a dominant religion.

St. George's Basilica also holds fairly regular evening concerts of classical favorites.

Lobkowicz Palace
(Lobkowiczký Palác)

Jiřská 3; tel. +420 702 201 145; www.lobkowicz.com; Thur-Fri 10am-5pm, Sat-Sun 10am-6pm; 200-300

CZK; tram: Pohořelec or Pražský hrad, metro: Malostranská

The 16th-century Lobkowicz Palace is the only privately owned building in the castle complex. After centuries of housing one of Prague's early noble families, the building now serves as a museum offering a taste of aristocratic elegance as well as an impressive collection of memorabilia showcasing the family's patronage toward artists and musicians. This is also the house where Polyxena Lobkowicz took in survivors of the 1618 Prague Defenstration from the Old Royal Palace.

Getting to the palace is possible without a castle ticket—just head downhill from St. George's Basilica on Jiřská street parallel to Golden Lane—but visitors will need to buy a ticket to enter the palace itself. Plan at least an hour to immerse yourself in the aristocratic atmosphere. At the time of writing, opening hours were reduced to four days a week as a result of COVID-19 conditions, but they may return to daily access by the time of your visit.

Inside, descendants of the 700-years-and-counting Lobkowicz family line take great pride in describing their family collection via the audio guide included with admission. The building and its elements were seized in recent decades by both the Nazis and Communists before finally returning to the family. Twenty-two decadent rooms include a massive collection of portraits (of both people and animals) as well as porcelain dishes, an armory of rifles, and chandelier-topped rooms draped with curtains. You may want to skip past some of the detailed family descriptions of the portraits in the first two rooms, simply pausing to admire and learn more about any that catch your eye.

Classical music fans will appreciate the music room, which displays Josef František Maxmilián's patronage of composers such as Mozart, Beethoven, and Handel.

1: St. George's Basilica 2: Golden Lane in the Prague Castle 3: Prague Castle South Gardens 4: St. Vitus Cathedral

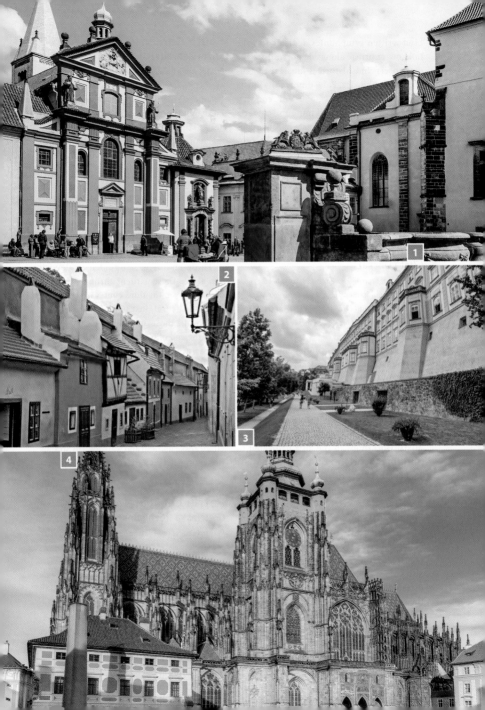

Find written symphonies dedicated to the Lobkowicz prince alongside portraits of the composers and historical musical instruments. Lobkowicz Palace normally hosts daily classical concerts (390 CZK concert, or 590 CZK concert and museum) under a frescoed ceiling in the intimate Baroque concert hall, but these were cancelled for coronavirus measures at the time of writing so double check availability before planning your visit.

The museum route ends on a stone balcony with a peaceful, panoramic view overlooking Prague.

Golden Lane
(Zlatá Ulička)

Zlatá ulička; tel. +420 224 372 423; www.hrad. cz; daily 10am-6pm Apr-Oct, 9am-4pm Nov-Mar; admission only with Circuit A (350 CZK) or B (250 CZK); tram stops Pohořelec or Pražský hrad, metro stop Malostranská

For a kitschy glimpse at 16th-century life in this area, choose a castle ticket that includes access to Golden Lane. The rows of 16 small houses built into the fortifying wall were inhabited by goldsmiths and members of the castle guard from the 16th century. Many tour guides offer speculation about alchemists' workshops in the area dedicated to fulfilling the whims of occult enthusiast Rudolph II, but these legends should be taken with a healthy dose of skepticism. The preserved and recreated residences now include Franz Kafka's former writing haunt (number 22) alongside souvenir and toy shops. Number 14 was the home of internationally renowned tarot-card reader Matylda Průšová, also known as "Madame de Thebes," who was arrested and died in custody for predicting the end of the Nazi regime. Climb the stairs into the White Tower (Bílá věž) to view suits of armor and a small torture chamber of brutal instruments.

The entire street is restricted by a ticketed turnstile during opening hours. Free access to walk down Golden Lane without entry to the buildings is possible only after 6pm.

South Gardens
(Jižní Zahrady)

Pražský hrad; www.hrad.cz; daily 6am-10pm Apr-Oct; free; tram: Pohořelec, Pražský hrad, or Malostranské náměstí, metro: Malostranská

For panoramic city views with no surcharge, head to the South Gardens. This long strip of manicured lawns and rounded staircases provides an obstacle-free view (if you ignore the selfie-takers) over Malá Strana's red-orange roofs, the Vltava River, Old Town, and the city beyond. Look along the castle walls outside the Old Royal Palace for the plaque at the base of the tower from which the officials were tossed during the Defenestration of Prague in 1618.

Those on a free, self-guided castle visit can access these gardens through the Bull Staircase from the third courtyard beside St. Vitus Cathedral, just opposite the Golden Gate, while those on a full tour can get here from the end of Golden Lane or Jiřská street after visiting the Lobkowicz Palace. The eastern end of these gardens marks the entrance to **St. Wenceslas' Vineyard,** named for the patron saint of the Czech lands, where you can recap your visit over a bottle of Riesling or Pinot Noir (500-900 CZK). You can also exit the South Gardens to the west onto Hradčanské náměstí and walk toward Strahov Brewery or Petřín Park and Lookout Tower.

PETŘÍN
Petřín Lookout Tower
(Petřínská Rozhledna)

Petřínské sady; tel. +420 257 320 112; www.prague. eu/en/object/places/116/petrin-lookout-tower-petrinska-rozhledna; daily 10am-9pm Jul-Sep. 10am-8pm Oct-Jun; 150 CZK; tram: Pohořelec

After visiting the newly unveiled Parisian Eiffel Tower in 1889, the Czech Tourist Club decided that the Prague skyline was missing something. The Petřín Lookout Tower was created for the General Land Centennial Exhibition in 1891, serving as a replica in tribute and admiration for its French inspiration. The tower also holds cheeky bragging rights as being technically higher than the Eiffel Tower due to its hilltop location. Climbing the 299 steps to the observation deck gives you one of the highest viewpoints in the city (note that social distancing can be difficult on the platform and staircases). There is an elevator (60 CZK), but at the time of writing the elevator was out of order. It is generally seen more as an option for visitors with limited mobility and for elderly visitors than for tired tourists.

The easiest way to reach the tower is an uphill funicular ride from the Petřín station located inside the park near the Újezd tram stop, and requires the same rules as a ride on any form of Prague's public transport—have a ticket and be sure to validate it before entering. For a simple, cost-free option, you could also walk through the park from the top of the hill after a visit to the Prague Castle or Strahov Monastery, both near the Pohořelec tram stop.

Petřín Funicular

Petřínské sady; www.dpp.cz; daily 9am-11:30pm, brief closures Mar and Oct; 24 CZK; tram: Újezd

This land-based version of a cable car is more than just the simplest way to ascend Petřín Hill. The Petřín Funicular offers panoramic window views from the base of the hill to the Petřín Lookout Tower, with a stop at one platform in between. This nostalgic hillside transport first ran on a water-based system in 1891, halting operations during World War I before switching to an electrical system when it resumed in 1932. The system took another 20-year break after a landslide in 1965. Since reopening in 1985, the ride has been part of the city's public transit network; access is included within a valid Prague transport ticket. Carriages leave every 15 minutes from November-March and every 10 minutes from April-October. Look for the Petřín funicular station just inside the grounds of the park when entering near the Újezd tram stop.

The Petřín Funicular does get crowded. There is a ticket machine on site, and a single ride (24 CZK) requires first buying a ticket and then stamping it in the yellow validation machines before boarding the funicular, to avoid a hefty fine from the controllers checking at either side of the ride.

Memorial to the Victims of Communism

Petřínské sady; free; tram: Újezd

Seven crumbling bronze men by sculptor Olbram Zoubek line the steps to Petřín Park as a Memorial to the Victims of Communism unveiled in 2002. The first man appears whole, while successive statues are each missing parts of their bodies, symbolizing a commitment to perseverance in the face of the damage inflicted from 1948-1989. The statistics running along the stairs spell out the effects in stark numbers: 205,486 people convicted, 248 executed, 4,500 died in prison, 327 died during illegal border crossings, and 170,938 people left their homes behind to emigrate. The figures are particularly harrowing when lit from below in the evening.

★ Smíchov Boardwalk (Smíchovská náplavka)

Smíchovská náplavka, between the Admiral Botel and Railway Bridge (Vyšehradský železniční most); tel. +420 222 013 618; www.prazskenaplavky.cz; free; tram: Na Knížecí or Zborovská

This roughly 350-meter (1,150-ft) riverside embankment, also known as the Hořejší Riverside, is located across from the busier New Town embankment that's simply known as Náplavka. An extensive renovation project completed in 2020 added enormous glass lenses that swivel to open a series of underground vaults lining the retaining walls. Most of these vaults on the Smíchov side hold cafés rather than gallery spaces, with additional tables that spill outdoors onto the large concrete walkway. Try a coffee, cocktail, or panini at **Dílna** (www.kafevdilne.cz; 2pm-midnight) near the middle of the boardwalk.

Smíchovská náplavka traditionally hosts a variety of international food and drink festivals throughout the summer and fall: See www.prazskenaplavky.cz for updates. The southern edge of the embankment also leads to a small patch of sand where you'll find a postcard-worthy backdrop of Vyšehrad and the Railway Bridge, likely with a bevy of swans floating in the foreground.

VINOHRADY

Peace Square
(Náměstí Míru)

free; metro: Náměstí Míru

This square is defined by the towering spires of the Neo-Gothic **Church of St. Ludmila** (Kostel svaté Ludmily). The church and Christmas markets in this square are among the city's most popular, when wooden stands fill the air with the sweet smell of crêpes (palačinky) and hot honey wine (medovina).

Jiřího z Poděbrad Square

free; metro: Jiřího z Poděbrad

Jiřího z Poděbrad Square is a popular outdoor hangout to enjoy a takeaway meal, browse the farmers market, admire the architecture, or toss a Frisbee in the grass in the heart of neighborhood life in Prague. The large clock face of the modern brown and white Catholic **Church of the Most Sacred Heart of Our Lord** (Kostel Nejsvětějšího Srdce Páně) marks the border where Vinohrady begins to blend into the neighborhood of Žižkov. Take a poll among your group to see how the majority feel about this love-it-or-hate-it piece of early 20th-century architecture. Wednesday-Saturday, a farmers market of fresh vegetables and flowers, plus ready-to-eat snacks, covers half the square from morning to late afternoon. The area is also surrounded by independent restaurants and coffee shops frequented by the neighborhood's international residents. Grab a seat on the benches lining the central path for some prime people-and-puppy watching before crossing the street to Beer Geek for a microbrew or to Cafefin for a Vietnamese meal.

ŽIŽKOV

★ Žižkov TV Tower
(Žižkovský Vysílač)

Mahlerovy sady 1; tel. +420 210 320 081; www. towerpark.cz; daily 9am-midnight; observation deck
250 CZK; tram: Lipanská or Jiřího z Poděbrad, metro: Jiřího z Poděbrad

It is a fitting testament to Prague's growth and fluctuation that the defining structure of the Žižkov neighborhood offers an array of posh experiences in an area known for its rough-and-tumble reputation. The Žižkov TV Tower, built between 1985 and 1992, holds the title of the tallest building in Prague, at more than 216 meters (700 ft) with a TV transmitter at its highest point. The interior contains an observation deck with panoramic views at roughly 93 meters (300 ft) as well as an exclusive hotel and the **Oblaca** fine dining restaurant and cocktail bar around 66 meters (215 ft). Swap your casual clothes for an upscale look to try a cocktail at the Oblaca bar (reservations recommended) before or after dinner at nearby **Martin's Bistro.**

Since its inception, controversies have surrounded the Žižkov TV Tower. The structure has proudly embraced being named the "Second-Ugliest Building in the World." Ten of David Černý's love-them-or-hate-them giant baby sculptures (similar to those beside Kampa Museum in Malá Strana) can also be seen climbing its walls. On a deeper cultural note, the tower stands on the previous site of a Jewish cemetery, with mounting community pressure to install a memorial at its base acknowledging that history exists amid the mini-golf course and playground.

Olšany Cemetery and New Jewish Cemetery
(Olšanské Hřbitov/ Nový Židovský Hřbitov)

tram and metro: Želivského

Two important burial grounds serving Prague's Jewish community are located on the outside edge of Žižkov. The massive **Olšany Cemetery** (Vinohradská 153; tel. +420 272 011 126; www.hrbitovy.cz; daily 8am-7pm May-Sep, 8am-6pm Mar-Apr and Oct, 8am-5pm Nov-Feb; free) was established in 1680 in response to the Plague epidemic sweeping Europe. Prague's oldest and largest graveyard holds the body of student protester

Vinohrady and Vršovice

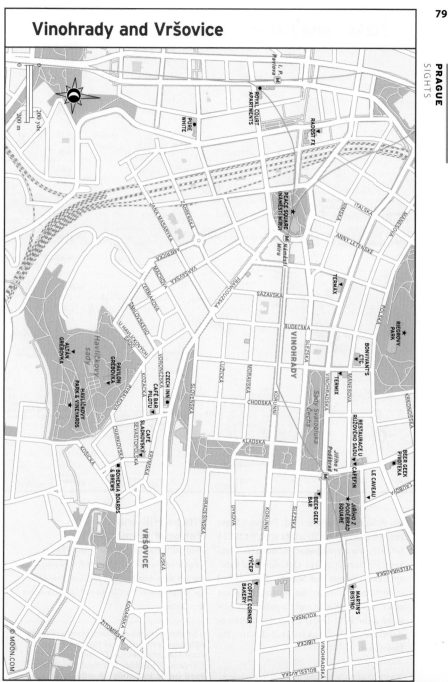

0
200 m
0
200 yds

I. P. Pavlova M

ROYAL COURT APARTMENTS

PURE WHITE

RADOST FX

PEACE SQUARE (NÁMĚSTÍ MÍRU) ★

M Náměstí Míru

ITALSKA

ŘÍMSKÁ

MÁNESOVA

ANNY LETENSKE

TERMAX

SAZAVSKA

RIEGROVY PARK ★

BUDEČSKÁ

VINOHRADY

SLEZSKA

POLSKÁ

JANA MASARYKA

ZÁBĚHLICKÁ

AMERICKÁ

VARŠAVSKÁ

MÁCHOVA

ČERMÁKOVA

FRANCOUZSKÁ

BONIVIVANT'S CTC

MÁNESOVA

TERMIX

KRKONOŠSKÁ

U HAVLÍČKOVÝCH SADŮ

SMETÁNKOVA

Havlíčkovy sady

VINOHRADSKÁ

Sady Svatopluka Čecha

RESTAURACE U RŮŽOVÉHO SADU

BEER GEEK PIVOTÉKA

ALTÁN GRÉBOVKA ▼

PAVILON GRÉBOVKA ▼

RYBALKOVA

VORONĚŽSKÁ

CZECH INN ●

CAFÉ BAR PILOTŮ ●

KOZÁCKÁ

LUŽICKÁ

MORAVSKÁ

CHODSKÁ

KORUNNÍ

LE CAVEAU

CAFEFIN ▼

JIŘÍHO Z PODĚBRAD

HAVLÍČKOVY PARK & VINEYARDS ★

CAFÉ SLADKOVSKÝ ▼

SEVASTOPOLSKÁ

KRYMSKÁ

SLOVENSKÁ

KLADSKÁ

M Jiřího z Poděbrad

JIŘÍHO Z PODĚBRAD SQUARE ★

KOSICKÁ

CHARKOVSKÁ

BOHEMIA BOARDS & BREWS ●

HŘADEŠINSKÁ

VRŠOVICE

RUSKÁ

DYKOVA

KORUNNÍ

SLEZSKÁ

BEER GEEK BAR ▼

KUBELÍKOVA

KODAŇSKÁ

VÝČEP ▼

VELEHRADSKÁ

ŽITOMÍRSKÁ

COFFEE CORNER BAKERY ▼

KOLÍNSKÁ

LÍBICKÁ

VINOHRADSKÁ

BOLESLAVSKÁ

MARTIN'S BISTRO ▼

© MOON.COM

Žižkov and Karlín

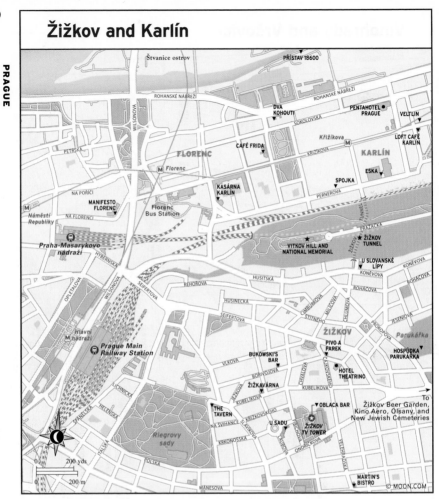

Jan Palach. Across the road, Prague's **New Jewish Cemetery** (Izraelská 1; tel. +420 224 800 812; www.synagogue.cz; Sun-Thu 9am-5pm, Fri 9am-2pm Apr-Oct, Sun-Thu 9am-4pm, Fri 9am-2pm Nov-Mar; free), established in 1890, is best known for housing the grave of writer Franz Kafka and his parents (tombstone number 21-14-21) along with a memorial to the Czechoslovak Jews killed during the Holocaust.

Vítkov Hill and National Memorial
(Národní Památník Na Vítkově)

U Památníku; tel. +420 732 947 509; www.nm.cz; Thu-Sun 10am-6pm Nov-Mar, Wed-Sun 10am-6pm Apr-Oct; memorial 120 CZK; tram: Biskupcova or bus stop Ohrada

---

1: Smíchov's recently renovated boardwalks come with great views. **2:** the stark Memorial to the Victims of Communism by Olbram Zoubek **3:** Church of St. Ludmila at Náměstí Míru **4:** Jiřího z Poděbrad Square and the Žižkov TV Tower

The Notorious David Černý

If you see a public sculpture in Prague, there is a good chance that David Černý is the artist behind it. The controversial artist was born just before the Prague Spring of 1968 and grew up in the subsequent era of Communist crackdown. When the Velvet Revolution opened Czechoslovakia's borders, Černý seized the opportunity to study in Switzerland and New York City.

The young artist grabbed attention in 1991 by painting a Soviet tank and war memorial bright pink. This earned him an arrest at age 23, but members of parliament repainted the tank pink in protest. Černý didn't stay imprisoned long and the tank was removed. The artist's work (and political statements) continue to decorate and provoke the city—he sent a giant blue middle finger entitled "Gesture" down the Vltava River when President Miloš Zeman was elected in 2013. Below are some of his pieces worth seeking out:

Three of David Černý's "Babies" stand outside Kampa Museum.

- A 2-meter (7-ft) Sigmund Freud entitled *Man Hanging Out* grips a rooftop outside the building at Na Perštýně 14 in Old Town (don't be fooled by the similar man hanging from an umbrella in front of the Mosaic House Hotel).

- The saint riding an upside-down horse suspended from the rooftop of Palac Lucerna in Wenceslas Square is also a David Černý creation.

- *Piss*—two mechanical men urinating into a Czech Republic-shaped pool in front of the Franz Kafka Museum—embodies his cheeky, provocative style.

- Three of his bronze **Babies** with barcodes for faces sit beside the Kampa Museum, while 10 of their siblings crawl the sides of the Žižkov TV Tower.

- A mirrored **head of Franz Kafka** sculpture, which rotates twice an hour, is located near the National Theater.

- A day trip to Liberec includes his *Giant's Feast,* a severed head and beverages decorating the top of a bus stop.

One of the most beautiful places to watch the sunset over Prague is from the National Memorial at Vítkov Hill. A roughly 20-minute walk up the hill from the Žižkov beer garden on the edge of Žižkov treats visitors to an open platform around a towering statue of Jan Žižka on horseback, with the Czech flag flying to your left and the Prague Castle framed by trees directly in front of you. History fans may want to peek inside the National Memorial for the exhibition on important events in 20th-century Czech history. Otherwise, skip the entrance fee and simply enjoy the view.

Žižkov Tunnel
(Žižkovský Tunel)

Žižkovský Tunel; free; bus: Tachovské náměstí

The nearly 300-meter-long (1,000-ft-long) Žižkov Tunnel connects the Žižkov neighborhood with Karlín, whose residents prefer to call it the Karlín Tunnel, underneath Vítkov Hill. The lengthy path is perfectly safe, even though you can't see from one side to the other, and is limited to pedestrians and bicycles. It was originally built for shelter from nuclear fallout. The echo is powerful, and you may often hear shouts or even music on your pilgrimage between the two very different districts of Prague. The tunnel is well lit at night, making it an easy connection for dinner at nearby U Slovanské Lípy on the Žižkov side and an evening drink at one of Karlín's sophisticated wine bars.

LETNÁ AND HOLEŠOVICE

National Gallery– Trade Fair Palace

(Veletržní Palác - Národní Galerie)

Dukelských hrdinů 47; tel. +420 224 301 122; www.ngprague.cz; Tue and Thurs-Sun 10am-6pm, Wed 10am-8pm; 220 CZK, free for children and visitors under 26; tram: Strossmayerovo náměstí or Veletržní palác

Prague's National Gallery includes a collection of exposition places scattered across Prague, but most people mentioning the National Gallery mean the Trade Fair Palace. A large collection of modern and contemporary art—including work by Vincent van Gogh, Gustav Klimt, Alfons Mucha, Zorka Ságlová, Toyen, Claude Monet, and Pablo Picasso—fills the walls and halls of this three-story exhibition space. Contemporary exhibitions often provide context for local life, such as a photography exhibit to mark the anniversary of the 1968 Soviet invasion or painted interpretations of Czech identity and national symbols. The 1920s building was the first example of Functionalist architecture in Prague, built for the Prague Sample Trade Fairs that inspired its name.

DOX Center for Contemporary Art

Poupětova 1; tel. +420 295 568 123; www.dox.cz; Wed 2pm-9pm Thu-Sun noon-6pm; 180 CZK; tram: Ortenovo náměstí

The mission of DOX Center for Contemporary Art includes using a variety of art forms to "create a space for research, presentation, and debate on important social issues." Thought-provoking exhibitions provide the starting point for panel discussions, film screenings, and interactive community events on topics ranging from big data and migration to the portrayal of war-torn countries. Recent exhibitions include Chinese contemporary artist Ai Weiwei's statement on refugees and human rights. This former 19th-century industrial space was converted to its present-day incarnation at the beginning of the millennium. A huge wooden airship, which hosts arts and literature events, rests on top of the building, adding to its photogenic appeal. Come with an open mind and decompress with a post-excursion discussion at the nearby Bitcoin Café. This place embodies a modern Czech sensibility, both literally and figuratively—Czechs of all ages aren't shy about talking politics or world events over a beer, and the gallery shows repurposed spaces and art among industry that characterizes the Holešovice neighborhood.

VYŠEHRAD

TOP EXPERIENCE

★ Vyšehrad Complex

V Pevnosti 159/5b; tel. +420 261 225 304; www.praha-vysehrad.cz; free; metro: Vyšehrad

Legend has it that this vast complex (and the city of Prague itself) was constructed after Princess Libuše looked out over the undeveloped landscape around the 8th century and declared, "Behold, I see a great city, whose fame will touch the stars."

You can enter the large grass-filled grounds of the Vyšehrad Complex after a short walk from the Vyšehrad metro, taking the exit toward the Congress Center and following the brown street signs pointing the way through a few residential streets. The grounds themselves include a maze of green spaces dotted with statues, alongside some of the city's oldest historic monuments. This quiet complex is far less crowded or touristy than the Prague Castle across the river, but filled with comparable levels of history and

Letná and Holešovice

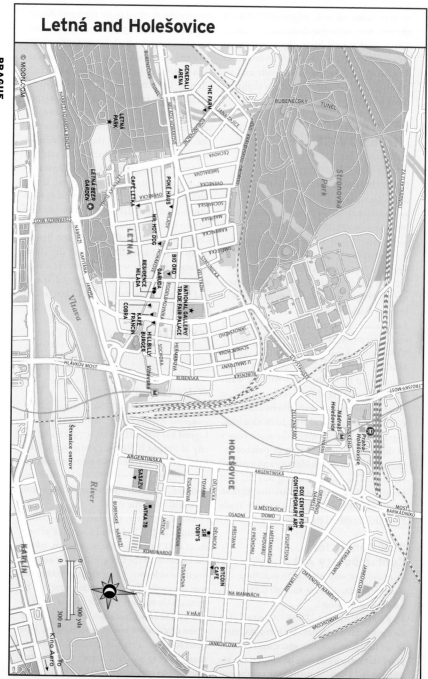

GENERALI
ARENA

THE FARM

LANA ZAJÍCE

Stromovka
Park

BUBENEČSKÝ TUNEL

LETNÁ
PARK

NÁBŘEŽÍ EDVARDA BENEŠE

NÁBŘEŽÍ KAPITÁNA JAROŠE

ŠTEFÁNIKŮV MOST

LETNÁ BEER
GARDEN

CAFÉ LETKA

POKÉ HAUS

MR. HOT DOG

RESIDENCE
MILADA

GARUDA

BIO OKO

COBRA

KAFE
FRANCIN

HILLBILLY
BURGER

NATIONAL GALLERY/
TRADE FAIR PALACE

LETNÁ

Vltava

HLÁVKŮV MOST

Štvanice ostrov

River

ARGENTINSKÁ

ARGENTINSKÁ

SASAZU

JATKA 78

SIR
TOBY'S

BITCOIN
CAFÉ

HOLEŠOVICE

Nádraží
Holešovice

Praha-
Holešovice

DOX CENTER FOR
CONTEMPORARY ART

MOST
BARIKÁDNÍKŮ

TROJSKÝ MOST

KARLÍN

0   300 yds
0   300 m

To
Kino Aero

TOP EXPERIENCE

Prague Off the Beaten Path

sunset in Riegrovy sady in Vinohrady

Prague's major sights are worth seeing, but the central neighborhoods can be packed with tourists. A good strategy is to visit the top sights that you can't bear to miss for as long as you can stand the crowds—then head to some of the lesser-known neighborhoods for the more undiscovered vibe that backpackers often associate with Prague of the 1990s and early 2000s. This adventure into fewer English-language menus, signage, and tourist-friendly customer service can give a more authentic picture of local life in Prague when approached with patience, preparation, and respect for the space.

Here's what some of Prague's lesser-known neighborhoods have to offer:

- **Vinohrady:** International, and just baby steps off the tourist path.

- **Žižkov:** Rowdy, and rumored to have the most bars per capita of any European district.

- **Karlín:** Sophisticated, and known for its food and wine bars, Karlín also embodies a spirit of revitalization, with repurposed spaces holding markets and entertainment venues.

- **Smíchov:** Riverside neighborhood in transition from industrial hub to independent restaurants and renovated spaces.

- **Holešovice:** Industrial and offbeat. Think: Theatrical space in a former slaughterhouse, or crypto-anarchist coffee shop.

beauty. Wander the edges of the park complex for stunning city-wide viewpoints from an alternate angle to those of Old Town or Malá Strana.

Visitors to both Vyšehrad (meaning "high castle") and the Prague Castle are often confused by the lack of Disneyland-style turrets and princess-worthy bedrooms. The term "castle" in Prague is not necessarily a single ornate building, but is used to describe fortified walls surrounding a seat of power, such as this royal base of King Vratislav II in the 11th century. Give yourself a few solid hours to explore the sights below and enjoy the peaceful greenery and sweeping city views that surround them.

ST. MARTIN'S ROTUNDA
(Rotunda Sv. Martina)

V Pevnosti; tel. +420 224 911 353; www.kkvys.cz;
free; metro: Vyšehrad

Shortly beyond the brick entrance of the Vyšehrad Complex you'll come upon a large circular building seemingly sprouting from the ground. St. Martin's Rotunda is arguably Prague's oldest intact building, dating from the 11th century. It has seen its fair share of battles, after being used as gunpowder storage during the Thirty Years' War from 1618-1648 (much like the Powder Tower of New Town in later years). The rotunda still holds a cannonball in its walls from the Prussians during the Battle of Prague in 1757. These days it maintains a more peaceful existence and is used for occasional religious services. It is not open to tourists, but signage in English in the surrounding courtyard can add context to the view. If you're ready for a break, the entrance to the **Hospůdka Na Hradbách** beer garden is hiding just behind the rotunda.

BASILICA OF STS. PETER AND PAUL
(Bazilika Sv. Petra A Pavla)

Štulcova; tel. +420 224 911 353; www.kkvys.cz;
90 CZK; metro: Vyšehrad

The tall neo-Gothic towers of the Basilica of Sts. Peter and Paul mirror the Prague Castle's St. Vitus Cathedral across the river. The interior of this 19th-century version (damaged and remodeled multiple times since its 11th-century founding by King Vratislav II) contains gorgeous art nouveau-style depictions of saints along its columns, along with flowered ceilings and stained-glass windows. Give yourself at least half an hour to browse the eye-catching decoration in soft, muted colors on every wall. The church was given the status of a "basilica minor" by Pope John Paul II, engraved in a plaque near the ornate doors, as a sign of its importance (as opposed to its architectural style).

The church is accessible to the public from 10am daily (except for 10:30am after mass on Sun), and stays open until 5pm in winter and 6pm on summer evenings except Thursday, when it shuts at 5:30pm to prepare for evening mass. This ornate beauty is far less crowded and more accessible than St. Vitus, drawing visitors on a tighter schedule and those wanting to experience a slice of history without elbowing their way through tour groups.

VYŠEHRAD CEMETERY

Štulcova; tel. +420 224 911 353; www.slavin.cz; daily
8am-7pm May-Sep, 8am-5pm Nov-Feb, 8am-6pm
Mar-Apr and Oct; free; metro: Vyšehrad

Many of Prague's final resting places are artfully decorated with intricate headstones and designed for visitors. In fact, the aisles of Vyšehrad's Cemetery hold many of Prague's celebrities who may enjoy an audience beyond the grave as much as they did while walking the earth. You can enter the cemetery through a gate to the left of the Basilica of Sts. Peter and Paul, where a list of famous graves is detailed by number, or from the back of the cemetery after a walk from the Vyšehrad metro station. Some of the names you may recognize include the classical composer Bedřich Smetana, whose resting place is surrounded by towering obelisks. A bust of Antonín Dvořák stands behind a gate along the northern wall. Art nouveau painter Alfons Mucha's plaque is tucked into a corner of the Slavin Tomb at the top of the stairs near the eastern entrance, and romantic poet Karel Hynek Mácha's name is written in gold on a headstone among the aisles. Literary fans take note that the Kafka buried here is Czech sculptor Bohumil Kafka, not the writer Franz Kafka, whose grave is in the New Jewish Cemetery in Žižkov. Also, "Rodina" is not the most popular Czech surname, but it means "family," so you'll find it on many of the tombstones marking familial plots.

1: decorative doors of Basilica of Sts. Peter and Paul at Vyšehrad 2: the ornate graves of Vyšehrad Cemetery 3: Olšany Cemetery in Žižkov

Local Legends

Franz Kafka, famous for his German-language writing, was born in Prague and has a Malá Strana museum dedicated to his work. But he's not the city's only claim to fame. Here is a short rundown of some famous Czechs that locals would be shocked to know you've never heard of:

- You will be forgiven for not knowing romantic poet **Karel Hynek Mácha** (1810-1836), but he will be familiar to anyone who visited his statue in Petřín Park. Mácha's most famous work, "Máj" ("May"), uses nature to share stories of life and love, and was translated into English on the 200th anniversary of the poet's birth in 2010.

- The music of **Bedřich Smetana** (1824-1884) is celebrated in his hometown of Litomyšl, about two hours east of Prague, with a festival every summer. The classical composer also lends his name to the great concert hall inside the Municipal House. This father of Bohemian music is best known for *Má vlast* (*My Homeland*), which opens the Prague Spring Music Festival each year and includes odes to the Vltava River and Vyšehrad.

grave of classical music legend Bedřich Smetana

- Smetana's younger contemporary **Antonín Dvořák** (1841-1904) gained international, or you could even say intergalactic, recognition for his classical compositions infused with Czech folk influences. Dvořák's "New World Symphony" accompanied American astronauts Neil Armstrong and Buzz Aldrin on their trip to the moon in 1969.

- Even if you don't immediately recognize his name, the swirling designs of art nouveau painter **Alfons Mucha** (1860-1939) will likely look familiar. While the artistic style is often connected to France, this hero of the movement is undeniably Czech. Mucha's work graces a window in St. Vitus Cathedral, the ceiling murals of Smetana Hall in the Municipal House, and an entire museum in New Town devoted to his posters, paintings, and interesting life story.

- Tennis legend **Martina Navrátilová** (1956-present) fled Communism in Prague to settle in the US in 1981. While many of her 59 tennis Grand Slam titles were won abroad, there is still plenty of local love for any Czech athletes who excel on a world stage.

- **Jaromír Jágr** (1972-present), one of the most beloved ice-hockey heroes of the modern Czech nation (even though he played many years for the NHL in the US), is an artist on the ice. The Kladno-born god of the sport went pro in the Czech Republic at age 15 and won two Stanley Cup championships with the Pittsburgh Penguins. You can also thank Jagr for helping to popularize the mullet hairstyle in the early 1990s, still embraced by some older Czech men to this day.

Recreation and Activities

Being in nature is a national Czech pastime. Whenever the weather is nice (and sometimes even when it isn't), a significant portion of Prague clears out of the city to spend time amongst the trees.

PARKS
Lesser Town
(Malá Strana)
WALLENSTEIN GARDENS
(Valdštejnská Zahrada)

Letenská 4; tel. +420 257 075 707;
daily 7:30am-5:30pm Apr-Oct; free;
tram or metro: Malostranská

Reasons to visit the manicured, Baroque-style Wallenstein Gardens: free-roaming peacocks, a carp-filled pond, a wall of gargoyle-like faces in a stalactite rock wall, an aviary of owls, outdoor summer evening concerts, the frescoed ceiling of Greek/Roman gods and Trojan War scenes in the Sala Pavilion, and a respite from Malá Strana's busy streets. The tall hedges lining the paths provide a labyrinth-like atmosphere between the pond and fountain at one end of this popular garden and the open courtyard and bench seating at the other. Do be on your best behavior—the buildings surrounding these gardens also house today's government officials of the Czech Senate. The entrance is tucked back from the street on the left side when facing the Malostranská metro station.

VOJAN GARDENS
(Vojanovy sady)

U Lužického semináře 17; daily 8am-4pm Dec-Jan,
8am-5pm Feb-Mar and Oct-Nov, 8am-7pm Apr-Sep;
free; tram or metro: Malostranská

Think of Vojanovy sady as a smaller, quieter version of the Wallenstein Gardens just one street away. While these former monastery gardens have fewer ornate statues and grand palaces, they offer a more peaceful vibe of tree-lined paths, rose-covered archways,

relaxing park benches, and free-roaming peacocks (with fewer visitors vying for their photographs). This park is walled in on all sides, insulating the air from the traffic and tourism of the Malá Strana streets. You can find the arched entrance tucked into the wall surrounding to the gardens on your right-hand side while walking south on U Lužického semináře street.

Petřín
PETŘÍN PARK AND GARDENS
(Petřínské sady)

Petřínské sady; free; lower tram: Újezd,
upper tram: Petřín

You could easily get lost for an afternoon among the curving pathways throughout this park that stretches across roughly 8 hectares (20 ac) of land. Start with a visit to the rose gardens surrounding the base of the Petřín Lookout Tower. Heading downhill, you'll pass a statue of Czech poet Karel Hynek Mácha, who wrote the locally famous poem "Máj" ("May"). Couples come to share a kiss in his presence (preferably under a birch or cherry tree) on the first of May (the day on which Czechs celebrate love, but with way less pressure or commercialization than Valentine's Day). The quiet Kinsky gardens cover the southern area of the park, divided by a castle fortification known as the Hunger Wall. This fortification was commissioned by Charles IV in the mid-14th century and named for the jobs providing an income to poor communities of the time.

Vinohrady
RIEGROVY PARK
(Riegrovy sady)

Riegrovy sady; free; Metro: Jiřího z Poděbrad,
tram: Vinohradská tržnice

One of the most popular places to watch the sunset, alongside nature-loving folks and couples cuddling on blankets, is the

Islands on the Vltava River

A number of small islands dotting the Vltava River offer secluded paths, outdoor activities, and interesting viewpoints to survey the surrounding skylines.

- **Slovanský ostrov:** This island just south of the National Theater is easy to spot, thanks to the pale yellow walls of the Žofín Palace standing in the center. Visitors can stroll the manicured gardens with views of the Prague Castle or look for stairs on the east side of the island that lead to boat rentals on the Vltava River. If you've got a 500 CZK note on hand, try comparing the statue of Czech author Božena Němcová on the north side of the island to her likeness on the bill. Enter via walkway near the Manes Exhibition Center (Masarykovo nábřeží 250) on the south or near the National Theater on the north side of the island.

- **Střelecký ostrov:** Depending on the day, you might find a quiet walk under the trees, crowds chatting around a pop-up café, or open-air concerts and events (see www.letnak.cz for events calendar). Access to this most central island in the Vltava River requires a walk to the middle of the Legion Bridge ("most Legií"

Look for the small goblin while walking along Kampa Island.

in Czech), which is just north of the National Theater, for stairs leading down to the island on the south side.

- **Dětský ostrov:** "Children's Island," beside the Smíchov neighborhood on the east side of the river, holds exactly what you'd expect—playgrounds and climbing structures. A bronze statue on top of a column on the island's northern point symbolizes the Vltava River and four women (around the sides of the column) represent its tributaries: Otava, Lužnice, Sázava, and Berounka. Enter via two walkways on the Smíchov side, one across the river from the Dancing House and just north of the Jiráskův Bridge, another just south of the Legion Bridge ("most Legií" in Czech).

- **Kampa Island:** For a relaxing alternative to Malá Strana's heavily trafficked streets, take the stairs just before the Lesser Town Bridge Tower down to Kampa Island. The small Čertovka canal separates this quiet strip from the mainland of Malá Strana. A footbridge beside the John Lennon Wall serves as a viewpoint to a tiny goblin beside a 15th-century mill, and the greenery of Park Kampa sets a relaxing tone on the southern end of the island.

- **Štvanice ostrov:** The small wooden ferry boat connecting Karlín and Holešovice on the north side of the river also makes one stop at this off-beat island. The sliver of land with a web of streets surrounding a tennis club and bicycle park is a popular spot for Prague runners.

great lawn of Riegrovy sady. The distant view of the Prague Castle over iconic red-orange rooftops in Malá Strana sets a peaceful scene, though you may get some residual crowd noise or live music from a nearby beer garden. Puppies and their human companions frequent the surrounding paths, which stretch from the main train station (hlavní nádraží) uphill toward Jiřího z Poděbrad Square.

HAVLÍČKOVY PARK AND VINEYARDS
(Havlíčkovy sady)

Havlíčkovy sady; daily 6am-10pm Nov-Mar, 6am-midnight Apr-Oct; free; tram: Jana Masaryka or Krymska

You might hear Havlíčkovy sady, the name of the park, and **Grébovka,** the internal vineyards, used interchangeably to describe this hilly green area on the southern edge of Vinohrady. The Stone Grotto's curved walls, arched doorways, and sculpted fountain are a photographer's dream. The summer and autumn months bring a variety of wine festivals to the grounds, and both the open-air Altán Grébovka gazebo wine bar (Havlíčkovy sady 1369; tel. +420 725 999 495; http://altangrebovka.com; daily 10am-10pm; wine 60-100 CZK) and Pavilon Grébovka café (Havlíčkovy sady 2188; tel. +420 725 000 858; www.pavilongrebovka.cz; daily 10am-10pm; wine 50-100 CZK) with an outdoor patio pour drinks all year long. This area offers a relaxing, sophisticated option for outdoor entertainment.

Letná and Holešovice
LETNÁ PARK
(Letenské sady)
Letenské sady; www.letenskyzamecek.cz; beer garden daily 11am-11pm depending on weather; tram: Čechův most, Letenské náměstí, or Strossmayerovo náměstí

The main draw for many of Letná Park's visitors is one of the city's largest beer gardens overlooking the Vltava River and the rooftops of Old Town. Outside of those imbibing around the rows of picnic benches, local residents come to the park to walk their dogs, admire the blooming flower beds, or tie a slackline between two trees and spend an afternoon testing their balance. Entrance to the park is possible via an uphill hike from the Vltava River banks near the Čechův most tram stop, or a more leisurely walk from the opposite side of the park around tram stops Letenské náměstí or Strossmayerovo náměstí.

CYCLING
If you're okay with the bumps of some cobblestone streets, cycling can be a fun way to get around Prague.

Bike Tours and Rentals
PRAHA BIKE
Dlouha 24; tel. +420 732 388 880; www.prahabike.cz; 9am-8pm Mar 15-Oct 15, 10am-5pm Oct 16-Mar 14; tram: Dlouhá třída

You can get an overview of the city with Praha Bike offering tours around the Prague Castle, the Vyšehrad Complex, beer gardens, or panoramic viewpoints (650-1250 CZK), or just rent a bike (220 CZK for two hours) and explore on your own.

Bike-Sharing
REKOLA
www.rekola.cz

You'll find pink ridesharing Rekola bikes around the city. These are available for rent by downloading a mobile app. Don't worry if the first two screens ask for your email and password in Czech—you can set the default language to English as soon as you're registered. The first 15 minutes are free and then users are charged 24 CZK per hour on their credit card.

BOATING
The Czech Republic may be a landlocked country, but there are plenty of water-based (or water-adjacent) sports to draw people to the Vltava River. The majority of boat rentals and beach volleyball games take place along the river's western curve, extending south from the National Theater, past Vyšehrad, down to more residential neighborhoods. Floating on top of the river provides a gorgeous perspective to take in the beauty of the skylines away from any crowds.

KAYAK BEACH BAR
Náplavka; tel. +420 608 584 961; kayakbeachbar. cz; Tue-Fri 4pm-11pm, Sat-Sun noon-11pm (weather permitting); tram: Výtoň

This combination cocktail bar and recreation center on a docked boat, located just south of the railway bridge at the end of the Náplavka boardwalk, offers a relatively secluded chance to work up a sweat on the Vltava River. Kayaks and paddleboards are available for rent by the hour (190 CZK) or as part of a guided tour (1,200-2,900 CZK per person). Small groups can also rent the beach volleyball court floating on the river itself (450 CZK first hour, plus 50 CZK ball). Call in advance to reserve a spot on the court.

Geek Culture in Prague

Historical Prague was all about the kings and castles, but modern-day Czech life embraces technology in all its many forms. The city has a thriving startup scene and pockets of the counter-culture vibe can be found among the crowds of its annual Comic Con. Fans of video games, innovation, or an evening of Settlers of Catan all have a place in Prague.

New Town's **Joystick Bar** (Jindřišská 5; tel. +420 732 473 788; www.joystickbar.cz) serves one of Prague's favorite microbrews, Unětický Pivovar, in a room filled with classic arcade games and pinball machines (10 CZK). This old-school gamers bar is open from 4pm to 2am Tuesday to Saturday, closing at midnight on Sundays and Mondays.

Prague's **Bitcoin Café** (Dělnická 43; tel. +420 608 088 822; www.paralelnipolis.cz; Mon-Fri 8am-8pm; prices vary with currency) in Holešovice provides a home for the local crypto-anarchist crew devoted to an open and decentralized internet. They don't take cash or cards, but the staff will teach you how to buy multiple cryptocurrencies using their onsite machine to pay for your specialty coffee and cake.

Bohemia Boards & Brews (Charkovská 18; tel. +420 252 548 435; www.bohemiaboardsandbrews.com; Mon-Fri 5pm-11pm, Sat 4pm-11pm, Sun 4-10pm) in Vršovice has a massive collection of board games available for a 60 CZK cover charge. A menu of sandwiches, snacks, and beverages ensure that players don't have to take a hunger break in between turns.

SLOVANKA BOAT RENTAL

Slovanský ostrov; tel. +420 777 870 511 or +420 777 800 003; www.slovanka.net; daily 11am-10pm (weather permitting); tram: Národní divadlo

Long-running and centrally located, Slovanka Boat Rental offers 2-5-person pedal boats (some in the shape of swans) and rowboats for 200-250 CZK per hour. Surrounding views include silhouettes of New Town, Old Town, and the Prague Castle. To find the docks, cross a small bridge to the island of Slovanský ostrov, just south of the National Theater.

SPECTATOR SPORTS

Many Czechs are more likely to play a sport themselves than to spend much time watching them. Lots of adults participate in organized leagues for ice hockey, floorball, soccer, and other active hobbies (with the requisite meeting in the pub afterward). However, when it comes to national and international championships or intercity rivalries, there are a few local sports that result in locals donning jerseys and hitting the streets.

Ice Hockey

Ice hockey is a top contender for the most popular national sport. Jaromir Jagr of NHL fame is a national hero, despite leaving the Czech Republic to play across the pond. Every pub in town will have multiple screens devoted to matches during the Winter Olympics or the World Hockey Championships in May—Czechs broke IHF attendance records with more than 11,000 fans per game when they hosted these championships in 2015.

Prague's two main teams are **HC Sparta Praha** (www.hcsparta.cz) and **HC Slavia Praha** (www.hc-slavia.cz), who play in the **Tipsport Arena** (Za Elektrárnou 419/1; tel. +420 266 727 411; www.tipsportarena-praha.cz; tickets 100-300 CZK) in Holešovice or the **O2 Arena** (Českomoravská 2345/17; tel. +420 266 771 351; www.o2arena.cz; tickets 100-300 CZK) east of the city center.

Football

On the world stage, where "football" means **soccer,** you'll know when the two biggest rivals in Prague are playing. Fans of **SK Slavia Praha** (www.slavia.cz) and **AC Sparta Prague** (www.sparta.cz) often get a police escort to march through the city before the

---

1: paddleboats on the Vltava River **2:** Rent a bike to see the city on wheels.

match. Slavia's home stadium is the **Sinobo Stadium** (U Slavie 1540/2a; tel. +420 725 875 438; www.slavia.cz; tickets 200-1,000 CZK), formerly known as Eden Arena, in Vršovice while AC Sparta calls Letná's **Generali Arena** (Milady Horakove 1066/98; tel. +420 296 111 400; www.sparta.cz; tickets 170-500 CZK) their home base. Rivalry games are a rowdy, beer-fueled glimpse into local fandom from an otherwise fairly subdued national culture.

Bars and Nightlife

"Nightlife" is almost the wrong term to use for Prague's beverage scene, considering a cold beer with lunch or an afternoon drinking in a beer garden is as much a part of life as a night on the town. Hikes and cycling trips include multiple pub stops along the way, and a steaming-hot adult beverage at an outdoor holiday market isn't limited to roped-off areas or wristbands. Recreation with a drink in hand is integrated into all hours of daily life.

That prevalence of adult beverages doesn't necessarily translate to a rowdy, shouty landscape. Prague overall has more of a mellow pub culture than a massive club scene. Most wine, beer, and cocktail bars stick to table service all night, as opposed to mingling around a bar and communicating directly with a bartender. Budget 30-65 CZK for a domestic beer, depending on the neighborhood, and 50-100 CZK for craft beer and imported microbrews. A glass of wine can vary from 35-150 CZK, and specialty cocktails generally fall into the 150-300 CZK range.

Servers often keep a tally of the drinks on a piece of paper at your table in a traditional pub, or use an automated system in other venues. Separate checks are expected, but it is the responsibility of the patrons to remember what they had and tell the server which food or drinks they want to pay for at the end of the night—something to note if you're the last one of your group to pay the bill! Credit cards are accepted in maybe 65 percent of venues, but many systems don't allow tips on cards, so carrying cash in the local currency is always a good backup plan.

Euros may be accepted in some touristy pubs around the center, but usually at an abysmal exchange rate.

The pub scene starts in the early evening around 4-7pm. Many venues and restaurants then transition from dinner to late-night drinks without much change to the atmosphere. A recent smoking ban has also put more patrons on the sidewalks in front of pubs and clubs, so noise ordinances in residential areas usually go into effect at 11pm or midnight. Nightlife in Prague is also fairly casual, and people generally don't worry about changing clothes to go from work, school, or the park to the pub.

NIGHTLIFE DISTRICTS

The pubs and small clubs lining **Krymská street** in the Vršovice district get a steady stream of business from the large Czech Inn hostel at the top of the hill and the local residents who live in the surrounding area. Lots of pubs spread across the **Žižkov** neighborhood make for a wide array of choices, but aren't consolidated around a single street.

Wine bars in **Karlín** and craft-beer pubs in **Vinohrady** allow for conversation over a quality beverage. Cocktail bars around **Old Town** tend to focus on flair, atmosphere, and gimmicks, while those in the **Letná, Vinohrady,** or **Žižkov** neighborhoods tend to have a more laid-back vibe.

Try a mini-pub crawl from **Letná Beer Garden** to **Café Letka** to **Bio Oko's** cinema bar, ending with a cocktail at **Cobra** to experience the walkable diversity of this neighborhood's nightlife scene.

Reservations... at the Bar?

Visitors may be surprised to find that local nightlife requires reservations. For a seat in a popular pub or a table at a wine or cocktail bar, channel your inner planner and call ahead with a name, time, and number in your party, or check the venue's website for an online reservation system. It is possible to bounce from bar to bar, but be prepared for about 50 percent of the places you try to have no seats available. Standing at the bar or in the aisles of a pub isn't generally done. But don't worry—this doesn't mean you have to spend your whole night sitting at a table. Alternative spaces such as the Náplavka boardwalks, Kasarna Karlín, Přístav 18600, or any of the city's beer gardens are your best chances to interact with younger locals and meet fellow international visitors.

Pubs often require reservations.

BARS AND PUBS
Old Town
(Staré Město)
★ SKAUTSKY INSTITUTE
Staroměstské náměstí 4; tel. +420 732 947 509; www.skautskyinstitut.cz; Mon-Sat 9am-10pm, Sun 1pm-6pm; metro: Staroměstská or Můstek

Skautsky Institute is a peaceful escape from Old Town crowds. The laid-back space, run by young adult members of Prague's local Boy and Girl Scouts organization, extends from the light-filled interior with minimalist wooden furniture to the wrap-around balcony in the quiet center of the building. Coffee, craft beer on draft, and light snacks are surprisingly budget-friendly for Old Town Square. This secret hideout is popular with students and location-independent workers.

New Town
(Nové Město)
KAVÁRNA LUCERNA
Vodičkova 36; www.restaurace-monarchie.cz; tel. +420 224 215 495; daily 10am-midnight; metro: Můstek, tram: Václavské náměstí

Sip a half-liter of Pilsner Urquell or the Czech spirit Becherovka in the glamorous First Republic style of dark wood and chandeliers. Request a seat along the tall arched windows for a view of David Černý's upside-down horse sculpture hanging underneath the domed ceiling of Palac Lucerna. This is the elegant side of Czech pub life.

U-PINKASU
Jungmannovo náměstí 16; tel. +420 221 111 152; www.upinkasu.com; daily 10am-10pm; metro: Můstek

Bartenders have kept the regulars of U-Pinkasu supplied with foam-topped pints of Pilsner—well, technically half-liters—since the mid-1800s. The pub has expanded over the decades, along with the crowds, into multiple floors of arched ceilings and wooden pub furniture. Try the afternoon for a coveted seat in the Gothic Summer Beer Garden between the stone walls. Reservations strongly recommended.

PROPAGANDA
Pštrossova 29, tel. +420 224 932 285; www.propagandabar.cz; Mon-Fri 11am-3am Mon-Fri. Sat-Sun 5pm-3am; tram: Národní divadlo

For the gruff and gritty Czech pub experience, pull up a bar seat, wooden bench, or low-to-the-ground lounge chair in this medium-sized bar near the National Theater. Late-night hours often attract regulars looking for one (or four) final beers before turning in for the night. Try a few Czech words (e.g., "jedno malé pivo, prosím" for "one small beer, please") to order your first round.

Lesser Town
(Malá Strana)
CRAFT BEER SPOT

Plaská 623/5; tel. +420 257 219 855; www.craftbeerprague.com; Mon-Fri 11:30am-11pm, Sat 3pm-11pm; tram: Újezd

Grab a spot in the 40-seat beer garden in good weather (or inside the two-story pub if not) to sample a rotating selection of craft beer on tap. The clean lines and minimalist décor keep the focus on the product, with in-depth, 90-minute beer tastings available for 10 Czech styles (500 CZK) or six styles paired with a multi-course Czech menu (1250 CZK).

KAVÁRNA MLÝNSKÁ

Všehrdova 14; tel. +420 257 313 222; daily noon-midnight; cash only; tram: Újezd

Kavárna Mlýnská on the edge of Park Kampa attracts a mellow, artsy crowd that occasionally includes notorious local artist David Černý. The muraled walls, cozy size, and affordable drinks create a fairly local space, so pull out a few Czech phrases, keep your conversations to a moderate volume, and pay in cash (no cards accepted) to blend in with the crowd.

Prague Castle District
(Hradčany)
STRAHOV MONASTERY BREWERY

Strahovské nádvoří 301; tel. +420 233 353 155; www.klasterni-pivovar.cz; Mon-Thu 11am-10pm, Fri-Sun 10am-8pm; tram: Pohořelec

The Strahov Monastery Brewery, known locally as "Klášterní pivovar Strahov," is centuries-old but refurbished in this millennium. While admittedly a little touristy, the 230-seat restaurant and beer hall serves delicious seasonal brews and Czech food with efficient, multi-lingual service and plenty of indoor and outdoor seating.

Vinohrady
★ BEER GEEK BAR

Vinohradská 62; tel. +420 776-827-068; www.beergeek.cz; daily 3pm-2am; metro or tram: Jiřího z Poděbrad

Beer Geek Bar was one of the earliest purveyors of microbrew culture in Prague. The 32 rotating taps across the street from Jiřího z Poděbrad square still draw an international crowd of locals and travelers to this mid-sized underground pub lined with banquette seating in primary colors. Order your beers and snacks (including 11 flavors of chicken wings and vegetarian bites) at the bar. The bottle shop of the same name two streets away (at Slavíkova 10) stocks a wide selection of souvenirs for the beer lover in your life. Reservations recommended by phone or email at rezervace@beergeek.cz.

VÝČEP

Korunní 92; tel. +420 720 120 100; www.vycepkorunni.cz; Mon-Fri 11am-10pm, Sat-Sun noon-10pm; tram: Perunova

This casual addition to the Vinohrady neighborhood is a rare Bohemian pub serving delicious Moravian beer from the Dalešice brewery. Part pub, part restaurant, the refreshing soundtrack of folk music instead of international pop tunes draws a slightly older crowd of neighborhood residents and tourists in for a drink or a meal. A semi-upscale selection of Moravian wine, homemade lemonades, and specialty coffee offer non-beer choices for mixed crowds. Reservations recommended.

Žižkov
★ PIVO A PÁREK

Bořivojova 58; tel. +420 731 457 910; www.pivoaparek.cz; Mon-Sat 3pm-11pm, Sun 3pm-10pm; tram: Lipanská

The limited menu of Pivo a párek is as simple as translating the name "beer and hot dogs." That casual simplicity extends to the

---

1: the inner balcony of the Skautský Institut 2: Pivo a párek pub in Žižkov 3: meal and beer at Dva Kohouti brewery and pub in Karlín 4: Beer Geek Bar

The Best Czech Beverages

In Prague, the local custom is to stick to the deliciously simple beer or wine by the glass, or indulge in high-end cocktails heavy on flair and presentation. Ordering a rum and Coke in a traditional Czech pub is likely to get you a shot of rum plus a bottle of cola (charged for both), and maybe a glass of ice to mix them yourself! (If you're looking for cocktails, choose a place specializing in mixology.)

BEER

Beer is the local beverage of choice, and cheaper than water (!) on most menus. A beer in Prague can range from 30 CZK for a half-liter in small neighborhood pubs, rising to around 50 CZK in more touristy areas around the city center or Malá Strana, and up to 75-100 CZK for an imported microbrew. Most locals prefer a foam-topped **Pilsner Urquell,** although the growing microbrewery scene caters to a broadening array of tastes—Matuška and Únětice are some popular up-and-coming brands.

Homemade lemonades (domácí limonády) come in all kinds of flavors.

WINE

Central Europe's climate and geography favor white wines and lighter, fruit-forward reds, with the eastern region of Moravia producing some of the best domestic labels.

Burčák is a sweet, cloudy glass of partially fermented grape juice. You won't find it on a lot of wine menus, but it starts to pop up in plastic bottles and wine festivals from around September until the end of November. Warning: This easy-to-drink autumn treat packs a killer headache upon overconsumption.

When the weather turns cold, gloved hands begin to clutch glasses of svařák, the local take on mulled wine sold at most Christmas markets and some traditional Czech pubs in winter. Svařák is less sweet and more citrusy than traditional mulled wine, and is often spiked with Czech rum or brandy.

To satisfy a sweet tooth at Christmas or Easter markets, try a small glass of medovina, a sugar-packed honey wine that can be served hot or cold.

SPIRITS

For a taste of local spirits, skip the absinthe and order a throat-burning shot of slivovice, a clear plum brandy. Alternatively, you could try some Becharovka, an herbal liqueur with hints of cinnamon and pine from a distillery in Karlovy Vary, best described with the phrase "it tastes like Christmas." In warmer weather, order it with tonic and a slice of lime to create a "Beton" cocktail.

NON-ALCOHOLIC

Domácí limonády translates literally to "homemade lemonade" but means a freshly mixed, sparkling drink infused with fresh fruit, cucumber, ginger, or mint, to name a few flavors. Prague's rapidly growing specialty coffee scene has sparked a generation of baristas who embrace the craft as a passion beyond a profession.

chalkboard-menu-and-wooden-table interior of this mid-sized staple. A lively summer beer garden in the inner courtyard has a residential feel in the shadow of the Žižkov TV Tower. If the closing time is early for your tastes, grab some takeaway bottles from their well-stocked beer fridges or head down the street to Bukowski's Bar for a late-night cocktail.

U SADU
Škroupovo náměstí 5; tel. +420 222 727 072; www.usadu.cz; Sun-Mon 8am-2am, Tue-Sat 8am-4am; metro or tram: Jiřího z Poděbrad

With pub food served late every night, this neighborhood watering hole near the base of the Žižkov TV Tower is a last stop for pubgoers on their way home (if they can find a seat among the regulars who have been there since early evening). The large, multi-floor interior has an eclectic, thrift-store style décor of globes, baskets, and random items hanging from the walls and ceilings, plus a number of picnic benches outdoors. Try a Svijany beer with some smažený sýr (fried cheese) and tartar sauce, potato pancakes, or a grilled steak to satisfy your late-night cravings.

Karlín
DVA KOHOUTI
Sokolovská 55; tel. +420 604 611 001; www.dvakohouti.cz; Mon-Fri 2pm-10pm, Sat-Sun noon-10pm; tram: Karlínské náměstí

The young guys behind the "two cocks" (as the name loosely translates) are well known in the local brewery scene, drawing crowds from the moment they opened in late 2018. The interior of this brewery and taproom is simple—wooden benches and tables on one side of the warehouse-style space, standing tables and exposed tanks on the other. The fence-enclosed cement beer garden attracts young professionals from the area in summer and smokers in winter. No reservations are taken, so arrive before 5pm on weekdays or try a weekend afternoon if you want a seat.

Letná and Holešovice
CAFÉ LETKA
Letohradská 44; tel. +420 777 444 035; www.cafeletka.cz; Mon-Fri 8am-midnight, Sat 9am-midnight, Sun 9am-10pm; cash only; tram: Letenské náměstí

Prague bars are usually split into two camps: great beer and a nondescript house wine, or an impressive wine selection and one decent beer. Café Letka serves the best of both worlds in an intimate setting of distressed wood, pillow-lined windows, and pastel accents. Quality coffee and a breakfast menu bring a morning crowd that blends seamlessly into leisurely lunches and post-work crowds unwinding over adult beverages and late-night snacks. This is a sophisticated alternative to the nearby Letná Beer Garden. Cash only; weekend reservations recommended.

TOP EXPERIENCE

BEER GARDENS
The phrase "Česká pohoda" is one of those tricky, untranslatable ideas, but is basically used to describe enjoying life in good weather. Combine two essential elements of Czech social life—beer and being in nature—and you've got the idea. The opening of beer gardens in nearly every neighborhood is a sure sign that the season of sunshine has arrived. Each of the city's beer gardens has a distinct character.

Žižkov
ŽIŽKOV BEER GARDEN
Koněvova; www.zizkovbg.cz; Mon-Fri 2pm-9pm (or later if busy), depending on weather, usually May-Sep; tram: Biskupcova

Žižkov Beer Garden, at the base of Vítkov Hill near the Ohrada bus stop, feels more like an outdoor barbeque or family reunion. Pop music from recent decades blasts from speakers of questionable quality and neighborhood dogs run free in the surrounding grass while local residents sip Pilsner and eat grilled meats under beach umbrellas. Live concerts and amusement park rides sometimes pop up in mid-summer. This residential favorite feels endearingly stuck in a previous era, a perfect beer stop before or after climbing Vítkov Hill to admire the view. Bring cash.

HOSPŮDKA PARUKÁŘKA

Vrch sv. Kříže Parukářka; tel. +420 776 366 410; www.parukarka.cz; daily 1pm-11pm, depending on weather, usually May-Sept; tram: Olšanské náměstí
The outdoor patio of this smallish pub-in-a-park has a relaxed, neighborhood vibe. Leave a 50 CZK deposit for your glass and grab a spot in the grass. The hilly landscape of the surrounding park includes impressive views of the Žižkov TV Tower and the city center in the distance. Time your visit around June when this park hosts the **Žižkovské pivobraní,** a neighborhood microbrew festival with tons of tents and live bands that draws an all-ages crowd.

Letná and Holešovice
★ LETNÁ BEER GARDEN

Letenské sady 341; tel. +420 233 378 200; daily 11am-midnight, depending on weather, usually May-Sep; lower tram: Čechův most, upper tram: Letenské náměstí
You can tell that Prague summer has begun when the drinks start flowing around Letná Beer Garden, located inside the park of the same name, with arguably the best view in town over the Vltava River and Old Town. Hundreds of international visitors line the picnic tables along the edge of the hillside park, with dogs and their humans often stopping here for a break on a walk through the park. Carts and stands along the edges serve primarily beer, with some vendors also offering cider, wine, and shots of liquor. Available snacks are largely meat-based dishes like grilled sausages. Feel free to bring a deck of cards or entertainment for your group, but no outside food or drink is allowed, so step into the grassy lawn of the surrounding park if you want to bring a picnic or vegetarian snacks.

Vyšehrad
HOSPŮDKA NA HRADBÁCH

V Pevnosti 2; tel. +420 734 112 214; Mon-Fri 2pm-midnight, Sat-Sun noon-midnight Sat-Sun; metro: Vyšehrad
This beer garden tucked inside the Vyšehrad Complex just behind St. Martin's Rotunda is a laid-back, all-ages space popular among locals. Picnic tables lining the outer edges offer a view of the city if you peek over the hedges.

Hospůdka Na Hradbách

Local Beer Culture

As one of the oldest brewing cultures around, Czechs take pivo (beer) very seriously, and the country ranks among the highest per-capita consumption rates in the world. A few things you should know:

- **Pilsner is king.** While local microbrews are starting to expand the national palate, don't expect to find stouts, reds, or IPAs outside of select beer pubs. Try a Pilsner Urquell for the classic experience, and if you spot a Svijany sign (my personal favorite beer) outside any neighborhood pubs, duck inside for at least one.

- **Foam is a sign of freshness.** You haven't been shortchanged if the liquid doesn't reach the brim of your glass. A typical pour has a frothy head that leaves rings below the rim with each sip.

- **Choose your size.** When ordering a beer, you'll be asked if you want a large (velké), which is a half-liter (almost 17 ounces), or small (malé) one of 0.3 liters (just over 10 ounces), particularly if you appear to be female.

A properly poured Czech beer includes a smooth layer of foam.

- **Practice your toast.** The Czech version of "cheers" is "Na zdraví" (literally meaning "to health") and pronounced roughly "NAH-straw-vee." Emphasizing the first syllable is important to differentiate it from the Russian "na zDROvvje" (being lumped in or confused with other Slavic-speaking countries is a pet peeve among many Czechs). Toasting in a Czech pub is common for the first round. To toast, each person at the table should make eye contact while clinking glasses. Reaching over or under another set of arms is not allowed. Yes, this takes some time for each pair to acknowledge everyone else—it's a ritual that highlights the personal connection of sharing a beverage.

- **Drink to your health.** If you share a pivo with a Czech friend, you might be surprised to hear people describe it as "healthy." Many Czechs like to tout the level of vitamins in their favorite beverage and will counter any health-conscious criticisms by pointing out the amount of sugar in most non-alcoholic options.

- **Take your time.** Prague is not a binge-drinking city, and you won't win any points for chugging in record time. In fact, many young people find it strange that the losers in American drinking games are punished with sips. In true Czech style, beer is to be enjoyed, savored, and revered all day long over lunch, dinner, and evenings with friends.

The center area of the two-tiered lawn offers more tables surrounding an open play space, drawing families and the stroller set to enjoy a drink within eyesight of their young ones. Beverage stands along the edges offer a wide selection of beer, wine, cider, and domácí limonády (a sparkling soft drink in various fruit and herb flavors), plus grilled meats and snacks. The small indoor pub on site can provide refuge in a rainstorm, but the beer garden is the star of this space.

WINE AND COCKTAIL BARS
New Town
(Nové Město)
★ STŘECHA LUCERNY

Palác Lucerna; tel. +420 604 707 686; https://strechalucerny.cz; May-Oct; 100 CZK entry; metro: Můstek, tram: Václavské náměstí

The 2019 opening of Palac Lucerna's rooftop bar drew an all-ages stream of visitors excited to see a new side of the historical building. The multiple terraces, sparsely decorated with potted plans and scattered furniture, come with gorgeous rooftop views and spires on all sides. Double check flexible opening hours when planning a visit; regular hours are Saturday-Monday around 2-3pm-10pm May-July, 9pm in August, 8pm in September, and 7pm in October. However, a varied events calendar (yoga Wednesdays, G&T and prosecco Thursdays, folk dance Fridays) often extends chances to visit. Enter beside the Grand Hall inside Palac Lucerna and take the continuously running paternoster elevator to avoid climbing five flights of stairs.

ANONYMOUS SHRINK'S OFFICE

Jungmannova 11; tel. +420 608 911 884;
www.shrinksoffice.cz; Sun-Thurs 6pm-2am,
Fri-Sat 6pm-3am; cocktails 205-235 CZK;
metro: Národní třída, tram: Vodičkova

The ingredients may be a mystery, but that's half the fun of ordering "cocktail therapy" based on a Rorschach-test menu at Anonymous Shrink's Office. Settle into a high-backed, brown leather chair in this candlelit, underground brick cave—or, if you're looking for a private table and you ask nicely as you enter, the bar staff might show you the secret room hidden behind a bookshelf. This quirky addition to the Prague cocktail scene attracts young professionals and international travelers, but the doorbell required for entry ensures that it's never overcrowded. Make your reservation online.

CHAMPAGNERIA

Průchodní 4; tel. +420 735 025 482;
htps://champagneria.cz; Mon-Sat 3pm-midnight, Sun
3pm-10pm; wine 85-300 CZK, bottle 400-1,850 CZK;
metro or tram: Národní třída

Imagine sipping red, white, rosé, or sparkling wines in a sparsely decorated apartment with plush sofas and wooden furniture scattered through multiple rooms. Tables in the outdoor garden are great for people-watching on this quiet side street near the National Theater.

The light menu of olives, bruschetta, cheese plates, and sandwiches will save you from ordering a second bottle on an empty stomach. Call or text for reservations.

Vinohrady and Vršovice
BONVIVANT'S CTC

Mánesova 55; tel. +420 604 958 311; +420 604 958
311; daily 4pm-1am; cocktails 185 CZK; metro or tram:
Jiřího z Poděbrad

Bonvivant's small cocktail and tapas café (the "CTC") is staffed by mixologists who take both their craft and the appearance of their crisp white uniforms seriously. Seasonal cocktail menus could feature blends of whiskey, ginger, and honey or a vodka, sake, and lavender martini. For a fun alternative to sitting in the small space, order a picnic basket of cocktails and baguettes to enjoy in the nearby Jiřího z Poděbrad Square.

LE CAVEAU

Náměstí Jiřího z Poděbrad 9; tel. +420 775 294 864;
www.broz-d.cz; Mon-Fri 8am-10:30pm,
Sat 9am-10:30pm, Sun 10am-8:30pm;
wine 100-150 CZK, bottle 250-1,400 CZK;
metro or tram: Jiřího z Poděbrad

Neighborhood wine lovers congregate for hours around the standing tables just outside this small French bakery, café, and wine bar on Jiřího z Poděbrad Square. This is a great place to sample multiple wines from the tasting menu before committing to a bottle. The smell of fresh bread from the onsite bakery may also inspire you to add a croissant or fruit tart to your order.

ALTÁN GRÉBOVKA

Havlíčkovy sady 1369; tel. +420 725 999 495;
http://altangrebovka.com; daily 10am-10pm;
bottle 350-1,500 CZK; tram and bus: Krymská

Indulge in a bottle of Czech, Slovak, Austrian, Hungarian, or Italian wine in this open-air gazebo located inside a Vršovice park. The nearby Vinohrady neighborhood was named for the rows of grapes stretching down the hillside toward Prague's famed red rooftops

Up-and-Coming Karlín

The Karlín neighborhood is known for food, wine, and being an ideal place to live, but is also a neighborhood in transition: There is construction around the neighborhood, such as the rebuilding of a railway bridge, completed in May 2020, and shops planned to fill the stone arches underneath it. The below venues are part of a trend toward artsy innovation in the area:

KASÁRNA KARLÍN

Prvního Pluku 2; www.kasarnakarlin.cz;
Mon-Fri 1pm-11:30pm, Sat-Sun 10am-11:30pm
Every corner of this outdoor space, located inside repurposed industrial barracks, is packed with entertainment, with rotating options like a volleyball court, outdoor cinema, view tower, and a metallic unicorn statue in the summer or an ice rink in winter. Mini-art galleries, cafés, bars, and live music are tucked into the various doorways surrounding the square, making it easy to drift from one space to the next for a change of scenery. This year-round hot spot attracts an ultra-cool, all-ages, international crowd. Come for a drink, or catch some un-

Kasárna Karlín, former army barracks turned bar and event space

structured live music performances. The live music shows are more like seeing a band in a friend's basement than a concert venue—people wander into the room, listen to a song, and then wander back out to the courtyard. Kasárna Karlín operates on a long-term temporary lease so double check opening hours before going.

PŘÍSTAV 18600

Rohanský ostrov 8; www.18600.cz; daily noon-10:30pm late April-Sept, weather permitting
A group of young architects created the laid-back hangout in 2014 to relax among wild plantlife instead of pristine parks. Tucked behind rows of industrial office buildings and down a dirt path beside the Vltava River, it exemplifies the neighborhood's vibe. It's an oasis of outdoor beer stands and picnic tables, with a volleyball court and a playground for families. A summertime ferry ride connects this spot to the Holešovice neighborhood and is a fun way to come and go. (Ferry stop below street level near the Pražská Tržnice tram stop.) Come for a mellow outdoor drink after spending an afternoon at DOX Center for Contemporary Art. Bring cash for a reusable-cup deposit.

and Vyšehrad in the distance. Double check the "svatby" tab on their website before visiting to ensure that this popular wedding venue isn't booked for the night.

CAFÉ BAR PILOTU

Dónská 19; tel. +420 739 765 694;
www.cafebarpilotu.cz; Mon-Thurs 5pm-midnight,
Sat-Sun 5pm-1am; cocktails 150-200 CZK;
tram and bus: Krymská

For craft cocktails and a casual atmosphere, head to Café Bar Pilotu near the top of bar-lined Krymská street in the trendy Vršovice neighborhood. Bookshelves and a grand piano establish a living-room vibe hosted by inventive mixologists. The creative cocktail list is inspired by neighboring businesses—think fresh ingredients for a vegetarian restaurant or an everything-on-the-shelves approach for the convenience shop.

Žižkov

★ BUKOWSKI'S BAR

Bořijovova 86; tel. +420 773 445 280;
daily 7pm-3am; cocktails 90-150 CZK;
tram: Lipanská or Husinecká

Bukowski's Bar is cool for all the same reasons as the Žižkov neighborhood. It's affordable, comfortable, non-judgmental, a little grungy, and always up for a party. The friendly staff at this long-standing, all-ages, local favorite know their way around the bar. Dim lighting and a candle-lined bookshelf covering one wall set a homey atmosphere to the multi-room venue, with conversations varying from intimate whispers to slurred debates from table to table.

OBLACA BAR

Mahlerovy sady 1; tel. +420 210 320 086;
www.towerpark.cz; daily 7pm-3am;
cocktails 250 CZK; metro: Jiřího z Poděbrad,
tram: Olšanské náměstí or Jiřího z Poděbrad

For a more upscale experience, try a cocktail with a panoramic view at Oblaca Bar inside the Žižkov TV Tower. The unofficial dress code in this sophisticated crowd is fashion forward, and you'll need to check in with a hostess on the ground floor to be allowed access to the elevator. Reservations required, especially on weekends or during peak seasons.

KINO AERO

Biskupcova 31; tel. +420 271 771 349;
www.kinoaero.cz; daily 2pm-midnight; wine 50 CZK;
tram: Biskupcova

You don't actually have to see a movie to join the eclectic crowds talking arts and culture in the courtyard of this 1930s art house cinema. Cinephiles of all ages mingle over wine and beer underneath twinkling lights strung above an outdoor patio of 10-15 tables. Stop by for an evening drink after watching the sunset on top of nearby Vítkov Hill.

Karlín

★ VELTLIN

Křižíkova 488/115; +420 725 535 395;
www.veltlin.cz; Mon-Sat 5pm-11pm;
glass 100-300 CZK; tram: Urxova

Natural wines at this 10-15-table Karlín wine bar come exclusively from countries of the former Austro-Hungarian Empire, illustrated by a large map drawn on one wall. Instead of a menu, the staff will chat (in many languages) about preferences and price points before recommending individual glasses or a bottle to share. Indoor and outdoor tables available. Make a reservation for a nightcap after having dinner at the nearby Eska restaurant.

Letná and Holešovice

COBRA

Milady Horákové 8; tel. +420 778 470 515; www.
barcobra.cz; Mon-Thu 8am-1am, Fri 8am-2am, Sat
9am-2am, Sun 9am-1am; cocktails 140-180 CZK;
tram: Strossmayerovo náměstí

The bar staff at Cobra like to get creative, so make sure to investigate the latest specialty cocktail list. This trendy, minimalist environment of exposed lightbulbs and bar-stool seating includes a rotating set of DJs from Thursday-Saturday nights. Take note of the address or look for the small door sign of this otherwise unmarked and easy-to-miss venue.

BIO OKO

Františka Křížka 15; tel. +420 233 382 606;
www.biooko.net; Mon-Fri 10am-1am, Sat-Sun
9am-1am; wine 50-100 CZK; tram: Strossmayerovo
náměstí or Kamenická

The lobby bar of this art-house cinema spills out onto the streets during warmer months with all-ages crowds around sidewalk tables scattered under the theater's name in neon lights. Film lovers and families flow in and out of the theater, sipping beer, wine, and spirits or coffee in between cigarette breaks. Seating inside the cinemas is equally quirky, including beanbags, beach chairs, and an old-time-y dentist's chair.

LGBTQ+ Prague

Prague's live-and-let-live attitude ranges from tolerance to celebration for the gay and lesbian community, with a popular Pride parade each summer, a Mezipatra film festival (www.mezipatra. cz) each fall, and Queer balls (www.queerball.cz) held in Prague and Brno in February or March. Czech culture is generally less accepting but usually not actively hostile or aggressive toward trans individuals. The overall landscape is generally safe for LGBTQ+ residents to enter any pub, dance in any nightclub, or hold hands while walking down the streets, but a romantic advance toward another patron outside of a designated gay club may not be well received. **Prague Pride** (www.praguepride.cz) can recommend hotels and bars where visitors should be welcomed with open arms.

- Prague's cis gay male club scene has historically centered around the Vinohrady neighborhood but has expanded into multiple neighborhoods. The small, neon-lit dance floor at Vinohrady's **Termix** (Třebízského 4a; tel. +420 222 710 462; www.club-termix.cz; Wed-Sat 10pm-6am) is generally packed with young men dancing to Top 40 hits, while **Termax** (Vinohradská 40; tel. +420 222 710 462; www.club-max.cz; Fri-Sat 10pm-6am), just a few streets away, claims the title of Prague's largest gay bar.

- **Freedom Night** parties (www.freedomnight.cz) cater to a cis lesbian crowd with monthly DJ dance parties around Prague every third Friday, plus additional events in Brno, Pilsen, and Bratislava, Slovakia. The Prague party is often hosted at **PM Club** (Trojická 10; tel. +420 222 518 097; www.pmclub.net; daily 4pm-4am) near the Vltava River and the base of Vyšehrad hill. **Jampa Dampa** (V Tůních 10; tel. +420 604 774 959; www.jampadampaprague.cz; Wed-Thurs 8pm-3am, Fri-Sat 8pm-5am) in New Town is also known to welcome a lesbian crowd.

- For a quieter vibe during daylight hours, head to **Q Cafe** (Opatovická 12; tel. +420 776 856 361; www.q-cafe.cz; daily 3pm-2am) for a relaxing atmosphere with subtle rainbow-themed touches around the bar and bench seating. This New Town location near Karlovo náměstí welcomes a mixed crowd of the LGBTQ+ community and allies.

- For further questions or advice, try **Trans*parent** (www.transparentprague.cz) for the trans community or Brno-based STUD (www.stud.cz) for the wider LGBTQ+ community.

Performing Arts

With glamorous interiors, affordable prices, and a rich history of classical music, there's good reason that Prague is ranked one of Europe's top cultural and creative destinations. When purchasing tickets in advance, read the cancellation policies carefully. At the time of writing, COVID-19 regulations could quickly alter the size of public events allowed to operate. For a more spontaneous approach, tickets are often available on the day of the performance, particularly if it's not the opening weekend of a particular show. All venues listed are wheelchair-accessible, but some historical buildings require alternative entrances as noted below.

CLASSICAL MUSIC
MUNICIPAL HOUSE

Náměstí Republiky 5; tel. +420 222 002 101; www.obecnidum.cz; tickets 500-1,500 CZK depending on event; tram or metro: Náměstí Republiky

Smetana Hall inside the Municipal House has the honor of opening the Prague Spring concert each year with a performance of its namesake's symphony *Má vlast* (*My Country*). Gorgeous murals encircle the domed ceiling of this home to the Prague Symphony Orchestra (FOK). More than 1,250 seats line the floor and surrounding balconies, with fantastic acoustics no matter which you choose. The smaller 300-seat **Sladkovsky Hall** and

1

2

150-seat **Gregr Hall** provide more intimate settings for chamber concerts.

RUDOLFINUM

Alšovo nábřeží 12; tel. +420 227 059 227;
www.rudolfinum.cz; box office Mon-Fri 10am-6pm
Sep-Jun, Mon-Fri 10am-3pm Jul-Aug; tickets
300-3,000 CZK depending on event;
tram or metro: Staroměstská

There are two concert halls housed inside the Rudolfinum—the stately Dvořák Hall, named for the renowned composer Antonin Dvořák, who conducted the first Czech Philharmonic concert in 1896, and the smaller chandeliered ceiling of the Suk Hall, added during the 1940s renovations. This home of the Czech Philharmonic also hosts concerts by the Prague Symphony Orchestra (FOK), Prague Philharmonia (PKF), smaller chamber ensembles, and visiting musicians during the Prague Spring Festival. A large flight of stairs marks the main entrance, but both concert halls are accessible via elevator, entering from 17 listopadu street to the right of the entrance for Dvořák Hall or using the Rudolfinum Gallery entrance to the left for Suk Hall.

THEATER, DANCE, AND OPERA

Enjoyment and appreciation for fine arts is an ingrained element of Czech culture—this is, after all, a country that elected a playwright as their first president. Prague is also one of the most affordable European capitals to take in a show; however, dressing up at the theater is a sign of respect. Tourists won't be turned away for wearing jeans or shorts, but they're definitely likely to get a few sideways glances. Instead, aim for wedding-appropriate attire: Cocktail dresses and a suit and tie (at least a collared shirt or unwrinkled top and trousers) are a safe bet. Opening nights and premieres may even inspire floor-length gowns and tuxedos among some regular theatergoers. Bonus points if you've got a

matching face mask, which could be required depending on COVID-19 regulations at the time of visiting. The more avant-garde theaters (e.g., Nová scéna or Jatka 78) can be a little more casual.

★ NATIONAL THEATER

Národní 2; tel. +420 224 901 448;
www.narodni-divadlo.cz; tickets 100-1,500 CZK
depending on event; tram: Národní divadlo,
metro: Národní třída

You can spot the golden-crowned rooftop of the National Theater from almost any point along the Vltava River. This queen of the cultural scene was built in the late 1800s, along with the National Museum, as part of the Czech National Revival—a movement that focused on reclaiming the Czech language and cultural identity from outside influences of the surrounding empires. Inside the columned walls of this Renaissance Revival building, the rows of plush red seats, the painted ceiling, and the golden detailed opera boxes create an aura of pure elegance. Get your tickets for ballet, opera, and theater performances online or at the box office next door, inside the New Stage. Wheelchair access to the National Theater is available through an entrance on Masarykovo nábřeží street, which is to the right and around the corner from the main entrance. Visitors using this entrance with limited mobility should contact the theater in advance to ensure smooth entry.

NEW STAGE
(Nová Scéna)

Národní 4; +420 224 901 448; www.narodni-divadlo.
cz; tickets 250-700 CZK depending on event; tram
stop Národní divadlo or metro stop Národní třída

The beehive-like glass building beside Prague's National Theater is the New Stage. A little more experimental than its stately neighbor, this theater started as the home of circus-arts troupe Laterna Magika before both were adopted by the National Theater in 2010. Today the stage is shared between dance, drama, and circus performances in a modern,

---

1: National Theater **2:** Václav Havel Square between the National Theater and New Stage

intimate setting. Young artistic types and audience members congregate at the casual (and Wi-Fi-free) Café Nona on the second floor. Stop by Václav Havel Square, the courtyard between the New Stage and National Theater, to see the glowing red heart memorial and signature of the first Czech president—appropriately surrounded by performance spaces, as Havel was a former playwright.

ESTATES THEATER
(Stavovské Divadlo)

Železná; tel. +420 224 901 448;
www.narodni-divadlo.cz; tickets 100-2,000 CZK
depending on event; metro: Můstek

Don't let anyone convince you that the cloaked statue outside of the Estates Theatre is connected to a *Harry Potter* dementor or to Emperor Palpatine from *Star Wars*. It actually represents the 1787 premiere of Mozart's opera *Don Giovanni* inside this Neoclassical 18th-century building. The Estates Theater was also the first place that the Czech national anthem "Where Is My Home?" was sung in 1843—marked by a plaque on the wall to the right of the main entrance. Today, the luxurious pale blue and gold interior hosts a full program of ballet, theater, and opera. Wheelchair access to the Estates Theater is around the corner to the right of the main entrance, through an unmarked door on Havířská street, and requires contacting the theater in advance to arrange access.

STATE OPERA

Wilsonova 4; tel. +420 224 901 448;
www.narodni-divadlo.cz; tickets 100-1,500 CZK
depending on event; metro or tram: Muzeum

Prague's State Opera began hosting performances under a different name from 1888-1935: The New German Theater. When World War II broke out, this artistic space was co-opted by the Nazis for political meetings and performances (much like the symphony halls at the Rudolfinum). Czech artists reclaimed the space after the war, and the State Opera was enveloped by Prague's network of National Theater buildings in the late 1940s.

Extensive renovations from 2016-2020 added an extra level of sparkle to the historical elegance inside. Muraled ceilings, plush red seats, and a sparkling chandelier set an atmosphere of glamour. Ballet and opera performances with complex sets fit perfectly on the largest stage in Prague (which also has the highest seating capacity when looking for last-minute tickets). Opera boxes lining the walls are worth the splurge for a private experience.

The entrance, across a highway from Wenceslas Square, can be tricky to access so plan an extra 15 minutes for your arrival. An underpass near the Muzeum metro stop or the crosswalk at the southeast corner of Wenceslas Square (near the National Museum) will lead pedestrians to the entrance. Visitors who use a wheelchair should contact the theater in advance for entrance assistance.

JATKA 78

Bubenské nábřeží 306; tel. +420 773 217 127;
www.jatka78.cz; Mon-Fri 10am-midnight, Sat
9am-midnight; tickets 100-550 CZK depending on
event; tram: Pražská tržnice, metro: stop Vltavská

Jatka 78 takes its playful name from the building's former life as a slaughterhouse. This gritty, multi-use performance space with an emphasis on circus performances opened its doors in 2015 inside the grounds of Holešovice's Prague City Market (Pražská tržnice). The artfully curated warehouse now houses resident theater, dance, and circus-arts companies, plus a bar and bistro.

Festivals and Events

NEW YEAR'S EVE
(Silvestr)

The local name for New Year's Eve, "Silvestr," takes its name from the Czech saints' days calendar (which can be found on the lower clock face of the Astronomical Clock in Old Town Square). Fireworks are traditionally the centerpiece of the party on December 31st—teenagers and young adults shoot bottle rockets at each other in the main squares, turning them into a bit of a war zone. However, a December 2020 ban of fireworks in the city has lessened the prevalence of this practice. You're likely to find a largely international presence in most Prague bars as Czech residents often celebrate Silvestr with a small group of friends in a countryside cabin. Some neighborhoods, bars, and restaurants across the city, especially those lining the **Vltava River,** have put on their own unofficial fireworks shows at midnight on December 31 (bundle up and head to Vyšehrad or **Letná Park** for a great view).

NEW YEAR'S DAY

New Year's Day marks the anniversary of the peaceful split between the Czech Republic and Slovakia, known as the Velvet Divorce, in 1993. One way to celebrate in Czech style is with a rigorous hike (whether hungover or not) to the top of a nearby hill. In 2019, the city government of Prague replaced official New Year's Day fireworks—usually held in the evening on January 1—with a video mapping show on the National Theater out of respect and safety concerns for local wildlife. Check www.prague.eu to confirm details on which form the celebrations will take when you visit.

ČARODEJNICE
("Witches Night")

April 30 is a family-friendly event marking the end of winter in the Czech Republic. Many of Prague's parks, particularly **Ladronka**

Park just west of the Anděl neighborhood, prepare bonfires topped with a wooden figure dressed in witch's clothing. Many local children attending the celebrations also don their pointed black hats and cloaks as part of the fun. From around noon to early evening, the areas around the bonfire entertain crowds with beer stands, grilled sausages, and free concert stages of local Czech bands. Around sundown everyone circles around the witch to watch the pile go up in flames and bid farewell to the cold months of winter.

PRAGUE SPRING
(Pražské Jaro)

www.festival.cz

The Prague Spring International Music Festival centers around a number of significant dates. It began in 1946 to celebrate one peaceful year since the end of World War II. A performance of Bedřich Smetana's *Má vlast* (*My Country*) kicks things off in the **Municipal House's Smetana Hall** every year on the anniversary of the composer's May 12 passing. The following three weeks fill Prague's concert halls, from the **Rudolfinum** to the **National Theater,** with international symphony orchestras and up-and-coming young musicians competing for prizes. Tickets (200-2,000 CZK depending on the show) for this late spring festival generally go on sale around Christmas the year before, but tickets for smaller ensembles and incredibly accomplished student performances are often available closer to the festival for more flexible planning.

PRAGUE FRINGE FESTIVAL

www.praguefringe.com

Fans of avant-garde theater, comedy, and cabaret should think about a trip in late May or early June to catch the Prague Fringe Festival. This English-language (or

Czech Holiday Traditions

In addition to festive markets that pop up around the city, Christmas and Easter are commemorated with some noteworthy local traditions.

EASTER

For a largely non-religious country, Easter (Velikonoce in Czech, which comes from "velká noc" meaning "great night") is a really big deal, with festive markets popping up around town. Many of the local traditions have roots in paganism rather than Christianity, so the holiday often feels more like a celebration of spring.

Easter in Prague is also accompanied by an unusual tradition. On Easter Monday (not Sunday) before noon, boys and men take braided, ribbon-covered whips made from young saplings and visit the women in their lives. They knock on their neighbors' doors and sing "Hody, hody doprovody, dejte vejce malovaný, nedáte-li malovaný, dejte aspoň bílý, slepička vám snese jiný…" which means

whips and colored eggs at Czech Easter markets

roughly "Give me a painted egg, or at least a plain one. The hen will give you another."

The boys then (gently) whip the women to ensure beauty, health, and fertility for the next year, and are rewarded with eggs, chocolate, or a shot of liquor for teens and fathers. The rules vary slightly between regions, but some also dictate that guys visiting after noon will be greeted with a bucket of water in the face rather than a reward.

While this tradition makes my feminist blood boil a bit (a feeling echoed by some Czech female friends), I am assured by other locals that the intention is lighthearted and nostalgic. You're unlikely to witness the tradition in the city center, but might spot groups of young men with their decorated sticks in some places outside Prague.

CHRISTMAS

Prague's Christmas season kicks off on December 5, which is the name day for St. Mikuláš (the Czech version of St. Nicholas). You might spot the costumed saint, accompanied by an angel and a devil, hanging around Prague's streets or shopping malls. In more residential neighborhoods, the trio goes door to door visiting children. Czech kids sing a song or recite a poem to show they've behaved and are rewarded with candy. The devil comes along to see if naughty children show fear (because good kids should have nothing to hide).

Another staple of Prague's street corners around Christmas, visible from about mid-December through the 24th, are fishmongers with mini-swimming pools of carp. These fish, breaded and fried, are the main course of a traditional Czech Christmas dinner, celebrated on the evening of December 24. Some families bring the fish home to live in the bathtub until the big day, while others have the fishmonger do the scaling and beheading right there on the corner (so watch your step in the messy sidewalks around these stands).

sometimes non-verbal) festival takes over the Malá Strana neighborhood for nine days of comedy, cabaret, music, dance, and theater. Performers come from England, the US, Australia, and all across Europe to play in various spaces, from traditional theaters to cafés and cave-like cellars. The shows (150-200 CZK) are roughly an hour long, with some family-friendly content in the afternoon and adults-only entertainment stretching into the evenings. Inspired by the Edinburgh Fringe, the Prague version is an intimate event where audiences and artists mingle until all hours at the bar inside **Malostranská beseda** (Malostranské náměstí 21; tel. +420 257 409 112; www.malostranska-beseda.cz) after the program finishes.

LETNÍ LETNÁ

www.letniletna.cz

Contemporary circus performers from across Europe descend upon the Letná neighborhood every August for the Letní Letná festival (a play on words combining the Czech word for summer and Letná Park). Troupes of tightrope walkers, acrobats, aerialists, and jugglers spend late summer days entertaining audiences in massive tents and open-air spaces on the west side of the park. Some outdoor performances are free while the more elaborate indoor events require advance tickets, available online.

PRAGUE SIGNAL FESTIVAL

www.signalfestival.com

The Czech Republic's largest cultural event takes place on the streets of Prague for one long weekend (usually Thu-Sun) each October. Signal Festival brings millions of visitors to witness the light installations and video mapping shows projected onto some of Prague's architectural beauties around the city. Vendors offering hot wine, beer, and snacks surround the most popular venues. Most of the exhibitions are free to enjoy, with a mobile app leading foot traffic through the various sites in different neighborhoods—recent years have included **Vinohrady, New Town, Old Town, Malá Strana, Holešovice,** and **Karlín.** Some interactive events require a small admission price (50-100 CZK). Video mapping on the Cathedral of St. Ludmila at **Náměstí Míru** is usually a crowd favorite, repeating between 7pm and midnight throughout the night.

ST. MARTIN'S DAY

The legend of St. Martin has historical roots, but the local wine and dining traditions have only developed in recent decades. According to the story, St. Martin rides into town on a white horse every **November 11** (his name day) and is meant to bring with him the first snow of the season. Winemakers and sommeliers across the country also pay close attention to the time—at 11:11am on November 11 they open and pour the first taste of that year's Svatomartinské young wine, which is on the sweet side. Almost every Czech restaurant in town offers a special menu of the St. Martin's meal: roast goose served with red cabbage and dumplings (usually 150-500 CZK depending on the venue).

Shopping

The retail landscape is not necessarily Prague's main attraction, but there are a few places worth heading to if you're looking for retail therapy or a souvenir.

SHOPPING DISTRICTS

Prague's one well-known shopping destination is **Pařížská ulice** (www.parizskastreet.cz). This fittingly translates to "Parisian street," where the most famous names in luxury fashion line the storefronts. The high-end shopping lane branches off from Old Town Square between St. Nicholas Church and the Tourist Information Center and runs through the Jewish Quarter of Josefov. Pařížská is where the visiting European fashion elite, decked out in designer shades in the summer and fur coats in winter, peruse collections from Tiffany's jewelers, Prada handbags, and Louis Vuitton luggage.

A walk around the edges of **Wenceslas Square** or **Na Příkopě street,** dividing Old Town and New Town, might be fun for some window shopping of Czech names interspersed with international chain stores that show Prague's identity as a modern cosmopolitan city as much as a historical European capital. Many of the souvenir shops around Old Town and Malá Strana fall distinctly into the tourist-trap category, so stick to recommendations below for truly local gifts and memorabilia hiding in plain sight in these areas.

GIFTS AND HOME DECOR
Old Town
(Staré Město)
MANUFAKTURA–ORIGINAL CZECH TRADITION

Karlova 26; tel. +420 601 310 605; www. manufaktura.cz; daily 10am-7pm; 100-1,000 CZK; metro or tram: Staroměstská

The Manufaktura—Original Czech Tradition concept grew out of a desire to offer truly local souvenirs. The company began in 1991 by collecting handmade goods from small towns across the country. More than 25 years later, they have kept a network of independent producers of wooden toys, candles, cosmetics, and household accessories in business and accessible to Prague tourists wanting to support local craftspeople. There are a variety of additional locations across the city, detailed online.

Lesser Town
(Malá Strana)
PRAGTIQUE

Mostecka Street 20; tel. +420 737 252 729; www. pragtique.cz; Mon-Fri noon-7pm, Sat-Sun 11am-7pm; 50-500 CZK; metro or tram: Malostranské náměstí

For a gift that supports local, independent designers, try this trendy boutique just off the Malá Strana side of the Charles Bridge. Modern designs on t-shirts, onesies, notebooks, postcards, magnets, tote bags, posters, and accessories are inspired by classic Czech symbols such as the Astronomical Clock, the Prague Castle, Golem, and the Týn Church in Old Town. Stop into neighboring Roesel—Beer and Cake for a post-shopping snack.

Prague Castle District
(Hradčany)
FROM PRAGUE WITH LOVE

Loretánská 13; tel. +420 736 751 012; www.frompraguewithlove.eu; 100-2,000 CZK; tram: Pohořelec

Want to grab a locally made t-shirt, tote bag, or kitchen accessories near the Prague Castle? Stop in From Prague with Love, just a few streets away from the main castle gates near Hradčanské náměstí. The family-owned shop of screen-printed cotton,

Best Souvenirs

There are some great options to bring a piece of Czech culture home with you:

- **Gingerbread:** Gingerbread has a local history dating at least to the 16th century, with the Czech recipe originating in the Pardubice region. You won't find a household without at least a few different designs around Christmas time, often baked in huge batches and shared with friends, neighbors, and coworkers in the weeks before the holiday season. Visit the family-owned **Perníčkův sen** (Haštalská 21; tel. +420 607 773 350; www.pernickuvsen.cz; daily 10am-6pm) in Old Town for a wide selection of adorably hand-designed sweets.

- **Pilsner Beer or Becherovka:** You can find bottles from most of the bigger breweries in any local supermarket, or hold off until duty-free shopping on your trip home. Many of the Czech Republic's big-name distilleries (e.g., Becherovka, Žufánek) are based in cities outside of Prague, so a supermarket or the airport is your best bet for spirits.

- **Wine:** Your best bet for wine in Prague is choosing from the wine bar scene, where most of those you taste are also available to take home. **Veltlin** (www.veltlin.cz) in the Karlín neighborhood focuses on small, independent wine producers. Gala wines are one of the most trusted names on the Czech wine landscape, available at **Vinotéka U Mouřenína** (www.vinotekaumourenina.cz) wine bar in Malá Strana or their smaller wine shop in Old Town.

- **No. 2 Pencils:** Czechs also had a hand in the popularity of No. 2 pencils. The 18th-century art supply company **Koh-i-noor** (Na Příkopě 26; tel. +420 739 329 019; www.koh-i-noor.cz; daily 10am-8pm, additional locations detailed online) patented the blend of lead inside and made the pencil yellow, which spread to copycats and became the industry standard. Their colored pencils and art supplies remain incredibly popular, particularly for fans of children's or adults' coloring books.

- **"The Little Mole":** An authentic choice for young ones is Krtek (or Krteček), the locally loved cartoon character known as "the Little Mole." In 2009, NASA astronaut Andrew Feustel, who is married to a Czech woman, took a toy version of Krtek into space in honor of a 1965 episode detailing a similar adventure. This Czech alternative to Mickey Mouse entered into a Chinese partnership in 2016, giving the character a reboot and new location, but the vintage look still dominates Czech toy shops. Buy the Little Mole and other toys at **Rocking Horse Toy Shop** (Loretánské náměstí 3; tel. +420 220 512 234 or +420 603 515 745; Fri-Wed 11am-6pm; 50-500 CZK) near the Prague Castle or at **Hugo chodí bos** (Milady Horákové 26; tel. +420 775 407 298; www.hugochodibos.cz; Mon-Fri 10am-6pm, Sat 10am-4pm; 100-600 CZK) in the Letná neighborhood.

One particular plea is to avoid purchasing the Soviet-era memorabilia that's sold in a number of shops. Czechoslovakia was forcefully occupied by the Soviet Union from 1968-1989 so any investment in Russian nesting dolls or trinkets and T-shirts with a hammer-and-sickle insignia is ultimately celebrating the oppression of Czech people.

porcelain, and wooden goods uses simple line drawings of Prague symbols, city maps, or the souvenir-appropriate name of their brand. At the time of writing, the brick-and-mortar shop was operating by appointment only under COVID-19 conditions, so double check the website for opening hours during your visit.

BOOKS
New Town
(Novy Město)
GLOBE BOOKSTORE & CAFE

Pštrossova 6; tel. +420 224 934 203; https://globebookstore.cz; Mon-Fri 10am-7pm, Sat 9:30am-7pm, Sun 9:30am-4pm; 100-500 CZK; tram: Myslíkova or Novoměstská radnice

The Globe Bookstore was founded as a haven

for English speakers by an early group of transplants in 1993, when Prague's landscape was fairly new to visitors beyond the Iron Curtain. Today the establishment is a staple of international life in the Czech capital and a reliable source of English-language books on Czech history, politics, legends, and fairy tales, alongside mainstream fiction and nonfiction. The bookstore area includes a few seats, but no reading is allowed unless you've purchased. The adjoining pub hosts regular reading and writing groups as well as a beloved pub quiz (50 CZK per person) every Wednesday at 7:30pm, with reservations essential at least a week in advance.

Lesser Town
(Malá Strana)
SHAKESPEARE & SONS
U Lužického semináře 91; tel. +420-257 531 894; www.shakes.cz; daily 11am-7pm; 150-500 CZK; metro or tram: Malostranské náměstí

This multi-story bookshop with a wide selection of Czech and English titles has that cozy, crowded feeling that makes you want to get lost in the aisles. Browse through translations of local authors like Franz Kafka, Karel Čapek, or Milan Kundera and use their e-shop to send your book home without taking up space in your luggage.

WINE, BEER, AND SPIRITS
Lesser Town
(Malá Strana)
VINOTÉKA U MOUŘENÍNA
Tržiště 17; tel. +420 606 483 087; www.vinotekaumourenina.cz; daily 2pm-10pm; bottles 200-5,000 CZK; metro or tram: Malostranské náměstí

The wooden cabinets lining the walls of Vinotéka U Mouřenína are stocked with Czech, Italian, and French wines and cognacs in a wide range of price points, with a few small tables in the front and rear of the store for tasting. When in doubt, look for bottles by Gala, one of the country's most celebrated winemakers. International shipping is available in store or on their website (only in Czech, so you'll need your preferred translation tool). There is also a second, smaller wine shop in Old Town (Dlouhá 39; tel. +420 601 666 650; Mon-Sat 1pm-10pm).

Vinohrady
BEER GEEK PIVOTEKA
Slavíkova 10; tel. +420 775 260 871; pivoteka. beergeek.cz; Mon-Sat 1pm-8pm, Sun 3pm-9pm; bottles 60-400 CZK; metro or tram: Jiřího z Poděbrad

Beer Geek Pivoteka is the place for microbrews in Prague. This beer-lover's boutique, arranged on shelves by country of origin, stocks over 500 different bottles from across Europe and the US. A few local Czech favorites include anything by Clock, Matuška, Raven, or Zichovec. You can find many of the local bottles on tap at nearby Beer Geek Pub if you want to try before you buy. International shipping is available online (only in Czech, so you'll need your preferred translation tool).

FASHION AND DESIGN
The most current Czech designs don't have a permanent home, but they do have a presence. **Mint Design Market** (www.mintmarket.cz) is an independent pop-up concept of fashion, design, and food that has been bouncing around the country—from Brno to Pilsen to Prague and beyond—since 2015. The collection of young and independent designers runs an e-shop and offers information on the time and location of their events on their website. Prague's **Dyzajn Market** (www.dyzajnmarket.com) also pops up quarterly with a curated collection of independent arts, crafts, and fashion designers. Dyzajn Market events usually take place on Václav Havel Square next to the National Theater or at the Prague Exhibition Center (Výstaviště Praha) in Holešovice.

1: Krtek ("Little Mole") is the Czech equivalent of Mickey Mouse. **2:** Shakespeare & Sons bookstore in Malá Strana **3:** Take home some Czech gingerbread from Perníčkův sen.

Easter and Christmas Markets

Prague is magical all year round, but the holiday markets around Christmas and Easter turn the volume up to eleven. Wooden stands fill every square in town with the smells of warm spiced wine (svařák), hot honey wine (medovina), and street-food blends of meats and potatoes. Old Town Square and Wenceslas Square Christmas markets run through most of December and into the New Year, while some of the smaller neighborhood markets may have more limited runs. The landscape is equally festive during the week before Easter in the same locations, just swapping Christmas decorations for pastel colors.

Prague's holiday markets are generally cheerful and family-friendly, with tourists dominating Old Town Square and locals sometimes stopping by locations near metro stops (e.g., Náměstí Miru or Náměstí Republiky) for a festive pre-commute drink or snack. Most market visitors spend their time browsing and chatting while occasionally picking up some presents. Delicately carved ornaments of wooden scenes and Christmas symbols (around 50-300 CZK) are traditional trinkets. At the Easter markets, you'll find intricately painted wooden eggs called kraslice (100-500 CZK) alongside one unusual element: a braided, ribbon-covered whip made from young saplings (50-300 CZK). (Wondering how this whip is used? See page 110.)

Holiday market stalls generally come to life around 10am and stay busy until 10pm, with food and drinks served in the city center until midnight. Details can change from year to year. Prague Markets (www.trhypraha.cz) and Prague Tourism (www.prage.eu) are good resources to double-check the dates and times around your visit. Fair warning: Prague markets have become an extremely popular tourist experience in the last decade. Head to Brno for Christmas markets with a more local feel.

OLD TOWN SQUARE
(Staroměstské Náměstí)

The markets on Old Town Square are the most crowded and commercial of the bunch, with a strong focus on consumable goods like sweets, hot drinks, and street food. The layout is designed for photo ops, including a large Christmas tree in front of the towers of the Church of Our Lady Before Týn plus stairs to a festive viewing platform in the center of it all.

WENCESLAS SQUARE
(Václavské Náměstí)

Wenceslas Square's market is a low-key experience, usually lined with more food and beverage stands than gifts or trinkets. Standing tables are also a limited commodity in this area, so eating and drinking festive beverages can require a bit of a balancing act.

Old Town
(Staré Město)

SMETANAQ

Smetanovo nábřeží 4; tel. +420 222 263 526;
www.smetanaq.cz; daily 10am-8pm;
tram: Národní divadlo; tram stop Národní divadlo

The SmetenaQ complex, which opened in 2016, houses a young group of independent furniture and accessories designers on its second floor, and a small Deelive Design Store selling their ideas come to life on the ground floor. The riverfront spot also includes a popular café and a gallery on the top level. Located next to Prague's prestigious FAMU school of TV and film, the crowd skews young, hip, and artsy.

PRAGUE CASTLE
(Pražský hrad)
Be prepared to pass through a security screening to enter the grounds for Prague Castle Christmas markets, which close earlier than most (around 6-7pm). That said, the magic of browsing and snacking in St. George's Square, next to St. Vitus Cathedral, may be worth it for some travelers, especially when paired with a visit to the rest of the castle grounds.

REPUBLIC SQUARE
(Náměstí Republiky)
Náměstí Republiky adds a lighthearted presence in front of the busy Palladium shopping mall. This medium-sized market wraps around a busy transportation corner and caters to shoppers grabbing a quick drink, bite, or small gift among their holiday errands at the mall. If you spot a Včelcovina stand, try a glass of their hot honey wine (medovina).

Old Town Square Christmas market

PEACE SQUARE
(Náměstí Míru)
Náměstí Míru draws a busy crowd of both residents and tourists with holiday treats and handmade crafts, plus a small Christmas tree, in the shadow of the Church of St. Ludmila. The pace at this market is slower, made for eating, browsing, and absorbing the atmosphere.

JIŘÍHO Z PODĚBRAD SQUARE
(Náměstí Jiřího z Poděbrad)
Vinohrady's small neighborhood market is less crowded than its central counterparts, with the tradeoff of fewer stalls to browse. Twinkling white lights set a festive scene over benches and wooden booths lining the park in front of the towering Church of the Most Sacred Heart of Our Lord. A temporary stage hosts Christmas choirs and children's performances throughout the day.

Food

Traditional Czech cuisine is hearty, meaty, and often covered in sauce. Local meals (including most daily lunch specials) are divided into grilled meats (pork, beef, game, chicken, or duck) with some form of potatoes or dumplings on the side. Vegetables are scarce and seafood is uncommon (or pricey) in this landlocked country. Enjoy the indulgence of comfort foods like svíčková (a national favorite) or a rich roast duck, or grab some chlebíčky (open-faced sandwiches) for a lighter lunch.

At the time of writing, many Prague restaurants were closing early and collecting customer information for potential contact tracing, so having your accommodation info on hand when dining out may be helpful (or even required). Double check hours for potentially extended late-night dining, depending on current conditions, on your visit.

OLD TOWN
(Staré Město)
Czech
SISTERS BISTRO

Dlouhá 39; tel. +420 775 991 975; www.sistersbistro. cz; Mon-Fri 8am-8pm, Sat-Sun 9am-6pm; s andwiches 50-75 CZK; tram: Dlouhá třída

When all you need is a quick bite between sightseeing, stop into Sisters Bistro for a fresh, modern take on traditional Czech chlebíčky (open-faced sandwiches). Instead of the old-fashioned classic of ham and potato salad on white bread, these artisan updates include beetroot with goat cheese or roast beef with sprouts, plus gluten-free options and service with a smile. Mix and match a selection to take across the river for a picnic in Letná Park.

U DVOU KOČEK

Uhelný trh 10; tel. +420 224 229 982; www.udvoukocek.cz; daily 11am-11pm; entrées 100-300 CZK; metro or tram: Národní třída

The historical U Dvou Koček ("At the Two Cats") is a cat-themed pub, with kitschy accents like cats sculpted into the beer taps and small murals on the walls. (It's not a cat café, so there are no live felines roaming the premises.) The menu features hearty, no-frills Czech cuisine. Try a beer from the onsite microbrewery, Kočka světlá (light) or tmavá (dark). Reservations recommended.

KRČMA

Kostečná 4; tel. +420 725 157 262; www.krcma.cz; daily 11am-11pm; entrées 175-300 CZK; metro or tram: Staroměstská

Krčma is an underground den of deliciousness (with limited outdoor seating) just steps from Old Town Square. Enjoy hearty portions of grilled meats, sauces, and dumplings in a medieval setting of cave-like brick walls. Vegetarian options are minimal in this old-style, traditional Czech tavern. Reservations recommended.

LOD' PIVOVAR

Dvořákovo nábřeží, kotviště č. 19; tel. +420 773 778 788; www.pivolod.cz; daily 11:30am-10pm; entrées 200-300 CZK; tram: Dlouhá třída

This microbrewery is on a boat! The main-floor restaurant of Lod' Pivovar offers fresh, modern takes on Czech cuisine—think rabbit, duck, or pork knee accompanied by more vegetables than you'd find in a traditional pub. The below-deck pub and 72 open-air seats on the top deck strike a more casual pub vibe with beer snacks and in-house microbrews.

Cafés and Cakes
★ GRAND CAFÉ ORIENT

Ovocný trh 19; tel. +420 224 224 240; www.grandcafeorient.cz; Mon-Fri 9am-10pm, Sat-Sun 10am-10pm; entrées 100-200 CZK; metro or tram: Náměstí Republiky

The only café in Prague with exclusively cubist décor takes its commitment to right angles down to the details. Everything from the coat hooks to the light fixtures is on point. Enjoy a slice of homemade cake, a breakfast croissant, or a toasted baguette on the second floor of Prague's historic House of the Black Madonna (named for the identifying marker outside) before climbing the nearby Powder Tower or touring the Municipal House.

KAVÁRNA KOČIČI

Michalská 3; tel. +420 223 008 284; www.kavarnakocici.cz; daily 11am-8pm; metro: Můstek, tram: Karlovy lázně

Feline residents roam freely across the laps (and laptops) of customers in wooden booths and soft sofas at this Old Town cat café. Coffee, quiches, soups, and cakes with gluten- and dairy-free options, plus strong Wi-Fi, keep the crowd of digital nomads and curious visitors in their seats for hours. Payment includes a 39 CZK "cat cover charge" per person.

Vegetarian
FORKY'S

Veleslavínova 10; tel. +420 773 080 337; www.forkys.eu; daily 11am-8pm; entrees 150-200 CZK; metro or tram: Staroměstská

For a quick, casual vegetarian meal in the city center, swing by this local chain just off Old Town Square. Choose from "Superbowls" of quinoa or kimchi and tons of plant-based burgers, wraps, and sides to mix and match in a simple cafeteria setting. A handful of tiny sidewalk tables offer limited outdoor dining.

★ LEHKA HLAVA

Boršov 2; tel. +420 222 220 665; www.lehkahlava.cz; Mon-Fri 11:30am-4pm and 5pm-10pm, Sat-Sun noon-4pm and 5pm-10pm; entrées 225-275 CZK; tram: Karlovy lázně

In a meat-heavy country, Lehka Hlava ("Clear Head") is a vegetarian oasis. One of the intimate dining rooms includes a dark blue ceiling and twinkling star lights, while another has warm, fiery walls and a calming fish tank to set the scene for a mellow meal. Browse the meat-free menu from Thai curry to quesadillas, with a glossary of potentially unfamiliar terms like tempeh or seitan. Reservations required.

NEW TOWN
(Nové Město)
Czech
KANTÝNA

Politických vězňů 5; www.kantyna.ambi.cz; daily 11:30am-10pm; entrees 100-250 CZK; metro: Hlavní nádraží, tram stops Jindřišská or Václavské náměstí

The meats are freshly sliced, diced, and grilled by highly trained butchers in the stark, marble beauty of this former bank building. Step one: Choose between a communal standing table in the lobby or one of two seat-yourself dining rooms. Step two: Fill out a paper ticket handed out upon entering. Step three: Head to the butchery counter to choose your meat and place your order. Fair warning that English communication is limited, so translating a few words in advance and sticking to simple orders will help navigate the process—try the carpaccio (same spelling in Czech) or beef tartare (Tatarák ze stařeného masa).

★ CAFÉ LOUVRE

Národní 22; tel.+420 724 054 055 or +420 224 930 949; www.cafelouvre.cz; Mon-Fri 8am-11:30pm, Sat-Sun 9am-11:30pm; entrées 150-300 CZK; metro or tram: Národní třída

Café Louvre has been satisfying local appetites since 1902 and can even claim Albert Einstein and Franz Kafka as former regulars. Enjoy Czech and Austro-Hungarian cuisine in the chandeliered elegance of the First Republic café style established in the early years of Czechoslovakia, located just down the street from the National Theater. This is a great place to try svíčková, a Czech favorite of sirloin beef in vegetable cream sauce with cranberries, cream, and bread dumplings, reminiscent of the rich blend of flavors in a Thanksgiving dinner. Select the kavarna (café) or restaurace (restaurant) when making your online reservation for the most ornately decorated rooms—you can order food in either.

International
PIZZERIA KMOTRA

V Jirchářích 12; tel. +420 224 934 100; www.kmotra.cz; daily 11am-11pm; entrées 150-200 CZK; metro or tram: Národní třída

The extensive menu of pizza, pasta, and salads at Pizzeria Kmotra caters to a budget-conscious crowd of university students and casual patrons on their way to the bars. Split one of their massive pizzas (ignore any recommendations that these are personal-sized) in an underground, brick-walled cavern setting with cutlery-inspired décor. Reservations recommended.

Breakfast and Brunch
CACAO

V Celnici 4; tel. +420 777 511 677; www.cacaoprague.cz; Mon-Fri 8:30am-10pm, Sat-Sun 9:30am-10pm; entrées 100-200 CZK; metro and tram: Náměstí Republiky

Health-conscious travelers and restricted diets are no problem for the staff at Cacao. The large, two-story dining room plus an outdoor patio near Náměstí Republiky

Czech Cuisine

roast duck with dumplings and cabbage

ENTRÉES

- **Svíčková:** A local favorite of thinly sliced sirloin beef in vegetable cream sauce with cranberries, cream, and bread dumplings, almost like a Czech take on Thanksgiving flavors. This is what every Czech child writes under "favorite food" in school and continues to love throughout adulthood. Try a classic one at **Café Louvre** (page 119), while local vegetarian favorite **Maitrea** (Týnská ulička 6; www.restaurace-maitrea.cz) in Old Town does make a soy-based, meat-free version.

- **Pražská šunka** (Prague ham): This cured, lightly smoked, boneless ham prepared with traditional butchery techniques is a regional specialty. Head to **Kantýna** (page 119) to try it, and avoid the stands in Old Town Square, known for scamming customers with prices by weight not portion.

- **Pečená kachní stehna** (roast duck leg): **U Modré Kachničky** (page 122) serves delicious duck-based dishes, including pečená kachní stehna, which is usually paired with red cabbage and dumplings. This hearty Bohemian-style classic is served on the bone, often in one-quarter or one-half portions.

- **Pečené vepřové koleno** (roast pork knuckle): Try pečené vepřové koleno at **Loď Pivovar** (page 118), a floating brewery on a boat focused on classic Czech dishes with quality ingredients. The potent flavors of a dark beer sauce, mustard, and horseradish are perfect for refueling on a winter evening.

- **Guláš** (goulash): The Czech version of this Hungarian classic involves less (or no) paprika and acts more as a thick sauce than soup. Pork, beef, and venison versions are available in different venues. Jan Macuch (a former food tour guide with culinary taste I trust) claims that Czech Slovak Restaurant (page 123) makes the best one in Prague.

- Smažený sýr (fried cheese): Traditional vegetarian "meals" in Prague tend to be cheese-based. Smažený sýr is a thick slice of white cheese (often a mild, white Edam) that is breaded, fried, and served with French fries and tartar sauce without a vegetable in sight.

- Nakládaný Hermelín (marinated cheese): Another vegetarian option is a pickled Camembert-style cheese marinated in oil and herbs and spread on bread. Try both greasy pub favorites at U Sadu (page 99).

SOUPS

In the same way that many people think of a small salad as a starter to a meal, a Czech lunch always begins with soup:

- Česneková polévka (garlic soup): Different versions of this fragrant and flavorful dish range from a creamy base to a light broth, often garnished with ham, cheese, potatoes, and croutons. Česnečka (the short name) is a fantastic cure for the common cold. Soup menus in Czech pubs often change daily, so keep an eye out for this classic when the weather turns cold.

- Kulajda (dill and vegetable soup): For a more unusual flavor, watch soup-of-the-day menus for kulajda, a blend of dill, mushroom, potato, and egg. You'll find this consistently on the menu at Staročeská restaurace V Ruthardce (page 151) if you take a day trip to Kutná Hora.

SMALL BITES AND PASTRIES

A quick snack in Prague usually centers around bread or a sweet shop:

- Chlebíčky (open-faced sandwiches): The traditional version of chlebíčky would be white bread topped with potato salad and sliced ham, possibly garnished with a radish or carrot. These simple hors d'oeuvres are particularly popular at Czech weddings or New Year's Eve parties at a cabin in the countryside. Sisters Bistro (page 118) makes incredible modern versions with fresh ingredients such as beetroot and goat cheese.

- Klobásy (sausage): This staple of any pub, beer garden, outdoor market, or food stand is the go-to solution for "we should probably serve some kind of food" at any Czech event. They can be pork or beef, grilled or smoked, and mild or spiced, and are usually served with mustard and a few slices of brown bread.

- Medovník (honey cake): Czech cakes and pastries offer a wide range of flavors (e.g., gingerbread, poppy seed, forest berries, and cream-filled dough) but one of my personal favorites is Medovník or Medovy Dort, which translates to "honey cake." Taste this light, flaky delight in cubist form at Old Town's Grand Café Orient (page 118).

- Trdelník (cinnamon-sugar pastry): This doughy spiral pastry cooked over coals and dipped in sugar and cinnamon is a delicious guilty pleasure sold at stands all around Old Town, but it is about as Czech as an "I ♥ NY" T-shirt—its prevalence is a pet peeve of the Honest Prague Guide on YouTube. With claimed roots in Romania, Hungary, Sweden, and Slovakia, it has become a popular tourist attraction across the former Austro-Hungarian Empire. Feel free to indulge, but to maintain your traveler's credibility and avoid dirty looks from locals, skip the Instagram-inspired, sugar-overload trend of filling it with ice cream or hashtagging #traditional.

serves bagels, egg breakfast, smoothies, acai bowls, and delicious espresso to start your day. The menu transitions into fresh soups, salads, and sandwiches for lunch or dinner. Homemade ice cream and a considerable array of cakes will placate the sweet tooth of anyone in your group.

Cafés and Cakes

CAFÉ ADASTRA

Podskalská 8; tel. +420 733 748 662; www.cafeadastra.cz; Mon-Sat 9am-8pm; entrees 100-150 CZK; tram: Výtoň

Proceeds from this nonprofit café near the Náplavka boardwalk help to support a neurodiverse staff. Come for the French wine, specialty coffee, and daily lunch menu in a cozy café with bookshelves lining the walls, then stick around for live piano music each night. Feel free to play a song yourself if the instrument is free.

STYL & INTERIER

Vodičkova 35; tel. +420 222 543 128; www.stylainterier.cz; Mon-Fri 8am-10pm, Sat-Sun 9am-10pm; entrées 125-200 CZK; tram: Václavské náměstí

It's easy to miss the entrance to Styl & Interier, tucked into a quiet courtyard just off the bustling streets around Wenceslas Square. This café doubles as an interior-design showroom of wicker home accessories and colorful accent pieces, plus a peaceful summer garden. The seasonal bistro menu of light egg breakfasts and quiches, colorful salads, and homemade desserts is popular with locals and tourists, so reservations are recommended. Try a sparkling, fruit-infused lemonade in the coveted garden seats during summer or some homemade svařák (hot spiced wine) and Christmas cookies in winter.

CAFÉ TRUHLÁRNA

Františkánská zahrada, Jungmannova 19; tel. +420 603 239 290; www.cafetruhlarna.cz; Mon-Fri 8:30am-8pm, 9:30am-8pm Sat-Sun Apr-Oct, Mon-Fri 8:30am-7pm, Sat-Sun 9:30am-7pm Nov-Mar; metro: Můstek, tram: Václavské náměstí

Complete a relaxing walk through the Franciscan Gardens with a pause for coffee and Czech pastries at this peaceful outdoor café surrounded by green leaves and sculpted hedges. Try a traditional buchtu (sweet bun), an affogato (espresso poured over ice cream) in a martini glass, or specialty coffee topped with photogenic latte art.

LESSER TOWN
(Malá Strana)
Czech
ST. MARTIN

Vítězná 5; tel. +420 257 219 728; www.stmartin.cz; daily noon-11pm; entrées 200-300 CZK; metro and tram: Malostranské náměstí

The brother-and-sister chef team at St. Martin blends traditional Czech recipes with French and Asian touches discovered through their travels. Mix-and-match from the seasonal menu of soups, salads, grilled meats, vegetarian dishes, and continental sides. The mini turkey burger plus a side dish makes a great light meal, and the wild boar burger is a carnivore favorite. Both the food and the white domed walls of the small dining room embody a classic, modern quality. A leafy outdoor patio extends the dining area in warmer months.

★ U MODRÉ KACHNIČKY

Nebovidská 6; tel. +420 602 353 559 or +420 257 320 308; www.umodrekachnicky.cz; daily noon-4pm and 6:30pm-11:30pm; entrées 500-600 CZK; tram: Hellichova

The tasting menus of duck or game at U Modré Kachničky are 100 percent worth the splurge. Five or seven courses of decadent flavors can also be paired with local wines and liquors in the most fashionable, old-world living room settings that you can imagine. The staff walk a talented tightrope of friendly professionalism for a clientele of primarily couples sharing romantic meals. Duck and game specials are also available a la carte, and the roast duck with apples, raisins, and honey is a standout. Reservations recommended.

International
★ ROESEL–BEER & FOOD

*Mostecká 20; tel. +420 777 119 368 or +420 212 241
552; roesel-beer-cake.business.site; daily 10am-10pm;
entrées 75-200 CZK; metro and tram: Malostranské
náměstí*

The quiet patio and low ceilings of this casual
café offer a hidden escape from the crowds
surrounding the Lesser Town entrance to
the Charles Bridge. In addition to craft beer
and homemade sweets, this small, friendly
spot with simple wooden furniture and a tiny
outdoor courtyard serves specialty coffee,
seasonal pâtés, and daily lunch and dinner
specials. The young, often multilingual staff
are patient with an international clientele of
locals, foreigners, and families.

PRAGUE CASTLE DISTRICT
(Hradčany)
Czech
KUCHYŇ

*Hradčanské nám. 2; tel. +420 736 152 891;
https://kuchyn.ambi.cz; daily 11am-8pm;
entrées 150-300 CZK; tram: Pražský hrad*

Most restaurants in and around the Prague
Castle serve high-priced food that falls short
on quality. The 2018 addition of Kuchyň is
still a little pricier than your average Czech
pub, but the cuisine and experience are worth
it. Try the vegetarian Koprová omáčka (dill
sauce served over boiled eggs and potatoes)
or řízek (schnitzel) with potato salad, preferably on the roughly 65-seat terrace with
incredible views over the city. Reservations
recommended.

PETŘÍN
Czech
KOLKOVNA OLYMPIA

*Vítězná 7; tel. +420 251 511 080; www.kolkovna.cz;
daily 11am-10pm; entrées 175-300 CZK; tram: Újezd*

Dark wood details and copper accents set
a traditional Czech pub scene in this 222-
seat member of the Pilsner Urquell Original
Restaurant group, where quality beer is a way
of life. Freshly poured pints (or technically,

half-liters) complement the menu, from bar
snacks of pickled sausage and marinated
cheeses to main courses like roast duck and
pork knee. The building has been serving
customers since 1903, and Kolkovna gave the
space a restorative makeover in 2003 without losing any of its historical charm. Grab
a hearty meal here after a walk along the
Smíchov boardwalk or through Petřín Park.

CZECH SLOVAK RESTAURANT

*Újezd 20; tel. +420 257 312 523; www.czechslovak.cz;
daily noon-11pm; entrées 250-400 CZK; tram: Újezd*

The trendy, dimly lit atmosphere of Czech
Slovak Restaurant surrounds an international
crowd enjoying modern twists on traditional
dishes. The menu includes Bohemian baked
snails, venison goulash, dill and mushroom
soup, wild rabbit, and a local-leaning wine list.
Reservations recommended.

International
MANIFESTO SMÍCHOV

*náměstí 14. října 16; tel. +420 702 011 638;
www.manifestomarket.com; daily 11am-10pm;
tram: Zborovská*

Pop-up food stands centered around a shallow wading pool and lots of plantlife serve
a wide selection of hummus, burgers, poké
bowls, Mexican meals, fresh cocktails, and
Pilsner Urquell in this outdoor food market.
Manifesto Markets are also built around sus-
tainability, meaning this non-smoking location runs on 100 percent green energy with
locally sourced furniture.

Cafés and Cakes
KAVÁRNA CO HLEDÁ JMÉNO

*Stroupežnického 10; tel. +420 770 165 561;
www.kavarnacohledajmeno.cz; Mon noon-10pm,
Tues-Fri 8am-10pm, Sat-Sun 9am-8pm;
metro: Anděl, tram: Na Knížecí*

The industrial vibe of Kavárna Co Hledá
Jméno ("Café in Search of a Name") is popular with young coffee lovers and remote workers—both the coffee and Wi-Fi are strong.
This large, multi-room café with an outdoor
garden is set back from the street, so if you're

walking down a driveway it's likely you're in the right place. Brunch is served until noon (or 3pm on weekends) and includes an impossibly fluffy eggs benedict soufflé.

VINOHRADY AND VRŠOVICE
Czech
RESTAURACE U RŮŽOVÉHO SADU

Mánesova 89; tel. +420 222 725 154; www.uruzovehosadu.cz; Mon-Thurs 10:30am-midnight, Fri 10:30am-1am, Sat 11am-midnight, Sun 11:30am-10pm; entrées 115-215 CZK; tram or metro: Jiřího z Poděbrad

Restaurace U Růžového Sadu serves classic, hearty, meat-and-potato meals in a comfortable 90-seat pub with an additional outdoor patio during sunny seasons. Work up an appetite with a walk through nearby Riegrovy sady, then stop in for one of the simple daily lunch specials (think pork schnitzel or grilled chicken with potatoes) served until 3pm at less than 100 CZK for a true taste of Czech-style dining.

International
CAFEFIN

nám. J. z Poděbrad 4; https://format.coffee; Mon-Sat 9am-8pm, Sun 9am-7pm; entrees 75-150 CZK; metro or tram: Jiřího z Poděbrad

The breakfast bowls, open-faced sandwiches, Vietnamese soups, and matcha lattes at Cafefin are as delicious as they are photogenic. Exposed brick walls, mismatched chairs, and lightbulbs hanging overhead complete the carefully curated aesthetic in this trendy café at the base of Jiřího z Poděbrad square.

CAFÉ SLADKOVSKY

Sevastopolská 17; tel. +420 776 772 478; www.cafesladkovsky.cz; Tues-Sun 11am-1am, Mon 4pm-1am; entrées 100-200 CZK; tram or bus: Krymská

Everything about this Vršovice staple is charmingly quirky, from the antique-style furniture to the menu. Mediterranean and Middle Eastern-inspired dishes mingle alongside organic beef or veggie burgers and English breakfasts. The décor channels First

Republic café style as seen in Café Louvre or Kavárna Lucerna but with a more lived-in, vintage vibe (it actually opened in 2011). Service can be on the slower side, but is generally patient and kind with English speakers. Food service finishes at 9:45pm when the bar starts slinging gin cocktails.

Cafés and Cakes
COFFEE CORNER BAKERY

Korunní 96; tel. +420 777 779 176; Mon 8am-7pm, Tue-Fri 8am-9pm, Sat 9am-9pm, Sun 9:30am-8pm; entrees 150-250 CZK; tram: Perunova

Grab a plush, high-backed seat in the far corner of this long L-shaped café to enjoy an espresso drink, eggs benedict, chicken burger, or homemade cakes from an eclectic menu. Freelance workers with laptops sip lattes for hours at one table, while a group of friends catches up over sandwiches and homemade lemonades at the next. The welcoming vibe in this easygoing, multilingual space is worth the slightly higher prices.

Vegetarian
RADOST FX

Bělehradská 12; tel. +420 224 254 776; www.radostfx.cz; Mon-Wed 11am-10pm, Thu-Fri 11am-midnight; Sat 10:30am-3pm and 5pm-midnight, Sun 10:30am-3pm; tram: IP Pavlova, metro: Náměstí Míru or IP Pavlova

Radost FX has been a dependable vegetarian haven in Prague since 1992. The eclectic menu jumps from nachos to gnocchi, stir-fry to salads (175-215 CZK), with salmon sneaking onto the brunch menu (100-200 CZK). The laid-back vibe extends from a small, quiet café out front to the crowds nursing hangovers and Bloody Marys in the high-backed booths of the windowless restaurant. Some hard-core diners may have not even made it home between breakfast and the all-hours dance party in the downstairs club on Thursday through Saturday nights. Brunch reservations recommended.

1: Kavárna Čekárna's backyard patio 2: Kuchyň's outdoor patio beside the Prague Castle 3: chlebíčky (open-faced sandwiches) of Sisters Bistro 4: Styl & Interier's patio

ŽIŽKOV
Czech
U SLOVANSKÉ LÍPY

Tachovské náměstí 6; tel. +420 734 743 094;
www.uslovanskelipy.cz; daily 11am-midnight;
entrées 175-225 CZK, cash only; bus: Rokycanova

This large, casual, traditional Czech pub near the Žižkov Tunnel offers hearty meals with no-nonsense service that keeps the pivo (beer) flowing. Slightly off the beaten path below Vítkov Hill and the Žižkov Beer Garden, this local favorite caters to a mixed crowd of residents and visitors (assisted by English-friendly menus). Choose from 10 rotating taps of Czech beers and a main course of flank steak or schnitzel with potato salad. Cash only.

International
★ MARTIN'S BISTRO

Velehradská 4; tel. +420 774 100 378; Mon-Sat
11:30am-10pm, Sun 10am-4pm; entrées 150-300 CZK;
metro or tram: Jiřího z Poděbrad

Friendly, multilingual service and seasonal, fresh-from-the-farmers-market ingredients define the vibe at Martin's Bistro. Choose from a weekly revamped menu that might include pasta tossed with fresh veggies and herbs, roast duck or pork entrées, Asian-inspired noodles and curries, or shrimp and cheese appetizers, plus soups, quiches, and desserts. Vegetarian options are almost always available. This local favorite fills up fast, so call for a reservation to ensure an available seat.

Breakfast and Brunch
ŽIŽKAVÁRNA

Kubelíkova 17; tel. +420 606 281 546; Mon-Fri
7:30am-9pm, Sat-Sun 8:30am-9pm; entrées 50-75
CZK; metro: Jiřího z Poděbrad, tram: Jiřího z
Poděbrad or Husinecká

This quiet neighborhood favorite of international residents and remote workers camped out for hours serves quality coffee and light homemade meals with a friendly, patient approach. The seasonal menu often includes omelets, sandwiches, granola, and a soup of the day, with a slice of carrot or honey cake for dessert. If you can't score one of the 10 tables, take your coffee to go for a short walk to the benches of Jiřího z Poděbrad square.

THE TAVERN

Chopinova 26; tel. +420 725 319 226; www.thetavern.
cz; Mon-Fri 11:30am-11pm, Sat-Sun 10:30am-11pm;
entrees 150-200 CZK; metro: Jiřího z Poděbrad,
tram: Jiřího z Poděbrad or Husinecká

A US couple hailing from Kentucky and Washington State opened The Tavern in 2014 to satisfy their cravings for classic American meals. Popular weekend brunches (11am-5pm), feature Southern US staples like biscuits and gravy or fried chicken and waffles, along with omelets, hash browns, and breakfast sliders, served in a cavernous dining room or an outdoor patio. Reservations available for dinner only.

KARLÍN
Czech
SPOJKA

Pernerova 35; tel. +420 226 203 888;
www.spojka-karlin.cz; Mon-Fri 8am-11pm, Sat
9am-11pm, Sun 9am-4pm; entrees 200-450 CZK;
metro or tram: Křižíkova

A group of friends opened Spojka in 2019 to fill a gap in the Prague restaurant scene. Meat eaters were often unsatisfied at vegetarian-only restaurants, and vegan diners found limited options in most establishments. Spojka aims to cater to all dietary choices, serving a flexitarian menu of cauliflower gnocchi with rabbit meat alongside lentil burgers, and lots of gluten-free options. All meats come from organic Czech farms, and vegetables and herbs are grown onsite. A dining room of glass walls, light wood, and potted plants hanging from the ceiling help create the overall sense of calm.

★ ESKA

Pernerova 49; tel. +420 731 140 884; www.eska.ambi.
cz; Mon-Fri 8am-10pm, Sat-Sun 9am-10pm; entrées
200-600 CZK; metro or tram: Křižíkova

Eska is internationally celebrated for serving great food at fair prices. The ground floor of this light, modern warehouse space is dominated by an in-house bakery. Upstairs, the dining room serves simple plates of seasonal vegetables and fresh meats in a laid-back atmosphere of structural support beams softened by hanging plants. Grab an open-faced sandwich for lunch or try the eight-course tasting menu for an indulgent dinner. Reservations recommended.

International
CAFÉ FRIDA

Karlínské náměstí 11; tel. +420 728 042 910;
www.cafefrida.cz; Mon-Fri 9am-midnight,
Sat-Sun 11am-midnight; entrées 125-200 CZK,
cash only; tram: Karlínské náměstí

This casual, colorful, Mexican-inspired restaurant is named for Frida Kahlo. Don't expect too much spice from the burritos, quesadillas, and burgers tailored to a milder local palate. Plenty of vegetarian and meat-lovers' options keep this popular establishment packed with a young, international crowd. Cash only. Reservations recommended.

MANIFESTO FLORENC

Na Florenci Street; tel. +420 702 048 247;
www.manifestomarket.com; daily 11am-10pm;
entrees 100-300 CZK, card only; metro: Florenc,
tram: Masarykovo nádraží

Restaurants and independent chefs looking to test out new concepts populate this open-air market on the border of New Town and Karlín. Individual booths made from shipping containers serve everything from poké bowls to burgers, tacos, and Czech open-faced sandwiches plus beer and cocktails. Reservations are available for outdoor tables (free) in summer or to rent dome-shaped, heated igloos (300-600 CZK) in colder months. Payment is by card only, with no cash accepted.

Cafés and Cakes
LOFT CAFÉ KARLÍN

Křižíkova 68; tel. +420 778 088 438; http://loftcafe.
cz; Mon-Fri 8am-8pm, Sat 10am-6pm, Sun 11am-6pm;
snacks 50-100 CZK; tram: Urxova or Křižíkova

Lots of non-dairy and vegan milk options for specialty coffee and desserts set this trendy industrial space apart from many Prague cafés. A largely local crowd occupies seats on the ground floor and the balcony of tables circling the room. Take your espresso to go for a walk through Barikádníků Park next door, located in front of a stately art nouveau primary school building.

LETNÁ AND HOLEŠOVICE
International
MR. HOT DOG

Kamenická 24; tel. +420 732 732 404;
www.mrhotdog.cz; daily 11:30am-10pm;
entrées 50-150 CZK; tram: Kamenická

For a quick bite, grab one of the namesake hot dogs or sliders at this low-key local favorite. The menu of American classics is supplemented with limited-time specials such as lobster rolls, plus a yearly eating contest. Indoor seating is limited, making take-out service before hitting nearby Letná Park a popular option.

HILLBILLY BURGER

Pplk Sochora 21; tel. +420 774 156 735;
www.hillbilly.cz; Tues-Fri noon-3pm and 5pm-10pm,
Sat noon-10pm, Sun noon-9pm; entrées 150-200
CZK; tram: Strossmayerovo náměstí

The guiding principle behind this Letná eatery is simple: "Just F*@¢ing Good Burgers". The below-ground dining room is decorated with chalkboard scrawls and exposed brick, with a long backyard patio where smokers congregate. The burgers are hearty, including veggie, pork, and chicken variations, and the coleslaw is delicious.

POKÉ HAUS

Milady Horákové 63; tel. +420 608 548 858;
https://poke.haus; daily 11am-10pm; entrees
175-250 CZK; tram: Letenské náměstí or Kamenická

These Hawaiian-inspired poké bowls provide the rare combination of fresh, non-fried, moderately priced seafood in Prague. Choose from ahi tuna, salmon, shrimp, and tofu tossed with your choice of vegetables, seaweed, and sauces in a fast-paced and casual setting. These light, fresh meals are perfect for take-away and a picnic in nearby Letná Park.

GARUDA

Milady Horákové 12; tel. +420 730 890 424; www.garudarestaurant.cz; daily 10:30am-10pm; entrées 150-275 CZK; tram: Strossmayerovo náměstí or Kamenická

The two-story café, restaurant, and "chill out zone" at Garuda blends relaxing elements (think water features and soft lighting) with a trendy, low-key vibe and delicious Indonesian food. Grab an early meal at a daily happy hour discount from 2:30-5:30pm before watching the sunset at nearby Letná Beer Garden.

SASAZU

Bubenské nábřeží 306; tel. +420 284 097 455; www.sasazu.com; Mon-Thurs noon-midnight, Fri-Sat noon-1am, Sun noon-11pm; entrées 300-1,000 CZK; tram: Pražská tržnice

High-end dining in Holešovice is rare, but SaSaZu breaks that rule with Southeast Asian-inspired cuisine in a dimly lit nightclub setting inside the Holešovice Market grounds (also referred to as Pražská tržnice): Shared plates are served family-style, with starters such as salmon tartar and lobster soup, and flavorful meat-based dishes from a stone oven or grilled in a wok. Glowing red lanterns and sculpted figurines set a vibe that blends elegance and kitsch. Follow up your meal with a performance at nearby circus arts venue Jatka 78. Dinner reservations required.

Breakfast and Brunch
★ THE FARM

Korunovacni 17; tel. +420 773 626 177; Mon-Fri 8am-10:30pm, Sat 9am-10:30pm, Sun 9am-8pm; entrées 100-175 CZK; tram: Letenské náměstí or Korunovační

If you're willing to venture a little further for breakfast, join the local crowd of young families and friend groups brunching on fresh eggs, omelets, and avocado-toast variations at The Farm. Add a Bloody Mary or mimosa to start your day in style. These fresh-from-the-farmers-market meals take full advantage of seasonal flavors in a tightly squeezed dining room and outdoor summer patio. Reservations required.

KAFÉ FRANCIN

Dukelských Hrdinů 35; tel. +420 778 719 217; www.francin.cz; Mon-Fri 7:30am-8pm, Sat-Sun 9am-7pm; entrées 125-185 CZK; tram: Strossmayerovo náměstí

Breakfast at Kafé Francin can fuel a full day of sightseeing. Try the massive sweet or savory crêpes, a hard-to-find bagel sandwich, or an egg and fresh bread breakfast with your morning coffee. Head to the back of the restaurant for plush sofa seating and a browsable bookshelf if space is available, or squeeze into one of the smaller tables in the front of this cozy café.

Cafés and Cakes
BITCOIN CAFÉ

Dělnická 43; tel. +420 608 088 822; www.paralelnipolis.cz; Mon-Fri 8am-8pm, Sat noon-6pm, Sun noon-8pm; cash or credit not accepted (cryptocurrency only); tram: Dělnická

As the name would imply, the only way to pay for your coffee in this café is with cryptocurrency (either Bitcoin or Litecoin). Luckily, there is a machine on site and staff on hand to show you how to purchase enough to cover your bill. The gimmick will get you in the door, but the yummy cakes and espresso drinks will keep you in the large, black leather sofas inside this building founded by the Institute for Cryptoanarchy. Observe the tech-focused crowd working to make the internet a place of free information to support a decentralized economy... or just enjoy some quality coffee and a comfortable seat.

VYŠEHRAD
Czech
HOSPŮDKA NA HRADBÁCH

V Pevnosti 2; tel. +420 734 112 214; daily noon-midnight; entrées 50-150 CZK; metro: Vyšehrad

The best way to enjoy a meal inside the Vyšehrad Complex is outdoors. This locally loved beer garden offers bar snacks like grilled Hermelin cheese or pickled sausages alongside heavier meals of grilled meats, to be eaten under the umbrella-topped picnic benches lining the garden. Imagine a casual, family BBQ setting with the added bonus of a panoramic view from the tables lining the perimeter.

U KROKA

Vratislavova 12; tel. +420 775 905 022; www.ukroka.cz; daily 11am-11pm; entrées 185-400 CZK; tram: Výtoň

Slightly higher prices at this Czech restaurant reflect a convenient location on the path to or from Vyšehrad hill as well as attentive, multilingual service. Try the kulajda (dill) soup with mushrooms and poached egg or roast duck with red cabbage and dumplings. Eat indoors in the exposed-brick dining room, or outside on the small patio.

International
YAM YAM VYŠEHRAD

Vyšehrad Metro Station 1670; tel. +420 774 844 443; www.yamyam.cz; daily 11am-11pm; entrées 150-200 CZK; metro: Vyšehrad

Yam Yam Vyšehrad's convenient location just outside the Vyšehrad Metro Station makes it an easy stop for a simple Thai food meal. The clean lines, stenciled vines, and splashes of red create a relaxed environment for an international clientele. The extensive, lighthearted menu includes "Ca-la-la-mari" and sections of main courses encouraging visitors to "Eat Some Meat" and "Curry On."

Cafés and Cakes
PURO GELATO

Na Hrobci 1; tel. +420 721 438 209; www.purogelato. cz; Mon-Fri 10am-10pm, Sat 9am-10pm, Sun 10am-9pm May-Sep, Mon-Sat 9am-8pm, Sun 9am-7pm Oct-Apr; 40-75 CZK; tram: Výtoň

This cozy gelato shop below Vyšehrad is a perfect stop before a stroll along the nearby Náplavka boardwalk beside the Vltava river (where you might have to hide your treat from a few hungry swans). Choose a scoop of your favorite from the daily-made and often unusual flavors (an orange scoop might be mango or carrot) including vegan options, or try the artfully designed cakes and tarts for some warm-weather indulgence.

KAVÁRNA ČEKÁRNA

Vratislavova 8; tel. +420 601 593 741; Mon-Fri 8am-10pm, Sat 10am-8pm, Sun 1pm-8pm; entrées 50-100 CZK; tram: Výtoň

The unassuming entrance to this casual café extends into long halls of cushions and simple wooden furniture, leading to a massive backyard garden at the base of Vyšehrad hill. Patio seating is tucked under brick arches and around patches of grass where the noise of the city disappears. Pair your specialty coffee with homemade cakes, quiches, or the soup of the day.

Accommodations

Prague's accommodation offerings reflect the distinctive personalities of its different neighborhoods. Malá Strana and Old Town are known for historical luxury hotels within steps of major sights. New Town and Vinohrady offer more apartments and trendy, boutique hotels—the Bohemian Hotels and Hostels Group is a local favorite for mid-range, modern style. Vyšehrad, Letná, and Karlín have a more peaceful neighborhood vibe, while Vršovice, Holešovice, and Žižkov tend to draw younger, budget-conscious crowds looking for nightlife and not afraid of public transport.

Some of Prague's older mid-range and budget hotels can feel quite dated, and payment in cash only is not unheard of, so read your booking details carefully when choosing a place. Renovation restrictions in public buildings and a prevalence of stairs also make it a less-accessible landscape for travelers with disabilities. Hotels that do offer specially equipped rooms are noted below when possible, but it's definitely not standard in all accommodation options, so ask about barrier-free travel or accessibility needs before booking.

The Prague landscape offers many alternatives beyond traditional hotel chains. Pensions and aparthotels provide more residential living environments with access to cooking facilities and family-friendly amenities. Design hotels cater to architecture lovers, and the luxury level maintains the outstanding service and modern touches that their clientele expect. At the time of writing, many hotels had modified check-in processes, increased cleaning measures, staff members supervising buffet breakfasts, and reduced access to communal gyms or spa areas in response to COVID-19. If you have any concerns about specifics that might make or break your stay, contact your hosts before booking to confirm your expectations.

OLD TOWN
(Staré Město)
Under 4,000 CZK
HOSTEL HOMER

Melantrichova 11; tel. +420 722 661 922;
www.hostelhomer.com; cash only; metro: Můstek
The 16th-century building of Hostel HOMEr is just steps from Old Town Square. Choose from 4-bed, female-only spaces (750 CZK) to mixed, 16-bed dorms (600 CZK) plus a few private double and triple rooms (2,500-3,500 CZK), all with shared bathrooms. The domed ceilings, historical décor, friendly 24-hour reception, plus free adapters and Wi-Fi make this a favorite for backpackers of all ages. Payment in cash only.

4,000-7,000 CZK
THE EMERALD

Žatecká 7; tel. +420 602 666 982; www.the-emerald-prague.com; 3,500 CZK s, 3,000-5,000 CZK d;
metro: Staroměstská

Every design detail of The Emerald tells a story inside this historical art nouveau building in the Josefov neighborhood. Thirteen individual rooms take inspiration from themes including the Orient Express, the Italian region of Tuscany, and Japanese principles of natural harmony. The original architecture is highlighted with copper-chain shower curtains, distressed walls, and natural wood touches. Rooms include a fridge, oven, and private bathroom among the minimal, customized furnishings. There is Wi-Fi but no elevator. These aparthotels cater to independent travelers looking for a familiar, photogenic alternative to hotel life.

Over 7,000 CZK
★ EMBLEM HOTEL

Platnéřská 19; tel. +420 226 202 500;
www.emblemprague.com; 5,000-10,000 CZK d,
10,000-20,000 CZK suites; metro: Staroměstská
The cozy rooms at the family-owned boutique Emblem Hotel make up for their size with comfortable public spaces for socializing. Fifty-nine small rooms (including one equipped for accessibility) are decked out in modern style and private bathrooms inside a 1908 building just one street off Old Town Square. A private, 30-minute (1,200 CZK for two people) or 60-minute (2,200 CZK for two people) reservation of the rooftop Jacuzzi and terrace includes a bottle of prosecco to toast the incredible view. Guests exchange travel tips over complimentary wine in the M Lounge from 6pm-8pm. Splurge on the Library Suite (around 20,000 CZK), with a huge copper bathtub and sliding bookshelf separating the bedroom from a reading lounge. At the time of writing, in response to the coronavirus, Emblem kept rooms empty for 72 hours between guests and offered 24/7 access to English-language medical advice.

1: rooftop terrace at Emblem Hotel 2: Corinthia Hotel pool with a view

NEW TOWN
(Nové Město)
Under 4,000 CZK
SOPHIE'S HOSTEL

Melounova 2; tel. +420 246 032 621;
www.sophieshostel.com; 400 CZK dorms;
metro: I.P. Pavlova, tram: I.P. Pavlova or Štěpánská

Sophie's Hostel is a peaceful alternative to the rowdy, bunk-bed dorm experience with 12 light, clean, private rooms (1,800 CZK) and apartments (2,500 CZK) with en suite bathrooms, or 17 shared dorm rooms for up to five people (women-only dorms available). This central location near Karlovo náměstí and Náměstí Miru provides an affordable place to lay your head, with buffet breakfast (150 CZK) or hot breakfast (200 CZK) options in the lobby bar. Seven-night maximum stay in any three-month period.

MOSAIC HOUSE

Odborů 4; tel. +420 277 016 880; www.mosaichouse.
com; 350-600 CZK dorms, 2,000-4,000 CZK d;
metro: Karlovo náměstí, tram: Novoměstská radnice

This nearly 100-room structure includes both a 38-room hostel ranging from four-bed to 26-bed shared dorms with bathrooms, plus a 55-room design hotel with one accessibility-equipped private double room. Mosaic House uses energy-efficient appliances, renewable energy sources, and a gray water system to make it Prague's greenest accommodation option. The décor is fun and funky including a Mediterranean-and-Middle-East-inspired restaurant and private spa and sauna for four to eight people. Look for the giant mushroom statues outside the entrance to find your way home to the southern edge of New Town and Vyšehrad. Rooms book out fast so make your reservation early.

BED & BOOKS ART HOTEL

Nekázanka 14; tel. +420 773 317 733; https://
bedbooks-art-hotel.prague-hotels.org; 1,250 CZK s,
2,000-5,000 CZK d, cash only; tram: Jindřišská

Between a boutique hotel and high-end hostel, Bed & Books offers peaceful comfort in an ethereal palette of distressed wood and pastels. Seven rooms across multiple floors (with no elevator) range from singles up to three-bedroom apartments with shared or en suite bathrooms and kitchens. The trade offs for a great price, central location, and free Wi-Fi are limited reception hours (check in outside of a 2pm-6pm window costs 250 CZK) and cash-only payments.

4,000-7,000 CZK
MISS SOPHIE'S NEW TOWN

Melounova 3; tel. +420 210 011 200;
www.miss-sophies.com; 4,000 CZK s, 4,500 CZK d

The casual chic of Miss Sophie's 16-room boutique hotel with en suite bathrooms combines a quiet side street location with the convenience of 10-minute walks to the Náplavka riverbank or Wenceslas Square. Try the private basement Jacuzzi and sauna (rent onsite for 1,500 CZK for 90 min, or 750 CZK with direct online booking), limited to no more than three people in your group. A simple buffet breakfast or hot brunch is served across the street at Sophie's Hostel for an extra 150-200 CZK. At the time of writing, free cancellation was available up to the day before arrival for direct bookings.

MISS SOPHIE'S DOWNTOWN

Opletalova 39; tel. +420 210 011 700;
www.miss-sophies.com; 4,000 CZK s, 4,000-6,000 d;
metro stop; metro stop Hlavní nádraží or tram
stop Jindřišská

Fifty-nine rooms spread across two historical buildings (renovated in 2020) just outside Prague's main train station offer convenience over quiet. The décor in warm reds, browns, and turquoise with lots of exposed pipes draws inspiration from train travel. Choose from twins, singles, and doubles with en suite bathrooms and potential balcony space, or suites ranging from doubles to quadruples for group travel. Continental breakfast and Wi-Fi included. At the time of writing, free cancellation was available up to the day before arrival for direct bookings.

★ DANCING HOUSE HOTEL

Jiraskovo Namesti 6; tel. +420 720 983 172;
www.dancinghousehotel.com; 3,000-8,000 CZK d;
tram: Jiráskovo náměstí

There is no comparison for sleeping inside one of the city's most famous sights, the Dancing House. Request a riverside room with floor-to-ceiling windows and wake up to a view of the Prague Castle. You set the mood inside these 40 spacious, modern rooms with en suite bathrooms and a choice of multi-colored LED lights. A welcome drink and buffet breakfast served under a sparkling chandelier are included from the Fred and Ginger restaurant on the top floor.

MOOO APARTMENTS

Myslikova 22; tel. +420 608 278 422;
www.mooo-apartments.com; 2,000-3,500 CZK s,
2,500-10,000 CZK d; metro: Karlovo náměstí,
tram: Novoměstská radnice

Treat yourself to a comfortable home-away-from-home decorated in bovine kitsch at MOOo Apartments. What's with the name? The designers wanted to combine the relaxing feel of the countryside with the urban energy of the city. New Town bars and restaurants, as well as the Náplavka Boardwalk, are within stumbling distance. Sixteen one-bedroom apartments (2,000-3,500 CZK) and five two-bedroom apartments (4,500-6,000 CZK) are available, plus two penthouse suites (10,000 CZK) for up to eight people, all with private bathrooms.

LESSER TOWN
(Malá Strana)
4,000-7,000 CZK
★ MISS SOPHIE'S
CHARLES BRIDGE

Malostranske namesti 5; tel. +420 210 011 500;
www.miss-sophies.com; 2,000 CZK d, 3,500-5,000
CZK suites; tram: Malostranské náměstí

The charming nine-room Miss Sophie's Charles Bridge (previously named Nicholas Hotel Residence) offers one of the most centrally located home bases in Malá Strana, just next door to the Church of St. Nicholas and the busy square of Malostranské náměstí. The expansive, comfortable furnishings include living-room spaces, well-equipped kitchen facilities, washer-dryer, and free Wi-Fi, great for families and couples of all ages. Toss on your robe for the continental breakfast buffet served in the hallways, where you can load up your plate and say "Dobré ráno" (good morning) to your neighbors before taking breakfast back to your room to enjoy. Twenty-four-hour reception is friendly and helpful, even if you've got an odd-hour arrival. At the time of writing, free cancellation was available up to the day before arrival for direct bookings.

Over 7,000 CZK
GOLDEN WELL HOTEL

U Zlaté studně 4; tel. +420 257 011 213;
www.goldenwell.cz; 6,500-8,000 CZK d;
metro or tram: Malostranská

The boutique Golden Well Hotel, known as U Zlaté Studné in Czech, is as well known for its impressive rooftop restaurant as the decadence of its 17 en suite rooms and two luxurious suites (around 15,000 CZK). This peaceful property tucked between the Prague Castle's lower gardens and Wallenstein Gardens, just slightly off the main tourist track through Malá Strana, was originally owned by Roman Emperor and Bohemian King Rudolf II and refurbished after decades of neglect to reopen in the new millennium. This splurge-worthy destination is made for a romantic weekend.

ARIA HOTEL

Trziste 9; tel. +420 225 334 111; www.ariahotel.net;
6,000 CZK d, 7,000-25,000 CZK suites; tram:
Malostranské náměstí

Aria Hotel's roughly 50 music-themed rooms with en suite bathrooms are dedicated to the greats of contemporary, classical, opera, and jazz music, ranging from Beethoven to the Beatles. Elegant touches include a rooftop terrace, fireplace lounge, small fitness center, free access to the neighboring Vrtba Garden, and a music concierge offering personal recommendations for local concerts. Buffet breakfast and Wi-Fi are complimentary.

THE ALCHYMIST GRAND HOTEL AND SPA

Trziste 19; tel. +420 257 286 011; www.alchymisthotel. com; 8,000 CZK d, 9,000-25,000 CZK suites; tram: Malostranské náměstí

The Alchymist Grand Hotel and Spa goes all-in on the historic charm of its 16th-century Baroque surroundings. Rich hues, ornate headboards, private bathrooms, and decorative details in every room and suite set a truly regal tone. The underground Ecsotica Spa includes a plunge pool, saunas, Indonesian-inspired massage and aromatherapy treatments, and a small, stone-walled fitness center. A buffet breakfast is included and can also be delivered to your room.

AUGUSTINE HOTEL

Letenská 33; tel. +420 266 112 233; www. augustinehotel.com; 10,000 CZK d, 15,000-40,000 CZK suites; metro or tram: Malostranská

The luxurious Augustine Hotel spreads 101 en suite rooms of historical ambience (with one equipped for accessibility) across seven historic buildings, including a 13th-century former monastery. The cubist details and a subtle color palette create a sense of regal calm just off the bustling square and transport hub of Malostranské náměstí, with individual suites offering tower views, historic frescoes, or custom glass designs. A 24-hour fitness center plus a wellness center of spa treatments and a Turkish hammam round out the menu of indulgent experiences.

★ MANDARIN ORIENTAL

Nebovidska 1; tel. +420 233 088 888; www. mandarinoriental.com; 10,000-20,000 CZK d, 20,000-40,000 CZK suites; tram: Hellichova

Attentive service, Spices Asian Restaurant, and a spa housed inside a Renaissance chapel keep the guests of Mandarin Oriental in a state of bliss. The quiet location, with 79 en suite guest rooms (one accessibility equipped)

plus 20 suites is tucked between the green lawns of Park Kampa and Petřín Hill. Guests are encouraged to relax and unplug, and Wi-Fi comes at a premium.

PRAGUE CASTLE DISTRICT

(Hradčany)

4,000-7,000 CZK

ROMANTIK HOTEL U RAKA

Černínská 10; tel. +420 220 511 100; www.hoteluraka. cz; 2,500-7,000 CZK d; tram: Brusnice

To mix a peaceful, residential vibe with the convenience of walking to the Prague Castle, book early for a spot in the six-room Romantik Hotel U Raka. This tiny, family-owned cottage at the top of hilly Hradčany is as cute as they come. Comfortable apartments with en suite bathrooms are decorated in deep reds and exposed brick, accented with the artistic family's own paintings and sculptures. Private residences surround a quiet cobble-stoned courtyard. Enjoy a light snack in the warm breakfast nook or outdoors on the terrace in summer months.

VINOHRADY AND VRŠOVICE

Under 4,000 CZK

CZECH INN

Francouzská 76; tel. +420 210 011 100; www.czech-inn.com; 125 CZK dorm, 1,500 CZK studio; tram or bus: Krymská

For lively budget accommodation in Vršovice, steps away from the trendy bistros and adult beverages of Krymská Street, check into the pun-intended Czech Inn. This massive, modern staple of the Bohemian Hostels group offers stylish rooms from private studios (1,500 CZK) to 36-bed mixed dorms and shared bathrooms (125 CZK) with free Wi-Fi throughout the building. There is a seven-night maximum stay. At the time of writing, dorm-room beds were blocked off for increased social distancing, and free cancellation was available up to the day before arrival for direct bookings.

PURE WHITE
Koubkova 12; tel. +420 220 992 569;
www.purewhitehotel.com; 2,500 CZK s, 3,500 CZK d;
tram: Bruselská

Pure White boutique hotel offers 37 en suite rooms of modern comfort on a quiet side street in Vinohrady. Reception is open 24 hours with a menu of pillow preferences, in-room Wi-Fi, and buffet breakfast included. Business travelers and sophisticated sightseers can decompress in the lobby bar.

★ ROYAL COURT APARTMENTS
Legerova 48; tel. +420 725 702 326;
www.royalcourthotel.cz; 3,000 CZK studio, 3,500 CZK suite; metro or tram: I.P. Pavlova

The boutique selection of 17 studios and family apartments at Royal Court Apartments comes decorated with brightly colored details, ranging from purple roses to American flags, that give each room a playful personality. With full kitchen amenities and private bedrooms and bathrooms, these spacious temporary residences are great for couples, small friend groups, and families traveling with teens. The lively surrounding area just off the IP Pavlova metro stop is flush with restaurants and public transport connections, with a tourist information center on the ground floor to answer any questions.

ŽIŽKOV
Under 4,000 CZK
HOTEL THEATRINO
Borivojova 53; tel. +420-227 031 894;
www.hoteltheatrino.cz; 1,750 CZK s, 3,000 CZK d;
tram: Lipanská

Hotel Theatrino sits in the heart of this pub-heavy residential neighborhood popular with international students, young professionals, and long-term local residents who remember its working-class roots. Far from the crowds of the city center, this large, five-story collection of simple rooms with rich red accents and a large, ornate conference hall caters to groups and business travelers. Free Wi-Fi, 24-hour

reception, and a private sauna for rent round out the offerings.

KARLÍN
4,000-7,000 CZK
PENTAHOTEL PRAGUE
Sokolovská 112; tel. +420 222 332 800;
www.pentahotels.com; 2,500 CZK s, 3,000-5,000 CZK d; tram: Křižíkova

The neon lighting and modern design of the seven-story Pentahotel Prague demonstrate the growing (and grown-up) nightlife scene of this neighborhood. The 227 en suite rooms are a bit outside the center, but right on a public transportation line in this largely residential area packed with restaurants and wine bars. Free Wi-Fi is natural for the trendy clientele, and the bar staff of the lobby's Penta Lounge perform double duty as the reception desk. At the time of writing, Penta Hotel required cashless payments as well as reservations to use the gym.

LETNÁ AND HOLEŠOVICE
Under 4,000 CZK
SIR TOBY'S
Dělnická 24; tel. +420 210 011 610; www.sirtobys.com; 250-750 CZK dorms; tram: Dělnická

Sir Toby's has been a favorite of the backpacking community and anyone looking to escape the traditional tourist track since its humble beginnings in 1999. Vintage-style 4-bed, or 12-bed dorm rooms with shared bathrooms are restricted to travelers ages 18-39, while the all-ages, private en suite rooms (1,500-3,500 CZK) upstairs are impressively insulated from noise. The Wi-Fi is strong, the staff are friendly, and your bunkmates are likely to stumble home at all hours. Buffet breakfast in the downstairs bar includes fruit, cereal, and a pancake station. At the time of writing, dorm-room beds were blocked off for increased social distancing, and free cancellation was available up to the day before arrival for direct bookings.

RESIDENCE MILADA

Milady Horákové 12; tel. +420 775 888 830; https://residencemilada.praguehotels.site; 2,500 CZK s, 3,500 CZK d; tram: Strossmayerovo náměstí

Rich red tones and eight multi-bed, en suite apartments in the boutique Residence Milada cater to families and close friends comfortable with shared sleeping areas. Deluxe and Family Apartments (5,000-9,000 CZK) with soundproof rooms can sleep up to five guests, and include a washing machine, modern bathroom facilities, and fully equipped kitchen and dining-room spaces. If you don't feel like cooking, grab breakfast nearby at Café Letka, or try a film brunch at independent cinema Bio Oko.

VYŠEHRAD
4,000-7,000 CZK
CORINTHIA HOTEL

Kongresová 1; tel. +420 261 191 111; www.corinthia.com; 3,500-5,000 CZK d, metro: Vyšehrad

You don't have to stay in the tourist center to enjoy five-star elegance in Prague. The towering Corinthia Hotel offers more than 500 rooms with private bathrooms and modern amenities, five of which are equipped for accessibility, and incredible views of the city skyline. Situated just off the Vyšehrad metro stop, this location is perfect for relaxing evening walks around the Vyšehrad Complex or exploring more of Prague's neighborhoods. The hotel itself houses four restaurants for breakfast, grilled meats and pizzas, Asian cuisine, and a cocktail lounge as well as a full swimming pool, top-floor spa, and gym facilities.

Information and Services

TOURIST INFORMATION

If you're looking for brochures of entertainment options and day trips, answers to lingering questions about transportation, or really just anything you want to ask in English, Prague's Tourist Information Centers are there to help. You'll find offices in some of the most popular tourist areas. The **Old Town Square location** (Staroměstské Náměstí 1; daily 9am-7pm) is at the Old Town Hall, next to the Astronomical Clock, while **Wenceslas Square's closest base** (Rytířská 12; daily 9am-7pm) is on the main street connecting it to Old Town—walk past the large New Yorker store at the base of the square and keep an eye out on your left-hand side. You'll also find a tourist-friendly base beside the **Charles Bridge Tower** (Mostecká 4; daily 9am-8pm) on the Malá Strana side of the Vltava River.

BUSINESS HOURS

While office workers may get an early start and fill public transport from 6am-9am, many independent shops don't open until 10am (although supermarkets and shopping malls tend to open earlier, at 8am-9am). Shops start to close down between 5pm-7pm. Most weekend hours are limited, but shops are not closed entirely.

Lunch hour is early during weekdays, and pubs may fill up as early as 11am. You can usually expect dinner service to last until at least 10pm. Many independent coffee shops don't cater to the pre-work crowd and instead open around 10am on weekdays and possibly even later on weekends.

EMERGENCY NUMBERS

The universal emergency number across Europe is **112,** and operators can direct you toward any specific emergency needs if you are unable to reach a police station. Additional numbers are available for fire (**150**) and ambulance (**155**), but these services are not guaranteed to speak English, so 112 is your safest bet to be redirected.

In case of emergency (e.g., lost or stolen possessions, criminal encounters) you'll want to file a police report for official documentation. English fluency among Prague police officers on the street is not guaranteed, but the following stations are intended to have an interpreter on site at all times for concerns in multiple languages.

- **New Town** (Jungmannovo námesti. 9; tel. +420 974 851 750)
- **New Town** (Krakovská 11; tel. +420 974 851 720)
- **Old Town** (Benediktská 1; tel. +420 974 889 210)
- **Malá Strana** (Vlašská 3; tel. +420 974 851 730)

CRIME

The Czech Republic was ranked 8th in the world in the 2020 Global Peace Index. Crime is low, threat of terror attacks is minimal, and solo travelers can walk almost all streets safely at any hour. However, travelers from some ethnic or religious backgrounds, particularly those with darker skin or wearing head coverings, may experience xenophobic attitudes and unwanted attention. Being alert and aware of your possessions while in large crowds or on public transportation is always a good idea.

One criminal act that has recently drawn international attention and consequences is graffiti. In 2019, two tourists spray painted the base of the Charles Bridge. The pair were charged 100,000 CZK (around $4,375) each and banned from the country for five years. Czechs take the preservation of their historic monuments seriously.

HOSPITALS AND PHARMACIES

In case of emergency, call 112. If you're in need of medical attention in the center of Prague, private clinics **Canadian Medical** (Na Poříčí 12; tel. +420 222 300 300; www.canadian.cz; metro or tram: Náměstí Republiky)

and **Poliklinika Na Národní** (Národní 9; tel. +420 222 075 119 or +420 222 075 120; metro or tram: Národní třída or tram: Národní divadlo) offer English-speaking reception and quality medical care.

Visitors will also find two hospital options just west of the Smíchov neighborhood, outside the center of Prague. **Na Homolce Hospital** (Roentgenova 2; tel. +420 257 273 289; www.homolka.cz; bus: Nemocnice Na Homolce) offers English-speaking service and a high standard of care. Public **Motol Hospital** (V Úvalu 84; www.fnmotol.cz; metro: Nemocnice Motol) has a specific, English-speaking emergency reception area for foreigners. Depending on the type of insurance you have, visitors may have to pay a deposit on arrival before seeing a doctor and then settle the bill after receiving treatment. It can also be helpful to have copies of insurance info on paper (rather than stored on a phone). Many hospitals operate by making paper copies of patient information.

You can spot pharmacies (lekarna in Czech) by looking for a green cross outside the buildings. **Lékárna U svaté Ludmily** (Belgická 37; www.lekbelgicka.cz; tel. +420 222 513 396) is located next to Náměstí Miru and open 24 hours a day.

Mental Health Services and Emergency Support

Local expat **Gail Whitmore** (tel. +420 775 248 363, www.counselinginprague.com) offers crisis support specializing in depression, sexual violence, domestic violence, and LGBTQI+ support to English speakers in Prague. Confidentiality is ensured and help is available at any hour of day or night.

FOREIGN CONSULATES

- **Embassy of the United States** (Tržiště 15; https://cz.usembassy.gov; tel. +420 257 022 000)
- **Canadian Embassy** (Ve Struhách 95/2; www.canadainternational.gc.ca; tel. +420 272 101 800)

- **British Embassy** (Thunovská 14; www.gov.uk; tel. +420 257 402 111)
- **Irish Embassy** (Tržiště 13; www.dfa.ie; tel. +420 257 011 280)
- **Embassy of South Africa** (Ruská 65; www.mzv.cz; tel. +420 267 311 114)
- **Australian Consulate** (Klimentska 10 sixth floor; www.dfat.gov.au; tel. +420 221 729 260)
- **Consulate of New Zealand** (Václavské náměstí 9; www.mfat.govt.nz; tel. +420 234 784 777)

CURRENCY EXCHANGE

Many of the city's currency exchange offices advertise zero-percent commission in large letters, but offer abysmal rates in small print when you actually hand over your cash. Two trusted offices to change money are **Visitor Change** (Na Můstku 2; 9am-7pm) at the information center or **eXchange** (Kaprova 14) just off Old Town Square past St. Nicholas Church. A wider map of honest exchange offices is available at https://honest.blog/cs/honest-exchange-places. ATMs generally offer a fair rate, but check with your bank about any fees for withdrawing money abroad.

LAUNDRY

Laundromats are not a common amenity in Prague.

ANDY'S LAUNDROMAT
Korunní 14; tel. +420 222 510 180 or +420 733 112 693; https://praguelaundromat.cz; daily 8am-8pm; metro or tram: Náměstí Míru

This is your best English-friendly option with detergent (20 CZK) and fabric softener (15 CZK) available. Choose from self-service with small (79 CZK), large (120 CZK), or extra-large (150 CZK) washers and dryers, plus free coffee, tea, and internet access while you wait. You can also drop off clothes for wash and dry with a turnaround of 2-3 days (300 CZK) or next day service (400 CZK). Final loads start no later than 6:30pm, and tokens to operate the machines are sold at the front desk with payment by cash or card.

DROP-OFF LAUNDRY SERVICE

Drop-off laundry service is also available at **Čistírna Oděvů A Kůží Laundromat** (Karolíny Světlé 11; tel. +420 739 775 255; https://cistirnapur1.webnode.cz; Mon-Fri 7:30am-7pm; tram: Národní divadlo) with 250 CZK load and 24-hour turnaround. Note that one "load" of laundry is often small by US standards, roughly the size of one shopping bag.

Laundry service is common (though often pricy) in Prague's larger luxury hotels but rare in most of the boutique hotels and hostels. Try apartment rentals at **Miss Sophie's Charles Bridge** or **Residence Milada** if you plan to do laundry in Prague, or book a hostel stay at **Hostel HOMEr** (250 CZK per load; 24 hours).

Transportation

GETTING THERE
Air
International flights will most likely arrive at **Vaclav Havel International Airport (PRG)** (Aviatická; www.prg.aero). There are two terminals, with Terminal 1 serving flights from outside the Schengen area (e.g., North America, the UK, Asia, Africa, and the Middle East) and Terminal 2 serving flights from within Europe's Schengen countries. The airport is small and reasonably easy to navigate, with hit-or-miss public Wi-Fi available. At the time of writing, free COVID-19 antigen testing was available at the Prague Airport with a reservation (www.ghcgenetics.cz; tel. +420 739 500 500).

Did You Know... ?

Every city has its fun facts and local secrets that define its personality. Here are a few nuggets of knowledge you should know about Prague and the Czech Republic:

- Prague has a number of **nicknames** including the Golden City, the Heart of Europe, and the City of a Hundred (or a Thousand) Spires.

- Despite all those spires, a large portion of the population identify as **atheist or agnostic,** followed by **Catholics** as the largest organized religion. There is also a sci-fi streak, with more than 15,000 Czechs identifying as **"Jedi Knights"** as their religious affiliation on the last census.

- The Czech Republic is the official name of the country, and **Czechia** was approved in 2016 as an official short version accepted on paperwork and uniforms for the national sports teams. The controversial decision is divisive among the locals, who either love it or hate it and refuse to use it.

- Decisions in Prague have had a galactic impact. The 2006 meeting of the International Astronomical Union that decided to demote **Pluto** was held in Prague.

- The US and the Czech Republic have been connected since the formation of Czechoslovakia in 1918. **Thomas Garrigue Masaryk,** the first Czechoslovak president, married an American woman and took her maiden name as his middle name—how's that for avant-garde feminism?

AIRPORT TRANSPORTATION

The airport is 17 kilometers (about 10.5 mi) east of the city center, and transportation from the airport to the city center is not always straightforward. There is no direct public transportation link, but you can catch **buses** from Terminal 1 or Terminal 2 (routes 100 or 119, 32 CZK transport ticket), which run frequently from about 4:45am until around 11pm. After about a 15-20-minute ride, transfer to the green metro line at the last bus stop, Nádraží Veleslavín. The trip between the airport and the city center takes roughly 35-55 minutes total.

For an easier (and usually slightly cheaper than a taxi) ride into the city, try local ridesharing providers **Liftago** (www.liftago.cz) or international operators **Bolt** (www.bolt.eu) and **Uber** (www.uber.com). These do require setting up a profile, so it's best to download and enter information before your trip. Rideshares pick up passengers along the strip of pavement in the short-term parking lot that sits in front of Terminal 1 and Terminal 2 (not at the sidewalk in front of arrivals). The ride

into the city takes roughly 20-30 minutes and costs 350-700 CZK.

There are no taxi stands at the Prague Airport, so if you want to take a taxi, ask one of the airport information desks (Fix Taxi or Taxi Praha) to arrange one for you or negotiate your fare in advance—Prague taxis have a reputation for overcharging foreigners. The ride into the city takes roughly 20-30 minutes and costs around 500-800 CZK in a taxi.

Train

The national rail company is called **České dráhy** (www.cd.cz), with unpredictable service varying between older models with minimal amenities and newer trains with Wi-Fi and electrical outlets. When booking a ticket in person or online, make sure to specify that you want a seat reservation unless you're okay standing in the train-car halls during peak seasons. Two private carriers, **Regiojet** (www.regiojet.com) and **Leo Express** (www.leoexpress.com), also run on the same lines with more consistently modern service and guaranteed seating at varying prices. Trains arrive and depart efficiently and reliably, so be sure to find your platform with plenty of time to spare. At the time of writing, face masks were required on trains and public transport in the Czech Republic. Double check requirements (or carry one with you just in case).

There are three train stations serving Prague. The Main Railway Station is called **Praha—Hlavní nádraží** (Wilsonova 8), and is often written as Praha hl. n in Czech. This station is located in the center of New Town and connects directly to the red Metro line C. This station serves both domestic and international destinations and is filled with restaurants, shopping, and even a supermarket. This is the most common station that international tourists will arrive or depart from.

Two smaller stations also offer connections to destinations abroad and within the Czech Republic: **Praha—Masarykovo nádraží** (Havlíčkova 2) is in New Town not far from Náměstí Republiky and next to tram stop Masarykovo nádraží. Indirect trains requiring transfers to other European destinations may depart from or arrive at this station.

Train station **Praha—Holešovice** (Partyzánská 26) is located along the red Metro line C at the metro stop with the same name. Some indirect trains to domestic or international destinations may stop at this local station, one stop outside of Prague's main central train station (Hlavní nádraží). This may be a more convenient place for travelers staying in Letná or Holešovice to board or depart these trains.

From Vienna: Trains to Prague (4 hours, €19-66) depart Vienna's Wien Hauptbahnhof station between 6:30am-10:10pm every one-two hours. Most trains are operated by **ÖBB Railjet** (www.oebb.at) or **RegioJet** (www.regiojet.com). Fares vary depending on the train company. (RegioJet tends to be cheaper, but ÖBB Railjet have some discounted tickets.) There is also a night train operated by **EuroNight** (an international night train that is run by various operators, like ÖBB Railjet; you can buy tickets on the ÖBB Railjet website) that

leaves Vienna around 10pm and arrives in Prague at 6am; tickets cost from €60.

From Budapest: Regiojet (www.regiojet.com) launched a new service connecting Prague and Budapest in 2020, running twice daily from 7:45am-3:45pm arriving roughly seven hours later (€16-35/5,500-12,500 HUF). Trains operated by EuroCity, a cross border train category running within the European intercity rail network run by more than one train company, run from Budapest Keleti every two hours between 5:40am-3:40pm (6.5 hours, €20-30/6175-9750 HUF). You can buy tickets from the MÁV website (www.mavcsoport.hu). There is also a night train available, but you need to book this in advance if you want a sleeper (€29-39/9,425-12,675 HUF).

Bus

Prague's main **Florenc Bus Station** (Křižíkova 6; www.florenc.cz) can be tricky to find. It is connected to the Florenc Metro station along the red Metro line C and yellow metro line B, but you have to follow signs for the specific exit to "Autobusové nádraží" or you may find yourself a few streets away. Multiple bus companies arrive and depart from Florenc at all hours, but the terminal building of fast food, indoor seating, carrier information counters, and luggage storage is only open between 6am-10pm. Travelers may have to wait outside for late-night connections and overnight buses. At the time of writing, face masks were required on buses and coaches in the Czech Republic.

Some buses may stop on the street above the Main Railway Station of **Praha—Hlavní nádraží** (Wilsonova 8). There are staircases and elevators to reach the station from the parking area. This stop is most common for international routes on private companies such as Flixbus or Eurolines.

The **Na Knížecí Bus Station** (Na Knížecí) in the Smíchov neighborhood serves domestic routes to places such as Český Krumlov or Karovy Vary. The outdoor platforms do not offer much customer service or shelter, so double-check your departure information and bundle up in winter if departing from this station. Na Knížecí is easily accessible on the yellow metro line—just follow the signs with a picture of a bus for the correct exit out of the large, underground Anděl metro stop. Na Knížecí is also accessible via tram 20 from Malá Strana (10-15 minutes) or tram 5 from Wenceslas Square (15-20 minutes). A taxi from Wenceslas Square takes 10-20 minutes, depending on traffic, and should cost 150-250 CZK.

The **Černý Most** bus station lies at the end of the yellow Metro line B. The bus stops are located downstairs from the subway platforms. Day trips to Liberec depart hourly from this outdoor station for most of the day, and there are a few fast-food options and a RegioJet information center on the lower level.

From Vienna: You can get the bus with **FlixBus** (www.flixbus.com) from Wien Erdberg or **RegioJet** (www.regiojet.com) from Wien Hauptbahnhof from Vienna to Prague 6am-11:30pm. Buses go every hour and a half for FlixBus, whereas for RegioJet there are services running six times a day. The journey takes around four-five hours and tickets cost €15-23.

From Budapest: FlixBus (www.flixbus.com) in collaboration with the domestic Volánbusz company (http://nemzetkozi.volanbusz.hu) has buses to Prague (7.5 hours, €15-26) several times a day, approximately every two hours, usually going from the Népliget bus station.

Car

An international license is required to drive in the Czech Republic. To access the highways, you'll need to purchase a sticker at a border crossing point, post office, or gas station and display it on your windshield. Prague's highways, particularly the D1 highway connecting Prague and Brno, are notorious for heavy traffic and construction delays. Satellite navigation or GPS is recommended for visitors navigating the Czech Republic by car.

From Vienna: Plan on three-and-a-half to five hours if you want to drive the roughly 250 kilometers (155 mi) from Vienna to Prague. Take the A5 north to Brno (a great place for lunch or a stopover) and then take the D1/E65 highway West to Prague. This route has roads with tolls so you will need a vignette for Austria (€9) and the Czech Republic (CZK 350).

From Budapest: Drive the M1 west from Budapest toward the Hungarian border and continue northwest toward Vienna. Follow the A5 north to Brno before heading west on the D1/E65 to Prague. The route is 525 kilometers (325 mi) long and takes five hours. There are tolls in both Austria (€9) and Hungary (HUF 3000), so you will need a vignette for each country.

GETTING AROUND

Prague's public transportation system, **Dopravní podnik hlavního města Prahy** (www.dpp.cz), is one of the best in the world, with easy access to almost every part of the city via metro and tram for most neighborhoods, or by bus for a few of the more residential areas or the outskirts. Prague's city center is also incredibly walkable (with comfortable shoes). The most popular sights are clustered in a few areas—the condensed Old Town, the ring of New Town wrapping around it, and the Malá Strana neighborhood sitting below the Prague Castle. Most surrounding neighborhoods such as Vinohrady, Žižkov, Letná, or Karlín are just one or two metro or tram stops outside the city center, making them easy to access or even to use as your home base.

One possible pitfall is that Prague's streets are not arranged in a grid, so carry or download an offline map to avoid getting turned around, especially in Old Town.

Transit Passes

Public transport tickets are sold in chunks of time, not single rides. They are valid from the moment they are validated, *not* when they are bought, so don't forget to stamp your ticket when you're ready to use it. Individual tickets are available for 30 minutes (24 CZK) or 90 minutes (32 CZK), as well as 24-hour passes

Transit Etiquette

color-coded signs in Prague metro stations

- **Noise:** The atmosphere on Prague's public transport is generally quiet, and loud conversations or phone calls will be met with dirty looks from the residents.

- **Seating:** There is a line of succession when it comes to seating—riders are expected to stand up and offer their spots at any stop to elderly people, injured individuals with crutches or a cane, pregnant women, and young children.

- **Boarding:** Always let the departing passengers exit before attempting to board. During rush hours, passengers near the doors often step off the train and stand near the doors to let passengers off before re-entering, so maintain an awareness of anyone needing to squeeze past, especially when traveling with luggage or a backpack.

- **Escalators:** When riding the escalator in metro stations, passengers who want to walk use the left side and those who want to stand stay to the right—the locals take this seriously, so don't block the path with luggage or a group of side-by-side riders.

- **Face masks:** At the time of writing, face masks were required on public transit and in transit stations. Always have one with you just in case.

(110 CZK) or 72-hour passes (310 CZK). There are no week passes, but a monthly unlimited pass is only 670 CZK. Prague transport tickets can be used on all metro, tram, and bus lines, and also include use of the funicular on Petřín Hill and the ferries crossing the Vltava River during warmer months. Tickets are valid for unlimited rides during the allotted time, including transfers between the various modes.

The PID Lítačka smartphone app (pidlitacka.cz) is one of the easier ways to purchase and keep public transport tickets using Wi-Fi or mobile data. Paper tickets are also available to purchase from yellow automated machines inside Metro stations and near some major tram stops, or in person at limited information desks (see www.dpp.cz for locations). Some updated machines accept credit cards, but many require cash in coins (not bills), so a multi-day pass can save the hassle of finding a machine plus the right change for every individual ride, especially if searching late at night. Many modern trams allow you to pay with a credit card at a contactless cash point onboard, but you'll need a contactless credit card that you can tap (not a chip) and if anything goes wrong then you're stuck without a ticket, which could still qualify you for a fine, if checked. Some corner stores around town also sell transport tickets, but availability is inconsistent. It is not possible to buy a ticket onboard most public transport in Prague.

Tickets work on an honor system. You validate your ticket before entering and then keep the ticket with you as proof of payment. Inspectors can do random checks at any time, and anyone caught without a ticket will be removed and required to pay a hefty 1,500 CZK fine on the spot—inspectors will accompany you to an ATM if you don't have cash on hand. Excuses such as ignorance or simply forgetting to stamp your ticket or contactless payment not working are not accepted, so be sure to validate every time and keep your ticket in a safe, accessible place.

Metro

Prague's underground subway system consists of three lines: the green **Metro line A** running from Dejvice through the Old Town and into Vinohrady and Žižkov, the yellow **Metro**

line B running from Anděl across Old Town and New Town and into Karlín, and the red **Metro line C** connecting Holešovice with the city center and Vyšehrad. Most stations have a single platform with service in both directions (Vyšehrad, Hlavní Nádraží, and Černý Most are exceptions). At the time of writing, face masks were required in all metro stations.

The metro runs from 5am-midnight daily, with trains arriving every two-three minutes in peak hours and 5-10 minutes in off-peak hours. Many stations have a digital display counting down until the arrival. Validate your ticket in the yellow boxes located at the entrance to the stations, usually at the top of stairs or escalators before you reach the platform.

Not all metro stations are accessible via elevator (see www.dpp.cz for barrier-free travel) and most stations combine escalators and stairs, so be prepared to lift any luggage that you're traveling with. Many of the escalators are quite steep and faster than travelers may be used to. The deepest station at Náměstí Miru takes over two minutes to travel 53 meters (almost 175 ft) down one of the longest escalators in all of Europe.

Trams with yellow trim have the most modern amenities.

Tram

The tram system runs 24 hours a day, switching to limited night-tram schedules at midnight. Tram 22 is particularly popular among tourists, connecting the Prague Castle to Malá Strana, Vinohrady, and New Town. Night trams generally begin with the number nine (e.g., 92, 97). If you have a single-ride paper ticket, be sure to validate it onboard in small yellow boxes near some of the doors. Tram rides can be a bit jerky, so hold on when the train starts to move to avoid tumbling down the aisles. At the time of writing, face masks were required for all passengers on trams.

Construction and maintenance on the tram lines are prevalent during the summer months, so many tram routes may be interrupted. Information is often posted at the stop, but not always in English, so having a map or data-enabled phone can be useful to tackle surprise route changes. The transit authority website (www.dpp.en) usually provides updates in English.

Bus

Prague's city buses connect to some of the more remote neighborhoods and trips to the Prague airport. Validate your ticket on board in small yellow boxes near some of the doors. Like trams, buses run at all hours, and night buses also begin with the number nine (e.g., 92, 97). At the time of writing, face masks were required on all buses.

Taxi and Ride-Sharing

Taxi service in Prague is notorious for taking indirect routes and overcharging foreigners, particularly if flagged down off the street near touristy areas. You may ask your hotel or restaurant to call a cab for you to be on the safe side. Smartphone travelers can also use local ride-sharing providers Liftago (www.liftago.cz) or international operators Bolt (www.bolt.eu) and Uber (www.uber.com) for a safe ride that is tracked on a map and doesn't require having the local currency on hand.

Public transport can generally take you anywhere that taxis could during the day, but a taxi can be helpful if you're out on the town after midnight, when the metro stops running and trams and buses switch to limited night routes.

Car

Driving in Prague is more trouble than it's worth: lots of one-way streets, confusing parking zones, and restrictions (see www.parkujvklidu.cz for details). Cars stick to the right side of the road in the Czech capital, so look right first at any intersections.

However, a car can be useful for day trips and seeing some of the countryside. You can find many international rental car companies, including Avis (www.avis.cz; tel. +420 221 851 225; Mon-Fri 7:30am-6pm, Sat-Sun 8am-noon) or Budget (www.budget.cz; tel. +420 602 165 108; daily 8am-8pm), at the Prague Airport.

Day Trips from Prague

Nearby towns and reliable public transport

make it easy to step outside of Prague for a day trip and experience life and culture across the Czech Republic. Kutná Hora delights the eyes with a combination of churches and contemporary Czech art. Liberec, just an hour north of Prague, offers a laid-back day of reservoir walks and café culture. Outdoor enthusiasts are drawn to the lush forests and rock formations in the protected natural landscape of Bohemian Paradise.

Spending one night outside of Prague opens up even more opportunity. The peaceful spa town of Karlovy Vary is made for relaxation, while travelers looking for quirky monuments and cocktail bars will enjoy the city of Brno. The medieval town of Český Krumlov is known

Highlights

Look for ★ to find recommended sights, activities, dining, and lodging.

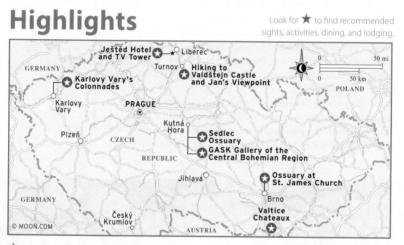

★ **Sedlec Ossuary:** Kutná Hora's famed "bone church" contains thousands of artfully arranged human skeletons. A recent photography ban has restored a more peaceful atmosphere to this sacred site (page 150).

★ **GASK Gallery of the Central Bohemian Region:** The GASK contemporary art gallery creatively curates Czech art by topics such as friendship, fear, and understanding for a fascinating cultural commentary (page 151).

★ **Ještěd Hotel and TV Tower:** It's hard to say what's more appealing about this architecturally renowned tower in the mountaintops of North Bohemia: the panoramic views stretching to Germany and Poland or the quirky, retro-futuristic décor (page 154).

★ **Hiking to Valdštejn Castle and Jan's Viewpoint:** Trek through a small town to reach Bohemian Paradise, a protected nature preserve with rock formations and impressive viewpoints (page 157).

★ **Karlovy Vary's Colonnades:** Fill your spa cup with mineral water from free-flowing fountains while strolling through gorgeous column-lined architecture (page 162).

★ **Ossuary at St. James Church:** Brno's ossuary—the second largest in Europe—isn't as famous as Kutná Hora's "bone church," but the local sculptures and classical music composed specifically for its halls make it a worthwhile sight in its own right (page 175).

★ **Valtice Chateau:** Tour grand royal residences and a Baroque theater before sampling the country's best wines straight from the barrel in this chateau's basement wine cellar (page 189).

for its fairy tale castle, cobblestoned streets, and summertime river rafting trips. The region of South Moravia includes royal residences and wine country around the town of Mikulov, a popular stopping point for travelers continuing to Vienna or Budapest.

PLANNING YOUR TIME

Kutná Hora, Liberec, and **Bohemian Paradise** are all easy day trips from Prague by train or bus. An overnight stay will help to make the most out of **Karlovy Vary** or **Český Krumlov,** allowing for the travel time without feeling rushed. If you head east to the Moravian region, it's worth spending a few days traveling between **Brno** and the **Lednice-Valtice Area,** which are connected to each other and to Prague by regular trains and buses or highways.

Bohemian Paradise and the **Mikulov-Lednice-Valtice area** are very much seasonal destinations, best visited in good weather from April-October. Summers in **Český Krumlov** have been bordering on overtourism in recent years, but the town is still a peaceful destination in spring, winter, and autumn. Book your tickets to see the interiors of the **Lednice and Valtice Châteaux** or tours of the **Český Krumlov Castle** at least a month in advance to ensure the availability of English tours.

You can store your luggage at Prague's **Main Train Station** (Praha hlavní nádraží) or **Florenc bus station** for up to 24 hours for 60-100 CZK per day. For longer, multi-day trips, try **Luggage Storage Prague** (www.luggagestorageprague.com), which maintains three locations near Náměstí Republiky, Praha hlavní nádraží, and Národní třída. Prices start at 150 CZK per piece for one day, with discounted rates of 105 CZK per piece for 2-7 days.

Kutná Hora

Less than an hour east of Prague is Kutná Hora, a city of fascinating architecture and historical importance. A quieter complement to the cosmopolitan capital city, Kutná Hora remains accessible for travelers on a tight schedule. The presence of silver mines established the city's royal status in the 14th century, while its "bone church" at the Sedlec Ossuary remains the most famous draw for tourists. The historic city center, St. Barbara's Cathedral, and Cathedral of the Assumption at Sedlec have earned their places on the UNESCO World Heritage List, and the GASK contemporary art gallery adds a dash of modern Czech perspective to the historical experience.

PLANNING YOUR TIME

Sightseeing in Kutná Hora works best if you start with the furthest sights in the outskirts of town (called Sedlec) then and work your way back to the city center. The short walk from Kutná Hora's main train station, Kutná Hora hl. n., to the Sedlec Ossuary passes by a lesser known architectural sight worth stepping inside, the lengthily named Church of the Assumption of Our Lady and Saint John the Baptist. Take your time exploring the artistic detail in every corner of this church while the first wave of train travelers makes their way straight to the Sedlec Ossuary. By the time you walk up the street after them, the crowds inside should be a little bit lighter.

An eight-person Tourist Shuttle Van (35 CZK) departs from the ossuary whenever

---

Previous: Bohemian Paradise is know for its sandstone rocks; Český Krumlov's castle gardens; Karlovy Vary's Park Spring in Dvořák's Park.

Day Trips from Prague

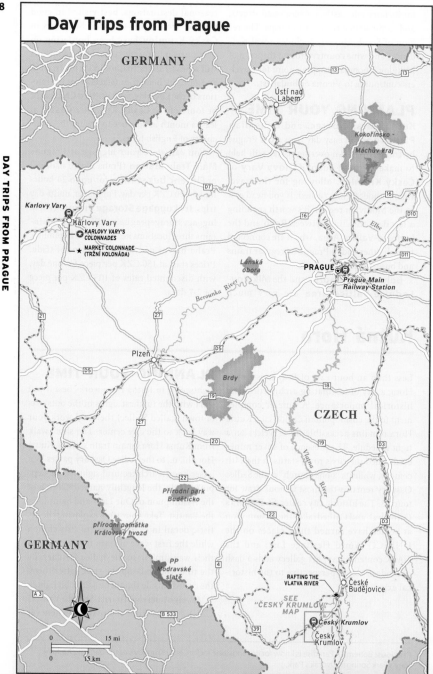

GERMANY

Ústí nad Labem

Kokořínsko - Máchův kraj

Karlovy Vary

Karlovy Vary

⊕ KARLOVY VARY'S COLONNADES

★ MARKET COLONNADE (TRŽNÍ KOLONÁDA)

Lánská obora

PRAGUE

Prague Main Railway Station

Vltava River

Elbe River

Berounka River

Plzeň

Brdy

CZECH

Přírodní park Buděticko

GERMANY

přírodní památka Královský hvozd

PP Modravské slatě

Vltava River

RAFTING THE VLTAVA RIVER

SEE "ČESKÝ KRUMLOV" MAP

České Budějovice

Český Krumlov

Český Krumlov

0   15 mi

0   15 km

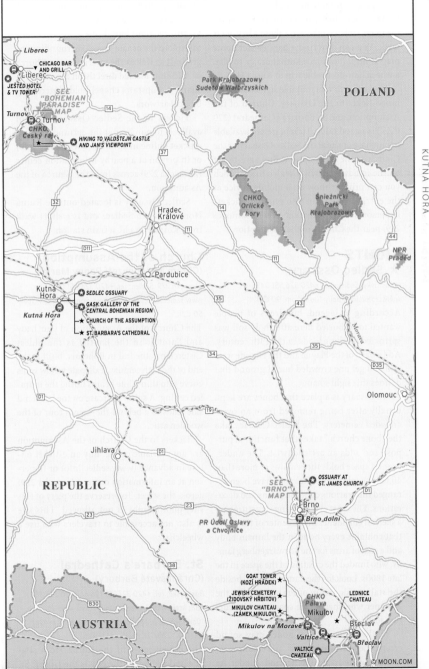

Liberec

CHICAGO BAR
AND GRILL

Liberec

JEŠTĚD HOTEL
& TV TOWER

SEE
"BOHEMIAN
PARADISE"
MAP

14

Turnov

Turnov

CHKO
Český ráj

HIKING TO VALDŠTEJN CASTLE
AND JAN'S VIEWPOINT

Park Krajobrazowy
Sudetów Wałbrzyskich

POLAND

37

32

14

CHKO
Orlické
hory

Śnieżnicki
Park
Krajobrazowy

Hradec
Králové

11

44

NPR
Praděd

D11

11

Pardubice

Kutná
Hora

SEDLEC OSSUARY

35

43

GASK GALLERY OF THE
CENTRAL BOHEMIAN REGION

Kutná Hora

CHURCH OF THE ASSUMPTION

ST. BARBARA'S CATHEDRAL

Morava

34

35

D35

D1

19

Olomouc

Jihlava

D1

REPUBLIC

OSSUARY AT
ST. JAMES CHURCH

SEE
"BRNO"
MAP

D1

Brno

23

23

Brno dolní

PR Údolí Oslavy
a Chvojnice

GOAT TOWER
(KOZÍ HRÁDEK)

38

JEWISH CEMETERY
(ŽIDOVSKÝ HŘBITOV)

MIKULOV CHATEAU
(ZÁMEK MIKULOV)

CHKO
Pálava

LEDNICE
CHATEAU

Mikulov

B30

Mikulov na Moravě

Břeclav

AUSTRIA

Valtice

Břeclav

VALTICE
CHATEAU

© MOON.COM

three people or more are ready to go. This is the best option to reach the historical center of the town, which is otherwise about a half-hour walk. You can also find a barrier-free route map at http://destinace.kutnahora.cz to plan a wheelchair-accessible trip to Kutná Hora.

If you plan to visit multiple sights, the combined ticket to the Ossuary, Church of the Assumption, and St. Barbara's Cathedral (220 CZK) is a good value. Tickets are not available to purchase onsite at the Sedlec Ossuary or the Church of the Assumption. Buy an e-ticket online in advance (www.sedlec.info), which you can print or show on a mobile device at the entrance. You can also purchase tickets in person at an information center (Zámecká 279) near the Church of the Assumption.

SIGHTS
★ Sedlec Ossuary

U Zastávky, Sedlec; tel. +420 326 551 049; www.sedlec.info; daily 10am-5pm; 90 CZK

According to legend, hundreds of people wanted to be buried here after holy soil was sprinkled on these lands in the 13th century. Add a dash of the Plague and the Hussite wars and you get one crowded burial ground that defines this sight's name.

An ossuary is a place that bones are kept, usually after being removed from an overcrowded cemetery. The Sedlec Ossuary, aka the "bone church," takes that functional purpose and adds an artistic twist. The underground space holds the remains of more than 40,000 people whose skeletons have been arranged into various configurations and decorations. The most eye-catching structures are a skeletal chandelier in the center of the room that contains every bone in the human body and a coat of arms for the Schwarzenberg family, who funded the creation of the space in the late 1800s. Look for the name "F. Rint" beside the stairs, a signature of František Rint, the designer who shaped the space into its current form.

While a room full of bones may sound creepy, the towers, pyramids, and columns actually provide an air of peace and wonder. As

of January 2020, photography is not allowed, to preserve a sense of reverence and respect for this religious burial site. Take some time to explore the ornate graves surrounding the grounds as well as the interior of the Church of All Saints located directly on top of the ossuary. An upstairs chapel holds interesting biblical artwork.

Tickets to the Sedlec Ossuary are not available to purchase at the entrance. Buy an e-ticket online in advance (www.sedlec.info) or in person at a nearby information center (Zámecká 279) across from the Church of the Assumption.

Sedlec Ossuary is located outside Kutná Hora proper in Sedlec, and is a short walk from Kutná Hora hl. n train station.

Church of the Assumption
(Chrám Nanebevzetí Panny Marie)

Zámecká 279, Sedlec; tel. +420 326 551 049; www.sedlec.info; Mon-Sat 10am-5pm, Sun 11am-5pm; 50 CZK

The Church of the Assumption of Our Lady and Saint John the Baptist is the oldest Cistercian cathedral in Bohemia, built at the end of the 12th century. Tall, pale yellow walls curve into thin white beams lining the muraled ceiling. A spiral staircase on the left-hand side leads to a behind-the-scenes tour of the wooden attic.

Tickets to the Church of the Assumption are not available onsite. Buy an e-ticket online in advance (www.sedlec.info) or in person at an information center (Zámecká 279) across the street. To preserve the piety of this site, photography is not allowed. This site is also not accessible to travelers who use a wheelchair.

St. Barbara's Cathedral
(Chrám svaté Barbory)

Barborská; tel. +420 327 515 796 or +420 775 363 938; https://khfarnost.cz; daily 10am-4pm Jan-Feb, 10am-5pm Mar, Nov, and Dec, 9am-6pm Apr-Oct; 160 CZK, 220 CZK combined ticket

The crown jewel of the Kutná Hora skyline and symbol of the city is the Gothic St.

Barbara's Cathedral, named after the patron saint of the miners who defined this town. Admiring every detail of the tall sloping curves of the exterior combined with the frescoed ceilings inside will give your neck a workout. The grass courtyard around the church provides a peaceful place to relax after a day of sightseeing. Outside the church, Barborská street is lined with stone statues and views over the town.

Purchase e-tickets in advance (https://tickets.khfarnost.cz) or in person at the nearby information center (Barborská 685). The church is about half an hour to an hour's walk from either Kutná Hora město or Kutná Hora hl.n, so you may want to take a taxi.

★ GASK Gallery of the Central Bohemian Region
(Galerie Středočeského Kraje)

Barborská 51-53; tel. +420 725 377 433; www.gask. cz; Tue-Sun 10am-6pm; 80-200 CZK admission

The multi-story GASK contemporary art gallery holds paintings, sculpture, and multimedia pieces from Czech artists of the 20th-21st centuries. I recommend a solid 90 minutes to take in the permanent exhibition of "States of Mind – Beyond the Image" (80 CZK), spread across two floors and organized into 21 pairs of emotions or ideas. Connected rooms and hallways house 5-10 pieces from different artists that explore opposing themes, such as solitude and friendship, fear and courage, gentleness and cruelty, and prejudice and understanding. Czech perspectives on confinement and freedom on the third floor offer particularly striking connections to world history.

Other sections of the gallery hold individually ticketed, rotating exhibitions (80 CZK each). An all-access gallery pass (200 CZK) is also available. Audio guides are only available in Czech, but captions are in English. The walls around the art are adorned with translated quotes by international artists, writers, and pop culture figures, from Czech cartoonists to Marcus Aurelius and John Lennon. There's an onsite bookstore and local design shop, along with a coin-operated locker and cloakroom.

FOOD
Czech
★ STAROČESKÁ RESTAURACE V RUTHARDCE

Dačického náměstí 10; tel. +420 607 286 298; www.v-ruthardce.cz; Sun-Thu noon-11pm, Fri-Sat noon-1am; entrées 150-300 CZK

No matter which wooden bench or chair you claim in the dimly lit dining room, glassed-enclosed winter garden, or casual outdoor courtyard, you can expect hearty meals and efficient service in this massive, multi-room Czech restaurant. Try the kulajda soup of dill, cream, potatoes, and a poached egg as a starter, or pair it with a beet root and goat cheese salad for a lighter meal. Hungrier visitors should stick to one of the many grilled meat dishes. Make a reservation online to request an outdoor (or indoor) seat.

International
BLUES CAFE

Jakubská 562; tel. +420 602 438 634; www. blues-caffe.cz; Tue-Thu 9am-7pm, Fri-Sat noon-8pm, Sun noon-6pm; entrées 50-100 CZK, cash only

Baguettes, quiches, soups, and sweets satisfy a multigenerational crowd at this music-themed café and bar. Gruff but efficient service includes multilingual menus and staff, and local cash is required to pay your bill. The dining room of mismatched wooden furniture surrounded by concert fliers and classic rock posters occasionally doubles as a live music venue on weekends. The entryway is also a small vintage music shop of classic records and CDs.

ČTYŘI SESTRY

Havlíčkovo náměstí 16; tel. +420 327 512 749 or +420 722 019 546; http://ctyrisestry.cz; Mon 11am-3pm, Tue-Thu 11am-10pm, Fri 11am-11pm, Sat noon-11pm, Sun noon-10pm; entrées 150-300 CZK

Choose from a small outdoor patio or pale pastels and light wood indoors at "Four Sisters" restaurant. The decor feels

sophisticated enough for date night, but solo travelers and families are welcomed just as warmly. Seasonal menus cover an array of seafood, steaks, soups, salads, and Czech specialties with sections for vegans, vegetarians, and children. Prices run a little higher than a typical Czech pub for filling portions and a refreshing amount of vegetables in carnivore country. Reservations recommended.

GETTING THERE
Train

You can reach Kutná Hora in about an hour on the national rail service **České dráhy** (www.cd.cz; 200-250 CZK round trip) leaving from Prague's main train station (Praha hl. n.) about once an hour from 4:30am, with the last trains departing to Prague around 10:15pm. Choose a direct train rather than one that requires a transfer in Kolín. There are three train stations around the area: Kutná Hora hl. n. is a good place to start with a short walk to sights in the Sedlec area, including Sedlec Ossuary. The regional Kutná Hora-Sedlec station is closest to tourist sights but requires transferring trains. Kutná Hora město is closest to the center of town, good for the return journey at the end of your trip.

Before purchasing your ticket, you have a decision to make: 1) buy a direct round-trip ticket to Kutná Hora hl.n. and walk for 10-15 minutes to the Sedlec Ossuary (recommended) or 2) purchase one round-trip ticket from Prague to Kutná Hora hl.n plus an additional regional ticket from Kutná Hora hl.n to Kutná Hora-Sedlec. Transfering to the small local train is not well signed, but does drop you off steps away from the Church of the Assumption and Sedlec Ossuary. Either way, you are likely to return to Prague from the Kutná Hora město station, closest to the center of town, which is included in a return ticket to either station.

Car

Kutná Hora is just over an hour east of Prague (roughly 80 km/50 mi) on highway D11, Route 2, or D1/E65. There is some free street parking around the Sedlec Ossuary and Cathedral of the Assumption at Sedlec and you can find a list of places to park in town at https://destinace.kutnahora.cz/d/parking.

GETTING AROUND

Because Kutná Hora's sights and train stations are spread across town, they are more easily reached with a little help from local transport options. The **Tourist Bus** (tel. +420 733 551 011) provides rides for 3-8 people from the Sedlec Ossuary to the city center, to St. Barbara's Cathedral, or to the main train station when time allows (at driver's discretion). For traditional taxi service, call **Taxi Kutná Hora** (tel. +420 800 100 512, +420 777 239 909, or +420 327 512 618).

LEAVING KUTNÁ HORA

The majority of travelers do this day trip as a Prague-Kutná Hora-Prague loop. The last two trains from Kutná Hora to Prague on the state railway depart around 9pm and 10:30pm. Kutná Hora could potentially provide drivers, or those okay with indirect trains on the state rail service, an eastern head start on the way to **Brno** (150 km/93 mi; 2-3 hours by car).

1: Vienna's Town Hall has a twin in Liberec. **2:** Kutná Hora's Sedlec Ossuary (or "bone church") **3:** Ještěd Tower defines the Liberec skyline.

Liberec

Liberec (pronounced LIB-er-ets, not lib-er-ECK), located an hour north of Prague by bus or car, falls somewhere between cosmopolitan and country life. This university town near the German border is filled with interesting architectural sights, international restaurants, café culture, and walking trails. History buffs and German-speakers may know it as Reichenburg, the capital of the Sudetenland—a region of Czechoslovakia annexed by Germany in 1938. Allied forces conceded the Sudetenland to Hitler in the 1938 Munich Pact, hoping to avoid WWII. Fast forward a few decades and Liberec today is the Czech Republic's fifth-largest city, offering a peek at local life with some tourist-friendly attractions thrown in.

SIGHTS

★ Ještěd Hotel and TV Tower

Horní Hanychov 153; tel. +420 485 104 291,
+420 605 292 563 (hotel), tel. +420 731 658 045
(restaurant), www.jested.cz; tram: Horní Hanychov

Liberec's most distinctive building overlooks the city from a perch on top of the surrounding mountain range. The slender point of the Ještěd Hotel and TV Tower has earned international architectural acclaim for its ability to blend seamlessly into the natural silhouette.

On a clear day, visitors can see beyond the borders of Germany and Poland from the surrounding courtyard. The bronze "Little Martian" statue by sculptor Jaroslav Róna spends a lifetime crying at the base of the tower, often compared to a spaceship. On the opposite side of the tower, a plaque embedded in bricks marks the location of the last free radio broadcast made by future president Vaclav Havel and Jan Tříska in 1968's Czechoslovakia before the next few decades of Russian occupation.

The hotel and restaurant housed inside the curved walls maintain a charmingly nostalgic imagination of futuristic design from a 1970s perspective. Rounded chandelier light fixtures hang overhead the visitors staring out the floor-to-ceiling windows of the 120-seat restaurant and 50-seat café. A spontaneous snack or afternoon drink is usually available, but reservations are recommended to enjoy dinner with a panoramic view among the stars.

The easiest way to reach the tower is a cable car ride, departing from the base of the hill, a short walk from the Horní Hanychov tram stop. Cable car service starts at 8am from Tuesday-Sunday but not until 2pm on Mondays, running roughly every 20 minutes, and finishing at 7pm April-October and 6pm November-March. In winter, the ride includes a view overlooking the small Ještěd ski slope, which reverts to green grass in the warmer months.

Town Hall

Náměstí Dr. E. Beneše 1; tel. +420 485 101 709; www.
visitliberec.eu; Mon-Fri 9am-3pm, Sat 9am-11am
Jun-Sep, Thu 9am-3pm Oct-May; English tour 170
CZK, tower access 30 CZK; tram: Šaldovo Náměstí

The Liberec Town Hall draws the eye of anyone setting foot on the main square. Designed by Austrian architect Franz von Neumann, the building draws comparisons to another of his Central European masterpieces—the Vienna Town Hall. The intricate Neo-Renaissance façade and turquoise-topped spires are a testament to the Austro-Hungarian rule of this area in the 19th century. Balcony access is fun for a bird's-eye view of the area. Otherwise, set up shop across the square next to the statue of Neptune and his trident and find the best angle to fit the entire building inside your camera lens. Around the holidays, the town hall overlooks Christmas and Easter markets on the square with homemade crafts, hot wine (svařák), and fresh pastries, while summer months bring food, beer, and music festivals. The lively, central location means easy access to lots of pubs and restaurants, including Radniční Sklípek in the town hall basement.

Feast of Giants
(Hostina Obrů)

Nám. Dr. E. Beneše 27; free; tram: Šaldovo Náměstí
A fairy tale scene from sculptor David Černý, in his signature controversial style, is designed to look like a bus stop, though no buses actually stop here. The sculpture, entitled *Hostina Obrů* or *Feast of Giants* is shaped like a table and topped with two beer mugs in Czech and German style on either side of a severed head on a plate. The head is rumored to symbolize Konrad Henlein, a German politician from the Sudetenland and member of the Nazi party. A menorah on its side refers to a local synagogue that was burned down in 1938. The vase and Venus flytrap are thought to symbolize the Liberec museum and botanical gardens along Masarykova street. A pair of Czech sausages sit beside a trash can on the sidewalk next to the stop. This quirky artistic statement is located just beyond F. X. Šalda Theatre and the Liberec Town Hall.

RECREATION
Liberec Reservoir
(Liberecká Přehrada)

tel. 485 101 709; bus: Poliklinika or Technická Univerzita
Students and young families sprawl across blankets on a grassy hill beside the Liberec Reservoir on any sunny day—fair warning that swimsuits are somewhat optional for the under six or 60-plus crowds. Sausages, cold beer, and soft drinks from the onsite snack bar keep the crowds in good spirits. Park bench seating is available under the shade of a wooden roof. Stop into nearby Kavarna Bez Konceptu in advance for homemade sandwiches, pastries, and specialty coffee. The 1.5-kilometer (just over a mile) pathway around the reservoir offers a peaceful walk—particularly around sunset—surrounded by a lush ring of evergreen trees and alongside runners, a few cyclists, and parents pushing baby strollers. The footpath draws consistent

traffic through all seasons, circling around ice skaters and hockey players if the reservoir freezes over in winter. The stone dam flanked with turrets on the west adds the requisite fairy tale backdrop to the photogenic scene.

Hiking
LIBEREC LOOKOUT TOWER
(Liberecká výšina)

Distance (round-trip): *2.5 km (1.5 mi)*
Duration (round-trip): *1 hour*
Effort: *easy*
Trailhead: *near Lidové sady tram stop*
The forested area of Lidové sady provides a nice, easy hike to a **lookout tower** (Wolkerova 251; tel. +420 728 945 990; www.liberecka-vysina.cz; daily 10:30am-8pm; entrance 30 CZK) that works within a day trip itinerary. Enter Lidové sady across the street from a cultural center of the same name and follow the path for about 30 minutes, watching for signs to turn right toward "Liberecká výšina" (Liberec Heights) or "rozhledna" (lookout tower). The 25-meter (82-ft) viewpoint, originally built in the 1900s to resemble a medieval castle, is now connected to a hotel and restaurant, perfect for a celebratory beer or snack afterward. Climb roughly 100 stairs for views over the Liberec skyline all the way to the Ještěd TV Tower in the distance.

FOOD
Czech
★ RADNIČNÍ SKLÍPEK

Náměstí Dr. E. Beneše 1; tel. +420 602 602 260; www.sklipekliberec.cz; Mon-Thu 11am-11pm, Fri-Sat 11am-midnight; entrées 125-300 CZK; tram: Šaldovo Náměstí
The translation of Radniční Sklípek—Town Hall Cellar—tells you exactly where to find this 250-seat, traditional Czech beer hall. Try the pork schnitzel (known locally as řízek) with a foam-topped glass of locally brewed Svijany beer, and glance up between bites to admire the stained glass windows and dark wooden details. Despite the massive dining room size, reservations are recommended, particularly on weekends.

BALADA

Moskevská 13; tel. +420 485 110 109;
www.balada-liberec.cz; Mon-Sat 10:30am-midnight,
Sun noon-10pm; entrées 125-300 CZK; tram: Šaldovo
Náměstí

For a cozier setting, head down Moskevská Street to Balada. Exposed-brick walls and eclectic wooden furniture set a warm, comfortable vibe across three small rooms, plus an outdoor patio. The garlic soup (česneková) is a perfect starter before a hearty Czech meal on a cold day.

International
CHICAGO BAR AND GRILL

Dr. Milady Horákové 1; tel. +420 484 800 080;
www.chicago-grill.cz; Mon-Thu 11am-midnight,
Fri-Sat 11am-1am, Sun 11:30am-11pm;
entrées 150-250 CZK; tram or bus: Fügnerova

A long-term Liberec transplant from Chicago opened this burger joint and taqueria, conveniently located near the Regiojet bus stop back to Prague, to satisfy cravings for flavors that are hard to find in Central Europe. Enjoy sandwiches, salads, burgers, ribs, and Mexican food inside the long dining room or at an outdoor balcony table. Online reservations recommended.

Cafés and Cakes

Café culture has become an established part of the Liberec landscape in the last decade, with local favorites serving delicious lattes and sparkling lemonades alongside homemade cakes and open-faced sandwiches.

KAVARNA BEZ KONCEPTU

Husova 87; tel. +420 485 111 947; www.bezkonceptu.
cz; Mon-Fri 8am-10pm, Sat-Sun 9am-10pm; bus:
Technická Univerzita

Kavarna Bez Konceptu offers a bright, relaxed atmosphere with outdoor seating near the Liberec Reservoir.

MIKYNA

5. května 62; tel. +420 482 710 746;
www.mikynapoint.cz; Mon-Fri 8am-7pm, Sat
9am-7pm, Sun 10am-6pm; tram: Průmyslová Škola or
Ulice 5. Května

Between the Lázně Regional Art Gallery and Town Hall, Mikyna's friendly baristas keep the brunch crowds satisfied.

GETTING THERE
Bus

Regiojet (www.regiojet.com) offers hourly service to Liberec from the Černý bus station located at the end of Prague's Yellow metro line B, for about 100 CZK. Download the Regiojet app for impressive flexibility—cancelling and rebooking is available online up to 15 minutes before departure for most tickets. Ride in comfortable style with reasonably reliable Wi-Fi, touch screen entertainment, and leather seats. Take note that buses run from Prague-Liberec from 7am-11pm, but the last Liberec-Prague bus usually departs at 8pm (sometimes 9pm Jun-Aug). Book your trip to Liberec-Fügnerova (instead of Liberec-AN) to be dropped off at the first stop in the center of town instead of the main bus terminal—the Fügnerova bus stop is smack in the middle of town.

Car

Liberec is located about 110 kilometers (70 mi) northeast of Prague on Route D10/E65. Large parking garages for both the Forum and Plaza shopping malls in the city center offer parking (free Sat-Sun, 20-30 CZK/hour Mon-Fri). Otherwise, paid street parking requires a semi-complicated system of registration with the city and a working smartphone (see www.parking.liberec.cz).

GETTING AROUND

From Fügnerova bus terminal, you can walk about 1 km (just over 0.5 mi) or take tram 3 to the town square. Almost every sight can also be reached on foot.

Liberec city transport (www.dpmlj.cz) consists of multiple bus lines and two trams, 2 and 3, that run along a single tram line. Both trams 2 and 3 run from Lidové sady on the northeast side of the city toward Ještěd in the southwest. Tram 2 connects 17 stops from Lidové sady to the Dolní Hanychov stop. Tram 3 runs from Lidové sady through 21 stops, ending at Horní Hanychov, a short walk from the cable car to Ještěd. At the time of writing, Liberec was conducting long-term repairs on the tram lines, so riders may need to switch to replacement bus service (X2 and X3) on some sections of the tram line.

Transport tickets in Liberec are valid for a set amount of time (just like in Prague), beginning when they are validated. Visitors can purchase single tickets (24 CZK, valid for 40 minutes Mon-Fri, 60 minutes Sat-Sun), a 24-hour bus and tram pass (80 CZK), or a 24-hour tourist tram ticket (50 CZK), which is valid only on trams 2 and 3 (and replacement buses X2 and X3). There are automated ticket machines at Fugnerova and a small newsstand that sells tickets at the center of the station. The tourist tram ticket is great for visiting Ještěd, while a bus and tram ticket might be useful for including the Liberec Reservoir.

If you need a taxi, try **City Taxi Liberec Ltd** (tel. +420 800 501 501) or local rideshare app **Liftago.**

LEAVING LIBEREC

Consider 8pm a deadline for the last Regiojet bus leaving Fügnerova. Regiojet buses run every 30-60 minutes from 5:30am to 8pm (sometimes 9pm in summer).

While Regiojet is the simplest connection from Prague, some travelers may want to use the Liberec Train Station for connections to Turnov to explore nearby Česky ráj ("Bohemian Paradise"). The main **Liberec train station** is located at Žitavská 2 near the Nádraží tram stop, about a 15-20-minute walk uphill or a three-minute tram 2 or 3 ride from the Fügnerova bus stop in the center of town. Direct train service from Liberec to **Turnov** on the national railway (www.cd.cz) takes around 40-45 minutes (64 CZK) and runs about every two hours from 4:30am-10:30pm.

DAY TRIPS FROM PRAGUE
BOHEMIAN PARADISE (ČESKÝ RÁJ)

Bohemian Paradise (Český ráj)

Spending time outdoors (or "in the nature" as Czechs like to say) is a national pastime. One of the most accessible places to explore on a day trip from Prague is the protected landscape area of Český ráj (tel. +420 481 540 253; www.cesky-raj.info/en/) known as either "Bohemian Paradise" or "Czech Paradise." This massive nature preserve stretches across roughly 181 kilometers (70 mi) of hiking paths, castle ruins, and sandstone rock formations. Most travelers arrive by train via the small, quiet town of Turnov, which sits on the edge of the protected area, before entering the hills of Bohemian Paradise.

★ HIKING TO VALDŠTEJN CASTLE AND JAN'S VIEWPOINT

Distance (round-trip): *10 km (6 mi)*
Duration (round-trip): *5-7 hours*
Effort: *moderate*
Trailhead: *Turnov Train Station*

You could return to Bohemian Paradise multiple times, taking multiple paths (over multiple days, even), and stumble upon something new on every visit. The below route, which focuses on an accessible route along the yellow, green, and red lines, is a good place to start. It includes the rock formations that the area is known for, multiple viewpoints of both civilization and natural landscapes, and one

Bohemian Paradise

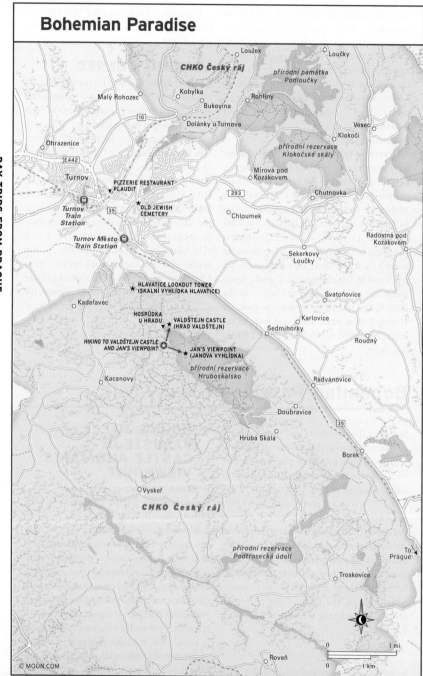

Loužek

Loučky

CHKO Český ráj

přírodní památka
Podloučky

Malý Rohozec

Kobylka

Bukovina

Rohliny

10

Dolánky u Turnova

Vesec

Klokoči

Ohrazenice

přírodní rezervace
Klokočské skály

E442

Turnov

Mírová pod
Kozákovem

PIZZERIE RESTAURANT
PLAUDIT

283

Chutnovka

Turnov
Train
Station

35

OLD JEWISH
CEMETERY

Chloumek

Radostná pod
Kozákovem

Turnov Město
Train Station

Sekerkovy
Loučky

HLAVATICE LOOKOUT TOWER
(SKALNÍ VYHLÍDKA HLAVATICE)

Svatoňovice

Kadeřavec

Karlovice

HOSPŮDKA
U HRADU

VALDŠTEJN CASTLE
(HRAD VALDŠTEJN)

Sedmihorky

Roudný

HIKING TO VALDŠTEJN CASTLE
AND JAN'S VIEWPOINT

JAN'S VIEWPOINT
(JANOVA VYHLÍDKA)

přírodní rezervace
Hruboskalsko

Radvánovice

Kacanovy

Doubravice

35

Hrubá Skála

Borek

Vyskeř

CHKO Český ráj

přírodní rezervace
Podtrosecká údolí

To
Prague

Troskovice

0   1 mi

0   1 km

© MOON.COM

Roveň

Tips for Hiking in Bohemian Paradise

- **Pack light** so that you can set off as soon as your train pulls into the station.

- Hiking boots aren't required for the recommended route, but **comfortable shoes that you don't mind getting a little dirty** are definitely recommended.

- Embrace navigating the **language barrier** as a part of your adventure. While this area draws many hikers, the level of signage and the amount of English spoken in shops and restaurants in Turnov is far more limited than in Prague.

- To help ensure you're going the right way, look for a large **map** just outside the train station; for **brown street signs** highlighting tourist sights; and for **colored stripes** on Turnov lampposts and the trees of Bohemian Paradise.

Follow color-coded paths to navigate Bohemian Paradise.

historic chateau, with no guide or overnight camping required. This route is not terribly well signed, so a paper map or phone with GPS can be handy, or keep your eyes out for colored stripes on light posts and gates along the way for reassurance.

Begin the Hike: Turnov Train Station

After arriving at Turnov Train Station, turn right out of the station and follow the yellow path down **Nádražní Street** and onto **Palackého Street** for about 10-15 minutes, crossing a beautiful flower-lined bridge over the **Jizera River.** After the bridge, ignore tree markings for the yellow path and continue straight on **Palackého** to reach **Sobotecká Street.** Turn right, walking another 5-10 minutes along the green line to find Turnov's Old Jewish Cemetery.

Old Jewish Cemetery
(Skalní vyhlídka Hlavatice)

Sobotecká, Turnov; www.synagoga-turnov.cz

The granite headstones at this 16th-century cemetery seem to arise out of nowhere in a grassy hill that was formerly located on the outskirts of town until the highway was added in the late 1980s. Only 19 Jewish citizens returned to Turnov after WWII and the local congregation ceased to exist in the 1960s. Today, the local synagogue is owned and run by the city and largely open for tourism purposes. It's not possible to enter and walk around the cemetery, but it's worth pausing as you pass by alongside to remember a community that was forced out of their homes, leaving behind evidence of centuries of existence along the German border.

After passing the cemetery: Continue along **Sobotecká Street** for five minutes to reach the small **Turnov město train station.** Turn left onto a cement road and watch for red stripes marking the trail through a residential area for about 25 minutes. Keep an eye out for a clearing of wooden sculptures marking the **Gate to Bohemian Paradise** on your left about 10 minutes after entering the woodsy area and continue uphill to reach the Hlavatice Lookout Tower.

Hlavatice Lookout Tower
(Skalní vyhlídka Hlavatice)

www.cesky-raj.info/en/; free

A 36-step, iron staircase spirals around the outside of this small sandstone rock serving as a viewpoint over the surrounding towns. A plaque at the top points out the skyline highlights, including the Jizera River and the Ještěd Tower over the city of Liberec. Spend 15 minutes relaxing on the benches and admiring the panoramic view of the town and surrounding mountains.

Leaving Hlavatice Lookout Tower: Keep walking along the red line for another 20 minutes to reach Valdštejn Castle.

Valdštejn Castle
(Hrad Valdštejn)

tel. +420 739 014 104 or +420 733 565 254; www.hrad-valdstejn.cz; daily 9am-6pm Jun-Aug, Tue-Sun 9:30am-5pm May, daily 9:30am-5pm Sep, Sat-Sun 10am-5pm Apr and Oct

The royal residence was established in the 13th century and—when it wasn't under attack—was owned by the Valdštejn (or Wallenstein) family, whose name you may recognize from the peaceful senate gardens below the Prague Castle. All visitors are free to admire the expressive stone sculptures of patron saints that line the cement bridge leading to the entrance. Take 15 minutes to enjoy these, and peek your head into the courtyard, but skip the self-guided tour of the interior (70 CZK, cash only, booked in advance for English) unless you're a major historical architecture fan.

The pub **Hospůdka U Hradu** is located next to Valdštejn Castle. Stop here to refuel on Czech hot dogs (párek) or fried cheese (smažený sýr) with French fries or grab a bench seat and dig into your own snacks.

Leaving Valdštejn Castle: Behind Hospůdka U Hradu, follow the red path for about 15 minutes keeping an eye to your left for signs to Jan's Viewpoint (Janova vyhlídka) along a blue path.

Jan's Viewpoint
(Janova vyhlídka)

Inside Český ráj; www.cesky-raj.info/en/; free

This railing-lined corner of the forest overlooks sandstone rock formations. Soak up the view of the rocks and look for a Czech flag flying on top or tiny rock climbers scaling the sides.

Bohemian Paradise near Turnov

Leaving Jan's Viewpoint: Backtrack the way you came to reach the rest area in front of **Valdštejn Castle,** then get ready for a 90-minute walk back into town, which follows a different path than the way you came in. Head down a path to the right of the castle and follow the green path to a parking lot. Then continue through residential streets along the red path to take you back to **Turnov město train station.** This time continue straight, following the train tracks over another bridge and past a soccer field. Turn right onto **Koškova** and left up one set of stairs to reach **Nádražní Street,** which should start to look familiar. Continue 5-10 minutes up the road to the main Turnov train station for a two-hour ride back to Prague.

FOOD

Many hikers prefer to pack a bag with snacks to eat along the hike. The walk through Turnov also offers plenty of small shops to grab a pre-made sandwich, pretzels, or a cold drink to toss into your backpack for a picnic later on.

Czech
HOSPŮDKA U HRADU

Kadeřavec 24, Turnov (inside Bohemian Paradise); tel. +420 773 686 064, www.hrad-valdstejn.cz; daily 10am-5pm May-Sep, Sat-Sun 10am-5pm Apr and Oct; entrées 100-200 CZK

If you prefer to pack light and don't mind a slightly touristy vibe, try the Hospůdka U Hradu or "Pub at the Castle" outside Valdštejn Castle. The hearty menu of traditional Czech cuisine, from fried cheese to grilled sausages, is best enjoyed outdoors on the surrounding picnic benches.

International
PIZZERIE RESTAURANT PLAUDIT

Bezručova 698, Turnov; tel. +420 481 311 288; www. plaudit.eu; Mon-Tue 11am-11pm, Wed-Thurs and Sat 11am-midnight, Fri 11am-1am, Sun 11am-10pm; pizzas 150-200 CZK

For a slightly more formal bite in town (though wearing hiking clothes is still totally acceptable), head to Pizzerie Restaurant Plaudit. This North Bohemian chain offers a wide selection of thin-crust pizzas with interesting toppings (think corn or a fried egg) alongside a full menu of chicken, steak, and pasta dishes. The 10-minute walk from the station allows for a leisurely meal to refuel after a day on your feet.

GETTING THERE
Train

The easiest way to explore Český ráj without a car is by train to the small town of Turnov. Trains depart from Prague's main train station (Praha hl. n.) or the centrally located Praha Masarykovo nádraží roughly every two hours via the national rail service **České dráhy** (www.cd.cz; 250-300 CZK round trip). Service to Turnov begins just before 6am with the last train from Turnov back to Prague departing shortly after 9pm. The direct journey with local stops takes just under two hours, while some routes require transfers of 2.5 hours or more so check the online schedule carefully.

Direct train service also runs from Liberec to Turnov on the national railway (www. cd.cz), with the 40-45-minute journey (64 CZK) running about every two hours from 4:30am-10:30pm.

Car

Český ráj is roughly 90 kilometers (55 mi) northeast of Prague on highway E65. The drive takes about an hour. Parking lots are available near some popular areas, including Turnov, usually for a fee around 50-100 CZK.

LEAVING BOHEMIAN PARADISE

The last train from Turnov back to Prague departs shortly after 9pm. The last train to Liberec departs Turnov just after 11pm.

Karlovy Vary

An aura of relaxation surrounds this peaceful valley town of pastel buildings and natural springs beside the Ohře River. The main attractions of Karlovy Vary (also known as Carlsbad in English) are the grand structures housing 15 thermal springs of drinking water, tapped and free-flowing for all pedestrians to taste. Tiny, decorative "spa cups" with a helpful spout are sold every few steps in shops and stands. The various temperatures and mineral contents give each spring a distinctive flavor and are believed by many to have healing powers. Join the ranks of King Charles IV, who founded the town in the 14th century, along with Russia's Peter the Great, Mozart and Beethoven, Franz Kafka, and many modern Hollywood stars who have come to "take the waters" over the centuries. Most facilities are open year-round, but spa season officially kicks off the first weekend of May, when a costumed King Charles IV rides a white horse through town and the mineral spas receive an annual blessing. Warm weather draws continuous crowds through September, while autumn, winter, and spring offer the same peaceful charm with quieter streets.

Once you get indoors, spa towns in the Czech Republic focus less on indulgence in white fluffy robes and more on natural treatments to improve your health. It's not unusual for local physicians to prescribe an extended stay for locals suffering from various illnesses and conditions. Services like mineral baths, salt caves, aromatherapy, and massages are usually accessible to travelers with a reservation in advance, but other services may require a physician's consultation, so read the fine print when booking online. The overall environment of these spas may also have a more clinical vibe than travelers are used to, but don't let that deter you from indulging in the local approach to wellness.

SIGHTS
★ Colonnades

To experience the most popular activity in Karlovy Vary, all you have to do is take a walk. The mineral springs that flow underground have been organized into a system of fountains housed inside gazebos and stone temples alongside the river. Many of these open-air structures are named "colonnade" for the rows of columns making up their architectural style.

Visitors are free to walk the city streets and sample most of the waters at all hours of the day. (Note: Don't drink too heavily—too much thermal water can cause digestive discomfort.) You can fill any container you like, although plastic bottles are not the best choice for the hottest of the springs. For the best experience, grab a porcelain spa cup (prices vary wildly depending on size and decoration, but expect between 100-1,000 CZK) from any of the vendors along the colonnades.

MILL COLONNADE
(Mlýnská kolonáda)

Mlýnské nábř; www.karlovyvary.cz

The 19th-century stone design of the Mill Colonnade embodies the royal atmosphere of Karlovy Vary's history. This temple of health is the largest and most popular in town, housing five separate springs between its symmetrical, arched halls. Some of the waters flow from taps emerging from the floor or walls, while others pool into shallow basins around the fountains. Twelve sandstone statues representing the calendar months line the rooftops of this open-air structure. Look for stairs near the northern side of the colonnade next to a large Becherovka bottle and climb five minutes to reach a quiet viewpoint just behind the roof for skyline views.

MARKET COLONNADE
(Tržní kolonáda)

Tržiště; www.karlovyvary.cz

The white latticed exterior of the Market Colonnade sets a more natural, delicate tone around the spring named for Charles IV as well the Market Spring and Lower Castle Spring. The building was designed in the late 1800s in a Swiss-inspired style.

As you continue along the river, keep an eye out for a musical patch of sidewalk, where stepping on the metal plates creates different tones. Take a moment to dance out a tune in front of Hotel Jessenius, about halfway between the Market Colonnade and the Grand Hotel Pupp.

Diana Observation Tower

Vrch přátelství 1; tel. +420 353 109 111; www.dianakv. cz; daily 9am-4:45pm Nov-Mar, 9am-5:45pm Apr and Oct, 9am-6:45pm May-Sep; free entry

Avid hikers can climb the hill to the Diana Observation Tower, but many travelers opt for an easy three-minute ride from the funicular beside the Grand Hotel Pupp (90 CZK return), saving their strength for the 150-step climb to the top of the tower (although elevator access is also available). The roughly 40-meter (130-ft) structure offers sweeping views of the city center and the surrounding forests in a remote area on the edge of town.

To hike to the tower, follow a path winding off Pod Jelením skokem street through the forest for about 2.2 kilometers (1.5 mi) to the west.

Grand Hotel Pupp

Mírové náměstí 2; tel. +420 353 109 111; www.pupp.cz

This stately building at the southern end of Karlovy Vary's spa center is as much a tourist destination as it is an accommodation option. Built in 1701, the glowing white palace wrapped around the bend of the Teplá River has hosted its fair share of both actual royalty (Empress Marie Therese, Napoleon Bonaparte) and Hollywood royalty (John Travolta, Scarlett Johansson, Sean Bean).

The hotel itself has held a cinematic spotlight as well, acting as backdrop for Queen Latifah's romantic comedy *Last Holiday*, impersonating a Montenegrin hotel in the James Bond film *Casino Royale*, and opening the Edith Piaf biopic in *La Vie en Rose*. The hotel plays host to both screenings and stars during Karlovy Vary's annual international film festival (www.kviff.com).

Stop by the outer courtyard to read some of the names and years etched in brick, offering a mini-Walk of Fame of the centuries of celebrities and historical figures who have stayed here. For a taste of the interior elegance without the hefty luxury hotel price tag (8,000 CZK s, 10,000-20,000 CZK d), try an afternoon drink at **Malá Dvorana** just off the lobby, where a portrait of Morgan Freeman keeps watch over the white tablecloths and French doors, or splurge on dinner at **Becher's Bar** decorated in deep red, green, and bronze tones.

Becherovka Museum & Factory

T. G. Masaryka 57; tel. +420 359 578 142; www.becherovka.com; Tue-Sun 9am-5pm; 150 CZK

Legend has it that the only two people in possession of the herbal recipe to make the Czech digestif Becherovka refuse to fly together in order to ensure its safety. The Jan Becher Museum holds more fun facts about the eventful history of this local cure-all liquor, created in 1807 and best described as "tasting like Christmas." Reserve a place online in advance to ensure a tour in English.

RECREATION
Parks

Stretches of landscaped lawns and sprawling parks are woven throughout the riverside valley, with hillside hiking paths lining the slopes behind the buildings in Karlovy Vary. You won't need to go out of your way and will likely pass through these parks on a walk through the town.

SMETANA'S GARDENS
(Smetanovy sady)

Colorful flowers are shaped daily to display the date at the entrance to these pristinely manicured gardens in front of the Elisabeth Spa, providing a fantastic photo op in spring and summer. Lime trees and benches line the long paths, offering a quick taste of nature at the busier northern edge of town, or a calming walk to your spa appointment.

DVOŘÁK'S PARK
(Dvořákovy sady)

The grassy area connecting the cement courtyard of Hotel Thermal to the grand Mill Colonnade marks the beginning of spa central. Dirt paths lined with benches curve around a peaceful pond, a statue of the park's namesake Czech composer, leading to the small Park Spring housed at the end of a cream-colored gazebo with a long, arched hallway. Most visitors bypass the park to head straight to the springs, but a leisurely 15-minute detour encompasses Karlovy Vary's stress-reducing approach to a slower pace of life.

DEER JUMP LOOKOUT
(Jelení skok)

The tree-lined hills behind the Mill and Market Colonnades hide a small bit of history between their branches. A statue of a deer (actually a chamois for any picky zoologists) symbolizes the 14th-century legend of the town's founding. Emperor Charles IV was supposedly hunting in the area when one of his dogs chased a deer off a cliff and fell into one of the thermal pools below. Charles was impressed that the waters cured his dog's injuries and dipped his own limbs into the pools with similar results. Thus, the healing powers of the spa town were born.

To reach the hillside lookout, look for a

1: Hlavatice Lookout Tower is built into the rocks. 2: Sip from a spa cup and you've got an automatic souvenir. 3: Karlovy Vary, a town of peaceful relaxation

yellow-marked path off Pod Jelením skokem street or take the funicular to Diana's Tower and follow a 10-minute path through the woods.

Spas
ELISABETH SPA

Mírové náměstí 2; tel. +420 353 222 536 or +420 353 222 5367; www.spa5.cz; Mon-Fri 8am-7pm, Sat 9am-7pm, Sun 10am-6pm; treatments 120-800 CZK

Entrance to Elisabeth Spa, named in the early 1900s for Austro-Hungarian Empress Sisi, starts with a walk through the pristinely manicured Smetana's Gardens. Inside, the individual treatment rooms feel more like doctor's offices that offer mineral baths, aromatherapy and hot stone massages, heat-, hydro- and electro-therapy treatments, and a swimming pool. Splurge on a relaxation package or spend an affordable 45 minutes wrapped in a blanket and breathing deeply in the salt caves to feel your stress melt away. This long-running local favorite combines relaxation with the historic ambiance that defines this town for a memorable wellness experience. Most spa treatments require advance booking.

FESTIVALS AND EVENTS

The **Karlovy Vary International Film Festival** (www.kviff.com) takes over the town and fills hotels in late June and early July each summer. The **Vary Září Festival** (vary-zari.karlovyvary.cz) brings light shows and video mapping to the city's historic buildings in September.

FOOD
Czech
PILSNER URQUELL ORIGINAL RESTAURANT - NÁRODÁK

T. G. Masaryka 24; tel. +420 353 408 523; www.narodak.eu; daily 11am-11pm daily; entrées 185-300 CZK

The Pilsner Urquell stamp of approval means the beer is fresh, the taps are sparkling clean, and the menu is mostly fried. Visitors mix with locals on their lunch break in the mid-sized dining area lined with wooden bar stools, green banquettes, and the signature copper tanks and light fixtures. For the best value, come early and stick to the daily lunch menu (100-150 CZK) of Czech specialties at this slightly touristy pub connected to the Ambassador Hotel.

International
★ LE MARCHE

Mariánskolázeňská 4; tel. +420 730 133 695; www.le-marche.cz; Mon-Sat noon-10pm; 490-1,290 CZK prix fixe menus

The mood at Le Marche is pure elegance in pale blue and white tones, with watercolor paintings and a sparkling chandelier decorating the dining room of roughly 25 seats. Three-course lunches (490 CZK) and multi-course dinner options (790-1,290 CZK) change daily based on seasonal flavors, often with a French twist. Reservations are essential for a luxurious lunch (noon-3pm) or an indulgent dinner (6pm-10pm) at the far end of town, around the river bend from the Grand Hotel Pupp.

Breakfast and Brunch
REPUBLICA COFFEE

T.G.Masaryka 28; tel. +420 720 347 166; Mon-Fri 7am-7pm, Sat-Sun 8am-7pm; entrées 100-150 CZK

Karlovy Vary's coffee connoisseurs frequent Republica Coffee for flat whites and breakfast pastries. The efficient baristas don't skimp on quality, so there may be a short wait at peak times. Grab a table in the pop-art balcony area or one of the candy-colored chairs on the outdoor terraces.

ACCOMMODATIONS

Grand Hotel Pupp may be the most luxurious option in town, but there are other good choices, too.

APARTMANY VICTORIA

Jugoslávská 10; tel. +420 222 532 547; https:// apartmany-victoria.worhot.com; 1,500 CZK d

Apartmany Victoria provides a comfortable home base and a helpful staff full of personal recommendations. These kitchen-equipped apartments with one-, two-, or three-bedroom options are decked out in clean, light-wood details. The convenient location is just around the corner from the Tržnice bus terminal and a 15-minute walk from the Mill Colonnade, surrounded by casual dining options. The one quirk of this quiet, mid-sized option with on-site massage services is the cash-only payment upon arrival.

HOTEL THERMAL

I.P. Pavlova 11; tel. +420 359 002 201; www.thermal. cz; 2,000-3,000 CZK s, 2,500-3,500 CZK d

This massive cement building of 273 rooms (three equipped for accessibility) offers river and forest views in the center of town. The beautifully renovated wellness area includes a mid-sized swimming pool, jacuzzi, and multiple saunas. Friendly, English-speaking staff on the second floor schedule spa treatments including salt chambers (165 CZK), whirlpool baths (450 CZK) and massages (500-1,300 CZK). A health-conscious buffet breakfast is included.

GETTING THERE

Buses are a better option than the train for getting to Karlovy Vary. Trains take longer, cost twice as much, and drop you off at a less convenient station.

Train

State-run **České dráhy** (www.cd.cz) trains depart from Prague's main train station (Praha hlavní nádraží) roughly every two hours from about 5am-7pm (3 hours; 300-350 CZK round trip). The train station is across the Ohře River from the center of town, requiring a 15-minute walk to hotels on the northern side of town and about half an hour's walk from the Grand Hotel Pupp at the opposite end.

Bus

Comfortable coach service from **Regiojet** (www.regiojet.com; 300-350 CZK round trip) or **Flixbus** (www.flixbus.com; 250-315

CZK) departs from Prague's Florenc bus station almost every hour 6am-10pm. The journey takes just over two hours, finishing at two stops both on the northern end of town. Regiojet service to Karlovy Vary also connects directly to Prague's Vaclav Havel airport, so visitors could easily start or finish their Czech trip in this destination. The first bus stop in Karlovy Vary, called Tržnice, will be more convenient for the majority of visitors walking 10 minutes into town. The main Terminál station just five minutes further down the river can be an easier place to find a taxi if you have large luggage or would like a ride to accommodation near the Grand Hotel Pupp at the opposite end of town.

Car

Karlovy Vary is located about two hours (roughly 130 km/80 mi) west of Prague on Route 6. www.karlovyvary.cz offers updated information and pricing on parking garages around town.

GETTING AROUND

With a compact city center lining the river, most of Karlovy Vary is designed to be walkable. If you need a taxi, try **KV Taxi** (tel. +420 777 141 413; www.kv-taxi.cz).

LEAVING KARLOVY VARY

Buses depart for Prague from the **Karlovy Vary, Terminál station** roughly every hour between 5am-8pm on **Regiojet,** and around 7am-6pm on **Flixbus.** Note that outgoing buses do not stop to pick up passengers at the Tržnice stop, where most passengers likely got off when they arrived. Tržnice is about five minutes closer to town than Terminál, so give yourself a few extra minutes to walk to the main station.

Český Krumlov

In many towns, the term "fairy tale atmosphere" can feel cliched, but the pastel colors and medieval atmosphere of Český Krumlov deserve full rights to the phrase. The main draws to this carefully preserved 13th-century city are the Český Krumlov Castle, encircled by the curves of the Vltava River, and the chance for some river rafting fun.

Expect heavy tourist traffic during summer months. A local artist even hired people to live "normal" lives in the summer of 2018 to draw attention to tourism pushing the locals out of town, so be aware that there may be some anti-tourist sentiment around town. Try using the local language whenever possible and visiting during one of the shoulder seasons. This popular city is equally beautiful and half as crowded in late spring and early autumn while the castle sights are still open, or even a peaceful day in winter when fewer sights are open but the city streets are dusted in snow. Many tour groups also treat the city as a day trip, so an overnight stay allows you to explore in a more peaceful evening setting. A **Český Krumlov card** (www.ckrumlov.info; 400 CZK) provides a single entrance to five sights for one year, including the Castle Tower and Museum, Fotoatelier Seidel, and Egon Schiele Gallery, and will save you money if you intend to see all three of these sights. Purchase the card at any included sight or at the Český Krumlov Tourist Information Center (nám. Svornosti 2; tel. +420 380 704 622; www.ckrumlov.info).

SIGHTS
Český Krumlov Castle
(Zámek Český Krumlov)
Zámek 59; tel. +420 380 704 721;
www.zamek-ceskykrumlov.cz
This castle and chateau served as a royal residence to a variety of aristocratic families—the Lords of Krumlov, the Rosenbergs, the Eggenbergs, and the

Český Krumlov

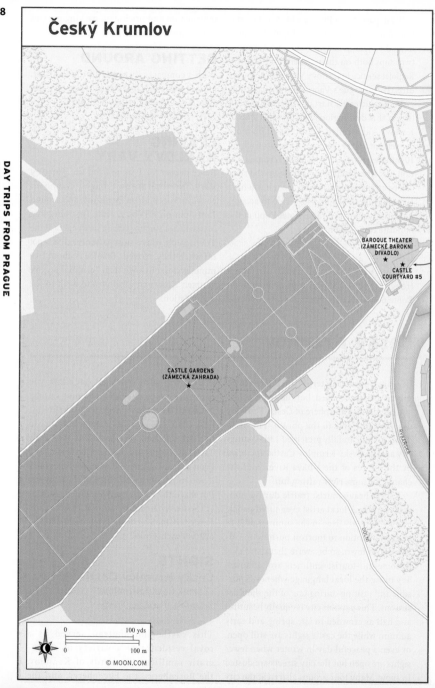

BAROQUE THEATER
(ZÁMECKÉ BAROKNÍ
DIVADLO)
★

★ CASTLE
COURTYARD #5

RYBÁŘSKÁ

CASTLE GARDENS
(ZÁMECKÁ ZAHRADA)
★

DLOUHÁ

0   100 yds

0   100 m

© MOON.COM

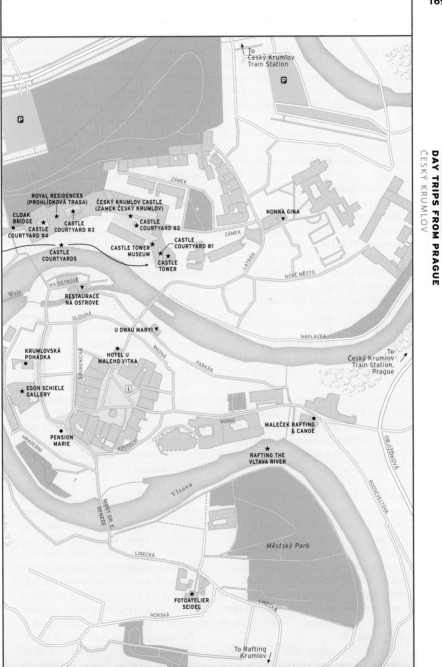

To
Český Krumlov
Train Station

P

P

ZÁMEK

ROYAL RESIDENCES
(PROHLÍDKOVÁ TRASA)
★

CLOAK
BRIDGE
■
★
CASTLE
COURTYARD #4
★
CASTLE
COURTYARD #3

ČESKÝ KRUMLOV CASTLE
(ZÁMEK ČESKÝ KRUMLOV)
★
CASTLE
COURTYARD #2

NONNA GINA
▼

ZÁMEK

★
CASTLE
COURTYARDS

★
CASTLE TOWER
MUSEUM
★
CASTLE
COURTYARD #1

★
CASTLE
TOWER

LATRÁN

NOVÉ MĚSTO

Weir

NA OSTROVĚ

▼
RESTAURACE
NA OSTROVE

DLOUHÁ

NÁPLAVKA

U DWAU MARYÍ ▼

SOUKENICKÁ

MASNÁ

PARKÁN

To
Český Krumlov
Train Station,
Prague

KRUMLOVSKÁ
POHÁDKA
●

★
HOTEL U
MALÉHO VITKA

i

★
EGON SCHIELE
GALLERY

HORNÍ

■
MALEČEK RAFTING
& CANOE

OBJÍŽĎKOVÁ

●
PENSION
MARIE

KOSTELNÍ

★
RAFTING THE
VLTAVA RIVER

HRADEBNÍ

ROOSEVELTOVA

Vltava

MOST DR. E.
BENEŠE

LINECKÁ

Městský Park

LINECKÁ

★
FOTOATELIER
SEIDEL

HORSKÁ

To Rafting
Krumlov ↙

Schwartzenbergs—between the 13th-19th century, and was privately owned up until the 1940s before becoming state property. The collection of 41 buildings includes private residences, theaters, wine cellars, and gorgeously manicured gardens. Entrance to the castle courtyards and bridges is free of charge, while tickets to individual attractions and tours are arranged onsite.

How much time you spend at the castle depends entirely on your interests. For a simple, budget-friendly overview of the atmosphere, go for the iconic view from the Castle Tower, a free walk through the open courtyards, and a stroll through the massive manicured gardens. Guided tours booked months in advance are the only way to gain access to the **Baroque Theater** (a worthwhile addition for performing arts fans) or for a glimpse of the **Royal Residences** (240-320 CZK). Visit www.ckrumlov.info for barrier-free accessibility information for travelers who use wheelchairs and suggested routes within the castle grounds.

The dug-out area below the castle grounds actually houses a few bears, which were introduced to the area as a form of defense as early as the 16th or 17th centuries. Some visitors jostle along a small bridge for the chance to see them from a distance, but they're located pretty far beneath the bridge and aren't all that easy to spot. It's also worth noting that animal rights activists have protested their treatment in recent years.

CASTLE TOWER AND MUSEUM

Tue-Sun 9am-4pm Jan-Mar, daily 9am-5pm Apr-May and Sep-Oct, daily 9am-6pm Jun-Aug, daily 9am-4pm Dec, closed Dec 18-Jan 4; 150 CZK

The Castle Tower dominates the silhouette of the hilltop fortress and symbolizes the city itself. A climb up 162 spiral stairs rewards visitors with impossibly wide panoramic views of the city. Arrive early or toward the end of the day to avoid the maximum limit of 50 people on the snug balcony.

While many visitors head straight to the top of the tower, the 14-room **museum** at its base (included in the ticket) is absolutely worth browsing. Ask for a free audio guide at the ticket counter for a more enjoyable experience. Wander through a collection of portrait halls, former administrative offices, and glass cases full of 19th-century artifacts including board games, glasses, and porcelain dining sets. Continue through a treasury of sacred art, an armory of weapons and soldiers' uniforms, and a collection of family photos from former castle residents the Schwarzenburg family. One hour is plenty of time to complete the self-guided tour. Hang onto your museum ticket, which also accesses the turnstile to the tower entrance.

This attraction comes with the added bonus of being open year-round (with the exception of Dec 18-Jan 4) with no reservations required. The lobby of the tower includes a reasonably priced gift shop and coin-operated lockers for a deposit of 10 CZK. The cozy onsite **Cafe Hrádek** offers a handful of wooden tables for a quick beer, wine, coffee, and cake before continuing further into the castle grounds.

CASTLE COURTYARDS

These five connected courtyards, open year-round, act as a long line of outdoor hallways running through the grounds. A stroll through them functions as a sort of self-guided tour of the grounds, giving some sense of the aristocratic atmosphere and beauty of the place without stepping foot inside any of the buildings.

The first fairly nondescript courtyard lies before the moat and holds the tourist information center as well as closeup exterior views of the Castle Tower. Entering the large second courtyard brings you officially inside the grounds, where you'll find the entrance to the Castle Tower and Museum on your immediate left and ticket offices in the far-left corner. This second courtyard is another gorgeous viewpoint to photograph the Castle Tower.

The smaller third and fourth courtyards are visual sights in their own right, with etched sgraffito designs on the walls surrounding the Royal Residences. Look for stairs on your right around the fourth courtyard to duck underground and explore "The Czech-Krumlov Surreality," a free (and somewhat eerie) sculpture exhibit in the cellars.

After the enclosed third and fourth courtyards you will cross the sculpture-lined **Cloak Bridge** (a favorite spot for selfies and skyline views) to reach a fifth outdoor courtyard, which holds a pricey outdoor café. Look up to your right to find a decorative sundial clock on the wall. Further ahead on the left, 26 stone windows lining the edge of the fifth courtyard create popular frames for photographs of the city.

The fifth courtyard acts as a pathway to the **Castle Gardens** (daily 8am-5pm Apr-Oct, 8am-7pm May-Sep), where the 17th-century landscape of geometric hedges, swirling flowers, and stair-lined fountains stretches far enough to feel secluded even in the busiest months.

BAROQUE THEATER
(Zámecké barokní divadlo)
Zámek 59; tel. +420 380 704 721;
www.zamek-ceskykrumlov.cz
The meticulously restored Baroque Theater inside the castle is renowned across Europe for its attention to historic detail. Dramatic performances were a part of castle life as early as the 1500s, but a 17th-century remodel created the appearance that has been maintained to this day. This theater and the Drottningholms Slottsteater in Sweden are the only two preserved Baroque theaters in existence in the world. The guided, forty-five-minute tour (380 CZK) is the only way to see the hand-painted scenery, the stark audience divisions between the aristocracy and the commoners, the wood-and-rope mechanics used to change sets, and the inventive machines used to create sound effects like wind and rain—raise your hand fast when the guide asks for volunteers to demonstrate the sounds.

English tours usually run at 10am from Tuesday-Sunday from May-October. Purchase your tickets in advance through www.

zamek-ceskykrumlov.cz or hit the box office early in the morning to reserve a space in person on the day you want to see it.

Fotoatelier Seidel
Linecká 272; tel. +420 736 503 871; www.seidel.cz;
Tues-Sun 9am-noon and 1pm-5pm, last entry at 4pm;
120 CZK plus 30 CZK for photography pass
Take a walk through early 20th century life of local photographer Josef Seidel in this restored art nouveau home and studio. Admission begins with a six-minute video detailing the life of the family before continuing an audio-guided walk in your chosen language through the home at your own pace (usually under an hour). The Seidel family's collection of 10,000 carefully labeled photos and negatives documenting local life and the natural beauty of the forests and hills of the Šumava area were confiscated under Communist rule, but luckily recovered intact and now displayed throughout the residence. Photography fans will love cases filled with classic camera equipment and accessories.

Make an online reservation in advance to arrange a souvenir photo shoot with a selection of period costumes (500-2,500 CZK depending on number of poses) in the light-filled portrait studio on the top floor.

Egon Schiele Gallery
Široká 71; tel. +420 380 704 011; www. schieleartcentrum.cz; daily 10am-6pm; 180 CZK
One of the most interesting sights outside the castle grounds is the three-story Egon Schiele Gallery. Schiele was an Austrian contemporary of Gustav Klimt in the early 1900s known for his nude figures and provocative approach. A permanent exhibit chronicles his life, including his adopted home of Český Krumlov and his success in Vienna, while the gallery rotates contemporary modern artists through the space.

RAFTING THE VLTAVA RIVER
The winding curves of the Vltava River through Český Krumlov can be as much a

draw as the human-made attractions on dry land. Largely during the summer months of July-August (but possible from May-Sep if weather permits), groups of Czechs and international travelers pile into rented boats (sometimes decked out in themed costumes) to spend the day floating and paddling downstream. This is one of the few times that the informal version of "ahoj" (meaning "hi") gets tossed at everyone you see.

Multiple boat rental companies cater to this hobby, with trips ranging from a short cruise through town (about 300-350 CZK pp) to an all-day journey from neighboring towns like Rožmberk or Vyšší Brod (about 600-750 CZK pp) on a large inflatable raft or canoe. The river is lined with pubs and restaurants for breaks and the occasional cocktail stand popping up in the middle of the water. Conditions are generally mild, but the slopes along the sides at various points can provide some excitement.

Storage is usually available at the rental office, where drivers shuttle groups to their starting points, and dry bags are provided—but to be on the safe side, leave electronics and sentimental valuables behind. You can spot the true pros with plastic bottles of beer attached with rope to the back of the boats and dragging along the water to stay cool.

MALEČEK RAFTING & CANOE

Kaplická 27; tel. +420 380 712 508; www.malecek.cz; daily 9am-6pm usually May-Sep (depending on weather)

The laid-back staff at Maleček offer short boat trips through the city center or longer day trips from the surrounding areas. Rental prices include boat rental of inflatable rafts or canoes, paddles, lifejackets, and a sealable bag for valuables. The staff will drive you to your starting point and collect the equipment at the end point of your trip.

RAFTING KRUMLOV

Pod Svatým Duchem 135; tel. +420 777 066 999 or +420 777 629 316; www.rafting-krumlov.cz; daily 9am-6pm usually May-Sep (depending on weather)

Rafting Krumlov offers similar services to Maleček of inflatable rafts and canoes with equipment and transport included for one-day excursions, plus the option to rent innertubes and paddleboards.

FOOD
Czech
RESTAURACE NA OSTROVE

Na Ostrově 171; tel. +420 608 731 606 or +420 606 698 382; www.naostroveck.cz; daily 10am-10pm; entrées 100-150 CZK

Restaurace na Ostrove is tucked onto a small pseudo-island just across the river from the Castle Tower. This casual, friendly pub setting can hold 20 guests inside and another 60 outdoors. Mixed salads, soups, baguettes, and bar snacks offer lighter alternatives with full meals of mostly grilled meats also available. The laid-back staff may take some time to get to each table, but they generally do so with a smile.

★ U DWAU MARYI

Parkán 104; tel. +420 380 717 228; www.2marie.cz; daily 11am-10pm daily; entrées 125-200 CZK

The riverside location of U Dwau Maryi is as much a draw as the fantastic Old Bohemian meals. On a warm day, the wooden tables along the grass-and-stone patio are filled with families and friends discussing the day's events as rafts pass by. During cooler months, the stone walls and cozy nooks indoors keep diners warm and dry. Try the Old Bohemian Feast of smoked meat and vegetables alongside your choice of chicken, rabbit, or pheasant.

International
NONNA GINA

Klášterní 52; tel. +420 380 717 187; daily 11am-11pm; entrées 150-250 CZK, cash only

Red checkered tablecloths and watercolor paintings set the Italian scene at this casual, two-story restaurant. Choose from more than

1: Český Krumlov town and Castle **2:** Český Krumlov Castle's fifth courtyard is a favorite photo spot. **3:** Old Bohemian Feast at U Dwau Maryi **4:** Cathedral of Sts. Peter & Paul in Brno

35 different pizzas served alongside soups, salads, pastas, and risotto. The attention to culinary detail, with spiced olive oils for dipping pizza crusts and sparkling lemonades infused with fresh fruit, draws a mixed crowd of solo travelers, locals on their lunch break, and international groups down this quiet side street below the castle gates. Save room for a slice of tiramisu. Cash only. Reservations recommended.

ACCOMMODATIONS
HOTEL U MALEHO VITKA
Radniční 27; tel. +420 380 711 925; www.hotelvitek.
cz; 1,500-1,725 CZK s, 2,200-3,200 CZK d

If you prefer a livelier environment, Hotel U Maleho Vitka attracts a slightly rowdier crowd to their 20 rooms of simple wood furnishings and exposed beams. The historic atmosphere comes with free Wi-Fi and a central location just off the town square. Each room of these three former residences combined into one large location has a slightly different character that you can browse online before booking.

PENSION MARIE
Kájovská 67; tel. +420 222 539 539;
www.pension-marie.cz; 2,000-2,500 CZK d

Pension Marie is a cozy, home-like setting for small groups and families. The 15th-century town house setting is decorated with simple, modern furnishings and brightly colored walls in a relatively quiet area just down the street from the Egon Schiele Gallery. Free Wi-Fi and breakfast in the on-site Italian restaurant are included.

★ KRUMLOVSKÁ POHÁDKA
Široká 74; tel. +420 777 127 982; www.
krumlovskapohadka.cz; 3,500-4,500 CZK d

This family-owned boutique hotel seamlessly mixes centuries of design elements. The 19th-century façade and preserved 16th-century ceiling murals set a medieval tone, complemented by modern in-room amenities (think rainforest showers and Netflix-equipped televisions). The nine individually designed

rooms range from a simple, functional single to a deluxe, three-room family suite. Breakfast in the onsite café or packed to go for early departures is included.

GETTING THERE
Train
The national rail service **České dráhy** (www.cd.cz; 200-350 CZK) runs one direct, three-hour train service from Prague daily around 8am. The main train station of Český Krumlov is a 30-minute downhill walk from the center of town, with local taxi service available.

Bus
Locally owned **Regiojet** (www.regiojet. com; 125-200 CZK) coaches depart from Prague's Na Knížecí station in the Smíchov neighborhood to Český Krumlov roughly every hour from 6am-9pm. The three-hour journey includes complimentary hot drinks and seat-back screens with English movies. Wi-Fi is solid near major cities, but less reliable in the countryside. Regiojet stops at both the Český Krumlov, Špičák and Český Krumlov, AN bus stations on opposite sides of the center. Both options are potentially convenient for a walk into town—Špičák through a hilly (and sometimes muddy) park and Český Krumlov, AN through cobblestoned streets—depending on the location of your accommodation.

Flixbus (www.flixbus.com; 200-385 CZK) also runs direct buses from multiple locations in Prague, so check your departure station carefully.

Car
Český Krumlov is a two-to-three-hour drive, about 160 kilometers (just over 100 mi) south of Prague on highway D3 and Route 3 or taking Route 4 and Route 20/E49. The historic center is a pedestrian area, but www.ckrumlov.info details some of the parking options surrounding the town that are available to visitors.

GETTING AROUND

The historic center of Český Krumlov is a compact, walkable area and a car-free zone, with exceptions for residents and certified taxis. If you need a taxi from the bus or train stations to your accommodation, try **Green Taxi** (tel. +420 800 712 712; www.greentaxi.cz).

LEAVING ČESKÝ KRUMLOV

Regiojet runs hourly bus service between Prague and Český Krumlov beginning around 6am, with the last bus to Prague departing Český Krumlov at 8pm daily. **Flixbus** service is a little less frequent, and usually includes a last departure from Český Krumlov to Prague at 6pm on weekends and 6:30pm on weekdays. The national rail service runs one direct train from Český Krumlov to Prague around 2pm daily.

Public transportation connections without connecting through Prague are somewhat limited, but the national rail service does run once-daily trains in the afternoon heading east to **Brno** (about 6 hours; 250 CZK), requiring a transfer in the town of České Budějovice.

Brno

The Czech Republic's second-largest city, Brno, is regularly referred to as the "capital of Moravia" for both its historical and modern importance. The town has a subtle sense of humor, with light-hearted legends hidden in the details of its historical sights. Brno's roughly 400,000 residents skew toward a young, university-aged crowd alongside an innovative startup scene. The active streets and underground sights of Brno make for an ideal stopping point between Prague and either Vienna or Budapest.

SIGHTS

★ **Ossuary at St. James Church**
(Kostnice u sv. Jakuba)

Jakubské náměstí; tel. +420 515 919 793;
www.ticbrno.cz; Tue-Sun 9:30am-6pm; 140 CZK;
tram: Náměstí Svobody or Česká

Overcrowded cemeteries in the 18th century often led to remains being excavated every 10-12 years and moved to underground ossuaries. The Ossuary at the Church of St. James was discovered in 2001, and is estimated to hold around 50,000 skeletal remains from residents lost to cholera, plague, the Thirty Years' War, and the Swedish siege of 1645.

This makes it Europe's second-largest ossuary behind the catacombs in Paris.

The underground space is organized into columns and pyramids built from bones with paths for visitors to observe and pay their respects. A curated selection of contemporary sculptures add to the display and a soundtrack composed specifically for the experience completes the serene scene, which has been open to the public since 2012. Candlelit night tours (140 CZK) also run Fridays in August from 10pm-1am. No more than 20 visitors are allowed to enter at one time, so reservations are recommended. This sight is not wheelchair accessible.

Church of St. James
(Kostel sv. Jakuba)

Jakubské náměstí 2; tel. +420 542 212 039;
www.svatyjakubbrno.wz.cz; daily 9am-6:30pm;
free; tram: Náměstí Svobody or Česká

One of Brno's (literally) cheeky monuments adorns the exterior walls of the Church of St. James. A small stone man called Nehaňba (meaning "Unashamed" or "Shameless") can be seen gripping the top of one of the exterior windows and exposing his bottom in the direction of Petrov Hill. One theory is that architect Anton Pilgram was poking fun at the

Brno

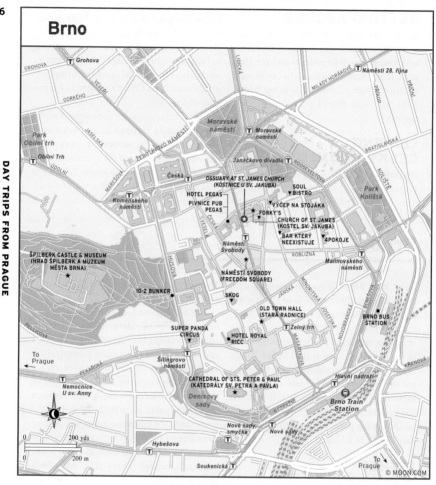

© MOON.COM

slow construction work on the Cathedral of Sts. Peter & Paul.

The interior of this bright 13th century church, renovated from Romanesque to Gothic to Baroque and to Gothic again over the centuries, is unusual for its three aisles of the same height. The décor is simpler than Brno's Cathedral of Sts. Peter & Paul, with tall arched windows and intricate patterns of wooden beams lining the vaulted ceilings and creating an aesthetic more serene than ostentatious.

Views from the 92-meter (300-ft) **church tower** over the center of town are worth an afternoon visit (Mon-Sat 10am-6pm, Sun 11am-6pm Jul-Aug, daily noon-5pm May-Jun and Sep, daily 1pm-5pm Apr and Oct, Fri-Sun 1pm-5pm Mar and Nov; 50 CZK).

Náměstí Svobody (Freedom Square)

free; tram: Náměstí Svobody

Business and trade have filled this market "square" (actually triangular) since at least the 13th century, when it was known as Dolní trh (Lower Market). Christmas and Easter markets cover the cobblestones in colder months, and summertime events bring lounge chairs and sidewalk seating ideal for people-watching into the open space. Visitors to Brno are likely to cross this square a few times while navigating the city, making it easy to enjoy as part of a walk to your next destination.

The city installed a large, black granite timepiece on the southern end of the square in 2010. This structure is often referred to as Brno's **"Astronomical Clock"** although it doesn't exactly display the positions of the sun, moon, and stars, or the time for that matter. I'll leave the shape open to the viewer's interpretation (the design was inspired by a bullet but often inspires phallic comparisons). Crowds start to gather as 11am approaches around the sculpture to watch a lucky few with their arms inside four holes around the sculpture. When the church bells of Sts. Peter & Paul's Cathedral chime 12 times to commemorate the defeat of the Swedish Army, a small glass marble drops from inside the clock. People show up to hold their spots for hours in advance, hoping for a chance to catch the once-a-day souvenir.

The rest of the square holds architectural monuments with more traditional, postcard-style beauty. If you look closely at **Dům U Čtyř mamlasů** (the House of Four Giants) just behind the Astronomical Clock, you'll spot four carved figures holding the façade of the building on their shoulders. A Baroque **Plague Column**—built in the late 17th century to express gratitude for surviving both the Thirty Years War and waves of plague outbreaks from the mid-to-late 1600s—stands tall in the northwest corner of the square. In summer months, **Česká Street** behind the column is often shaded by a canopy of colorful umbrellas, auctioned off each year to support various charities.

Old Town Hall
(Stará radnice)

Radnická 2; tel. +420 542 427 150; www.ticbrno.cz; Mon-Fri noon-7pm, Sat-Sun noon-8pm May, Mon-Fri noon-7pm, Sat-Sun 10am-8pm Jun, daily 10am-10pm Jul-Aug; 75 CZK; tram: Zelný trh

The Old Town Hall holds more of the city's fantastical tales. The Brno Dragon (okay, so it's actually a taxidermy crocodile) hangs from the ceiling just inside the entrance. One theory on the longstanding legend posits that the exotic beast was imported by a wealthy resident in the city's early days, meaning the creature could easily have been mistaken for a monster by locals who had never seen one. Anyway, the crocodile terrorized the town until a visiting butcher came up with a plan. He wrapped limes in an ox fur (or squeezed them onto it, depending on who tells the tale) and left it for the dragon to eat. The crocodile then drank from the river, and his stomach expanded and burst, slaying the dragon that now decorates the municipal building.

The wagon wheel on the wall beside him has a less incredible origin story. Georg Birck from the town of Lednice bet a group of his friends (likely over many beers) that he could cut down a tree, carve it into a wagon wheel, and roll it to Brno in less than a day. His skeptical friends accepted, and were shocked when he pulled off the task. Spoiler alert: This wheel on the wall didn't actually come from a single tree, but the legend did inspire an annual event of rolling wooden wheels between the two towns each October.

The final fantastical tale of the Old Town Hall explains the front of the building. If you look closely at the sculpted turrets over the entrance, you'll find that one appears to twist off track. This is supposedly because architect Anton Pilgram was unhappy about not being paid. Of course, the other side counters that it was actually a result of the architect drinking too much. Either way, don't let structural concerns stop you from climbing the tower for a panoramic view from the city center.

These days, the Town Hall functions largely as a draw for visitors with an information center and a panoramic view of the city center rewarding visitors climbing the stairs of its 63-meter (200-ft) tower (75 CZK). It's open regularly May-August, but individual access may be possible to arrange year-round (tel. +420 542 427 150; info@ticbrno.cz).

Cathedral of Sts. Peter & Paul
(Katedrály sv. Petra a Pavla)

Petrov 9; tel. +420 543 235 031; Mon-Sat 8:15am-6:30pm, Sun 7am-6:30pm; free; tram: Zelný trh

The towering shape of the Cathedral of Sts. Peter & Paul, also called Petrov for the hill it sits on, might look familiar to any visitors who have looked at their Czech currency. The neo-Gothic cathedral graces the face of the 10 CZK coin and is an icon of the Brno skyline. Renovations expanded the 13th-century Romanesque Basilica that previously stood on this sight. The unusual central location of the towers, crowdfunded and added to the building in the early 1900s, are the result of limited space on the top of Petrov Hill. Highlights of the ornate Baroque interior include stained glass windows that depict the life of Jesus, and climbing 30 steps to the top of the tower (daily noon-5pm Oct-Apr, noon-6:30pm May-Sep; 40 CZK), which gives you an incredible vantage point to admire the city.

When you leave the cathedral, keep your eyes peeled for another pair of saints, Cyril and Methodius, carved in minimalist, postmodern style of two faceless bodies marked with crosses. This statue on a small platform just downhill from the entrance of the cathedral was unveiled in 2013 marking the 1,150th anniversary of the pair's arrival in Moravia. Cyril and Methodius are credited with bringing Christianity to the region in a Slavic language.

Don't be confused if you hear the cathedral's clock chime 12 times on the 11:00 hour. Legend has it that in 1645, during the Thirty Years' War, the Swedish army was frustrated after months of unsuccessful attacks. The general declared that if they didn't take the city by noon, they would turn around and go home. An enterprising local decided to reset the bells to one hour earlier and the Swedish army stuck to their word and retreated.

Špilberk Castle & Museum
(Hrad Špilberk a Muzeum města Brna)

Špilberk 1; tel. +420 515 919 793; www.spilberk.cz; daily 10am-6pm April-Sep, 9am-5pm Oct-Mar; 90 CZK; tram: Komenského náměstí

Just outside the city center on a hill beside Petrov sits the Špilberk Castle & Museum of the City of Brno. Czech King Přemysl Otakar II established the fortified castle in the 13th century to give Moravian rulers a residence that commanded respect. The building changed hands throughout the

views over Brno from Špilberk Castle & Museum

centuries, owned by the city of Brno in the 16th century, confiscated by the Habsburg empire in the 17th century, and converted to a prison in the 17th and 18th centuries to be used later by the Nazis. Today the building is back in the hands of the city and houses the Museum of the City of Brno with the surrounding grounds offering yet another perspective to view the city from above. The permanent exhibits of the former prison grounds and historical photographs charting the city's architectural development make the castle interior a worthy draw alongside the hilltop views.

10-Z Bunker

Husova ulice; tel. +420 542 210 622; https://10-z.cz; Tue-Sun 11:30am-6:45pm; 150-240 CZK; tram: Šilingrovo náměstí

The purpose of this underground shelter has varied from wartime protection to recreation and education over the last century. Neighborhood residents raced inside to hide from WWII bombings in November of 1944. The bunker enjoyed a brief stint as a wholesale wine shop in the mid-1940s before being seized by Communists in 1948. The space was then converted to a 500-person nuclear fallout shelter and cloaked in confidentiality for decades until its declassification in 1993. The title "10-Z" a holdover from its top-secret code name.

Today, neon orange signs welcome visitors inside. Historian and academic Pavel Paleček has worked to create an educational space that defies its oppressive past. The resulting museum and hostel opened in 2016, decorated with multimedia exhibits, artifacts donated by local residents, and Wi-Fi powered by the only functioning wires of an original switchboard. A 40-60-minute guided tour in English (240 CZK per person), limited to nine people, can be booked online in advance. These tours are customized to guests' interests, offering a bit more context and technical insight than wandering the maze of hallways on your own (150 CZK), which is also enjoyable.

NIGHTLIFE

Thanks to a population of university students, residents who stick around after graduation, and international visitors, Brno's landscape of laid-back pubs and craft cocktail bars is rarely short of customers. The streets around Jakubské náměstí in particular are lined in almost every direction (and continuously expanding) with restaurants and bars to choose from.

BAR KTERÝ NEEXISTUJE

Dvořákova 1; tel. +420 734 878 602; www. barkteryneexistuje.cz; Sun-Tue 5pm-2am, Wed-Thu 5pm-3am, Fri-Sat 5pm-4am; cocktails 100-150 CZK; tram: Náměstí Svobody or Malinovského náměstí

Despite its name, Bar který neexistuje or "The Bar That Doesn't Exist" is absolutely real. Passionate mixologists serve craft cocktails on two floors. Choose from a specialty cocktail list, an extensive-is-an-understatement list of spirits, or just describe your mood to the staff for a custom-made order. Reservations recommended to snag a seat in this busy sophisticated space where brightly lit liquor bottles serve as the backdrop.

SUPER PANDA CIRCUS

Šilingrovo náměstí 3; tel. +420 734 878 603; www.superpandacircus.cz; Mon-Sat 6pm-2am; cocktails 125-150 CZK; tram: Šilingrovo náměstí

In the words of Super Panda Circus this is "a completely different world where nothing makes sense." The cocktail experience involves surprise flavors and unusual containers in a speakeasy-style environment where patrons have to ring a doorbell and wait for an available seat. Join an upbeat, international crowd, preferably at the bar where you can watch the staff show off their flair for flipping bottles and passion for the craft.

VÝČEP NA STOJÁKA

Běhounská 16; tel. +420 702 202 048; www.vycepnastojaka.cz; Mon-Fri noon-midnight, Sat-Sun 2pm-midnight; beer 45-65 CZK; tram: Náměstí Svobody or Česká

The local beer-drinking crowd spills out of

Christmas Markets Beyond Prague

Prague's Christmas markets have grown from charming cultural experiences into huge tourist draws in recent decades. Try a holiday trip to another Czech city for a little more regional character and fewer crowds. Festivities usually run daily throughout December, with local choirs and other activities common on weekends.

- Advent markets in **Liberec** (www.trhyvliberci.cz) fill the main Town Hall square with wooden booths of hot wine, snacks, and handmade gifts. Residents pack the square to watch the Christmas tree lighting each year.

- In **Brno** (www.brnenskevanoce.cz), the holiday atmosphere spreads across multiple squares, with a holiday tram covered in lights circling the center. A Ferris wheel and skating rink add some physical fun alongside stalls of street food, spiced wine, craft beer, handmade gifts, and commemorative mugs.

- Christmas in **Karlovy Vary** is a more peaceful experience, with sparkling lights strung over small stalls of sweets, warm drinks, and trinkets in front of Hotel Thermal. A small, kitschy Christmas House and Teddy Bear Museum (Studentská 1; tel. +420 353 220 091; daily 10am-8pm Nov-Dec, 1pm-6pm Jan-Oct; 120 CZK) offers a touch of holiday cheer in Karlovy Vary year-round.

Výčep Na Stojáka and onto the surrounding streets of Jakubské náměstí. The name roughly translates to "A Place for Standing" with the minimally decorated interior of tall tables and no stools in sight. The selection of rotating microbrews brings a steady stream of the local university crowds and young professionals meeting after work.

FESTIVALS AND EVENTS

The **Ignis Brunensis fireworks festival** (www.ignisbrunensis.cz) lights up the sky in late May and June each summer, the **Marathon of Music festival** (www.maratonhudby.cz) brightens August with multigenre concerts and buskers performing across the city, **Christmas markets** twinkle in city squares in December, and a **Queer Ball** (www.queerball.cz) celebrates the LGBTQ+ community in February or March.

FOOD

This cosmopolitan dining destination caters to a variety of tastes, including an exceptional array of vegetarian-friendly options and a specialty coffee scene so good that it inspired the

creation of the **European Coffee Trip** blog (www.europeancoffeetrip.com).

Czech
PIVNICE PUB PEGAS

Jakubská 4; tel. +420 542 210 104 or +420 542 211 232; www.brnopivovar.hotelpegas.com; Mon-Thu and Sat 10am-midnight, Fri 10am-1am, Sun 11am-11pm; entrées 175-350 CZK; tram: Náměstí Svobody or Česká

Pivnice Pub Pegas, located inside the hotel of the same name, is a tourist-friendly environment with the accessibility of English menus and vegetarian options (try the risotto). The staff are friendly and multi-lingual, and the décor of dark wooden tables and arched doorways sets a traditional Czech pub vibe. Try a Pegas beer from the first on-site microbrewery to open in Moravia in 1989.

International
SOUL BISTRO

Jezuitská 7; tel. +420 773 179 212; Mon-Thu 8am-10pm; Fri 8am-11pm, Sat 10am-11pm; entrées 100-200 CZK; bus: Janáčkovo divadlo, tram: Náměstí Svobody

Stop by the casually cool Soul Bistro for a breakfast bagel in the morning or a selection of seasonal lunch specials ranging from fish & chips to stir fried rice. The dining room is divided into intimate spaces with minimalist, Scandinavian-inspired design. Soul Bistro is just off the busy square around St. Jacob's church, pairing nicely with a visit to the Ossuary or a beer at Výčep Na Stojáka.

4POKOJE

Vachova 6; tel. +420 770 122 102; www.miluju4pokoje.cz; Sun-Tue 7am-3am, Wed-Thu 7am-4am, Fri-Sat 7am-5am; entrées 150-250 CZK, tram: Malinovského náměstí

The atmosphere, menu, soundtrack, and prices at 4pokoje change nine times throughout the day. In other words, every visit in the 22 hours the venue is open is a different experience. The name, meaning "four rooms" describes the café, bistro, bar, and nightclub spread across multiple floors, each with distinct, brightly colored and neon-lit personalities. The rotating menu has plenty of international and vegetarian options like pancakes and breakfast sandwiches, hot dogs, and specialty cocktails. You'll get hearty comfort food in winter and refreshing fare on a hot day.

Cafés and Cakes
SKOG

Dominikánské náměstí 5; tel. +420 607 098 557; www.skog.cz; Mon-Thu 8am-1am, Fri 8am-2am, Sat 10am-2am, Sun noon-10pm; tram: Zelný trh

SKOG is the embodiment of modern coffee culture: pallet-based furniture and wooden spool tables, minimalist touches of fresh flowers and exposed lightbulbs, solid Wi-Fi for the freelance crowd, and a purist approach to specialty coffee. The two-story space just around the corner from the Town Hall offers plenty of seating spread across creaky wood floors. Seasonal food options are strictly vegan and vegetarian.

Vegetarian
★ FORKY'S

Jakubské Náměstí 1; tel. +420 515 908 665; www.forkys.eu; Mon-Fri 11am-9pm, Sat noon-9pm,

Sun noon-6pm; entrées 75-150 CZK; tram: Náměstí Svobody or Česká

Forky's is an entirely plant-based, vegan concept. Their 2018 move into a large, multistory space with outdoor tables on Jakubské náměstí emphasizes the growing demand for ethical, health-conscious cuisine (including no plastic packaging) among a younger generation of Czechs and international residents. Try one of the Asian-inspired noodle dishes, veggie burgers for a hearty meal, or build your own Superbowl of fresh vegetables. One coveted table at the upstairs picture window offers prime people-watching for a small donation to a monthly rotating charitable cause.

ACCOMMODATIONS
10-Z BUNKER

Husova ulice; tel. +420 542 210 622; https://10-z.cz

Spending the night inside 10-Z Bunker's former nuclear fallout shelter is an extraordinary historical experience. Rooms range from 30-bed dorms (around 625 CZK) to 4-to-5-person private rooms (1,800-2,200 CZK), 2-person quarters (1,250 CZK), or single officer's quarters (850 CZK) all with shared bathrooms. Park warm PJs for a night in a sleeping bag on military-grade bunks with décor of desks, lockers, and artifacts. A modest but yummy breakfast from the cafeteria is included.

Note: Amazing though this experience may be, it's worth noting that beds are in close quarters in a space that's not necessarily well ventilated and, at the time of writing, the bunker was closed due to the coronavirus pandemic.

★ HOTEL ROYAL RICC

Starobrněnská 10; tel. +420 542 219 262; www.royalricc.cz; 2,000-2,500 CZK d; tram: Zelný trh or Šilingrovo náměstí

The family-run Hotel Royal Ricc combines old-world charm and a convenient location just off Brno's cabbage market square. Exposed beams, rich dark wood furnishing, and muraled staircases add an air of elegance to a comfortable atmosphere with 24-hour reception happy to answer questions. Don't skip the beautifully presented breakfast buffet before heading uphill to the Cathedral of Sts. Peter & Paul or a few streets down to the town hall.

HOTEL PEGAS

Jakubská 4; tel. +420 542 210 104 or +420 542 211 232; https://brnohotel.hotelpegas.com; 2,000 CZK s, 2,500 CZK d; tram: Náměstí Svobody or Česká

Hotel Pegas, located just down the street from the Church of St. James, offers more convenience than ambiance. Twenty-four rooms range from singles to triples decorated in simple wood and white linens. Free Wi-Fi, en suite bathrooms, air-conditioning, and breakfast are included. The lobby holds a quality Czech restaurant and Moravia's oldest microbrewery.

GETTING THERE

A train ride from Prague to Brno offers the most comfortable ride for a reasonable price.

From Prague
TRAIN

The national rail service **České dráhy** (www. cd.cz; 125-350 CZK) takes about 2.5 hours from Prague's main train station (Praha hl. n.) to Brno's main train station (Brno hl. n.) leaving roughly twice an hour from 4:45am until almost midnight.

I prefer local providers **Regiojet** (www. regiojet.com), who run comfortable, direct, 2.5-hour train rides (100-175 CZK) roughly every two hours from around 5:30am until roughly 8:30pm. Splurge on business class (250-450 CZK) for a reserved leather seat in a four-person compartment, free sparkling wine and coffee on departure, food available for purchase, and solid Wi-Fi.

The main Brno train station is located just off the center of town, with a moderate walk to most accommodation options.

BUS

Czech company **Regiojet** (www.regiojet. com) runs three-and-a-half-hour coach service (150-200 CZK) from Prague's Florenc Bus Station to Brno's Grand Hotel, located directly in front of the main train station. Service usually includes an attendant offering complimentary hot drinks and in-ride entertainment with English movies on seat-back TV screens. Wi-Fi is solid near major cities, but less reliable in the countryside.

Leo Express (www.leoexpress.com) and **Flixbus** (www.flixbus.com) also offer regular bus connections (150-375 CZK) from Florenc.

Brno's main bus stops are both located in the city center offering an easy walk to most accommodation options.

CAR

Brno is located about 210 kilometers (130 mi) and between two-three hours (depending on traffic) southeast of Prague on highway D1/E65. As of 2018, visitors to Brno are only allowed to drive or use street parking (20-40 CZK per hour) in limited areas outside the center—see www.parkovanivbrne. cz for details. Many parking garages have limited daytime hours or a 24-hour limit, but **Pinki Park** (www.bkom.cz) offers multi-day parking of 88 spaces for around 300 CZK per day.

From Vienna
TRAIN

Trains from Vienna to Brno (www.cd.cz; 350-650 CZK) run almost hourly around 7am-10pm from Wien Hbf to Brno's main train station, with some routes transferring at Břeclav for the 90-minute journey. **Regiojet** (www.regiojet.com) launched a 90-minute service connecting Vienna (Wien Hbf) to Brno's main train station (175-350 CZK) in 2020, running four times daily between 6:30am-8pm.

BUS

Regiojet (www.regiojet.com) coach service also runs from Wien Hbf to Brno's AN u hotelu Grand stop (1.5-2 hours; 175-350 CZK) about 7-8 times a day from 4:30am-11:45pm. This centrally located bus station is within walking distance to most accommodation options. **Flixbus** (www.flixbus.com) runs one late-night connection departing outside the center from Vienna Erdberg (VIB) at 3:15am to Brno's AN u hotelu Grand at 5am on Saturdays and Sundays (450 CZK).

CAR

Brno is located about 130 kilometers (80 mi) north of Vienna, between two-three hours (depending on traffic) on highway D1/E65 and A5.

From Budapest

TRAIN

Regiojet (www.regiojet.com) launched a new service connecting Budapest and Brno in 2020, running twice daily at 7:45am and 3:45pm arriving roughly seven hours later (400-900 CZK).

From Mikulov

Regional bus service is available for travelers with light hand luggage only. Local bus 105 is run by the **South Moravian Integrated Public Transport System** locally known as Integrovaný Dopravní Systém Jihomoravského Kraje (www.idsjmk.cz; just over an hour's journey; 60 CZK). Buses depart from Mikulov's main train station around once an hour, stopping at Mikulov's u parku bus stop in the south and the Brněnská stop on the northwestern side of town before continuing to Brno. Cash-only payment requires exact change.

GETTING AROUND

Brno's city center is fairly flat and walkable with easy public transport options (www.dpmb.cz; 16 CZK) that include a tram line running through the center of town. Local rideshare app **Liftago** offers local service around Brno, or you can use the **City Taxi** service (tel. +420 777 014 004; www.citytaxi-brno.cz).

LEAVING BRNO

Buses and trains to Prague run consistently from around 2am-midnight via **Regiojet** (2.5-3 hours; buses 200-250 CZK, trains 100-400 CZK), every 1-2 hours from about 7:30am-5:40pm on **LeoExpress** (buses 2.5-3 hours; 100-150 CZK), and three times a day on **Flixbus** (2.5 hours; buses 200-350 CZK). A private Regiojet lounge (daily 6am-6pm) in Brno's main train station offers free Wi-Fi, coffee, soda, and restrooms to all train ticketholders for two hours before their departure. The Czech national rail service runs hourly direct service from around 4:30am-9:30pm (trains 2.5-3 hours; 200-300 CZK).

Travelers with luggage should use the Czech national rail service with indirect service to Mikulov from around 4am-8:30pm (1.5 hours; 100-125 CZK trains), changing in Břeclav. Local regional buses from the South Moravian Integrated Public Transport System run every 1-2 hours from around 5am-10:30pm (1 hour; 60 CZK), for travelers with light hand luggage only.

Lednice and Valtice Chateaux

Think of Mikulov, Lednice, and Valtice as a sort of tri-city area, often referred to as the Lednice-Valtice Area or Complex. The strategic location of this trio on the southern border of the Czech Republic and Austria, roughly halfway between Vienna and Brno, made it an important historic center of trade routes and military observation. Today the area is best known for the majestic chateaux that

once housed the aristocracy of the Austro-Hungarian Empire.

These chateaux served as royal residences and summer homes, particularly for the Liechtenstein family. Although this family name is now associated with a smaller European country far to the west, the family acquired and renovated many of the properties across this Central Europe region. Each of these distinctive chateaux grounds and gardens are open to visitors, with interior access provided by guided tours of individual areas.

In addition to grand chateaux, South Moravia also holds some of the country's best vineyards. The Wine Salon of the Czech Republic (located in the cellar of Valtice Chateau) ranks and pours the 100 best Czech wines every year, while smaller wine bars in Mikulov offer a more intimate environment for a taste.

Note that this region was hit with a rare tornado in June 2021, damaging both the Břeclav train station and Valtice Chateau. All sights and train routes should be operational, but you may experience signs of ongoing repairs.

MIKULOV

Czech poet Jan Skácel famously compared the town of Mikulov to a piece of Italy that God moved to Moravia, making it a beautiful home base for day trips to the surrounding area. The center of this small town is easily walkable with regular public transport connections to the neighboring chateaux.

Sights
MIKULOV CHATEAU
(Zámek Mikulov)
Zámek 1; tel. +420 519 309 014; www.rmm.cz; Tue-Sun 9am-5pm May-Jun and Sep, daily 9am-6pm Jul-Aug, Fri-Sun 9am-4pm Apr and Oct-Nov

When approaching the town from the train station, the red rooftops and single tower of the Mikulov Chateau may not exactly stun observers. However, this gift from Otakar II of the royal Přemysl dynasty to the Liechtenstein family in the 13th century was an influential move. The Liechtensteins completed construction and used Mikulov as a home base to spread their influence across South Moravia, including the area's other more famous (and arguably more impressive) chateaux.

Entering through the main gate from the center of town opens up views of manicured gardens, curved archways, detailed sculptures, and a lookout point from the edge of the gardens over the city that will take your breath away. The interior is semi-accessible with a mix-and-match package of guided tours through various exhibits located inside the chateau. A stroll through the courtyard may be enough for visitors on a tight schedule or saving their chateau enthusiasm for Lednice and Valtice, but the indoor exhibitions, including an 18th-century library (60 CZK), octagonal chapel (30 CZK), and an enormous barrel from 1643 in the wine cellar (60 CZK) may appeal to curious history buffs.

CHURCH TOWER OF ST. WENCESLAS
(Kostel sv. Václava)
Kostelní náměstí 4; www.farnostimikulovska.cz; 50 CZK

At first glance, it would be easy to assume that the tower of this Roman Catholic church was part of the neighboring Mikulov Chateau. Its cream-colored walls extending skyward toward a balcony of curved arches definitely give off a regal vibe, but the religious roots of this location run deep. A 12th-century Romanesque church, destroyed by a fire in the 1500s, previously stood on the grounds that now hold the Church of St. Wenceslas. This led to renovations in the Mannerism era of architecture, an inventive departure from the symmetry of Renaissance buildings. The following Baroque architecture era also added some influence in 1768 with the curved dome on top of the clock tower.

Similar to the St. Nicholas Bell Tower in Prague, this tower historically played a role in town safety. The fourth-floor balcony level once housed an apartment for the tower keeper, and its 360-degree views allowed them to survey the skyline for any signs of fire or impending attacks. Today's tower visitors are more likely to admire Holy Hill or take an overhead look at the Mikulov Chateau grounds after the 135-step climb. The lower landings are also worth a browse: Read the history of the building on the first level, see the bells on the second, and spend some time in a small art gallery that extends across the third and fourth landings.

In this largely wine tourism-fueled town, summer and autumn opening hours are the most consistent. The tower is open daily at 10am from June-October, closing at 6pm in October, 7pm in September, 8pm in August and June, and 9pm in July. You can also visit on April weekends (Fri-Sun) from 10am-6pm and May weekends (Fri-Sun) from 10am-7pm. This sight is not accessible for travelers who use wheelchairs.

JEWISH CEMETERY
(Židovský hřbitov)

Kozí hrádek 11; tel. +420 519 512 368 or +420 731 484 500; www.zidovskyhrbitovmikulov.cz; daily 10am-5pm May-Jun, 10am-6pm July-Sep, Tue-Sun 10am-4pm Apr and Oct; 30 CZK

Mikulov's Jewish Cemetery, the largest in the Czech Republic, stands in sharp contrast to the cramped headstones of Prague's Old Jewish Cemetery. This quiet hillside resting place has easy paths that wind between more than 4,000 graves.

In previous centuries, Mikulov provided sanctuary to Jews who were fleeing from religious persecution in Austria. Rabbi Loew, the infamous creator of the Golem hiding in Prague's Old-New Synagogue, served the area in the mid-16th century, bringing even more importance to the town. The Jewish population grew to nearly half of the town in the 1800s, with Jews and Christians co-existing in peace and tolerance. Tragically, a combination of emigration and the horrors or WWII left no Jewish residents in the area today.

Wine Bars
VINOTÉKA VOLAŘÍK

Kostelní náměstí 9; tel. +420 353 230 797; Mon-Sat noon-midnight, Sun 10am-10pm; glass 45-75 CZK

Vinotéka Volařík's handful of indoor tables and covered, lantern-lit terrace seat wine connoisseurs comfortably, even during the occasional summer storm. This intimate wine shop next door to Hotel Piano also serves as a tasting room with a mid-sized wine list of local varietals available by the glass. The relaxed, award-winning wine bar is a great place to enjoy an evening al fresco. Smoking is permitted on the outdoor terrace.

(NE)VINNÁ KAVÁRNA

Náměstí 18; tel. +420 776 257 829; www.nevinnakavarna.cz; Sun-Thu 9am-6pm, Fri-Sat 9am-11pm; glass 50-100 CZK

Despite its name, (Ne)Vinná Kavárna meaning "(No) Wine Café" actually has plenty of vino to offer alongside specialty coffee and sweet homemade treats. The walls are lined with wooden china cabinets, typewriters, a piano, and other homey touches. Twenty-five wooden terrace seats outdoors make for great people watching while sampling a glass of the local Riesling.

Hiking
GOAT TOWER
(Kozí Hrádek)

Distance (round-trip): *0.8 km (0.5 mi)*
Duration (round-trip): *20 minutes*
Effort: *easy*
Trailhead: *Mikulov Town Center*

The easy incline of a 10-minute walk from the town center or five-minute journey from the Jewish Cemetery to the **"Goat Tower"** (Na Jámě; tel. +420 608 002 976; www.mikulov.cz; free) of Kozí hrádek makes a hilltop vantage point accessible to even the most novice hikers. This 15th-century structure served as strategic defensive surveillance of the surrounding trade routes leading to Vienna, Brno, and Prague. The inconsistent opening hours are signaled manually when the flag is flying, but entrance to the small building is secondary to the panoramic views of the city from its base.

HOLY HILL
(Svatý kopeček)

Distance (round-trip): *2 km (1.25 mi)*
Duration (round-trip): *1 hour*
Effort: *moderate*
Trailhead: *Novokopečná Street*

Mikulov's Holy Hill is sometimes referred

to as Tanzberg or Taneční hora (meaning "Dancing Mountain"), named for the pagan ceremonies held here in pre-Christian times. The hill then became a pilgrimage sight in the 17th century. Today, it's the stunning, unobstructed, views over Mikulov and the surrounding countryside that draw travelers of all faiths and backgrounds. The roughly 30-minute journey from the center of town to the hill's peak includes a moderate path lined with benches and rest areas. As you hike, keep an eye out for small purple irises on the hillside, one of the rare plant species that helped to classify this area as a protected nature reserve.

To begin the hike, follow the blue hiking path at the base of Holy Hill from Novokopečná Street for about 15-20 minutes to pass **14 small chapels** representing the Stations of the Cross. Seven of these (1, 8, 10, 11, 12, 13, 14) originally sat on the top of Holy Hill. The remaining seven were added between 1750-1776, when the religious community later came to a consensus that 14 was the appropriate number. If you peek through the metal bars lining their gates, you can get a shadowy glimpse of the religious statues inside these small Baroque structures.

Two dominant buildings stand on top of Holy Hill: the Greek-style domed roof of **St. Sebastian's Chapel,** and the freestanding 17th-century **Bell Tower** beside it. Cardinal Franz von Dietrichstein built the chapel to promote the spread of Catholicism and express his appreciation for making it through the plague of 1622. Sebastian, the patron saint often associated with survival, is usually depicted as defiantly living through a barrage of arrow-inflicted wounds. Visitors can enter St. Sebastian's Chapel and the Bell Tower on summer weekends from July to mid-September, 10am-4pm on Saturdays and 10am-2pm on Sundays. The grassy area in front of the chapel is a popular viewpoint for photographers and couples, especially around sunset, with unobstructed views over the entire town of Mikulov.

Many visitors miss the quieter plateau behind the religious monuments, where swirling rocks line the grounds and the skylines offer a more natural landscape of vineyards and countryside.

Food

Mikulov's city center is quite compact, with dining options lining Náměstí (which in Miklov is more of a street than a "square") along the center of town, plus a few outlying favorites worth a five-minute walk.

AMICI MIEI

Alfonse Muchy 10; tel. +420 608 822 348; www.amicimiei.eu; Sun-Thu 9am-11pm, Fri-Sat 9am-midnight; entrées 150-200 CZK, cash only

Italian flags and red and green décor set the bright, kitschy scene at Amici Miei, which is Italian for "my friends." This small restaurant and wine bar just downhill from the main restaurant row of Náměstí street draws Czechs as well as international travelers. Choose from a small selection of pasta dishes and bruschetta with seasonal toppings. In the summer, grab an outdoor table in front of the restaurant or across the street on the covered patio. This is a great place to pair your meal with a local glass of sweet white Pálava wine indigenous to this region. Cash only payments. Some staff speak English.

★ RESTAURACE TEMPL

Husova 50; tel. +420 721 095 111; www.templ.cz; Mon-Thu 11am-11pm, Fri-Sat 11am-midnight, Sun 11am-11:30pm; entrées 150-300 CZK

Restaurace Templ inside the hotel of the same name, blends regional Czech flavors with modern style in a variety of indoor and outdoor spaces—a 20-seat, Renaissance-style restaurant, a bright 22-person bistro, and a relaxing outdoor patio in the summer. The seasonal menu skews toward meats like grilled pork loin, bacon-wrapped rabbit, and beef tartare, often with more adventurous vegetarian options (cauliflower burgers or

---

1: Lednice Chateau **2:** the aristocratic beauty of Valtice Chateau **3:** Mikulov's Holy Hill **4:** historical town of Mikulov in Moravia

mushroom ragout) than you'll find elsewhere. Reservations recommended.

BISTRO KUK
Kostelní náměstí 4; tel. +420 728 332 485; Sun-Thu 8am-10pm

The bright, geometric design and upbeat soundtrack at Bistro KUK sets a modern vibe for the young crowd of coffee lovers and fans of fresh-baked goods. This is one of the few places in town that you'll find any non-dairy milk options. Menus are available in Czech and English.

Accommodations
★ HOTEL PIANO
Česká 2; tel. +420 519 512 076; www.mhmikulov.cz; 1,300 CZK d

Whoever trains the staff at Hotel Piano should teach a worldwide master class on cultivating friendly service. This smack-in-the-center boutique hotel of 13 double rooms plus family suites (1,800 CZK) makes full use of the available space. Super comfy beds, free Wi-Fi and hints of subtle elegance, like mini-chandeliers or framed fine art prints, enhance the modest appeal along with bonus views of the small chapels sitting on top of the grass-covered Holy Hill to the east or the Mikulov Chateau to the southwest. The impressive breakfast buffet includes eggs, sausage, and bacon alongside cereal, fresh bread, fruit, tea, and coffee to be enjoyed in the jazz-themed dining room or quiet terrace. Stays beyond two nights are treated to a complimentary bottle from neighboring wine bar Vinotéka Volařík.

HOTEL GALANT MIKULOV
Mlýnská 2; tel. +420 519 510 692; www.mikulov.galant.cz; 2,500-3,000 CZK d

Families and groups fill these 125 en suite rooms, with free Wi-Fi, a buffet breakfast, on-site winery and microbrewery, 24-hour reception, and one multi-floor family suite (3,500 CZK). A glass-enclosed lap pool and rooftop jacuzzis require a surcharge, but the views are worth the splurge. Take a post-breakfast soak at 150 CZK for two hours between 9am-3pm or 300 CZK between 4pm-10pm for adults only. Additional spa services are available by appointment. This eco-friendly hotel is also committed to energy-efficient design and sustainable practices.

Getting There
FROM PRAGUE
The easiest way to get from Prague to Mikulov is by train. The national rail service **České dráhy** (www.cd.cz; 450-500 CZK) runs hourly, transferring at Břeclav for the four-hour journey. Trains depart from just before 6am until around 6pm, with a few late-night options requiring multiple transfers. **Regiojet** (www.regiojet.com; 150-550 CZK) also runs between Prague and Břeclav every two hours from about 5:30am-5:30pm, but this requires a transfer to České dráhy to reach Mikulov. The main train station of Mikulov na Moravě is a 15-20-minute walk from the center of town, with local taxi service available.

There is no direct bus connection from Prague to Mikulov.

If you're driving, Mikulov is roughly three-four hours (about 240 km/150 mi) southeast of Prague on highway D1/E65.

FROM BRNO
Regional bus 105 run by the **South Moravian Integrated Public Transport System** locally known as Integrovaný Dopravní Systém Jihomoravského Kraje (www.idsjmk.cz; just over an hour's journey; 60 CZK) departs from Brno's ÚAN Zvonařka stop just south of the main train station around once an hour. Local service in Mikulov stops at the Brněnská bus stop on the northwestern side of town before continuing to the u parku bus stop to the south. This option is only appropriate for travelers with light hand luggage.

Travelers with luggage should use the Czech national rail service with indirect service to Mikulov from around 4am-8:30pm (1.5 hours; 100-125 CZK trains), changing in Břeclav.

If you're driving, Mikulov is located about 55 kilometers (35 mi) south of Brno, which takes about an hour on Routs 52/E65.

FROM VIENNA

Trains from Vienna to Mikulov (www.cd.cz; 350-550 CZK) run almost hourly from around 8am-7pm from Wien Hbf, transferring at Břeclav for the 2-to-3-hour journey (depending on connections). **Regiojet** (www.regiojet.com) train service also runs from Wien Hbf to Břeclav (150-375 CZK) about four times a day from 6:30am-6:30pm but requires a transfer to České dráhy to reach Mikulov.

If you're driving, Mikulov is located about 85 kilometers (50 mi) north of Vienna, which takes about 60-90 minutes on highway A5.

Getting Around

The compact center of Mikulov is entirely walkable, with multiple bus stops connecting Mikulov to the surrounding chateaux in Lednice and Valtice. For taxi service, try **Nejlevnější Taxi Mikulov** (tel. +420 607 856 205; www.nejlevnejsi-taxi-mikulov.cz) or **Taxi Mikulov** (tel. +420 606 707 770; www.taxi-mikulov.cz).

★ VALTICE CHATEAU

Zámek 1, Valtice; tel. +420 778 743 754;
www.zamek-valtice.cz; bus stop Valtice, Aut.St
The Liechtenstein family helped to establish the splendid, 100-room Valtice Chateau in the 14th century. In 1945, it was confiscated to be used for various labor camps under Communist rule. Ongoing renovations since the 1970s have maintained the beauty of the building, which is only available through a one-hour basic guided tour (320 CZK) running every 1-2 hours either in English or with printed English text provided. Small groups don slippers over their shoes to protect the floors and swish through around 25 staged rooms and halls of royal portraits, muraled ceilings, and canopy beds. The chateau opens at 9am from late March through the end of October, closing at 3pm in October, 4pm in March and April, and 5pm from May to

September. Monday entry is only available during the months of July and August. The chateau interior is barrier-free, but wheelchair users will need assistance to navigate one flight of stairs to reach the tour starting point.

Beyond the basic chateau, theater fans will enjoy a behind-the-scenes tour of the newly reconstructed **Baroque Theater** (90 CZK), modeled after the historically preserved Baroque Theater in Český Krumlov. The 45-minute theater tour runs every 1-2 hours based on demand, either in English or with English text provided. Note that the theater tour is not wheelchair accessible. Be sure to save time to visit the National Wine Cellar in the basement of the chateau, pouring tastes of the country's 100 most prized wines.

Wine Cellar
NATIONAL WINE CELLAR
Zamek 1, Valtice; tel. +420 519 352 744;
www.vinarskecentrum.cz; Tue-Thu 9:30am-5pm,
Fri-Sat 10:30am-6pm Feb-Dec, Sun 10:30am-5pm
Jun-Sep only; tastings 100-500 CZK
Every August, a professional panel selects the hundred best wines in the country. The winners are available to taste in this cellar located in the basement of Valtice Chateau, arranged by varietal along the long brick halls. Tasting packages are based on time: Taste as many wines as you like in 90 minutes (399 CZK) or 150 minutes (499 CZK) or choose 16 pre-paid pours on a shorter time limit (a hearty lunch before visiting is a good idea to avoid getting overly tipsy). Descriptive charts in multiple languages offer detailed information including the varietal, winemaker, regions, and the number of bottles produced. Grab a bottle for purchase from below these posters. Call in advance to arrange wheelchair access.

Food
AVALON KELTIC RESTAURANT
Příční 46; tel. +420 721 095 111; www.avalonvaltice.com; Tue-Sun 11am-11pm; 125-250 CZK
Plan time for a quick lunch at Avalon Keltic Restaurant as part of your day trip to the Valtice Chateau. The light-hearted, medieval

hunting lodge decor indoors is accented by patches of exposed brick and swords fastened to the walls. The outdoor summer garden is cloaked in ivy around a serene waterfall and a fish pond dotted with water lilies, with Celtic music keeping the mood light and fun. This is a popular stop for cyclists crisscrossing the Moravian wine trails. The menu items resemble Czech specialties but with a lighter twist— grilled chicken and cranberry sauce or duck confit with beet root and potato dumplings, and vegetarian options available. Try a cold Svijany (my personal favorite Czech beer) with your meal before walking around the corner to the Valtice Chateau gates.

Getting There

Bus route 585 (20 CZK) on the **South Moravian Integrated Public Transport System** locally known as Integrovaný Dopravní Systém Jihomoravského Kraje (www.idsjmk.cz) departs at least once every hour between 5:30am-3pm from Mikulov to Valtice. The ride takes about 20 minutes with multiple stops in Mikulov, terminating at bus stop Valtice, Aut.St. just a few streets away from the chateau entrance. Return service on Route 585 to Mikulov from the Valtice, Aut. St stop runs about once an hour until around 7pm. Bus route x58 runs more often, but with fewer stops in Mikulov, so it may require a longer walk.

LEDNICE CHATEAU

Zámek 1, Lednice; tel. +420 519 340 128;
www.zamek-lednice.com; bus: Lednice náměstí

Lednice Chateau provides the most striking exterior silhouette of the three stately homes in this region. The Lichtenstein family, who dominated the area from the 13th century onward, renovated the existing structure into a bright, neo-Gothic summer palace in the mid-1800s, smaller in size than Valtice but with much more expansive gardens and equally ornate interiors. A stroll through the swirling floral patterns takes visitors to the 62-meter (200-ft) Minaret (80 CZK), also called the Turkish Tower, which gives you an aerial view of the entire grounds.

Different guided tours are the only opportunity for visitors to explore the chateau's interior and surrounding buildings. Highlights include the one-hour Representative Rooms tour (330 CZK), which explores the ground floor's distinctively color-coded décor, including the Blue Room, Turquoise Hall, and Red Smoking Hall. Gardening fans will want unlimited, non-guided access to the greenhouse (80 CZK), to see the plantlife housed in steel, iron, and glass design that was ahead of its time in 1842. Additional tour options focus on Princely apartments (300 CZK) and marionettes (300 CZK). The Lednice Chateau opens at 9am from late March until the end of October, closing at 4pm from October-April, and 5pm from May-September. Monday entry is only available during the months of July and August.

Getting There

Bus number 570 (25 CZK) on the **South Moravian Integrated Public Transport System** locally known as Integrovaný Dopravní Systém Jihomoravského Kraje (www.idsjmk.cz) takes just under an hour to get to from multiple stops around Mikulov (see www.idsjmk.idos.cz for route details) to the Lednice náměstí bus stop just outside the chateau. Route 570 runs every 1-2 hours from around 6:30am-7:30pm.

Vienna

Once the imperial capital of the Austro-

Hungarian Empire, Vienna doesn't skimp on opulence. Beneath gilded and damask-upholstered interiors, Vienna is a city that has music in its soul and psychoanalysis in its blood. Beyond the Habsburg grandeur, the waltzes composed by the Strauss family, the nostalgic coffeehouses, and gold-clad Klimt paintings adorning Vienna's galleries and museums, it's a city that bursts with history and stories. Vienna invites you to look closer at the details, to glance up at the intricate façades of Otto Wagner's buildings, and admire the colorful geometric fantasies by architect Friedensreich Hundertwasser. You can wander over the cobbles that once led to a 14th-century synagogue, ride a 100-year-old Ferris wheel that still turns above the city, or take a tram up into the

Highlights

Look for ★ to find recommended sights, activities, dining, and lodging.

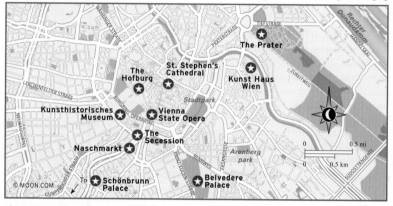

★ **St. Stephen's Cathedral:** Vienna's Gothic masterpiece towers over the historic center. Climb up to the top for the great views, or head below ground to its macabre skull-clad catacombs (page 204).

★ **The Hofburg:** The resplendent base for the Habsburg rulers is worth exploring for its exquisite architecture alone. It also houses a diverse set of museums (page 209).

★ **Vienna State Opera:** One of the most esteemed opera houses in the world is also a recognizable landmark, thanks to its neo-Renaissance architecture (page 214).

★ **Kunsthistorisches Museum:** One of the world's most important art museums houses a vast selection of Bruegel pieces and works by Raphael, Velazquez, Rubens, Rembrandt, and more (page 217).

★ **Naschmarkt:** This cluster of stalls and gourmet bistros peppers a long stretch along the Weinzeile. Come on Saturday when the flea market is also trading (page 221).

★ **The Secession:** The world's oldest exhibition space dedicated to contemporary art was once the stomping ground of Vienna's avant-garde artists. Klimt's *Beethoven Frieze* is its most popular piece (page 221).

★ **Belvedere Palace:** The former Habsburg residence. Enclosed within its frescoed halls is one of Vienna's best art museums, which features Klimt's *The Kiss* as well as an excellent collection of work by Schiele and Kokoschka (page 227).

★ **Kunst Haus Wien:** This Hundertwasser-designed building with undulating floors and colorful ceramic columns contains the largest permanent collection of Hundertwasser's paintings (page 231).

★ **The Prater:** Vienna's biggest park encompasses woodlands, meadows, and boulevards, hemmed in by chestnut trees. You'll also find the giant Ferris wheel that was immortalized in Orson Welles's *The Third Man* (page 231).

★ **Schönbrunn Palace:** The former summer residence of the Habsburg dynasty is now a museum where the opulent grandeur from the former Austrian Empire is on full display (page 239).

hills for an afternoon of wine and song in one of the many taverns near the city's vineyards.

If you're a music lover, you won't tire of things to do in Vienna. Take a tour of the Staatsoper (the Vienna Opera House) or see a concert at the Musikverein (Vienna's best-known concert hall). You can even make a pilgrimage to the Vienna Central Cemetery to see where some of the city's most famous musical residents are buried.

Setting aside some time to sit in Vienna's smoky cafés and sip a Melange (a local foamy coffee) or tuck into a succulent pastry is a must. You may find yourself lost in people-watching as locals come to read the paper and meet up with old friends. Then, you may feel the urge to relax in the city's lush green parks under the shadow of Baroque palaces. The more you uncover Vienna, it seems, the deeper the rabbit hole goes.

HISTORY

The area surrounding the Danube just outside today's Austrian capital once housed a thriving prehistoric civilization before the city became a Celtic trading post. In the first century A.D., the **Romans** arrived and named their camp Vindobona. The town flourished, and around this time, the Romans introduced vineyards to the surrounding hills; Emperor Marcus Aurelius died in Vindobona in 180 A.D.

In the ninth century, Wenia surfaced as a city from the ruins of Vindobona, and from that time Vienna as a city changed hands frequently. First, the Babenbergs ruled before the territory passed into Habsburg control. Times were turbulent in Vienna until the 18th century: The city was besieged by the Turks in the 16th century (and again in the 17th century), and it dealt with the backlash from the Reformation and Counter-Reformation—and then the devastation of the Plague at the end of the 17th century.

The 18th century became Vienna's golden age, when civil reform, architecture, and classical music rose to its zenith in the era of Maria Theresa and her son Joseph II. Classical music exploded from the capital of the Habsburg Empire, leaving Vienna with a musical legacy that pervades to this day.

Vienna saw another wave of art and culture after Napoleon occupied the city twice. The fin de siècle became another golden era for Vienna, with the rise of Austria's own brand of art nouveau and the foundation of **the Secession,** which included noted figures such as Klimt, Moser, and Schiele. This period also brought Otto Wagner's Stadtbahn (today's U-Bahn, the subway, lines 4 and 6) and buildings, along with the newly constructed **Ringstraße** (also known as the Ring) defining the cityscape. Emperor Franz Joseph I ruled the Austro-Hungarian Empire and encouraged the city's development. This era also ushered in the birth of psychoanalysis from Sigmund Freud's apartment in Alsergrund.

The 20th century also saw considerable shifts in Vienna. First, the assassination of Archduke Franz Ferdinand ushered in World War I—and signaled the end of Habsburg rule and the breakup of the Austro-Hungarian Empire. In 1938, the Anschluss (the occupation and annexation of Austria by Nazi Germany) took place, locking Vienna into Axis hands until the end of World War II.

A few days following the war, the Allied Forces occupied Austria, and Britain, France, Russia, and the U.S. partitioned Vienna into quadrants (except for the 1st district, which was equally controlled by all four countries) until 1955. Austria then grew as an independent republic that lay on the western border of the Iron Curtain. More recently, Vienna has gained attention as one of the world's most livable cities, and it is a fascinating European capital patched together by its history and culture.

Previous: Natural History Museum; view from the rooftop of St. Stephen's Cathedral; the Hofburg.

Vienna

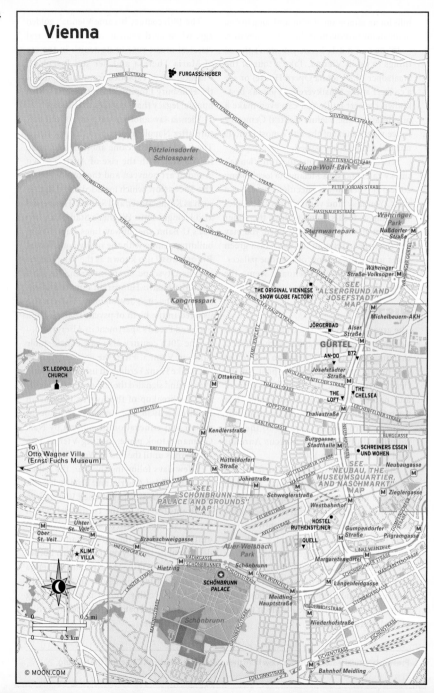

FURGASSL-HUBER

HAMEAUSTRASSE

KROTTENBACHSTRASSE

SIEVERINGER STRASSE

Pötzleinsdorfer Schlosspark

KROTTENBACHSTRASSE

POTZLEINSDORFER STRASSE

Hugo-Wolf-Park

MELNALDEGGER STRASSE

PETER-JORDAN-STRASSE

CZARTORYSKIGASSE

HASENAUERSTRASSE

Währinger Park

Sternwartepark

Nußdorfer Straße Ⓜ

DORNBACHER STRASSE

Kongresspark

KREUZGASSE

Währinger Straße-Volksoper Ⓜ

WÄHRINGER GÜRTEL

SEE "ALSERGRUND AND JOSEFSTADT" MAP

THE ORIGINAL VIENNESE SNOW GLOBE FACTORY

HERNALSER HAUPTSTRASSE

FAMILIENPLATZ

Michelbeuern-AKH

JÖRGERBAD

Alser Straße Ⓜ

GÜRTEL

AN-DO

B72

Josefstädter Straße Ⓜ

NEULERCHENFELDER STRASSE

ST. LEOPOLD CHURCH

Ottakring Ⓜ

THALIASTRASSE

THE LOFT

THE CHELSEA

FLOTZERSTEIG

KOPPSTRASSE

LERCHENFELDER STRASSE

Thaliastraße Ⓜ

GABLENZGASSE

To Otto Wagner Villa (Ernst Fuchs Museum)

Kendlerstraße Ⓜ

BREITENSEER STRASSE

Burggasse-Stadthalle Ⓜ

BURGGASSE

NEUBAUGURTEL

SCHREINERS ESSEN UND WOHEN

Hütteldorfer Straße Ⓜ

HÜTTELDORFER STRASSE

MARZSTRASSE

SEE "NEUBAU, THE MUSEUMSQUARTIER, AND NASCHMARKT" MAP

Neubaugasse

Johnstraße Ⓜ

Zieglergasse Ⓜ

SEE "SCHÖNBRUNN PALACE AND GROUNDS" MAP

Schweglerstraße Ⓜ

FELBERSTRASSE

Westbahnhof Ⓜ

Unter St. Veit Ⓜ

AVEDIKSTRASSE

HOSTEL RUTHENSTEINER

Gumpendorfer Straße Ⓜ

Pilgramgasse Ⓜ

Ober St. Veit Ⓜ

Braunschweiggasse

Auer-Welsbach Park

QUELL

LINKE WIENZEILE

Margaretengürtel Ⓜ

MARGARETENSTRASSE

KLIMT VILLA

HIETZINGER KAI

HADIKGASSE

SCHÖNBRUNNER STRASSE

Schönbrunn

SCHÖNBRUNNER STRASSE

LINKE WIENZEILE

SCHÖNBRUNNER STRASSE

Hietzing

Längenfeldgasse Ⓜ

STEINBAUERGASSE

LAINZER STRASSE

MAXINGSTRASSE

☉ SCHÖNBRUNN PALACE

Meidling Hauptstraße Ⓜ

GRÜNBERGSTRASSE

NIEDERHOFSTRASSE

Niederhofstraße Ⓜ

Schönbrunn

EICHENSTRASSE

Bahnhof Meidling Ⓜ

EDELSINNSTRASSE

0   0.5 mi

0   0.5 km

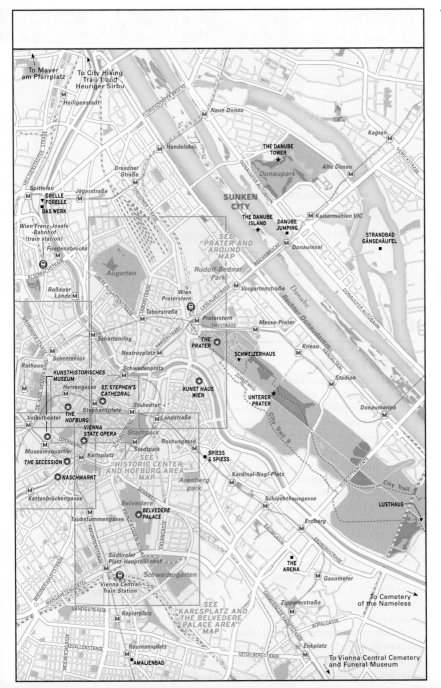

To Mayer am Pfarrplatz

To City Hiking Trail 1 and Heuriger Sirbu

Heiligenstadt

FLORIDSDORFER BRÜCKE

Neue Donau

Kagran

HEILIGENSTÄDTER STRASSE

SIEBECKSTRASSE

Handelskai

THE DANUBE TOWER

Alte Donau

Dresdner Straße

DONAUUFER AUTOBAHN

Donaupark

Jägerstraße

Spittelau

GRELLE FORELLE

DAS WERK

SUNKEN CITY

Kaisermühlen VIC

Wien Franz-Josefs- -Bahnhof (train station)

THE DANUBE ISLAND

DANUBE JUMPING

STRANDBAD GÄNSEHÄUFEL

Friedensbrücke

REICHSBRÜCKE

Donauinsel

SEE "PRATER AND AROUND" MAP

ALSERBACHSTRASSE

Roßauer Lände

Augarten

Rudolf-Bednar- Park

OBERE AUGARTENSTRASSE

Danube

DONAUUFER AUTOBAHN

WÄHRINGER STRASSE

Schottenring

TABORSTRASSE

Wien Praterstern

Vorgartenstraße

Rechter Donauzeile HANDELSKAI

Schottentor

LASSALLESTRASSE

Praterstern

Messe-Prater

Nestroyplatz

PRATERSTRASSE

TIEFSTRASSE

Krieau

Rathaus

Taborstraße

THE PRATER

Stadion

DIE KÄRNTNER STRASSE

KUNSTHISTORISCHES MUSEUM

Schwedenplatz

SCHWEIZERHAUS

Herrengasse

ST. STEPHEN'S CATHEDRAL

KUNST HAUS WIEN

ZUREITWEG

UNTERER PRATER

Donaumarina

Stephansplatz

Stubentor

Volkstheater

THE HOFBURG

Landstraße

City Trail 8

VIENNA STATE OPERA

Stadtpark

OPERNRING

Rochusgasse

Museumsquartier

Karlsplatz

Stadtpark

SPIESS & SPIESS

SÜDOSTTANGENTE

City Trail

THE SECESSION

SEE "HISTORIC CENTER AND HOFBURG AREA" MAP

Kardinal-Nagl-Platz

NASCHMARKT

Arenberg park

Kettenbrückengasse

RENNWEG

Schlachthausgasse

LUSTHAUS

Belvedere

PRINZ-EUGEN-STRASSE

BELVEDERE PALACE

Taubstummengasse

FAVORITENSTRASSE

FASANGASSE

Erdberg

BAUMGASSE

ERDBERGSTRASSE

Südtiroler Platz-Hauptbahnhof

THE ARENA

Gasometer

WIEDNER HAUPTSTRASSE

Schweizgarten

Vienna Central Train Station

To Cemetery of the Nameless

MARGARETENGÜRTEL

SEE "KARLSPLATZ AND THE BELVEDERE PALACE AREA" MAP

Zippererstraße

SIMMERINGER HAUPTSTRASSE

KOPALGASSE

LANDGUTGASSE

Landgutgasse

Keplerplatz

To Vienna Central Cemetery and Funeral Museum

NEILREICHGASSE

QUELLENSTRASSE

Reumannplatz

GEISELBERGSTRASSE

Enkplatz

AMALIENBAD

Budgeting

- **Beer:** €3.50-5
- **Glass of wine:** €3.50-10
- **Cocktail:** €11-18
- **Soft drink:** €3.50-5
- **Melange or cappuccino:** €3.50-5
- **Lunch or dinner:** €8-30 per person
- **Hostel dorm bed:** €17-40 per night
- **Hotel room:** €50-300 per night
- **Car rental:** €60-250 per day
- **Gasoline:** €1.10-1.50 per liter, €4.15-5.70 per gallon
- **Parking:** €4-5 per hour, €4-48 per day
- **Public transport pass:** €16 per day

Orientation and Planning

ORIENTATION

Vienna's "downtown" area is very compact, but many historical sites are spread out, so you will likely need to use public transport. Vienna has a great public transport network run by **Wiener Linien** (www.wienerlinien.at) that includes five U-Bahn (subway) lines, which sometimes runs above ground on bridges, (often referred to just by the letter "U" and followed by the number of the line); the straßenbahn (trams); and buses. A little fun fact, despite there being a U6 U-bahn line, there is no U5. This line was planned for a long time, but by the time it's successor the U6 was built, the construction of the U5 was scrapped for financial reasons.

Today's U-Bahn line U4 was designed at the turn of the 20th century as one of the city's Stadtbahns and has some beautiful art nouveau details.

Budapest and Prague are centered around their rivers, but in Vienna, the Danube flows through the suburbs toward the east of the city; you can easily spend a few days seeing the main sites without ever spotting it. (In fact, the Danube splits in Vienna, partly making its way toward the center in a small canal, which divides the 1st District from the 2nd.) Downtown Vienna is mostly situated within the **Ringstraße,** a circular road that traces the city walls that formerly enclosed the Old Town—today's 1st District. There are 23 districts, and they can be referred to by the district name (for example, the 2nd District is Leopoldstadt). You can tell which district you're in from the street signs, which usually have a number before the street name (for example, 2. Praterstraße is in District 2).

Street names usually end with -straße or -gasse (usually a narrower street). You'll also see platz (or square), and -ring, which is part of the Ringstraße.

Historic Center and Hofburg Area
(1st District)

The **oldest part of Vienna** lies inside the

1st District, clustered around the Gothic **St. Stephen's Cathedral** and **the Hofburg,** the former residence of the Habsburg emperors. Despite its compact size, you could spend days in the Historic Center and only uncover a fraction of the stories of the Baroque houses, 15th-century frescoes, medieval courtyards, and streets that were once part of the Jewish Quarter. The U-Bahn to Stephansplatz will take you right to the heart of this district, but the best way to get around is to walk. The area is bordered by the Danube Canal, the Ringstraße, and the Hofburg. **The Graben,** one of Vienna's most famous pedestrianized streets, is lined with shops, cafés, and restaurants that run from the Kohlmarkt to Stephansplatz, cutting through the center of the district.

Neubau and the MuseumsQuartier
(7th District)

Art lovers will adore the MuseumsQuartier, an area set in the former Imperial Stables that's densely packed with Vienna's **top museums, restaurants, theaters,** and **cafés.** Just on the other side of Museumsplatz (which, despite the name, is a busy road), you'll find the **Kunsthistorisches (Art History) Museum** and the **Naturhistorisches (Natural History) Museum.**

Southwest of the MuseumsQuartier, the vibrant Neubau district is populated with quirky **design shops, trendy restaurants,** and **cobbled alleyways.** In the evenings, young people spill out of tiny exhibitions or sit in small bars and café terraces with a spritzer (wine with carbonated water). **Mariahilferstraße** is the main shopping artery, along with lively **Neubaugasse** (with smaller shops) that runs adjacent to it.

Around Naschmarkt
(6th District)

Just southwest of the golden-domed **Secession,** the Naschmarkt begins, a **large open-air market** that runs for about half a kilometer (approx. 1,800 ft), ending at

Kettenbrückengasse, where the famous flea market sets up shop on Saturdays. The neighborhood north of the market is marked by **winding hilly streets** interconnected with beautiful staircases, while the area south is home to **quirky cafés** and **student hangouts.**

Karlsplatz and the Belvedere Palace Area
(1st, 3rd, and 4th Districts)

Three different districts convene around **Karlsplatz,** a transport hub in the inner city where three metro lines meet. This large square is covered with pockets of parkland. To the southeast is the grand **Belvedere Palace,** whose surrounding area is characterized by **eclectic architecture.** Near the palace, you'll find lively street art and intimate cafés.

Prater and Around
(2nd and 22nd Districts)

Across the Danube Canal from the Historic Center, the 2nd District (also known as **Leopoldstadt**) lies on an island in the Danube. Most come to this part of Vienna for the **Prater,** a large green area famous for its historic amusement park, the **Würstelprater.** The 2nd district is also home to the **Augarten,** a 52-hectare (129-ac) public park with a variety of French Baroque-inspired public buildings. Meanwhile, on the southern banks of the Danube Canal, a vibrant residential area with surreal, colorful architecture by Friedensreich Hundertwasser (like the **Hundertwasserhaus** and **Kunst Haus Wien**) is worth exploring.

Alsergrund and Josefstadt
(9th and 8th Districts)

Alsergrund and Josefstadt lie just northwest of the Ringstraße. Josefstadt is a small district, where **independent shops and cafés** dot the upward-angled streets. Neighboring Alsergrund, just north of Josefstadt, was once the former stomping ground of Sigmund Freud (whose apartment you can still visit today).

If you visit this district, you'll discover a **student area** with three universities, and you'll also find many large old hospitals—including the grounds of the former **Vienna General Hospital** (now a university) where Freud began his medical career. It's a youthful area, with plenty of cheap eateries and **student bars.**

Running parallel to the Ringstraße is the **Gürtel,** an important main road that divides the inner and outer districts. The outer borders of Josefstadt and Alsergrund feature viaducts built for the Stadtbahn (now used for the U6 line). You'll also find some of the city's **hottest nightlife** under the railway arches.

Schönbrunn Palace and Grounds
(13th and 14th Districts)
The imperial summer palace of Schönbrunn is dominated by **parkland.** You could spend a day lounging in the beautiful landscaped park, visiting the oldest **zoo** in Europe, or strolling through the **Palm House** for a botanical fix. Outside the park, the area is filled with **luxurious villas,** including the villa built around Klimt's old garden house and studio. Head farther up into the hills to see **Kirche am Steinhof (St. Leopold Church),** a stunning art nouveau church by Wagner, and beautiful high-level views of Vienna.

PLANNING YOUR TIME
You can see the highlights of Vienna in **three days,** but you'll really need to prioritize based on your interests (don't be surprised to leave with a yearning to come back for more). If your schedule is tight, hone in on the Habsburgs, go on a pilgrimage to the great artistic haunts of the 1900s Vienna of Klimt and Otto Wagner, or follow in the footsteps of Hollywood stars.

Daily Reminders
Some of Vienna's most popular museums and attractions are not open daily.

- The **Secession** is closed on Monday.
- The **Kunsthistorisches** is closed Monday between September and May.
- The **Leopold Museum** is closed on Tuesdays.
- The **Naschmarkt** does not open on Sundays.
- Some museums (such as the Kunsthistorisches, Belvedere, or the Museum of Applied Arts) stay open as late as 9pm or 10pm on certain days.

Vienna's trams rattling through Neubau

Some of the more niche attractions only open a few days out of the week, such as the **Narrenturm** (Wed, Sat), **St. Leopold Church** (Sat and Sun only, but worth seeing for the exterior), and the **Klimt Villa** (Thu-Sun).

MONDAY

Many museums, including the following, are closed:

- Kunsthistorisches Museum (but open Monday Jun-Aug)
- The Secession
- The Literature Museum
- The Viennese Clock Museum
- Chapel of St. Virgil
- Austrian National Library
- Museum of Illusions
- Leopold Museum
- mumok
- Kunsthalle
- ZOOM Children's Museum
- Imperial Furniture Collection
- Museum of Applied Arts
- Johann Strauss Residence
- Criminal Museum
- Beethoven Pasqualatihaus
- Otto Wagner Villa (Ernst Fuchs Museum)

TUESDAY

The following are closed:

- Leopold Museum
- Imperial Treasury
- Natural History Museum
- mumok

SATURDAY

The following are closed:

- The Jewish Museum Vienna Judenplatz
- The Jewish Museum Vienna Dorotheergasse

The following attractions are open only on Saturday:

- Third Man Museum
- Flohmarkt flea market

SUNDAY

Many shops close on Sundays, as do the following sights:

- Naschmarkt
- Funeral Museum
- Augarten Porcelain Manufactory and Museum

CLOSED ON HOLIDAYS

- Hofburg Chapel at the Imperial Palace

Also note that most museums and sights are closed December 25 and January 1, and some even close May 1. In some cases, museums will be open on public holidays, even if they would be normally closed, so check before going if you are not sure.

Advanced Bookings and Time-Saving Tips

It's a good idea to book tickets in advance for tours of the **Spanish Riding School** or the **Third Man Tour of the Vienna Sewers** as they often sell out. Many museums will have queues during the high season, but they move pretty quickly. If you have large bags (approximately 30 cm/12 in or larger) most museums require you to use a storage locker during your visit. Keep a euro or 50 cent coin on you as you may need a deposit.

Sightseeing Passes

There are two cards to choose from. First, the **Vienna City Card** (www.viennacitycard.at) from the Vienna Tourism Board. The Vienna City Card gives you free transport and discounts for over 200 sights, shops, bars, and restaurants.

Current pricing is:

- 24 hours: €17

- 48 hours: €25
- 72 hours: €29

The **Vienna Pass** (www.viennapass.com) costs more but includes free entrance to 60-plus sites as well as use of the Hop-On Hop-Off Bus (www.viennasightseeing.at/hop-on-hop-off) and city boat cruises (www.viennasightseeing.at/hop-on-hop-off/boat-ride). The Vienna Pass also grants you fast-track access to some of the most popular sites, like the Belvedere and Schönbrunn Palace, so you can skip the lines. Pricing is as follows:

- 1 day: €79
- 2 day: €99
- 3 day: €129

If you're literarily inclined, you can purchase a **Universal Week Ticket** (€19) that gets you into the National Library, the Literature Museum, and also the Esperanto, Globe and Papyrus Museums and the House of Austrian History museum over the course of a week. You can buy a ticket online at https://ticket.onb.ac.at/week_ticket or at one of the museum service desks.

The **MQ FAB 4 Ticket** (€29.90) will get you into all the museums in the MuseumsQuartier, with a discount on the ZOOM Children's Museum and the Tanzquartier Wien and Halle G Studios.

Itinerary Ideas

You really need more than three days to appreciate Vienna fully—you could easily spend an entire day at either the **Kunsthistorisches Museum** (not included in the below itineraries) or the **MuseumsQuartier** alone. However, if you just want a taste of the city, these three days will show you a few popular highlights as well as a few hidden local secrets to whet your appetite to return to Vienna for more.

DAY 1
Before heading out, reserve a table for lunch at Figlmüller around 1pm.

1 Before you get ready to walk around the kernel of the old city, grab a coffee at one of Vienna's classic downtown coffeehouses, like **Café Hawelka.**

2 Wander down the cobbled streets 5 minutes away to the **Hofburg.** You can get a Sisi ticket for the museums in the Hofburg—hold onto the ticket if you plan to go to Schönbrunn Palace—to see how the Habsburg-half lived.

3 Walk 10 minutes down Kohlmarkt and the Graben to **St. Stephen's Cathedral.** Look inside Vienna's most famous landmark or take the elevator or the stairs up to one of the towers for panoramic views over the historic center and the colorful tiled roof.

4 Try a Schnitzel or some other Austrian special at **Figlmüller** in the historic center—just make sure you reserve a table first.

5 Head over to the **Stadtpark** on a 10-minute walk southeast down Bäckerstraße—see if you can find the golden Strauss statue in the park.

6 Get on the tram D just 10 minutes away and get off at the Schloss Belvedere for the **Belvedere Palace** to see Klimt's famous *The Kiss.*

7 From the Belvedere Palace, take the S-Bahn S1, S2, S3, or S4 from the Quartier Belvedere station at the southern entrance to the palace to the Praterstern station for an evening at the **Prater.** Ride the iconic Riesenrad for vistas over the Danube, Old Vienna, and sometimes even the mountains beyond. The best time to come is at sunset.

8 If it's the summer, head back on the U1—or walk—to Schwedenplatz for the riverside bars at the Danube Canal, like the **Strandbar Herrmann,** which is open till 1am.

DAY 2

1 Start off in Karlsplatz and wander over to the **Secession.** Stop and admire the golden dome before popping inside to admire Klimt's stunning *Beethoven Frieze.* You only need about an hour to explore this small museum.

2 Walk over to the **Naschmarkt,** right next to the Secession. Head into one of the trendy market restaurants for a hearty brunch, then take some time to wander through this vibrant market, but don't forget to look up at the flower and gold covered art nouveau apartment blocks on the Wienzeile by Otto Wagner. If it's a Saturday, check out the flea market nearby.

3 Get on the metro at Kettenbrückengasse to Schönbrunn. Explore **Schönbrunn Palace,** the famous Habsburg summer residence.

4 After you've explored the palace, head out into the park beyond, and hike up the hill to the **Gloriette** for magnificent vistas of the Schönbrunn. Exploring the palace and park together will take a total of a couple hours.

5 Take the U-Bahn from Hietzing—see if you can spot the exclusive train station built for Emperor Franz Joseph I by Otto Wagner—to Schottenring. It's only a short walk from here to the **Sigmund Freud Museum,** the former residence of the famous psychoanalyst.

6 Walk over or take the U-Bahn to the Rathaus and explore the Josefstadt area for its culinary scene. For a recommended dish, try the Backhendl (fried chicken) at **Café Hummel.**

7 In the evening, check out the live music scene around the **Gürtel,** like the Chelsea and B72.

VIENNA LIKE A LOCAL

Although it's easy to lose yourself in Vienna's grand downtown sites, there is more to the city than the area enclosed by the Ringstraße. You can still fit some spectacular sights in while slipping into some of the outer districts away from the crowds for a taste of local Viennese life.

1 Head down to the area around Schwedenplatz and the Danube Canal in the morning. You'll find plenty of breakfast options here, like **KLYO** in the old Urania observatory.

2 Saunter 10 minutes due east over to the **Kunst Haus Wien** to explore the art and architecture of one of Vienna's most experimental architects, Friedensreich Hundertwasser.

3 After you've done the museum, have your camera ready to see Hundertwasser's most spectacular building in Vienna—the **Hundertwasserhaus**—which is a five-minute walk away.

4 Take the bus 4A to Karlsplatz and walk 5 minutes to Albertinaplatz to the **Bitzinger Würstelstand** for a light lunch. Try the Käsekrainer, a sausage filled with cheese. Don't forget to order a couple of slices of bread and some pickles to go with it.

5 Follow up with a coffee at **Café Bräunerhof** just 5 minutes away to fuel up at this traditional Viennese café without the crowds. Try their strudel!

Itinerary Ideas

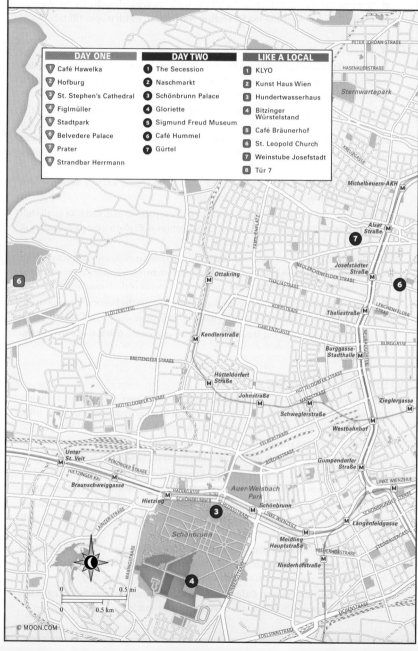

DAY ONE
1. Café Hawelka
2. Hofburg
3. St. Stephen's Cathedral
4. Figlmüller
5. Stadtpark
6. Belvedere Palace
7. Prater
8. Strandbar Herrmann

DAY TWO
1. The Secession
2. Naschmarkt
3. Schönbrunn Palace
4. Gloriette
5. Sigmund Freud Museum
6. Café Hummel
7. Gürtel

LIKE A LOCAL
1. KLYO
2. Kunst Haus Wien
3. Hundertwasserhaus
4. Bitzinger Würstelstand
5. Café Bräunerhof
6. St. Leopold Church
7. Weinstube Josefstadt
8. Tür 7

© MOON.COM

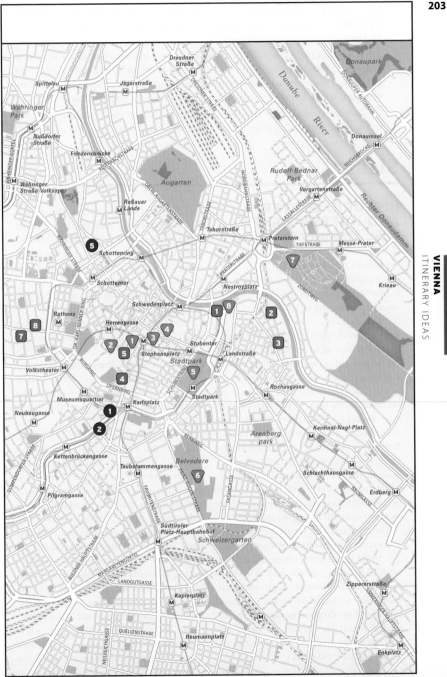

6 Take the U3 U-Bahn to Ottakring and then transfer onto the bus 48A and get off at the Spital Otto Wagner. Wander uphill following the signs to the stunning art nouveau **St. Leopold Church** by Otto Wagner.

7 To get back to the center, return the way you came and jump back to the 48A bus to Burggasse/Neubaugasse for dinner at **Weinstube Josefstadt,** a hidden Stadtheuriger tucked away in a secret courtyard in the Josefstadt neighborhood. It's popular with locals, so be sure to book ahead, especially if you want a table in the magical garden!

8 Ring the doorbell to get into **Tür 7,** a hidden bar only 10 minutes away on foot, and try one of their cocktails (make sure you've reserved in advance).

Sights

HISTORIC CENTER AND HOFBURG AREA
★ St. Stephen's Cathedral
(Stephansdom)

Stephansplatz 3; tel. 01/51552-3054; www.stephanskirche.at; Mon-Sat 6am-10pm, Sun 7am-10pm; €6 individual entry to North Tower, catacombs, or cathedral, €5 South Tower; U1, U3: Stephansplatz

You can spot the Gothic spires of St. Stephen's Cathedral from as far as the hills surrounding the city, rising high above all of Vienna's downtown buildings. Construction began in the 12th century, but most of what you'll see today dates back to the 14th century, after Rudolf IV, the Duke of Austria, built the cathedral on the foundations of the older Romanesque church. It's become a symbol of the city, not only as its most important religious monument, but also as the site of imperial weddings and royal funerals. (Its crypt became the resting place for the organs from members of the Habsburg dynasty.)

The cathedral itself is a tapestry of Gothic architecture superimposed by Baroque style. You could spend hours inside and still not catch all the quirky details, such as the stone basilisks, snakes, dragons, eagles and lions, toads, and salamanders carved into royal tombs and on display throughout the cathedral. (See if you can spot the cheeky self-portrait of the sculptor staring out of the window beneath the stairs.)

Real beasts once wandered Vienna. The **Giant's Gate,** the main entrance, gets its name not just from its grand size, but also from the mastodon thigh bone unearthed when the foundations for the North Tower were built in 1443. At the time, people believed the bone belonged to a giant that perished in Noah's great flood.

You'll appreciate the cathedral's colorful tiled rooftop and the view of the old town—which is why it's worth the hike up the 343 steps to the **South Tower** even after a few too many decadent cakes. Alternatively, save your energy by taking the lift in the **North Tower,** which provides a view just as spectacular.

To truly appreciate St. Stephen's Cathedral, you don't just need the view from above—you need to go deep below. Tours of the **catacombs** run five to nine times a day, depending on demand (check the cathedral website for the timetable), and last around half an hour. At first, you may think you're just in a musty chapel with whitewashed walls. You'll see the final resting places of the bishops who once served the cathedral. But as the guide leads you into the crypts, things get interesting. First, you'll come upon the 70 copper urns that house the Habsburgs' internal organs, "preserved" in alcohol. (Their bodies rest in the Kaisergruft, while their hearts lie in the crypt of the Augustiner Church, a few streets away.) Passing the lapidarium of broken stone sculptures, the temperature drops as the tunnel swerves into the unrenovated part of the crypt where the bones of thousands of plague victims from the 18th century lie stacked up behind iron bars.

The cathedral can get crowded during the high season, but you can escape the hordes if you head out early in the morning.

Once you've had your fill of the cathedral, head next door to the **Dommuseum** (Stephansplatz 6; tel. 01/51552-5300; www.dommuseum.at; Wed-Sun 10am-6pm, Thu 10am-8pm; €8) for a treasure trove of religious art.

Mozarthaus

Domgasse 5; tel. 01/512-1791; www.mozarthausvienna. at; daily 10am-7pm; €11; U1, U3: Stephansplatz

Mozart moved frequently during his stay in Vienna, but the first floor of this three-story home (now a museum) is one of the few surviving apartments where the famous composer lived. He resided in the space for two and a half years, and it is where he penned his most famous opera, *The Marriage of Figaro*. Today, the entire house is dedicated to Mozart, and is a must for music lovers interested in the life of the child prodigy who rose to fame, then crashed into debt and sickness. He passed away at the age of 35.

Once you get your ticket, the museum will give you a worthwhile audio guide, and you can either climb the stairs or take the lift to the top floor, where the exhibit illustrates Mozart's life in Vienna. You can see original music scores, instruments and other collections in the museum, but the museum also explores Mozart's involvement with the Freemasons, as well as his vices, such as his escapades with women and gambling. Before you head down to the residential part of the flat, make sure you check out the mesmerizing holographic presentation with a scene from the *Magic Flute*, the last opera Mozart ever composed.

The Literature Museum (Grillparzerhaus)

Johannesgasse 6; www.onb.ac.at/literaturmuseum; Tue-Sun 10am-6pm; €7; U1, U3: Stephansplatz

Book lovers will love this interactive museum dedicated to Austrian literature, whether or not they've read Joseph Roth's *Radetzky March* or Robert Musil's *A Man Without Qualities*. Although the exhibition is in German, you'll get a tablet computer at the ticket office that will let you scan the barcodes around the exhibit for English translations. You can get to know the literary life of the city from the 18th century to the present, with an interesting collection of books, letters, artifacts, photographs, and multimedia installations. Compare Rilke's elegant handwriting to Kafka's scrawl, or learn about how Alma Mahler's salons influenced the literary scene of Fin de Siècle Vienna. The permanent collection of the museum is fairly extensive; expect to spend two hours here, especially if you want to read all the notes provided via the tablet.

The Jewish Museum Vienna Dorotheergasse

Dorotheergasse 11; Sun-Fri 10am-6pm; €12 combined ticket with Dorotheergasse Museum; U3: Herrengasse or U1, U3: Stephansplatz

This museum, renovated within the last few years, is set in a former palace that once belonged to a Jewish family, and it charts the history of Jewish Vienna where the Jewish Museum Vienna Judenplatz leaves off. The permanent "Our City!" exhibition traces Jewish life through Vienna under the Habsburgs, at the Fin de Siécle, and through the dark times of the Holocaust and World War II through to the present day. The museum also offers a mix of artifacts interspersed with contemporary art installations and personal stories. On the top floor, you'll find relics and ceremonial art rescued from Vienna's destroyed synagogues. Expect to spend a couple hours exploring this museum.

Historic Center and Hofburg Area

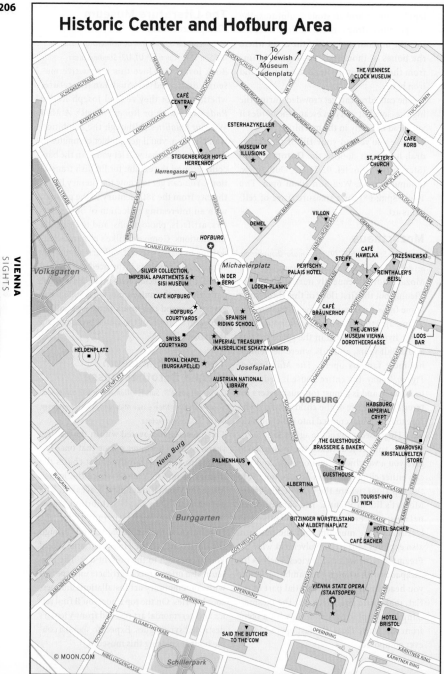

To
The Jewish
Museum
Judenplatz

THE VIENNESE
CLOCK MUSEUM

CAFÉ
CENTRAL

ESTERHAZYKELLER

CAFÉ
KORB

MUSEUM OF
ILLUSIONS

STEIGENBERGER HOTEL
HERRENHOF

ST. PETER'S
CHURCH

Herrengasse Ⓜ

VILLON

DEMEL

HOFBURG

CAFÉ
HAWELKA

STEIFF

TRZEŚNIEWSKI

Michaelerplatz

PERTSCHY
PALAIS HOTEL

REINTHALER'S
BEISL

Volksgarten

SILVER COLLECTION,
IMPERIAL APARTMENTS &
SISI MUSEUM

IN DER
BERG

LODEN-PLANKL

CAFÉ HOFBURG

CAFÉ
BRÄUNERHOF

HOFBURG
COURTYARDS

SPANISH
RIDING SCHOOL

THE JEWISH
MUSEUM VIENNA
DOROTHEERGASSE

LOOS
BAR

SWISS
COURTYARD

IMPERIAL TREASURY
(KAISERLICHE SCHATZKAMMER)

HELDENPLATZ

ROYAL CHAPEL
(BURGKAPELLE)

Josefsplatz

AUSTRIAN NATIONAL
LIBRARY

HOFBURG

HABSBURG
IMPERIAL
CRYPT

Neue Burg

THE GUESTHOUSE
BRASSERIE & BAKERY

SWAROVSKI
KRISTALLWELTEN
STORE

PALMENHAUS

THE
GUESTHOUSE

ALBERTINA

TOURIST-INFO
WIEN

Burggarten

BITZINGER WÜRSTELSTAND
AM ALBERTINAPLATZ

HOTEL SACHER

CAFÉ SACHER

VIENNA STATE OPERA
(STAATSOPER)

SAID THE BUTCHER
TO THE COW

HOTEL
BRISTOL

© MOON.COM

Schillerpark

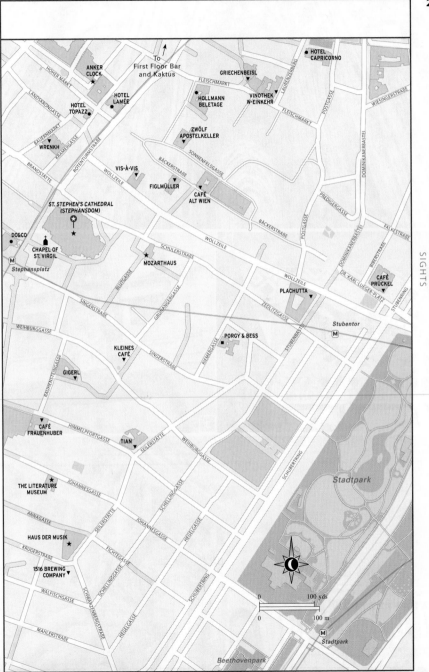

ANKER CLOCK

To First Floor Bar and Kaktus

HOTEL CAPRICORNO

GRIECHENBEISL

HOTEL LAMÉE

HOLLMANN BELETAGE

VINOTHEK W-EINKEHR

HOTEL TOPAZZ

WRENKH

ZWÖLF APOSTELKELLER

VIS-À-VIS

FIGLMÜLLER

CAFÉ ALT WIEN

ST. STEPHEN'S CATHEDRAL (STEPHANSDOM)

DO&CO

CHAPEL OF ST. VIRGIL

MOZARTHAUS

Stephansplatz

CAFÉ PRÜCKEL

PLACHUTTA

Stubentor

PORGY & BESS

KLEINES CAFÉ

GIGERL

CAFÉ FRAUENHUBER

TIAN

THE LITERATURE MUSEUM

Stadtpark

HAUS DER MUSIK

1516 BREWING COMPANY

0   100 yds

0   100 m

Stadtpark

Beethovenpark

The Viennese Clock Museum
(Uhrenmuseum)

Schulhof 2; tel. 01/533-2265; www.wienmuseum. at/en/locations/uhrenmuseum; Tue-Sun and public holidays 10am-6pm; €7; U3: Herrengasse

The Vienna Clock Museum occupies one of Vienna's oldest buildings, on a quiet square where horse carriages move along the cobbled street. This tower-like building contains over 20,000 curious timepieces, including 15th-century painted Gothic clocks, the world's smallest pendulum clock (the size of a thimble), musical clocks, computer clocks, and intricate astronomical clocks. The museum allows visitors to see how measuring time has evolved over the centuries, from the 700-kg (approx. 1.5-ton) clock movement taken from St. Stephen's Tower, as well as grandfather clocks, and on to tiny pocket watches and digital wristwatches. Try to be there on the hour, when every clock strikes on the hour in choral unison.

Anker Clock

Hoher Markt 10-11; free; U1, U4: Schwedenplatz, U1, U3: Stephansplatz

A few streets down from St. Stephen's Cathedral, the Anker Clock is an art nouveau masterpiece that's worth a look if you're passing by. Franz von Matsch created this copper green and gold clock, constructed 1911-1914. It adorns the bridge between two buildings currently owned by the Anker Insurance Company. At noon, with music playing, its figurines move across the clock face. Each character represents a historical figure from Austrian history, like Roman Emperor Marcus Aurelius, and Maria Theresa. The precession of 12 figures lasts around 10 minutes, and the organ music you'll hear is made up of excerpts representative of the time periods in which the famous figures lived.

1: interior of St. Stephen's Cathedral 2: detail of St. Stephen's Cathedral's roof 3: The art nouveau Anker Clock is one of the quirkier landmarks in Vienna's historic center. 4: The Hofburg was the permanent powerhouse of the Habsburg emperors.

St. Peter's Church

Petersplatz; tel. 01/533-6433; www.peterskirche.at/ home; Mon-Fri 7am-8pm, Sat-Sun 9am-9pm; U1, U3: Stephansplatz

As you walk down the Graben, a pedestrianized street lined with shops and restaurants, you will pass St. Peter's Church. Its imposing turreted green dome and Baroque façade are inspired by St. Peter's Cathedral in Rome. This Catholic church has been in the hands of the Opus Dei since the 1970s, and it's worth stepping inside just to see the rich, bright frescoes of cherub-like figures and toga-clad saints painted by JM Rottmayer which decorate the ceiling and dome. Try to get there at 3pm Monday to Friday for one of their free organ concerts.

Chapel of St. Virgil

Stephansplatz; tel. 01/664-882-93930; www.wienmuseum.at/en/locations/virgilkapelle; Tue-Sun 10am-6pm; €5; U1, U3: Stephansplatz

As you leave the U-Bahn at Stephansplatz, make sure you look to the right before going up the escalator to the square for a glimpse of one of Vienna's most fascinating places: the Chapel of St. Virgil. This medieval chapel was built in the early 13th century, and now exists where the Chapel of St. Mary Magdalene (built in the late 14th century), once stood. The Chapel of St. Mary Magdalene was destroyed completely in a fire in 1781.

Upon entering the chapel, you can use one of the tablet computers there which works as an interactive audio guide. When you descend the iron staircase into the heart of the chapel, it's easy to lose yourself in the dimly lit chamber, accented with crusade-like crosses (which have faded over the centuries into a light pink) painted into the alcoves of the chapel. A small museum in the back of the chapel covers Vienna's medieval history.

★ The Hofburg

Michaelerkuppel; http://hofburg-wien.at/; U3: Herrengasse

This palatial complex, home to the Habsburgs from 1273 to 1918, was the epicenter of life

Jews in Vienna

Judenplatz was once part of the Medieval Jewish Quarter; today a memorial covers the historic synagogue, which can be visited via the Jewish Museum.

The first written record of Jews in Vienna dates back to the 12th century, with a mint master named Schlom—but there was little to no evidence of an established community until 1230. In a compact area in today's 1st District, 70 two-story houses were once home to around 800 Jews in the Middle Ages; the community congregated around the synagogue (whose ruins you can see in the Jewish Museum in Judenplatz). Jewish life thrived here until the Wiener Gesera, when King Albert V ordered the annihilation of the city's Jews in the 1420s. And after being allowed to settle again two centuries later, they were expelled by Leopold I (circa 1670).

Under Emperor Joseph II, Jews acquired more rights, although forming a religious community was still forbidden. It was only in the mid-19th century that the community was allowed to flourish; by 1900 it became the largest German-speaking Jewish community in the world (around 185,000). Prominent figures like Sigmund Freud, Gustav Mahler, Stefan Zweig, Arnold Schoenberg, and Theodor Herzl made significant contributions to that community and to the world. Until 1938, Jews in Vienna were an integral part of society. Following the Holocaust, only 9,000 Jews were part of that community—and out of the 94 temples that once stood, only one survived the war.

for the European royals. It now offers numerous museums, Café Hofburg, libraries, and more—and it serves as the residence of the Austrian president. It is a historical tapestry, where Renaissance details mingle with Baroque grandeur. The oldest section is the 13th-century Swiss Courtyard. (Various additions to the building were created by monarchs trying to outdo previous rulers.)

Some of Vienna's best museums, such as the Albertina, are located at this site. The Hofburg also features the Imperial Apartments and the Spanish Riding School. Take some time to walk through the grand courtyards, which are open for free to the public, and take in the architectural splendor.

Most of the below mentioned sites are reachable through the gate at the Michaelerkuppel (Michael dome) at Michaelerplatz, located just next to Herrengasse, with the exception of the National Austrian Library (on the neighboring square as you head south along Reitschulegasse from Michaelerplatz) and the

Albertina, which is set in the outer part of the Hofburg facing the Staatsoper. All the sites are best accessed from the Herrengasse U-Bahn station, except the Albertina, which is close to the Oper, Karlsplatz U-Bahn.

SILVER COLLECTION, IMPERIAL APARTMENTS & SISI MUSEUM

Michaelerkuppel; tel. 01/533-7570;
http://hofburg-wien.at; daily 9am-5pm; €15

The best way to experience the Hofburg in its imperial glory is to head to the three-in-one museum at this location—comprising the Silver Collection, Imperial Apartments, and the Sisi Museum. One ticket will get you into all three. Expect to spend a few hours immersed in Habsburg opulence. You can also take a guided tour (€17), which runs daily in the Sisi Museum and the Imperial Apartments at 2pm.

You'll begin at the **Silver Collection** (which despite the name is more than just silverware). It offers fascinating insight into daily life in the Hofburg. You'll see imperial kitchen items ranging from copper jelly molds to linen and tableware—some used on a daily basis, others only for special occasions. You'll also see rococo-style golden candles and orientalist porcelain and ceramics. An audio guide (included with your ticket) accompanies you on your journey.

The next stop is the **Sisi Museum,** located one floor above the Silver Collection. The Sisi Museum is dedicated to the legendary Empress Elizabeth, more affectionately known as Sisi, who was the wife of Emperor Franz Joseph I and ruled alongside her husband in the second half of the 19th century. She was renowned for her looks and is still famed for her legacy in popular culture. You'll get insights into her life as a young girl through to her more independent jaunts across Europe. The museum offers an interesting peek into the woman behind the chocolate boxes and postcards—a woman who used raw meat facials to maintain her beauty and lived with an insatiable curiosity. (She once begged a ship's captain to tie her to a chair during a storm so she could experience it like Odysseus from Greek mythology.)

The Sisi Museum leads into the **Imperial Apartments,** where Sisi lived with her husband, the Emperor Franz Joseph. The imperial couple lived separately, and their apartments reflect their character and express their personalities. Franz Joseph's rooms are traditional, with deep-red damask walls and furniture accented with gold; Franz Joseph's study holds several intimate portraits of Sisi.

Sisi's apartments are airy and light, decorated with frescoes, and include a personal gym with small weights and workout areas that were not in vogue for women of her time.

IMPERIAL TREASURY (Kaiserliche Schatzkammer)

Schweizerhof; tel. 01/525-244031; www.kaiserliche-schatzkammer.at; Wed-Mon 9am-5:30pm; €12

The Imperial Treasury takes you on a journey through 1,000 years of royal and ecclesiastical history. Items on display include robes, scepters, and royal jewels, but the highlight of the collection is a golden crown encrusted with rubies, emeralds and other precious gems. If you're fascinated by religious treasures, you won't want to miss the piece of the cross on which Jesus was allegedly crucified, a tooth of St. John the Baptist, and another from St. Peter, as well as a scrap from the tablecloth used at the Last Supper.

You can easily spend one to two hours here in this literal treasure trove. The audio guide (€5) is a worthwhile tool for understanding the historical context of the precious objects.

ROYAL CHAPEL (Burgkapelle)

Schweizerhof; tel. 01/533-9927;
www.hofmusikkapelle.gv.at; Mon-Tue 10am-2pm,
Fri 11am-1pm; free entry to visit

Originally built in the 13th century, this chapel is the oldest part of the Hofburg. Over the centuries, it has undergone numerous makeovers and additions, particularly in the 15th century and then later in the Baroque period. The Royal Chapel is perhaps most famous for the Vienna Boys' Choir performances at Sunday Holy Mass.

HOFBURG COURTYARDS

The Hofburg is a labyrinth of courtyards and gates. If you start at Augustinerstraße, then you'll come to Josefsplatz.

Movie lovers may recognize the entrance of the Austrian National Library, which was part of the scene of Harry Lime's accident in the film *The Third Man*, starring Orson Welles. Continue down Reitschulgasse, past the Spanish Riding School stables to Michaelerplatz, and take the path under the arches of the main gate to the first grand courtyard, **In der Berg,** a large enclosed square with a statue of Emperor Franz I, the last Holy Roman Emperor, and the founder of the Austrian Empire. The ornate red and black 16th-century Swiss Gate leads into the oldest part of the Hofburg, the 13th-century **Swiss Courtyard** (Schweitzerhof), named for the Swiss guards who once protected the palace.

Continuing toward the gate from In der Berg brings you out to **Heldenplatz** (Hero's Square), which connects with the Ringsraße.

SPANISH RIDING SCHOOL

Michaelerplatz 1; tel. 01/533-9031; www.srs.at; daily 9am-4pm; tours €18

The Spanish Riding School, inside the Hofburg, maintains a 16th-century tradition, with equestrian shows twice a week featuring the stable's 70 Lipizzaner stallions, a Baroque breed of horse descended from the Andalusians mixed in with other horse breeds. Although shows are a little pricey (starting from €53 for individual seats), you can get a sneak peek at the morning exercises on most weekdays from 10am to midday (check the calendar on the website as this varies by season), which is much more affordable with tickets going for €16-26. You can't explore the riding school or the stables without a guide, but you can catch a glimpse of the horses through the stable windows as you walk down Reitschulgasse.

It's also possible to pay a visit to the horses in the Stable Castles (the stables where the horses live and sleep) across the road on a tour of the riding school (€19). Inside the Stable Castles, you may catch sight of a few white stallions peering out of their boxes into the colonnaded courtyard. Stallions stand inside their own spacious pen. The stallions come in varying shades of gray (most Lipizzaners turn white as they age) and come with first and last names—the first from the stud father, the second from the brood mare.

Tricks the horses perform actually have origins in the military, with roots in Ancient Greece. Each horse specializes in a particular exercise. During the tour, you'll likely see a rare black Lipizzaner. (It's said that while there is a black Lipizzaner in the stables, the Spanish Riding School will keep going.)

AUSTRIAN NATIONAL LIBRARY (Österreichische Nationalbibliothek)

Joseph Platz 1; tel. 01/534-10; www.onb.ac.at; Tue-Wed and Fri-Sun 10am-6pm, Thu 10am-9pm; €8, Universal week ticket with Literature Museum, Esperanto, Globe and Papyrus Museums €19

Between the Albertina and the museums in the Hofburg is the Austrian National Library, in the palace building. It was once the Imperial Library. The Ceremonial Hall is a work of art, with frescoes by court painter Daniel Gran. Over 200,000 grand tomes line the dark wooden bookshelves, punctuated by Venetian Baroque globes, Corinthian marble columns, and glass cabinets full of rare texts opened up at colorful pages. The library was built in the early 1700s, after Emperor Karl VI ordered its construction. It was built as a private wing of the Hofburg, but today it belongs to the Austrian National Library.

ALBERTINA

Albertinaplatz 1; tel. 01/534-83540; www.albertina. at; Mon, Tue, Thu, Sat-Sun 10am-6pm, Wed and Fri 10am-9pm; €16.90; U1, U2, U4: Karlsplatz, trams 1, 2, 71, D: Oper, Karlsplatz

Ringstraße Tram Tour

Vienna's State Opera House on the Ringstraße

The Ringstraße, a 5.3-kilometer (3.3-mi) boulevard that ranks as one of the most beautiful streets in the world, is now a fixture in Vienna's cityscape.

A tram tour of the Ringstraße is a good way to see most of Vienna's best sites. Get on the **number 1 tram at Schwedenplatz** in the direction of Stefan-Fadinger-Platz and change to **the number 2 at the Oper, Karlsplatz** stop from the same platform (it'll go in the direction of Friedrich-Engels-Platz) for a full tour around the Ringstraße. The journey takes around 30-40 minutes, depending on how long you'll need to wait between trams when changing.

If you begin with tram 1 from Schwedenplatz, you'll pass the following, in this order: the Votive Church, Town Hall, the Parliament (all on the right), the Hofburg grounds (on the left), the Kunsthistorisches, the Naturhistorisches (both on the right), the State Opera House (on the left), and the Stadtpark (right). Also keep a look out for beautiful theaters, palaces, cafés, and luxury hotels along the way, noticing the melting pot of architectural influences drawn from classical Greece, Gothic Flanders, Renaissance Italy, and Baroque Central Europe, as well as some art nouveau styles, mixing up into an eclectic style that is unique to the boulevard.

Trams 1 and 2 don't have commentary on board, so if you want to know what you're seeing you can take the nonstop 25-minute **Ring Tram Tour** (€12), which includes an audio guide that has explanations in English. This runs every 30 minutes from Schwedenplatz 10am-5:30pm (www. viennasightseeing.at) on Saturday and Sunday.

Today, the Albertina is home to one of the greatest art collections in the world, so vast that rotating exhibitions are required. The permanent exhibition covering avant-garde art is impressive and goes from Monet to Picasso. You'll also be able to view pieces from pointillism, expressionism, fauvism, surrealism, and cubism.

You can get a standard audio guide (€4) when you buy your ticket, but there is the option to turn your smartphone into an audio guide. Just ask for a code at the ticket counter (€3), and you can listen to it all again at home. You can also install the Artvive app on your smartphone (make sure you bring headphones!) and hold your phone up to designated paintings for augmented reality views and more information.

Museum of Illusions

Wallnerstraße 4; tel. 01/532-2255;
www.museumderillusionen.at; Tue-Thu 10am-6pm,
Fri-Sun 10am-7:30pm; €12; U3: Herrengasse

This small museum in the heart of the city opened in the summer of 2017 and has quickly become popular with locals and tourists of all ages. The museum specializes in visual illusions, from classic trippy posters that spin before your eyes to inverted faces of Albert Einstein that change expression, depending on your vantage point. The best illusions are the larger installations, like a room with a bridge above a spinning display that tricks you into thinking you're inside a spaceship zipping through outer space. There are also plenty of photo opportunities.

Habsburg Imperial Crypt
(Kaisergruft)

Tegetthoffstraße 2; tel. 01/512-685-316;
www.kaisergruft.at; daily 10am-6pm;
€7.50; U1, U3: Stephansplatz

Set underneath the triangle-shaped Capuchin Church in the city center, the Habsburg Imperial Crypt is the resting place for the members of the Habsburg family. The crypt spreads out over 10 subterranean vaulted rooms; 149 Habsburgs have been buried here, from the 17th century up until the death of Otto Habsburg in 2011. This building holds pieces of 400 years of Austria's imperial history, and the sarcophagi for 12 emperors and 19 empresses and queens. Most impressive of the tombs is the double sarcophagus for Maria Theresa and her husband Emperor Franz I, a theatrical piece by Balthasar Ferdinand Moll, with the imperial couple represented on the top gazing into each other's eyes. The tombs of Franz Joseph and Elizabeth in the next room are simpler. Tours in English (€3.50) run daily at 3:30pm, however at the time of writing, these were unavailable due to Covid-19.

Haus der Musik

Seilerstätte 30; tel. 01/513-4850; www.hdm.at;
daily 10am-10pm; €14; U1, U2, U4: Karlsplatz, tram 2,
D: Schwarzenbergplatz

The Haus der Musik (which means House of Music in German) is a unique museum that combines Vienna's music history with the science of sound. The museum is located in a tall townhouse in the heart of the city.

The first floor is accessible by a set of stairs that doubles as piano keys (there is also a lift if needed). The first floor covers the history of the Vienna Philharmonic. This floor is a classic museum, with personal relics like conductors' letters, old watches, photographs, and scribbled sheets of music. There are also interactive listening stations.

On the second floor, devoted to the science of sound, is the Sonisphere, which is like an interactive art installation—with screens that demonstrate how your ear works, and exhibitions like an indented globe you can duck your head inside and hear music and sounds from around the world. Another feature allows you to perform specific experiments with your voice.

The third floor is a walkthrough, tactile installation on Vienna's most famous composers, beginning with Mozart and moving up to 20th-century composers like Schönberg, Berg, and Webern. Each room has a theme that ties in with the spirit of the composer.

On the fourth floor, you can experience what it's like to be a conductor. Virtual conductor rooms let you see if you've got what it takes to take over the Vienna Philharmonic.

★ Vienna State Opera
(Staatsoper)

Opernring 2; tel. 01/514-442-250; www.wiener-
staatsoper.at; English language tours run 1-3 times
a day, see website for times; tours €10; U1, U2, U4:
Karlsplatz, trams 1, 2, 71, D: Oper, Karlsplatz

The Vienna State Opera is a cathedral to classical music. The best way to experience one of the world's most prestigious opera houses is to get a ticket for a production. But if you can't, it's worth taking the 45-minute guided tour for a behind-the-scenes peek into a world hidden away from regular operagoers. You don't need to register for the tour, but I recommend coming 20 minutes before the tour time given

Neubau, the MuseumsQuartier, and Naschmarkt

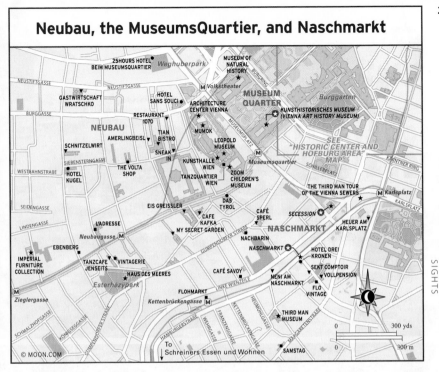

on the website (www.wiener-staatsoper.at/en/service/guided-tours) to the entrance on the Opernring/Operngasse corner so you can get a spot before the tour fills up.

Only a third of the original opera house built in 1869 remains (after bombs in World War II devastated the iconic building), but the building has been beautifully restored. One of the few intact rooms is the tearoom, where Emperor Franz Joseph sipped tea near golden silk wall panels and marble cladding. The tearoom is only open during tours of the opera house, and not during productions—unless you want to hire it for 20 minutes in a break during a show for €500.

The tours also take you through the maze-like passages beyond the gilded Grand Staircase to the main auditorium or the stage area, where you can see the set designers getting ready for the latest production.

The Vienna State Opera runs shows virtually every night. Each night brings a different opera or ballet production. Sets are mounted on the six platforms on the revolving stage. The tour gives insight into just how much work goes into each production. Approximately 120 stagehands work day and night to ensure flawless shows.

NEUBAU AND THE MUSEUMSQUARTIER

Vienna's MuseumsQuartier combines 60 cultural institutions in over 100,000 square yards of territory. This ambitious cultural hub is one of the city's biggest tourist draws, and you can easily spend days exploring these world-class museums. If you need a little orientation, head to the **MQ Point**, the quarter's information center located by the main entrance. You can get an **MQ Kombi ticket** here (€29.90, includes entry into all the museums, except Zoom—you'll get a discount), or you can purchase an **MQ FAB 4 Ticket,** which includes the Leopold Museum (covering art

from the late 19th century and the early 20th century), the mumok, and the Kunsthalle Wien (€22.90).

★ Kunsthistorisches Museum

Maria-Theresien-Platz; tel. 01/525-240; www.khm.at; Fri-Wed 10am-6pm, Thu 10am-9pm Jun-Aug, closed Mon Sep-May; €16; U3: Museumsquartier, U2, U3: Volkstheater, trams 1, 2, 71, D: Burgring

If you only visit one museum in Vienna on your trip, make it the Kunsthistorisches Museum, the largest art history museum in the country—with pieces spanning chronologically from the Ancient Egyptians to the masters of the Renaissance and Baroque periods.

The idea for the museum originated with Emperor Franz Joseph I, who wanted to create a home for the extensive imperial art collection. Plans to construct the Ringstraße began in 1857. A competition to design the new museum was held a decade later, in 1867. The winner, architect Gottfried Semper, worked on two museums (the Kunsthistorisches and the Naturhistorisches) whose semicircular façades mirror each other. The two museums opened to the public in 1891 and 1889, respectively.

Expect to spend five hours here unless you prioritize the section you're interested in. Crowds can get heavy at the museum in the early afternoon. It's best to head out in the morning when the museum opens at 10am to get the most out of your visit. You can also skip the lines by buying your tickets online via the museum website, but do factor in some extra time for security checks as you enter the museum.

If you need refueling from all the art, the café and restaurant in the Kunsthistorisches Museum Cupola Hall (www.genussimmuseum.at; Tue-Sun 10am-5:30pm) offers plush red seating. The museum also runs gourmet evenings (Thu 6:30pm-10pm, €44).

Museum highlights include:

MEZZANINE FLOOR

Kunstkammer Collections: What you see here may seem like a mishmash of objects at first glance, but it's a fascinating collection of curiosities that never quite found a definitive functional place in history. The more than 2,200 items include odd wind-up figurines, ball-operated gilded clocks, secret boxes, and much, much more. The items span the fields of natural history, geology, ethnography, archaeology, religious or historical relics, and arts and antiquity.

Egyptian, Near Eastern, Greek, and Roman Collection: You can easily spend a couple of hours in the Egyptian, Near-Eastern, Greek and Roman Collection, appreciating the exhibits as well as the exquisite decor that complements the art on display. In the Egyptian wing, Egyptian-style frescoes adorn the walls and the ceiling, which is propped up with authentic Egyptian columns. In the rooms featuring Roman and Greek sculpture, you feel like you're in a villa Nero himself would have been proud to call home.

FIRST FLOOR

Picture Gallery: The vast picture gallery looks like something out of a Wes Anderson movie, probably why the director decided to curate his own exhibition here in 2018-19—with classic paintings piled up upon each other in quirky symmetry against a backdrop of pastel-colored walls. Classics from the Renaissance, ranging from Raphael to Titian, plus Baroque painting from Italy, Flanders, and the Netherlands, and an exquisite collection of Pieter Bruegel the Elder occupy the walls of the labyrinthine Picture Gallery.

GRAND STAIRCASE

The Grand Staircase connects the ground floor and the mezzanine floor with the first floor. No matter which section you prioritize, do not miss the **"Stairway to Klimt,"** the authentic frescoes painted in Egyptian style by the artist that hang above the Grand Staircase.

1: See Vienna differently by taking a rooftop tour of the Natural History Museum. **2:** Drink a Melange at the iconic café in the Kunsthistorisches Museum.

Natural History Museum
(Naturhistorisches Museum)

Maria-Theresien Platz; tel. 01/521-770;
www.nhm-wien.ac.at; Thu-Mon 9am-6:30pm,
Wed 9am-9pm; €12; U3: Museumsquartier, U2,
U3: Volkstheater, trams 1, 2, 71, D: Burgring

The Natural History Museum features near-identical façades and a similar interior layout to the Kunsthistorisches. The museum decor features impressive art and sculpture that capture the themes of the rooms, from maidens representing various crystals to scenes from prehistory and under the sea.

You could spend days examining all the mineral samples and kaleidoscopic crystals before you even get to the fossils in the connecting wing. The highlight is a huge room with giant dinosaur skeletons—and there is even a realistic-looking robot of a T-Rex that moves and growls. Three rooms exhibit items from prehistory, like flint arrowheads and Iron Age torques, but the real treasure is the voluptuous stone figure of the 11.1 cm (4 3/8 in) Venus of Willendorf, an over 25,000-year-old masterpiece that became one of the most famous archaeological discoveries in the world.

If you're only planning on spending a couple of hours in the museum, you may want to skim the first floor (unless you're passionate about taxidermy). The second floor is home to temporary exhibitions.

I highly recommend the one-hour English-language **View from the Roof Tour** (Fri-Sun 3pm, €8). This guided tour will take you to rooms that are typically off limits, such as the anthropology rooms on the top floor, which contain rows of curious skulls, then onto the rooftop for a fantastic view over Vienna.

Leopold Museum

Museumsplatz 1; tel. 01/525-700;
www.leopoldmuseum.org; Wed-Sun 10am-6pm; €14;
U3: Museumsquartier, U2, U3: Volkstheater, trams 1,
2, 71, D: Burgring

Don't be surprised if you need to queue at the ticket office or the cloakroom—this is one of Vienna's most popular museums. The Leopold collection is one of the most important collections of modern Austrian art, amassed by Rudolf and Elisabeth Leopold over a period of five decades. It features the Viennese avant-garde, with works from Klimt, Schiele, Moser and other great artists.

You can expect to immerse yourself in art for a few hours in this extensive museum. Varying exhibitions shift around, but you'll find the largest collection of Egon Schiele's

The MuseumsQuartier was once the Habsburg stables.

work on display, from distorted landscapes to poignant portraits of mothers with children, and expressive nudes. (Of course, don't miss Klimt's allegorical *Death and Life*.)

The museum contains a café (don't lose your museum ticket as you will need it to get in and out of the café).

Afternoons see a lot of traffic, so try to come in the morning, and if you want to save extra time, buy a ticket online.

mumok

Museumsplatz 1; tel. 01/525-000; www.mumok.at; Wed and Fri-Sun 10am-6pm, Thu 10am-9pm; €13, U3: Museumsquartier, U2, U3: Volkstheater, trams 1, 2, 71, D: Burgring

From the inside out, mumok—the world's largest museum dedicated to Central European modern art—pushes the boundaries. It's an imposing structure in the MuseumsQuartier. There is no permanent exhibition here; instead, there's a rotating exhibition from its extensive 9,000-piece collection that consistently looks ahead—whether the pieces are a throwback to the Actionist avant-gardes of 1960s Vienna, like Günter Brus, Hermann Nitsch, and Otto Mühl, or the works represent early 20th-century modernism, with more global names like Pablo Picasso and René Magritte, or today's media and art. Sometimes, mumok offers space for other temporary exhibits, so check the website to see the current program.

There are also 300 works on show by 48 women artists from Europe and North and South America, such as Ana Mendieta, Cindy Sherman, and ORLAN, as well as Austrian artists such as Renate Bertlmann, Linda Christanell, VALIE EXPORT, Birgit Jürgenssen, Brigitte Lang, Karin Mack, Friederike Pezold, and Margot Pilz.

In the basement, two floors below the entry level, you'll find the mumok cinema. The films are sometimes grotesque, shocking and explicit. Most films are silent, or in German with subtitles. They are sometimes in English, depending on the work being shown. Expect to spend at least two hours here.

(You may want to skip this museum if you're with kids—a good portion of the content is intended for mature audiences.)

ZOOM Children's Museum

Museumsplatz 1; tel. 01/524-7908; www. kindermuseum.at; Tue-Sun 12:45pm-5pm Jul-Aug, Tue-Fri 8:30am-4pm, Sat-Sun 9:45am-4pm Sep-Jun; programs €5-6; U3: Museumsquartier, U2, U3: Volkstheater, trams 1, 2, 71, D: Burgring

ZOOM children's museum is not a museum in the classic sense of the word. Instead of paintings or installations, children can participate in activities that range from an hour to 90 minutes in length. Activities target different age groups and sometimes tackle weighty subject matter: In 2018, one exhibition dealt with forced displacement of young refugees, showing the lives of Syrian children through activities like rug weaving. Other themes focus on creativity, like filmmaking. They may also be academic, like a study of the alphabet. See the website for the programs on offer and make sure you book in advance over the phone. Programs are available in English.

Architecture Center Vienna

Museumsplatz 1; tel. 01/522-3115; www.azw.at; daily 10am-7pm; €9; U3: Museumsquartier, U2, U3: Volkstheater, trams 1, 2, 71, D: Burgring

This niche museum in the MuseumsQuartier is dedicated to the architectural development of Vienna. If you're interested in learning how the city has evolved, Architecture Center Vienna delivers with blueprints, old photographs and documents, and interactive displays. The museum follows the development of Vienna's architectural history in comparison with famous landmarks built in other parts of the world. This museum is an immersion in the nuances of Austrian architecture. If you'd like to visit, plan for at least an hour.

Kunsthalle Wien

Museumsplatz 1; tel. 01/521-890; www.kunsthallewien. at; Tue-Wed and Fri-Sun 11am-7pm, Thu 11am-9pm; €8; U3: Museumsquartier, U2, U3: Volkstheater, trams 1, 2, 71, D: Burgring

Biedermeier Vienna

The term "Biedermeier" is used often around Vienna and Austria. It refers to the period in Central Europe between 1815 and 1848, when there was a boom in the region's middle class, and it describes art, design, music, and literature from this time.

Growing urbanization and industrialization, along with political stability following the end of the Napoleonic Wars led to a thriving middle class hungry for the arts. Interior and furniture design blossomed with the market demand for a comfortable home life. Biedermeier style was simple, utilitarian, and drew subtle influences from Roman Empire styles. It would go on to influence other styles like Bauhaus. Locally used materials like oak, cherry, and ash wood were favored in place of imported timbers. Art during the Biedermeier period reinforced the feeling of security through everyday realism and eschewed political commentary. Portraits became increasingly popular, as well as landscapes and contemporary scenes from daily life. The Biedermeier period ended in 1848 with the wave of political unrest sweeping Europe.

You can see examples of Biedermeier art in the **Upper Belvedere** (page 229), and furniture and design in the **Museum of Applied Arts** (page 235) or the **Imperial Furniture Collection** (page 220).

The Kunsthalle is a series of exhibition halls for contemporary and international art. The industrial, windowless setting with high ceilings is a perfect black box, and one of the best exhibition spaces in Europe. Check the website before visiting to determine whether the current exhibition sparks your interest. Programs usually rely on video, film, installations, and photography. If you're only interested in the space, head up to the café on the top floor for a coffee or a light meal.

Imperial Furniture Collection
(Hofmobiliendepot)

Andreasgasse 7; tel. 01/524-3357;
www.hofmobiliendepot.at; Tue-Sun 10am-5pm;
€10.50; U3: Neubaugasse

The Habsburgs owned several palatial residences around the Austro-Hungarian Empire. With the exception of the Hofburg, which was permanently furnished, every piece for the other imperial residences was stashed in the Hofmobiliendepot, the Imperial Furniture Storehouse. Once the royals came up with a wishlist, the depot shipped the items off to the desired location: Schönbrunn Palace, Gödöllő chateaux in Hungary, the Castello Miramare in Italy in the summer, or hunting lodges within Austria for the hunting season, usually in autumn.

The storehouse (now museum) holds the Imperial Furniture Collection, made up of 165,000 objects (some carefully arranged, others behind locked-up cages), offering time-travel through regal furniture history, from the Baroque furniture used during Maria Theresa's reign to Biedermeier pieces from well-to-do Viennese households. At the end of the tour, you'll find furniture from post-Habsburg days, such as curved art nouveau chairs and a 1960s café setup and apartments.

It's easy to spend an hour or two wandering the rooms and pondering the evolution of Austrian life, from Habsburg grandeur to daily life in late 20th-century Vienna. If you're a fan of the old Sissi films with Romy Schneider, look for some of the authentic furniture used in the films, like a Baroque writing desk, or the imperial bed. Until the 1970s, furniture from the collection was loaned out for film productions; but after damage and losses, the museum cut its ties with the film industry. However, when Queen Elizabeth II was in town in 1969, the hotel where she stayed brought in a bed from the collection just for the British monarch. Audio guides are available in English free of charge.

AROUND NASCHMARKT
★ Naschmarkt

Wienzeile; www.wienernaschmarkt.eu; Mon-Fri 6am-7:30pm; Sat 6am-6pm; U4: Kettenbrückengasse

More than a market for shopping or dining, Naschmarkt is a sight in its own right, and it's worth spending a morning or an afternoon negotiating crowds of local shoppers and tourists to grab some great food and soak in the atmosphere at this large, open-air market. It starts just across the road from the golden-domed Secession and goes on for about 1.5 kilometers (just under 1 mi) alongside the Wienzeile main road. There are no less than 120 market stalls, where you'll find fresh vegetables, dried fruit, cheese, cold cuts, and much more. The best time to come is in the morning in the middle of the week if you want to skip the crowds and get your hands on the best produce and enjoy a good breakfast.

The market is split into two lanes. The north side lane is made up of trendy global restaurants. You'll find what you're craving, whether it's Turkish home cooking, an Indian thali, pad thai, sushi, or Wiener Schnitzel. The lane on the southern side is lined with stalls selling fresh seasonal vegetables, cured meats, olives, vats of hummus, freshly cooked falafel balls, dried fruit, and artisanal cheeses.

In the 16th century, the market specialized in selling milk bottles made from ash wood. (It gets most of its name from the word Aschenmarkt.) It became closer to the market we know today in the 18th century when a law decreeing that produce brought in by cart rather than boat had to be sold on-site. (More recent urban legends tell of stall vendors who hid cocaine in vats of sauerkraut.)

The market gets its look from the Fin de Siècle, in true art nouveau style. If you're a fan of Vienna's art nouveau, you'll definitely want to hike up to the end by Kettenbrückengasse and look up at Otto Wagner's Majolica Wienzeile—a beautiful apartment block with tiles depicting roses and floral motifs—or the neighboring Medallion House with elaborate gold ornamentation decorating the façade.

If you come the market on Saturday, keep walking and you'll find a fascinating antique flea market, the **Flohmarkt** (see page 268).

★ The Secession

Friedrichstraße 12; tel. 01/587-5307; www.secession. at; Tue-Sun 2pm-6pm; €9.50; U1, U2, U4: Karlsplatz

The Secession building, by Joseph Maria Olbrich, after the movement of the same name, is the Secession's architectural manifesto. It may be a symbol of the city today, but the exhibition hall caused a scandal when it was built in 1897. Its austere block-like shape topped with a dome of gold leaves was dubbed the "Golden Cabbage," and pushed the boundaries of the traditional art scene—which is exactly what its founders and members wanted. Artists such as Klimt, Kolo Moser, Joseph M. Olbrich, and Josef Hoffman wanted to break away from the mainstream and create a space where art broke the shackles of convention.

The building has suffered over the years. It functioned as a hospital in World War I. It was later torched by the Germans in retreat in World War II. But today, it once again functions as an exhibition hall. The ground floor and top floor host temporary, contemporary art exhibitions, but the biggest draw is Klimt's *Beethoven Frieze*. The fragmented frieze is one of Klimt's most recognized works. The top left corner of the frieze is an artistic symphony based on Richard Wagner's interpretation of Beethoven's *Ninth Symphony*, with allegories and personification of three sins: lust, gluttony, and unchastity. It was only meant to be a temporary exhibit back in 1902, but since the 1980s, it's become a fixture in the Secession.

There are audio guides available in English (€3). The Secession is smaller than other Vienna museums—you only need 45 minutes to an hour to see it. It's also less crowded, but with the opening hours reduced as of August 2020, it's best to come when it opens at 2pm, or just before it closes at 5pm, so you have some time to enjoy it before it closes at 6pm.

The Golden Age of the Secession

When the Secession was built, its avant-garde design and golden dome caused a scandal.

In 1897, a group of artists, including Gustav Klimt and Koloman Moser, broke away from Vienna's mainstream art scene and founded the Secession in a bid to escape the conservatism that they felt was suffocating mainstream art. This new movement, which was philosophical as well as aesthetic, is embodied in the motto that's still inscribed above the entrance to the Secession: "Der Zeit ihre Kunst. Der Kunst ihre Freiheit." ("To every age its art. To every art its freedom.")

The work of various Secession artists ranges from Klimt's seductive golden portraits of femme fatales to Schiele's disjointed lines and organic color palette. Aesthetically, these works, some of

The Third Man Tour of the Vienna Sewers

Karlsplatz/Girardi Park; tel. 01/4000-3033;
www.thirdmantour.at; English tours daily 3pm
May-Oct; €10; U1, U2, U4: Karlsplatz

If you're a fan of *The Third Man* or you love exploring weird and wonderful places, then sign up for one of these one-hour tours that run from May to October. Although the film is the main theme of the tour, you'll also see the sewers. The sewers themselves are spectacular, especially the banks of the covered Vienna River.

The Vienna sewers are a subterranean labyrinth that run below the city in a complex network of tunnels. As sewers go, it doesn't smell that bad, and you also get to see part of the Vienna River (Wien River) which was forced underground during the time of

Franz Joseph, when the sewer system was built. Since then, the sewers have served as a backdrop for movies and music videos, the most famous of which is the finale of Orson Welles's *The Third Man*.

First, you'll don your provided hard hat with flashlight, then follow the sewer workers down into the Viennese underworld. You'll learn what it's like to work in the sewers—from the 13-pound steel-cap boots worn by sewer workers to pranks played on newcomers. You'll also watch a surreal screening of *The Third Man* projected on the wall right where the memorable scene was shot. You'll also get a chance to see the underground river before resurfacing. Wear sensible shoes, and don't panic if you see a sewer rat on your subterranean journey. Disinfectant is provided when you return to the surface. (You won't

which are graphically sexual in nature, may not have much in common. But what united these artists was a manifesto of artistic freedom and a hunger for modernity and new ideas—like the psychoanalytic writings of Sigmund Freud, who was a contemporary of the artists. Otto Wagner's thirst for modernity and modern application of architecture fit into the philosophy of the Secession as well.

Here's a summary of some of the best work that captures the spirit of the Secession in Vienna:

- **The Secession Building:** Joseph Maria Olbrich's daring building, nicknamed the "Golden Cabbage" when it was built, became an architectural manifesto for the movement, and a space for artists who chose to break away from the status quo to exhibit.

- **The *Beethoven Frieze*:** Located in the Secession, Klimt's *Beethoven Frieze* captures the spirit of the Secession by embodying the idea of the Gesamtkunstwerk, a total artistic environment. For the Secessionists, it was not only the visual arts that were reflected in the movement, but also music. For example, at the launch of the exhibition where the piece was presented, Gustav Mahler adapted Beethoven's *Ninth Symphony*. You may not hear Mahler play in the background when you visit the work, but you can still see the Gesamtkunstwerk, like the real gems incorporated into the fresco details.

- **The Stadtbahn Pavilions:** Otto Wagner's Stadtbahn Pavilions embrace the modern spirit of the Secession by incorporating technology with aesthetics. Wagner did not only break from classical art in form, but also sought functionality in his art with his metro line and its gilded pavilions. The pavilions rely on three colors—green, gold, and white—in a similar style to the lithographs by Kolo Moser and other contemporaries, showing a continued exchange between the artists.

- **Egon Schiele's Self Portrait:** If any artist broke away from the respected forms of classical art, it was Egon Schiele, whose jagged lines and intense colors captured the Expressionist form of art that rose up after the Secessionist movement. Schiele was a contemporary of Klimt, Moser, and Wagner, and his intense, eroticized self-portrait on display at the Leopold Museum captures the movement's rebellious spirit.

really get dirty, but I wouldn't dress for the opera before going on this tour.)

In 2020, there were no tours running due to the COVID-19 pandemic, however, there are plans to run again from May 2021. Check the website first.

Third Man Museum

Preßgasse 25; tel. 01/586-4872; www.3mpc.net; Sat 2-6pm; €9.50; U4: Kettenbrückengasse

Even if you're not a movie buff, it's worth visiting this eccentric and special museum to learn more about the strange and turbulent time in Vienna in which *The Third Man* with Orson Welles was set, when the black market was thriving and people lived in a city with borders.

The museum's collection is a passion project by married couple Gerhard and Karin, who put the museum together without outside help. The museum's collection started in 1997 and keeps growing. Today, it spans three separate buildings.

In the first building, you're submerged in an eccentric collection of movie memorabilia, photographs and newspaper cutouts and stories of both the famous and local actors in the film. You'll get a glimpse of rare items like pages of the original script.

In the second building, you can watch two minutes of the film, via a projector from 1936. The iconic zither theme by Anton Karas gets its own dedication in a small room with pictures from the tavern the musician played in.

The third building is a museum of Vienna just before and after World War II, with rare photos of the devastation the city endured, as well as memorabilia, including soldiers'

uniforms and newspaper clippings from the time Vienna was partitioned into American, British, French, and Russian zones.

The museum was at risk from closure due to COVID-19, but after a crowdfunding initiative, the museum has kept its doors open to date. Check their website before visiting.

Haus des Meeres

Fritz-Grünbaum-Platz 1; tel. 01/587-1417;
www.haus-des-meeres.at; daily 9am-8pm; €20;
U3: Neubaugasse

If you've ever wanted to visit an aquarium and a zoo in a former Nazi Flak Tower (an anti-aircraft tower), now is your chance. The Haus des Meeres ("House of the Sea") spans more than 10 floors of a repurposed concrete structure built by the Nazis, where each floor is occupied by aquarium tanks filled with curious marine life, from luminescent jellyfish and sea horses to hammerhead sharks and tropical fish. Various sections—some taking up a whole floor, some only a room or two—represent different regions of the world. There are more than 10,000 animals in this vertical zoo, including birds, primates, and reptiles as well as fish and other water-dwellers.

Glass extensions on the north-eastern and south-western side of the concrete flak tower create a hanging greenhouse. You'll find the crocodile park on the north-eastern side and a tropical hot house on the south-western one. Take care in the latter not to put your hand in exotic bird droppings, as superb glossy-starlings and eastern yellow-billed hornbills fly freely in this suspended greenhouse. You'll also spot a few curious primates, like Goeldi's marmosets and white faced sakis, clambering about the tropical vegetation.

A couple rooms on the 10th floor function as a mini-museum to the building's history as a Flak Tower, with items like radios, typewriters, helmets and everyday items used by the personnel working in the tower during WWII dotting the dark concrete room. And don't miss the stunning rooftop terrace, with amazing views over downtown Vienna.

Despite there being a lot of stairs, Haus des Meeres is accessible with elevators leading to every floor.

KARLSPLATZ AND THE BELVEDERE PALACE AREA
Stadtbahn Pavilions

Karlsplatz; U1, U2, U4: Karlsplatz

Otto Wagner left his mark on Vienna. The Jugendstil (the German word for art nouveau) artist fused modern function and architecture to create buildings for a new age—among them his metro stations. The twin Stadtbahn Pavilions on Karlsplatz are his most beautiful, with floral designs enhanced by gold trim on white marble that complements the apple green of the Stadtbahn (the tram or metro railway). One pavilion has reopened as a small museum, the **Otto Wagner Pavilion Karlsplatz** (Karlsplatz; www.wienmuseum. at; Tue-Sun 10am-1pm and 2pm-6pm Aug-Oct; €5) devoted to Wagner's principle works, like the gold-domed Kirche am Steinhof in the hills above Vienna. The building opposite is a café and a club, the **Café Restaurant Karl-Otto im Otto Wagner Pavilion** (tel. 01/505-9904; 9am-4am) and **Club U** (tel. 01/505-9904; 10pm-4am).

Karlskirche

Karlsplatz; www.karlskirche.at; Mon-Sat 9am-6pm,
Sun midday-7pm; €8; U1, U2, U4: Karlsplatz

Rising above Karlsplatz, this Baroque church, built between 1716 and 1736, is one of Vienna's most beautiful churches and one of the most famous landmarks in the city. You can take an elevator up to the dome ceiling, which towers at over 70 meters (230 ft). Inside, you'll get a close-up of the beautiful frescoes of the Glory of St. Charles Borromeo (the leading figure of the counter-reformation against the Protestant Reformation), along with an abundant collection of fleshy cherubs by Johann Michael Rottmayr. The lift to

1: staircase in Vienna State Opera House
2: Karlskirche, perched on Karlsplatz **3:** interesting shopping and dining at the Naschmarkt

Karlsplatz and the Belvedere Palace Area

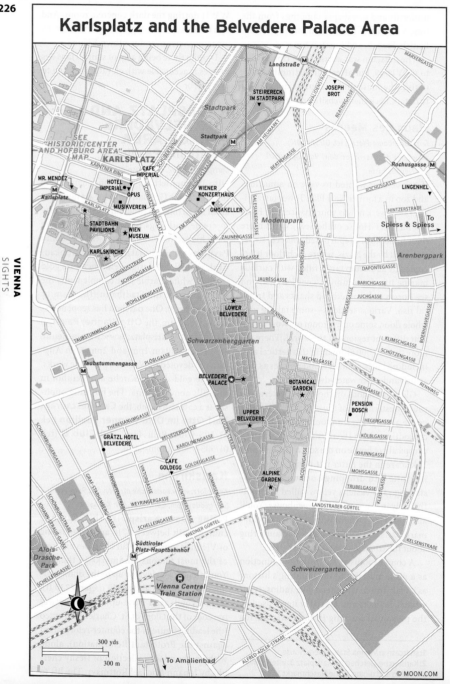

© MOON.COM

the dome is included in the admission price, but expect to queue for as long as an hour. To avoid lines, come as soon as the church opens its doors.

Even if you don't go inside, make sure you stop and admire Karlskirche from the outside (including the enormous twin columns that were modeled on Trajan's Column in Rome). Look closely at these columns to see scenes from the life of Charles Borromeo, from whom the church gets its name, and who helped plague victims in Italy.

★ Belvedere Palace

Prinz Eugen-straße 27; tel. 01/795-570; www.belvedere.at; daily 10am-6pm; €16 for Unteres Belvedere; tram D: Schloss Belvedere, S1, S2, S3, S4 tram 1, 18, O: Wien Quartier Belvedere

The Belvedere Palace was designed by Johann Lukas von Hildebrandt as the summer residence for Prince Eugene of Savoy, the general of the Imperial Army, who beat back the Turks at the beginning of the 18th century. It is one of the most spectacular examples of Baroque architecture you can explore.

The Belvedere offers the main palace building, and state and ceremonial rooms that serve as spaces for fine art, including Klimt's famous piece *The Kiss*. You need at least half a day to really get the most out of both. The museum is always busy, but if you arrive when it opens or after 4pm in the afternoon (especially on weekdays), the crowds thin out slightly. Buying tickets online also can help cut down time spent in line.

You can rent audio guides (€6) for both parts of the museums, but if you want the VIP treatment, sign up for one of their themed tours for a flat rate of €75 (not including admission price) for groups up to 10. Note that the ticket office is not in the palace, but in an outbuilding to the west, just after the gate from Prinz Eugen Straße (it is signposted, so just follow the arrows). There is also a ticket office in the Lower Belvedere from Rennweg (the entrance here is also marked).

LOWER BELVEDERE
(Unteres Belvedere)

Lower Belvedere was built in the early 1700s and lies at the northern end of the garden, at the bottom of the slope. The U-shaped palace's grand ceremonial salons and state apartments, along with the adjoining buildings, the former horse stables, and the Orangerie (a building once used to store citrus and other exotic plants in the winter), are home to the museum's temporary collections and a permanent collection of Gothic art.

As you approach the museum from Upper Belvedere, you'll find the entrance on the western side of the palace, which leads into the Hall of Grotesques, an entrance hall decorated with allegorical figures from Greco-Roman mythology. Turn right, and this will take you into the main wings of the former residential palace, now home to temporary exhibitions across its 14 rooms, with the Marble Hall, a grand hall clad in marble friezes and frescoes, at the center of the palace. However, if you go straight ahead in the Hall of Grotesques, this takes you through the lavish ceremonial rooms, first into the Marble Gallery, an ornamental hall lined with marble statues, mirrors, and carved stuccos, and then into the spectacular Golden Cabinet, originally a conversation room later clad out all in gold and mirrors. Beyond the Golden Cabinet a covered walkway will lead you to the Orangerie and the stables, the latter of which now hold an exquisite collection of 150 medieval paintings, sculptures, and triptychs. If you want to visit the stables, make sure arrive between 10am and noon when it is open. The Orangerie, on the other hand, also hosts temporary exhibitions in a large hall.

Although the Lower Belvedere is worth visiting for the spectacular Marble Hall, Marble Gallery, and Golden Cabinet, check the program for the exhibitions that are on to see if these would be of interest to you. If you plan to visit the Lower Belvedere, you could easily spend one to two hours.

1

2

3

At the time of updating, the Lower Belvedere was closed for renovations until summer 2021.

UPPER BELVEDERE
(Oberes Belvedere)

Whereas the Lower Belvedere was meant as a residence, Prince Eugene of Savoy built the impressive Upper Belvedere largely for show and ceremonial purposes. This is where you'll find the palace's permanent art collection chronicling the history of art from medieval times to the early 20th century.

The museum's exhibitions spread out over the three palatial floors. The entrance on the ground floor opens into the Sala Terrena, a brilliant white lobby decorated with stucco and columns sculpted into muscular Atlas figures that appear to be holding up the ceiling. Turn right at the entrance and you enter Carlone Hall in the west wing, covered entirely with extravagant Baroque frescoes. It was originally used in the hot summer months for guests to stay cool. From the Carlone Hall, there are four halls filled with medieval art. And on the other side of the Sala Terrena, in the east wing, you'll find rooms for temporary exhibitions and two rooms devoted to the history of the palace.

Take the Grand Staircase to the first floor (there are also lifts available on both sides of the staircase), which leads into the Marble Hall at the top. This magnificent antechamber occupies two stories, resplendent in reddish marble, gold leaf accents, dangling crystal chandeliers, and elaborate frescoes depicting the glorious Prince Eugene as the Greek god Apollo. In the west wing, the rooms are filled with excellent Baroque paintings and sculptures that glorify the Habsburg legend. The east wing on the first floor offers an impressive collection of Viennese art from the 1900s.

The star of the show is Klimt's *The Kiss.* You'll also find Klimt's *Judith*, a seductive golden portrait rich with detail. Works by contemporaries like Schiele, Kokoschka, and Moser also line the grand walls, and explore themes like psychoanalysis and mortality.

On the second floor, the four rooms open in the west wing have some nice Biedermeier landscapes, impressionist works from Monet and Degas, and in the four rooms in the east wing there is also a great collection of post-World War I art, with works from the expressionist movement.

A good time to visit the Upper Belvedere is first thing in the morning before the midday crowds hit, or toward the end of the day.

GARDENS

If you find you're oversaturated with art, take a break in the beautiful gardens.

The name Belvedere means "beautiful view." When you take a stroll through the landscaped Baroque gardens, you'll see statues inspired by Greek mythology, along with winged, voluptuous Sphynxes, sculpted hedges, ornate parterres (flat stretches of garden populated with ornate flower beds), and cascading fountains. The garden links the Upper and Lower Belvedere palaces.

Entry to the garden is free. On the southern end, you can walk into the neighboring **Botanical Garden** (Rennweg 14; www.botanik.univie.ac.at; daily from 10am-1 hr before dusk; free admission) and the **Alpine Garden** (Prinz Eugen Straße 27; www.bundesgaerten.at; Mar-Aug 10am-6pm; €4) to the east of the garden walls.

PRATER AND AROUND
Hundertwasserhaus

Hundertwasserhaus Kegelgasse 37-39; U3, U4: Landstraße

Architect Hundertwasser built this house in the 1980s, drawing inspiration from his love of color, curved lines and incorporating nature. A private residence, the building is not open to the public, but you could spend hours looking at the façade, snapping photos, or simply admiring the details from the bench opposite. This building is a kaleidoscope of

---

1: gardens of the Belvedere Palace **2:** Klimt's *The Kiss* is the highlight of the Belvedere Palace. **3:** Belvedere Palace

Prater and Around

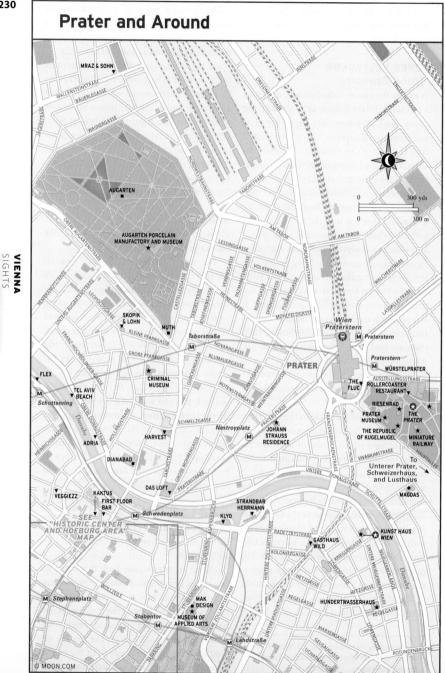

MRAZ & SOHN

WALLENSTEINSTRASSE
BAUERLEGASSE
JÄGERSTRASSE
WASNERGASSE

NORDWESTBAHNSTRASSE

DRESDNER STRASSE

INNSTRASSE

TABORSTRASSE

ENGERTHSTRASSE

AUGARTEN

TABORSTRASSE

0   300 yds
0   300 m

OBERE AUGARTENSTRASSE

AUGARTEN PORCELAIN
MANUFACTORY AND MUSEUM

AM TABOR

LESSINGGASSE

VOLKERTSTRASSE

NORDBAHNSTRASSE

AM TABOR

WALCHERSTRASSE

LASSALLESTRASSE

REMBRANDTSTRASSE
LEOPOLDGASSE
UNTERE AUGARTENSTRASSE
FRANZ-HOCHEDLINGER-GASSE

VERDINGASSE
PAZMANITENGASSE
HEINESTRASSE
RUEPPGASSE
SPRINGERGASSE
FUGBACHGASSE
MÜHLFELDGASSE

CASTELLEZGASSE
JOSEFINENGASSE
TABORSTRASSE

SKOPIK
& LOHN
MUTH
KLEINE PFARRGASSE

Taborstraße

NOVARAGASSE
BLUMAUERGASSE

Wien
Praterstern

Praterstern

FLEX

TEL AVIV
BEACH

Schottenring

HEINRICHSGASSE

Donaukanal

OBERE DONAUSTRASSE

CRIMINAL
MUSEUM

GROBE PFARRGASSE

GLOCKENGASSE

ROTENSTERNGASSE

TRAUGASSE

WEINTRAUBENGASSE

PRATER

PRATERSTRASSE

FRANZENSBRÜCKENSTRASSE

Praterstern
WÜRSTELPRATER

AUSSTELLUNGSSTRASSE
THE
FLUC
ROLLERCOASTER
RESTAURANT

RIESENRAD

PRATER
MUSEUM
THE REPUBLIC
OF KUGELMUGEL

THE
PRATER

MINIATURE
RAILWAY

HOLLANDSTRASSE

ADRIA

DIANABAD

HARVEST

SCHMELZGASSE

GROBE MOHRENGASSE
TABORSTRASSE
PRATERSTRASSE

Nestroyplatz

JOHANN
STRAUSS
RESIDENCE

VIVARIUMSTRASSE

UNTERE DONAUSTRASSE

SCHÜTTELSTRASSE

HAUPTALLEE

To
Unterer Prater,
Schweizerhaus,
and Lusthaus

MAGDAS

VEGGIEZZ

KAKTUS
FIRST FLOOR
BAR

DAS LOFT

Schwedenplatz

STRANDBAR
HERRMANN

KLYO

STUBENRING
ASPERNBRÜCKE
UNTERE VIADUKTSTRASSE

RADETZKYSTRASSE

ZOLLAMTSSTRASSE

KOLONITZGASSE

GASTHAUS
WILD

HETZGASSE

KRIEGERGASSE
LÖWENGASSE
HETZGASSE

UNTERE WEIBGERBERSTRASSE

WEIBGERBERLÄNDE

HAUPTALLEE

KUNST HAUS
WIEN

Donau

SEE
"HISTORIC CENTER
AND HOFBURG AREA"
MAP

WOLLZEILE

Stephansplatz

Stubentor

MAK
DESIGN
MUSEUM OF
APPLIED ARTS

VORDERE ZOLLAMTSSTRASSE

Landstraße

KEGELGASSE

MARXERGASSE

GEUSAUGASSE

UCHATIUSGASSE

HUNDERTWASSERHAUS

KEGELGASSE

LÖWENGASSE

ROTUNDENBRÜCKE

PARKING

© MOON.COM

colors, lines and some 200 trees and shrubs sprouting from the roof, terraces, alcoves, and anywhere else plants can grow.

You can drop by the **Kunst und Cafe coffeehouse** (daily 10am-6pm) on the ground floor for a free short film about the architect shown continuously on a loop or head to **Hundertwasser Village** (a former tire workshop turned into a shopping quarter that Hundertwasser also designed) which now houses a shopping center with bars and souvenir shops. If you need a public toilet, the "Public Toilet of Modern Art" is on display with its colorful mosaics and ceramics, and is a good way to spend any loose change.

★ Kunst Haus Wien

Untere Weissgerberstraße 13; tel. 01/712-049512;
www.kunsthauswien.com; daily 10am-6pm;
€12; U3, U4: Landstraße

If you're hungry for more Hundertwasser, take the five-minute walk from the Hundertwasserhaus to the Kunst Haus Wien, a museum set in one of his apartment blocks that scales three floors. Not only do you get a peek inside one of his buildings, with undulating floors and rooms propped up by colorful columns in glazed ceramics, but you can see the largest permanent collection of Hundertwasser's paintings. His style emulates his architecture, with irregular, organic forms playing with color and texture (you'll see his use of silver and gold foil). Hundertwasser established the museum in a 19th-century building he reconstructed in the 1990s. It's one of the top places to visit in Vienna, particularly if you love modern art and architecture. There are also temporary photography exhibitions held on the top floor. Expect to spend between an hour to two hours here.

★ The Prater

Prater; tel. 01/728-0516; www.prater.at;
open 24 hours; free; U1, U2: Praterstern

The Prater is Vienna's largest park, stretching 60 square kilometers (about 40 sq mi). The Prater is all about fun, whether that means being thrown about like laundry in a centrifuge on one of the rides at the Würstelprater or having a beer at Schweizerhaus, a breezy biergarten. Joggers run along the tree-lined Hauptallee, the main promenade that cuts through the Prater, and locals regularly relax in the meadows and grassy patches away from the mayhem of the city. There is also a hiking trail that will take you through the woods and wilder parts of the green Prater.

The Prater has been a place of pleasure for more than 200 years, declared as a place for public enjoyment in 1766—first as a retreat, but in true Viennese fashion, it has turned into a place populated by taverns, cafés, swings, carousels, and the huge Ferris wheel (the iconic Riesenrad) that dominated the skyline in the 19th century.

WÜRSTELPRATER

Free; open 24 hours

At the northern end of Prater lies this retro amusement park, the Würstelprater, which is one of the city's most iconic spots. There are some 250 attractions here, including roller coasters, ghost trains, and bumper cars. Buy your ticket for rides (usually €1.50-10) at the ride booth. You can also invest in a **Prater Highlights Card** for €45 that will get you access to the 20 most famous attractions, you can buy it online (www.praterhighlights.at; note the site is only in German) or at the information office at the entrance (daily 10:30am-10pm Mar-Oct).

Access to the Würstelprater grounds is free and the park itself is open 24 hours, but most attractions operate from 10am-midnight or 1am.

As you walk around, notice the architecture, which has an old-world carnival feel, with painted statues, cardboard cutouts, and Jugendstil buildings. You may also want to ride on the nostalgic pastel-hued **Luftikus Carousel** that has exhausted riders for decades (don't worry, it's been restored with state-of-the-art technology). Or you may want to ride on the 115-meter (380-ft) tall **Praterturm** that will whisk you around at

60 kilometers per hour (38 mph) for a huge adrenaline rush (don't eat before riding).

RIESENRAD

Prater 90; tel. 01/729-5430; www.wienerriesenrad. com; Sun-Thu 10am-8pm, Fri-Sat 10am-10pm, winter has shorter hours, can be closed in Jan; €12

Rising above the Prater over 200 feet (60 m), the Riesenrad, or Giant Ferris Wheel, is a symbol of the city. (You may have seen it in movies like Orson Welles' *The Third Man* or in *Before Sunrise*). It's absolutely worth taking a ride on this 110-year-old Ferris wheel (unless you have a fear or heights or enclosed spaces!).

Once you've bought your ticket, you enter a circular room enclosed by a wall of mirrors and filled with vintage carriages. Each carriage features insights into Vienna's history, including a model of the Prater. From here, exit through a door (which may take you a moment to find) and get in line to board the red carriage, which fits around 15 people. Although the Riesenrad is the gentlest of the rides in the Prater, its height can induce vertigo (you can always sit down on the wooden bench inside the carriage if it gets too much.) The wheel moves incredibly slowly and is stable, and you are secure inside. The ride takes approximately 20 minutes. The view from the top is worth it: You'll see most of the city's most prominent landmarks from above, like St. Stephen's Cathedral, and also beyond to the Danube and the hills surrounding Vienna.

The Riesenrad has been part of the cityscape since 1897 (marking the 50th year of Emperor Franz Joseph's rule). It can also be booked for special events, like dinners, weddings or breakfasts. Weekday mornings and evenings after 9pm are generally quiet, but if you come during the weekend, especially in the afternoon, expect queues.

PRATER MUSEUM

Oswald-Thomas-Platz 1 (inside the Planetarium); tel. 01/726-7683; www.wienmuseum.at; Fri-Sun 10am-1pm and 2pm-6pm; €5

Theater and circus beat at the heart of the Prater, and this museum, set in the same building as the planetarium, depicts the evolution into the amusement park we see today. Highlights include the dragon from the grotto railway from the 1950s, the tall centerpiece from a 19th-century merry-go-round, coin-operated machines from the early 1900s, and a somewhat creepy collection of ventriloquist dummies and puppets. The park's dark history is on display as well, with former human zoos depicted in black and white photographs from the early 1900s, along with pictures and objects, such as tiny shoes, from little people who once resided in the "Lilliputian cities" within the Prater and held theater performances. It's worth the visit to this one-room museum for the historical context.

UNTERER PRATER

Away from the bright lights of the amusement park, the Unterer Prater relaxes into grassy meadows, and woodlands filled with slender poplar and chestnut trees and lakes. You'll spot families and groups of friends picnicking away from the chaos of the city in the summer, along with joggers, cyclists, and in-line skaters along the 4.3-kilometer-long (2-mi-long) Hauptallee, which begins up by the Praterstern and ends at the Lusthaus, a 16th-century hunting lodge that's now a restaurant set next to a golf course and a riding school. Nature lovers should hike toward the water meadow at Freudenau at the southern end of the Prater on the Stadtwanderweg 9 hiking trail, or relax and stroll by the water at the Heustadlwasser, a channel-like lake that once linked up with the Danube at the middle of the Hauptallee.

1: Hundertwasserhaus 2: Danube Canal 3: The Narrenturm was once an asylum that is now a museum of pathology. 4: Riesenrad, the giant Ferris wheel in the Prater

MINIATURE RAILWAY

Prater 99; tel. 01/726-8236; www.liliputbahn.com; daily 10am-5pm Oct and Mar, 10am-6pm Apr and Sep, 10am-7pm May and Jun, 10am-8pm Jul and Aug; €5

This tiny railway trundles through the Prater for 4 kilometers (2.5 mi), taking you on a 20-minute roundtrip from the foot of the Riesenrad to the edge of the Prater, and to the Hauptallee—a tree-lined boulevard that is the closest the Prater has to a main road. The train even plunges into woodland before making its turn and bringing you back to the amusement park. The railway is great fun for the kids, and a vertigo-free alternative to the Giant Ferris Wheel. Get your tickets from the kiosk by the train platform before getting on.

THE REPUBLIC OF KUGELMUGEL

Antifaschismus Platz; www.kugelmugel.at

While you're in the Prater, you'll want to stop by the world's smallest micronation, the Republic of Kugelmugel, a tiny 35-square-yard republic created by Edwin Lipburger following a dispute with the Austrian government in 1984 after he built his house without a permit. (He almost went to jail for refusing to pay taxes and for printing his own stamps.) The republic is essentially a spherical house that looks like something from a 1960s UFO film. It's surrounded by a barbed border, so unless there is an exhibition on, you won't be able to cross.

The Republic of Kugelmugel wasn't always in the Prater, making it one of the few mobile nations. Stop by while you're in the Prater and see if you can get a glimpse inside this surreal nation (which is mostly made up of artists working inside the spherical house). The republic now holds 650 non-resident Kugelmugel citizens.

Johann Strauss Residence

Praterstraße 54; tel. 01/214-0121; www.wienmuseum.at; Tue-Sun 10am-1pm and 2pm-6pm; €5; U2: Taborstraße

Johann Strauss immortalized the Danube River (a notable natural feature in the neighborhood of Leopoldstadt, where this residence is located) in his waltz *The Blue Danube*. The compact museum occupies the seven rooms once part of the original apartment (a section of the Strauss apartment lies in a private residence). The museum holds some of the composer's original scores, with handwritten notes like, "Please forgive the bad and untidy handwriting, I had to finish this off in a few minutes," scribbled in the margins. Make sure you look over the caricatures, not only those of the composer but by the composer himself, who drew them as a way to relax.

Criminal Museum

Große Sperlgasse 24; tel. 06/64-300-6577; http:// wien.kriminalmuseum.at; Thu-Sun 10am-5pm; €8 including the short guide in English; U2: Taborstraße

This morbid collection of criminal documents, skeletons, and torture equipment resides in a 17th-century town house with a labyrinth-like interior winding through 15 rooms and corridors. The museum details the evolution of Vienna's justice system from the 17th century, when a dismembered corpse was found close to today's museum, up to postwar Vienna. The museum covers forensics in the 19th century, attempted assassinations on the Emperor Franz Joseph I, and photographic documentation of gruesome crimes. There are plenty of skulls, a mummified head, and uncensored photographic evidence. Anyone fascinated with the history of crime could easily spend hours perusing old newspaper cuttings, murder weapons and vintage forensic tools. (Note: This museum is not appropriate for children.)

Augarten Porcelain Manufactory and Museum

Obere Augartenstraße 1; tel. 06/1-211-24-200; www.augarten.com; Mon-Sat 11am-5pm; €7; U2: Taborstraße

Porcelain production began in the Augarten in 1718, making this factory (located in an 18th-century former imperial pleasure palace) the second oldest of its kind in Europe. The museum takes you through the history of porcelain and its various uses—in excessively ornamented rococo pieces up through modern times, as designers draw inspiration from the simple lines of the 1920s. The exhibition includes the original kilns (no longer in use) used to make porcelain. If you're interested to learn more about how quartz, white kaolin, feldspar can be molded, cast and luted into the creations you'll see in the exhibition and the shop, you can take an hour-long tour, only available upon request (you can book by calling the number above or by emailing augarten@augarten.at). Make sure you check out the shop if you want to take some unique porcelain pieces, such dishes, cups, dining sets, and figurines home with you.

Museum of Applied Arts

Stubenring 5; tel. 01/711-360; www.mak.at;
Tue 10am-9pm, Wed-Sun 10am-6pm; €14; U3:
Stubentor, S1, S2, S3, S4: Wien Mitte-Landstraße,
U3, U4: Landstraße, tram 2, D: Stubentor

It's worth stepping inside the Museum of Applied Arts for the architecture alone—the huge central courtyard looks like a Roman palace. You'll want to stay for the exhibits delving into Vienna's history with arts and crafts. This museum is more than just a collection of pretty objects; it will leave you thinking about how you perceive design and its function.

The museum spreads over three floors. The ground floor displays rococo style furniture, with the porcelain room originally in the Palais Dubsky as the highlight. In the 1700s, it became fashionable to decorate rooms as "porcelain cabinets," such as this room, with cups and vases set into the wall as decoration. This porcelain room, once located in Brno during the 1740s, has been reconstructed inside a block in the middle of the museum hall with golden damask upholstery, rococo furniture and porcelain accents. There is also an exquisite collection of art from East Asia, porcelain from China, Korea,

and Japan, as well as carpets from the Middle East. On the other side of the hall you'll find furniture from the Biedermeier era, as well as wooden art nouveau chairs and benches. The Jugendstil creations are backlit behind a white screen, which really brings out their curved forms.

For more art nouveau, head up to the first floor, where you'll see examples of Viennese pieces along with contemporary pieces from France, Belgium, Hungary, as well as ceramics influenced by motifs drawn from Japanese art, which was fashionable at the turn of the 20th century.

The basement charts the history of design across time and cultures. Many displays are tactile, allowing you to touch and feel, like the replica of the world's first fitted kitchen—the Frankfurter Küche—designed by Austria's first female student of architecture, Margarete Schütte-Lihotzky. There are also documentaries playing on a loop with English subtitles, and creative installations about the future of design and how it will affect how we eat, cook, and sit as we progress into the digital age.

ALSERGRUND AND JOSEFSTADT
Vienna City Hall
(Rathaus)

Rathausplatz 1; www.wien.gv.at; guided tours take
place Mon, Wed, Fri 1pm; U2: Rathaus, U2, U3:
Volkstheater, tram 1, 71, D: Rathausplatz/Burgtheater

The Rathaus rises up above the Ringstraße in a dramatic architectural symphony of spires and Gothic arches. This City Hall was built in 1883 by Friedrich von Schmidt in the neo-Gothic style and is one of the Ringstraße's finest buildings. It still functions as an official seat of the mayor and houses the provincial government. You can take tours inside on Mondays, Wednesdays and Fridays for free in German (audio guides are available in English for no extra cost), but you're better off saving the time and just appreciating the building from the outside when you're strolling past.

Alsergrund and Josefstadt

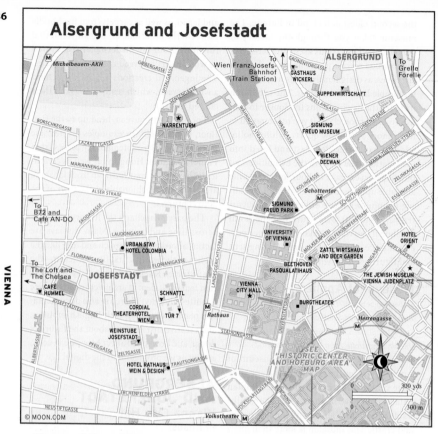

Sigmund Freud Museum

Berggasse 19; tel. 01/319-1596; www.freud-museum.
at; Thu-Tue 10am-6pm, Wed 10am-9pm; €14; U2:
Schottentor, tram 1, D: Schlickgasse

Whether or not you agree with his theories in psychoanalysis, Sigmund Freud's theories on symbols, dreams and sexuality are deeply woven into the cultural fabric of Vienna—and the world, so if you're in Vienna, it's worth paying a visit to his former home, the epicenter of his most famous theories, and of course, that infamous couch. The museum occupies three floors of the building and reopened in the fall of 2020 following a renovation that opened even more rooms to the public (previously only the first floor was open to visitors). The ticket desk, café, and shop reside on the ground floor, where Freud's former

first surgery (on the right as you go up the stairs) is a space for conceptual art of a psychoanalytical nature. If you turn left, you'll find the former apartment where the "Father of Psychoanalysis" lived and practiced most of his life till he was forcefully exiled to Britain by the Nazis in 1938. This part of the museum spreads out across the first-floor apartment. Some of the rooms capture Freud's daily life, such as the cramped entrance hall where one of his iconic bronze ashtrays is on display, and his furnished waiting room. In the next room, you'll find a cabinet of antique curiosities in the corner, stacked with Greek and Egyptian statuettes, along with other archaeological relics. Freud's study and the rooms where Freud held consultations are presented more as an exhibition to his life and his work, with letters, notes and photographs along with first editions of his most famous books. Freud's youngest daughter, Anna Freud—also a noted psychoanalyst in her own right—helped put the museum together in the 1970s, and there is even a room dedicated to her.

The next floor up houses the Library of Psychoanalysis, with more than 40,000 works, including the Sigmund Freud archive. You can see a little bit about the history of the building—which were used by the Nazis to round up Jews before being deported to concentration camps—in the stairwell leading to the library.

You can spend a couple of hours in this curious museum, but if you'd like to delve deeper into Freud's world of psychoanalysis, email tours@freud-museum.at to book a tour for an extra €4 per person.

Narrenturm

Uni Campus, Spitalgasse 2; tel. 01/521-77606; www.nhm-wien.ac.at/narrenturm; Wed 10am-6pm; €8 entrance, an extra €4 for the tour; U2: Schottentor, tram 37, 38, 40, 41, 42: Sessengasse, tram 5, 33: Lazarettgasse

Looming above the former grounds of the Vienna General Hospital where Freud began his career, the Narrenturm, which translates as "the Fools Tower," is an imposing structure. It was built in 1784 and was Continental Europe's oldest insane asylum. Neither the Narrenturm nor the grounds surrounding it currently function as a hospital (in fact, the surrounding hospital buildings now make up the campus grounds for the University of Vienna). Today you'll find a pathological museum in the claustrophobic rooms and tight circular corridor of the infamous tower. The ground floor gives you an overview of the collection, a few musty apothecary cabinets, deformed baby skeletons, and some waxworks of skin diseases, but to get the gruesome details, make sure you register for the one hour-long tour in English (which runs depending on demand on the hour, so contact the museum to arrange a tour before).

The tour takes you to the normally closed first floor, where one of the medical students from the university guides you through the collection of waxworks graphically depicting diseases, skeletons of conjoined twins, and organs preserved in formaldehyde. This graphic collection was once intended to teach medical students about diseases in a time before color photography, with some pieces dating back to the 18th century. It's informative for anyone fascinated with pathology and medical history, but it is graphic, and may be upsetting for some.

Beethoven Pasqualatihaus

Mölker Bastei 8; tel. 01/535-8905; www.wienmuseum. at; Tue-Sun 10am-1pm and 2pm-6pm; €5; U2: Schottentor, tram 1, 71, D: Schottentor

The Beethoven Pasqualatihaus was once the composer's favorite residence. Its transformation into a museum began in the 1930s, when the Nazis expelled the Jewish family living in this residence and turned the apartment into a memorial to the composer in 1941. (Some members of that family, the Ecksteins, died in Auschwitz, while the children escaped to England in in 1938.)

The museum you see today was redesigned in the 1990s. The museum occupies an apartment on the fourth floor of the old townhouse perched on the former city wall that resembles a bastion. Beethoven loved living here and composed his only opera, *Fidelio*, in this house. You'll find a collection of scores handwritten by Beethoven, as well as his piano, and portraits of Beethoven and his family scattered around the six-room apartment. You can also sit down at one of the desks and put a pair of headphones on to listen to the composer's most famous work.

The Jewish Museum Vienna Judenplatz

Judenplatz 8; tel. 01/535-0431; www.jmw.at; Sun-Thu 10am-6pm, Fri 10am-5pm, closed Jewish Holidays; €12 combined ticket with Dorotheergasse Museum; U3: Herrengasse or U1, U3: Stephansplatz

The area surrounding Judenplatz was once the center of medieval Jewish life. Today, the only traces of the historic community are in

Schönbrunn Palace and Grounds

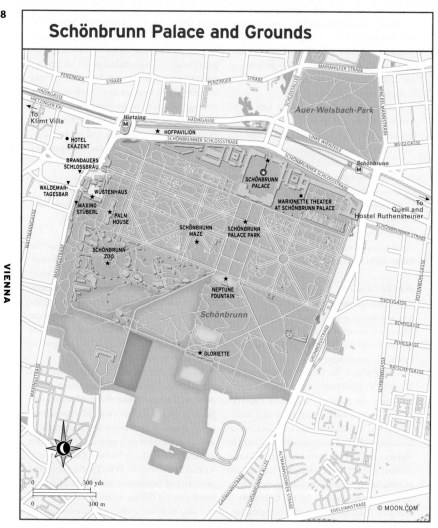

the ruins of the synagogue lying under the poignant Holocaust memorial by Rachel Whiteread. It's a concrete block formed in the shape of an inverted library, where the spines of the books are invisible—a metaphor for Jews as the "People of the Book"; each book symbolizes a Holocaust victim. Next to the memorial on the square lies the entrance to this branch of the Jewish Museum (the other branch is on Dorotheergasse). It focuses on Jewish life in the neighborhood in the 14th

century up to the Wiener Gesera in the early 15th century, when the Jews were expelled, and the quarter destroyed. The permanent exhibition, depicting relics and excavations dating back to the 14th century, is underground. One of the most poignant things you'll see are the ruins of the synagogue, accessible by a subterranean passage running under the square that takes you up inside the memorial.

A ticket to the museum, which can be used within four days of issue, includes both branches of the Jewish Museum. Although the Jewish Museum in Judenplatz is quite small, most travelers visit it in conjunction with the Jewish Museum on Dorotheergasse, which is a 10-minute walk away.

SCHÖNBRUNN PALACE AND GROUNDS
★ Schönbrunn Palace

Schönbrunner Schloßstraße; tel. 01/811-13-239; www. schoenbrunn.at; daily 9:30am-5pm; €18-22; U4: Schönbrunn, tram 10, 52, 60 Schloss Schönbrunn

The Hofburg may have been the permanent home of the Habsburgs, but the imperial family preferred to summer farther out in the leafy suburbs in the brilliant yellow Schönbrunn Palace, with 1,441 rooms—only 40 of which can be visited.

This palace is the centerpiece of Habsburg grandeur. Most of the rooms are rococo. Some are clad with porcelain, others are inspired by ancient Chinese art, and still others feature original Indian and embedded Persian miniatures. Most of the palace dates back to the 18th century, and it became the heart of court life during Maria Theresa's reign. The stylistic influences of the different eras of the Habsburg monarchy are clear as you wander through its maze of rooms.

There are two ways to visit the palace. The self-guided **Imperial Tour** (€18; 30-40 minutes) will guide you through 22 rooms, which include the state rooms and Sisi and Franz Joseph's apartments. The **Grand Tour** (€22; 50-60 minutes) takes you through 40 rooms, with some of the older apartments dating back to Maria Theresa's reign, and is self-guided with an audio guide. Although the Palace itself is one of Vienna's wonders, you'll want to visit the gardens that surround it with lush vegetation, secret nooks, and amazing views over the palace. I recommend a **Classic Pass** (€28.50), which not only gets you on the Grand Tour but includes the Orangerie, Privy Garden, Gloriette, and Maze.

This is one of Austria's most visited sites (with good reason) so plan your visit carefully. Buy your ticket online to skip the long lines in high season. A good tip is to get there early on a weekday, especially in the summer. Your ticket will come with an allocated time of entry, so get in immediately and explore the park afterward. Even with a ticket, you may need to wait a long time to enter the palace.

Schönbrunn Palace was the summer palace for the Habsburgs and is one of the top attractions in Vienna.

PALACE HIGHLIGHTS

Each room will leave you gawking at something, especially the **Great Gallery** occupying the center of the palace between the two wings, with its hall of mirrors, chandeliers, and gold underneath a colorful fresco depicting the Habsburgs and their lands. The 40-meter-long (131-ft-long) hall once served court functions like balls, banquets, and receptions.

Just off the Great Gallery on the south-facing side of the palace, take a peek into the **East Asian Cabinets,** two rooms flanking the Small Gallery (adjoining the Great Gallery) decked out in rococo grandeur, accented by lacquer panels and porcelain from China and Japan; these small, intimate rooms once served Maria Theresa's small gatherings, either for a game of cards or more discrete conferences.

Both of these can be visited on the Imperial Tour, but the **Millions Room** in the east wing can only be seen with the Grand Tour. This room is fitted with rich rosewood paneling.

Schönbrunn Palace Park (Schlosspark)

Schönbrunner Schlossstraße; tel. 01/811-130; www. schoenbrunn.at; daily 6:30am-5:30pm Nov-Feb, 6:30am-7pm Mar and Oct, 6:30am-8pm Apr-Sep; free; U4: Schönbrunn, Hietzing, tram 10, 52, 60: Schloss Schönbrunn, Hietzing

Even if you're on a budget, you should still pay a visit to Schönbrunn, if only for the magnificent park grounds surrounding the palace. Most of the park is free, but with the Classic Pass, you can also enter the Maze—a labyrinth of shrubs, fountains, statues and woodland paths that extend for about a 1.5 kilometers (about 1 mi) east to west, and just under one kilometer (just over half a mile) north to south. The best time to come is in the morning, when you'll generally only see joggers on the winding graveled pathways.

There's more than one way to enter the park. The Hietzinger Tor (Gate), the gateway on the western end of the park, is perhaps closest to the U-Bahn and tram networks, and brings you into the park around the Palm

House and the zoo. The gate on the southeastern end of the park on the hill brings you out to the Gloriette, a triumphal arch flanked by arcaded wings facing the palace from the hill opposite. There are also a couple of gateways around the palace itself.

The best way to visit the park is simply to explore and let it surprise you, but if you want some orientation, head over to the **Great Parterre,** a large open stretch that lies between Schönbrunn Palace and the Gloriette, surrounded by statues, high hedges and patches of flower-covered lawns that sometimes draw their designs from embroidery patterns. This is the backbone of the garden and one of the best places to get your bearings. Facing the Gloriette, you'll find the Columbary (a gorgeous aviary full of pigeons—which you can see from the outside for free—that looks like a gigantic lantern) and the Roman Ruins (fake, but beautiful). To the right are the maze, Palm House and the zoo. Straight ahead, you'll find the Neptune Fountain, one of the highlights of the garden, commissioned by Maria Theresa in the 1770s.

GLORIETTE

Facing Schönbrunn Palace, this elaborate pavilion crowns Schönbrunn Park. Built in 1775 during the reign of Emperor Joseph II and Maria Theresa, the Gloriette, with its triumphal arch flanked by arcaded wings, is renowned for its impressive views over the Habsburg summer palace and the surrounding grounds, and is a major focal point in the garden. It functioned as a dining and festival hall for the Habsburg monarchy, but today its café, **Cafe Gloriette** (tel. 01/879-1311; www. gloriette-café.at; daily 9am-sunset) is not only recommended, but reservations must be made four weeks in advance). You can traipse up the spiral staircase to the **viewing platform** (daily 10am-5pm Oct; €4.50).

SCHÖNBRUNN ZOO

Maxingstraße 13b; tel. 01/877-93940; www. zoovienna.at; daily 9am-4:30pm Nov-Jan, 9am-5pm Feb, 9am-5:30pm Mar and Oct (until end of daylight

An Imperial Metro Stop

Otto Wagner built his Stadtbahn for everyone, including the Emperor Franz Joseph I, whose imperial station can be found at Schönbrunn.

When you go to Schönbrunn Palace Park or the zoo and get off the metro at Hietzing, you can also check out Otto Wagner's **Hofpavilion** (Schönbrunner Schloßstraße; tel. 01/877-1571; www.wienmuseum.at; Sat-Sun 10am-1pm and 2pm-6pm Mar-Oct; €5, also run by the Wien Museum), which he made for the Emperor so he could use the innovative metro like everyone else. (Despite the plush carpets, wood paneling, and private entrance, Franz Joseph only attended the opening.) You can visit the pavilion from street level and take a look inside the lush waiting room and cloak rooms. The entrance down to the U-Bahn is, however, closed.

savings time), 9am-6:30pm Apr-Sep; €22; U4: Hietzing, tram 10, 52, 60: Hietzing
Schönbrunn Zoo (Tiergarten in German), is the oldest zoo in the world. It's also large, so expect to spend a few hours here.

The best way to enter is from the Hietzing Entrance, which will bring you right into the heart of the action. You'll have the koala house to your left and the giraffes to the right, and straight ahead is the Kaiser Pavilion, a café set inside a pavilion, which is a lunch stop fit for a Habsburg with its frescoed interior and gold leaf accents on dark wooden panels.

The animals here have plenty of room to roam. The Vienna Zoo celebrated the first panda babies born in a zoo in 2007, and celebrated twin baby pandas again in 2016. In 2020, the zoo added a new member to the family when their first baby koala was also born on the premises. Don't miss the tropical house, with tropical birds and bats. Head into the cave on the lower level if you're brave: The tiny bats there fly around your head so closely you can almost feel the flap of their wings.

Head into Franz Josef Land to catch a glimpse of the polar bears in the 5,500-square-meter (18,000-sq-ft) enclosure, or the playful penguins nearby. You can catch a little Dotto train at the Kaiser Pavilion from 10am to 6pm; the journey takes around 20 minutes and runs every 45 minutes, taking you from the pavilion to the Elephant House and the Tirolerhof, the exit gate on the southern end of the zoo near the Gloriette.

PALM HOUSE (Palmenhaus)

Schlosspark; tel. 01/877-5087; daily 9:30am-5pm Oct-Apr, 9:30am-6pm May-Sep; €7; U4: Hietzing, tram 10, 52, 60: Hietzing

The Palm House, the largest in continental Europe, built from elegant green iron beams and 45,000 panes of glass, is split into three pavilions to accommodate different climate zones that are connected by glass corridors: one representing Mediterranean climate, another with plants from Asia and New Zealand, and one dedicated to tropical and subtropical flora. The largest palm stands 23 meters (75 ft) high. You can also visit a jungle populated with blooming flowers, carnivorous plants, various smaller palms, and the world's largest water lily. Opposite, **Wüstenhaus** (the desert house; daily 9am-5pm Oct-Apr, 9am-6pm May-Sep; €7) resides in a less impressive building, but contains a broad range of arid specimens like cacti and other water-retentive plants.

SCHÖNBRUNN MAZE

Schlosspark; daily 10am-5pm; €6; U4: Hietzing, tram 10, 52, 60: Hietzing

This maze (two mazes, actually) of tall hedges sits on the site of an old maze from the 18th century. One of the two mazes is smaller and easier to navigate. The other takes you round dead ends and repetitive turns until you finally reach the middle where you can clamber up to the viewing platform to watch others fumbling their way through the labyrinth. When it's time to leave, you're given the option for the short way out (easier) or the long way, which will plunge you back into the heart of the maze. Depending on how good you are at getting in and out of mazes, you can expect to spend 30 to 40 minutes here.

NEPTUNE FOUNTAIN

At the heart of Schönbrunn Park between the palace and the Gloriette, the Neptune Fountain, carved out of white marble, rises up in all its Greco-Roman glory. The sea god Neptune with his trademark trident in hand towers over a cascade of water, with the sea goddess Thetis kneeling beside him, and a nymph reclining opposite, against the rocks. Below the main figures, Tritons, mythological creatures who are half fish and half men, frolic on the level below on backs of "sea horses" that pull Neptune's chariot across the sea. This impressive folly makes for great photo opportunities.

Klimt Villa

Feldmühlgasse 11; tel. 01/876-1125; www.klimtvilla.at; Thu-Sun 10am-6pm Apr-Dec; €10; tram 10: Verbindungsbahn

Take the tram 10 a few stops from Schönbrunn Park to Verbindungsbahn and you'll find yourself in an area populated with residential villas, one of which has a prominent connection to one of Vienna's most iconic artists. Klimt lived and worked in this single-story garden house. The wealthy family who bought the property after his passing built a whole new villa surrounding it. Fortunately, the original rooms Klimt resided in are still present.

Today, the villa is privately owned, and functions as a museum that mixes permanent installations with temporary exhibits. The most interesting parts are the two rooms where Klimt lived and worked, which the curators reconstructed by studying old photos. One is filled with Japanese art loved by the artist, while the other (Klimt's bedroom) is filled with copies of Klimt's original paintings. You can wander through his model room, leading into the bedroom, or through the garden that inspired his rose garden paintings—which the museum's owners replanted using the paintings for inspiration. If you're a Klimt fan, it's worth the trek out to this small, special museum dedicated to the final years of Klimt's life.

GREATER VIENNA
The Danube Tower
(Donauturm)

Donauturmstraße 4; www.donauturm.at; Mon-Fri 11:30am-11pm, Sat-Sun. 10am-11pm; €14.50; U6: Neue Donau

Rising out of Donaupark, the 250-meter (825-ft) Danube Tower, Donauturm, is the tallest building in the city. Ride the lift up to the viewing platform for 360-degree views look over the Danube and toward the old part of the city and the hills beyond. There is a revolving restaurant at the top serving Viennese food, and there's also a café.

The Danube Island
(Donauinsel)

www.wien.gv.at; open 24 hours; free; U1: Donauinsel

This slender island cleaves Vienna's Danube landscape in two and runs about 21 kilometers (13 mi). The Danube Island is a place of leisure, with cycling paths, not-so-sandy patches of Danube beaches, stretches of parkland hugging the waterfront, and also watersports, like boating. (Note that parts of the island marked FKK are nudist areas.)

Close to the U-Bahn stop, bars and restaurants cluster together in an area known as the **Sunken City,** with some bars set on little islands in the river accessible by jetties.

Death in Vienna

The Viennese have a unique fascination with death, and the idea of the "beautiful corpse," or **"Schöne Leich,"** celebrates the idea that death is a part of life. The concept of the Schöne Leich became immortalized in songs, poetry and in the funerary arts of Vienna in the mid-19th century. When the Austro-Hungarian Empire was at its height, Vienna experienced a large influx of wealth, and extravagant funerals became a status symbol and a festive occasion. Viennese funerals were a form of art and theater, with each funeral trying to surpass the next.

Some odd traditions also tie in with a fear of being buried alive, like attaching a bell-like device to the corpse inside the coffin so should the worst case happen, someone would be alerted.

The tradition of death lies all around Vienna, whether it's in the grand cemeteries of the city or the Habsburg resting places. Within literature, art, music, death is very much on the forefront of Viennese minds.

The Cemetery of the Nameless is a small cemetery dedicated to anonymous bodies pulled from the Danube.

Grab a cocktail and recline in a hammock or a deck chair among the palm trees or under the fairy lights once the sun goes down, and you'll feel like you're on holiday in a tropical resort. There is also a 0.5-hectare (1-ac) water playground that's free, and if you head toward Reichsbrücke, the main bridge that stretches to the island from the city center, you can find **Danube Jumping** (www.danubejumping.at; Mar and Oct 1pm-7pm; Apr 1pm-8pm, Sep 1pm-9pm, May-Aug 1pm-11pm, €3 per 10 minutes) a huge trampoline center that's fun for adults and kids alike. And in June, **Donauinselfest** usually takes over the island.

Vienna Central Cemetery
(Wiener Zentralfriedhof)

Simmeringer Hauptstraße 234; tel.
01/534-692-8405; www.friedhoefewien.at; daily
7am-6pm; free; tram 11, 71: Zentralfriedhof 2.Tor
Vienna's main cemetery captures the essence of Vienna and its former residents. It's one of Europe's largest cemeteries, with over 330,000 graves within its grounds that spread out over 250 hectares (620 ac). The resting places represent all religious denominations.

If you take tram 6 or 71 to Zentralfriedhof tor. 2 from the Simmering U-Bahn, you will arrive right at the main gate—the most impressive entrance. Since Austrians value their cakes as much as their respect for the dead, you'll find an **Oberlaa** café and patisserie just inside (Simmeringer Hauptstraße 232; tel. 01/767-1768-0; www.oberlaa-wien.at; daily 8am-4:30pm Jan-Feb and Nov-Dec, 8am-5:30pm Mar and Oct, 8am-6:30pm Apr-Sep), so you can grab a Melange and a Sachertorte before heading out to discover the graves.

As you take the main pathway to the **St. Charles Borromeo Church** (Karl-Borromäus-Kirche) at the heart of the cemetery, to the left there is an area dedicated to composers and musicians. This is where you'll find the graves of Beethoven, Johann Strauss (father and son), Brahms, Schubert, and a memorial grave to Mozart.

Don't skip the church. From the outside, it seems simple (white and square with a green dome), but inside, it's an art nouveau masterpiece. The cupola strikes you with its intense turquoise blue and painted gold stars. The white-walled interior of the church also has colorful stained glass and mosaic work.

Before leaving the cemetery, head over to the old part of the Jewish Cemetery in the northwest corner. This is the most atmospheric part of the cemetery, with romantic neoclassical mausoleums and overgrown tombstones inscribed in Hebrew.

If you want to get more context for the cemetery as you explore, download the Hearonymus-App (free from the App Store or Google Play) and get the audio guide (€7, or €5 on-site).

Funeral Museum

Simmeringer Hauptstraße 234; tel. 01/76-067; www.bestattungsmuseum.at; Mon-Fri 9am-4:30pm, Sat 10am-5:30pm Mar-Nov; €7; tram 11, 71: Zentralfriedhof 2.Tor

This quirky museum set just next to the main entrance inside the cemetery offers insight into Vienna's decadent traditions surrounding death. From the role of the undertaker to funerary haute couture for elegant widows, this interactive museum with touchscreen displays and audio collections of popular funeral songs spreads out in a 1,000-square-meter (3,200-sq-ft) basement underneath a chapel. There are all kinds morbid curiosities on display, from death masks to Joseph II's "foldaway coffin" (an unpopular idea proposed by the Emperor to recycle coffins) as well as photographic material depicting grand funerals for Vienna's bourgeoisie. All aspects of Viennese funerary life can be traced in this near blacked-out basement, showing an evolution of funerals and how they became a status symbol. You can expect to spend around 40 minutes to an hour in this museum.

Cemetery of the Nameless

Alberner Hafenzufahrtsstraße; tel. 06/60-600-3023; http://friedhof-der-namenlosen.at; daily 7am-5pm Nov-Feb, 7am-6pm Mar and Oct, 7am-7pm Apr-Sep, 7am-8pm May-Aug; free; bus 76A, 76B: Abner Hafen

It feels like a pilgrimage to get to this cemetery just off the Danube shore. The 76A bus puts you down next to industrial buildings and silos—and you may feel you're in the middle of nowhere. But take the path next to the bus stop and turn left at the train tracks and you'll see a signpost to the cemetery. There are around 100 graves here, marked by black iron crosses, some adorned with flowers, others with children's toys. Few have names, but most bear Namenlos, or nameless.

Even though the last burial here was in the 1940s, all the graves are lovingly tended with fresh flowers. Film buffs may recognize this moving cemetery from the movie *Before Sunrise*, when Julie Delpy and Ethan Hawke's characters find themselves at the graveyard. (The movie is a bit misleading—don't expect it to be a short stroll to the Riesenrad of the Prater afterward.)

If you love cemeteries, it's worth combining a trip with the Vienna Central Cemetery and taking a taxi or public transport over.

St. Leopold Church
(Kirche am Steinhof)

Kirche am Steinhof, Baumgartner Höhe 1; tel. 01/910-601-1007; Sat 4pm-5pm, Sun midday-4pm; €8; bus 47A, 48A: Klinik Penzing

If you're an architecture lover, visit this art nouveau church built by Otto Wagner, up in the hills above Vienna. The church is perhaps Otto Wagner's masterpiece, built between 1904 and 1907. It's one of the first churches in Europe to embrace this bold modern style, echoing the design of the Secession with its cube-like structure and golden dome. You'll find art nouveau angels with gold wings guarding the entrance, and glass mosaics on the windows by Koloman Moser.

The inside of the church is only open Saturdays from 4-5pm or Sunday noon-4pm. Guided tours are in German. However, at the time of updating the church itself is closed due to COVID-19.

The interior is strikingly simple compared to the drama you'll feel when you see it first from the outside. Consider enjoying a picnic in the park behind the church, where you'll have flawless views over the hills surrounding Vienna.

Otto Wagner

Otto Wagner's former villa on the edge of the Vienna Woods

If there is one architect who captures the spirit of Fin de Siècle, Vienna's journey into modernity, it's Otto Wagner. Otto Wagner blended modernity with an art nouveau aesthetic into beautifully simple design. His work is visible in his golden-domed Kirche am Steinhof up in the hills, the flower-inscribed apartment block close to the Naschmarkt, and infrastructure like the U-Bahn stations and bridges.

Wagner also was the designer behind the first Stadtbahn, the city train which became part of today's U-Bahn. The most famous monuments as part of his legacy include the Stadtbahn Pavilions in Karlsplatz and the Hofpavilion. He believed in advancing the city for the better. When he built his U-Bahn stations, his vision was inclusive of all classes, including the Emperor—which is why he opened the royal Stadtbahn Pavilion in Hietzing near Schönbrunn Palace. (Emperor Franz Joseph I used it once during the grand opening, but never again.)

You can get to the church in two ways. One option is to go to the Otto Wagner Spital, either by taxi or by bus 47A from U-Bahn stop Unter-St.-Weit (two stops from Hietzing), or by bus 48A from Ottakring (if coming from Stephansplatz). Both routes take around 30 minutes. Once you reach the psychiatric institute, it's a 10-minute climb up to the church along the path that's signposted from the entrance.

Alternatively, you can take bus 46A from Ottakring to Feuerwache Am Steinhof, lasting 15 minutes, and cross the meadows and the Park Steinhofgründe to get to the golden-domed church.

If you arrive via the hospital route and leave through the park, you get to meet the church at the most dramatic vantage point, towering above the hospital in architectural splendor.

If you have a pass for public transport, the journey should be free on all modes of transport, otherwise a single ticket of €2.40 should cover you for the journey.

Otto Wagner Villa (Ernst Fuchs Museum)

Hüttelbergstraße 26; tel. 01/91-48-575; www. ernstfuchsmuseum.at; Tue-Sun 10am-4pm; €11; bus 43B, 52A, 52B: Campingplatz Wien-West 1

If Otto Wagner's architecture has enchanted you or you have a taste for contemporary art with a surreal flair, it's worth the trek into the suburbs on the borders with the Vienna Woods for this curious museum. This lavish Palladian style villa with a Secessionist twist was not only built by Otto Wagner, but was his home for a time, where he entertained Vienna's crème de la crème, with illustrious names like Gustav Klimt, Adolf Loos, and Gustav Mahler, making the guestlist in the early 1900s. The highlight of Otto Wagner's villa is undoubtedly the Adolf-Böhm Parlor with its Tiffany-glass windows depicting the Vienna Woods in Jugendstil style.

The villa had been left abandoned for decades until artist Ernst Fuchs—who founded the Vienna School of Fantastic Realism in 1946—acquired it in 1971 and restored this Secessionist jewel box. Today the villa doubles up as a museum to the artist, whose surreal paintings feature Jewish imagery and generously voluptuous women (the curvy goddess-like figure added to the colonnaded façade is Fuchs's addition) in equal measure. This villa and museum is a synesthesia-inducing sensory overload, blending Wagner's Secessionist vision with Fuchs's unique colorful style. Another highlight is the kaleidoscopic fountain house in the surrounding garden built by Fuchs in the 1990s.

Recreation and Activities

Vienna is a green city: You can escape to a vineyard, a water forest, or the woods without even having to leave the city limits. If you head to the north or the western outskirts of the city, you'll come to the Vienna Woods with numerous hiking trails. The south and western part of the Viennese suburbs are marshier and lined with water forests and meadows around the Danube.

The best way to experience the Danube in Vienna is to either head down to the Danube Canal for its canal-side bars and hangouts, or head out to Old Danube in the north-eastern part of the city, which is a peaceful and recreational area famed for its beaches and gentler watersports like SUP. If you want to do a Danube cruise, I suggest saving it for Budapest (which is far more spectacular).

PARKS

If you're looking to pick up some snacks from the Naschmarkt and want to find a wonderful picnic spot close to the city center, you have plenty of parks and gardens to choose from. The obvious are **Schönbrunn Park,** or the parkland around the **Prater,** or the **Danube Island,** but if you need more inspiration, the following parks are worth spending a lazy afternoon in.

AUGARTEN

U2, tram 2: Taborstraße, tram 31: Obere Augartenstraße

Out of all the parks in Vienna, there is something really special about the Augarten—52 hectares (129 ac) enclosed inside an old wall just northwest of the Prater. The Augarten began as a pleasure garden in the 18th century and was loved so much by Emperor Joseph II that he released a flock of nightingales on the grounds every year. In 1775, the gardens opened to the public, and Mozart conducted the first Augarten concert here.

The Augarten, accessible through five gates open from dawn till dusk, mixes French landscaped gardens with elegant rows of chestnut trees and trimmed hedges, and meadow-like lawns where locals sunbathe or practice yoga under the shadow of the imposing and sinister Flak Towers (air defense towers built by the Nazis) that still haunt the grounds. In the summer, the Augarten comes to life with picnicking Viennese carrying bottles of Grüner Veltliner in coolers, old men playing boules, or youths lounging in hammocks they bring to the park. If you prefer to sit at a proper table and admire the park, head to the **Café Augarten Restaurant** (daily 9am-10pm Apr-Oct, 9am-6pm Nov-Mar) on the terrace

Lobau: Vienna's Water Forest

Inside Vienna, you can still visit an ancient water forest that branches off the Danube.

Vienna is an unusual city when it comes to its abundance of green spaces, but the Lobau is particularly special. This water forest and wetlands in the eastern suburbs of the city cover 2,300 hectares (5,700 acres) and make up a rich ecosystem with diverse species of plants, mammals, birds, reptiles, fish, and amphibians. Taking a walk through the Lobau, you'll be accompanied by an active, noisy chorus of birdsong echoing among the trees. Other signs of life include chewed pieces of wood (the work of the local beavers). The Lobau is not only loved as Vienna's "jungle"—locals also come here to canoe, hike, ride their bikes, and swim (some areas are particularly loved by nudist bathers).

If you want a taste of the Lobau, take the daily **boat tour** in the summer. Booking is a must as the boat is pretty tiny. It can be reserved online (www.donauauen.at/events/mit-dem-national-parkboot-von-der-city-in-die-au-2020/33550). Tours (€13) last 4.5 hours, leaving at 9am from the banks of the river next to the bridge called the Salztorbrücke, near Schwedenplatz. Tours are in German, but it's a convenient and cheap way to get out to this unique nature reserve from the city center. You'll get a ride up the Danube Canal for an hour before taking an hour-long walking tour in the Lobau with a guide, and hopping back on the boat. Plus, you get a boat ride down the Danube Canal at a fraction of the price of most boat tours (usually around €24) as a bonus!

of the Augarten Porcelain Factory and the Augarten.

STADTPARK

U4: Stadtpark, U3, U4: Landstraße, S1, S2, S3, S4: Wien Mitte-Landstraße tram 2, D: Weihburgstrasse

Stadtpark, Vienna's first public park, opened in 1862 and lies just to the south of the Museum of Applied Arts. It's a popular spot for picnics and evening strolls as the sun sets in the summer. It's one of Vienna's most elegant parks, flanked with art nouveau architecture at the U-Bahn pavilions, the bridge across the Vienna River as it emerges from being forced underground before Karlsplatz, and of course, the famous golden statue of Johann Strauss on his fiddle (which is one of the most photographed memorials in Vienna). Coffee and ice cream trucks are conveniently parked around this gorgeous park, but the best way to experience it is to head to Naschmarkt, gather ingredients for a picnic, and hop on U-Bahn line 4, then get off at the Stadtpark station.

There are plenty of benches for seating if you need them.

VOLKSGARTEN AND BURGGARTEN

U2, U3: Volksteater, U1, U2, U4: Karlsplatz, tram 1, 2, 71, D: Burgring, Ring, Volkstheater

These large gardens on the grounds of the Hofburg lie next to each other, but they have their own histories. The Volksgarten (meaning "the people's garden") was built over the 16th-century fortifications destroyed by Napoleon in 1809 and opened to the public in the 1820s, becoming Vienna's first public garden. It's a stunning landscaped garden with monuments like the neoclassical Theseus Temple, a small-scale replica based on the Temple of Hephaestus in Athens. You'll also see sculpture clad fountains and rose gardens.

Nearby, the Burggarten was once the private grounds of the Emperor Franz Joseph I. It opened to the public in 1919. You'll find the art nouveau Palm House here, which is now a trendy bar and a **butterfly house** (tel. 01/533-8570; www.schmetterlinghaus.at; Mon-Fri 10am-4:45pm, Sat-Sun 10am-6:15pm Apr-Oct, daily 10am-3:45pm Nov-Mar; €7).

SIGMUND FREUD PARK

U2: Schottentor, tram 1, 37, 38, 40, 41, 42, 43, 44, 71, D: Schottentor

Reachable just across from Vienna's main university, lounging students are a common sight at this park named after the famous psychoanalyst. The towers of the Votive Church dominate the sky, but the church's presence doesn't deter sunbathers who camp out on the grass. In the summer, around 100 sun loungers are delivered each morning and collected around 9pm. You can visit free of charge. Free Wi-Fi is also available here.

DONAUPARK

U1: Kaisermühlen VIC

There is 99 hectares of parkland here in this new part of the city in the 22nd district. Set between the Danube Island and the Old Danube—a crescent shaped arm of the Danube populated with boats, canoes, and

waterside promenades, this park rose out of a 1960s garbage dump to become an oasis filled with flowers, paths, playgrounds and an aviary. The main landmark is the 250 meter (830 ft) high Danube Tower (Donauturm), and there are thousands of roses that bloom in the summer months in the **Rosarium** (in the southeastern corner of the park; open all hours; free). You can explore the park on foot or hop on the **Donauparkbahn,** a small train that will take you around the park every half an hour for €4. You can board at numerous locations, including the Donauturm or the Rosarium.

HIKING

Draped in green meadows and woodlands—even within city limits—Vienna is the perfect destination for the outdoor-loving traveler. All the city's 11 hiking trails (Stadtwanderweg) are well marked—just look for the wooden sign with the word Stadtwanderweg plus the number of the hiking trail at every turn of the route. It's nearly impossible to get lost, but if you're worried, just download the free Vienna city map (Stadt Wien in the app stores) and allow it to track your location.

The full list of the hiking paths, plus maps, are available online (www.wien.gv.at/english/leisure/hiking/paths.html). The most popular trails for visitors are the City Hiking Trail 1/1A (see page 306), and City Hiking Trail 9.

CITY HIKING TRAIL 9

Distance (round-trip): *13 km (8 mi)*
Duration (round-trip): *3-4 hours*
Effort: *easy*
Trailhead: *Praterstern*

Best known for its retro amusement park, the Prater is also a popular hiking destination. Just get off at the Praterstern U-Bahn stop and follow the signs for the City Hiking Trail 9, a long, mostly flat, trek deep into the water

---

1: The Old Danube is a popular summer spot for boating. **2:** Wooden "Stadtwanderweg" signs mark Vienna's hiking trails. **3:** The Burggarten is home to an art nouveau Butterfly House and the trendy Palmenhaus bar.

meadows and wooded areas of a former imperial hunting ground. The trail loops back to where you started.

To find the trailhead, come out of the Praterstern train/U-bahn station and take the underpass leading to the beginning of the Hauptallee (the main promenade that cuts through the Prater), where you'll see a map of the trail on a large board. Continue along the Hauptallee on the righthand side until you see the Stadtwanderweg 9 sign, and continue following the Stadtwanderweg 9 signs along the route.

CYCLING

Vienna is a bike-friendly city with 1,300 kilometers (800 mi) of cycle paths and a bike-sharing program known as Vienna Citybike.

Bike-Sharing
CITYBIKES

www.citybikewien.at

Vienna's bike-sharing program can be used at over 120 stations around the city. Register online, or just use your credit card (Visa or MasterCard) at any of the Citybike terminals across the city. You pay a one-time fee of one euro; then, the charges go up depending on how long you rent the bike. The first hour is free—after that, it's €1 per second hour, €2 in the third hour, and so on. If you go over 120 hours, there is a flat fee of €600.

When you're done using the bike and you're ready to return it, you'll see a green light come on when the bike is placed in the rack correctly.

Bike Paths
SIGHTSEEING BICYCLE PATH RINGSTRASSE

Head down to Urania (an old observatory on the Danube Canal where the Vienna River flows into the canal) and you can cycle along the paved, traffic free Sightseeing Bicycle Path Ringstraße (Ring-Rund-Radweg) that will take you along the old city and past some of the most famous landmarks, like the Staatsoper (Opera House) and the Parliament

along a five-kilometer (3-mi) route. You can begin by the Urania Kino—either take tram 1 to Julius-Raab Platz, or from Schwedenplatz by U-Bahn, or just take your bike.

HAUPTALLEE TO LOBAU WATER FOREST

Nature lovers can cross the Aspern Bridge and take the bike route down the Praterstraße and Prater Hauptallee (the main promenade that cuts through the Prater) and cycle all the way down to the Lobau water forest. Cycle eight kilometers (5 miles) down the Hauptallee into the Unterer Prater and turn left. Take the road to the Donaustadtbrücke (the bridge crossing Danube Island and over the river), then turn right when you get off the bridge. The route along the Hauptallee is paved, flat, and lined with trees, taking you past woods and meadows. The bridge runs along the A23 road so it is a little busier, but on the other side, you'll be treated to a Danube-side cycle.

DANUBE ISLAND

There are also cycle paths running along the length of the 21-kilometer (13-mi) long Danube Island. Cycle across Leopoldstadt and just take any of the bridges, like Brigittenauerbrücke, to reach the island.

BEACHES
STRANDBAD GÄNSEHÄUFEL (GÄNSEHÄUFEL LIDO)

Sommerbad Moissigasse 21, Gänsehäufel; tel. 01/269-9016; www.gaensehaeufel.at; Mon-Fri 9am-7pm, Sat-Sun 8am-7pm, May-Aug Mon-Fri 9am-8pm, Sat-Sun 8am-8pm May and Sep; €3; U1: Kaisermühlen

Situated in an arm of the Old Danube, northwest of the city center, and east of Danube Island, 30-hectare (74-ac) **Gänsehäufel Island** is occupied by a lido (a complex of beaches and outdoor pools). Locals flock to it in the summer to bake in the sun, so it can get crowded, but luckily there is enough space and shade (thanks to the island's 4,000 trees) for everyone.

There is a sense of retro nostalgia across

the island, with its 1950s cabin blocks (rented out by dedicated locals for the summer), curving lookout tower, and kiosks selling snacks and ice cream at reasonable prices. The bathing areas are split into family areas, but there are also nudist zones, designated by signs marked as FKK, meaning Freikörperkulture, or free body culture, hidden discretely behind dense reed fencing. (When you arrive at the entrance, these areas are also marked on the map, but you'll notice entrances with clearly marked glyphs saying "no clothes.")

You can easily spend most of the day here swimming and relaxing. If swimming in the Danube doesn't appeal to you, there are a number of swimming pools that are included in the entrance price, some with slides. One of them (the largest pool just south of the clock tower) even has a wave machine. There are also lockers on the island stationed close to the cabins that you can use with a €1 or €2 coin.

To get here, take the free shuttle service from the U-Bahn station Kaisermühlen to the beach. (The shuttle was not running in 2020, but you can also take the 92A or 92B buses from the station, or walk). There is also bike and car parking (€5 for the day) available on the island by the entrance.

BOATING AND WATER SPORTS
GÄNSEHÄUFEL ISLAND
On the southern end of Gänsehäufel Island, you have the chance to do **stand-up paddling (SUP)** or **kayaking.** Just find the kiosk marked with the signs for SUP and pay at the cash deck (cards accepted). Prices for an hour's SUP is €13, while kayaking costs €10.

OLD DANUBE
U1: Alte Donau
Viennese come to the Old Danube—a former arm of the Danube that's cut off from today's river, so is more like a lake—for boating and water sports. As soon as you get out of the U1 stop named Alte Donau you're treated to a view of boats and canoes spreading out across the reed-lined waters. It won't take

long to find a place to get sailing. **Marina Hofbauer** (www.marina-hofbauer.at; Mon-Thu noon-10pm, Fri-Sun 11am-10pm Apr-end of summer) offers private boating opportunities, with rowboats priced €18 per hour, paddle boats from €18 per hour and motorboats from €22 per hour.

If you prefer SUP, check out **Flotus** (www.flotus.at; summer season Mon-Fri noon-7pm, Sat-Sun 11am-7pm). Hourly rates for SUP is €13, while kayaking prices start at €13. They also organize SUP yoga and SUP Pilates, as well as concerts on their private waterfront.

SWIMMING POOLS
JÖRGERBAD
Jörgerstraße 42-44; tel. 01/406-4305; Tue 9am-6pm, Wed and Fri 9am-9:30pm, Thu and Sun 8am-7pm, Sat 8am-8pm; €3; tram 1, 43: Palffygasse
Among one of Vienna's oldest indoor swimming pools, Jörgerbad was built before World War I and is an art nouveau-style pool with tiles in shades of rusty orange and sky blue. If you love architecture and want to grab a swim before or after sightseeing, then check out this stunning pool.

AMALIENBAD
Reumannplatz 23; Mon 12:30pm-3pm (senior citizens only), Tue 9am-6pm, Wed 9am-9:30pm, Thu 7am-9:30pm, Sat 7am-8pm, Sun 7am-6pm; €3; U1: Reumannplatz
For a local experience, head over to the Amalienbad. Inside, the Amalienbad looks like something out of a Wes Anderson movie. You'll find the pool under a tiled glass ceiling with accents of art nouveau and art deco styles.

Get your ticket at the cash desk, then hand it in at the desk by the entrance to the baths to get your wristband. Chances are you have a locker and not a private cabin (cabins have to be requested), so instead of slipping into one of the elegant changing cabins surrounding the pool, look for the women's and men's lockers and changing rooms sign. When you're ready to swim, just hold the wristband to the lock and press, and it's locked.

The Amalienbad also offers saunas, a restaurant, and more for a day of elegant relaxation.

DIANABAD

Lilienbrunngasse 7-9; tel. 01/219-81810; www.dianabad.at; Mon-Sat 10am-9:30pm, Sun 10am-7:30pm; €18-26.10 bath and sauna depending on the day and duration; tram 1, 2: Salztorbrücke

The Dianabad lies just off the Danube Canal in Leopoldstadt, and is home to the city's largest adventure pool, themed water slides (from wild stream to dinosaurs), a wave pool and a pirate boat, and also a sauna area for adults to detox while the kids (or adults with adventurous hearts) splash around. Palm trees and a controlled balmy temperature keeps things feeling tropical, so if you're in Vienna in the winter or it happens to rain, you can escape to the tropics for a bit in the city center.

SPA

THERME WIEN

Kurbadstraße 14; tel. 01/680-09; www.thermewien. at; daily 9am-10pm, Sun 8am-10pm; €21 for a 3-hour ticket; U1: Oberlaa

If you take U-Bahn line 1 to the end of the line to Oberlaa, in just 20 minutes, you'll make it out to one of the largest and most modern city spas in Europe. Unlike pools in the inner city, Therme Wien uses sulfur springs once loved by the Romans for their healing properties. With multiple areas in the complex featuring pools, sauna and steam rooms, aquatic gymnastics, lounge areas, health and fitness, meals, rehabilitation programs, and much more, you may never want to leave.

TOURS

GOOD VIENNA TOURS

www.goodviennatours.eu

Get your bearings in Vienna with a free walking tour of the city center hosted by Good Vienna Tours. These tours last just under three hours and take you around the 1st District. You'll see details of the city you might otherwise miss, like the curious medieval mural on the façade of the Hare House of a cow wearing glasses playing backgammon with a wolf, or the story behind the name of the Albertina (which is where the tour starts). If you like their free tour, they have other tours (paid) like the 2 hour and 30 minute walking tour of Hitler's Vienna (€25).

CONTEXT TRAVEL

www.contexttravel.com/cities/vienna; prices range €284-1,117 per person for a private tour

Context Travel tours offer you the unique opportunity to see the city with a docent who has an academic background in the topic of your choice, whether you're interested in Sigmund Freud or Vienna's culinary history. Small group tours may be available for a lower price. Check the website for more information.

Bars and Nightlife

Vienna may not have the same lively reputation as Budapest and Prague when it comes to bars and nightlife, but there's plenty of nocturnal activity to keep you dancing or drinking until dawn (at the time of writing, due to COVID-19, most places only stayed open till 1am). Vienna's nightlife comes with its own unique flavor, with repurposed venues underneath railway arches, old factories, former bordellos, or in summertime pop-up bars along the Danube Canal. For a truly Viennese experience, you can also while away the hours in the city's Heurige, rustic wine taverns serving local wine from vineyards within the Austrian capital's limits.

A domestic beer will set you back around €4 (perhaps more for a craft beer), and a cocktail is around €11-15. In the summer, try the Spritzer, a drink made by mixing white wine or rosé with soda water (carbonated water). Most venues won't have a cover charge unless there is a special event or a concert.

Many venues only take cash, so it's a good idea to have some euros with you.

Despite Vienna's less-wild reputation, drinking laws set the drinking age at 16 (18 in some other parts of Austria). Drunk and disorderly behavior, however, can result in heavy fines. Some bars and clubs do permit smoking or have indoor smoking areas.

NIGHTLIFE DISTRICTS
Bermudadreieck

Nicknamed the "Bermuda Triangle" in German, this small area in the historic center, close to Schwedenplatz, earned its title for the countless forgotten nights enjoyed by locals and tourists in the area. This party district rose in the 1980s, but its overpriced downtown bars draw in the tourists more than the locals looking for a night out, but there are a few bars worth visiting. Do note that most of the bars here do not have outdoor spaces.

Gürtel

If you're in the mood for live music, make a beeline to the arches under the elevated U-Bahn rails at the Gürtel ring road between Thaliastraße and Nussdorferstraße, where classic bars and new music venues jostle together under the rumbling metro. The vibe around Gürtel is gritty—it's a red light district with sex shops—but over the past few years, it's become a happening night spot, particularly for live music.

Naschmarkt to Mariahilferstraße

By day, the Naschmarkt bustles with foodies, but when the day is over, it's great for a night out. Whether you pick the trendy bistros for an evening cocktail or you head into the side streets, you'll find stretches of bars, cafés and clubs on the cobbled roads between Mariahilferstrasse. The clubs and bars here appeal to students and young creatives, like Café Kafka or Tanzcafé Jenseits.

Around the Danube Canal

When summer comes around, the Danube Canal is the place to be. Beach bars line the grassy embankments, and if you take a stroll along here, make sure you stop to admire the street art at Vienna's largest legal graffiti zone. Afternoons are lazy; by night the clubs start to kick off and energy buzzes in venues like Flex. Even in the summer of 2020, this part of Vienna was heaving with al fresco activity from sunset onward.

BARS AND PUBS
Historic Center and Hofburg Area
PALMENHAUS

Burggarten 1; tel. 01/533-1033; www.palmenhaus.at; Mon-Fri 10am-11pm, Sat-Sun 9am-11pm; U1, U2, U4: Karlsplatz, tram 1, 2, 71, D: Oper, Karlsplatz

Not many bars are housed in an art nouveau palm house, so when it comes to location, the Palmenhaus (not to be confused with the Palmenhaus at Schönbrunn) is pretty special. The interior, with high arched ceilings, abundant palm trees, and glass-paneled walls, is stunning. In the summer, people gather on its terrace overlooking the Burggarten that once belonged to the Hofburg. This chilled-out bar serves food throughout the day, and on Friday nights or weekends, try the Palmenhaus Pimm's No. 1, which is Pimm's with lime juice, basil, cucumber, and ginger beer. If you want a table, it's a good idea to reserve in advance. They have a spacious outdoor terrace overlooking the grounds of the Burggarten.

★ LOOS BAR

Kärntner Durchgang 10; tel. 01/512-3283; www.loosbar.at; daily noon-1am; U1, U3: Stefansplatz

Sip on a classic dry martini in this tiny 27-square-meter (32-sq-yd) American-style cocktail bar that opened in 1908. What it lacks in size, it makes up for in style with onyx panels, brass details and mirrored walls. The bar was designed by and named for modernist architect Adolf Loos, whose architectural mission was to break down Vienna's obsessive love for ornamentation. This bar is a piece in Vienna's architectural history. The vibe is both classy and classic, so you may want to dress up. They have a small terrace on the street.

Around Naschmarkt
★ TANZCAFÉ JENSEITS
Nelkengasse 3; tel. 01/587-1233;
www.tanzcafé-jenseits.com; Tue-Sat 8pm-4am;
U3: Neubaugasse

Cozy, with red damask-upholstered walls and low lighting, this bar was once the site of a brothel. It still keeps its old-world seedy charm—just without the sex work. The name translates as the "Afterlife Dance Café," and the place comes to life around 11pm and stays lively until the early hours (in pre-COVID times at least). DJs start to play after midnight, and people crowd onto the tiny dance floor. There is usually a special cocktail menu written up on the chalkboard above the bar, and you can ask for a cigar menu, too, if you're feeling fancy. The main bar area is still smoker-friendly, but there is a non-smoking room to the side. At the time of writing, the bar was closed due to COVID-19, but scheduled to reopen once the situation improves. Check the website or their Facebook page for updates.

CAFE KAFKA
Capistrangasse 8; tel. 01/586-1317; Mon-Sat
8am-11pm, Sun 10am-11pm; U3: Neubaugasse,
U2: Museumsquartier

Café Kafka is a popular student hangout, with worn-looking walls plastered with film festival posters, exhibition openings and other art. Seating is in the form of welcoming vintage furniture. It's one of the few cafés that still allows smokers. During the day, young creatives gather to collaborate on projects, but in the evening, it turns into a trendy bar packed with 20-something hip Viennese. The vibe is laid-back, and a good place to start the evening with a few drinks. They have a tiny street terrace.

HEUER AM KARLSPLATZ
Treitl straße 2; tel. 01/890-0590; www.heuer-
amkarlsplatz.com; Mon-Wed 5pm-11pm, Thu
5pm-1am, Fri-Sat 3pm-1am; U1, U2, U4: Karlsplatz,
tram 1, 62, WLB: Karlsplatz

This trendy bar shares the building with the Kunsthalle Wien in downtown Vienna. It blends old and new with Thonet chairs and green leather benches, and there is even an outdoor terrace area. The shelves are lined with apothecary-like jars filled with cocktail ingredients like homemade pickles, preserves and syrups, some of which are used to make "shrubs," surprisingly refreshing vinegar-based drinks. Cocktails here are made from a selection of 350 spirits from the world over. Try an original creation like Bob Dill'n, made with dill-infused vodka, lemongrass syrup and cucumber.

Karlsplatz and the Belvedere Palace Area
MR. MENDÉZ
Karlsplatz 2; tel. 06/76-511-3099; www.mendez.at;
Thu-Sat 4pm-11pm; U1, U2, U4: Karlsplatz, tram 1, 62,
WLB: Karlsplatz

From the front, it looks like a café, but cross the Cafe Mendéz and there is a "secret" room in the back of the café decorated with Mexican-inspired murals depicting colorful flowers and *calavera* and luchador masks, where you'll find a hidden craft cocktail bar: Mr. Mendéz. The staff are friendly, and the cocktail menu is creative—many of the cocktail ingredients here are homemade. Try their tequila-based cocktails, or ask the bartenders to prepare your favorite concoction. You can get nachos and other spicy snacks with your beverages of choice.

Prater and Around
FIRST FLOOR BAR
Seitenstettengasse 5; tel. 01/532-1163;
http://firstfloorbar.at; daily 6pm-1am; U1,
U4: Schwedenplatz, tram 1, 2: Schwedenplatz

In the heart of the infamous "Bermuda Triangle," there's the First Floor Bar, a mainstay for 20 years. As its name suggests, you need to head up to the first floor to reach this cocktail bar. A fishless aquarium filled with swaying plants sits behind the bar, and the cocktail menu contains more than 200 drinks. Try the champagne cocktails or the more robust Whiskey Business, made with bourbon, rye, cocoa syrup and port. Jazz music floats in the background—it's sometimes live, too, usually on Thursdays. In the winter, you'll need to check your coats into the cloakroom.

KAKTUS

Seitenstettengasse 5; tel. 06/76-670-4405;
www.kaktusbar.at; daily 6pm-1am; U1, U4:
Schwedenplatz, tram 1, 2: Schwedenplatz

Kaktus is another venue to lose yourself in within Vienna's Bermudadreieck, with a solid reputation as one of the city's most exciting night spots. You won't find a quiet night here—parties rock late into the night (however, since COVID-19 the opening hours were cut down to 1am from 4am) with a young and energetic crowd dancing to local and guest DJs. With flashing neon and primary colors, bare bricks, spiral metal staircases and robust tables that have a history of being danced on, the décor adds to this bar's club atmosphere.

DAS LOFT

Praterstraße 1; tel. 01/90-616-8110; www.dasloftwien.
at; Sun-Thu 6pm-midnight; U1, U4: Schwedenplatz,
tram 1, 2: Schwedenplatz

You can't beat the view at Das Loft, set on the 18th floor of the Sofitel Hotel. You'll need to take the lift to get to this swanky, backlit bar. Das Loft serves a variety of cocktails that cater to more serious drinkers. (For example, the "Last Word" is made with Tanqueray no. 10 gin, chartreuse, maraschino, absinthe and lime.) The dress code is to impress, so put on your fanciest dress or suit. The city seems tiny from the 18th floor.

Alsergrund and Josefstadt
TÜR 7

Buchfeldgasse 7; tel. 06/64-54-63-717;
http://tuer7.at; Mon-Wed, Fri 9pm-1am, Thu 5pm-1am;
U2: Rathaus, tram 2: Rathaus

It takes a little sleuthing to find, but this little speakeasy-type bar is worth the hunt. It fits no more than 35 people. (Because it's hidden away and not advertised, there aren't queues out the door, but you may want to book a table, just in case.) You need to ring the doorbell to get in. They can prepare any classic cocktail for you, or make you a surprise concoction based on your tastes if you want something more unusual. Prices are fixed at €20 per drink. The bar is non-smoking. Look for the door marked with a seven—at 7 Buchfeldgasse.

WINE BARS

Wine is a big part of Viennese culture, with vineyards sprawling within the city limits and being cultivated nearby. Try some of the classics, like the Grüner Veltliner, a white wine with hints of fruit like citrus and pear, or the Blauburgunder, the local, complex pinot noir red. There's also the Riesling, a bold fruity white with plenty of acidity, or the Zweigelt, a bold red with aromas recalling cherries.

Historic Center and Hofburg Area
VIS-À-VIS

Wollzeile 5; tel. 01/512-9350; www.weibel.at;
Tue-Fri 4pm-10:30pm and Sat 3pm-10:30pm;
U1, U3: Stephansplatz

Set in a tiny venue that fits around 10 people tucked inside a tiny passage connecting Wollzeile and Bäckerstraße, this wine bar may be small, but it offers a massive collection of 350 wines. The focus is on Austrian wine, but you can also try international varieties. Order some antipasti to help the tasting go more smoothly.

VINOTHEK W-EINKEHR

Laurenzerberg 1; tel. 06/764-082854;
www.w-einkehr.at; Tue-Sat 4pm-10pm;
U4: Schwedenplatz, tram 1, 2: Schwedenplatz

This small wine bar has only 15 seats indoors, with eight more on the terrace, so get here early to snag a seat. Austrian wines from around the country dominate the menu.

Heurige

Head up into the Vienna Woods to a Heuriger like Furgassl-Huber for some young wine in the fall.

Head out toward the Vienna Woods, and you'll see row upon row of vines being cultivated within the city limits, taking up around 700 hectares (1,800 ac) of land. Where there is a vineyard, there will be a Viennese Heuriger nearby. These rustic wine taverns fill with locals and visitors who come to drink the local tipple, eat heavy portions of rich Austrian food, and have a good time. Only local wines are served in Heurige (plural for Heuriger), and the experience is as Viennese as riding the Riesenrad in the Prater or looking at portraits of Sisi hanging in the Hofburg. Songs have immortalized these wine taverns, which are legendary for their homey feel, and—unlike the grumpy charm of Viennese coffeehouse—have a welcoming atmosphere.

Usually drinking and dining in the Heuriger is al fresco, in the breezy courtyards and gardens, making it perfect on a hot summer or fall day—but most will have a cozy parlor, so the elements won't get in the way of your drinking. The wine served in the Heuriger is made by the owner (each Heuriger has its own vineyard) and the wine will also be just around a year old—in fact the word Heuriger actually means "this year's wine." If you prefer your wine more mature, you can ask for a bouteille, higher-quality wines that are bottled in 0.75-liter bottles. Sometimes, things can get a little festive and you may even be treated to live violin or accordion music.

FURGASSL-HUBER
Neustift am Walde 68; tel. 01/440-1405; www.fuhrgassl-huber.at; Mon-Sat 2pm-11pm, Sun midday-11pm; glass of wine €2-4; bus 35A: Neustift am Walde

Reserve a table if you want to make an afternoon of your visit or drop in for a taste if you're downtown. Come for the unpretentious atmosphere and dedication to serving the best Austrian wines available.

VILLON
Habsburgergasse 4; www.villon.at; Wed-Sat 2pm-11pm; U1, U3: Stephansplatz

Right below the city center, plunging 52 feet (16 m) below ground, this cellar dating back to 1701 is a place to forget the outside world. The wine bar is elegant and modern. You can order wine by the glass or by the bottle, and also order snacks for pairing. Keep your appetite at bay with goose liver pâté or truffle crostini.

This Heuriger on the outskirts of Vienna has been running for 40 years and it's personally one of my favorites. When the weather is good, grab a glass or two of the Heuriger's own wine and sit down to one of the green wooden benches on the terrace overlooking the vineyards and the Vienna Woods behind the garden. If the weather goes off, you can while away the cold and the rain inside this old, rustic house dating back to the 17th century with a glass of Wiener Gemischter Satz—a white cuvee that is slightly sweet and fruity—and a few traditional Heurigen dishes, such as Kümmelbraten, a pork roast with crispy skin, vegetable strudel, grilled chicken, and vinegary potato salad, which you can choose from behind the glass counter.

You can reach this Heuriger by taking the 35A bus from the Nussdorferstrasse or the Spittelau U-Bahn stations. They also own a charming hotel in an old manor house (**Landhaus Fuhrgassl-Huber;** Rathstraße 24; www.landhaus-fuhrgassl-huber.at; doubles with breakfast €145-185) conveniently located five minutes down the road if you prefer not to rush back to the city.

MAYER AM PFARRPLATZ

Pfarrplatz 2; tel. 01/370-1287; www.pfarrplatz.at; Mon-Sat 4pm-midnight, Sun noon-midnight; glass of wine €3-5; tram D: Grinzingerstraße

This Heuriger is famous for two things: Beethoven and wine. In 1817 Ludwig van Beethoven resided on the first floor of this charming house, which today is home to one of Vienna's most famous Heurige. In the summer, its vine-clad inner courtyard fills up with locals and tourists who come here to sample the wine from the nearby Mayer winery. Try the Heuriger wine, a young wine like the Mayer's Grüner Veltliner, a crisp dry white, or one of their more mature wines. You can even try a red like their fruity Pinot Noir. When it comes to food, order the crispy and succulent Backhendl, golden fried chicken—and accompany it with the traditional potato salad.

From the Heiligenstadt U-Bahn station, take the 38A bus to Fernsprechamt Heiligenstadt stop, which puts you three minutes away from the Heuriger.

HEURIGER SIRBU

Kahlenberger straße 210; tel. 01/320-5928; www.sirbu.at; Apr-Oct Mon-Fri 4pm-11pm, Sat 3pm-11pm, Sun 1pm-7pm (in cases of bad weather call to check if open); glass of wine €3-4; bus 38A: Kahlenberg

Grab a bench on the wooden picnic-style tables on the slopes of the vineyards overlooking the Danube. Sirbu is perhaps Vienna's most beautiful Heuriger and worth the journey for a glass of wine on its panoramic terrace. Pair your wine with a cheese plate or an assortment of meat cuts, and just make your way through the wine list trying this year's specials. You'll find the usual Viennese wines such as Grüner Veltliner and the Gemischter Satz cuvee, but try some of the winery's special wines, such as their Gemischter Satz Rot, a red cuvee, or the Frizzante Schweizerberg, a sparkling wine. It's a good idea to book a table here in the summer!

From the Heiligenstadt station, take the 38A bus to the end of the line at Kahlenberg and then walk down hill (it's a bit of a trek and will take you around 20 minutes), first down Höhenstraße and then down Kahlenberger straße till you reach the Heuriger.

Around Naschmarkt
SEKT COMPTOIR

Schleifmühlgasse 19; www.sektcomptoir.at; Wed-Thu 5pm-11pm, Fri 3pm-11pm, Sat noon-11pm; U4: Kettenbrückengasse

Sparkling wine lovers should head down to this bar by the Naschmarkt to try a glass of the Burgenland Sekt, a local Austrian, award-winning bubbly from the bar's vineyard, Szigeti. This cozy bar is popular with locals.

STADTHEURIGEN

Keep an eye out for sign that reads Stadtheuriger, meaning a city wine tavern. These taverns are the urban form of Heurige, traditional taverns located near vineyards on the outskirts of the city, where visitors can sip wine in a large yard with bench seating. Stadtheurigen are located in the city center and lack the atmospheric proximity to vineyards, but the wine is excellent.

Historic Center and Hofburg Area
GIGERL

Rauhensteingasse 3; tel. 01/513-4431; www.gigerl.at; daily 3pm-midnight; U1, U3: Stephansplatz

Tucked in a cobbled side street in the inner city, Gigerl has a rustic feel, with low, arched ceilings and wooden tables, and waitresses outfitted in traditional dirndl dresses. Despite being in the heart of the city, it still has that Heuriger feel, with local wines from surrounding vineyards in Vienna and Austria. You can also order substantial Austrian food like Schnitzel and Heurigenplatten to share, with cold cuts, pickles, and salads. This downtown spot is popular with locals and tourists alike.

ESTERHAZYKELLER

Haarhof 1; tel. 01/533-3482; www.esterhazykeller.at; open Oct-Jun Mon-Fri 11am-11pm, Sat-Sun 11am-11pm Oct-Jun; U1: Stephansplatz, U3: Herrengasse

This wine cellar has a unique history that dates back to 1683. As soldiers defended the city from the Turkish siege, they were supplied with wine before the fight to give them courage—and that was the first wine tasting in the Esterhazy Cellar. Its handmade bricks date back to the 15th century. The wine offered here bears the Esterhazy name—the name of a Hungarian aristocratic family who resided in Vienna. You can try wines from the Weingut Esterhazy winery, with classic Austrian wines like Grüner Veltliner and Blaufränkisch. Mains and snacks are also available with the usual suspects like Schnitzel, but there are also spicy sausages on offer.

Alsergrund and Josefstadt
WEINSTUBE JOSEFSTADT

Piaristengasse 27; tel. 01/406-4628; daily 4pm-midnight Apr-Dec; tram 2: Lederergasse

This Stadtheuriger is a true local's secret. You could walk down the street and pass the door without noticing. Just look for the green wreath on the doorway to uncover the entrance, which will lead you into its magic urban garden. You can easily lose an afternoon in this secluded sanctuary in the city center, where local wine flows liberally—and at good prices too. You can also get good food to go. If you want a table in the garden, I highly recommend making a booking. Although its location is hidden, locals know and love this charmingly rustic city oasis.

BEER

Beer is just as popular in Austria as wine. In fact, if you head away from the vine-clad hills around Vienna toward the Alps, you'll notice beer becomes more popular. Typical Austrian beers include Dunkel, dark beer with an intense flavor; Helles, light and hoppy; Pils, a crisp, strong beer inspired by Pilsner; Zwickel, unfiltered beer with a cloudy complexion (which also tastes good in non-alcoholic varieties); and finally, Märzen, a red beer with a malty taste.

If you're looking for something Viennese, beer from the Ottakringer brewery, the largest brewery still working in Vienna, is available all over the city. Beyond the traditional beers, craft beers are slowly gaining popularity, so if you really want a good IPA or Porter, you can find some great local concoctions made in local microbreweries.

Historic Center and Hofburg Area
1516 BREWING COMPANY

Schwarzenbergstraße 2; tel. 01/961-1516; www.1516brewingcompany.com; daily 10am-1am; U1, U2, U4: Karlsplatz, tram 2, 71, D: Schwarzenbergerplatz

If you love beer and want to try a local microbrewery, you can't go wrong with this one. The 1516 Brewing Company brews a tasty selection of seasonal brews made on the premises without filtering or additives, including ales and beers using malted barley, as well as malted and unmalted wheat, rye, and rice. Beers from the tap are served in units of 0.1 liters (from €2.10), 0.25 liters (from €2.90), 0.4 liters (from €3.70), and even 1.5 liters (from €12.40). The industrial chic décor, with exposed bricks and pipes, along with huge chrome tanks, give this brewery an industrial feel. Worth trying if you love your beer!

BEACH BARS

Austria is a landlocked country, but like Budapest, there's plenty of activity going on alongside the river. Around the Danube Canal and the Danube, Vienna heats up in the summer with beaches—some even complete with their own sand—that pop up for the season along the waterfront.

Prater and Around
TEL AVIV BEACH
Obere Donaustraße 65; https://neni.at/restaurants/ tel-aviv-beach-bar; Mon-Thu 4pm-midnight, Fri-Sun noon-midnight Apr-Oct; U2, U4: Schottenring, tram 1, 31: Schottenring

Head down to the Danube Canal when the sun comes out for summery drinks and great Middle Eastern food and staple burgers. Tel Aviv Beach (a seasonal bar complete with sand and shirtless men) popped up along the canal

banks and was supposed to be temporary, but it has decided to stay and has become a summer fixture in the city. Grab a TLV Beach Teller with generous amounts of hummus, falafel, tahini, pickled vegetables and pita bread, and try their cocktails, like the TLV Beach Mule, with vodka infused with lemongrass, fresh ginger, cucumber, ginger beer and lime juice.

★ STRANDBAR HERRMANN
Herrmannpark; tel. 07/20-229-996; www. strandbarherrmann.at; daily (in good weather) Mon-Fri 2pm-1am, Sat-Sun 10am-1am; U1, U4: Schwedenplatz, tram 1, 2: Julius-Raab-Platz

Facing the Urania Observatory where the Vienna River meets the Danube Canal, this bar is kaleidoscope of color with deckchairs, hammocks and an abundance of sand. It also offers amazing views of the Canal while sunbathing. Once the sun goes down, the DJs normally supply dance music until the early hours of the morning (when permitted). Cocktails and beer are the most popular drinks, and if you're hungry you can always grab a burger or one of the daily specials. If you come between 10am-2pm on weekends, you can get a great brunch (€16.90) with a wide range of favorites to choose from like scrambled eggs, jams, cereal, granola,

Head to the Danube Canal at sunset in summer to one of the "beach bars" like Strandbar Herrmann.

salad, and more. It's usually a bit quiet when it opens but fills up close to sundown.

ADRIA

Obere Donaustraße 77; tel. 06/60-127-1784; www.adriawien.at; daily 10am-1am; tram 1, 2: Salztorbrücke

If you're looking to find the party on the Canal after sundown, Adria is the place to be. This bar has an indoor area, set in a glasshouse, that is filled with quirky upcycled sofas and chandeliers. There's also a sprawling terrace that extends along the banks of the river. Young, hip, and artsy Viennese congregate here (even in the summer of 2020 this place was packed) to catch up over a drink in the balmy summer evening.

CLUBS

When it comes to electronic music, Vienna has venues reaching cult status. The area down by the Danube Canal is a hot nightlife spot, featuring clubs that pair well with the beach bars (some seasonal, some more temporary) along the embankment or up by the Gürtel. To get you started, here are a few clubs to check out.

Prater and Around
FLEX

Donaukanal - Augartenbrücke; tel. 01/533-7525; www.flex.at; Mon-Sat 7pm-1am, cover charge €8-10; U2, U4: Schottenring, tram 1, 31: Schottenring

Since Flex relocated to a former metro tunnel by the Danube Canal in 1995, it's become one of Europe's hottest clubs. Its state-of-the-art sound system and atmosphere mixes dance culture and alternative music, including rock, drum and bass, and dub. Clubbers spill out onto the bank of the Danube Canal to cool down on balmy summer nights. Music genres are mixed, and it's worth checking the program out on the website and the opening times.

Alsergrund and Josefstadt
THE LOFT

Lerchenfelder Gürtel 37; www.theloft.at; Wed-Thu 7pm-1am, Fri-Sat 8pm-1am; cover charge free-€10; U6: Thaliastraße, tram 45: Thaliastraße

This club occupies three levels of a former wooden floor factory, with a café on the ground floor (where you'll probably stumble into an exhibition or a concert), a dance floor in the basement, and a bar with plenty of seating on the first floor. The action happens in the basement, with techno and house beats going until late night. The atmosphere here is chill—so if you love your electronic dance music without going somewhere too fancy, this is the spot for you. It tends to open on an event-by-event basis (particularly with COVID-19), so keep an eye on their website or check out their Facebook page.

Greater Vienna
GRELLE FORELLE

Spittelauer Lände 12; www.grelleforelle.com; times depend on events, cover charge depends on the event but usually around €12; U4, U6: Spittelau, tram D: Spittelau

Located next door to Werk, this club on the Danube Canal focuses on house, techno and other electronic music categories. Famous international DJs from the underground scene play here and take advantage of the fantastic sound system. Finding the club is almost like a rite of passage: Follow the fish symbols that resemble arrows on the Danube Canal. Check their website or Facebook page to see what events are on.

Note: admission here is 21 and above, and photography is forbidden.

DAS WERK

Spittelauer Lände 12, Stadtbahnbogen 331; www.daswerk.org; events 7pm-1am, terrace Thu-Sun 4pm-11pm in summer; cover charge €7-10; terrace free; U4, U6: Spittelau, tram D: Spittelau

Go here for heavy electronic music and industrial ambience. This club has roots in a cultural association and can now be found under the arches of a former railway. It has a raw, work-in-progress look. Locals come here on the weekends for legendary parties with the best DJs from Vienna's underground electronic scene. Apart from epic club nights, this is also a place for theater productions, concerts, readings and screenings, so expect an alternative artistic crowd. In the summer you can grab a riverside drink at the **KuturTerrase WERK** (free entry), the club's al-fresco sister space, located on its terrace by the Danube Canal. There is usually some kind of activity going on, from shows and workshops to DJ sessions and even flea markets.

LIVE MUSIC
Prater and Around
THE FLUC
Praterstern 5; www.fluc.at; Wed-Sat 4pm-1am; cover charge free-€15; S1, S2, S3, S4, U1: Praterstern

When you're done with the adrenaline-fueled rides at the Prater, head over to the Fluc, a unique fixture in Leopoldstadt's nightlife and music scene by the entrance of the Prater at Praterstern. There is something going on every day here. Entrance to parties and concerts is free upstairs, and admission to club nights and concerts downstairs depends on the act, but generally ranges from €5-15. Rock concerts and electronic club nights make some noise, but among the live music there are usually readings and art exhibitions as well. Regulars are mostly young and bohemian.

Alsergrund and Josefstadt
THE CHELSEA
Lerchenfelder Gürtel, Stadtbahnbögen 29-30; tel. 01/407-9309; www.chelsea.co.at; daily 6pm-4am; concert tickets €12-25; U6: Thaliastraße, tram 45: Thaliastraße

This club, owned by a former professional soccer player, hosts both live soccer broadcasts and rock music shows. It's an institution on Vienna's Gürtel, occupying three interconnected railway arches, and hosting rock, indie and alternative concerts, but they also hold club nights. You can see the full list of entertainment on The Chelsea's website. The club has a soccer-themed interior and a great selection of British beers and ales. The venue can fit around 250 people (standing) for concerts.

B72
Hernalser Gürtel, Stadtbahnbögen 72; tel. 01/409-2128; www.b72.at; Sun-Thu 8pm-4am, Fri-Sat 8pm-6am; cover charge free-€15; U6: Alser Straße, tram 44: Hernalser Gürtel

Not far from The Chelsea, you'll also find B72 also under two U-Bahn arches—it's a club with a focus on rock and alternative performances. Gigs here are from up-and-coming and better-known Austrian and international bands. Unlike other bars on the Gürtel, B72 occupies two stories. The ground floor is home to the bar, stage and dance floor, and the mezzanine is a chillout area with tables, chairs and a good view of the stage. This hip venue draws young, passionate music lovers and is a great place if you want to catch a good live music.

Performing Arts

TOP EXPERIENCE

CLASSICAL MUSIC AND OPERA

More famous composers have lived and worked in Vienna than anywhere else in the world, with names like Mozart, Beethoven, Strauss, Schubert, and more. Still today, Vienna is world-renowned for the Vienna Philharmonic Opera (Staatsoper) and its flawless productions.

During the coronavirus pandemic in 2020, some venues, including the Vienna State Opera and the Musikverein, instituted compulsory safety precautions such as mandatory masking, social distancing measures, and a pause on the sale of standing tickets. Check each venue's website for updated requirements. It may also be harder to get tickets in general, as fewer are being sold due to social distancing requirements.

VIENNA STATE OPERA
(Staatsoper)

Opernring 2; tel. 01/514-442-250;
www.wiener-staatsoper.at; U1, U2, U4: Karlsplatz,
tram 1, 2, 71, D: Oper, Karlsplatz

This grand opera house never rests. There are different productions on each night—over 60 shows and performances take place at this legendary opera house, 350 days of the year. The members of the orchestra are also musicians in the famous Vienna Philharmonic Orchestra.

The opera has capacity for 1,700 viewers, and there are 567 standing tickets available. Getting a seat at the Staatsoper can cost over €40 (or even over €100 for seats in the mid-price range); there are tickets for as low as €14, but note these have restricted views of the stage, so you might not see much. To get these tickets, you need to be in line at the standing room ticket office *at least* 80 minutes before the curtain goes up. (You will find the office under the arcades at Operngasse.) Tickets are first come, first served. (It's a good idea to bring a scarf or something you can tie on the railing at your standing position to reserve your spot.)

If you want to delve deeper into the lives of Vienna's composers, the **Staatsoper shop** (Arcadia Opera Shop, Kärntnerstraße 40, Mon-Sat 9:30am-7pm, Sun 10am-7pm) sells plenty of interesting reading material and music.

MUSIKVEREIN

Musikvereinsplatz 1; tel. 01/505-8190;
www.musikverein.at; €20-72; U1, U2, U4: Karlsplatz,
tram 2, 71, D: Schwarzenbergerplatz

Famed for its New Year's Day Concert, the Musikverein is one of Vienna's best-known classical music halls. The Vienna Philharmonic Orchestra is often found in this elegant building constructed and decorated with neoclassical columns, statues of Apollo and the Muses, and liberal quantities of gold leaf. This is also one of the best places in the world for spatial acoustics. There are shows 364 days of the year in its five halls. Away from the famous Golden Hall, there is the Glass Hall, Metal Hall, Stone Hall, and Wood Hall—each of these smaller halls focuses on young artists, jazz and literary performances.

WIENER KONZERTHAUS

Lothringerstraße 20; tel. 01/242-002;
www.konzerthaus.at; €30-142; U4: Stadtpark,
tram 2, 71, D: Schwarzenbergerplatz

The Wiener Konzerthaus caters to a wide range of musical tastes, going beyond Classical. It also taps into Baroque and medieval through to jazz and world music performances. It's set in an art nouveau building that opened in 1913. Emperor Franz Joseph I attended the first gala concert, and the concert house has played a varied repertoire ever since. There are three concert halls on one level, which fill up over the season, running from September to June. On average, Wiener Konzerthaus houses 750 events, 2,500 compositions, and around 600,000 visitors over a season. Check the website for the program and for COVID-19 rules.

MUTH

Obere Augartenstraße 1e; tel. 01/347-8080;
www.muth.at; tickets for Boys' Choir performance
€39-89; U2: Taborstraße, tram 2: Taborstraße

MuTH (which stands for music and theater) is the home of the world-famous Vienna Boys' Choir (Wiener Sängerknaben), who once only performed at the Hofburg. You can see the choir during Friday afternoon choral sessions from 5:00pm to 6:45pm in this 400-seat auditorium.

MuTH also stages theater and dance productions, as well as various classical music and jazz performances.

THEATER AND DANCE
BURGTHEATER

Universitätsring 2; tel. 01/51-444-4545;
www.burgtheater.at; tickets €8-64; tram 1, 71,
D: Rathausplatz/Burgtheater

The grandiose Burgtheater is not only Vienna's most popular theater, but one of the

Vienna Boys' Choir

Emperor Maximilian I founded the imperial Vienna Boys' Choir in the 15th century, and it has since become one of the most famous choirs in the world. The young male singers in the choir range in age from 10-14. If you want to see the choir perform, you have some options:

On Friday afternoons, the choir performs 5pm to 6:45pm in **MuTH,** a Baroque concert hall. Tickets range from €39-89. Between September and June, the choir also performs at Sunday Holy Mass in the **Royal Chapel** (www.culturall.com/ticket/hmk; 9:15am; box office open Fri 11am-1pm and 3-5pm, Sun 8-8:45am; tickets €12-38; tickets can also be bought online) in the Hofburg. Booking in advance is required.

most pivotal in the German-speaking world. There are over 530 people working at the theater producing some 20 premieres each year, from Shakespeare and Goethe to contemporary work. Architecturally, this over 1,000-seat theater is a work of art, from the Historicist-style exterior to the Klimt frescos inside. Selected performances are subtitled in English. See the website for the program and to check for any COVID-19 measure you need to take.

MARIONETTE THEATER AT SCHÖNBRUNN PALACE

Schloss Schönbrunn, Hofratstrakt; tel. 01/817-3247; www.marionettentheater.at; tickets €20-39; U4: Schönbrunn

Take the kids to see a production of Mozart's *The Magic Flute* performed by wooden marionette puppets. Even adults will love these delightful productions with ornately dressed puppets in this small theater. All the marionettes, costumes, stage technology and scenery are produced with prominent directors and top designers. (There is a reason this little theater has won awards.) The performances are in German, but English-speaking guests can get a program with the synopsis in English. In the summer there are open-air performances.

TANZQUARTIER WIEN

MuseumsQuartier, Museumsplatz 1; tel. 01/581-3591; www.tqw.at; tickets €15-30; U2: Museumsquartier

The Tanzquartier Wien is Austria's hub for contemporary dance. Part of the MuseumsQuartier, this theater stages around 120 performances a year, with productions from local and international artists. Some of the performances are performed in the large Halle G and Halle E in the MuseumsQuartier. Check the website for the program. During COVID outbreaks, limited seating is available and you will need to wear a mask indoors.

CONCERT VENUES

Vienna is more than just waltzes and Mozart. Get a great feel for live music at these unique and much-loved venues, whether you're up for jazz or something heavier.

PORGY & BESS

Riemergasse 11; tel. 01/512-8811; www.porgy.at; performances from 9pm; tickets €8-50; U3: Stubentor, tram 2: Stubentor

Named after George Gershwin's iconic jazz opera of the same name, Porgy & Bess captures the best in Vienna's jazz scene, while retaining that feel of the music it hosted as part of the "underworld" of the city in the 1940s. The area was replete with bars, clubs and cabarets for more than a 100 years. This dimly lit Jazz club, which fits 350 (but due to COVID-19 safety measures only 130 people are allowed at the time of writing), captures that original spirit; today, it's a non-profit club that serves as a musical hub for local arts. Top jazz acts perform here alongside up-and-coming young performers from the area. Booking ahead is recommended.

THE ARENA

Baumgasse 80; tel. 01/798-8595;
www.arena.co.at; tickets free-€30; U3: Erdberg

Set in a former slaughterhouse under the shadow of the old Gasometer towers, the Arena has become one of Vienna's hottest venues, with 450 events per year. Local and international punk bands, pop groups, rock bands, and drum and bass DJs play here. The history of the Arena goes back to the 1970s, when a neighboring slaughterhouse was occupied by activists, kickstarting a countercultural movement in the city. Though the original site was destroyed with wrecking balls, the neighboring slaughterhouse became today's Arena. Leonard Cohen once described it as "the best place in Vienna."

Festivals and Events

EASTER MARKETS

www.oestermarkt.co.at; dates vary

Schönbrunn Palace is home to the city's most romantic Easter market, with some 60-plus exhibitors offering decorative Easter decorations and Austrian Handicrafts daily 10am-6pm; dates vary each year, so see the website.

DONAUINSELFEST

https://donauinselfest.at; June

The Donauinselfest is one of the largest open-air music festivals in the world, with three million visitors flocking to the five-kilometer (3-mi) stretch of the Danube Island each year. There are usually 10 open-air stages and 18 tented areas, featuring local bands, international acts like Billy Idol and Simple Minds, and DJs. This festival has been active since 1984 and is still a summer highlight. Book your accommodation as early as possible. Bringing your own alcohol is a huge no-no (there are plenty of bars at the festival), and security may also stop you from entering with a large backpack or bag.

The festival usually takes place in late June. In 2020, a scaled-back version took place in front of a limited audience (chosen by raffle) in September, and it seemed that later date may be permanent. Check the website ahead of time before making plans.

Christmas Market in front of the Vienna Rathaus

REGENBOGEN PARADE

https://viennapride.at/regenbogenparade; June

Vienna's Regenbogen Parade paints the Ringstraße rainbow as one of the headlining events of the year on the LGBTQ calendar. Although the parade is the highlight, the weeks surrounding the event also get the city in the mood with parties, events, performances and a Pride Beach set up along the Danube Canal. The parade is usually held in mid-June. Check the website for details.

CHRISTMAS MARKETS

Nov.-Jan.

From mid-November into the New Year, Vienna turns festive with Christmas markets that pop up on pretty much any free town square. The most spectacular are the Christmas markets by the Rathaus (mid-November to 26 December; www.wienerweihnachtstraum.at; Sun-Thu 10am-9:30pm, Fri-Sat 10am-10pm) and Schönbrunn Palace (daily 10am-9pm end of November-26 December; www.weihnachtsmarkt.at).

Expect cute wooden stalls selling ornaments, mulled wine, roasted chestnuts, artisanal goods, strudel, and more. It's essentially an open-air market with a strong festive flair, but you won't find tackiness here—in fact, Vienna's authorities and the organizers behind the iconic market have put strict rules on quality and taste, so you won't find disposable plastic gifts, but rather artisanal goods made from sustainable and quality materials like wood, glass, wax, and fabric.

Even if you don't plan on doing any shopping, it's still worth perusing this living Christmas postcard. Grab some Glühwein—spiced hot wine—and some snacks and take a walk around the market. If you want the perfect festive Instagram post, I recommend heading over to the steps of the Burgtheater (Universitätsring 2) to take in the scene.

VIENNA OPERA BALL

www.wiener-staatsoper.at; year-round

Vienna hosts around 450 balls every year. The most famous is the Vienna Opera Ball at the end of February. The entire opera house is transformed into a spectacular ballroom, with over 5,000 guests. The crème de la crème of Viennese society attends this illustrious occasion. Tickets go on sale as early as two years prior, and usually sell out fast. Tickets begin at €315, but only really get you in through the door. The tickets don't include a seat (reserving a box will set you back €11,000—at least). However, you'll find numerous bars, a casino and a spectacular dance floor.

Shopping

When it comes to shopping for souvenirs in Vienna, there's plenty to choose from. If you want to take home a Sachertorte (whether large or small), there is no need to worry about transporting this decadent cake as it stays fresh (the Sacher Hotel, where the cake was invented, even ships the cake abroad by mail). The same goes for the Imperial Torte.

If you or your loved ones would rather not return home with a stack of cakes and pastries, then you might choose a bottle of pumpkin seed oil, a dark green, cold-pressed oil that is nutty and uniquely Austrian, which you can pick up from one of the stalls in the Naschmarkt, supermarkets, or certain souvenir shops.

On a different note, did you know that Austria invented the snow globe? If you or someone you know is a fan, you're in the right pace to pick up one or two (or more). If you have the opportunity to spend, you may want to consider some Swarovski crystal or a beautiful piece of porcelain from the Augarten Porcelain Factory. For something different, explore Vienna's design scene and discover original and contemporary art pieces or décor that are uniquely Viennese.

Note: If shopping is on your itinerary, please be aware that many shops are closed on Sundays.

SHOPPING DISTRICTS

Downtown Vienna is threaded with pedestrianized zones, shopping streets, design shops and quirky markets. Some, like the flea market, happen only on specific days. Popular souvenirs like a Klimt handbag or boxes of chocolates with Sisi's or Mozart's portrait usually pop up in the typical souvenir shops around the Hofburg and Schönbrunn.

If you want to shop where the locals go, head to the following neighborhoods.

Kärtnerstraße

U1, U3: Stephansplatz, U1, U2, U4: Karlsplatz

Kärtnerstraße lies right in the heart of the 1st district. This almost kilometer-long (0.5-mi-long) shopping artery (which stretches between St. Stephen's Cathedral and the Staatsoper) is one of Vienna's longest shopping streets, and this pedestrianized zone is always busy with locals heading into popular European mainstream fashion stores like H&M, Zara, or Mango. There are also few designer shops thrown into the mix, like Austria's flagship Swarovski store, and labels like Hugo Boss and Karl Lagerfeld.

Goldenes Quartier

U1, U3: Stephansplatz

Just like Paris' Champs Elyseés and London's Bond Street, Vienna also has its quarter of luxury boutiques and stores set in the in the heart of the old city, only a short distance from St. Stephen's Cathedral. The Goldenes Quartier offers luxury blended with the historical character of the neighborhood. It lies between the streets of Tuchlauben, Am Hof, and Bognergasse. You can shop designer labels here like Prada, Armani, Louis Vuitton, Chanel, and other big names.

Kohlmarkt

U3: Herrengasse, U1, U3: Stephansplatz

A few streets down toward the Hofburg, the Kohlmarkt is Empress Elizabeth's favorite confectionary, Demel. This pedestrianized zone of shops is where you come if you're looking to buy jewelry and gems from the likes of Tiffany and Cartier. High fashion houses you may have missed in the Goldenes Quartier set up shop with a more imperial view here, like Gucci and Dior.

Mariahilferstraße

U2: Museumsquartier, U3: Neubaugasse, Zieglergasse

The 1st District may bring in the rich hitting up the luxury boutiques and tourists shopping for souvenirs, but young locals prefer to cross the Ringstraße to the trendy 6th District to Mariahilferstraße, a lively shopping street running for over three kilometers (2 mi) between the MuseumsQuartier and Schönbrunn Palace. It's one of Vienna's longest streets, and much of the shopping action takes place between the Ringstraße and the Westbahnhof. Browse the department stores, malls and small boutiques in and around this shopping metropolis, and don't be afraid of stumbling into the side streets, like Neubaugasse or Zollergasse.

Naschmarkt

U1, U2, U4: Karlsplatz, U4: Kettenbrückengasse

Naschmarkt has such an iconic status in Vienna it's become a sight in its own right. Naschmarkt is more of an experience than a place to buy souvenirs, but if you want to grab some cheese, freshly cooked falafels, and slices of smoked sausage and head to the Stadtpark for a picnic, this is the place to come. The customers here are a mix of tourists and local foodies, but on Saturdays, the crowd is more eclectic when the Flohmarkt (flea market) is on.

DESIGN SHOPS AND MARKETS

Neubau and the MuseumsQuartier

THE VOLTA SHOP

Siebensterngasse 28; www.thevoltashop.com; Tue-Fri 10am-6:30pm, Sat 11am-6pm; U3: Neubaugasse, tram 49: Siebensterngasse

Volta bills itself as the "palace of minimalism" for interior design, arts and crafts, and accessories, such as copper mugs, natural linens, and amber glass bulbs. Volta's minimalist design with stark white walls, meticulously lined with dark wooden shelves stacked with textiles and ceramics keeps the focus on product. If you love light bulbs, you'll find an amazing selection of filters, settings and filaments.

Prater and Around

MAK DESIGN

Stubenring 5; www.makdesignshop.at; Tue 10am-10pm, Wed-Sun 10am-6pm, Tue 10am-9pm; U3: Stubentor, tram 2: Stubentor

This shop, set inside Vienna's Museum of Applied Arts, has been around since 1991, and it was the very first design shop in the city. You won't need a museum ticket to get into the shop—there is a separate entrance from the outside via the Österreicher Restaurant. MAK is packed with great gifts for any design lover, from notebooks and crockery to more left-field souvenirs that make for great conversation pieces, like designer eye patches made by a local goldsmith and sculptor, or a breadbasket made with a stainless-steel mesh that you can form into any shape you want.

CLOTHING AND ACCESSORIES

Historic Center and Hofburg Area

LODEN-PLANKL

Michaelerplatz 6; www.loden-plankl.at; Mon-Sat 10am-5pm; U3: Herrengasse, U1, U3: Stephansplatz

For something authentically Austrian, you can don traditional clothing at this 180-year-old tailoring and clothing shop. You'll find handmade dirndls (traditional Austrian dresses for women), along with loden (fabric made of wool that's been combed and boiled), as well as blouses and coats. This quality clothing shop also offers contemporary designs.

Around Naschmarkt

NACHBARIN

Gumpendorferstraße 17; www.nachbarin.co.at; Mon midday-6:30pm, Tue-Wed, Fri 11am-4pm, Thu 2pm-6pm; U4: Kettenbrückengasse

Nachbarin is a local favorite with Viennese fashionistas. The inventory of women's designer fashion and shoes is made up of hot names from the European design scene, like Veronique Leroy and Anita Moser. Whether you're shopping for clothes, accessories, bags or jewelry, you can be sure of the quality and cult status of each item stacked up in the wood-paneled shop.

SAMSTAG

Margaretenstraße 46; www.samstag-shop.com; Wed-Fri midday-7pm, Sat 10am-6pm; U4: Kettenbrückengasse

Close to the Naschmarkt, this high-fashion store for men and women, run by designers Peter and Christian, focuses on young Austrian designers, but you'll also find international labels. Everything about this shop is a collaboration, including the fun black and white graffiti that animates the facade. The entire boutique lives and breathes the Vienna design scene and is worth dropping by if you want to find something truly local and contemporary.

FLO VINTAGE

Schleifmühlgasse 15a; www.flovintage.com; Mon-Fri 10am-6:30pm, Sat 10am-3:30pm; U4: Kettenbrückengasse

Love vintage? Then check out Flo Vintage, with an excellent collection of women's clothing, dating from 1880 and up to 1980. This store been running since the 1970s. The stock here is substantial, and most of it is meticulously preserved and seldom worn. If you want a pearl-studded dress from the Fin de Siecle, an authentic Flapper dress, or something from the 1950s, you'll find it in this boutique.

EBENBERG

Neubaugasse 4; tel. 06/99-1528-7226; Tue-Fri 1pm-6pm, Sat 11am-4pm; U3: Neubaugasse

This tiny ethical fashion concept store on Neubaugasse is the passion project of designer Laura Ebenberg, who is dedicated to sustainable and ethical fashion. She handpicks items from the European sustainable fashion scene, like Austrian organic brand anzüglich and Berlin-based fair trade fashion company SlowMo—but Ebenberg also presents her own creations in this intimate boutique. Here, you can pick up shoes made from organic ingredients and bags made from recycled sails.

L'ADRESSE

Zollergasse 4; tel. 06/76-653-7911; www.ladresseconceptstore.com; Mon-Fri 11am-7pm, Sat 10am-6pm; U3: Neubaugasse

Founded by French mother-daughter duo Anne and Hanae, these two ladies decided to open this boutique in the trendy Neubau district. The concept? That each item has a story to tell. The bright, airy boutique sells both women's and men's fashion, with items ranging from bags to pajamas and lingerie.

ANTIQUE SHOPS AND MARKETS
Around Naschmarkt
FLOHMARKT

Linke Wienzeile 48-52; Sat 6:30am-2pm; U4: Kettenbrückengasse

If you're in Vienna on a Saturday, make sure you venture one block west of the Naschmarkt for the weekly flea market with some 400 sellers. The chaos of stalls selling everything from

antique chandeliers to old vinyl records and clothing takes place in the vicinity of Otto Wagner's residential Linke Wienzeile building. Even if you don't plan on buying, it's worth heading down to the market just to immerse yourself in this Viennese experience. Brush up on your German numbers if you're the kind of person who likes to negotiate the price.

VINTAGERIE

Nelkengasse 4; www.vintagerie.at; Mon-Fri noon-7pm, Sat 11am-6pm; U3: Neubaugasse

This unique shop occupies a former hair salon on a side street close to Mariahilferstraße. It's a junket of rare furniture and once-loved items from yesterday. If you're a collector, you'll love the design pieces that make their way into the collection as well as vintage items from the 1930s to the 1980s. You may be able to squeeze a 1960s lamp or a designer clock in your suitcase; if not, you may be tempted to ship something home. It's worth it for the experience alone to stop by. There are no price tags, meaning you can negotiate within reason.

GIFTS
Historic Center and Hofburg Area
STEIFF

Bräunerstraße 3; www.steiffinwien.eu; Mon-Fri 10am-12:30pm and 1:30-6pm, Sat 10am-12:30pm and 1:30-5pml U1, U3: Stephansplatz

Steiff—founded by the inventor of the teddy bear, Richard Steiff—has its origins in 19th-century Germany. Its main Austrian shop is worth the visit. When you step inside this nostalgic shop, you'll and find yourself surrounded by rows upon rows of cute cuddly toys, from the classic teddy bear to other members of the animal kingdom, like pandas and puppies, and some of them may be waiting for you to take them home.

1: the Saturday flea market just next to the Naschmarkt 2: Vienna's cafés and bars are the life of the city, and there is no institution quite like Café Sperl.

1

2

Greater Vienna
THE ORIGINAL VIENNESE SNOW GLOBE FACTORY

Schumanngasse 87; tel. 01/486-4341; www.viennasnowglobe.at; Mon-Thu 9am-3pm; U6: Michelbeuern – AKH, tram 9, 42: Sommaraugagasse

At the end of the 19th century, Erwin Perzy, a producer of surgical instruments, received the first patent for his invention of the Schneekugel (snow globe). You can head out to the original Viennese snow globe factory in a suburban house in Hernals, the neighborhood just outside the Gürtel near the Alsergrund. Today the factory is run by the grandson of the inventor, Erwin Perzy III. You can peruse rows upon rows of snow globes with miniature, snowy landscapes of the Riesenrad, Schönbrunn Palace, and Stephansdom inside. There is also a small museum (free entry) that illustrates how they're made, along with the workshop where the snow globe was invented. If you have a special gift in mind, you can request custom snow globes to order. Snow globes cost from €7-25, depending on the size.

SWAROVSKI CRYSTAL
Historic Center and Hofburg Area
SWAROVSKI KRISTALLWELTEN STORE

Kärtner Straße 24; tel. 01/324-0000; www.swarovski.com; Mon-Fri 10am-7pm, Sat 10am-6pm; U1, U3: Stephansplatz

If you're strolling down Kärtner Straße in the evening, you may see the Swarovski Kristallwelten store's façade lit up by LED crystal light modules and art installations. Go inside and immerse yourself in the dazzling world of cut and polished crystal from the iconic Austrian crystal manufacturer. It's more than just a place to take home crystal jewelry, watches, and Christmas ornaments—it also features crystal installations by different designers and artists. You can find everything crystal here in all colors, styles, and shapes.

Viennese Coffeehouses

TOP EXPERIENCE

Even more essential than a visit to the Hofburg is a trip to an authentic Kaffeehaus. Although some have morphed into "museums," you can still find classic coffeehouses that capture the Viennese spirit. Each café has its own character and style, and some are more opulent than others, but they will usually have cozy booths and marble tables where you could comfortably sip coffee all day, newspapers, coat stands by the door, and elegantly dressed waiters. Some have quirky features as a nod back to their late 19th-century/early 20th-century heritage, like old telephone boxes in the back.

Some of the traditional coffeehouses also serve classic Austrian dishes like Schnitzel and have strudels and cakes. These cafés are all have waiter service, but don't expect a service with a smile—the waiters' grumpy demeanor (or perhaps grumpy by American standards) is part of the coffeehouse experience.

The best thing about Vienna's cafés is the people watching. Put down your phone and watch some of the eccentric characters come and go, from elegantly dressed old men to art students sketching in the corner.

HISTORIC CENTER AND HOFBURG AREA
CAFÉ ALT WIEN

Bäckerstraße 9; tel 01/512-5222; www.kaffeealtwien.at; Sun-Thu 9am-midnight, Fri-Sat 10am-1am; U1, U4: Schwedenplatz, U3: Stubentor

The Alt Wien is plastered wall-to-wall with movie, exhibition and event posters, and it's an institution locals love. It's a cozy place to forget the world, with a Melange at hand as

What to Order in a Kaffeehaus

When you arrive at a coffeehouse, slip into one of the cushioned booths and choose the coffee of your choice from the menu (which may include more than 30 choices). The classics are:

- **Kleiner/Großer Schwarzer:** Single or double espresso, depending on whether you order small (kleiner) or large (großer).

- **Kleiner/Großer Brauner:** Similar to the Schwarzer, except you get a little cream on the side, so you can tailor your coffee as you like it.

- **Verlängerter:** Close to the classic Americano: a small cup of espresso served in a large cup with hot water added. Sometimes you'll get cream or milk on the side.

- **Melange:** The ultimate Viennese coffee drink—a small espresso topped half with steamed milk and milk froth.

- **Franziskaner:** Like a Melange, but with whipped cream on the top in place of milk foam.

- **Einspänner:** Double espresso topped with a dollop of fresh whipped cream. The name in English is "hansom" (a one-horse carriage typical for 19th-century Vienna). Legend has it that the drink was once a favorite with the carriage drivers who used the cream to stop the coffee from getting cold.

you recline in your chair and observe the regulars who frequent the café like their second home.

CAFÉ PRÜCKEL

Stubenring 24; tel. 01/512-6115; http://prueckel.at; daily 8:30am-10pm; U3: Stubentor, tram 2: Stubentor
Some cafés take pride in their historic literary legacy, and the Prückel is still a hangout for writers in Vienna's contemporary literary scene. The café dates back to 1904—you'll see the odd art nouveau detail here and there, but most of it bears a pink and tan look from the 1950s. You should come to Prückel for the sumptuous cakes, apple strudel, colorful fruit-based cakes or rich chocolate.

CAFÉ FRAUENHUBER

Himmelpfortgasse 6; tel. 01/512-5353; www.caféfrauenhuber.at; Mon-Sat 8am-8pm; U1, U3: Stephansplatz
Vienna's oldest kaffeehaus dates back to the 18th century, and it carries a classical cache since Mozart and Beethoven performed here. This café is cozy and refined, with low, arched ceilings and red damask armchairs. Grab one

of their house strudels with a coffee and bask in the ambience.

★ CAFÉ HAWELKA

Dorotheergasse 6; tel. 01/512-8230; www.hawelka.at; Sun-Wed 9am-7pm, Thu-Sat 9am-11pm; U1, U3: Stephansplatz
Hawelka is perhaps the most iconic of the Viennese cafés. It's dark and a bit moody, with faded upholstered booths, wooden coat stands and local art on the wall. It was opened in 1939 by Leopold and Josephine Hawelka (who formerly ran the Alt Wien). It has catered to an artistic clientele, counting Hundertwasser, Andy Warhol and Arthur Miller among its former regulars. Go after 8pm when freshly made Buchteln, baked dumplings filled with jam (Josephine's family recipe) are available, fresh out of the oven. They have a street side terrace if you prefer to sit outside.

★ CAFÉ BRÄUNERHOF

Stallburggasse 2; tel. 01/512-3893; Mon-Fri 8am-7:30pm, Sat 8am-6:30pm, Sun 10am-6:30pm; U1, U3: Stephansplatz
A street away from the Hofburg, Bräunerhof

still retains its timeless local charm. It was once the haunt of Thomas Bernhard (author of *Wittgenstein's Nephew*). You won't see Bernhard today, but if you're lucky, you may see actor Christoph Waltz sitting in one of the booths. Otherwise just enjoy the old-world charm of this café with a classic Viennese coffee like an Einspänner, a black coffee topped with cream.

KLEINES CAFÉ

Franziskanerplatz 3; Mon-Sat 10am-2am,
Sun 1pm-midnight; U1, U3: Stephansplatz

If you've seen *Before Sunrise* you'll recognize this tiny and charming café on Franziskanerplatz. There are a handful of marble tables in the tiny indoor section (and more space in the newer extension toward the back), but the main appeal is the generous outdoor area, where tables spread up to the fountain. Dating to the 1970s, it's a fixture on the Viennese café scene, and perfect if you're looking for a traditional style café with a charming outdoor space.

AROUND NASCHMARKT

★ CAFÉ SPERL

Gumpendorferstraße 11; tel. 01/586-4158;
www.cafésperl.at; Mon-Sat 7am-10pm,
Sun 10am-8pm; U3: Museumsquartier,
U4: Kettenbrückengasse

Sperl, which opened in 1880, has hardly changed—and without turning into a caricature of itself. It's a cozy café you could easily lose an afternoon inside, just sitting in one of the upholstered booths reading the paper, playing a game of billiards, or drinking from the menu of 34 coffees. You may want to try the house cake, the Sperl Schnitte, a rich chocolate wafer.

CAFÉ SAVOY

Linke Wienzeile 36; tel. 06/60-798-2623;
https://cafe-savoy.at; Sun-Fri 10am-1am,
Sat 9am-1am; U4: Kettenbrückengasse

Parked next to the Naschmarkt, next to Otto Wagner's floral and golden houses on the Wienzeile, Café Savoy captures the spirit of old Viennese coffeehouses with a glamourous twist. This café resides in an old palace once belonging to a textile baron. It opened in 1896 as the Café Wienzeile and was renamed Café Savoy in 1983. Since then it has become an iconic gay-friendly hangout. Come and grab a coffee under the bronze chandeliers and high ceilings, or on its terrace overlooking the gold Medallion house next door.

KARLSPLATZ AND THE BELVEDERE PALACE AREA

CAFE GOLDEGG

Argentinierstraße 49; tel. 01/505-9162; www.
cafégoldegg.at; Mon-Fri 8am-8pm, Sat 9am-8pm,
Sun 9am-7pm; S1, S2, S3, S4: Wien Quartier
Belvedere, tram 1, 18, O: Wien Quartier Belvedere

You won't find crowds of tourists in this café (opened in 1910, close to Belvedere). Instead, you'll find a coterie of locals who come here for their ritualistic coffee. It's quiet at times—the only noise you might hear are cooking sounds from kitchen. If you're looking for a moment of peace and quiet, head to this demure café painted in tones of burgundy, green and gold. (Note: Smokers have their own section here.)

Food

Austrian food is rich and hearty, and meat and cakes dominate menus around the city. Unless you're vegetarian, it would be a crime to miss out on the famous Wiener Schnitzel in its many varieties here—most traditionally veal. If you're hungry for Wiener Schnitzel, look for the word "Beisl," the name for a typical Viennese tavern that cooks up good Austrian comfort food. These cozy pubs tend to be old fashioned with dark wood paneling, plain, undecorated wooden tables, and low lighting.

Breakfasts in Austria are a feast. A traditional breakfast usually features Semmeln, white bread rolls that are crusty on the outside and soft and spongy on the inside (the singular noun is Semmel), along with butter and coffee. You may also find cold cuts, boiled eggs, cakes and pastries, jams, and orange juice. Most hotels in Vienna will offer a luxurious buffet you can fill up on in the morning. If you choose to go into a café, many will offer a breakfast menus. You may notice something called a Viennese Breakfast in a café—this is a portion for a single person, with a Semmel, jam, coffee, butter, and a glass of orange juice. You can also get a savory breakfast with slices of cheese and ham, or a boiled egg. Breakfast is usually served until noon and sometimes to 2pm. Cafés mostly buzz with crowds around 9-10am.

In general, portions are generous, and unless you're in a fine dining place it's okay to ask for a container for leftovers.

Viennese Eateries
BEISL

These unique Viennese bistros serve hearty local cuisine and have their origins in the 18th-century inns. The word "Beisl" perhaps originates from the Yiddish word for house, "Bajiss." Most Beisln, the plural in German for Beisl, are simple on the inside, with dark painted wood paneling and plain tables that sometimes sprawl out onto the cobbled streets on the outside or into a courtyard. Food is hearty, dense, and focuses on local specials, think Schnitzel, goulash, pastries, and clear consumes served with strips of pancakes. Although most Beisln root themselves in tradition, a new wave of Beisl has taken over the city known as neo-Beisln, where old recipes get a modern twist.

HEURIGER

For something genuinely Viennese, visit a Heuriger, one of the rustic wine taverns you'll usually find on the outskirts of the city, like Grinzing or Oberlaa. Legends and songs have sprung up in honor of these taverns, it would be a crime to miss one on your trip. They are the perfect place to try local, Viennese wines with the ideal food to go with them. Look out for the signs with the pine branches on them and the word "Ausgsteckt," with the time the tavern opens. The most important feature of any Heuriger is the Heuriger Wine, usually made by the owner of the inn and often a very young wine, around a year old. In the Heuriger, food is sold by the decagram, with a mix of warm and cold food. You can usually get roast pork, blood sausage, cured meats and other dishes that go well with the local wine.

WÜRSTELSTAND

Try some Viennese street food for something local and on a budget—or for a late-night snack—at one of the many sausage stands scattered around the city. Give the Käsekrainer, sausage stuffed with cheese, a taste for something unique, but you can also go for the usual Frankfurters, Bratwurst, and other sausage specials. Order a slice of bread, pickles, fries, and even a beer. These quirky kiosks where all walks of life come to snack—from taxi drivers to the drunken elite in their opera gowns—are meant to be dined at standing. Have some mustard (strong or sweet) with your meat, but don't ask for mayonnaise unless you're having fries.

KAFFEEHAUS AND KONDITOREI

It would be a crime to leave Vienna without visiting an iconic Kaffeehaus. You could spend a day in Vienna's coffeehouses sipping Melanges and people watching. Another establishment to look out for is the Konditorei, confectionary shops with beautiful cakes with generous layers of marzipan or jellied fruit toppings, or lashings of cream. Vienna is famous for its pastries so make sure you order a strudel or a Sachertorte while you're here.

HISTORIC CENTER AND HOFBURG AREA
Austrian
ZWÖLF APOSTELKELLER

Sonnenfelsgasse 3; tel. 01/512-6777; www.zwoelf-apostelkeller.at; Mon-Fri 4pm-11pm, Sat-Sun 11am-11pm; mains €8-20; U1, U3: Stephansplatz, U1, U4: Schwedenplatz, tram 1, 2: Schwedenplatz

Zwölf Apostelkeller (12 Apostles Cellar) lies deep in a gorgeous vaulted 14th-century cellar below the old city; it can seat over 300 people. Time seems to stop here as you dine on traditional Austrian cuisine made with local ingredients. Try their Fiakergulasch, a beef goulash stew with sausage and fried egg, along with one of their beers on tap, or local Viennese white wines, like the Gemischter Satz, a special Viennese blend. You may get lucky and be treated to a concert of Heurigen Musik, Austrian tavern music.

REINTHALER'S BEISL

Dorotheergasse 2-4; tel. 01/513-1249; www.reinthalersbeisl.com; daily 11am-11pm; mains €9.80-16.20; U1, U3: Stephansplatz

If you're looking for the traditional Beisl experience, Reinthaler's has it. Complete with dusky wood paneling, low-hanging lights and packed with locals tucking into a plate of *Tafelspitz* or smoked pork, you should find the Viennese atmosphere you're looking for here. Food is good, hearty, inexpensive, and the service is prompt and friendly.

CAFÉ HOFBURG

Innerer Burghof 1; tel. 01/241-00400; www.cafe-hofburg.at; daily 10am-6pm; mains €13-16; U3: Herrengasse

Set inside the Hofburg, this café and bistro serves classic Austrian cuisine like Viennese beef consommé, Schnitzel, goulash, and sausages. A classic Viennese coffeehouse environment, with plush velvet seating and decadent cakes on display behind a glass cabinet adds to the cozy atmosphere, making it a good place to stop in for lunch after a long tour (though it is a bit of a tourist trap).

★ FIGLMÜLLER

Wollzeile 5; tel. 01/512-6177; www.figlmueller.at; daily 11am-10pm; mains €10-20.50; U1, U3: Stephansplatz

Figlmüller is a Viennese institution—a traditional Beisl that serves some of the biggest Schnitzels in the city. (At 30 cm/12 in in diameter, you won't leave hungry.) The owner has his own vineyard, so try local varieties like the Grüner Veltliner if you like whites, or the Blaufränkischer if you prefer spicy reds. This atmospheric old wine tavern is hidden in an alleyway just off the Wollzeile. It's a popular place (reservations are a must!), but you can also try your luck at Bäckerstraße, Figlmüller's second location.

GRIECHENBEISL

Fleischmarkt 11; tel. 01/533-1977; www.griechenbeisl.at; daily 4pm-11:30pm; mains €15-30; U1, U4: Schwedenplatz; tram 1, 2: Schwedenplatz

Beethoven, Brahms, Strauss, and even Mark Twain once frequented this traditional Viennese restaurant (one of the city's oldest, dating back to the 15th century). You can enjoy all the classic meat-heavy Viennese favorites, like Schnitzel, Tafelspitz and goulash. (There are options for vegetarians as well.) Take a seat in the garden if you can, but if the weather is not on your side, try to get a table in the oldest section, like the Zither Stüberl rooms, where you can view famous autographs displayed on the walls.

Austrian Specialties

Viennese specials often revolve around two things: meat and sweets. Expect food to be heavy, hearty, and filling. You may feel the urge to resist the cakes and chocolates, but I highly discourage this—the Austrians make some of the best cakes and pastries in the world. (Did you know the croissant is actually Austrian?)

RESTAURANT ENTRÉES

- **Tafelspitz:** A classic dish featuring boiled beef with horseradish, potatoes, and apples.

- **Schnitzel:** A slice of pork or veal (a true Wiener Schnitzel is made with veal) that's been hammered into a thin disc, then coated with breadcrumbs and fried, and usually drizzled with lemon.

- **Backhendl:** Made from the succulent Austrian Styrian chicken, this half or whole chicken is coated in breadcrumbs and fried until golden. The chicken is best eaten with a vinegary potato salad drizzled with pumpkin seed oil, and served with a side of lingonberry jam.

Try a Käsekrainer at an iconic Viennese Würstelstand.

STREET FOOD

- **Bratwurst:** Fried sausage, available from Würstelstand—sausage stands you'll see around the city. Slice it up and eat it with a side of mustard, or ask for an extra slice of bread.

- **Käsekrainer:** Another hit at the Würstelstand, these fried and grilled sausages are filled with cheese. Eat these with a white bread roll or a slice of dark bread with a dash of mustard.

DESSERT AND CAKES

- **Sachertorte:** This iconic cake, invented at the famous Sacher Hotel, is a dense, rich chocolate sponge with a thin spread of apricot jam in the middle layer. The whole cake is covered in a layer of chocolate icing and served with whipped cream.

- **Imperial Torte:** The Sacher is not the only hotel with a signature cake. The nearby Imperial also has a legendary cake: The Imperial Torte. The cake is made with layers of whipped chocolate cream, sliced almonds, covered with marzipan and topped with a chocolate glaze.

- **Apfelstrudel:** This hearty Austrian classic is a rich, flaky pastry filled with a stewed apple filling. It comes with a serving of cream on the side.

PLACHUTTA

Wollzeile 38; tel. 01/512-1577; www.plachutta.at; daily 11:30am-11:15pm; mains €16.50-30; U3: Stubentor, tram 2: Stubentor

This restaurant is the place to try Franz Joseph's favorite dish: Tafelspitz, boiled cuts of beef served over three courses: beef broth, beef marrow, on toast, and finally the meat itself. An international crowd dines here. There are other items on the menu, but with 13 varieties of Austrian-reared beef cuts to choose from for inclusion in your Tafelspitz, ordering anything else would be waste of a visit. Waiters bring out the Tafelspitz in copper pots that are kept warm throughout your meal, along with accompaniments like cream of spinach, roasted grated potatoes, plus horseradish and applesauce. Plachutta gets pretty packed around lunchtime, so book ahead.

International
SAID THE BUTCHER TO THE COW

*Opernring 11; tel. 01/535-69696; http://butcher-cow.
at; Tue-Sat 4pm-1am; mains €11-32; U1, U2, U4:
Karlsplatz, tram 1, 2, 71, D: Oper, Karlsplatz*

If you're craving a burger, head over to this joint, where the burgers live up to the hype. Served with brioche buns, you'll find innovative options such as grilled octopus tentacles, or chicken teriyaki with mango chutney. Vegetarians should try the marinated halloumi burger or the black bean burger. You can also get great steaks, and there is a gin bar with over 30 varieties, plus a selection of tonics. For something different, try the saffron gin.

Fine Dining
★ TIAN

*Himmelpfortgasse 23; tel. 01/890-46652; www.
tian-restaurant.com; Wed-Sat 6pm-11pm; 8-10 courses
€121-137; U4: Stadtpark, tram 2: Weihburggasse*

Tian is unique in the Michelin-starred restaurant world for its exclusively vegetarian culinary creations. Set aside two hours to pace yourself through 8-10 creative courses that will make you see cauliflower, cabbage and kohlrabi in a new light. Christian Halper and chef Paul Ivić use organic, locally sourced and seasonal produce—some from Tian's own garden. When you arrive, you'll be led down into the low-lit basement and welcomed on their culinary journey. Each course resembles a piece of modern art. Your server will not only deconstruct the ingredients but explain how to taste each dish, whether it's composed of a single vegetable or designed with creative pairings like dark chocolate and beetroot. (Don't skip the raw cheese plate.)

The menu is a great experience even if you aren't vegetarian, and it can be tailored for vegans upon request. If you don't have the budget to dine here, you can head over to Tian's sister restaurant, **Tian Bistro**, in Neubau.

Brunch
THE GUESTHOUSE
BRASSERIE & BAKERY

*Führichgasse 10; tel. 01/512-1320;
www.theguesthouse.at/breakfast.html; daily
6:30am-11pm; breakfasts €9-21; U1, U2, U4:
Karlsplatz, tram 1, 2, 71, D: Oper, Karlsplatz*

You don't have to be a hotel guest to enjoy the breakfasts at The Guesthouse: This bistro occupying the ground floor of the boutique hotel overlooking the Albertina is popular with locals and tourists alike. Many come for the all-day breakfasts, served with homemade bread and pastries. The Eggs Benedict and Eggs Florentine are house favorites, but for a more indulgent spread, opt for the Guesthouse Breakfast, which comes with delicacies like smoked salmon, dry cured ham, soft and hard cheeses, and more. The coffee served here is the hotel's special roast. Book a table if you plan to come in the morning.

Street Food
★ TRZEŚNIEWSKI

*Dorotheergasse 1; www.trzesniewski.at; Mon-Fri
9am-7pm, Sat 10am-6pm, Sun 10am-5pm;
sandwiches €1.40; U1, U3: Stephansplatz*

With windows of opaque glass, Trześniewski may look like a clandestine establishment from the outside—but inside, it's a popular sandwich bar where you can get small open-faced sandwiches topped with local produce, paprika-laced cream cheese or pates—for just over a euro each. Just point to the sandwiches you want to order. Ask for a beer when you pay and you'll get a poker chip to hand to the person pulling Hobbit-sized "pints." There are a few tables, but it's mostly standing room only. Other branches of Trześniewski can be found around Vienna, but the atmosphere here is special.

★ BITZINGER WÜRSTELSTAND
AM ALBERTINAPLATZ

*Albertinaplatz; www.bitzinger-wien.at; Sun-Wed
9am-10pm, Thu-Sat 9am-11pm; sausages €4-5; U1,
U2, U4: Karlsplatz; tram 1, 2, 71, D: Oper, Karlsplatz*

Sausage stands are iconic in Vienna, and

you'll see them all across the city, but this Würstelstand sandwiched between the Albertina and the Opera House has cult status. Before the pandemic, it wasn't uncommon to see people dressed for the opera standing around drinking champagne and eating inexpensive sausages late night after a show, but even with the reduced opening hours, it makes the perfect al fresco dining option. Go for the Bratwurst (fried sausage) or the Käsekrainer (sausage infused with cheese), with a slice of bread and some sweet (süß) or spicy (scharf) mustard. You can also grab some beer or wine for a few euros, of if you're feeling fancy, a 0.2-liter (just under 7-oz) bottle of champagne (around €23), and enjoy the view of the Staatsoper while eating.

Cafés and Cakes

DEMEL

Kohlmarkt 14; www.demel.at; daily 9am-7pm; coffees €6, cakes €4-6; U1, U3: Stephansplatz, U3: Herrengasse

This legendary café and cake shop just a short stroll from the Hofburg was once a favorite hangout of Empress Sisi. (One story tells of a tunnel that ran from the palace to the patisserie so the Empress could have her cake incognito. It's also said that the waitresses wear black to mourn their beloved patron, who was stabbed on Lake Geneva.) Grab an indulgent cake or a coffee in the café's elegant mirror lined salon. Favorites include the decadent chocolate-nougat house cake, the Anna Demel Torte. You can also try the Demel's Sachertorte—the cake that launched a lawsuit between the Sacher Hotel and the café. (Sacher was once a pastry chef at Demel, and there was a decade long dispute as to who had the rights to the cake.) If you want to take something special home, buy a box of candied violets from the shop on the way out. (They were one of Sisi's favorite sweets!) At the time of writing Demel was temporarily closed due to COVID-19, so it's worth checking the website before you plan to go.

★ CAFÉ CENTRAL

Herrengasse 14; tel. 01/533-3763-24; www. cafécentral.wien; Mon-Sat 8:30am-8pm, Sun 10am-8pm; coffees €3.50-7.30, cakes €4.20-6; U3: Herrengasse, tram 1, 71, D: Rathausplatz/Burgtheater

With arched ceilings, marble columns, decadent cakes and literary history, Café Central (set in a former stock exchange) draws in tourists in droves. Locals prefer less-touristy venues, but if you're in Vienna, you may as well have a coffee where Trotsky played chess and Freud smoked cigars. Order a Melange, pick out one of the colorful cakes behind the glass casing, and let your waiter do the rest. Expect queues out the doors in the afternoon, especially weekends. You can book a table on weekdays, or just come early for breakfast (€6.70-18.90).

CAFE KORB

Brandstätte 9; tel. 01/533-1526; www.cafékorb. at; Mon-Sat 8am-midnight, Sun 10am-11pm; mains €6-10; U1, U3: Stephansplatz, U3: Herrengasse

This café has a couple of claims to fame. The first: It was one of Sigmund Freud's many hangouts. The second: it's Apfelstrudel (apple strudel). This café has a retro 1960s look, with faded photographs and cozy booths. This coffeehouse also serves Schnitzel and sausages, but most come here for the strudel and to relax with a coffee. The crowd here is eclectic and artistic; literary and other creative events are held in the basement from time to time. There is a big street terrace if you prefer to sit outside.

CAFÉ SACHER

Philharmonikerstraße 4; tel. 01/514-561-053; www.sacher.com; daily 8am-7pm; original Sachertorte €8; U1, U2, U4: Karlsplatz, tram 1, 2, 71, D: Oper, Karlsplatz

Try Vienna's most famous cake in its namesake café—but you may have to queue to get in at peak times or book a table on certain day for breakfast via the website. The café has an imperial feel, with red damask fabrics on the walls and white wood paneling, marble tables, and plush burgundy carpets.

VIENNA
FOOD

The Sachertorte is a dark chocolate, layered cake with a glazing of apricot in the middle, topped with chocolate fondant icing. It is best served with a Melange to cut the sweetness.

The café may not be the least expensive place to try the Sachertorte, but considering the recipe is tightly guarded by the hotel (having been passed down through the Sacher family), it's worth it. If you can't get into the original café, head to the other side of the hotel to the Sacher Eck, another café located within the hotel, where you'll find a shop selling the cakes and a more modern café.

Vegetarian, Vegan, and Gluten-Free
WRENKH
Bauernmarkt 10; tel. 01/533-1526; www.wrenkh-wien. at; Mon-Sat 11am-11pm; mains €8-25; U1, U3: Stephansplatz, U1, U4: Schwedenplatz, tram 1, 2: Schwedenplatz
This friendly downtown bistro specializes in seasonal vegetable-based dishes, like pumpkin seed oil Spätzle, an Austrian pasta dish served with ewe cheese and roasted pumpkin seeds in the fall, or creative soups like saffron-fruit consommé in the summer. The menu changes weekly and you also have a street side terrace if you prefer outdoor dining.

Wrenkh also offers cooking courses.

The best time to drop in is at lunchtime on weekdays, when you can get a two or three-course lunch for around €10. The service here comes with a smile. Reservations are a must.

NEUBAU AND THE MUSEUMSQUARTIER
Austrian
GASTWIRTSCHAFT WRATSCHKO
Neustiftgasse 51; tel. 01/523-7161; www.wratschko. wien; Mon-Sat 5pm-1am; mains €7-20; U2, U3: Volkstheater, tram 46: Strozzigasse, tram 49: Volkstheater
Satisfying Austrian cuisine made with organic produce awaits here. You can try some interesting Austrian dishes, like Gröstl, meat and potatoes cooked together in a pan, or creative takes on classics like their peach strudel.

(Note: This pub is smoker-friendly, with only one non-smoking section in the back of the restaurant.)

If you plan on visiting here on the weekend, make sure you book ahead.

AMERLINGBEISL
Stiftgasse 8; tel. 01/526-1660; www.amerlingbeisl. at; Mon-Fri 11:30am-1am, Sat-Sun 10am-1am; mains €10-20; U2, U3: Volkstheater, tram 49: Stiftgasse
For a more modern Beisl experience, head to this Austrian-fusion restaurant in the heart of the Neubau area. You'll get Austrian specials like organic pork Schnitzel, beef goulash, Brettljause (a Heurigen platter with cold cuts, cheese, pickles and rye bread), along with Mediterranean-inspired dishes such as pasta and hummus plates. (If the organic veal Schnitzel is on the daily specials list, I highly recommend ordering it!) The real charm of Amerlingbeisl is its magical vine-clad garden strewn with parasols and Moroccan lanterns. Best to book ahead, but if you don't, you can just sit in the bar with glass of Wiener Gemischter Satz until a table frees up.

SCHNITZELWIRT
Neubaugasse 52; tel. 01/523-3771; www.schnitzelwirt.co.at; Tue-Sat 11am-10pm; mains €11-20; U3: Neubaugasse
This restaurant is huge. It's popular with the locals for its traditional food—especially the Schnitzels (which no one finishes, apparently, but the good news is the waiters will wrap it up in wax paper and a bag so you can take it home and have it later). The Schnitzels don't come with sides; you need to ask for fries, sauerkraut, salad, or potato salad as an extra. There are other options on the menu, but this place is about the Schnitzel.

Bistros
RESTAURANT 1070
Gutenberggasse 28; tel. 01/676-566-1774; www.restaurant-1070.com; Wed-Sun 5:30pm-1am; 3 courses €30; U2, U3: Volkstheater, tram 49: Volkstheater
Restaurant 1070 (named after its postal code)

is tucked away on a cobbled backstreet in the 7th District. This bistro, set in a quaint, cozy old townhouse, serves Mediterranean and Austrian recipes with a modern twist. All the dishes are prepared fresh daily from seasonal ingredients. Don't expect a menu: the default is three courses, but the food is so good most people ask for a fourth. The experience is slightly theatrical without being pretentious. There are only around eight tables inside, with limited outdoor seating, so make sure you book ahead (the online form on the website makes this easy). Let the server know if you have any dietary requirements, and they'll take care of the rest.

Brunch
SNEAK IN

Siebensterngasse 12; www.sneakin.at; Tue-Fri 9am-11pm (breakfast until 2pm), Sat 10am-midday (brunch) 3pm-11pm (drinks and bites), Sun 12:30pm-3pm; brunch €19; U2, U3: Volkstheater, tram 49: Stiftgasse

If you want an Instagrammable brunch, Sneak In offers spectacular brunches in building that serves as a bar, café and sneaker store with a gallery. It's popular with trendy young locals living in the area who come for the ambience. The food is served up on wooden boards. Brunch menus include a hot beverage and a buffet, where you'll find salads, cold cuts, cheeses, various breads and tasty dips. If you plan on coming on a weekend, make sure you reserve your spot!

Vegetarian, Vegan, and Gluten-Free
TIAN BISTRO

Schrankgasse 4; tel. 01/890-466-532; www. tian-bistro.com; Wed-Fri 5:30pm-10pm, Sat-Sun 10am-3pm and 5:30pm-10pm; courses €15-22; U2, U3: Volkstheater, tram 49: Stiftgasse

Tian Bistro (the less expensive sister restaurant of fine dining spot Tian) serves delicious vegan and vegetarian dishes, both indoors and on a spacious patio (weather permitting). Breakfast is served until 2pm on the weekends. Try the savory Tian Raphaello, a creative dish made from white polenta, or their vegan tarte flambée.

AROUND NASCHMARKT
International
NENI AM NASCHMARKT

Naschmarkt 510; tel. 01/585-2020; https://neni.at; Mon-Sat 8am-11pm; mains €13-18; U4: Kettenbrückengasse

You'll find NENI by the cheese mongers and the baklava stand in the heart of the Naschmarkt. This industrial-looking restaurant dishes out delicious and nutritious breakfasts, tasty Middle Eastern specials like shakshuka and hummus, along with creative dishes like spicy caramelized eggplant or the Israeli dessert Knafeh, a sweet pastry filled with cheese. Afternoons and evenings are packed, especially if there's a DJ—so it's smart to book in advance. It's also worth coming in the morning when things are quiet: Order the avocado breakfast toast served on sourdough bread, topped with pickled carrots and served with hard-boiled organic eggs.

Cafés and Cakes
★ VOLLPENSION

Schleifmühlgasse 16; tel. 01/585-0464; Mon-Sat 7:30am-10pm, Sun 8am-8pm; mains €7-9; U4: Kettenbrückengasse

This cozy café is welcoming, with bare brick walls adorned with family portraits, and old, mismatched armchairs. The coffee shop is open to everyone. And here, young people and senior citizens working side-by-side. Vollpension serves home cooking and cakes made with love. The menu changes regularly. (Soups, stews and sandwiches are among the staples.)

Head up to the counter to place your order, and the food will be delivered to your table. Try the cakes of the day (there are over 200 in this establishment's repertoire). Your options include everything from classic carrot cakes to strudels. You can also get a great breakfast here with cold cuts, cheese and rolls.

EIS GREISSLER

Mariahilferstraße 33; www.eis-greissler.at;
daily 11am-10pm; scoop €1.50; U3: Neubaugasse

Just look for the queue to find this ice cream parlor. When the sun comes out, locals line up to try Eis Greissler's ice cream, made from organic milk, cream and yogurt from its very own farm in nearby Lower Austria. (You can also get vegan friendly scoops made from oat or soy milk.) The flavors come and go seasonally, and it's worth popping in and seeing what's on offer the day you decide to go—chocolate, butter caramel, strawberry, raspberry, or pear.

Vegetarian, Vegan, and Gluten-Free

MY SECRET GARDEN

Mariahilferstraße 45; tel. 01/586-2839; www.
secretgardenrestaurant.at; Mon-Sat 9:30am-7pm,
Sun 10am-3pm; courses €8-13; U3: Neubaugasse

My Secret Garden definitely lives up to its name. This tiny little vegan and gluten-free friendly haven resides in a central courtyard within a hidden passage running between Mariahilferstraße and Windmühlgasse. The menu changes daily, offering a soup of the day, curry of the day and daily specials—all at a very reasonable price. The shady courtyard garden offers the perfect respite from the business of the downtown city. Do note that it's not wheelchair friendly, with three are steps within sloped the passage required to access it.

KARLSPLATZ AND THE BELVEDERE PALACE AREA

Austrian

GMOAKELLER

Am Heumarkt 25; tel. 01/712-5310; www.gmoakeller.
at; Mon-Sat 11am-11pm, Sun 11am-3pm; mains €9-18;
U4: Stadtpark, tram 2, 71, D: Schwarzenbergplatz

If you want a taste of authentic local cuisine Gmoakeller is a good choice. Brick vaults, parquet floors, and wooden panels lining the walls give it a cozy, feel, but it's the food that's worth the visit. They've been cooking up Austrian specials since 1858. Try the Zwiebelrostbraten, a Viennese dish made with roast beef, topped with onions, and served with potatoes, or the roasted or baked veal with parsley potatoes or mayonnaise salad. Above all, make sure you try the crisp and aromatic Austrian wines on the menu, like the red Zweigelt or the white Viennese cuvee, the Gemischter Satz. You can also grab a table outdoors here.

CAFE IMPERIAL

Kärntner Ring 16; tel. 01/501-10389; www.
café-imperial.at; daily 7am-11pm; mains €20-30; U1,
U2, U4: Karlsplatz, tram 1, 2, 71, D: Oper, Karlsplatz

Café Imperial, first opened in 1873, can be found on the ground floor of the grand hotel of the same name, boasts a guestbook of illustrious guests like Sigmund Freud, Gustav Mahler, and Stefan Zweig. It's elegant and modern with contemporary chandeliers and plush velvet booths. Despite being set inside a hotel, its sumptuous buffet champagne breakfasts (€41), and other meals are open to non-hotel guests. The chefs here cook up Austrian classics like Wiener Schnitzel (some argue it's the best in the city). And don't miss the house cake (the Imperial Torte), made with layers of marzipan and chocolate. If you're a fan of dark chocolate, they also have a wonderful chocolate orange or the raspberry version.

Bistros

JOSEPH BROT

Landstraßer Hauptstraße 4; http://www.joseph.co.at;
Mon-Fri 8am-9pm, Sat-Sun 8am-6pm; mains €13-18;
S1, S2, S3, S4: Wien Mitte-Landstraße Bahnhof, U3,
U4: Landstraße, tram 1, O: Landstraße, Wien Mitte

Joseph Brot is one of the best bakers in Vienna, baking creative loaves (like rye-honey-lavender or olive and tomato ciabatta). This bistro is ideal for a hearty breakfast, but you can also get smoothies, tea and coffee, and pastries to die for. The breakfast menu is diverse, with items like eggs benedict, and options like whole grain bread with avocado cream and chia pudding. Later in the day, you can get seasonal bistro dishes, including soups, salads, quinoa bowls or a classic burger. There are a few tables on the street if you prefer outdoor dining.

LINGENHEL

Landstraßer Hauptstraße 74; tel. 01/710-1566; www.lingenhel.com; Mon-Fri 9am-5pm, Sat 8am-3pm; mains €20-25; U3: Rochusgasse

This deli-bar-restaurant that also houses a shop has taken over a manor house dating back to 1795 and brings in the crowd for the cheeses produced in their own dairy, along with fine wines and salami cold cuts. Asides from picks of deli cuts, this restaurant with whitewashed walls also serves gourmet dishes, like gazpacho with avocado cream or burrata with passionfruit. You can also simply pop in before dinner for an aperitif with a glass of the house vermouth. But if you love cheese, this establishment worth the detour. Sample the buffalo mozzarella if you can, or try to get into one of their cheese-making workshops.

Fine Dining
STEIRERECK IM STADTPARK

Am Heumarkt 2a; tel. 01/713-3168; http://steirerek.at; Mon-Fri 8am-6pm; mains €50-55; 6 or 7 course menus, €155/169, U4: Stadtpark

Set in a former 20th-century dairy in the elegant Stadtpark, Steirereck im Stadtpark has two Michelin stars. You really need to try the tasting menus here to get the full experience. Menus vary with the season, and they also get creative with international flavors. For example, you can try reinanke, a type of fish, with coconut, fennel pollen and sorrel, or pigs trotter with wild chervil, woodruff and black caraway. Do save space for the cheese plate and tempting desserts. You can opt to add in wine pairing for €88-98. Reservations are a must.

OPUS

Kärntner Ring 16; tel. 01/501-10389; www.restaurant-opus.at; daily 6pm-11pm; 4-6 course tasting menus €69-120; U1, U2, U4: Karlsplatz, tram 1, 2, 71, D: Oper, Karlsplatz

This cozy Michelin-starred restaurant is hidden inside the Hotel Imperial behind the Cafe Imperial. The decor dates back to the 1930s and is decorated with restored furniture and elaborately paneled walls—and with a wide choice of tasting menus and main courses it's an experience. All dishes are inspired by Austrian cuisine and have a modern and playful take. (There is a vegetarian tasting menu available.) Dishes vary by season, but can include razor clam with fennel, sirloin of dry-aged beef with polenta and porcini mushrooms, or zucchini blossoms with artichoke and red pepper.

Cafés and Cakes
★ KONDITOREI OBERLAA AT THE ZENTRALFRIEDHOF

Wiener Zentralfriedhof, Simmeringer Hauptstraße 234; tel. 01/767-1768; www.oberlaa-wien.at; daily 8am-4:30pm Jan-Feb and Nov-Dec, 8am-5:30pm Mar and Oct, 8am-6:30pm Apr-Sep; cakes €4-5; tram 11, 71: Zentralfriedhof 2. Tor

Oberlaa is one of the best-known confectionery and cake shops in Vienna and is now a chain with multiple locations across the city.

This branch is perhaps the most surreal and Viennese—it's located inside the gates of Vienna's Central Cemetery. Once you're done with the Funeral Museum or wandering the graves, you can come back to this large, grand café (whose terrace is packed in the summer with visitors to the cemetery) and savor one of their many cakes. You can try the house cake, the Oberlaa Kurbad Torte—made with layers of spongy nut-based dough and chocolate mousse, covered with a nougat glaze. (For those with gluten allergies, Oberlaa carries plenty of gluten-free alternatives.)

PRATER AND AROUND
Austrian
SCHWEIZERHAUS

Prater 116; tel. 01/728-01520; www.schweizerhaus.at; daily 11am-11pm Mar-Oct; mains €9-21; S1, S2, S3, S4, U1, U2: Praterstern, tram 5, O: Praterstern

This huge beer garden at the heart of the Prater is the perfect place to fuel up after the carnival rides. The specialty here is the pork knuckle, but there are other great local delicacies, such as the fried cheese with lingonberry jam.

The beer here is also great, with a selection of draft and bottled beers from Austria and Bavaria, as well as a gluten-free option from Salzburg. With over 2,100 seats outdoors, Schweizerhaus is vast. Take a seat and let your server take care of the rest.

GASTHAUS WILD

*Radetzkyplatz 1; tel. 01/920-9477; http://
gasthaus-wild.at; Mon-Sat 10am-midnight, Sun
10am-10pm; mains €13-29; tram 1, O: Radetzkyplatz*

Hundred-year-old Gasthaus Wild rebranded itself in 2002 as a modern Beisl, offering a new take of the classic Viennese inn. It still looks like a traditional Beisl, with the trademark dark wood interior you'll find in inns across the city, but Viennese dishes are served with Mediterranean touches and updated recipes. You'll find the usual suspects, like veal Schnitzel and goulash, but also a range of vegetarian dishes, like vegetable curry or a delicious cheese plate with pineapple-chili marmalade. There is also a lovely terrace.

International
ROLLERCOASTER RESTAURANT

*Riesenradplatz 6/1; tel. 06/60-244-3823; www.
rollercoaster.rest; Fri 5pm-10pm, Sat 11:30am-10pm,
Sun 11:30am-9pm; mains €10-15; S1, S2, S3, S4, U1,
U2: Praterstern, tram 5, O: Praterstern*

Continue the amusement park festivities at the Rollercoaster Restaurant in the heart of the Prater. (The restaurant has its own small-scale rattling rollercoaster to go with the flashing lights and the techno soundtrack!) Order your food from a menu on a touchpad tablet, and it will come sealed, sliding down (on rails) to your table. Cocktails are mixed by robots, then delivered by rollercoaster (drink containers are strapped down, so they won't go flying). The food here is typical burgers, pasta, or salad, but this is more a place for a fun experience.

SKOPIK & LOHN

*Leopoldsgasse 17; tel. 01/219-8977;
www.skopikundlohn.at; Tue-Sat 6pm-1am; mains
€15-32; U2: Taborstraße, tram 2: Taborstraße*

The culinary focus here is to blend French dishes with a Mediterranean accent. The menu stars creations like pasta leaves with monkfish ragout and truffle, or corn-fed chicken served with pickled grapes, cranberry jus, and black salsify. Apart from the experimental cuisine, in the main indoor dining area, globe lights hang from the ceiling—which is decorated with abstract ink-like markings. You'll also find a space with red walls covered with sculptures of flying geese, making this an adventurous and modern dining experience.

Fine Dining
MRAZ & SOHN

*Wallensteinstraße 59; tel. 01/330-4594;
www.mraz-sohn.at; Mon-Fri 7pm-midnight;
15 course menus €145; U6: Jägerstraße, tram 5,
O: Rauscherstraße*

A restaurant with two Michelin stars, Mraz & Sohn stays true to its family-owned roots. Chef Markus Mraz is the creative brains behind the kitchen, with innovative combinations, like razor clams with elderflower sauerkraut, wild asparagus with umeboshi, or venison with shiso. The food here is inspired by fusion, with exotic ingredients thrown into the mix. The wine here is excellent and comes from small-scale wineries where the wines are handmade. You can add a wine pairing for €85.

Brunch
KLYO

*Uraniastraße 1; tel. 01/710-5946; www.klyo.at;
Sun-Wed 9am-11pm, Thu-Sat 9am-1am; breakfasts
€6.50-10.50; mains €10-35; U1, U4: Schwedenplatz,
tram 2: Julius-Raab-Platz*

KLYO serves up delicious breakfasts until 10:30pm, like poached eggs with saffron hollandaise and avocado mash, or various muesli and porridge, as well as vegan options. You'll also find mains and tempting desserts. Try their turmeric and ginger water.

This café and restaurant is located in the Urania building, an observatory built at the beginning of the 20th century in the art nouveau style. There's also a cinema there, a puppet theater and lecture halls. The café has amazing views of the Danube Canal from the terrace.

Vegetarian, Vegan, and Gluten-Free

HARVEST

Karmeliterplatz 1; tel. 06/76-492-7790; www. harvest-bistrot.at; Mon-Fri 11am-11pm, Sat-Sun 10am-11pm; mains €10-15; tram 2: Karmeliterplatz

Offering vegan and vegetarian dishes, Harvest is a cozy place with a quirky living-room feel. Mismatched furniture and soft lighting contribute to the ambience, and in the summer you can sit out on the terrace. The menu changes on a daily basis and keeps up with the season, but you can expect creations such as vegetable curries, and homemade vegan cakes, along with freshly roasted coffee. Go for the daily menu on weekdays, €10.80 for a soup and a main dish. There is a cute little terrace.

VEGGIEZZ

Salzgries 9; tel. 01/532-2650; https://veggiezz.at; Mon-Fri 11am-10pm, Sat-Sun midday-11pm; mains €10-15; U1, U4: Schwedenplatz, tram 1, 2: Schwedenplatz

Veggies, vegans, and those on a gluten-free or carb-free diet will love this casual dining restaurant. The menu offers a range of healthy dishes, including "superfood" soups and vegan gourmet burgers (with or without the bun). This is a good bet if you have special dietary needs (or if you've overdone the Schnitzel and Sachertorte).

ALSERGRUND AND JOSEFSTADT
Austrian
★ CAFÉ HUMMEL

Josefstädter straße 66; tel. 01/405-5314; http://caféhummel.at; Mon-Fri 7am-11pm, Sat-Sun

8am-11pm; mains €10-20; U6: Josefstädter straße, tram 2: Lederergasse, tram 5: Blindengasse

This Viennese café-restaurant has classic café ambience without the tourist crowd. Their fried chicken (Backhendl) comes with a vinegary potato salad, and don't forget to ask for a side of lingonberry (Preiselbeeren) jam as an accompaniment. You can also get other Austrian dishes, like Schnitzel and Austrian goulash. Give their homemade cakes a try if you can. This is also a great place to pop in for breakfast, which is served until 2pm.

ZATTL WIRTSHAUS AND BEER GARDEN

Freyung 6; tel. 01/533-7262; www.zattl.at; Mon-Sat 11:30am-midnight; mains €12-18; U2: Schottentor, tram 1, 37, 38, 40, 41, 42, 43, 44, 71, D: Schottentor

This Austrian restaurant and beer garden is best enjoyed in the summer, when you can sit out in the leafy courtyard with one of the traditional Czech or Bavarian beers they have on tap and try some good Austrian food. The Schnitzels here are massive! But you can also try the Tafelspitz (boiled beef), the fried chicken, or the meatless käsespätzle, dumplings cooked with cheese. In the winter or if it's raining, there is a huge indoor section with wooden benches and a nice cellar. The space is huge, so you really don't need a booking.

GASTHAUS WICKERL

Porzellangasse 24a; tel. 01/317-7489; www.wickerl. at; Mon-Sat 11:30am-3:30pm and 5:30pm-11pm, Sun 11am-10pm; mains €12-22; tram 1, D: Bauernfeldplatz

This Beisl captures the Viennese tavern tradition without the kitsch. This traditional small tavern welcomes guests with a seasonal menu of Austrian specials, like Spargel (white asparagus) in the spring and pumpkin goulash in the fall, as well as the universal favorites like Tafelspitz and Schnitzel. This Beisl is popular—it gets packed with locals around mealtimes. Pack your phrasebook to make communicating with the staff easier.

SCHNATTL

Lange Gasse 40; tel. 01/405-3400; www.schnattl. com; Mon-Thu 11:30am-4pm, Fri 11:30am-4pm and 6pm-midnight; mains €25-30; U2: Rathaus

Open only on weekdays, this restaurant pulls in the local artists living in Josefstadt, and you can expect to see them hanging out in the warm, inviting space full of tables with white tablecloths, or in the courtyard. Dishes are cooked on a seasonal basis. You can see specials like pumpkin and black chanterelle risotto in the fall, or brown trout fillet with lemon cucumber gnocchi in the summer.

International
WIENER DEEWAN

Liechtensteinstraße 11; tel. 01/925-1185; www.deewan. at; Mon-Sat 11am-11pm; pay what you can; U2: Schottentor, tram 1, 37, 38, 40, 41, 42, 43, 44, 71, D: Schottentor

Wiener Deewan is popular with students, and with good reason. This Pakistani restaurant cooks up three vegetarian and three meat dishes per day, plus one dessert, and is set up like an "eat as much as you like" buffet. There is a great spirit of generosity here: there are no fixed prices, instead you pay what you feel the meal is worth. Please be aware that the proprietors don't like food being wasted, so try to only take what you feel you can actually eat.

Brunch
CAFÉ AN-DO

Brunnenmarkt Stand 169; tel. 01/308-7575; www. caféando.at; Mon-Sat 9am-11pm, mains €7-15; U6: Josefstädter straße, tram 44: Yppengasse

You can find all kinds of trendy restaurants around the Brunnenmarkt, a lively open-air market with 170 stalls, just outside the Josefstadt in the 16th district, but AN-DO stands out for its breakfasts, which are served until 4pm. You can get traditional Austrian breakfasts with rolls, boiled egg, coffee and jam, but there are more adventurous dishes like halloumi cheese served with runny eggs and guacamole or more

Mediterranean-inspired choices with feta, olives and hummus.

Street Food
SUPPENWIRTSCHAFT

Servitengasse 6; www.suppenwirtschaft.at; Mon-Fri 11:30am-4pm; soups and snacks €5-7; U2: Schottentor, tram 1, D: Schlickgasse

This dine-in and takeaway venue focuses on soups, salads, and a few curries that alternate on a weekly menu. All the ingredients are carefully picked out from the Naschmarkt, so you can eat good food on a budget—especially if you go between 5pm and 6pm when prices are slashed in half. This is a great option if you're traveling on a budget.

SCHÖNBRUNN PALACE AND GROUNDS
Austrian
QUELL

Raindorfgasse 19; tel. 01/893-2407; www.gasthausquell.at; Mon-Fri 11am-midnight; mains €7-15; U6: Gumpendorfer Straße, tram 5, 9, 18, 49, 52, 60: Rustengasse

Quell captures the feel of a traditional Beisl, an Austrian tavern with ceramic stoves and wooden chandeliers. Regulars pack the place around lunch, and the Viennese menu comes with all the usual suspects like Schnitzel and goulash soup; however, there are also meat-free alternatives and fish dishes.

MAXING STÜBERL

Maxingstraße 7; www.maxingstuberl.at; Mon and Wed 6pm-11pm, Thu-Sun midday-11pm; mains €10-20; U4: Hietzing, trams 10, 52, 60: Hietzing

You can't get more Viennese than a former haunt of Johann Strauss. Maxing Stüberl prepares Austrian dishes with a gourmet twist, using local produce from the owner's home region. In the evening, you can dine by candlelight, and if there's live music, you may be serenaded. Try some local specials like the fried blood sausage with sauerkraut, or curd dumplings accompanied by stewed berries.

However, do note that service is slow and not a place to head to if you're in a hurry.

BRANDAUERS SCHLOSSBRÄU

Am Platz 5; tel. 01/879-5970; www.bierig.at; daily 10am-11pm; mains €10-20, U4: Hietzing, trams 10, 52, 60: Hietzing

This microbrewery not only sells great house brews and specialty beers—it also serves a menu of tasty Austrian food. Expect heavy meat dishes like spareribs with potatoes on the side, goulash stews, Schnitzel, and also vegetarian dishes. Come for lunch, when you can get a buffet on a budget for €10.90 between 11:30am-3pm on weekdays. When the sun comes out, head to the beer garden in the extensive courtyard.

Cafés and Cakes
WALDEMAR-TAGESBAR

Altgasse 6; tel. 06/643-616127; www.waldemar-tagesbar.at; Mon-Fri 8am-8pm, Sat-Sun 9am-3pm; mains €5-10; U4: Hietzing, trams 10, 52, 60: Hietzing

Drop into Waldemar-Tagesbar to grab breakfast, a light lunch or a sandwich to go. Breakfast lasts until 3pm, and there are daily lunch specials with a seasonal slant, like curries or quinoa bowls for dine-in or takeout. The space is modern and clean, the coffee is good.

GREATER VIENNA
Austrian
LUSTHAUS

Freudenau 254; tel. 01/728-9565; Mon-Tue and Thu-Sat midday-10pm, Sun midday-5pm, shortened hours in the winter; mains €11-20; bus 77A, 79B: Lusthaus/Aspernallee

Head deep into the more rural part of the Prater to find this 16th-century hunting lodge, which hosted Habsburg imperial festivities in the 18th century and now houses an Austrian restaurant that captures the old-world feel of the Prater. Try the Schnitzel or other Viennese classics such as the apricot dumplings. The Lusthaus is far southwest, deep in the Unterer Prater, and you can either get here by bus, take the 77A from the Donaumarina U-Bahn stop, or stop by if you find yourself cycling or hiking down this part of the Prater.

Accommodations

When it comes to picking a neighborhood to stay in Vienna, if you want to be within walking distance from the main sights and classic Viennese cafés, you can't go wrong with the Historic Center or the Hofburg area—but staying in this area does come at a price. Budget-conscious travelers can do better by booking a hotel or a hostel in the outer neighborhoods, like Alsergrund, or around the Prater. Nightlife lovers may prefer to stay in Josefstadt close to the Gürtel (although this area may feel a little seedy once the sun goes down).

Foodies may want to book something close to the Naschmarkt to pick up fresh produce, or dine out in one of the many restaurants near or along the market. And art lovers may want to camp out in Neubau, within easy reach of the MuseumsQuartier and the Kunsthistorisches Museum. Each neighborhood in Vienna has its own character and price tag, so where to book ultimately depends on your budget and needs.

HISTORIC CENTER AND HOFBURG AREA
€150-250
HOTEL CAPRICORNO

Schwedenplatz 3-4; tel. 01/533-31040; www.hotelcapricorno.wien; €150-200 d; U1, U4: Schwedenplatz, tram 1, 2: Schwedenplatz

The Hotel Capricorno stands by the Danube Canal in the old inner city. Inside, it's a burst of color and modern design. There are 42 rooms, with some overlooking the canal, others the quiet courtyard (some rooms have balconies) and there's a delicious buffet breakfast included in the price. If you're arriving or leaving by air, an airport shuttle is available upon request for €45-50.

PERTSCHY PALAIS HOTEL

Habsburgergasse 5; tel. 01/534-490; www.pertschy. com; €145-210 d; U1, U3: Stephansplatz

Get the Hofburg experience by staying in an 18th-century palace just minutes away from the Habsburg imperial monuments. The hotel's 55 rooms maintain an old world feel with white silk wallpaper, red damask curtains, and Baroque-style furniture, while still sporting a modern look. The price includes a lavish Viennese buffet breakfast with a substantial selection of organic produce.

HOLLMANN BELETAGE

Köllnerhofgasse 6; tel. 01/961-1960; www.hollmann-beletage.at; €169-250 d; U1, U4: Schwedenplatz, tram 1, 2: Schwedenplatz

There are only 26 rooms and suites in this downtown design boutique hotel, but staying here means only a two-minute walk from St. Stephen's Cathedral. The decor with classic yet comfortable furniture manages to be modern yet cozy at the same time. Guests can use the terrace and the lounge, and free snacks are offered around 2pm. A delicious buffet breakfast, which goes on until 11:30am, is included in the price. As a great bonus, there is a small cinema in the hotel, and you can also request a free iPad to use for the duration of your stay.

Over €250

★ HOTEL LAMÉE

Rotenturmstraße 15; tel. 01/532-2240; www.hotellamee.com; €150-280 d; U1, U3: Stephansplatz

Located between St. Stephen's Cathedral and the Danube Canal, the Lamée is centrally located. This boutique hotel with 32 rooms and suites evokes the feel of old Hollywood with dark paneling, and delicate gold and plush hot pink fabrics. Some rooms include spacious marble bathtubs. The buffet breakfast is extra (€21), with a wide selection of cold cuts, cheeses, smoked salmon, rolls and muesli. (It's possible to get a deal that includes breakfast when you book online, or directly through the hotel website.) The best part is the colorful rooftop bar with stunning views over the city. The hotel has its own vineyard, so make sure you try a bottle of house wine.

STEIGENBERGER HOTEL HERRENHOF

Herrengasse 10; tel. 01/534-4040; www.steigenberger.com/en/hotels/all-hotels/austria/vienna/steigenberger-hotel-herrenhof; €149-300 d; U3: Herrengasse

Only footsteps away from the Hofburg, the Steigenberger Hotel Herrenhof has a spacious 196 rooms decorated in a modern palette of white, eggplant and lime green. There is a wellness area in the hotel with a sauna and a steam room, as well as a fitness center. Buffet breakfast is extra at €30.

DO&CO

Stephansplatz 12; tel. 01/241-88; www.docohotel.com; €175-300 d; U1, U3: Stephansplatz

A five-star hotel in modern steel and glass, DO&CO stands just opposite St. Stephen's Cathedral. The interior is luxuriously modern and clean, and the 43 rooms designed in warm, earthy colors. Some rooms have Jacuzzis, but all have a seating area with a mini bar and a state-of-the-art entertainment system with large flat-screen TVs and DVD players. Some views let you see the cathedral; others overlook the surrounding streets. Head up to the rooftop bar for drinks. Breakfast is extra at €35.

HOTEL TOPAZZ

Lichtensteig 3; tel. 01/532-2250; www.hoteltopazz.com; €170-380 d; U1, U3: Stephansplatz

Opposite the Lamée, the Hotel Topazz blends early 20th-century Jugendstil design with a modern look. There are 32 rooms in this luxury boutique hotel. The rooms have oval-shaped windows. Some rooms come with a small balcony. Breakfast is extra (€21) and is available at the sister Hotel Lamée across the street; however, the Topazz has its own salon, with coffee and tea available for guests.

★ THE GUESTHOUSE

Führichgasse 10; tel. 01/512-1320;
www.theguesthouse.at; €265-325 d; U1, U2, U4:
Karlsplatz, tram 1, 2, 71, D, WLB: Oper, Karlsplatz

This boutique hotel has 39 rooms overlooking the Albertina. Most of the rooms offer window seats that give you both a view of the city square and a great place to catch up on some reading. The Guesthouse also provides a free wine bar in each room. Breakfast is a la carte, so it's not included in the price, but their breakfast is one of the most popular in the city, known for its bakery items and eggs benedict.

HOTEL BRISTOL

Kärntner Ring 1; tel. 01/515-5160; www.bristolvienna.
com; €350-550 d; U1, U2, U4: Karlsplatz, tram 1, 2,
71, D, WLB: Oper, Karlsplatz

The Hotel Bristol stands next to the Vienna State Opera and within walking distance of the main sites of the city. This luxury hotel opened in 1892 and has 150 rooms and 24 suites. The styles of the rooms range from Biedermeier to Art Deco. Guests can use the business center and the in-house gym 24 hours a day. If you love food, this hotel offers plenty of local and international dishes to enjoy. The Bristol Bar is in the heart of the hotel and is the oldest American-style bar in Vienna.

★ HOTEL SACHER

Philharmonikerstraße 4; tel. 01/514-560; www.sacher.
com; €400-600 d; U1, U2, U4: Karlsplatz, tram 1, 2,
71, D, WLB: Oper, Karlsplatz

The Hotel Sacher is a Viennese institution that is as much part of the city's history as the Staatsoper and the Hofburg. The iconic hotel lies just across the road from the opera house (request a room looking over the Staatsoper if you like). Stepping into the lobby is like

being transported to another era. The hotel's 149 rooms and suites, however, are an eclectic mix of traditional Viennese and modern design—particularly the rooms on the top floors. There is a wonderful boutique spa on-site with saunas, steam and aroma rooms, and massages are available. The in-house Blue Bar, Red Bar, and Green Bar serve food and cocktails, and the famous Café Sacher is located here as well (guests get to skip the line). Breakfast (€41 extra) is a decadent spread that includes champagne, the famous Sachertorte, wonderful cheeses, and freshly prepared egg dishes.

NEUBAU AND THE MUSEUMSQUARTIER

Under €150

HOTEL KUGEL

Siebensterngasse 43; tel. 01/523-3355;
www.hotelkugel.at; €110-130 d; U3: Zieglergasse,
tram 49: Westbahn str., Neubaugasse

Cozy, romantic and feminine, the Hotel Kugel is a family-owned hotel in the trendy Neubau district just 10 minutes' walking distance from the MuseumsQuartier. This boutique hotel has 25 rooms and 2 junior suites, each individually designed with different colors. Most of the rooms have a large canopy bed decked out in floral motifs and comfy pillows. A buffet breakfast is included in the price, and offers the usual cheese, ham, bread, yogurt, and cereal selection, but what makes Kugel stand out is its selection of local produce, delicious jams, and local honey. Since COVID-19, it's also possible to get your breakfast brought directly to your room at no extra charge.

€150-250

25HOURS HOTEL BEIM MUSEUMSQUARTIER

Lerchenfelder straße 1-3; tel. 01/521-510;
www.25hours-hotels.com/hotels/wien/
museumsquartier; €114-224 d; U2, U3: Volkstheater,
tram 46: Auerspergstraße

Minutes from the trendy MuseumsQuartier,

Hotel Orient

The **Hotel Orient** (Tiefer Graben 30; tel. 01/533-7307; www.hotel-orient.at) has been a secret sanctuary for lovers since it opened in the 17th century, when the street it's located on was not a street at all, but a side branch of the Danube Canal. This channel became a place where contraband—like spices, fabrics, and jewels—sailed up the Danube from the East and made its way into the heart of Vienna—which is how the hotel (which began life as a boatman's tavern) came to be called "The Orient." The hotel grew up into its current form in 1896, when discrete "rent by the hour" hotels, Stundenhotels, became popular with bourgeoisie looking for privacy. Though rent by the hour hotels often have a certain reputation, the Orient is not associated with sex work. There's usually a line of Mercedes and Porches parked outside the hotel, which still rents rooms on a three-hourly, or occasionally nightly, basis. This opulent hotel clad in crimson drapes, accented with hints of gold, gilded mirrors, and Baroque splendor has its regulars, but each visitor is a first timer the moment they step through the door.

Part of the Orient's charm is its discretion, but that doesn't mean that illustrious figures aren't known to have visited here, like the Emperor Franz Joseph I (without his wife Sisi) or more artistic figures like Orson Welles and Graham Greene. The hotel is walk-in. Aliases are not only acceptable but encouraged. Stays are normally three hours (but you can extend your hours upon request). Breakfast is served all day. There are six suites, and each room has its own theme, from Habsburgesque opulence to *One Thousand and One Nights*.

Prices range €63 to €95 for three hours.

this hotel makes a great base to explore Vienna's museums, but you don't have to wait to go out the door for art. Stepping inside this 217-room and 34-suite hotel, you're treated to bold colors, murals and playful design mixed in with vintage finds. The hotel's highlight the rooftop terrace with views over the MuseumsQuartier, where you can order cocktails or Italian food. There is also a spa area, the Mermaid's Cave, with a sauna and relaxation area. The hotel also organizes bike tours and electric bike rentals.

Over €250
★ SCHREINERS ESSEN UND WOHNEN
Westbahnstraße 42; tel. 01/676-4754060;
www.schreiners.cc/index_full.php; €240-360 d;
U6: Burggasse-Stadthalle, tram 5, 49: Westbahnstr./
Kaiserstr.

Schreiners Essen und Wohnen is the ultimate urban sanctuary. The setting is reminiscent of a Biedermeier-era garden house, each spacious room in this hotel has its own balcony or terrace overlooking the lush, vine-covered grounds. The rooms have oak flooring, wood furniture and white walls, and comfy king-size beds. There is a Viennese restaurant on-site, but breakfast is included in the price, and served in the garden or in the breakfast room. It includes locally sourced produce, freshly baked bread, free-range eggs, natural fruit juices, and more.

HOTEL SANS SOUCI
Burggasse 2; tel. 01/522-2520;
www.sanssouci-wien.com; €280-420 d;
U2, U3: Volkstheater, tram 49: Volkstheater

Hotel Sans Souci combines luxury with a central location near the city's museums. There is a spa as well as indoor pool. The 63 rooms are airy with large windows letting in a lot of light. Purple accents dominate, and modern design is mixed with antique furniture and fine art. A sumptuous breakfast (included in the price) is served on the veranda with eggs benedict, freshly squeezed juices, and a buffet.

AROUND NASCHMARKT
€150-250
HOTEL DREI KRONEN
Schleifmühlgasse 25; tel. 01/587-3289;
www.hotel3kronen.at; €109-200 d;
U4: Kettenbrückengasse

Art nouveau lovers should book the Hotel Drei Kronen, set in a building constructed in 1897 in the Jugendstil style, right next to the Naschmarkt and the Secession. The building's highlights include the beautiful golden spiral staircase and art nouveau details, like the murals in the entrance. The historic hotel and its 41 rooms were renovated in 2008 and given a modern, comfortable style with pale hues splashed with accents of colors. An excellent Austrian buffet breakfast is included in the price.

Over €250
DAS TYROL
Mariahilferstraße 15; tel. 01/587-54150; www.
das-tyrol.at; €295-355 d; U2: Museumsquarter

Within Vienna's shopping artery, Das Tyrol is at the center of the action, and gives you convenient walking distance from the Naschmarkt and the MuseumsQuartier, as well as downtown happenings in Neubau. Renovated in 2018, this is a modern art hotel with 30 rooms and five studios, featuring original artwork and classic furniture from noted Viennese manufacturers like Thonet. Despite being a boutique hotel, Das Tyrol has a spa in on the premises, with a Finnish sauna and steam bath, plus a light therapy shower and relaxation areas. You can even rent out a private spa for yourself if you like. Luxurious breakfast spreads are available for an extra €21 but may require advance reservations.

KARLSPLATZ AND THE BELVEDERE PALACE AREA
Under €150
PENSION BOSCH
Keilgasse 13; tel. 01/798-6179;
http://hotelpensionbosch.com; €85-95 d; tram 1,
O: Köblgasse

Pension Bosch occupies the first floor of a residential apartment block in a Jugendstil building. The interior is like a time capsule of art nouveau furniture and porcelain figurines. If you're looking for old, creaky charm, this hotel is for you. It's simple and comfortable.

Do note when booking that some of the

rooms may have a shared bathroom in the lower price category.

A good buffet breakfast is included in the price, with fresh rolls, cheese and ham slices, jam, and of course, freshly brewed coffee and tea.

GRÄTZL HOTEL BELVEDERE

Central office at Favoritenstraße 17/3-5; tel. 01/208-3904; www.graetzlhotel.com/home/ graetzl/belvedere; €85-130 d; U1: Taubstummengasse

The Grätzl Hotel is actually a set of ground-floor suites throughout Vienna, occupying former shops which have been renovated by a group of young architects. There is a central office where you can leave luggage and have questions answered; there's also a help number 24/7 and daily room cleaning service. Breakfast is not included, but the staff is happy to give local recommendations. There are four sui tes around the Belvedere Palace, plus more in other neighborhoods, including Leopoldstadt, and close to Schönbrunn. Check-in is easy: Punch the code (provided in your booking email) into the key box outside your apartment to get your key.

€150-250
SPIESS & SPIESS

Hainburger straße; tel. 01/714-8505; www.spiess-vienna.at; €150-220 d; U3: Rochusgasse

Travelers with allergies can be sure of a good night's sleep at Hotel Spiess & Spiess, which has been certified by the European Center for Allergy Research Foundation. This family-owned hotel close to the Danube Canal on a quiet backstreet offers guests elegant and crisp white rooms—some with balconies and fireplaces. Breakfast is included, and is a feast of high-quality, regionally produced organic products. Expect freshly squeezed orange juice, fresh bread and rolls, cold cuts, cheese spreads, jams, fresh fruit and yogurt, and more.

Over €250
★ HOTEL IMPERIAL

Kärntner Ring 16; tel. 01/501-1100; www.imperialvienna.com; €380-520 d; U1, U2, U4: Karlsplatz, tram 1, 2, 71, D, WLB: Oper, Karlsplatz

Hotel Imperial towers over the Ringstraße. Inside, the hotel is opulent, with marble colonnades and staircases and silk-upholstered rooms. The guest book at this legendary five-star hotel is inscribed with the names

deluxe room, Hotel Imperial, a Luxury Collection Hotel

of royalty and politicians. The Imperial was originally built as a palace in 1863 for the Prince of Württemberg but became a hotel 10 years later. Some of the rooms overlook the Musikverein classical music hall; top floor rooms and suites look out onto the dome of the Karlskirche. If you want an extra dash of luxury, the Imperial also offers butler service. Breakfast is sometimes included in the price (depending on the package you book when reserving a hotel room online). See the website for current pricing.

PRATER AND AROUND
Under €150
★ MAGDAS

Laufbergergasse 12; tel. 01/720-0288; www.magdas-hotel.at; €70-130 d; S1, S2, S3, S4, U1, U2: Praterstern, tram O: Franzensbrücke, tram 1: Prater Hauptallee

Magdas is a hotel with a mission—begun by architect Johanna Aufner and the charity Caritas. This is Austria's first hotel operated by refugees (in conjunction with local tourism professionals). It opened in 2015 in a former Leopoldstadt retirement home. This boutique hotel is colorful and modern. Rooms are fitted with upcycled furniture, and some look out onto the famous Riesenrad in the nearby Prater. There is also a beautiful garden with rainbow-colored benches, and an open-air cinema, where movies are occasionally screened on summer nights. You can request a tablet for use for the duration of your stay, or you can rent a bicycle. Breakfast (an extra €14), is served in the Green Salon, and it includes fair trade organic coffee. If the weather is nice, you can take your breakfast in the garden.

ALSERGRUND AND JOSEFSTADT
Under €150
CORDIAL THEATERHOTEL WIEN

Josephstädter straße 22; tel. 01/405-3648; www.theaterhotel-wien.at; €80-140 d; U2: Rathaus, tram 2: Rathaus

This hotel next to the famous German-language Theater in Josefstadt lies within walking distance from the Ringstraße. There are 54 comfortable and simply furnished rooms and suites, each with a flat-screen TV, radio, and minibar (some rooms come with a kitchenette). There is even a sauna, and massages are available on request. Underground parking is available. It's great for the location, but without the premium prices you'd find across the Ringstraße.

€150-250
URBAN STAY HOTEL COLOMBIA

Kochgasse 9; tel. 01/405-6757; www.urban-stay.at/de/wien; €90-160 d; U2: Rathaus, tram 5, 33: Laudongasse

This family-run guest house occupies the ground and first floors in a 120-year-old residential building just behind the Town Hall. Its 10 rooms feature bright colors, cutting-edge design and a clean, modern feel. You won't have a minibar in your room, but there is a communal fridge in the public area with drinks for sale. Some prices include breakfast; otherwise the buffet breakfast from local producers and suppliers, like locally baked bread or homemade cakes and jams, costs €11.

HOTEL RATHAUS WEIN & DESIGN

Lange Gasse 13; tel. 01/400-1122; www.hotel-rathaus-wien.at; €120-220 d; U2: Rathaus, tram 2: Rathaus, tram 46: Auerspergstraße

Wine lovers will love this hotel. Each of the 39 rooms in this old former residential building is dedicated to an Austrian winemaker. The bar here has over 450 Austrian wines, and some of which are available in the minibar in each room. The buffet breakfast, including regional specials like local cheeses, egg dishes and antipasti is an extra €18.

SCHÖNBRUNN PALACE AND GROUNDS
Under €150
HOTEL EKAZENT

Hietzinger Hauptstraße 22; tel. 01/877-7401; www.birghotels.com/hotel_ekazent; €44 d; U4: Hietzing, tram 10, 52, 60: Hietzing

For a hotel that meets your needs as a traveler

and that's close to the Schönbrunn Palace and Palace Gardens, Hotel Ekazent does the job on a budget. You'll find this hotel on the top floors of a shopping center, but the views from the terrace over the hills and the Vienna Woods make you forget you're staying in a shopping center. In minutes from the hotel, you're in the park or at the Hietzing U-Bahn station with connections to the city center. There are 40 en suite bedrooms and they are simple, classic rooms. Buffet breakfast is extra at €8.

HOSTEL RUTHENSTEINER

Robert-Hamerlinggasse 24; tel. 01/893-4202; www.hostelruthensteiner.com; €60-80 d, €20-30

for dorms; U6: Gumpendorfer Straße, tram 5, 9, 18, 49, 52, 60: Staglgasse

The Hostel Ruthensteiner has been open since 1968, offering travelers a refuge in the city with art-covered common areas, garden spaces with large homemade wooden chess sets on the patio and even musical instruments for the impromptu jam. There is also a fully equipped kitchen for guests, and there are always friendly staff on hand to help with any inquiries you may have. Backpackers and travelers love coming here for the community spirit. Minimum stay is two nights.

Information and Services

TOURIST INFORMATION

Vienna's main tourist information office can be found in Albertinaplatz. **Tourist Info Wien** (Albertinaplatz 1; tel. 01/245-55; www.wien.info; daily 10am-6pm) can help you get oriented and organize tickets for sites and shows, get your plan set up with maps, and they can also help with hotel booking. Their website has every single piece of information you need on Vienna—what to see, where to eat and stay, and you'll find topical articles about events in the city.

Other information offices around Vienna include the **Airport Information Center** (9am-3:30pm) located within the airport, with full tourist information services. This is also a place where you can get hotel booking and a Vienna City Card. Just look for the information center when you get to the arrival hall.

You can also find help at the City Hall, via the **Rathaus Information Office** (Rathaus, Friedrich-Schmidt-Platz 1; tel. 01/4000-4001; www.wien.gv.at; Mon-Fri 7:30am-3:30pm). You can get information on events around the city here, like cultural events, and information that's both useful for tourists and locals.

BUSINESS HOURS

Count on the shops being closed on a Sunday or public holidays in Vienna. However, if you urgently need supplies, the main railway stations, the airport and museum shops are usually open.

EMERGENCY NUMBERS

The emergency number in Austria is **112,** and it's also possible to call this number without a SIM card. Operators speak English. If you need an ambulance, called **144;** the fire brigade, **122;** or the police, **133.** There is also a 24-hour English speaking medical hotline, **ViennaMed:** 01/513-9595, and an emergency drugstore—dial **1455.**

CRIME

Vienna has been ranked as one of the world's safest cities, but as with any unfamiliar city, it's best to exercise caution. Take care of valuables in large, busy public spaces or on public transport.

HOSPITALS AND PHARMACIES

Vienna has a range of hospitals all across the city, the largest being the **Vienna General Hospital** (Währinger Gürtel 18-20; tel. 01/404-000; www.akhwien.at), with more than 1,900 beds. There are also a number of English-speaking clinics, like the **Ambulatorium Augarten** (Untere Augartenstraße 1-3; tel. 01/330-3468; www.ambulatorium.com).

There are pharmacies all over Vienna. In German, the word you're looking for is "apotheke." Be careful not to confuse this with "drogerie," which may sound like drugstore but actually stocks shampoos and toiletries. Most pharmacies are open during shop hours, but Vienna's pharmacies take turns opening at night or on the weekends. You can find a list posted outside each pharmacy for the week, marking the closest one open.

FOREIGN CONSULATES

If you have an emergency, like losing your passport, or if you need consular help, you can head over to the **United States Embassy** (Boltzmanngasse 16; tel. 01/313-390) which is located in Alsergrund (9th District). The **Canadian Embassy** (Laurenzerberg 2; tel. 01/531-383-000) can be found in the Inner City; the **British Embassy** (Jauresgasse 12; tel. 01/716-130) is next to the Belvedere Palace; and the **South African Embassy** (Sandgasse 33; tel. 01/320-6493) is outside the center in the 19th district. You can find the **Australian** (Mattiellistraße 2-4; tel. +43-1-506-740) and **New Zealand Embassy** (Mattiellistraße 2-4; tel. +43-1-505-3021) in Vienna as well.

LAUNDRY

If you're staying in one of the top hotels—like the Sacher or the Imperial—you'll have a laundry service in house. Finding a laundromat, especially inside the Ringstraße, can be a struggle (most Austrians have their own washing machines), but there are a few scattered around the city: Look out for a "Münzwäscherei" and "Waschsalon," which are the German words for laundry service or launderette. There are two reliable chains—Green & Clean, and Waschtreff—both with branches in different parts of the city. Some laundromats take cash (both coins and notes), while others can be paid by card or even with GPay or Apple Pay.

- **Green & Clean** (Favoritenstraße 36; www.greenandclean.store; daily 6am-10pm; washing €7-16, drying €2-9; U1: Taubstummengasse)

- **Waschtreff** (Margaretenplatz 6-7; www.waschsalon.wien; open daily 6am-10pm; washing €5-13, drying €3-16.50; U4: Pilgrimgasse)

Transportation

GETTING THERE
Air

Vienna International Airport (VIE; tel. 01/700-722-233; www.viennaairport.com) is 16 kilometers (10 mi) southwest of the city center. There are four terminal buildings, 1, 1A, 2, and 3, and two runways.

Flights between Budapest and Vienna take 45 minutes and between Prague and Vienna 1 hour (but once you factor in the time to check in, getting to the airport and so on, you're better off taking the train, especially now there are direct rail routes connecting the cities). **Austrian Airlines** (www.austrian.com) does connect Vienna with both cities.

AIRPORT TRANSPORTATION

From the airport, it's easy to get to Vienna on public transit. The most direct option is the **City Airport Train** (CAT; www.

cityairporttrain.com; €11 one way, €19 return, valid for 6 months). This brings you into the Wien Mitte train station. It takes 16 minutes and runs every half hour from 6am to 11:30pm daily (from the airport to Wien Mitte) and from 5:30am to 11pm (from Wien Mitte to the airport). Select airlines allow you to check in your luggage at the train station, so you don't have to worry about getting the suitcases on and off the train. However, during the COVID-19 pandemic, this trainline has been suspended so do check the website nearer the time of travel.

Another option is to take the ÖBB Raijet (www.oebb.at) from the Flughafen Wien Bahnhof (the airport train station) to Wien Hauptbahnhof (the city's main train station). From Wien Hauptbahnhof, it takes 15 minutes and costs €4.20 to get to the city center. You can get tickets from the ticket counter or from the ÖBB (Austrian Federal Railways) ticket terminals in the train stations. If you're using this option to get back to the airport, make sure you get on the right train at Hauptbahnhof—often the airport train splits here with one side going onto Budapest or another city.

Vienna Airport Lines (www.viennaairportlines.at) runs direct buses from the airport to various spots in Vienna (€8, 20 minutes to the city center). Buy tickets from the driver, from the ticket machines near the stop, or online (if buying online, show your ticket on your phone via the app).

Taxis to and from the airport cost €25-50 and take 20-30 minutes to reach the city center. As you come out of Arrivals, the yellow **Taxi 40100** (tel. 01/401-00; www.taxi40100.at) offers a fixed rate of €36, or you can go with the **C&K Airport Service** (tel. 01/444-44; www.cundk.at); you can find their desk at arrivals.

Train

Vienna has four train stations. **Wien Hauptbahnhof** (Main Train Station), the **Wien Meidling, Westbahnhof,** and **Wien Mitte.** All four train stations are close to the city center and are connected via the U-Bahn, tram and bus lines. Most international departures go from Wien Hauptbahnhof (some pass through Meidling as well).

From Prague: Trains run by **Ceske Drahy** (www.cd.cz), **Regiojet** (www.regiojet.com) or **Leo Express** (www.leoexpress.com) depart for Vienna (Wien) from Hlavní nádraží every 1-2 hours from about 6am to 7pm with a few late night options until midnight. The journey takes about 4 hours during the day and about 8-10 hours for an overnight train. Prices range roughly 238-1,200 CZK on different carriers and direct trains or transfers, with Regiojet offering the best prices.

From Budapest: Trains run from Budapest Keleti to Vienna every one to two hours (2.5-3 hours, €9-50/3300-18,300 HUF). Trains are operated by multiple companies, like **ÖBB Railjet** (www.oebb.at) or **MÁV** (www.mavcsoport.hu)—you can buy tickets online, but note that international tickets must be printed out at one of the ticket machines you will only find in one of the main Hungarian train stations, such as Budapest Keleti or Nyugati. In addition, since summer 2020 there is now a direct train route by **Regiojet** (www.regiojet.com) going from Budapest Déli to Vienna and then directly onto Prague. This is the cheapest way to travel by train, and you get a free bottle of water and steward service in the price. This route departs Budapest twice a day, once in the morning (7:45am) and once in the afternoon (3:45pm), and stops in Wien Meidling before continuing to Wien Hauptbahnhof.

One thing to note is that not all trains going to Vienna are going to be the same. ÖBB Railjet trains begin in Budapest Keleti and usually depart on time, and will go onto further destinations like Munich or Zurich, but there are also trains coming from Romania, Záhony (which begins in Hungary just across the Ukrainian border but connects with passengers coming on the train from Kiev), and

Serbia. A word of caution about the train coming from Belgrade (Serbia): It can be up to an hour late, as it is coming from outside the EU and gets held up at customs.

Bus

If you're coming to Vienna by bus from another country, you'll arrive at the **Vienna International Bus Terminal** (Erdbergstraße 200A; www.vib-wien.at; U Erdberg). You can reach the city center by U-Bahn (U3 to Stephansplatz) in under 10 minutes. **Eurolines** (tel. 09/001-28712; www.eurolines. at) has routes to Vienna from all over Europe, including Budapest and Prague.

From Prague: Buses from Prague Florenc to Vienna (Wien) depart almost every hour between 5am-8pm with a few late-night options closer to midnight. The journey takes about 5 to 6 hours and ranges from 350-550 CZK with different carriers, like **Eurolines** (www.eurolines.eu) and **FlixBus** (www.flixbus.com).

From Budapest: FlixBus in collaboration with the domestic **Volánbusz** company (http://nemzetkozi.volanbusz.hu) has several buses per day, once an hour or more (3 hours, €9-14/2925-4550 HUF).

Car

Driving to Austria is easy, as there are well-maintained highways in the country and the surrounding region.

Note that all highways, Autobahn, require a vignette or a toll. Display your highway vignette (toll sticker; www.asfinag.at/toll/vignette; €9.40 for 10 days) as you enter Austria—or if you have a digital sticker, this is tied to your number plate. You can either buy these online or at borders, gas stations, or post offices. Rental agencies may also be able organize a sticker for you.

From Prague: If you're driving from Prague, you'll drive 320 kilometers (200 mi) for 3.5 hours. You need to head south on the E50 toward Brno, and then take the E461 toward the Austrian border and then the A5 to Vienna. There are tolls on parts of the route

(CZK 310 in the Czech Republic for 10-day stickers).

From Budapest: Drive 90 kilometers (150 mi) northwest on the M1 and A4 highways to reach Vienna (tolls apply, in addition for the Hungarian motorway vignette, which is HUF 3500, you'll also need the Austrian one, which costs €9 for a 10-day sticker). The drive takes around 2.5 hours.

GETTING AROUND

Vienna is quite spread out, but it has impeccable public transport which makes it easy and quick to get around. The public transport network, run by **Wiener Linien** (www. wienerlinien.at), includes the U-Bahn (subway), trams, S-bahn (suburban railway), and buses. Buses take you more into the suburban parts of the city, which is useful if you're going off the beaten track a bit, but in general you're more likely to use the U-Bahn or the tram to get around. The S-Bahn is useful to get between stations like the Hauptbahnhof, Praterstern, Wien Mitte, and Wien Meidling. You can also take it for daytrip destinations, like Mödling.

Transit Passes

Buy transit passes at the red kiosks in the metro, from ticket offices in the main metro stations, or any of the city's tobacconists. You can even buy tickets online (shop.wienerlinien.at) or via an app. Passes can come in 24 hours (€8), 48 hours (€14.10), or 72 hours (€17.10) and are valid on all forms of public transport. Single tickets cost €2.40—valid on all forms of transport, including changes, but only for uninterrupted journeys. Make sure you validate your tickets and passes when you enter the U-Bahn (these are boxes as you enter the subway), or on the tram or bus on your first journey. You can also download the Wien Linien app and buy your ticket online. This is a useful hack if you want to avoid the queues at the train or bus station when you arrive. You just need to show the QR code to the inspector if you're asked to show a valid ticket or travel pass.

U-Bahn

Vienna has five subway lines, known as the U-Bahn (short for Untergrundbahn—underground train) and lines are denoted by numbers and colors. Although these mostly run underground, sometimes they cross bridges, raised platforms, or just run along open "ditches" below the city. The red U1 line runs from Orberlaa to Leopoldau, crossing the city center before heading out to Leopoldstadt, the Danube Island and the Old Danube. The purple U2 line begins in Karlsplatz, goes under the MuseumsQuartier and under the Ringstraße before crossing the Danube Canal and the Danube. The orange U3 line runs from Simmering in the south of the city to the Ottakering, also going under the inner city. The green U4 line is one of the most beautiful (it's one of the famous train lines built by Otto Wagner). It goes from Heiligenstadt in the north down to Karlsplatz and Schönbrunn, all the way to Hütteldorf. The brown U6 from Floridsdorf near the New Danube skims the city center over the arches of the Gürtel to Siebenhirten. And what about U5? This missing subway was planned in the 1960s, but never actually got built.

You can change between U-Bahn lines at various locations, the busiest being Karlsplatz (U1, U2, U4). The U-Bahn runs between 5am and midnight on weekdays, but goes all night on Fridays, Saturdays and days before national holidays.

Tram and Bus

There are 29 tram lines and 127 bus lines. Between 12:30am and 5am, 24 of these routes become night lines. The tram is an easy way of getting around the city, and you can even ride around the Ringstraße by combining tram lines 1 and 2, changing at the Oper, Burgring, or Volkstheater stops. You can buy tickets from the bus or tram driver.

WLB (Wiener Lokalbahnen)

The WLB (Wiener Lokalbahnen) is a tram-train service that takes you from the Staatsoper to the nearby town of Baden bei Wien. This electrified railway runs along the tramline in the city until the Schedifkaplatz in the Meidling district, before moving onto a light track rail. Within Vienna, you can treat it like a tram, and if you need to go south from Oper, it follows the same route as the 1 and 62 for 8 and 9 stops respectively.

Taxi

Vienna has a few taxi companies you can call on, like Taxi 60160 (tel. 01/60-160), Taxi 40100 (tel. 01/40-100), Taxi 31300 (tel. 01/31-300), or you can use an app like mytaxi.

Car

Vienna is an easy city to get around on foot or on public transport, but should you want to head out into the countryside, it may be worth renting a car. Your best bet is to rent cars from international rental companies such as Hertz (tel. 01/795-32 for local reservations; www.hertz.at). There are other options with Sixt (tel. 01/505-264000; www.sixt.at) and Avis (tel. 01/402-5592; www.avis.com/en/locations/at/vienna). Avis also has a rental office at the airport.

Day Trips from Vienna

Austria is not a big country, which makes it easy to explore in a few day trips from Vienna, whether you take a quick jaunt into the Vienna Woods or a longer trip out to Salzburg.

Day trips near Vienna include hiking trails through the Vienna Woods and vineyards, or a slightly longer excursion to the Wachau Valley. The Danube cuts through this valley, and on a boat trip you'll be surrounded by vine-clad hills topped with ruined castles and Baroque monasteries.

Some travelers want to throw in another country into their travels, which is why the day trip to Bratislava is so popular. The small Slovak capital is only an hour away, so many just hop on the train and cross the border for the day—or take scenic route by catamaran.

Despite being on the other side of Austria, Salzburg is still one of

Highlights

Look for ★ to find recommended
sights, activities, dining, and lodging.

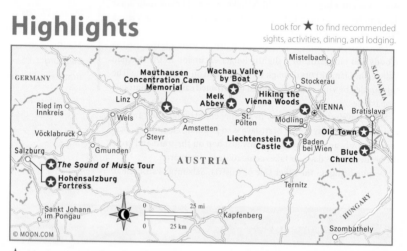

★ **Liechtenstein Castle:** This spectacular Medieval bastion perched up in the hills is outside Vienna. The castle is packed with historic details and offers sweeping views over the Vienna Woods (page 302).

★ **Hiking the Vienna Woods:** Hike the Stadtwanderweg 1 (City Hiking Path 1) or Stadtwanderweg 1a (City Hiking Path 1a) up into the Vienna Woods and through lush vineyards (page 306).

★ **Wachau Valley by Boat:** The banks of the Danube in the Wachau Valley are lined with vineyards and castles that are best viewed by boat (page 310).

★ **Melk Abbey:** Look out over the Danube from the impressive terrace of this tangerine-colored abbey (page 312).

★ **Mauthausen Concentration Camp Memorial:** This former concentration camp is a moving and poignant reminder of the horrors of the Holocaust (page 318).

★ **Hohensalzburg Fortress:** This 11th-century fortress in Salzburg, one of Europe's largest fortifications, offers impressive views from its free viewing terrace. There is also a cluster of museums within the fortress (page 320).

★ *The Sound of Music* **Tour:** Ride a bus to famous locations from the movie, including locations in the stunning countryside surrounding Salzburg (page 323).

★ **Old Town Bratislava:** The historic center of Slovakia's capital includes historic buildings as well as tempting cafés and quirky design shops (page 326).

★ **Blue Church:** Hungarian architect Ödön Lechner designed this stunning art nouveau church in Bratislava in no less than 50 shades of blue (page 327).

Austria's most popular destinations outside Vienna, with its dramatic Alpine landscape, striking castles, connections to Mozart, and, of course, being the home of *The Sound of Music.*

PLANNING YOUR TIME

When it comes to choosing a day trip, think about the time you're prepared to travel, the time of year, and what you're interested in. Most destinations can be visited year-round, but if you want to take a boat down the Wachau Valley, this only runs from April to October, so take seasonality into account.

If you don't want to spend a whole day away from Vienna, exploring the countryside around **Mödling** or **Baden bei Wien,** towns set in the hills of the **Vienna Woods,** is a good option, and can be reached in 20-30 minutes by train.

One of the most popular trips is nearby **Wachau Valley,** where boat rides down the Danube are popular. **Melk** is a good starting place along the River Danube, and reachable on a one-hour train ride from Vienna. From Melk, you can cruise down to **Krems an der Donau** on a boat or bike, then take the train back to Vienna from there in the evening.

Bratislava, the capital of Slovakia, is just an hour away by train—or take scenic route by catamaran. A more somber day trip option that's just over an hour away by train is the poignant **Mauthausen Concentration Camp.** Mauthausen is best experienced as part of a tour, but it can also be done solo.

Salzburg, known for Mozart and *The Sound of Music,* is 2.5 hours from Vienna by train. Salzburg can be done in a day, but you may want take an overnight trip to get the most out of it.

With the exception of the Baden be Wein train station and Krems and der Donau, **luggage storage** options are limited in the Vienna Woods and Wachau Valley. Lockers are available in Vienna in the Wien Hauptbahnhof, Westbahnhof, Wien Mitte, Meidling, or Praterstern stations (€2-5 depending on size) for up to 24 hours. Salzburg, Mathausen, and Bratislava all have luggage storage options.

Vienna Woods

The Vienna Woods (Wienerwald in German) lie on the western edge the Austrian capital, stretching beyond the city limits into Lower Austria, covering an area of about 1350 square kilometers (520 square miles). The northern part of the Vienna Woods skirting the suburbs of the Austrian Capital is densely packed with stretches of oak and beech trees punctuated by grassy meadows and vineyards, whereas evergreens and pine trees dominate the southern part around Mödling and Baden bei Wien. This branch of the woods making up the foothills of the Alps is not only popular for hiking, but is also designated as a Biosphere Reserve by UNESCO and home to 2,000 plant species and 150 bird species—including the nearly extinct Ural Owl.

Getting to the Vienna Woods is easy by public transport. You can go as part of a day trip to areas in Lower Austria, such as Mödling, around the Liechtenstein Castle. Another memorable option is to take one of the many hiking trails in the city, which you can reach easily by taking tram D from the city center.

AROUND MÖDLING

Mödling (pop. 20,500) is a charming historic town with tight streets among its thick-stoned medieval buildings. Mödling backs on to the

Day Trips from Vienna

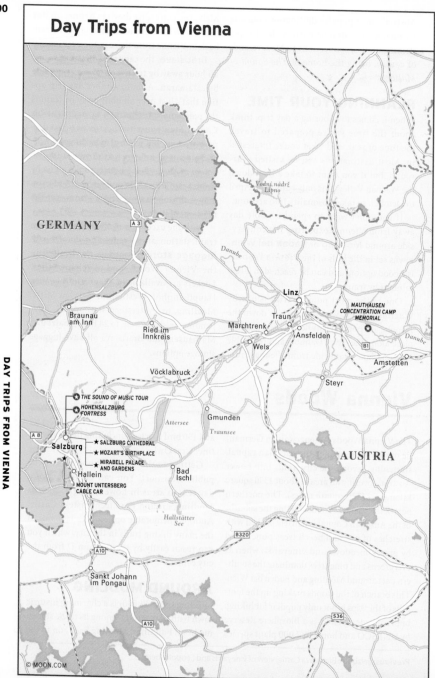

GERMANY

A 3

Vodní nádrž
Lipno

Danube

Linz

MAUTHAUSEN
CONCENTRATION CAMP
MEMORIAL

Braunau
am Inn

Ried im
Innkreis

Marchtrenk

Traun

Ansfelden

Danube

B1

Wels

Amstetten

Vöcklabruck

Steyr

★ THE SOUND OF MUSIC TOUR

★ HOHENSALZBURG
FORTRESS

Attersee

Gmunden

Traunsee

AUSTRIA

A 8

★ SALZBURG CATHEDRAL
★ MOZART'S BIRTHPLACE
★ MIRABELL PALACE
  AND GARDENS

Salzburg

Bad
Ischl

Hallein

MOUNT UNTERSBERG
CABLE CAR

Hallstätter
See

B320

A10

Sankt Johann
im Pongau

A10

S36

© MOON.COM

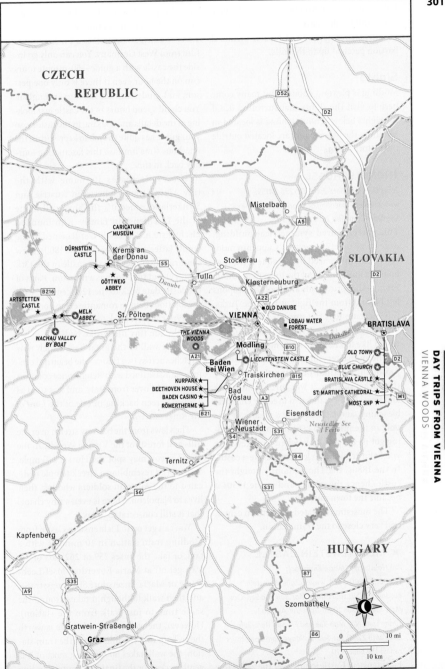

CZECH
REPUBLIC

D52

D2

Mistelbach

A5

CARICATURE
MUSEUM
★

DÜRNSTEIN
CASTLE
★

Krems an
der Donau

Stockerau

SLOVAKIA

D2

★
GÖTTWEIG
ABBEY

S5

Danube

Tulln

Klosterneuburg

A22

B216

ARTSTETTEN
CASTLE
★

★ ★ ☆ MELK
ABBEY

St. Pölten

VIENNA ☆

● OLD DANUBE

LOBAU WATER
FOREST

BRATISLAVA
☆

WACHAU VALLEY
BY BOAT

THE VIENNA
WOODS

Danube

OLD TOWN ◉

A21

Mödling

☆ LIECHTENSTEIN CASTLE

B10

BLUE CHURCH ◉

D2

Baden
bei Wien

Traiskirchen

B15

BRATISLAVA CASTLE ★

KURPARK ★
BEETHOVEN HOUSE ★
BADEN CASINO ★
RÖMERTHERME ★

Bad
Vöslau

A3

ST. MARTIN'S CATHEDRAL ★

M1

MOST SNP ★

B21

Eisenstadt

Wiener
Neustadt

S31

Neusiedler See
/ Fertő

S4

B4

Ternitz ○

S31

S6

Kapfenberg ○

HUNGARY

S35

B7

A9

Szombathely ○

Gratwein-Straßengel ○

B6

0   10 mi

Graz ●

0   10 km

hills of the Vienna Woods, packed with castle ruins and hidden caves. Most come to visit Liechtenstein Castle, a spectacular medieval bastion perched up in the hills.

Sights

Mödling is pleasant enough, but many come here to visit the sights that surround it. Of the sights below, Thonetschössl is located in Mödling; the other sights are located outside the historic town.

THONETSCHÖSSL

Josef Deutsch-Platz 2; tel. 02/236-24159; www.museum-moedling.at; Mon-Thu 9am-1pm, Sat 10am-2pm, Sun 2pm-6pm; €3

This three-floored symmetrical building, once home to a 17th-century Capuchin monastery and influenced by Baroque style, now houses a museum about the town of Mödling. From prehistoric fossils and tools to weapons left behind from the fight against the Turks, this museum tells the story of Mödling over the centuries. It's worth dropping in if you would like to know the town more.

The monastery building was rebuilt on top of the original building destroyed by the Turks. In 1686, it was turned into a silk and towel factory, and also used for chemical bleaching, and later became a theater. It was only in the mid-19th century that the building got its current look, when Countess Eise von Salm rebuilt it to look more like a castle. In the 1880s, the Thonet family bought the castle (hence the name), and in the 1930s it became the town museum.

The museum is located in the town center, and very close to the train station.

★ LIECHTENSTEIN CASTLE

Am Hausberg 2, Maria Enzerdorf; tel. 06/50-680-3901; www.burgliechtenstein. eu; Jan-Feb Sat tours 11am, Mar-Jun and Sep-Oct Mon-Tue, Fri-Sun 10am-4pm, Jul-Aug daily 10am-5pm, Nov Mon-Tue and Fri-Sun 11am-2pm, Dec (until 22nd) Sat-Sun, holidays 11am-2pm, tours run on the hour; €10

Liechtenstein Castle looms over the valley like something from a movie—which is why it's been used as a film location in the 1990s *The Three Musketeers*, as well as a 1970s vampire film from West Germany. You can only go inside the castle with a guide—50-minute tours run on the hour even if there is only one person, and guides can do the tour in English. You could spend hours in the castle just looking at the details and soaking in the history, so your guide has quite the job to keep within the one-hour time limit on this fascinating journey back in time.

The castle shares its name with the tiny Alpine country between Austria and Switzerland, since it's the ancestral home of the Liechtenstein family, who founded Liechtenstein. The castle is still owned by the family (after getting it back in the 1800s, a few centuries after they lost the castle in the 13th century), but functions as a museum. Parts of the castle date back to the 12th century, with the top floor being a romantic extension from the 19th century. Look for traces of medieval life, like the tiny niche-like beds for guests set in the wall of the great hall, which now stretches across two floors. The beautiful century staircase lined with Renaissance columns was brought over from Italy, and was used as a green-screen backing in one of the *Lord of the Rings* movies.

The views from the balcony stretch over the hills and forests of the Vienna Woods. In the distance you may spot the Hussar's Temple, a memorial resembling a Greek temple dedicated to the Austrian soldiers who lost their lives to Napoleon. There is even a tiny chapel that is still consecrated today.

You can get up to Lichtenstein Castle from Mödling train station in 10 minutes with a taxi, or take the buses 259 or 262 part of the way, get off at Maria Enzerdorf Josef-Leeb-Gasse or Maria Enzersdorf Siedlungsstraße, and then walk (although it takes around the same time to just walk from the station). However, the well-preserved castle is worth the trek up into the hills. From the train station, the walk takes 50 minutes; most of it is gentle except for the final 20 minutes winding up the hill, but the whole route is paved and follows the same road as the cars.

MÖDLING CASTLE RUINS

Jägerhausgasse 11; open 24 hours; free

The ruins of this 11th-century castle are worth the hike up into the hills—in fact, it's a popular hiking destination for locals. Much of the castle was damaged during the Turkish siege in 1529, and it was completely destroyed when it burned down after being struck by lightning 27 years later. The walls of the old castle still stand, but the whole sight is open to the elements. The best thing about the castle is the romantic view through the ruins over to the woods and the hills surrounding the site.

From the train station in Mödling to the castle, it'll take you around 40 minutes to walk it.

Food

MAUT WIRTSHAUS

Kaiserin Elisabeth-Strasse 22; tel. 02/236-24481; www.mauts.at; daily 10am-midnight; €8-16

Come for the good, home cooked Austrian food in this single-story townhouse that opens onto a terrace in the summer. The menu is in German, but you can't go wrong with Schnitzel. For something different try the Tyrolean liver with bacon and apple (Tiroler Leber mit Speck und Apfel)! Note that some of the rooms indoors are smoking, so you may want to book for the non-smoking section. This restaurant is close to the station, which makes it a good pitstop before visiting Liechtenstein Castle. Booking a table is highly advised.

PINO

Brühler Strasse 6; tel. 02/236-860187; http://pino-ristorante.at; Tue-Sat midday-2:30pm, 6pm-10pm; €15-25

This restaurant follows the "Slow Food" movement with local, fresh, and seasonal ingredients used to make Italian classics. You'll find incredible pizzas and freshly made pastas as well as daily specials, fish, and meat dishes. Booking is highly recommended (in the summer try to get a seat on the leafy terrace). Take your time to dine here, as the food is slow cooked to perfection and you need time to savor. You will find this restaurant 15 minutes walking from the main train station.

EIS PETER

Hauptstrasse 17; tel. 02/236-865151; www.eispeter.at; Feb-Oct daily 10am-10pm; €2 per scoop

This small ice cream parlor specializes in traditional gelato, you can try them served up in scoops to take on the go, but if you sit down try their creative sundaes named after Habsburg royals with imperial lashings of cream. In the summer, there is often a queue out the door made up of both visitors and locals eagerly waiting for a cone on the go—or a much-coveted table. Being just a five-minute walk from the train station, you may want to fuel up if you're planning to hike up to Liechtenstein Castle.

Getting There

From Vienna, train is the easiest way to get to Mödling. Bus tickets cost €4.80 one way—the same as the train—so unless you are near the bus station, it's easier and more comfortable to take the train.

TRAIN

There are frequent train connections from Vienna to Mödling, with local trains and suburban trains, both operated by **ÖBB Railjet** (www.oebb.at), running every 10 minutes from Wien Hauptbahnhof. You can take the regional trains, which take 20 minutes, or the S2 or S3 suburban trains (S-bahn) which take 25 minutes. These also stop in other parts of the city, like the Praterstern (30 minutes) or Wien Mitte (26 minutes). Tickets cost €4.80 one way.

Mödling's train station is located in the center of town.

BUS

From Vienna, a few buses also run to the train station in Mödling. Take the U6 to Siebenhirten, then take the bus 269 or 270

from there. The bus ride takes around half an hour.

Getting Around

You can get around Mödling easily on foot, but its most famous attractions lie beyond walking distance outside the town, such as Liechtenstein Castle. You'll usually find a taxi just next to the train station, but you can also call **City Taxi Mödling** (tel. 02/236-29000) if there are no cabs parked outside. Fares to Liechtenstein Castle are around €13. Uber also works as far out as Mödling.

Leaving Mödling

The last train back to Vienna from Mödling leaves around 12:40am. The last direct bus runs back to Vienna at 12:15am.

BADEN BEI WIEN

Set in the foothills around the Vienna Woods, Baden bei Wien (pop. 25,000) with its temple-dotted parkland, Biedermeier-era houses, repurposed neoclassical bathhouses, rose gardens, and of course, the thermal water, has been a popular place to escape for centuries. This classic Central European spa town captures a bygone era, and makes a pleasant day trip from Vienna for wellness lovers, or for anyone wanting to walk in the footsteps of Beethoven, who visited the town often for his health.

Baden bei Wien is half an hour by train from Vienna, but there is also an S-Bahn running from the Staatsoper taking an hour to get to town. If you want to get the full spa town experience, it's best to spend the night in one of the town's luxury hotels.

Sights
RÖMERTHERME

Brusattiplatz 4; tel. 02/252-45030;
www.roemertherme.at; daily 10am-10pm;
3-hour ticket weekdays €15.20, weekends €17.40

The alleged curative properties of its sulfur-rich water have made Baden bei Wien popular for centuries. If you stroll the town you'll spot various colonnaded buildings with the word "bad" in it, meaning bath, but only the Römertherme ("Roman Bath")—along with a smaller, more luxurious Turkish bath—operate today.

Although the original 19th-century facade of this bath house still exists, most of the Römertherme lies inside a huge, modern glass covered complex where you can swim or relax in 900 square meters (9700 sq ft) of pools. One of the small pools accessible through a water channel leading outside is filled with the thermal water, whereas the rest are Jacuzzis, whirlpools, pools with massage jets, and classic swimming pools. There is a separate section (€7.60 extra) for the saunas and steam baths, but note, you must go naked in this section and it's coed, so it may not be for everyone and at the time of writing was closed due to COVID-19. You can rent towels and bath sheets at the cash desk, but you'd probably want to bring your own bathers and shower slippers.

BADEN CASINO

Kaiser Franz-Ring 1; tel. 02/252-44496;
www.casinos.at; daily 3pm-3am; free entrance

Gambling and taking the waters often went hand in hand all across Central Europe's spa towns, and Baden bei Wien is no exception. This beautiful casino, built in the 1880s on the site of an old bath house, is one of the big draws to the town, offering all the classic games from blackjack and roulette to slots and poker. There is a smart dress code, but if you pop in spontaneously you can rent a jacket from the casino. Admission is strictly from the age of 18, so make sure you bring ID with you. When you arrive, buy your chips at reception and hit the tables or the slots. There is a fine dining restaurant on site, so you can dine before hitting the casino games.

1: Baden bei Wien **2:** Liechtenstein Castle in Mödling **3:** temple to Beethoven in Baden bei Wien's Kurpark

☆ Hiking in the Vienna Woods

a hiking trail in the Vienna Woods

Vienna has hiking trails going for more than 240 kilometers (150 mi), called the Stadtwanderwege (City Hiking Paths), most of which you can reach easily by public transport. Some of these trails wind through the **Vienna Woods,** which, despite the name, are not just stretches of wooded hills: Open meadows and vineyards add a little diversity to the landscape.

From Vienna, tram D leads to the first two hiking trails below. The last tram D leaves Beethovengang tram stop back to the city center at 12:35am—handy if you end up having a good time out in a Heuriger by the Vienna Woods!

CITY HIKING PATH 1

Distance (round-trip): *11 km (7 mi)*
Duration (round-trip): *3-4 hours*
Effort: *moderate*
Trailhead: *Nußdorf, Beethovengang tramstop*

One of the most famous trails, City Hiking Path 1 (Stadtwanderweg 1), begins at the end of tram D, at Nußdorf. The trail goes through the Vienna Woods, trailing past vineyards and overlooks the Danube before looping back to Nußdorf. Restaurants and vineyards—like the **Heuriger Sirbu** (page 257) and the sister winery of Mayer am Pfarrplatz, (**Mayer am Nussberg;** Kahlenberger straße 210; www.mayermnussberg.at)—dot the trail, so you can take this route at your leisure. At the top of Kahlenberg—Vienna's highest hill—you also also have lunch options at the self-service **Café Kahlenberg** (Am Kahlenberg 3; www.kahlenberg.wien/cafekahlenberg), located at the trail's approximate halfway point.

Most of the trail is paved and signposted. It's a gentle trek that doesn't require any hiking off the beaten track, but there is a lot of walking uphill.

CITY HIKING PATH 1A

Distance (round-trip): *11 km (7 mi)*
Duration (round-trip): *3-4 hours*
Effort: *moderate*
Trailhead: *Nußdorfer Platz*

This hiking trail takes you close to City Hiking Path 1, and even intersects at parts, but will also take you up to Leopoldsberg—one of Vienna's most famous hills—and along the Danube River.

To reach the trailhead, take the tram D and get off at the station Nußdorfer Platz. You'll see a signpost marking the route with Stadtwanderweg 1a, directing you under the bridge. The route here starts along the Danube to your left, but before starting your hike, you may want to check out Otto Wagner's famous Schemerl Bridge—more affectionately known as Löwenbrücke (Lion bridge) for its imposing bronze lions—at the Nußdorfer weir and lock (the point where the Danube Canal and the Danube meet) to your right.

The route will take you along the Danube for 2 kilometers (1 mi) before you turn to go uphill toward Leopoldsberg. I highly recommend stopping at one of the Heurige at the base of the hill for a refreshment before hiking Leopoldsberg, as there isn't anything else till you reach Kahlenberg. When you reach this village-like area and its Heurige, follow the sign up the hill, which is quite a hike, as you'll scale 435 meters (1394 ft) up various steps and inclined paths through the woods to the top of the hill. It's worth getting a bit out of breath for the view on the way up overlooking the Danube and the vineyards alone!

Leopoldsberg is the most eastern foothill of the Alps (the Vienna Woods belong to the Alpine foothills) and it's also topped with the Baroque Leopoldskirche, a church. From the top of Leopoldsberg, it's quite a gentle uphill stroll through the woods to the neighborhing Kahlenberg, Vienna's highest point, before the trail loops down to the vineyards of Nussberg (passing both Heuriger Sirbu and Mayer am Nussberg) and back down to the river again.

COBENZL TO GRINZING

Distance (round-trip): *2.5 km (1.5 mi)*
Duration (round-trip): *30 minutes*
Effort: *easy*
Trailhead: *Parkplatz Cobenzl*

For a gentler walk through the vines, take the 38A bus from Wien Heiligenstadt to the end of the U4 line in Vienna and get off at Parkplatz Cobenzl, and wander down hill taking the Oberer Reisenbergweg—a paved road taking you right past the vineyards—for beautiful vine-clad views over the city, which will take you back to the picturesque suburb of Grinzing, with single-story Baroque houses. From here you can take the 38A back to Heiligenstadt or the 38 tram which will take you back to Schottentor in the city center. This downhill walk is approximately 2.5 kilometers (1.5 mi).

BEETHOVEN HOUSE

Rathausgasse 10; tel. 02/252-868-00630; www. beethovenhaus-baden.at; Tue-Sun 10am-6pm; €6

Beethoven came to Baden bei Wien frequently for his health and spent most of his time at this two-story town house in Rathausgasse at the center of the town. The composer even wrote part of the famous *9th Symphony* here. This small museum commemorates Beethoven's life and his compositions through eccentric curiosities, like his death mask, a wax or plaster cast made of a person's face just after they die, and a lock of hair behind a glass cabinet. Sit down at the listening stations to hear recordings of his most famous pieces upstairs in the museum. There is also a sound lab in the basement that explores Beethoven's deafness and how he composed using bone conduction. You can even try bone conduction for yourself by placing the specially made headphones against your temple, wrist, and other parts of your body to experience the *9th Symphony* and Beethoven's other works through vibration in place of sound.

Parks and Gardens
KURPARK

Kaiser Franz-Ring; tel. 01/234-56789; open 24 hours; free

This charming park scaling up the hill is one of my favorite parts of Baden bei Wien. The garden was created in the 18th century to honor the Empress Maria Theresa, but its monuments are instead dedicated to composers, like the temple to Mozart and Beethoven. The best view point is from the Beethoven Temple, a neoclassical structure overlooking the town from the side of the hill. Make sure you look up at the allegorical frescoes under the dome. The scent of pines and flowers perfume the tree-clad gravel paths winding up the hillside. At the base of the Kurpark, close to the casino, there are plenty of benches for sunbathing, along with a small kiosk selling coffees and cakes. Deckchairs are nearby, too, that you can simply recline in to enjoy the sun. Make sure you also check out the beautiful art nouveau theater between the casino and

the park. If you're lucky, you may even catch a concert on the bandstand.

DOBLHOFF PARK AND ROSARIUM

Doblhoffpark; open 24 hours; free

Baden bei Wien is full of parkland, and if you head over to the other side of the town to the Doblhoff Park in June, prepare for a sensory overload when the 75,000-square-meter (90,000-square-yard) park is filled with 30,000 roses in bloom—and over 600 types. The centerpiece of the park is the Baroque orangery, a house used to store citrus trees and other exotic plants in the winter built in the 18th century, making the perfect photo backdrop against the rose carpet. Even when the roses are not in bloom, Doblhoff Park and the Rosarium are charming enough for a stroll. If you have time only for one, go for the Kurpark, especially if you come off season.

Food
BADENER ECK

Heiligenkreuzer Gasse 2; tel. 02/252-86695; daily 10am-11pm; €9.50-20

This tavern just behind the Römertherme serves up all the Austrian specials, such as Schnitzel, Tafelspitz, and sausages at a good price. It's a simple restaurant with a retro look, as seen in its brown wooden panels and slightly yellowed walls. Locals pack the place at lunchtime, and dining here feels authentically Austrian. Just note that smoking is allowed indoors, which can inhibit your dining enjoyment. Go for the daily menu (11am-2pm) priced at €8.50 for three courses.

EL GRECO

Theresiengasse 1; tel. 02/252-253071; www.restaurantelgreco.at; daily 11am-10pm; mains €9.50-20

You can spot this Greek restaurant from the outside easily by the classical-style statues in the doorway leading to the courtyard. The main restaurant lies in a basement decorated with Cretan paintings, Greek painted plates and small statues, and the menu has all the classics, including meze plates with an assortment of stuffed vine leaves, Tzatziki and other cold starters, as well as cooked dishes like moussaka, and souvlaki. You can wash down all the freshly prepared Greek food with ouzo, retsina, or other Hellenic wines.

EL GAUCHO

Josefsplatz 2; tel. 02/252-80399; www.elgaucho.at; daily 11:30am-11pm; mains €16-40

Housed in a former bath house that looks like a neoclassical temple, El Gaucho is a premium steak house inspired by Argentinian cuisine. The interior is modern and cozy, with leatherette booths and an open kitchen. Aside from delicious cuts of steak—including dry aged beef—you can find a mix of international fusion dishes such as grilled lamb chops, scallops, fish, and even burgers. The desserts are creative, especially the coconut cream sorbet with marinated pineapple, and if you're really feeling fancy go for the amazing cheese plate with a glass of tawny port. El Gaucho also has an excellent wine selection, and the Austrian wines served here are especially good.

CAFE CENTRAL

Hauptplatz 19; tel. 06/80-2004508; http:// cafe-central.at; daily 8am-8pm; cakes €3.70-5

Even when you're not in Vienna you can find a classic Viennese café. Cafe Central in Baden bei Wien is the ultimate people-watching spot, whether you grab a table on the plaza overlooking the town hall or sit inside besides one of the large windows or mirrored walls. This is a place where you can spend a good hour or two with a coffee or a cake—try the house cake, the Cafe Central Torte, made with white chocolate mousse and passion fruit.

CAFE KONDITOREI ULLMANN

Schlossergässchen 16; tel. 02/252-48665; Thu-Tue 8am-6pm; cakes €3-5

Hidden at the end of a picturesque alley lined with shops and alternative therapy clinics close to the Rosarium, Cafe Konditorei Ullmann is like stepping back in time a century. This café with its white wood-paneled

interior, portraits of Sisi, and dainty chandeliers has an old-world charm that adds to the flavor of the cakes. Try the cream cake with a Melange and just savor the experience. It's toward the edge of town, but on the way to the Rosarium and the park if you find yourself heading this direction.

Accommodations

HOTEL ADMIRAL AM KURPARK

Renngasse 8; tel. 02/252-86799; www.hotel-admiral.at; €125-150

Hotel Admiral has the best views in town, overlooking the casino and the Kurpark. Ideal for anyone wanting to spend the day strolling among the trees and hitting the roulette wheel at night. And if you don't want to trek out to the thermal bath, you can get some wellness treatments at the in-house sauna, steam bath, and sun bed. The rooms are modern and simple, with a palette of beiges, browns, and gold, and allergy tested bedding. A buffet breakfast spread is included in the price of the room. There are 17 rooms and 4 suites stretching over 3 floors.

HOTEL SCHLOSS WEIKERSDORF

Schloßgasse 9-11; tel. 02/252-48301; www.hotelschlossweikersdorf.at; €95-150 d

This 4-star hotel in a restored Renaissance castle overlooks the Rosarium. The hotel has 164 rooms and spreads out through the old part of the buildings and parts of the former converted stables, backing onto the ground of the Doblhoff Park. A buffet breakfast—included in the price—is served in the old part of the castle, and if the weather is good you can even sit out with a coffee and a croissant on the colonnaded terrace and watch the roses (whether in bloom or not). There is also a spa on site with a swimming pool and sauna, which offers massages and other treatments.

Luggage Storage

You can store your luggage in the Baden train station. Prices for lockers range €2-5 for a 24-hour period depending on size.

Cruising through the Wachau Valley

Danube River boat

The best way to take in the Wachau Valley is by boat between the towns of Krems and der Donau and Melk, but you can also take a bicycle and cycle along the river, or go by car and stop on the way.

There is also a bus running between Melk and Krems. **ÖBB Postbus** (www.postbus.at) goes once to twice an hour and takes just over an hour. Tickets cost €9.60.

★ BY BOAT

Brandner (www.brandner.at; Apr-Oct 10:05am Krems-Melk, 13:45 Melk-Krems; €27 one way) runs boats down the Danube daily from April to the end of October. You can start from Krems or Melk (or any of the stops in between). The boat is very comfortable, with an indoor area plus an outdoor terrace that's nice and breezy on warm days. There is a restaurant and a bar on board, so

Getting There

All public transit options from Vienna to Baden bei Wien cost €6 one way. The train is the fastest option. The Badner Bahn long-distance tram takes longer but is convenient, as it drops you in the center of Baden bei Wien.

TRAIN

The fastest way to get to Baden bei Wien from Vienna is to take the local train (30 minutes) operated by **ÖBB Railjet** (www.oebb.at) from Wien Hauptbahnhof, which run at least every

half an hour. There are also S-Bahn services that take longer (50 minutes), also running from Wien Hauptbahnhof once an hour from 5am-1am, and will also drop you off at the Baden bei Wien Bahnhof. The train station in Baden is 10-15 minutes walking from town center. You can also get a taxi, which you will usually find parked outside the train station, or call **Funktaxi Baden** (tel. 02/252-88500). Taxis will cost around €7.50 for the 5-minute drive into town.

However, if you simply want to hop on a train from the city center, grab the Badner

all you need to do is sit back and relax and watch the river go by. It's best to go out on the terrace rather than choosing a seat inside as you won't know which side to look as you sail past Schön-bühel Castle, Spitz, and Dürnstein on the way down the valley. A return ticket is only €5 more, and if you choose to return that way, just make sure you're on the other side of the boat for the trip back. It takes around an hour and a half downstream (from Melk to Krems); upstream (Krems to Melk) takes around 3 hours, stopping at Spitz, Weißenkirchen, and Dürnstein en route. Ships have around 290 seats inside spread over two decks and 200 seats on the sun deck.

BY BIKE

Cycling down the Wachau Valley between Melk and Krems is one of the most popular activities in the region. The route runs for 39 kilometers (24 mi) and follows a relatively flat bike path, which even goes downhill if you're cycling in the direction of Melk to Krems.

First take the train to Melk, and pick up a bike to rent at the Nextbike (www.nextbike.at). Once you've got your bike, follow the signs marked "Donauradweg." (You can also find a map with bike trails here at www.donau-oesterreich.at). There are two bike paths, one on the north side of the river and another on the south. For the most scenic route, ride along the south for around one and a half hours until you reach the cable ferry going across to Spitz (ferries go regularly upon request between Mon-Fri 6:15am-7pm, Sat-Sun 8:15am-7:30pm May-Sep, Mon-Fri 6:15am-6pm, Sat-Sun 8:15am-6pm Apr and Oct, Mon-Fri 6:15am-11:15am and 3:30pm-6pm Nov-Mar; €1.80 per person and another €1.20 per bike). You can also take another cable ferry farther along at Rossatz to Dürnstein (also on request 9:30am-6pm daily May-Sept, Fri-Sun 10am-5pm Apr and Oct; €2.70 per person and another €1.20 per bike). From the north side continue cycling down to Krems. Riding without stopping will take you 3-4 hours, but if you want to sightsee and have lunch, budget around 7-8 hours. You can just deposit the bike at the Nextbike station next to the train station in Krems. You can take the train directly back to Vienna from Krems.

BY CAR

The drive from Melk to Krems takes around 35-40 minutes and will take you along the northern banks of the Danube through the picturesque towns of Spitz and Dürnstein. From Melk take the Donaubrücke Melk across the river to Emmersdorf and turn onto the Donau Bundesstraße and continue northeast toward Krems following the river. This route will take you through Spitz and Dürnstein before you finally reach Krems.

Bahn (WLB) a long-distance tram run by the **Wiener Lokalbahnen** (www.wlb.at) from next to the Staatsoper which will take you into the center of Baden bei Wien. These trains run every 15 minutes to half an hour from around 5:30am-11:40pm. This takes just over an hour, but is more convenient when you add the time it takes to get to and from the main stations at each end.

BUS

Bus 360 goes from the Wien Oper stop next to the Staatsoper Baden bei Wien (40 minutes, €6 one way). These buses operated by Wiener Lokalbahnen (www.wlb.at) run once to twice an hour from 7am-3am, and will take you into the city center to Josefplatz and the Bahnhof.

CAR

Baden bei Wien is a 40-minute drive from Vienna, and the best way to reach the town is to take the Süd Autobahn E59 southward. Note that this road has tolls, so make sure your car has the correct vignette for Austria. If you rent a car in Austria, this should come with a vignette, but if you're bringing a rental car from abroad, like Hungary or Czech Republic, you may not have the appropriate vignette. Make sure to confirm with your rental company.

Leaving Baden bei Wien

From Baden, the last train back to Vienna departs at 12:30am, but there are buses going as late as 2:47am (running once an hour after midnight). The last Badner Bahn (WLB) departs Baden Josefsplatz at 11pm.

The Wachau Valley

The Danube River runs through the Wachau Valley and is lined with ruined castles, vineyards, and rolling hills, making it the perfect day trip from Vienna—especially if you choose to experience it by boat. The valley has been settled since prehistoric times and is immersed in ancient history. It's even the original home of the Venus of Willendorf, a small statue dating back to 30,000 BC, which you can visit in the Naturhistorisches Museum—so plenty of stories and historic sites await, including the castle that imprisoned Richard the Lionheart and one of the most beautiful Baroque abbeys in Europe.

The easiest way to reach the Wachau Valley from Vienna is by train to Melk or Krems, where you get on a boat to cruise down the Danube. If you're going from Melk to Krems, you'll pass the castle of Schönbühel perched on a rock one the southern shore, recognizable from the single tower with the onion shaped dome. Shortly after, you'll reach the town of Spitz, famed for its Gothic church and vineyards on the northern shore, and then you pass by Dürnstein, a spectacular small town with its pastel-blue abbey and ruined medieval castle, and then finally you will arrive at Krems an der Donau.

If you plan to travel from Vienna to Melk, then Krems an der Donau for the day—a very doable plan—I recommend traveling light and leaving your luggage at your accommodation in Vienna. You could store luggage at the train station in Vienna, but do note you won't be returning to the same train station in Vienna if you go to Melk and come back from Krems. There are no luggage storage options at the train station in Melk.

MELK AND VICINITY

Melk (pop. 5,300) is a pretty town with wood-beamed old houses lining cobbled streets looking like something you'd find on a confectionary box, but towering over the valley, it's the tangerine-colored abbey that dominates the town. You can spend a good three hours or more in Melk just exploring the abbey and the grounds with some time for lunch as well, so bear that in mind if you're planning on starting in Melk and then taking the boat down the river.

Sights
★ MELK ABBEY
Abt-Berthold-Dietmayr-Straße 1; tel. 02/752-5550; www.stiftmelk.at; 9am-5:30pm Apr-Oct, 9:30am-4:30pm Oct-Nov, 11am-12:30pm, 1:30pm-3pm Nov-Mar; €12.50

Crowning the town of Melk in hues of oranges and yellow, Melk Abbey is one of the most spectacular sites along the Danube. Although the abbey was founded in the 11th century, it gets its current look from the 18th century and is a huge complex that's still in use as an abbey today. One part still houses a group of monks, another courtyard encloses a school, and another wing is the museum—which along with the church is the only part of the abbey open to the public. The museum presents the history of the abbey with an immersive mix of art installations and historic objects, such as an 11th-century portable altar, books from the 16th century, and plenty of jewel-clad crosses from the abbey's past. But the main highlight is the stunning terrace overlooking the Danube, which leads into the equally beautiful library with 16,000 ancient books and its brightly colored ceiling frescoes. At midday, you can also see the monks perform the midday prayer in the golden Baroque church—which usually coincides with the end of the morning guided tour. You can also visit the abbey gardens just behind the complex.

The Benedictine abbey is a short hike from the train station and the boat dock, and worth the climb. At the time of writing, due to COVID-19 guided tours are only available upon request for your own group (up to 10 people; €60 per group plus €12.50 for the admission per person).

ARTSTETTEN CASTLE

Schlossplatz 1; tel. 07/413-8006; www.schloss-artstetten.at; museum and family crypt Thu-Sun 10am-5pm Apr-Nov, castle nature park Tue-Sun 10am-1pm Apr-Nov; €9 for the museum, €3.50 castle nature park

If you're interested in the legacy of the crown prince Franz Ferdinand, who was assassinated in Sarajevo—the event that kick-started World War I—then you may find this castle, his former home, worth a stop. Set in an enchanting verdant parkland high up in the hills above the Danube, this seven-turreted castle that wouldn't be out of place in a fairytale is the resting place for Franz Ferdinand and his wife. History buffs should check out the museum in the castle about the crown prince and his family, or you can simply just get a ticket to the lush gardens surrounding the historic castle.

If you're traveling the Wachau Valley by public transport, it may not be worth the trip to this castle, unless you have a fascination with the Habsburg family. Should you want to visit, the best way is to take the train from Melk to Pöchlarn Bahnhof (trains run three times an hour and take 5-7 minutes; €2.40) and then take the bus NG1A to Artstetten Ortsmitte (Mon.-Fri. 8:40am, 1:40pm, 4:40pm, taking 15 minutes; €2.40, but note there are no buses on the weekends). If you are driving, it takes 20 minutes from Melk, and is more worth the detour.

Bike-Sharing
NEXTBIKE

www.nextbike.at

If you want to cycle down the Danube from Melk to Krems, the NextBike bike rental station right next to the railway station is the place get a bike. There are also locations in Abt-Karl Straße, Sparkassengasse, and outside the Konditorei Mistlbacher. You just need to download the Nextbike app, register online, or call the hotline. Once you're registered via the app you will either get a bike number to enter on the back of the bike, or a QR code to scan on the bike, after which you will get a code via SMS to unlock it. To avoid using the app, call the hotline (02/742-229-901) to rent the bike, and receive the code via SMS. You can just deposit the bike at the Nextbike station next to the train station in Krems. The app and website will also show you other locations where you can rent bikes (there are other locations in Melk if you can't find any free bikes at the station). Hourly rental rates are €1, or you can rent a bike for 24 hours at €10.

Food
RATHAUSKELLER MELK

Rathausplatz 13; tel. 02/752-20460; www.rathauskeller-melk.at; daily 11am-9pm; mains €11-30

In the summer, this vaulted cellar in the center of Melk makes the perfect refuge from the heat—it's also quite cozy and warm in the winter. The menu serves all the usual Austrian favorites, from different types of Schnitzel to goulash stews with dumplings, but you can also get some vegetarian and vegan dishes. Central location, large portions and reasonable prices. You can also sit out in the streetside terrace if you prefer dining in the sun.

MADAR CAFE RESTAURANT ZUM FURSTEN

Rathausplatz 3; tel. 02/752-52343; www.kaffeehaustradition.at; daily 7am-11pm; mains €7-10

Despite its setting in a beautiful historic building on Rathausplatz, the prices at Madar Cafe are budget friendly. You can spot this restaurant—which is more like a traditional inn with a few hotel rooms on hand too—as it presents the perfect photo op, set in a cute, 16th-century town house with a frescoed facade. It's not a place for fine dining, but the food here is cheap and cheerful, featuring pizzas and breaded meat dishes. Do stay for a coffee and a cake; cakes are homemade and the coffee comes from the café's own roastery (tours of the roaster are available on demand). There is a scenic terrace overlooking the historic center.

BACKEREI KONDITOREI MISTLBACHER

Hauptstrasse 1; tel. 02/752-52350; www.mistlbacher. com; Mon-Sat 8am-6pm, Sun 1pm-6pm; cakes €2.90-4

Grab a coffee and a cake at this traditional café at the foot of the Melk Abbey. This huge café complex occupies a townhouse, with an 80-seater garden, and also has two indoor areas split into smoking and non-smoking that can seat 50 guests each. Come for the homemade pastries and ice cream and try some of the local specials. Taste a slice of the Melker Torte, a rich cake made with almonds, dark chocolate, and a filling of apricot jam.

Getting There

The easiest way to reach the Wachau Valley from Vienna is by train served by **ÖBB Railjet** (www.oebb.at). The best option is to take a train to Melk from the Wien Westbahnhof (1 hour; €19). Trains are direct and run once an hour from 6:20am-1am.

To reach Melk by car from Vienna, take the A1 due west for approximately an hour.

Leaving Melk

The last direct train back to Vienna from Melk leaves at 10:38pm. (There are also trains leaving after 11pm, but you'll need to change in St. Pölten.) The last boat for Krems an der Donau leaves Melk at 1:45pm April to October.

DÜRNSTEIN CASTLE

Dürnstein; tel. 02/711-200; www.duernstein.at; open 24 hours; free

If you take the Danube boat cruise, you'll surely be tempted to disembark when you float by the picturesque town of Dürnstein, with its pastel blue abbey and ruined castle. If you do decide to take a detour in this beautiful riverside town, then take the steep but short 20-minute hike from the town center up to the 12th-century ruined castle. The castle became famous because of Richard the Lionheart, the legendary English King who even gets a mention in the Robin Hood folklore. Local legend says the king was imprisoned in this very castle after he tore up the Austrian flag and refused to share his spoils of war. The castle is entirely ruined and exposed to the elements, so you won't find any museums here, but the ruins are romantic, and you can clamber around the walls to get a sense of the old castle that occupies 17 square kilometers (6.5 sq mi). Although the castle is lit up at night, if you're planning to head there after dark, take a flashlight as the paths are not well lit. It's worth the hike if you love history or simply want amazing views over the Danube from above.

Getting There

The **ÖBB Postbus** (www.oebb.at) that runs between Melk and Krems will also take you to Dürnstein (45 minutes; €8.40).

If you're driving from Melk, drive over the Danube taking the Donaubrücke Melk and take the road northeast in the direction of Krems. The drive will take around 30 minutes. Coming from Krems, it's only a 10-minute drive on the B3 road southwest to Dürnstein.

Leaving Dürnstein Castle

The last bus from Dürnstein to Krems an der Donau departs at 10:24pm Monday through

---

1: Dürnstein Abbey in Wachau Valley **2:** the historic town Krems an der Donau **3:** the town of Melk

1

2

3

Saturday. On Sunday, the last bus departs 9:24pm.

KREMS AN DER DONAU

Connected to Melk by boat, Krems (also known by its longer name Krems an der Donau) lies at the eastern stretch of the Wachau Valley. It's a large, historic town dotted with winding cobbled streets, modern art galleries, historic churches and wine bars, but is a little bit of a come down after Melk and Dürnstein. In the summer, it draws in crowds of tourists from the riverboats, along with and trendy arts crowds who come for avant-garde events. The best thing to do is when you get off the train or the boat in Krems is just wander around aimlessly (along the Danube, if you like), or grab a coffee in the historic streets. However, I would recommend spending more time in Dürnstein or Melk and just using Krems as a base to get the train back to Vienna.

Sights
KUNSTHALLE KREMS

Franz-Zeller-Platz 3; tel. 02/732-908-010; www.kunsthalle.at; Tue-Sun 10am-6pm Mar-Oct, Tue-Sun 10am-5pm Nov-Feb; €10

If you're interested in the contemporary art scene outside Vienna, then check out the Kunsthalle Krems. This art hall resides in a former tobacco factory built in the mid-19th century and functions as an exhibition space stretching over 1,400 square meters (15,000 sq ft). Exhibitions here are temporary and feature art created after 1945 and showcase work from young Austrian artists as well as international ones. The Kunsthalle Krems curates exhibitions usually centered around a theme, like sculptures made out of paper or work by an artist in residence, covering all forms of artistic media, whether it's more traditional forms like painting or sculpture through to video, photography, performance arts and installations. Each April and May it is one of the hosts of the Donaufestival (www.donaufestival.at), a large contemporary art festival that lasts a couple of weeks.

FORUM FROHNER

Minoritenplatz 4; tel. 02/32-908-010; www.forum-frohner.at; Tue-Sun 11am-5pm; €5

You'll find art lovers congregating at this art space housed inside a former Minorite Monastery. The Forum Frohner, named after artist Adolf Frohner, holds regular exhibitions and events, and you'll usually find hip young Austrians hanging around the cool stone corridors or in the white, cube-like exhibition space inside. Sometimes when there is an event on, or the Donaufestival is in full swing, you may find street food carts in the square outside selling craft beer and snacks, or a pop-up coffee bar inside. Exhibitions and events continually change, so you can either look at the program on the website (in German) or just pass by and see what's happening.

CARICATURE MUSEUM

Steiner Landstraße 3a; tel. 02/32-908-010; www.karikaturmuseum.at; daily 10am-6pm Mar-Oct, daily 10am-5pm Nov-Feb; €10

Krems is home to Austria's only museum dedicated to caricatures. The museum stretches over 780 square meters (8,400 sq ft) over the three-story building (only the ground floor and the upper floor are open to the public) and is loyally dedicated to satirical art, comics, cartoons, and caricatures. The museum is split up into sections, mostly covering temporary exhibitions, with permanent collections including the IRONIMUS Cabinet on the ground floor with its collection of political caricatures, and the upper floor with work by cartoonist Manfred Deix.

Food
2STEIN

Dr.-Karl-Dorrek-Straße 23; tel. 02/732-71615; www.2stein.at; Wed-Thu 11am-11pm, Fri-Sat 11am-midnight, Sun 11am-10pm; mains €8-30

2STEIN is a restaurant with a modern edge and a varied menu, offering everything from dry aged steak to gourmet burgers and vegan dishes. Design lovers will adore 2STEIN with its glass conservatory, contemporary chandeliers and randomly placed bicycle parts that accent the walls. Many come for the gourmet burgers, which include those made with dry-aged beef, Wagyu beef, and also veggie and vegan options, such as the Vegan Spicy, a Cajun-style patty made with a mix of grains, vegan mayo, and hot pickles. Pastas, curries, and other international fusion favorites all make the menu. Reservations highly recommended.

MOYOME
Obere Landstrasse 10; tel. 06/64-5144686; www.moyome.com; Mon-Fri 8am-7pm, Sat 8:30am-6pm, Sun 9am-5pm; dishes €5-9

This popular and cozy café spills out onto the street-side terrace in the summer. You'll find an extensive selection of all-day vegetarian and vegan breakfasts and dishes inspired by Middle Eastern and Asian cuisine. Try one of their curries or their breakfast dishes. Most of the dishes on the menu are vegetarian or vegan—which are marked respectively—but there is the odd meat dish as well. Don't be shy about checking out their daily menu, which is very reasonably priced, good for the budget traveler. Do order the coffee here, which comes from a local roastery in a nearby town.

Luggage Storage
Lockers for luggage storage are available at the train station in Krems an der Donau, ranging €2-5 depending on size for a 24-hour period.

Getting There
From Wien Franz-Josefs-Bahnhof, a train station in Alsergrund in the 9th District, you can take a train with **ÖBB Railjet** (www.oebb.at) to Krems an der Donau once an hour from 5:05am-12:05am, which takes just over an hour, costing €19.

If you want to drive to Krems an der Donau from Vienna take the A22 north and then onto the S5 in the west direction. The drive will take around an hour.

The boat operated by **Brandner** (www.brandner.at) departs Melk for Krems an der

Donau at 1:45pm daily from April to October, costing €27 per person.

Leaving Krems an der Donau
The last direct train from Krems an der Donau departs for Vienna at 9:50pm. (There are also trains leaving after 11pm, but you'll need to change in St. Pölten.)

GÖTTWEIG ABBEY
Stift Göttweig 1, Furth bei Göttweig; tel. 02/732-85581; www.stiftgoettweig.at; daily 10am-5:30pm Jun-Nov, daily 10am-4:30pm Nov-Dec; €10.50

Rising above the river in the hills with maroon turrets, the Göttweig Abbey sits on a mountain side overlooking the surrounding vineyards of the Wachau Valley. It was founded in the 11th century, but like Melk, this Benedictine Abbey gets its look from the 18th century. It's worth the trip for the view across the surrounding valleys and the Imperial Staircase crowned with a ceiling fresco painted by Paul Troger with intense colors, rococo drama, and cherub dotted blue skies. You can also shop for fruit brandy and other fruit products made by the monks from produce grown on the surrounding grounds.

Getting There
The easiest way to get to this working abbey is to take the bus 723 to Göttweig Abbey (Göttweig Stift) from Krems an der Donau, running every 3 hours from 7:20am to 4:20pm on weekends and holidays (this bus does not run on weekdays) April to October (15 minutes, €2.40). This will take you up to the abbey. You can also take a train to Furth bei Göttweig, which goes once an hour (6 minutes, €2.40), but you will need to hike a good 40 minutes up to the abbey.

Leaving Göttweig Abbey
The last bus 723 leaving Göttweig Stift for Krems an der Donau departs at 5:20pm (Sat-Sun only). The last train from Furth bei Göttweig departs for Krems an der Donau at 12:38am.

Mauthausen

Just outside the city of Linz lies a small, sleepy village (pop. 4,800) with a dark history, set up in the undulating hills overlooking the Danube. Even as you take the wooded paths up the hill on the way to the Mauthausen Concentration Camp memorial, it's hard to imagine that thousands met their death here and in the neighboring village of Gusen under the Nazi regime. Many make the journey to Mauthausen alone or on a tour from Vienna, to remember those who were sent here.

★ MAUTHAUSEN CONCENTRATION CAMP MEMORIAL

Erinnerungsstraße 1; tel. 07/238-22690;
www.mauthausen-memorial.org; daily 9am-5:30pm
Mar-Oct; Tue-Sun 9am-3:45pm Nov-Feb; free

Mauthausen may not have an instantly recognizable name like Auschwitz, but a few hours at this former concentration camp will leave an impact. On first impression, it's a peaceful place with wonderful views stretching as far as the Alps on a clear day and bird song coming from the surrounding trees, but it's a haunting place where Jews, Roma, homosexuals, and political prisoners were imprisoned, worked to death, and following the 1940s, gassed.

Initially, Mauthausen was used as a labor camp for the nearby quarry, and only German and Austrian men were imprisoned here. The complex resembles a barracks when you walk through the towering brick gates, with green-painted containers once crammed with prisoners living in squalor. To get some context, head over to the Infirmary where a well-curated museum with personal artifacts, uniforms, documents, photographs, and footage narrates the story of the camp from 1938-1945. Afterward, descend into the basement and head toward the Room of Names, a moving installation where the names of those sent to their death are inscribed on huge backlit blocks. There are a couple of tomes recording names and personal details—date of birth, hometown, date of death—in the room. The crematorium and the killing facilities in the adjacent room may distress you, as it did me, although nothing graphic is shown.

In July and August, English language tours

The Mauthausen Concentration Camp is a poignant reminder of the horrors of the 20th century.

run at 2pm lasting two hours for €5, no booking required. You can also get an audio guide for €3 from the information center at the entrance.

FOOD
MOSTSTUBE FRELLERHOF
Frellerhofweg 13; tel. 07/238-2789; www.frellerhof.

at; Tue-Fri 3pm-10pm May-Aug, 11am-10pm Sat-Sun, Thu-Fri 3pm-10pm Sep-Apr, 11am-10pm Sat-Sun; mains €10-20

Up on the hill, just a five-minute walk from the Mauthausen Memorial, Moststube Frellerhof has a wonderful garden and terrace in the summer, but also has a rustic indoor section if the weather is a bit off. Try their cold plates, with a selection of cheese, cured meats, and pickles, and if you're drinking, you'll want to try their homemade spirits!

INFORMATION AND SERVICES

If you have any luggage that needs storing, your best option is to store them at the luggage lockers in Linz train station, which costs from €2-5 depending on the size of your bags for a period of 24 hours.

GETTING THERE
Train and Bus

To get to Mauthausen, you first need to take the train with **ÖBB Railjet** (www.oebb.at) to Linz from Vienna (a little over an hour; €38.50 one way). Trains run 3 times an hour.

In Linz, change to the bus 361 run by **OÖVV** (www.ooevv.at) to Mauthausen Linzerstraße/Neue Mittelschule (40 minutes; €5.80 one way). These buses run from 10am from Linz Hauptbahnhof hourly on weekdays, and on even numbered hours on weekends.

From here, just follow the signposts up the hill to the Mauthausen Memorial, which takes an additional 20 minutes on foot.

Another option is to take another train from Linz to Mauthausen OÖ, costing €5.80 one way, but note that direct trains are less frequent than the bus, with sometimes as much as a four-hour gap between trains. You can also take the train and change at St. Valentin which go more frequently and costs the same. From the train station take a taxi the 4 kilometers (2.5 mi) to reach the memorial. There are three taxi firms in Mauthausen: **Taxi Brixner** (07/238-2439), **EasyCab** (06/64-57-12100), **4 You Taxi St. Georgen** (06/60-63-64-657).

Car

It's a two-hour drive from Vienna to Mauthausen. Take the A1 westward in the direction of Linz. Once you reach St. Valentin take the B123, which will lead you over the Donaubrücke Mauthausen, and follow the signs to the town. You will need a vignette for Austria as the highways have tolls. There is a parking place at the memorial, which is free for four hours and then €2 per additional hour.

Tours

Vienna à la Carte (www.vienna-alacarte. com; 8.5 hours; €148 per person) run group tour to Mauthausen three times a week from Vienna.

LEAVING MAUTHAUSEN

The last bus leaving Mauthausen Linzerstraße/Neue Mittelschule departs at 10:10pm and arrives back in Linz at 10:50pm. This gives you enough time to catch the last train back to Vienna going at 11:19pm.

Salzburg

"The hills are alive with the sound of music" may sound cliché, but it rings true in Salzburg (pop. 150,000). Mozart's hometown as well as the setting for *The Sound of Music*, Salzburg carries plenty of musical cachet, and with its fortress perched up on the top of a rocky outcrop and the Alpine views surrounding the town, it's easy to see why it's one of the most visited places in Austria.

You can hop on a train in Vienna and be in Salzburg two and a half hours later, making it possible to do it as a day trip. However, to really appreciate everything Salzburg has to offer, it's ideal to spend a night or two.

SIGHTS

Salzburg Old Town

Salzburg Old Town spreads out on both sides of the River Salzach, over an area of 236 hectares (close to a sq mi), and is a cocktail of Medieval and Baroque buildings. You could find your way to the Old Town just by looking out for the Hohensalzburg Fortress, which towers over the city at an altitude of 506 meters (1660 ft).

The whole Old Town is a UNESCO World Heritage Site, and when you stroll through the cobbled alleys and wander past its domed churches, through its open squares, it's easy to see why. The Old Town covers a large area on both sides of the river. On the south bank, it includes winding streets around the Cathedral, the Hohensalzburg Fortress, and the hill running northward from the fortress. On the northern side of the river, the Old Town also stretches to the Capuchin Monastery and the Mirabell Palace and Gardens. But don't let all that history fool you into thinking this is a living museum— there are 2,500 stores and 300 restaurants in the Old Town, not to mention the concerts, street festivals, and markets that add some color to the cobbled streets and open squares. The best thing to do is just wander, whether

it's exploring a church and the surrounding cemetery, stepping into some of the shops set into narrow alleyways, or taking a stroll beside the river.

★ Hohensalzburg Fortress

Mönchsberg 34; www.salzburg-burgen.at; daily 9:30am-5pm Jan-Apr and Oct-Dec, 8:30am-8pm May-Sep; all-inclusive ticket €15.70

Crowning Salzburg from above, the 11th-century Hohensalzburg Fortress is one of Europe's largest fortifications—and one of the most photogenic places in Central Europe. Hohensalzburg Fortress is striking from any viewpoint in the city, especially from afar on the pedestrianized Makartsteg Bridge or from Kapitalplatz, the square besides Salzburg Cathedral. But to experience it best you'll want to make it up to the top of the hill that it sits on, to visit the museums and wander the ramparts for a stunning panorama over the Alps and the city.

You can walk most of the castle grounds including the viewing terrace for free, but to go into the museums you'll need your ticket. There are also two restaurants and two souvenir shops within the complex. Expect to spend a good couple of hours up here going through the museums and enjoying the view.

GETTING TO THE FORTRESS

You have a couple options for getting there: You can hike up the 400-meter (1,300-ft), steep, rocky outcrop from Kapitalplatz, which will take around 15 minutes. Take the cobbled streets up Festungsgasse until you reach Oskar-Kokoschka Weg and follow the sign posts to the top. Alternatively, if you get an all-inclusive ticket—just buy this at the entrance to the funicular on Festungsgasse—you can hop on the funicular railway, which goes at the speed of a roller coaster up and down the steep 45-degree rail tracks, dropping you off right at the fortress entrance.

VIEWING TERRACE

Once you arrive at the viewing terrace, take in the amazing panoramas over the Alps in both Austria and across the border in Germany, as well as over rooftops and church domes down in the old city itself.

MUSEUMS

To head into the museums, follow the signs within the fortress. Most of the museums—the Castle Museum and the Rainer Regiment museum—occupy the Hoher Stock, the top floor of the Prince-Bishop's apartments in the inner courtyard.

The Castle Museum covers 1,000 years of the castle's history, leading you from its archaeological finds discovered in the area (a Roman fort stood here centuries before the current fortress) to the more than 900 years of history of the current castle. Highlights here are the brightly colored Gothic state rooms once belonging to the prince archbishop, which link to the Castle Museum.

The Rainer Regiment Museum on the military history of the imperial and royal infantry regiment also occupies nine rooms in the Hoher Stock, next to the Castle Museum.

The Puppet Museum (you'll find this on the northwest side of the fortress on the ground floor of the Hoher Stock building) and the observation tower (the west side of the castle), which will take you through the old torture chambers and includes an audio guide in the tour.

You can also visit the Medieval Prince's Chambers and the Golden Hall, which is worth the entrance fee, with its gold-speckled ceiling resembling a starry sky.

Mozart's Birthplace

Getreidegasse 9; tel. 06/62-844313; www.mozarteum.at; daily 9am-5:30pm Sep-Jun; daily 8:30am-7pm Jul-Aug; €12

This canary-yellow five-story house where Mozart was born is home to a museum dedicated to Mozart's life and the life of his family. Rooms are filled with portraits, personal artifacts—such as a lock of the composer's hair—and music scores. The museum, which spans the three floors of the building, offers fascinating insight into the composer's early life in Salzburg before he went to Vienna to find glory. If you visit the Mozart House in Vienna, this is an interesting contrast. There is a strict no photography policy and the museum can get crowded. Expect to spend around an hour to an hour and a half here.

Mirabell Palace and Gardens

Mirabellplatz; tel. 06/62-80720; daily 8am-6pm; free

Across the river from the Hohensalzburg Fortress, the flamboyant Mirabell Palace, built in 1606 by the reigning prince-archbishop Wolf Dietrich, is one of Salzburg's most popular sites. Aside from stunning views up to the castle from afar, the gardens are filled with roses, playful classical statues and atmospheric fountains. If you've seen The Sound of Music, these gardens will look familiar, especially the "Dwarf Garden" and the Pegasus fountain—all of which are featured in the "do-re-mi" song sequence. You can also go inside the palace for free to climb the cherub clad "Angel Staircase" and take a peek inside the Marble Hall, where Leopold Mozart and his children, including Wolfgang, once played.

Salzburg Cathedral

Domplatz 1a; tel. 06/62-80477950; www.salzburger-dom.at; Mon-Sat 8am-5pm, Sun 1pm-5pm Jan-Feb Mon-Sat 8am-6pm, Sun 1pm-6pm Mar-Apr and Oct, Mon-Sat 8pm-7pm, Sun 1pm-7pm May-Sep; free

Salzburg Cathedral with its cupola and twin spires is as much part of Salzburg's cityscape as the fortress. Although today's cathedral dates back to the 16th century, you can find traces of its predecessors in the crypt, with the oldest parts being from the 8th century. It's worth going inside to look at the ceiling frescoes depicting the Passion of Christ, then head down into the crypt for the resting places of the Salzburg bishops, subterranean chapels, and parts of the Romanesque cathedral.

★ *The Sound of Music* Tour

www.panoramatours.com; daily 9:15am and 2pm; €50

Many come to Salzburg to walk in the steps of Julie Andrews, Christopher Plummer, and the von Trapp children and take *The Sound of Music* Tour, one of the most popular excursions in Austria. The four-hour tour takes you to the most famous locations, such as the gazebo, the lake where the kids and Maria fall from the boat, and then up into the hills to the stunning lake district in the company of a guide who will give you the backstory of each location (both its role in the movie and in real life). Salzburg is a stunning town; however, one of the best things about following in the footsteps of the movie is getting out into the countryside surrounding it. You head up the hills alive with the sound of music, and if they're not, you can be sure people on the bus will start to sing along to the soundtrack playing on the 40-minute scenic bus tour between Salzburg and Mondsee in the nearby lake district.

RECREATION

MOUNT UNTERSBERG CABLE CAR

Dr.-Friedrich-Ödlweg 2, Gartenau;
tel. 06/246-724-770; www.untersbergbahn.at;
daily 8:30am-5pm; €27

Majestic Mount Untersberg, which hovers in the distance beyond Salzburg, is a popular destination for year-round Alpine adventures. This cable car soars up 1,320 meters (4330 ft) to the summit station of the famous mountain in just 8 and a half minutes. In the winter, winter sports lovers take the cable car to the top and ski or snowboard down the 7.5 km (4.7 mi) slope to the valley station in the village of Fürstenbrunn (only a short bus ride away from the cable car station). It's just as popular in summer, as the view from the top offers a stunning panorama not only over Austria but also Germany's stunning

Berchtesgadener Land region in Bavaria. You can hike along the ridge at the top or just enjoy the view.

The cable car departs on the hour and half past 8:30am-5pm daily. (It does close for maintenance periods occasionally so check the website in advance.) Wear warm clothing and hiking shoes. You will also need to wear a facemask in the cable car due to Covid-19 measures.

You can reach the base of the mountain and the cable car easily with public transport. Take buses 5, 25 and 28 from Salzburg Marktplatz or 840 from Salzburg Rathaus to Grödig Untersbergbahn (30 minutes; €3). Via car, it's a 20 minute drive on the A10 exiting Grödig-Anif in the direction toward Berchtesgaden.

FOOD

Austrian

GASTHOF GOLDGASSE

Goldgasse 10; tel. 06/62-848-200;
www.gasthofgoldgasse.at; Thu-Mon 7am-11pm;
€15.90-24.90

Tucked on the ground floor of a 700-year-old house, in a narrow street in the Old Town, Gasthof Goldgasse is a cozy inn serving excellent Austrian dishes made with fresh, seasonal, and locally sourced ingredients from regional farmers. Gasthof Goldgasse updates the traditional look with clean, cream-colored walls and light wood paneling accompanied by modern purple lampshades and chandeliers along with artfully presented cuisine. You can't go wrong with their Veal Wiener Schnitzel and Bratwurst, which always get rave reviews.

AUGUSTINER BRAUSTUBL

Lindhofstrasse 7; tel. 06/62-431246;
www.augustinerbier.at; Mon-Fri 3pm-11pm,
Sat-Sun 2:30pm-11pm; dishes €5-10

You won't want to miss this brewery in an Augustinian Monastery that's been making potent beers since 1621. It's a little outside the city center, but worth the detour. In the summer, you can sit out in the huge 1,400 seat beer garden, one of the largest in Austria. There are

---

1: Mozart's birthplace in Salzburg **2:** Mirabell Palace and Gardens **3:** The Hohensalzburg is a highlight of Salzburg.

various little snack stands scattered around the courtyard to choose from once you've grabbed your beer at the foyer pump. You also buy pretzels, fried fish, ham hocks, fries, and other local snacks served in carton trays that go perfectly with the local brew. It's worth the visit to this beer garden if only for the vibrant atmosphere in the summer, but the good news is in the winter there is a 5,000-square-meter (54,000-sq-ft) hall, so you can keep drinking beer even when the weather goes off.

International
ORGANIC PIZZA SALZBURG
Franz-Josef-Strasse 24A; tel. 06/64-5974470; www.organicpizza-salzburg.com; Wed-Fri 5pm-10pm, Sat-Sun noon-10pm; pizzas €10-18

For delicious, organic pizzas, head straight to Organic Pizza Salzburg. Vegan pizzas are available, but meat eaters, have no fear: You can still get prosciutto-topped specials. This tiny, cozy place, with friendly staff, makes all their pizzas with organic, fresh and seasonal ingredients. And if you're not drinking, they also have the best non-alcoholic beer ready to serve by the bottle! You can also ask for a pizza crust made out of spelt flour or gluten free. Even the cola here is organic!

Cafés and Cakes
CAFE AM KAI
Müllner Hauptstraße 4; tel. 06/64-1707899; www.cafeamkai.eu; Wed-Mon 8:30am-11:30pm (closing time depends on the weather); cakes €3.90-4.20

A favorite with locals, especially in the summer, this café on the riverside is the perfect spot for cake, coffee, or breakfast. Try to grab a table on the terrace overlooking the river and the Hohensalzburg Fortress in the distance. And it's not just the view that makes it worth the riverside stroll to this café, but the fact that everything is made with organic, locally sourced products, including eggs from the café's own farm. Don't miss the homemade strudel.

ACCOMMODATIONS
HOTEL GOLDENER HIRSCH
Getreidegasse 37; tel. 06/62-80840; www.goldenerhirsch.com, €240-435 d

Only minutes away from Mozart's birthplace in Salzburg, Hotel Goldener Hirsch is one of the oldest hotels in Vienna, with 600 years of hospitality in its history, making it as much of Salzburg's legacy as Mozart. Set in a stone town house dating back to the 1400s, and, later, functioning as an inn in 1564, today this is a luxury hotel with hunting trophies and old prints lining the whitewashed walls. There are 70 rustic-style rooms, with hand-painted antiques rescued from the nearby farms following World War II. You still have the comforts of the 21st century, like the modern bathrooms and flat screen televisions. There are gourmet restaurants serving Austrian food inside the hotel, and for an extra €34 you can indulge in a luxury breakfast buffet spread including artisanal cheeses, breads, and egg dishes made to order, such as eggs Benedict, or try some Palatschinken (Austrian pancakes).

★ VILLA TRAPP
Traunstraße 34; tel. 06/62-630860; www.villa-trapp.com; €109-275 d

If you're a *Sound of Music* fan, you may want to stay in the house once belonging to the real von Trapp family. Although the movie used various mansions in the area, this 19th century villa has now opened as a low-key bed and breakfast. Set behind a walled garden in the city suburbs, its location may not be central, but it's a fascinating place to stay, especially with all the family memorabilia decorating the walls and rooms. There are 15 rooms in this small bed and breakfast (some have shared bathrooms), and breakfast is an extra €18 including a copious buffet with fresh fruit, bread, jam, cheese, and cold cuts. Guests can also take advantage of a 45-minute tour of the old house. Do note that this hotel doesn't grant refunds for cancellations.

ARTHOTEL BLAUE GANS

Herbert-von-Karajan-Platz 3; tel. 06/62-8424910;
www.blaue-gans.com; €129-400 d

Even though the artHOTEL occupies a 14th-century house that's been an inn for centuries, it blends the old and new world flawlessly with more than 100 pieces of contemporary art, sculptures, and photographs dotting the individually decorated 35 rooms in the hotel. It lies at the foot of the Hohensalzburg Fortress, making it the ideal location to explore the old town. Breakfast is usually included in the price, but there is also a traditional Austrian restaurant on the premises and a bar filled with plush armchairs. Check out the herb garden on the first floor, or see if you can grab a jazz gig in the cellar during the Fall.

INFORMATION AND SERVICES

If you are staying in a hotel, you can request they hold your luggage once you check out, or leave your luggage at the Salzburg main train station with lockers ranging €2-5 for a 24-hour period depending on the size of your bags.

GETTING THERE

The best way to get from Vienna to Salzburg is to take the train, as the bus trip takes around 8-10 hours.

Train

ÖBB Railjet (www.oebb.at) operates regular train services to Salzburg from Wien Hauptbahnhof (2.5 hours); trains run approximately every half hour. One-way tickets usually cost €56.80, but check out the ÖBB Railjet website and buy a ticket in advance for special offers, as low as €39.90 a ticket if bought in advance.

From the train station, it takes 10 minutes to reach the Old Town in Salzburg on foot, 25 minutes to Salzburg Cathedral. There are also regular bus services operated by **Salzburg Verkehrsbund** (salzburg-verkehr.at) running outside the station (single tickets cost €2.90) that will take you into the city center. **Salzburg Taxi** (06/76-3347-141) is one of the taxi firms to use from the station.

Car

Going to Salzburg by car won't save you time compared to the train, as the journey will take around three hours. Take the A1 running west from Vienna for the fastest route, but make sure your car has a vignette as this route has tolls.

GETTING AROUND

Salzburg has a good public transport system, but the city center is compact enough to get around on foot. It's best to get a taxi from the front of the train station if you're not familiar with the city.

LEAVING SALZBURG

The last train leaving Salzburg Hauptbahnhof for Vienna leaves just after 10pm, getting into the Austrian capital around 12:30am.

Bratislava, Slovakia

If you fancy including another country and capital to your Central European itinerary, you can easily add Bratislava (pop. 420,000) as a day trip from Vienna. It's rare that you have two capital cities only an hour's ride from each other, so you can just hop on a train or bus and visit Slovakia and be back in Vienna by the evening.

Although Bratislava is not as spectacular as Prague and Budapest, nor as interesting and complex as Vienna, it still has plenty of charm, with medieval streets winding up to the whitewashed castle overlooking the Danube, or wide boulevards taking you just streets away to Ödön Lechner's Blue Church. Bratislava also has a very chilled-out, new wave café culture filled with hip and young creatives, and you could easily spend the day just hopping between coffee shops.

Slovakia is also in the EU and in the Schengen Zone, so there won't be border checks on the way, but still bring your passport or ID card with you, just in case. Like Austria, Slovakia uses the euro. Slovak is the official language spoken in Slovakia, a Slavic language similar to Czech, but you will find that many speak English in the capital.

You can use Bratislava as a base to break the journey between Budapest and Prague (it's located on the same train route), but if you choose to visit Bratislava when traveling between the two cities, it's best to spend the night. If you're looking to add Bratislava in your Budapest-Vienna itinerary, I would advise doing Bratislava as a day trip from Vienna rather than taking the detour with all that luggage.

SIGHTS
★ Old Town

Bratislava's compact historic nucleus is the old heart of the city. It's also the site of the festivals and vibrant cafés that keep the Slovak capital's blood pumping. The area in the Old Town around Hlavné námestie, the Main Square, is worth visiting for the Old Town Hall, whose stone tower dates as far back as the 14th century, and for the 16th century Roland Fountain featuring the Habsburg king Maximilian II depicted as a knight on the column towering above the fountain. From the Main Square, head up Michalská to the St. Michael's Tower, one of the only preserved gate towers dotted around the original city wall. Or turn down to the intersection of Panská and Rybárska Brána and see if you can catch sight of the bronze sculpture: a man peeking out from under a manhole cover. Keep your eyes peeled as you wander through the district for little architectural details, quirky design shops, and tempting little cafés.

Bratislava Castle

Bratislava Hrad; tel. 02/544-114-44;
www.bratislava-hrad.sk; daily 9am-5pm
Nov-Mar, daily 10am-6pm Apr-Oct; €10

Bratislava Castle is a symbol of the city. A huge cube-like structure with four stocky turreted towers topped with terracotta tiles sits on top of a hill overlooking the whole town. The original castle dates back to the 9th century, but the building you see today is actually a 1960s reconstruction based on

evening in Old Town Bratislava

a Renaissance style, as the original castle burned down in 1811.

You can climb up to the castle grounds for wonderful views over Bratislava, and there is also a museum inside the castle that will take you back in time through history of the castle. Climb up the Crown Tower for amazing views, and make sure you stop to look at the *Assumption of the Virgin Mary* painting by Anton Schmidt in the Music Hall, which is a wonderful example of local Baroque art. It's a good idea to hit the castle first thing in the morning if you want to avoid the crowds coming with the Danube cruises and the tour buses. Due to COVID-19, face masks are compulsory and social distancing measures are enforced.

★ Blue Church

Bezručova 2534/2; tel. 02/527-335-72;
www.modrykostol.fara.sk; Mon-Sat 6:30am-7:30am,
5:30pm-7pm, Sun 7:30am-midday, 5:30pm-7pm; free
This stunning art nouveau church in various shades of blue by Hungarian architect Ödön Lechner is worth the short detour out of the Old Town. Its official name is the Church of St. Elizabeth of Hungary—named after Empress Elizabeth, "Sisi," Franz Joseph I's wife—but its blue hues earned it the more common "Blue Church" title. Although the opening hours are sporadic, and only really open for services (and at the time of writing, the church was closed indefinitely due to COVID-19), you can admire the marzipan-like building from the outside where even the roof is lined with blue-glazed ceramics. If you can make it inside, then you'll notice even the interior is entirely blue, with pews painted in baby blue tones decorated with gold accents.

Most SNP

Viedenská cesta; tel. 02/6252-0300;
www.u-f-o.sk; daily 10am-11pm; €8.90
Towering nearly 95 meters (312 ft), the UFO Bridge (as it's known in English) offers amazing views over Bratislava. From afar the viewing platform looks like a flying saucer, and is a rather an odd sight in the capital. Built in 1972, the bridge and the highway running over it has left a bittersweet taste in locals' mouths after its construction took many historic buildings as casualties. Today, it's become integrated into Bratislava's cityscape and there is a pedestrian walkway across the river from the Old Town. Take the elevator—which takes 45 seconds to rocket up—to the observation deck, from which on a clear day you can see

Blue Church

as far as 100 kilometers (62 mi) into the distance. On good days, make sure you check out the beach just below the bridge where you can grab street food and drinks, or later in the evening catch some DJs spinning on hot summer nights.

St. Martin's Cathedral

Rudnayovo námestie 1; tel. 02/30-544334; http://dom.fara.sk; Mon-Fri 9am-11:30am and 1pm-6pm, Sat 9am-11:30am, Sun 1:30pm-4pm; free

Like many Central European churches, St. Martin's Cathedral is a tapestry of architectural styles from different time periods. It was built on the site of an earlier Romanesque church. The Gothic tower juts up 85 meters (280 ft), which once functioned as a lookout point and is topped by 300 kilograms (660 lbs) of real gold. Much of the cathedral dates back to the 14th century and despite the humble interior has held 19 coronations over the centuries. On the outside, it's worth taking a look at the walls of the house next to the cathedral that's filled with colorful artwork in the stone niches. Make sure you bring a scarf or a cardigan to cover bare shoulders before entering.

FOOD

Slovak food is influenced by its Czech, Austrian, and Hungarian neighbors. Local ingredients that could withstand the hot Slovakian summers and cold winters dominate the dishes, like potatoes, wheat, dairy products, sauerkraut, onion, and pork. Dumplings made from bread, wheat, or potato are popular, as are pork products like sausages, smoked bacon, and lard.

When you're in Slovakia you must try the Bryndzové halušky, potato dumplings with a tangy local sheep's cheese called bryndza, or the Bryndzové pirohy, cheese-filled boiled dumplings. Another local special is the Segedin goulash, which, despite the name, is actually nothing like the Hungarian gulyás or Viennese goulash, but a pork stew made with sauerkraut and cream, and served with dumplings.

Due to COVID-19, opening times may be volatile, or you may be required to give proof of vaccination, so check the websites and the situation before booking or going. You can also check the **Bratislava Tourist Information Center**'s website (www.visit-bratislava.com) for updates.

Slovak
MODRÁ HVIEZDA

Beblavého 292/14; tel. 0948 703 070; http://modrahviezda.sk; daily 11am-11pm; mains €10-20

Try some Slovak specials at Modrá Hviezda, which means "Blue Star." You'll find this brick-lined restaurant in a cellar in the back streets winding up toward Bratislava Castle, where you can sample Slovak specials like rabbit in red wine or locally caught baked trout. The menu changes with the seasons, but this cozy restaurant with antique wooden farming equipment on the wall and brick-lined cellar is inviting all year round.

BRATISLAVSKÝ MEŠTIANSKY PIVOVAR

Drevená 8; tel. 09/44-512-265; www.mestianskypivovar.sk; Mon-Sat 11am-midnight, Sun 11am-11pm; mains €7-30

This vaulted microbrewery is worth the visit for the in-house beers and hearty Slovak food. The beer here is unfiltered, unpasteurized, and served fresh from the tap, with a mix of lagers, dark beer, and German style Weissbier. If you're thirsty, you can get beers by the liter as well. Food includes cold cut and cheese plates, or you can try their special beef goulash made with beer, roasted pork knuckle, Schnitzel, and other Central European specials.

HOUDINI RESTAURANT

Tobrucká 6953/4; tel. 02/577-846-00; www.restauranthoudini.sk; Mon-Fri noon-10pm, Sat-Sun 6pm-10pm; mains €15-35

Set in the ground floor of the Marrol Hotel, Houdini Restaurant offers fine dining at affordable prices. You can order a la carte, but a four-course tasting menu with wine pairings won't break the bank at €40, with beautifully presented dishes such as rabbit leg confit and cheese risotto. The setting strikes a balance between elegant and cozy, with library-like shelves stocked with bottles of wine and wood paneling. The dishes here are Slovak with an international twist and a Mediterranean accent.

International
BISTRO KUBISTA

Grösslingová 2524/26; tel. 09/48-077-845; www.kubista.sk; Mon-Fri 8am-10pm, Sat 10am-10pm, Sun 10am-5pm; mains €12-15

If you're looking for great fusion food made with local, organic ingredients and freshly cooked dishes, then this trendy modern bistro just streets away from the Blue Church is a hit. You can get hearty soups, seasonal dishes like daily game specials, braised chicken in white wine, as well as vegetarian friendly soups and bites. The design is clean and modern with white walls, large windows and Edison bulbs, and in the summer there are outdoor tables too.

Cafés and Cakes
ŠTÚR

Štúrova 8; tel. 09/44-960-352; www.sturcafe.sk; Mon-Fri 8:30am-10pm, Sat 9am-10pm, Sat 9am-10pm, Sun 9am-9pm; snacks €4-7

Štúr is a trendy café named after the Slovak poet and linguist Ľudovít Štúr, whose face you'll find all over the walls of the modern-looking café. It pulls in a young crowd in the evening, but people of all ages come during the day for its freshly baked range of cakes. It's a relaxed place to grab a snack or a light lunch.

CAFE VERNE

Hviezdoslavovo námestie 175/18; tel. 02/544-305-14; https://cafeverne.sk; Mon-Thu 9am-midnight, Fri 9am-1am, Sat 10am-1am, Sun 10am-midnight; mains €4-11

In the summer, Cafe Verne spills out onto the square at Hviezdoslavovo námestie in the Old Town, and in the winter you can escape into this colorful basement with red velvet booths, lace curtains and old books. It's a great place

to hop in for a coffee—especially if the terrace is out—and despite its central location it's a place where even the locals come here to catch up with friends or read the morning paper. If you're hungry, grab something from the daily menu for some simple, yet hearty home cooking. Try the pancake filled with sweet cottage cheese!

ACCOMMODATIONS
ARCADIA BOUTIQUE HOTEL

Františkánska 3; tel. 02/594-905-00; www.arcadiahotel.sk; €80-135 d

Set in a 13th century building in the heart of Bratislava's Old Town, this charming 4-star boutique hotel makes the perfect base to explore the Slovak's capital's historic heart. There are 34 rooms and suites decked out in fabrics and plush carpets in rich reds or bold emerald greens. At the heart of the hotel, the lobby lies within a colonnaded courtyard enclosed by a stained-glass ceiling. There is a small wellness area set up in a former medieval prison with a plunge pool, saunas and gym. Guests are treated to a full breakfast buffet included in the price.

LOFT HOTEL BRATISLAVA

Štefánikova 4; tel. 02/575-110-00; www.lofthotel.sk; €65-146 d

The 4-star LOFT Hotel overlooks the Presidential Palace in the center of the city. There are 111 modern rooms with LCD TVs and a daily refilled minibars. If you love industrial chic go for one of the premium rooms with its exposed brick and brass lamps. Beer lovers will want to check out the Fabrika Beer Pub where you can get beer brewed on site. You can also get a rich buffet breakfast (included in most room packages, otherwise it's an additional €14) with full view of the brewery behind the Plexiglass.

INFORMATION AND SERVICES

If you are planning to stop by Bratislava on the way from Vienna to Budapest or Prague, you can store your luggage for the day at the lockers at the train station or the bus station. The luggage storage office in the main train station operates Monday-Friday 4am-11:55pm, with several 15-minute breaks during the day. Luggage is weighed and charged by the weight. Less than 15 kilograms (33 lbs) will cost €2 and more than 15 kilograms (33 lbs) will cost €2.50. Prices are charged per day.

There are also self-storage lockers by platform 1, which are available at any time. Prices start from €2—just insert the coin, close the locker, remove the key and take it with you. You can only use €1 and €2 coins.

You can also store luggage in the lockers in the train station, from 7am-6pm Monday-Friday, and 8am-6pm Saturday-Sunday, with prices going for a day at €1.50.

GETTING THERE
From Vienna
TRAIN

You can catch trains every half an hour from Wien Hauptbahnhof to Bratislava main station with **ÖBB Railjet** (www.oebb.at). The train journey takes approximately an hour, with tickets costing €11.20-18 one way, depending on the train.

From the main train station, get tram number 1 to the Old Town, which will take around 10 minutes to reach the city center, departing every 10-15 minutes. Single tickets cost €0.70.

BUS

For €5-10 one way, you can also grab the bus from Wien Erdberg to Bratislava, which also takes around an hour. Tickets can be bought on the Flixbus website (www.flixbus.com) which has regular bus services between the two cities. However, at the time of writing, due to COVID-19, this bus service has been temporarily stopped.

Bratislava Central Bus Station is a 20-minute walk out of town, but you can take a local bus 202, 208, 212 every 10 minutes and it takes 10 minutes to reach the center. Single tickets cost €0.70. You can also get

off the bus at Most SNP, which will leave you close to the center.

BOAT

Take the scenic route between Vienna and Bratislava with the catamaran run by **Twin City Liner** (www.twincityliner.com). It takes 75 minutes and you get a Danube cruise thrown in. You also have the added advantage of being dropped off right in Bratislava's Old Town.

Boat services run five times a day and start from the Vienna City ship station on the Danube Canal between Marienbrücke and Schedenbrücke. Tickets cost €30 one way. You can see more information about boat services, timetables and buy tickets online at the Twin City Liner website. Due to COVID-19, all boat journeys have been cancelled, so make sure you check the website before considering this option.

CAR

Take the A4 southeast from Vienna and then turn onto the A6 toward the Slovak border. The drive takes around an hour, but note that the highways have tolls within Austria and partial tolls in Slovakia.

From Budapest
TRAIN

You can catch trains hourly or every two hours from Budapest's Nyugati Train Station to Bratislava main station with **EuroCity** (www.bahn.de). The train journey takes approximately two and a half hours, with tickets costing €9-32.40 one way, depending on the train.

From the main train station, get tram number 1 to the Old Town, which will take around 10 minutes to reach the city center, departing every 10-15 minutes. Single tickets cost €0.70.

BUS

For €10-17 one way, you can grab the bus from Budapest Népliget to Bratislava, which also takes around two and a half hours. Tickets can be bought on the **Flixbus** website (www. flixbus.com) which has regular bus services between the two cities.

Bratislava Central Bus Station is a 20-minute walk out of town, but you can take a local bus 202, 208, 212 every 10 minutes and it takes 10 minutes to reach the center. Single tickets cost €0.70. You can also get off the bus at Most SNP, which will leave you close to the center.

CAR

Take the M1 northwest from Budapest following signs for Ausztria/Slovákia/Bécs-Wien-Győr, until you take the exit 166 to take the M15 toward Pozsony-Bratislava to the Slovak border. Once you cross the border take the E75 and follow the signs for Bratislava. The drive takes around two hours, but note that the highways have tolls within Hungary and partial tolls in Slovakia.

From Prague

TRAIN

The fastest and most comfortable way to travel is by taking the **RegioJet train** (www.regiojet.com). The train journey takes approximately 4 hours, with tickets costing from €12 one way, depending on the train.

BUS

If you do choose to travel by bus, the **RegioJet** (www.regiojet.com) is another convenient and popular choice. This bus is comfortable and is set up with Wi-Fi, and coffee and tea are included in price. The ticket is cheaper than a train ticket.

CAR

Take 5. května to Brněnská in Praha 11. Follow D1/E65 to Lamačská cesta/Route 2 in Bratislava, Slovensko. Take the exit toward Centrum Patrónka from E65. Continue on Lamačská cesta/Route 2. Take Route 572 to Hodžovo námestie in Staré Mesto. The drive takes around three hours and 20 minutes, but note that the highways have tolls.

GETTING AROUND

Dopravný podnik Bratislava (DPB; www. dpb.sk—Slovak only, but you can check out the time tables and information in public transport on imhd.sk in English) runs the public transport in Bratislava, which is well connected with a network of trams, buses and trolley buses. Like Vienna, Prague and Budapest, public transport operates on a trust system, so make sure you validate your tickets (€0.70 for a single ticket, no transfers allowed) otherwise you could get fined by plain clothes inspectors who check the trams and buses at random. You cannot buy tickets from the drivers, so your best bet is to buy from the yellow ticket machines at most tram or bus stops.

The good news once you're in the Old Town, you can get around Bratislava on foot pretty easily.

LEAVING BRATISLAVA

The last train going to Vienna departs at 11:15pm, 10:10pm to Prague, and 8pm to Budapest. At the time of writing, FlixBus was not operating buses from Bratislava due to COVID-19, so please check the FlixBus website for the final departures.

Budapest

Divided by the Danube River, Budapest is a city with two personalities. On the Buda side, hills curve up from the river, topped with palaces and citadels. Game-filled forests and ivy-covered villas stand above an underworld of caves. The Pest side spreads out on a plane built up with wide boulevards and grand monuments.

Budapest began as three separate towns: Buda, Pest, and Óbuda. Built on the Roman ruins of the city of Aquincum, modern Budapest is punctuated by medieval relics, Ottoman monuments, Habsburg grandeur, ceramic-clad art nouveau buildings, and Communist brutalism. It's this architectural diversity, along with an attractive tax incentive, that draws Hollywood producers to Budapest to shoot on location. But you don't need to go to the movies for compelling stories—Budapest's

Highlights

Look for ★ to find recommended sights, activities, dining, and lodging.

★ **Buda Castle:** This Habsburg palace houses the Hungarian National Gallery and Budapest History Museum. It stands on the ruins of castles that have been razed and rebuilt over time (page 344).

★ **Fisherman's Bastion:** This neo-Gothic lookout platform offers spectacular views over the Danube (page 348).

★ **Hungarian Parliament Building:** Whether you view it from the Danube or take a tour, the country's political powerhouse dominates the cityscape with its towering spires and claret-hued rooftop (page 351).

★ **St. Stephen's Basilica:** Climb the dome for 360-degree views over Budapest. Then, stop to see the mummified hand of St. Stephen in a jewel-encrusted box (page 356).

★ **Dohány Street Synagogue:** The second-largest synagogue in the world is the heart of the historic Jewish Quarter (page 358).

★ **Hungarian State Opera:** A bastion of Hungary's excellent classical music scene, this is one of the most important buildings on the UNESCO-protected Andrássy Avenue (page 359).

★ **Gellért Hill:** Take a hike up this hill beside the Danube for the best views over Budapest (page 370).

★ **Hungarian National Museum:** The largest museum in the country houses an eclectic collection of artifacts from Roman times to the 19th century (page 373).

★ **Memento Park:** This graveyard for Communist statues turned open-air museum is the best place to visit to glimpse Hungary's Communist past (page 379).

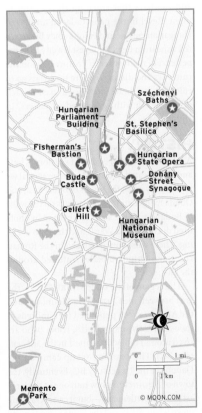

★ **Széchenyi Baths:** Budapest's most famous thermal bath with its canary-yellow pools is one of Central Europe's largest thermal bath complexes. It's also notorious for its "Sparties," raucous parties held on summer weekends (page 382).

complex and diverse history is written on its bullet-scarred walls and within the memories of its residents.

While rougher around the edges than Prague and Vienna, Budapest has famously made dilapidation part of its attraction (as evidenced by its "ruin bars,", unique watering holes housed in flaking buildings). Get to know the city by wandering the winding streets of the Castle District. Stop for views over the Danube, or ride a boat on the river. Explore the Jewish District's synagogues and the bars that spice up the quarter at night. Revel in the paprika-laden aromas of Hungarian cuisine and enjoy a spicy Bikavér, a red wine from Eger. Budapest is a city to be experienced, not just seen. Venture beyond the ruin bars and discover where the locals go to enjoy life, celebrate, and give a toast to each other's health with egészségedre ("cheers" in Hungarian).

HISTORY

A tale of three cities, Budapest's history is long and complicated. It unified into the capital we know today when the towns of Buda, Pest, and Óbuda merged in 1873. History is on the walls of Budapest, in the scars left behind by shots fired during World War II and the 1956 uprising. There's also much to learn in the Roman ruins and Ottoman baths scattered around the city.

The region of the **Carpathian Basin** (the area between the Carpathian Mountains and the Alps) has been populated for hundreds of thousands of years by **Celtic** tribes (who arrived around today's Budapest in the 3rd century BC). The **Romans** set up camp on the Danube in the 1st century BC. Eventually, the town of **Aquincum** grew into one of the largest Roman settlements—but it came crashing down when Attila and the Huns razed the city in the 5th century AD. (Despite the English name for the country, the Huns played only a short part in Hungary's history.) Following

Attila's death, Germanic tribes occupied the region for a century. The Avars (Eurasian nomads) controlled the Carpathian Basin in the 6th century. Charlemagne later conquered the area around today's Budapest and incorporated it into the Frankish Empire.

The **Magyars,** a nomadic people, arrived in the Carpathian Basin around the 9th century, conquering and settling the land under the leadership of Árpád, a chief military commander. In 1000, King Stephen I founded the Hungarian State and embraced Christianity as the new country's religion. The cities of Buda and Pest were villages at the time; they only became a principal seat of the nation following the Mongol invasion in the 13th century. King Béla IV rebuilt the devastated country and founded a fortress in the Buda Hills, but Buda saw most of its development during the Renaissance under the rule of King Matthias, who transformed Hungary into one of the leading powers in Europe at the time.

In the 16th century, the **Turks** invaded Hungary and defeated the Hungarian army in the southern town of Mohács in 1526. Large parts of Hungary, including Buda (occupied in 1541), existed under Ottoman rule for 150 years.

After the Ottomans came the **Habsburgs,** who liberated Buda and Pest in 1686, and Austria absorbed Hungary into the Habsburg Empire. Buda and Pest were rebuilt in the Baroque style, shaping the Castle District's current look. Pest also grew rapidly around the Inner City in today's V District.

A strengthening desire for Hungarian independence surfaced, but the failed **Hungarian Revolution of 1848** against the Habsburgs shook the empire. Austria weakened after its defeat by Prussia in 1866. The Austro-Hungarian Compromise of 1867 sought to strengthen the empire. It allowed for two self-governing states to be created under a dual monarchy with two capitals, Vienna and Budapest. Emperor Franz Joseph I provided

Previous: view of Budapest and the Fisherman's Bastion; Dohány Street Synagogue; tour boat on the Danube.

Hungary full autonomy. Following the compromise, Budapest flourished, with the streets of Pest rebuilt with Paris as its model, featuring wide boulevards and grand, eclectic buildings. By the end of the 1900s, Budapest had become one of Europe's most significant cultural centers.

Budapest suffered severe economic setbacks after World War I, the collapse of the Habsburg Empire, and the Treaty of Trianon (1920) that redrew the boundaries of the new, smaller Republic of Hungary. Trying to reclaim some of its territory, Hungary ended up on the side of Nazi Germany in World War II. However, when leftists attempted to negotiate peace, Germany stormed in and occupied the country in 1944. The Hungarian fascist Arrow Cross Party rose to power and rounded up Budapest's Jews—and immediately began deporting hundreds of thousands to Auschwitz. In 1945, Hungary was liberated by the Soviet Army, but not before the Germans blew up all the bridges upon retreating following the 50-day-long Siege of Budapest by the Red Army.

Communists had assumed full control of the country by 1949. Industry became nationalized, and estates were divided among the proletariat. The next revolution, however, was percolating—and it came to a head on October 23, 1956, when student demonstrators demanded the withdrawal of Soviet troops, and shots were fired. On November 4, Soviet tanks moved into Budapest and violently crushed the uprising. The fighting ended just one week later, on November 11. Some 25,000 people died within that short time. Over 20,000 were arrested in the aftermath, and 250,000 fled the country. Over time, Hungary's branch of Communism loosened into a limited market system, and by 1989, the Iron Curtain fell.

Once Communism fell in 1989, Hungary became a republic once again, and the first democratic elections were held in 1990. The last Soviet troops left in 1991. Hungary became a member of the EU in 2004 and entered the Schengen Area in 2007.

Orientation and Planning

ORIENTATION

The Danube River divides the city into **Buda** (western side) and **Pest** (eastern side). Budapest is also split up into 23 numbered municipal districts (kerület) that spiral out almost clockwise from the Castle District. White placards on street corners are labeled with the Roman numeral district number, the neighborhood name (Erzsébetváros), followed by the street name and the numbering of the houses on the block. If you're asking for directions, you can refer to the district number (for example, ask where "the seventh district" is if you're trying to get to VII District).

With street names, it's important to know your utca (street) from your út (boulevard or avenue), so you don't, for example, confuse Váci utca (a shopping artery in the Inner City) with Váci út (a long road leading to industrial suburbs). Other names are tér (square), körút (ring road or boulevard), sor (row), and rakpart (embankment). In some locations, you may notice street signs crossed out in red, which denote former place names that have been changed following the Communist regime; these have been replaced with the new name on the placard below.

Castle District (I District)

Budapest's I District (on the Buda side of the river) centers on Castle Hill, which rises sharply above the Danube, and is crowned by **Buda Castle.** The Castle District packs history into a dense space. Traces of the old medieval city can be seen in the excavated ruins near Buda Castle, but much of the original Buda lies in rubble or is hidden away. Much of the district is dominated by **cobbled, narrow**

Budapest

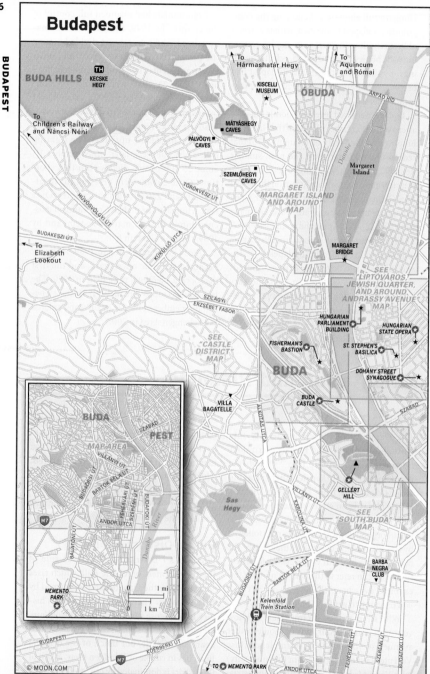

BUDA HILLS

KECSKE HEGY

To Hármashatár Hegy

To Aquincum and Római

KISCELLI MUSEUM

ÓBUDA

ÁRPÁD HÍD

To Children's Railway and Náncsi Néni

MÁTYÁSHEGY CAVES

PÁLVÖLGYI CAVES

SZEMLŐHEGYI CAVES

Margaret Island

TÖRÖKVÉSZ ÚT

SEE "MARGARET ISLAND AND AROUND" MAP

HŰVÖSVÖLGYI ÚT

BUDAKESZI ÚT

To Elizabeth Lookout

KŐKÜLLŐ UTCA

MARGARET BRIDGE

SEE "LIPTOVÁROS, JEWISH QUARTER, AND AROUND ANDRÁSSY AVENUE" MAP

SZILÁGYI ERZSÉBET FASOR

HUNGARIAN PARLIAMENT BUILDING

HUNGARIAN STATE OPERA

SEE "CASTLE DISTRICT" MAP

FISHERMAN'S BASTION

ST. STEPHEN'S BASILICA

DOHÁNY STREET SYNAGOGUE

BUDA

VILLA BAGATELLE

BUDA CASTLE

ALKOTÁS UTCA

SZABAD

BUDA

PEST

MAP AREA

SZABAD

VILLÁNYI ÚT

BUDAÖRSI ÚT

BARTÓK BÉLA ÚT

FEHÉRVÁRI ÚT

SZERÉMI ÚT

BUDAFOKI ÚT

GELLÉRT HILL

VILLÁNYI ÚT

KAROLINA ÚT

SEE "SOUTH BUDA" MAP

M7

BALATONI ÚT

ANDOR UTCA

Danube River

Sas Hegy

MEMENTO PARK

0   1 mi

0   1 km

BARBA NEGRA CLUB

BUDAÖRSI ÚT

BARTÓK BÉLA ÚT

Kelenföld Train Station

BUDAPESTI

KŐÉRBERKI ÚT

M7

TO MEMENTO PARK

ANDOR UTCA

FEHÉRVÁRI ÚT

SZERÉMI ÚT

BUDAFOKI ÚT

© MOON.COM

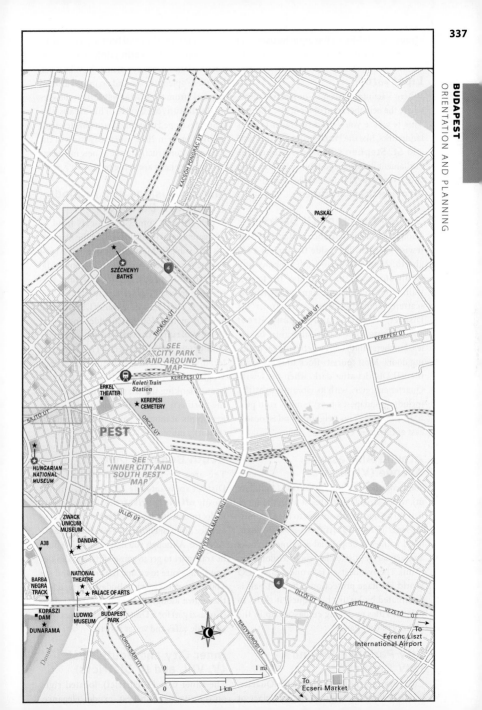

streets, pastel-hued Baroque houses, and romantic stone staircases that lead up the hill.

Lipótváros

Where Váci utca ends (at Vörösmarty tér) is where the neighborhood of Lipótváros begins. This is where you'll find the most famous landmarks, like the **Hungarian Parliament** and **St. Stephen's Basilica.** Around the Parliament Building and Liberty Square, keep your eyes peeled for incredible specimens of **art nouveau architecture.**

Jewish Quarter (VII District)

Though the neighborhood itself is older, the Jewish Quarter lies inside the former 1944 ghetto. **Memorials** on both Dohány and Király utca mark the location of the former wall. You can still find signs of Jewish life scattered about the streets of the inner VII District, from the grand **Dohány Street Synagogue** to kosher restaurants, bakeries, butchers, and Hebrew lettering on building doors. Most tourists flock to this part of the VII District after dark, when the Jewish Quarter energizes with its vibrant **nightlife,** including Budapest's most famous ruin pub, **Szimpla Kert.** This neighborhood is located east of the Inner City.

Around Andrássy Avenue (VI District)

Some consider **Andrássy Avenue** (Andrássy út), which stretches northeast from the Inner City, to be Budapest's answer to the Champs-Élysées. This **elegant, wide boulevard,** lined with eclectic palatial apartment blocks and slender trees, stretches about 3 kilometers (2 mi). The avenue itself falls under UNESCO World Heritage protection. The first half is dominated by luxury boutiques; it shifts to palatial villas enclosing embassies up in the vicinity of City Park.

City Park and Around (XIV District)

City Park, northeast of the Jewish Quarter, is one of Pest's main green lungs, a place of recreation with **thermal baths,** picnic spots, and a popular **ice-skating rink** in the winter. City Park lies in the residential XIV District, but there's plenty to see and do in and around the park, from the **Budapest Zoo** to the sites at **Vajdahunyad Castle.** This area is also being developed into a museum quarter, with plans to open in 2022. Currently parts of the park are a construction zone as new museums and concert halls are being built.

Margaret Island and Around (II and XIII Districts)

When the sun comes out, locals head to Margaret Island (Margitsziget) in the Danube. It's accessible by Margaret Bridge and Árpád Bridge for picnics, strolls, and sunbathing. The island is mostly **car-free** (though it is serviced by local bus service and taxis). The island is over 2.5 kilometers (1.5 mi) long and 500 meters (550 yards) wide. You'll find **medieval ruins, thermal baths,** and abundant **green parkland** here. (This is also allegedly where German composer Richard Wagner almost drowned after falling from a boat.) Flanking the island on the mainland, the northern parts of Buda and Pest have a few points of interest, from Turkish remains to quirky museums.

South Buda (XI District)

The area stretching south of the Castle District spills into the XI District, and it's mostly **off the tourist track.** There's plenty to do, from **hiking up Gellért Hill** to sipping a coffee in a trendy café on lively **Bartók Béla Avenue.** Although you may need to use public transport to get to some of the area's sites, you can be sure to escape the crowds and see a bit more of less touristy Budapest. Head further down along the river to **Kopaszi dam** (Kopaszi gát) for a **Danube beach** area with riverside cafés and water sports.

Inner City and South Pest (V, VIII, and IX Districts)

The Inner City (V District), located right on the riverbank in Pest, exudes elegance,

Budgeting

Hungary uses the Hungarian forint (HUF) instead of the euro, but many places, such as hotels, accept payment in euros.

- **Beer:** HUF 400-900
- **Glass of wine:** HUF 400-1,500
- **Lunch or dinner:** HUF 2,500-6,000
- **Hotel:** HUF 10,000-200,000 per night
- **Car rental:** HUF 10,000-25,000 per day
- **Gasoline:** HUF 365-415 (per liter)
- **Parking:** HUF 265-440 per hour
- **Public transport ticket:** HUF 350-450
- **Museum entry:** HUF 800-2800
- **Thermal bath entry:** HUF 2,500-6,500

from its promenades dotted with **riverside cafés** to **grand buildings** with elaborate friezes, columns, and wrought iron façades. Pedestrianized **Váci utca** is the main road for shopping and dining.

Stretching south of the Jewish Quarter and the Inner City, the VIII and IX Districts lie slightly **off the beaten track** for most tourists. However, you can take a walk past the grand, palatial apartments of the **Palace District** or head down to the Danube banks around the formerly industrial IX District, where old factories have been converted into **cultural centers** or **craft beer bars,** and you'll find a different, more laid-back side of Budapest.

The **Millennium Quarter** along Soroksári út, up by Rákóczi híd, is a new cultural hub for the city, with the **Palace of Art,** the **Ludwig Museum,** and the **National Theater.**

Óbuda (III District)

Óbuda (meaning Old Buda) was once a city in its own right, and it's outside the boundaries of historic Buda and Pest. Today,

Roman ruins lie beneath **Communist-era apartment blocks,** and two-story Baroque townhouses back onto industrial complexes. It has a different character from the rest of Budapest. While far-flung from the center, it has plenty to offer, from dining around **Kolosy tér** to **beaches** and **riverside bars at Római Part.** Meanwhile, **Óbuda Island** hosts one of Europe's largest music festivals—**Sziget**—in August.

Buda Hills
(II, III, and XII Districts)

What distinguishes Buda from mostly flat Pest is its hills. Gellért Hill and Castle Hill are the most prominent in the city center; the hills out in the II, III, and XII districts feel like they belong somewhere in the countryside and not in a capital city. You'll find **lookout points** offering views over the city, **hiking trails,** and even networks of **caves** running below the city for miles on end. The **Children's Railway,** a small railway run by children as a relic left over from Communist times, is located here.

PLANNING YOUR TIME

You can easily see the main sights in Budapest in **two days,** with one day in Buda and another in Pest. But **three days** will give you time to fully appreciate the city's charm, unique nightlife, and culture.

Daily Reminders

Most museums close on **Mondays,** and all Jewish sites, such as synagogues, close on **Saturdays.** Some churches close to visitors during Mass, and outdoor sites like the Budapest Zoo or Memento Park shift their opening hours based on the hour the sun sets.

Budapest's thermal baths are open daily.

SATURDAY

All Jewish sights, such as synagogues, are closed. "Sparties," on the other hand, only take place Saturday nights.

SUNDAY

A farmers market is typically held weekly in Szimpla Kert ruin bar. Klauzál Square Market (an antiques market) is open.

These attractions are closed:

- National Széchényi Library
- Hungarian House of Art Nouveau (Bedő House)
- Cave Church
- Central Market Hall
- Zwack Unicum Museum

MONDAY

Most museums are closed, including:

- Hungarian National Gallery
- Budapest History Museum
- National Széchényi Library
- House of Terror
- Vajdahunyad Castle

- Miksa Róth Memorial House
- Budapest Pinball Museum
- Hungarian National Museum
- Holocaust Memorial Center
- Ludwig Museum
- Aquincum
- Kiscelli Museum

Advance Reservations and Time-Saving Tips

You can buy tickets online for popular sites like the Hungarian National Gallery or the Hungarian Parliament Building. Buying online will help you skip the queues, but at most of the sites, you can just buy tickets when you arrive without any issues. Some places (like the Parliament or the synagogues and Jewish museums) may want you to put your bags through a security check, so account for a little extra time for that as well.

If you want to go to a "Sparty" (a rowdy party in a thermal bath; www.spartybooking. com; €50; over 18 only), make sure you buy a ticket in advance from the website, as these sell out fast. Sparties ceased with the coronavirus in 2020; however, there were plans to resume them at the time of writing.

Sightseeing Passes

The **Budapest Card** (www.budapest-card. com; €19 for 24-hours, €29 for 48-hours, €37 for 72-hours) includes public transport, free entrance to 13 museums (including the museums in Buda Castle, the Hungarian National Museum, and Memento Park), two walking tours, free entrance to the Lukács Baths, and discounts. The Budapest Card is available at Budapestinfo Points, and you can also buy it online. If you're planning to pack a number of museums into your trip and use the public transport often it's worth investing in a card.

Itinerary Ideas

Budapest is compact and you can divide the main sites between the Buda and Pest sides. To get away from the crowds, explore the Buda Hills to see a different side of the city.

And you will want to save one of Budapest's iconic experiences—soaking in a thermal bath—for the last day. It'll be a relaxing end to your trip.

DAY 1: THE CASTLE DISTRICT

1 Start the day at one of Budapest's most spectacular bridges, the **Chain Bridge,** with amazing views over the river.

2 From the bridge and Clark Ádám Square take Hunyadi János út heading uphill north of the Chain Bridge and keep walking till you reach the stairs leading up to **Fisherman's Bastion.** Usually, this is one of Budapest's most crowded sites, but early in the morning there are only a few people here, and it's the perfect spot for snapping a few photos of the river.

3 There are plenty of breakfast options up in the Castle District. **Baltazár,** which is a five-minute walk down Országút, will keep you fueled up for the morning.

4 Return to **Matthias Church** next to Fisherman's Bastion for its incredible frescoes. If you make it on the hour, get a ticket and go up the church tower.

5 For something offbeat, head over to the **Hospital in the Rock** just five minutes away for a subterranean journey back in time to World War II, the 1956 revolution, and the Cold War.

6 Stop at **Ruszwurm,** the oldest café and confectionary in Budapest, which you will have passed on the way to the museum.

7 In the afternoon, you'll want to spend a couple of hours at the **Hungarian National Gallery** in the Royal Palace, just a 10-minute walk away.

8 Once you're done learning about the history of Hungarian art, take the elevator in the Castle Garden down to the **Castle Garden Bazaar** and get on the 41 or 19 tram to Gárdonyi tér.

9 Have dinner and drinks at **Hadik,** a former literary hangout in the early 1900s that's now a trendy bistro.

DAY 2: PARLIAMENT AND INNER CITY

1 Kick-start your morning with breakfast in a classic café, like **Centrál Kávéház és Etterem 1887** in the old part of the Inner City.

2 Walk five minutes toward the Danube and get on the number 2 tram. Get off at **Széchenyi István tér** and turn around and take some pictures of the Royal Palace, the river, and Chain Bridge from the Pest side of the city.

3 Turn into Zrínyi street and pay a visit to **St. Stephen's Basilica.** Make sure you head up to the top inside to the dome, where amazing 360-degree views await.

4 It's a good time for a lunch break, and restaurants and cafés spill out onto the squares and streets surrounding the Basilica. **Zeller Bistro** on Hercegprímás utca is a good option.

5 Once you've eaten, stroll over to Hold utca for the **Postal Savings Bank** by Ödön

Itinerary Ideas

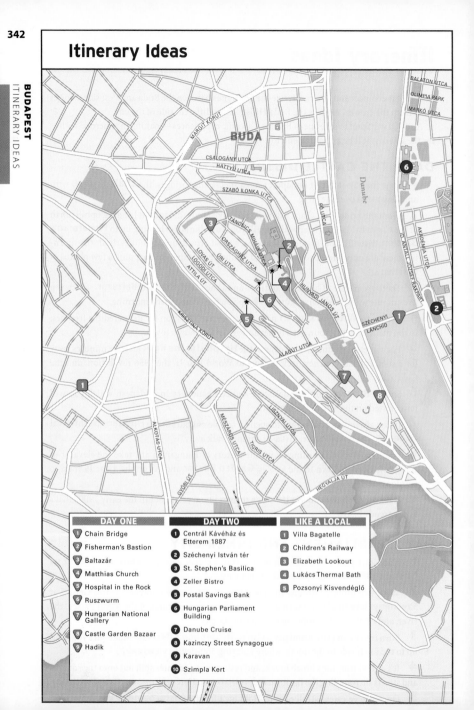

DAY ONE	DAY TWO	LIKE A LOCAL
1 Chain Bridge	1 Centrál Kávéház és Etterem 1887	1 Villa Bagatelle
2 Fisherman's Bastion	2 Széchenyi István tér	2 Children's Railway
3 Baltazár	3 St. Stephen's Basilica	3 Elizabeth Lookout
4 Matthias Church	4 Zeller Bistro	4 Lukács Thermal Bath
5 Hospital in the Rock	5 Postal Savings Bank	5 Pozsonyi Kisvendéglő
6 Ruszwurm	6 Hungarian Parliament Building	
7 Hungarian National Gallery	7 Danube Cruise	
8 Castle Garden Bazaar	8 Kazinczy Street Synagogue	
9 Hadik	9 Karavan	
	10 Szimpla Kert	

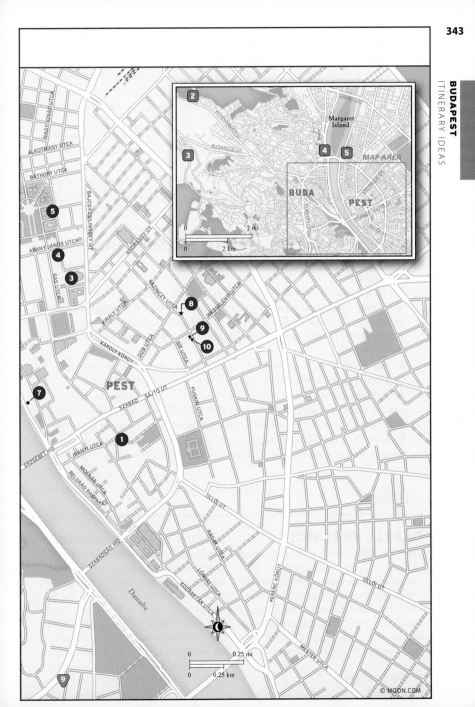

Lechner two blocks away. If you want to see the rooftop from above, go into the Hotel President across the street to the rooftop café—it's worth it for the view.

6   Stroll over to Freedom Square and head over to the Hungarian Parliament Building. Take one of the English-language tours—it's easiest to book online—to see inside this amazing building.

7   Get yourself on a Danube cruise. Take the tram number 2 to Vígadó and get on a boat organized by Legenda.

8   Once the boat docks, walk up to Vörösmarty tér and take the metro to Opera. Turn into Székely Mihály utca and then Kazinczy utca, passing the art nouveau Kazinczy Street Synagogue.

9   Grab a bite to eat at the Karavan, a street food court at the end of Kazinczy utca.

10   End the night at Budapest's most famous ruin bar, Szimpla Kert, located just next door.

BUDAPEST LIKE A LOCAL: INTO THE BUDA HILLS

1   Start with a decadent breakfast at the beautiful Villa Bagatelle at the base of the Buda Hills.

2   Walk down the hill five minutes and take the 61 tram to the end of the line at Hűvösvölgy. Take the carved wooden staircase leading up the hill pointing you in the direction of the Children's Railway and hop on this retro locomotive operated by children under 14 (drivers and engineers excepted) that will take you through the wilderness of the Buda Hills.

3   Get off the train at János Hegy and hike 20-30 minutes from the train station up to the Elizabeth Lookout, following the signposts up to Budapest's highest point.

4   At the base of the tower, take the chairlift down to Zugliget, where you can connect with the 291 bus and get off at the Margit híd, Budai hídfő stop. Cross the road and head north through Elvis Presley Park to the Lukács Thermal Bath for a soak and swim.

5   After relaxing a little at the baths, take the number 9 bus to Jászai Mari tér and walk 10 minutes north to the Pozsonyi Kisvendéglő for a hearty Hungarian dinner.

Sights

CASTLE DISTRICT

The Castle District was razed and rebuilt, occupied by Turks for over a century, left in ruins following the Habsburg liberation in the 17th century, besieged again in the 1849 revolution, and then damaged during the Siege of Budapest in 1945. When exploring, think of the district as a patchwork of history, where you'll find stories within the details.

★ Buda Castle

Buda Castle is a symbol of the city, perched on top of the hill overlooking the Danube. Its neo-Baroque façade spreads out in columns under a copper-green dome, and it's worth the hike up for the views from the terrace.

Despite centuries of history, the palace you see today is fairly new in the Budapest cityscape. The original Gothic and Renaissance palace was destroyed during the liberation from the Turkish occupation in 1686, then rebuilt from scratch in a Baroque style. Much of today's façade, including its iconic dome, comes from a post-World

Castle District

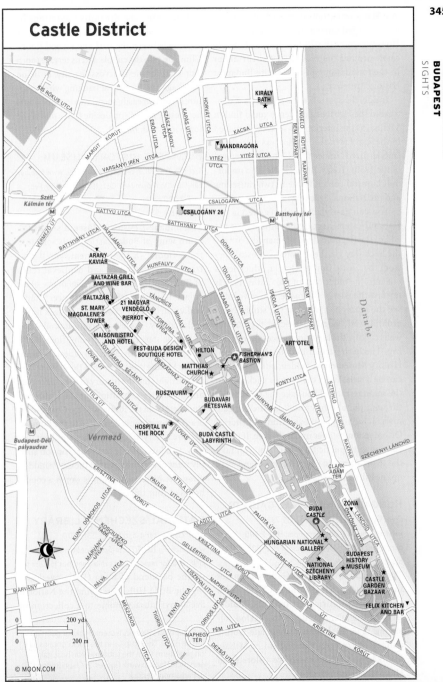

© MOON.COM

War II reconstruction after much of the castle was damaged during the Siege of Budapest. However, you can still find traces of the old castle around the reconstructed turrets or in the foundations in the on-site Budapest History Museum.

Inside, the spartan walls offer a stark contrast to the Habsburg opulence you'd find in Vienna, as the interior was severely damaged in the war. Later, the interior was gutted and "modernized" under the Communist regime of the 1950s. Today, Buda Castle is an important cultural center, home to two museums and the National Széchenyi Library.

You can easily access the castle via the Habsburg steps next to the funicular, at the end of the flagpole-lined promenade, or take the back way via the elevator and escalators from the Castle Garden Bazaar, which leads out into the older part of the castle. This is my favorite part of the castle, where you can see the layers of history in the stones lying around, and the reconstructed turrets and walls capture the historic essence of the building. The herb garden next to the Budapest History Museum is a hidden, quiet spot that can be a relief from the crowds packed onto the main terrace. If you take the steps down through the old tower and out the old gate toward Tabán, you'll even find a cluster of Ottoman tombstones under the tree. If you're coming with public transport, you can take the 16 or 105 bus to Clark Ádám tér and walk up the hill or take the funicular.

HUNGARIAN NATIONAL GALLERY

Szent György tér 2; tel. 06/20-439-7331; www.mng.hu; Tue-Sun 10am-6pm; HUF 2,800 permanent exhibition, audio guides HUF 800; bus 16, 105: Dísz tér

The Hungarian National Gallery occupies the river-facing wings of Buda Castle, and it chronicles Hungarian art from the Middle Ages to the avant-garde in the period following 1945. Highlights include late-Gothic winged altarpieces, the realism of Mihály Munkácsy, and the explosive colors from Hungarian Expressionists.

Don't miss the dreamlike paintings by Tivadar Csontváry Kosztka on the staircase landing between the first and second floors. Climb up into the cupola and its terrace (open Apr-Oct) for views across the city, or lie on beanbags and look up at hanging wire sculptures. You can easily spend two to three hours here, especially if you decide to see one of the temporary exhibitions.

BUDAPEST HISTORY MUSEUM

Szent György tér 2; tel. 06/1-487-8800; www.btm.hu; Tue-Sun 10am-6pm Mar-Oct, 10am-4pm Nov-Feb; HUF 2,000 entrance, HUF 1,200 audio guide; bus 16: Dísz tér

The Budapest History Museum sits in the south wing of Buda Castle and is split into three floors. In the basement, you'll find traces of Renaissance and medieval relics of Buda Castle, including parts of the older palace like the 14th-century tower chapel and vaulted palace rooms dating back to the 15th century. There is an exquisite collection of Gothic statues on the ground floor, and a unique Hungarian-Angevin tapestry dating to the Middle Ages. The first floor offers further insight into the history of the palace plus an interactive exhibition on the history of Budapest from the Romans to the Communist era. The top floor is dedicated to the Romans and prehistory. If you're passionate about history, you love Gothic sculpture, or you simply want to explore a part of the castle hidden away, the history museum is worth a couple hours of your time.

NATIONAL SZÉCHÉNYI LIBRARY

Szent György tér 4-6; tel. 06/1-224-3700; www.oszk.hu; Tue-Fri 9am-5pm, Sat 9am-2pm; HUF 400 for museum and exhibitions; bus 16: Dísz tér

At the back end of Buda Castle overlooking the Buda Hills, you'll find the National Széchényi Library, home to a collection of

---

1: Fisherman's Bastion, a scenic lookout point on Castle Hill 2: The Hospital in the Rock contains all original items from the subterranean hospital, enhanced by waxwork figures. 3: Chain Bridge 4: Parliament at dusk

Budapest by Boat

the view of Buda Castle from a boat on the Danube

Budapest is best seen from the Danube, especially on hot summer days when there's a refreshing breeze to keep you cool. The water is generally calm. From the perspective of a boat, you can really appreciate the differences between Buda and Pest and get close to monuments like the Hungarian Parliament Building in a way you can't on land.

RIVER CRUISES

Options in this category include a classic sightseeing cruise, speedboat tour, or amphibious bus:

- **Legenda** (Dock 7 Jane Haining rakpart; tel. 06/1-317-2203; www.legenda.hu; HUF 4,200; tram 2: Vigadó tér) offers a classic 70-minute-long sightseeing cruise with a glass of sparkling wine, beer, or soft drink included. The boats fit 150-180 people and they are adaptable to the weather. If you're interested in knowing more about the various sites, audio guides are

codices, manuscripts, and everything that has been published in Hungary. It's only open to members of the library for research purposes. So unless you're a traveling academic looking to delve into a historic manuscript, most of the library will be inaccessible. However, if you really want a peek inside, there are some temporary exhibitions to view, along with a permanent library museum.

★ Fisherman's Bastion
(Halászbástya)

Szentháromság tér; Mar-Apr 9am-7pm, May-Oct 9am-8pm; HUF 1,000; bus 16: Szentháromság tér

Glimmering white above the Danube, the romantic Fisherman's Bastion overlooks the Hungarian Parliament Building and the rooftops of Pest. Built as a spectacular viewing platform by Frigyes Schulek between 1890-1905, it's still one of Budapest's most beautiful structures. Its seven turrets represent the seven tribes that came to the Carpathian Basin back in the 9th century. With winding staircases and arched colonnades, it may look medieval, but it's a 19th century folly.

Why the odd-sounding name? In the Middle Ages, it was very close to a fish market. The Guild of Fisherman defended that portion of the castle wall.

In the summer, the colonnade below turns

available. Otherwise, just sit and relax. Once you get to Margaret Island, you can get off the boat for 90 minutes before being picked up, or you can decide to stay on board.

- **RiverRide** (Széchenyi István tér 7-8; tel. 06/1-332-2555; www.riverride.com; HUF 9,000; tram 2: Széchenyi István tér) operates an amphibious bus tour. After taking an on-road tour through the Inner City, you'll see the Danube on a water bus. The tour takes around 95 minutes and starts on Széchenyi István tér near the Chain Bridge.

- **Dunarama** (tel. 06/70-942-2613; www.dunarama.hu; HUF 39,000-72,000 for 25- or 50-minute cruises without a guide) is a speedboat tour down the Danube. This luxury water limousine fits only 10 people in its closed cabins and open platform, so this is an option if you're traveling with a small group or you're really feeling fancy.

CRUISING ON A BUDGET

From March through October, public **BKK** boats run from Kopaszi gát in the south to Margaret Island, or even as far as Rómaifürdő in the north. The route (HUF 750, or free with a city transport pass on weekdays) takes two hours. These boats stop at a variety of docks en route, including the Castle Garden Bazaar, the Hungarian Parliament Building, and on weekends Margaret Island.

A word of caution: These boats can be unreliable (i.e., not on schedule), and if the boat is already full, it won't dock. Your best bet is to embark at one of the first ports of call, like Kopaszi gát, the National Theatre, or Rómaifürdő, if you want a good seat and a guarantee to board.

Boats are packed on weekends, but weekday mornings are quiet (for locals, it's not the fastest commute). The boats are a little rustier than the touring boats, but the view is still the same. If you're lucky, there is a working bar or toilet on board.

One thing that public boats have over the sightseeing cruises (other than the price tag) is that they go further than the central part of the river, taking you down into the Millennium Quarter and the Kopaszi Dam to the south, and up past Margaret Island and Óbuda Island to the north—beyond the usual sites like Buda Castle, the Parliament, and the Chain Bridge. The boat north passes offbeat sites like the Óbuda Gas Works, which looks more like a turreted castle than an old factory.

In 2020, this boat service did not operate due to COVID-19 restrictions. Check the BKK website (https://bkk.hu) to make sure it's sailing on your visit.

into a café. It certainly has one of the best views in the city, but let's say it's not necessarily a place locals would go to hang out.

If you want to skip the crowds and the price tag that comes with getting to the top of the viewing platform, then head to the main staircase in the middle—you'll see medieval-style carvings in the arches. The view through those arches is one of the most beautiful over the bastion.

Matthias Church
(Mátyás Templom)

Szentháromság ter 2; tel. 06/1-488-7716;
www.matyas-templom.hu; Mon-Fri 9am-5pm, Sat

9am-noon, Sun 1pm-5pm; HUF 1,800
church admission, HUF 1,800 tower visit;
bus 16: Szentháromság tér

The Church of Our Lady of Buda Castle (more colloquially known as Matthias Church after the Renaissance monarch was married twice in this church) presents an eclectic architectural tapestry, beginning as early as the 1200s. The colorful interior, painted with frescoes of angels, saints, and floral and leaf motifs, can be traced back to the 19th century. Like the rest of the historic district, Matthias Church has seen significant damage (at one point, the Turks turned it into a mosque, stripped it bare, and painted its

Sightseeing on the Number 2 Tram

Budapest's yellow trams make it easy to navigate the city, and some lines even offer the perfect sightseeing vantage point. Hop on the number 2 tram, beginning at Jászai Mari tér near Margaret Bridge. The tram will take you past the Hungarian Parliament Building, down the Danube banks past the Chain Bridge, the Vigadó (a gorgeous concert hall), and the city's most famous bridges. Get off at Fővám tér by the Central Market Hall, or continue to the Bálna cultural center or the Müpa-Nemzeti Színház stop for the Millennium cultural complex. Around Christmas, the tram may be dressed up with thousands of festive fairy lights.

the 2 tram on the riverbank

walls). For a different perspective, climb the intricately carved neo-Gothic stairway to the gallery for views across the church and to see exquisite stained-glass windows illuminating the nave from above.

Hospital in the Rock

Lovas út 4/C; tel. 06/70-701-0101; www.sziklakorhaz. eu; daily 7am-10pm, English language tours depart on the hour or every 30 minutes in peak season; HUF 4,000; bus 16: Szentháromság tér

Hospital in the Rock is a curiosity built into the caves under Castle Hill. After beginning life as a wine cellar, it was reinforced with concrete in the 1930s and was used as an underground military hospital during World War II (and again in the 1956 Uprising). Later, it was used as a prison for revolutionaries and then as a secret nuclear bunker during the Cold War. Declassified in 2002, it now houses one of Budapest's most fascinating museums. All the medical equipment on display is original, and the eerie waxwork figures give a lifelike depiction of the hospital. You can only visit the hospital with a guide, but tours run on the hour for English speakers. The tour ends in the decontamination chambers of the shelter (reinforced to withstand nuclear and chemical attack).

St. Mary Magdalene's Tower

Kapisztran tér 6; www.budatower.hu; daily 10am-6pm Mar-Dec, Sat-Sun 10am-6pm Jan-Feb; HUF 1,500; bus 16: Bécsi kapu tér

Take a stroll around the Castle District and you may notice a lone church tower hovering above the two-story houses at the corner between Kapisztrán tér and Országház utca. The original church was built in the 13th century as a Franciscan church for Hungarian-speaking worshippers. Under the Ottoman occupation, it was the only place of worship for Christians in Buda, as the rest of the churches had been converted into mosques. Catholics were confined to the chancel and the Protestants to the nave, both of which were destroyed in World War II. Only the 15th-century bell tower and a reconstructed window survived the bombing. You can go up the tower if you want a view over Castle Hill; otherwise, it's enough to see the grounds from below.

Buda Castle Labyrinth (Labirintus)

Úri utca 9; tel. 06/1-212-0207; www.labirintus.eu; daily 10am-7pm; HUF 3,000 (cash only); bus 16: Szentháromság tér

The entire Castle District sits on top of

hollow marl and limestone caves, and underneath each street is a tunnel of similar length. Initially, these natural subterranean pockets were used only as cellars, storage rooms, and wells. The Turks later connected many of these underground chambers for strategic reasons, digging more than a kilometer (almost a mile) of tunnels.

Today, you can visit a section of this labyrinth at Buda Castle. The labyrinth winds past a surreal waxwork exhibition with figures dressed in costumes once belonging to the Hungarian State Opera House. You'll then wander into smoky chambers illuminated with eerie blue light where Vlad the Impaler was allegedly imprisoned.

You'll also see marble and limestone relics from Buda's medieval past, along with Turkish tombstones. For an adrenaline-pumping experience, head to the ticket office at 6pm and pick up an oil lantern to guide you through the tunnels when the lights go out. (This is something I do not recommend doing alone—unless stumbling around a dark labyrinth alone sounds like an enjoyable experience).

Castle Garden Bazaar
(Várkert Bazár)

Ybl Miklós tér 6; tel. 06/1-225-0554; www.varkertbazar.hu; tram 41, 19: Várkert Bazár

Originally built in the 19th century as a pleasure park along the Danube, the Castle Garden Bazaar fell into decay over the decades—but it was renovated in 2014. Today, this neo-Renaissance stretch of sloping promenades featuring statues, fountains, and elegant pavilions has reopened as a cultural center with exhibition halls, film screening space, and restaurants and shops. Head up the walkway and you'll come to the neo-Renaissance gardens. You'll find an escalator and an elevator (if needed) that can carry you up to Buda Castle without having to hike up or take the bus or the funicular railway.

LIPÓTVÁROS
★ Hungarian Parliament Building

Kossúth tér 1-3; tel. 06/1-441-4904; http:// latogatokozpont.parlament.hu; daily 8am-6pm Apr-Oct, daily 8am-4pm Nov-Mar, tours daily 10am-4pm; HUF 6,700 non-EU citizens including guide; metro 2, tram 2: Kossuth Lajos tér

Facing the Danube, in carved blocks of white Hungarian marble and topped with neo-Gothic spires on a wine-hued rooftop crowned with a dome, the Hungarian Parliament Building is a symbol of the city. An architectural wonder designed by Imre Steindl and completed in 1902, its 691 rooms exist in a labyrinth of gilded corridors and grand staircases. It's still in use today, which is why you'll only see part of the building on the tour (and only with a guide).

You can head to the visitor center underground to join a 45-minute tour—but first, you'll want to guarantee your place by buying a ticket online (www.jegymester.hu) because openings fill quickly. You'll have a time allocated for your English-language tour, and you'll need to go through a security checkpoint (similar to an airport check) before you're handed a headset.

The tour takes you up a golden staircase (there is an elevator as an alternative to the 100-plus stairs). The staircase leads to a corridor lined with stained-glass windows and accents of real gold. (More than 40 kg/88 lbs of gold were used to create the gold leaf that covers the Parliament Building.)

In the hall under the dome, you'll see the Hungarian Crown Jewels, which once belonged to the canonized King Stephen, the first monarch of Hungary. The crown has led an adventurous life over the past 1,000 years—it has been lost, stolen, and was locked up in Fort Knox at one point until its return to Hungary in 1978. It resided in the Hungarian National Museum until 2000, and then found a new home under the iconic dome.

The tour will take you into the Lobby Room, where you'll spot statues dedicated to Hungarian shepherds, doctors, and

Liptóváros, Jewish Quarter, and Around Andrássy Avenue

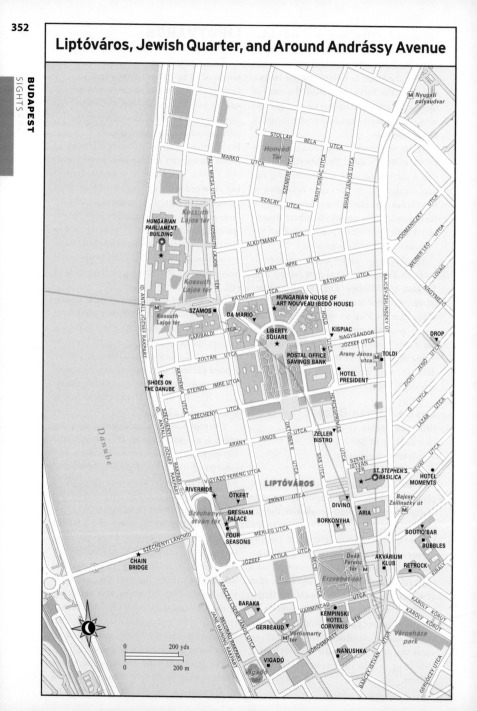

M Nyugati
palyaudvar

STOLLÁR   BÉLA   UTCA

Honvéd
Tér

MARKO   UTCA   SZEMERE UTCA   NAGY IGNÁC UTCA   BIHARI JÁNOS UTCA

FALK MIKSA UTCA

SZALAY   UTCA

PODMANICZKY   UTCA

WEINER LEÓ   UTCA

LOVÁG

NAGYMEZŐ

Kossuth
Lajos tér

HUNGARIAN
PARLIAMENT
BUILDING

ALKOTMÁNY   UTCA

KOSSUTH LAJOS   TÉR

KÁLMÁN   IMRE   UTCA

BÁTHORY   UTCA

BAJCSY-ZSILINSZKY ÚT

Kossuth
Lajos tér

ID. ANTALL JÓZSEF RAKPART

BATHORY   UTCA

HUNGARIAN HOUSE OF
ART NOUVEAU (BEDŐ HOUSE)

HOLD

M   SZAMOS   DA MARIO

KISPIAC
NAGYSÁNDOR
JÓZSEF UTCA

DROP

Kossuth
Lajos tér

GARIBALDI   UTCA

LIBERTY
SQUARE

ZICHY JENŐ UTCA

ZOLTÁN   UTCA

POSTAL OFFICE
SAVINGS BANK

Arany János
utca   M   TOLDI

Ő   UTCA   UTCA

AKADEMIA UTCA

SHOES ON
THE DANUBE

STEINDL   IMRE   UTCA

HOTEL
PRESIDENT

LÁZÁR   UTCA

ID. SZÉCHENYI ANTALL JÓZSEF RAKPART

SZÉCHENYI   UTCA

HERCEGPRÍMÁS

Danube

ARANY   JÁNOS   UTCA

OKTÓBER 6   UTCA

ZELLER
BISTRO

SAS UTCA

RÉVAY   UTCA

SZENT
ISTVÁN
TÉR

ST. STEPHEN'S
BASILICA

HOTEL
MOMENTS

VIGYÁZÓ FERENC UTCA

LIPTÓVÁROS

RIVERRIDE   ÖTKERT

ZRÍNYI   UTCA

DIVINO

Bajcsy-
Zsilinszky út
M

Széchenyi
István tér

GRESHAM
PALACE

MERLEG UTCA

BORKONYHA

ARIA

BOUTIQ'BAR

FOUR
SEASONS

BUBBLES

CHAIN
BRIDGE

SZÉCHENYI LÁNCHÍD

JÓZSEF   ATTILA   UTCA

BÉCSI

Deák
Ferenc
tér   M

AKVÁRIUM
KLUB

RETROCK

KIRÁLY

Erzsébet tér

APÁCZAI CSERE JÁNOS UTCA

JANE HAINING RAKPART

BELGRÁD RAKPART

BARAKA

HARMINCAD   UTCA

KÁROLY   KÖRÚT

KÁROLY   KÖRÚT

KEMPINSKI
HOTEL
CORVINUS

GERBEAUD

Vörösmarty
M   tér

TÉR

Városháza
park

VÖRÖSMARTY

NANUSHKA

BÁRCZY ISTVÁN UTCA

GERLÓCZY UTCA

VIGADÓ

Vigadó
tér

0   200 yds
0   200 m

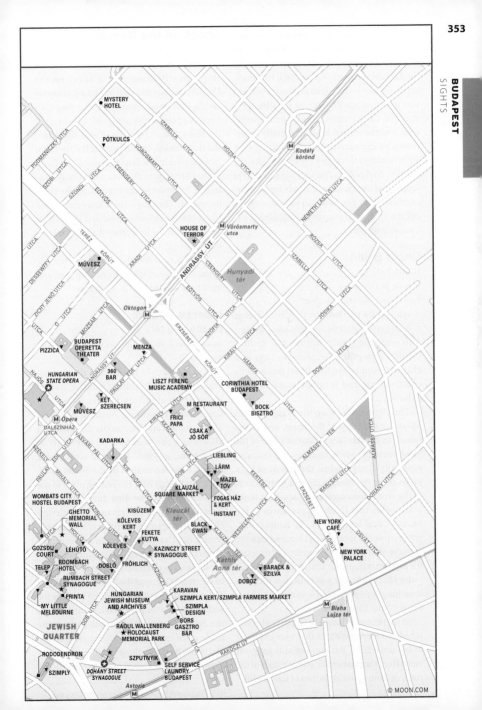

MYSTERY HOTEL

PÓTKULCS

Kodály körönd (M)

HOUSE OF TERROR ★

Vörösmarty utca (M)

MŰVÉSZ

Hunyadi tér

ANDRÁSSY ÚT

Oktogon (M)

PIZZICA

BUDAPEST OPERETTA THEATER

MENZA

HUNGARIAN STATE OPERA ★

360 BAR

LISZT FERENC MUSIC ACADEMY

CORINTHIA HOTEL BUDAPEST

MŰVÉSZ

KÉT SZERECSEN

M RESTAURANT

BOCK BISZTRÓ

Opera (M)
DALSZÍNHÁZ UTCA

FRICI PAPA

KADARKA

CSAK A JÓ SÖR

LIEBLING

LÁRM

MAZEL TOV

WOMBATS CITY HOSTEL BUDAPEST

KLAUZÁL SQUARE MARKET

FOGAS HÁZ & KERT

GHETTO MEMORIAL WALL

KISÜZEM

Klauzál tér

INSTANT

KÖLEVES KERT

FEKETE KUTYA

BLACK SWAN

NEW YORK CAFÉ

GOZSDU COURT

LÉHÚTÓ

KÖLEVES

KAZINCZY STREET SYNAGOGUE

NEW YORK PALACE

TELEP

ROOMBACH HOTEL

DOBLÓ

FRÖHLICH

Kéthly Anna tér

RUMBACH STREET SYNAGOGUE

BARACK & SZILVA

PRINTA

DOBOZ

MY LITTLE MELBOURNE

HUNGARIAN JEWISH MUSEUM AND ARCHIVES ★

KARAVAN

SZIMPLA KERT/SZIMPLA FARMERS MARKET

SZIMPLA DESIGN

Blaha Lujza tér (M)

JEWISH QUARTER

RAOUL WALLENBERG HOLOCAUST MEMORIAL PARK ★

BORS GASZTRO BÁR

RODODENDRON

SZPUTNYIK

SELF SERVICE LAUNDRY BUDAPEST

SZIMPLY

DOHÁNY STREET SYNAGOGUE ★

Astoria (M)

RÁKÓCZI ÚT

© MOON.COM

theologians. You'll then enter the Session Hall and the north gallery overlooking the Danube. Make sure you take some time in the final exhibition room, where you'll find interactive screens and curious information about Budapest and the Parliament Building. (For example, there are no chimneys on the structure, and the central heating actually comes from a boiler room in a nearby building—hot air is funneled through a series of shafts and tunnels. And cold air from ice wells under the square was once used as an early form of air-conditioning.) You can also see the original red star that was on top of the building in the Communist era.

Chain Bridge
(Lánc híd)

Tram 41, 19: Clark Ádám tér (Buda),

tram 2: Széchenyi István tér (Pest)

A symbol of a unified city, the Chain Bridge is Budapest's oldest permanent stone bridge. This suspension bridge features two vaulted, classical-style pillars connected by large iron chains. Count István Széchenyi financed its construction, and it took almost 50 years to build.

The Germans blew up the bridge in 1945 following the Siege of Budapest, and it was rebuilt in the late '40s. Today, it's one of the most romantic spots to cross the Danube, especially at night when thousands of light bulbs come on. Make sure you stop to look at the stone lions created by sculptor János Marschalkó that flank the entrances to the bridge. Local legend says the sculptor forgot to carve the tongues and jumped into the Danube after being mocked for it. However, it's just hearsay, as the sculptor lived for decades after the bridge was built, and the lions have tongues—they can be seen from above but not from the sidewalk.

At the time of writing, the Chain Bridge was scheduled for renovations that were expected to last until 2023. But you can still get great views from the promenade on both sides of the river, or from above at the top of Castle Hill.

Shoes on the Danube

metro 2, tram 2: Kossúth Lajos tér

Set on the embankment just in front of the Hungarian Parliament, the Shoes on the Danube memorial, envisioned by sculptor Gyula Pauer and filmmaker and poet Can Toga, is a poignant reminder of the horrors of the Holocaust. Sixty pairs of iron shoes face the river bank to commemorate the Jews shot into the river by the fascist Arrow Cross Party in the 1940s. Sadly, this was not the only location in Budapest where executions like these happened. The shoes—men's, women's, and small children's—were modeled after 1940s designs, with the iron creased and folded like leather.

To get here, follow the stairs down the side of the Parliament, take the crossing over, and walk back toward the Chain Bridge.

Liberty Square
(Szabadság tér)

metro 2, tram 2: Kossúth Lajos tér, metro 3: Arany János utca

This green patch in the heart of the city, enclosed by grand buildings housing banks, embassies, and offices, was once the location of an 18th-century Austrian barracks. Today, statues and memorials can be found all around the square. The **Soviet War Memorial,** an obelisk topped with a gold star, was erected in 1946 by the Soviet army. It stands directly over the resting place of the Russian soldiers who died during the city's liberation from the Germans. Considering Hungary's communist history, it's controversial, but Hungary signed an agreement to protect the monument. On the other side of the square, a newer memorial to the "Victims of German Occupation" appeared in 2014. The memorial has been criticized by some for whitewashing Hungary's collaboration with the Nazis. A moving **protest memorial** made up of candles, personal memorabilia, and letters by those whose families died in the Holocaust can be visited just a few feet away.

1: St. Stephen's Basilica **2:** Shoes on the Danube

Postal Savings Bank
(Postatakarék)

Hold utca; metro 3: Arany János utca

Just behind Liberty Square is the former Postal Savings Bank. It is not open to the public but is worth passing by. Designed by Ödön Lechner and completed in 1901, this striking example of Hungarian art nouveau is an architectural symphony of Hungarian folk ornamentation, with sprouting flowers and ceramic bees "flying" up to a ceramic beehive. The design culminates with a tapestry-like rooftop made from glazed green-and-yellow octagonal tiles, topped with serpents, angel wings, and dragon tails.

For an excellent view of the Postal Savings Bank, head across the street to the rooftop terrace of the **Hotel President.**

Hungarian House of Art Nouveau
(Bedő House)

Honvéd utca 3; tel. 06/1-269-4622; www.magyarszecessziohaza.hu; Mon-Sat 10am-5pm; HUF 2,000 for the museum; metro 2: Kossuth Lajos tér

From the outside, the Hungarian House of Art Nouveau (also known as Bedő House) looks like it was piped out of a bag full of icing. Designed by Hungarian art nouveau architect Emil Viador for the Bedő family, the building has a style more in line with French, Belgian, or German Jugendstil than Lechner's orientalist creations. Although residential apartments and offices occupy most of the building, the rest is a shrine to all things art nouveau. You'll find a café and museum filled with period furniture, ceramics, and artwork. The space is more like a curious antique shop than a curated museum. It offers a fascinating collection for anyone wanting a glance into a past world and the way the Hungarian upper middle class lived in the early 1900s.

Gresham Palace

Széchenyi István tér 5; tram 2: Szechenyi István tér

The building that is now the **Four Seasons Hotel** was once a block of luxury apartments and offices, built between 1905 and 1907 by the London Gresham Insurance Company, which used the building as its headquarters. The gently undulating façade is typical art nouveau style, with ceramic accents, intricate wrought ironwork, friezes, and floral motifs. Take a peek into the lobby at the intricate curved arcade made with tiles of lead glass, and the beautiful mosaic flooring.

★ St. Stephen's Basilica

Szent István tér; www.bazilika.biz; Mon-Fri 9am-5pm, Sat 9am-1pm, Sun 1pm-5pm; HUF 200 recommended donation; metro 1: Bajcsy-Zsilinsky út

It took half a century to build this basilica, partly because its iconic dome collapsed halfway through construction, and the work began again almost from scratch. Today, this impressive neoclassical cathedral stands at the same height as the Hungarian Parliament. (Both are the tallest buildings in downtown Budapest.) You can scale over 300 stairs (or take an elevator) to the viewing platform (daily 10am-4:30pm Nov-Mar, 10am-5:30pm Apr, May, Oct, 10am-6:30pm June-Sep; HUF 600) outside the dome for 360-degree views of Budapest's most famous sites.

The interior of the cathedral—laid out in a Greek cross—is intricate, with frescoes adorning the gold-accented walls. In the chapel on the right-hand side from the entrance, head over to see a mummified relic: the holy right hand of St. Stephen, which is kept inside a gilded box. It gets taken for a yearly "walk" on August 20, during the St. Stephen's Day procession. Throw a coin in the slot, and the gilded box will light up so you can see the relic in its full glory.

Why is there a mummified limb in the basilica? Legend has it that when the Hungarian king was canonized in 1083, part of making him a saint involved exhuming his body; his right arm was found as fresh as the day he was buried (although apparently not the rest of him). His right arm was chopped off and preserved as a Catholic relic. The hand has

Ödön Lechner

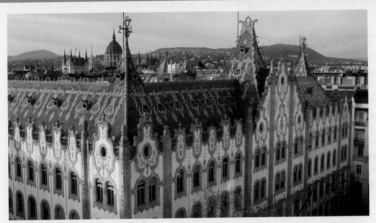

the rooftop of the Postal Savings Bank

Ödön Lechner may be known as the Hungarian Gaudí, but the architect who defined **Hungarian Secession** (or art nouveau) created his most extravagant buildings a couple of years before Gaudí built his most colorful creations. Searching for a style that he could call uniquely Hungarian, and rebelling against the architectural norms of the Habsburg styles, Lechner turned to Hungarian folk art expressed through embroidery and wood painting. He also turned toward the East—following the anthropological theory popular at the time that the Hungarians were an Asiatic race. His architecture blended Indian and Persian influences, Hungarian folk art, and modern technological innovations like iron, steel, fortified concrete, and colorful glazed ceramics and tiles from the Zsolnay factory in Pécs. (Zsolnay was one of the first porcelain, ceramics, and tile manufacturers to develop pyrogranite, a durable type of ornamental ceramic fired under high temperature that could withstand the elements, like frost, making them perfect for architectural details and roof tiles.)

Lechner is regarded as the master of Secession and the father of modern Hungarian architecture. His work was a departure from the traditional Habsburg style visible all across Central Europe (which draws its inspiration from rococo, Baroque, and Western Historicism). Hungarian Secessionism followed the art nouveau trends popping up in Europe, but it applied its own Eastern accent, whether in floral motifs inspired by embroidery or in the intricate details from Islamic architecture. His work, which can look like it's been made from gingerbread, is characterized by glazed ceramics and tiles in greens, blues, and yellows. His most beautiful buildings can be found in Budapest, including the former **Postal Savings Bank** (page 356) and the **Geological Institute of Hungary** (page 365).

traveled to Bosnia, Dubrovnik, Vienna, and Salzburg. (A priest from the American army returned it to Budapest in 1945.)

Outside the entrance, opposite the stairs heading up to the dome, you can take the elevator to the **treasury** (daily 10am-6:30pm July-Sep, 10am-4:30pm Oct-Jun; HUF 400) to see some of the fine silver, gold, and textiles that are the property of this opulent cathedral.

If you want to get to know the basilica better, take a guided tour between 10am-3pm, but you need to book in advance on the phone (06/1-338-2151). Guided tours in English cost HUF 12,700 for a group of one to five persons.

If you're fascinated with the huge pipe organ inside (www.organconcert.hu), you can hear it in action on Monday nights (HUF 3,500) and Friday nights (HUF 4,500-7,000).

JEWISH QUARTER
★ Dohány Street Synagogue

Dohány utca 2; tel. 06/1-413-5585; www.jewishtourhungary.com; Sun-Thu 10am-6pm, Fri 10am-4pm Mar-Oct, Sun-Thu 10am-4pm, Fri 10am-2pm Nov-Feb; HUF 4,500 (with guide); metro 2, tram 47, 49: Astoria

Above Károly körút at the intersection with Dohány utca is the Grand Synagogue, more colloquially known as the Dohány Street Synagogue. Its twin towers, topped with onion-shaped domes (covered in intricate gold leaf), rise over 42 meters (140 ft).

The Grand Synagogue is Europe's largest. The architecture deviates from traditional synagogues—the architects were not Jewish, and the inspiration for the building came from Christian basilicas. It includes a stunning rose window and a cluster of stars made out of stained glass; an orientalist Moorish twist symbolizes both the Jews' Eastern origins and the Neolog interest in integrating into the local community.

German-Austrian architect Ludwig Förster, along with Hungarian architect Frigyes Feszl, built this 3,000-seat synagogue in the 1850s. Inside, the seating is divided in two, with the men taking the ground floor (gilded with golden columns) and the women meant to sit in the gallery above, beneath dripping chandeliers.

The arcaded garden outside was a makeshift cemetery during the Holocaust. The 2,000 bodies buried here are commemorated with graves and memorials. Beyond, the Heroes' Temple, also known as the Winter Synagogue, is used for weekday services. In the courtyard before the exit, you'll find the **Raoul Wallenberg Holocaust Memorial Park,** dedicated to the Swedish diplomat who saved tens of thousands of Jews during World War II. You'll see the profound metallic sculpture of a weeping willow by Imre Varga, which was placed directly above a mass grave; victims' names and tattoo numbers glint on the sculpture's dangling metal leaves. You'll also find the **Hungarian Jewish Museum and Archives** (Dohány utca 2; tel. 06/1-462-0477; www.milev.hu; Sun-Thu 10am-6pm, Fri 10am-4pm Mar-Apr and Oct, Sun-Thu 10am-8pm, Fri 10am-4pm May-Sep, Sun-Thu 10am-4pm, Fri 10am-2pm Nov-Feb; HUF 4,000). It includes a collection

ceiling in the Grand Synagogue

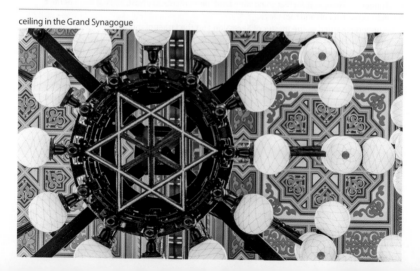

of objects from religious and daily Hungarian Jewish life.

Kazinczy Street Synagogue

Kazinczy utca 29-31; tel. 06/1-351-0524; Sun-Thu 10am-6pm Mar-Oct, Fri 10am-1pm Mar, Fri 10am-4pm Apr-Oct, Sun-Thu 10am-4pm, Fri 10am-1pm Nov-Feb; HUF 1,000; metro 1: Opera

The Kazinczy Street Synagogue, also known as the Orthodox Synagogue, stands in the corner of the cobbled portion of Kazinczy utca. You need to look up to see the Hebrew lettering on the ashlar above the exposed brick façade. The Secessionist-style interior, drawing influences from Hungarian folk art (such as Transylvanian wood carvings and Hungarian floral motifs), is surprising—it is the heart of Orthodox Jewry in Budapest. The complex, designed by Béla and Sándor Löffler in 1912-1913, expands into a courtyard where there is a kosher restaurant and a shop.

Rumbach Street Synagogue

Rumbach Sebestyén utca 11-13; metro 1, 2, 3, tram 47, 49: Deák Ferenc tér

A few blocks away from the Kazinczy and Dohány utca synagogue, the minaret-like spires of the Rumbach Street Synagogue tower over the design shops, vibrant street art, and avant-garde underground theaters that characterize the Jewish Quarter today. This Moorish-style synagogue, designed by Viennese architect Otto Wagner in 1872, is a museum and cultural hall.

Inside the synagogue, seven striking rose windows in a kaleidoscope of colors can be seen in its domed ceiling, and the walls are covered in ornate lavender-, fuchsia-, and lapis-toned friezes. The synagogue fell into disuse following the war and then stood as a semi-derelict, pigeon-infested ruin after a partial reconstruction in the late 1980s and early 1990s. (The work had to be aborted when the private corporation that bought the building went bankrupt.) But at the time of this writing, it's now back in Jewish hands and is being restored to its former glory.

Ghetto Memorial Wall

15 Király utca; metro 1, 2, 3, tram 47, 49: Deák Ferenc tér

In the winter of 1944, more than 50,000 Jews were moved into the ghetto, an area fortified with wooden fencing and stone walls topped with barbed wire. A local conservation group working to protect the Jewish Quarter's cultural heritage has reconstructed the original ghetto wall as a memorial. Take a walk down Király utca and peek through the bars of the gate at number 15 to see it—it's at the back of a courtyard of residential houses. The memorial was constructed from stones from the original ghetto wall and is topped with barbed wire.

AROUND ANDRÁSSY AVENUE

★ Hungarian State Opera

Andrássy út 22; tel. 06/1-814-7100; www.opera.hu; metro 1: Opera

As you're strolling down Andrássy Avenue, stop to admire the Hungarian State Opera House, one of the world's most beautiful opera houses. This neo-Renaissance structure was built in 1884 by Miklós Ybl, with the financial support of Emperor Franz Joseph I. Its exterior is decorated with stone sphinxes, muses between the columns, and images of famous opera composers on the roof terrace. Marble columns, vaulted ceilings, and chandeliers adorn the interior. The gold-covered auditorium seats over 1,200, and at the time of this writing, the building is undergoing a major renovation to improve its acoustics and staging, allowing it to compete with other great European opera houses. (It's expected to re-open for the season of 2021/2022.) If you can't catch a show, you can still join one of the daily tours (HUF 2,990) at 2pm, 3pm, or 4pm. The tours include a mini concert at the end.

House of Terror

Andrássy út 60; tel. 06/1-374-2600; www.terrorhaza.hu; Tue-Sun 10am-6pm; HUF 3,000; metro 1: Vörösmarty utca

This infamous four-story apartment block on a corner of Andrássy Avenue was once the

Budapest's Jews of the VII District

the Star of David on the fencing at the Dohány Street Synagogue

Unlike Prague, Venice, or Krakow, Budapest has never had an exclusively Jewish neighborhood. Jews have long lived side by side in Hungary with non-Jews. (The most famous Jewish area in the VII District received the name "Jewish Quarter" after becoming a ghetto in the 1940s.)

The story behind the Jews of the VII District ties in with the segregation rules of the 18th century—Jews could not even spend the night in the Inner City at that time. So the community grew outside the city walls. Many Jews worked as merchants, typically trading grain, cattle, leather goods, and textiles in the market just outside, in today's **Deák Ferenc tér** (a large downtown central square bordering on the Inner City where three metro lines meet).

As the community prospered in the 19th century, Budapest's Jews split into two factions: **Neolog Jews,** a socially liberal group inclined toward integrating into Hungary that preferred to speak Hungarian over Yiddish, and the **Orthodox** community, a conservative group that resisted the modern and secular leanings of the Neolog community.

Budapest's Jewish population peaked following World War I. At that time, there were 125 synagogues and over 200,000 Jews in the city. Tragically, nearly 50 percent of the city's Jews died in the Holocaust, and the community never fully recovered.

Today, a walk around this district reveals signs of Jewish heritage. But you won't find signs of Jewish life only in this district. In the **VIII District, XIII District,** and in **Buda** today, you'll find active synagogues and prayer houses with tightly knit Jewish communities. Some synagogues are visible from the outside, like the **Grand Synagogue** on Dohány utca, or they may be tucked away in a private apartment, like the prayer house on Teleki tér in the VIII District.

headquarters of the secret police and a place where many were held captive, tortured, and killed. Today, its imposing roof with the word "TERROR" punched out in the metal overhang dominates this part of the avenue. Inside is a unique museum—a monument to the victims of Hungary's fascist and communist regimes—that opened in 2002. The interactive museum contains chilling reconstructed prison cells in the basement, rooms lined with propaganda posters, and installations from the darkest moments in Hungarian

---

1: the Hungarian State Opera on Andrássy Avenue **2:** the Geological Institute of Hungary **3:** Vajdahunyad Castle in City Park **4:** Heroes' Square

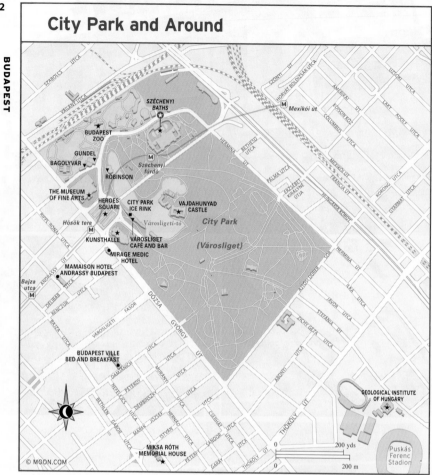

City Park and Around

history. The museum spreads from the basement to the second floor, and it's worth taking two to three hours to go through, especially if you watch the poignant interactive video displays, where you can listen to firsthand stories of victims and survivors.

How did the infamous number 60 turn into a tourist attraction? In late 2000, the Public Foundation for the Research of Central and East European History and Society bought the building and spent a year reconstructing the interior to create a memorial and museum to the victims of the regimes.

CITY PARK AND AROUND
Vajdahunyad Castle

Városliget; tel. 06/1-422-0765; Tue-Fri 10am-5pm;
HUF 2,100 combined ticket for museum and towers;
metro 1: Széchenyi fürdő

The spires of Vajdahunyad Castle may look like something out of *Dracula* (it has been a film location in an adaptation). But look closely and you'll notice that this castle, built at the end of the 19th century, is an eclectic mixture of architectural styles. Medieval towers share space with Baroque statues.

You get the best views from the gate tower (enter through the door on the left as you go through the gate) or the Apostle's Tower, which is accessible from inside the Museum of Agriculture with a guide. The interior of the castle is just as spectacular, with ornate rococo ballrooms, crystal chandeliers, Renaissance-inspired frescoes in hues of blue and maroon, and stained-glass windows.

The interior of the castle houses the **Museum of Agriculture** (www.mezogaz-dasagimuzeum.hu), which showcases the history of Hungarian agriculture with reconstructed yurts and dwellings, antique plows, farming equipment, and an impressive collection of taxidermy and antlers. Upstairs, next to the intricate staircase, is an interesting photographic exhibition displaying the architectural inspirations for the castle.

The castle grounds are free of charge to roam. You can even go up to the hooded statue of Anonymous, the unknown chronicler who penned the history of the early Magyars in the court of King Béla III, and rub the bronze pen for literary inspiration.

Budapest Zoo

Állatkerti körút 6-12; tel. 06/1-273-4900;
www.zoobudapest.com; daily 9am-sunset;
HUF 3,300, metro 1: Széchenyi fürdő

Founded in 1866, Budapest Zoo is one of Europe's oldest zoos. Located near City Park, the zoo is a vast complex with two artificial mountains, 500 species of animals, and 4,000 plant species. You can explore greenhouses dedicated to Madagascar and an Australia section where kangaroos hop right past you. Pay a visit to the turn-of-the-20th-century palm houses built by the Eiffel Company in Paris; they feature a replica rainforest complete with sprinkler-generated "rain." The neighboring butterfly house is also a great stop.

The main highlights of the zoo include the "Magic Mountain" set inside a hollow, artificial rocky outcrop where you'll find a life-school made up of an aquarium, games, educational experiments, and 3D documentary screenings. The art nouveau elephant house, another highlight, is a spectacular piece of architecture, with mosque-like domes covered in scaly turquoise Zsolnay tiles.

On the way in and out, notice the gate of the zoo, created by the architect who designed the elephant house. It's flanked by elephants, topped with polar bears, and decorated with intricate botanical murals. (The zoo's art nouveau buildings have been listed as national landmarks.)

Budapest Zoo is also expanding its territory to include a 1.7-hectare (4.2-acre) Biodome (still under construction at the time of writing), complete with a rich community of animals, plants, and even an aquarium.

The Museum of Fine Arts
(Szépművészeti Múzeum)

Dózsa György út 41; tel. 01/469-7100;
www.szepmuveszeti.hu; Tue-Sun 10am-6pm;
HUF 2,800; metro 1: Hősök tere

The Museum of Fine Arts, which resembles a Greek temple, lies on the northern side of Heroes' Square. After three years of construction work, it reopened to the public in the fall of 2018. The permanent collection spans five floors, so expect to spend over three hours if you want to explore the whole museum—and that's without the temporary exhibitions thrown in.

Start in the basement for the museum's exquisite collection of Egyptian art and Classical antiquities. The collection features bronze statuettes of Egyptian gods, painted pottery, colorful sarcophagi, Hellenic sculpture, and Roman glass, which could keep any history lover occupied for a couple of hours.

The ground floor is exciting because this is where you will find the Romanesque Hall—which was closed to the public for 70 years after a bomb damaged the museum in 1945—a stunning hall designed to showcase Hungarian Romanesque art. The Romanesque Hall is covered wall-to-wall with colorful frescoes inspired by the art from medieval churches with a vibrant cast of characters like kings and angels, and mythological figures such as dragons, painted in hues of royal reds, lapis blues, wood green, and accents of gold leaf. It had been built to house medieval plaster casts, but now the hall itself is an exhibition in its own right.

The first floor is now home to European art from 1250-1600, with work from Europe's greatest Renaissance and Baroque masters like Raphael, Titian, Tintoretto, van Dyck, Holbein, El Greco, and Goya. However, if you're passionate about sculpture, head to the second floor to the display of European sculpture 1350-1800, including a statue of a horse attributed to Leonardo da Vinci.

Level three is dedicated to Hungarian Baroque art from 1600-1800. This collection was originally housed in the Hungarian National Gallery, in the Royal Palace in Buda, and now gets a new home here in the museum.

Kunsthalle
(Műcsarnok)

Dózsa György út 37; tel. 06/1-460-7000;
www.mucsarnok.hu; Tue-Wed, Fri-Sun 10am-6pm,
Thu noon-8pm; HUF 2,900 combined ticket for all
exhibitions; metro 1: Hősök tere

Since the 19th century, the Kunsthalle has been the main hub of contemporary art in Hungary. Flanking Heroes' Square, opposite the Museum of Fine Arts, the Kunsthalle looks more like a Greek temple than an exhibition hall, with gold-gilded Corinthian columns. Kunsthalle is one of Budapest's largest exhibition spaces focusing on visual and contemporary art. Top international exhibitions change with the seasons—examples include photography from Steve McCurry and Sandro Miller, installations by Shilpa Gupta, and video installations and photography on social and women's issues in Iran by Shirin Neshat.

Heroes' Square

metro 1: Hősök tere

Heroes' Square, marked by the towering pillar topped by the angel Gabriel holding the holy crown, can be seen all the way down Andrássy Avenue. The square itself was erected in 1896 to celebrate the millennium of the conquest of the Carpathian Basin. (The rest of the work on the square was completed in 1929.) The features of the square are packed with Hungarian symbolism, from the chieftains of the seven Magyar tribes at the base of the pillar to the two semicircular colonnades featuring bronze statues of Hungarian kings and leaders. You'll find statues of Hungarian heroes like Lajos Kossuth, a revolutionary who struggled for independence from Austrian rule during the 1848 uprising against the Habsburgs.

You can get up close to the monuments, including the tomb of the unknown soldier, a cenotaph remembering the soldiers from multiple wars. Next to the tomb is a cast-iron manhole covering (originally made out of wood) for the first thermal water well used for a thermal bath that once stood on the square.

Today, you'll only find locals on Heroes' Square during protests and marches, like Budapest Pride, or for public events like the National Gallop, a large Hungarian cultural festival centered on horse racing. Otherwise, the square is filled with tourists.

Miksa Róth Memorial House

Nefelejcs utca 26; 06/1-341-6789;
www.rothmuzeum.hu; 2pm-6pm Tue-Sun;
HUF 750; metro 2: Keleti Pályaudvar

Tucked inside a courtyard in the outer VII District, the Miksa Róth Memorial House is a fascinating and underrated museum dedicated to the life and work of stained-glass artist Miksa Róth. The entrance from the street will bring you into the courtyard. Take the door on the left to get into the museum.

The former Róth residence occupies part of the museum here, so you'll get a glimpse into the way the Róth family lived. The top floor of the building contains an exhibition of Róth's work, with beautiful panels of stained glass and stunning art nouveau mosaics. Sometimes the museum closes for August.

Miksa Róth's Stained Glass

stained glass by Miksa Róth

Miksa Róth (1865-1944) was one of Hungary's most prolific and famous artists. Working for half a century, he became a master of stained glass and mosaic art. Róth's style evolved through the Secession and beyond with the Renaissance of stained-glass art at the end of the 19th century. Following World War I, his art declined while Hungary suffered social and economic challenges.

Róth was Jewish, and his work suffered again during World War II. Although baptized as a Roman Catholic in 1897, Róth still struggled under the anti-Semitic law passed in 1939 that limited Jewish public and economic life. Eventually, he closed his workshop and transferred his house and possessions to his Roman Catholic wife. He died of natural causes in Budapest in 1944 at 89.

His stained-glass art can be found as far away as Oslo and Mexico City, but only in Budapest is his craft embedded into the architectural landscape of the city. Look for his work in the stained-glass windows of the **Hungarian Parliament Building** (page 351) and inside the stairwell of the **Gresham Palace** building housing the Four Seasons Hotel (page 356). Beyond stained glass, Róth also created architectural mosaics, like those in the **Liszt Ferenc Music Academy** (page 399) and adorning the dome inside the intricate entrance of the **Széchenyi Baths** (page 382).

Geological Institute of Hungary

Stefánia út 14; email muzeum@mbfsz.gov.hu one week in advance to visit the geological museum and the interior; free; bus 5, 7, 110, 112: Stefánia út/ Thököly út

It's worth going off the beaten track to see the Geological Institute of Hungary, arguably one of Ödön Lechner's most spectacular buildings. Its two-toned blue tiled roof is topped with four Atlas figures holding up a terrestrial globe. Fittingly, the building incorporates geological elements: the roof represents the Thetis Sea, and the building is embedded with fossil-shaped ceramics. Emperor Franz Josef I approved the founding of the institute, but Lechner, who won a competition for the commission, began work on the building in 1896, finishing in 1899. The institute features the typical Lechner qualities, including folk motifs in the architectural ceramics and flowers carved into the windows. The institute also houses a geology museum, which can be visited by appointment.

MARGARET ISLAND AND AROUND
Water Tower

Margitsziget; tel. 06/20-383-6352; lookout platform daily 11:30am-7pm May-Oct; HUF 600; bus 26: Szabadtéri Színpad

Towering above trees and grassy lawns, the Water Tower on Margaret Island is visible from both Buda and Pest. A beautiful piece of architecture embodying the Hungarian Secessionist style, the tower was also one of the first structures of its kind in Europe that employed innovative ferro-concrete engineering. Designed by Szilárd Zielinski and built by architect Rezső Vilmos Ray in 1911, it reaches over 55 meters (180 ft) into the air.

The tower can be admired from most spots on the island, whether you're relaxing with a book or riding a quadracycle. To get into the tower you must buy a ticket at the ticket office (which is also the box office for the open-air theater in the area). Then you can hike up 153 steps to the lookout platform for 360-degree views across the island, the river, and the city.

Dominican Convent Ruins

Margitsziget; bus 26: Palatinus fürdő

King Béla IV is responsible for this convent's construction. He promised God he would build a convent on the island and send his daughter Margaret there if Hungary survived the Mongol invasion in 1241. The Mongols withdrew, and his daughter, then nine years old, became a nun. She was later canonized.

The ruins of the Dominican Convent still stand on Margaret Island, and they consist mostly of excavated stone walls with a few Gothic features. The ruins are available for public view for free, so anyone can stroll among them. Margaret's remains were taken off the island when the nuns fled the Turkish invasion in the 16th century, but you can still see her sepulcher marked by a slab of red marble. Nearby, a memorial enclosed in red bricks contains pictures of the saint, and you'll likely see candles left behind by devout Catholic locals. There are metal lookout points positioned among the ruins that allow a better overview of the former convent's layout.

If you're interested in medieval history, there are more ruins scattered on the island. Just north of the convent, there is the reconstructed **Romanesque Premonstratensian Church,** dating back to the 12th century.

Budapest Pinball Museum

Radnóti Miklós utca 18; www.flippermuzeum. hu; Wed-Fri 4pm-midnight, Sat 2pm-midnight, Sun 10am-10pm; HUF 3,000; metro 3: Nyugati Pályaudvar

Over on mainland Pest, the Budapest Pinball Museum (officially Europe's largest ongoing interactive museum dedicated to pinball machines) draws visitors from the world over. Tucked away in a 400-square-meter (4,300-sq-ft) basement, the museum's 130 vintage pinball machines are are not just for show; they are available for play. There is no need to bring any coins—playing on the machines is included in the museum's admission price. The oldest pieces in the collection are bagatelles from the 1880s, a 1920s table hockey game, and a Humpty Dumpty game from the 1940s (one of the first pinball machines to include flipper bumpers).

Margaret Bridge

tram 4, 6: Margitsziget/Margit híd

Margaret Bridge is Budapest's second permanent bridge, built in 1876 by French engineer Ernest Gouin. The iron structure painted in pale yellow is suspended on seven stone pillars with statues of winged, bare-breasted women (created by French sculptor Adolphe Thabard). This bridge doesn't stretch across the river in a completely straight line; it stands at angles to converge with Margaret Island's southern tip. It begins from the edge of the Grand Boulevard and goes over to Buda, where the middle prong (which was added in 1900) also runs down to the island. You can

---

1: a cemetery for old communist statues in Memento Park 2: the Margaret Island Water Tower, a symbol of the island 3: The top of Gellért Hill has some of the best views over Budapest.

Margaret Island and Around

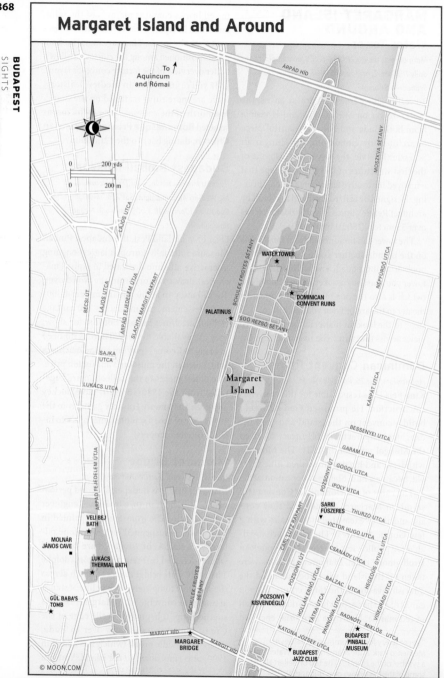

To
Aquincum
and Római

ÁRPÁD HÍD

0   200 yds
0   200 m

MOSZKVA SÉTÁNY

WATER TOWER

DOMINICAN
CONVENT RUINS

PALATINUS

SCHULEK FRIGYES SÉTÁNY

SOÓ REZSŐ SÉTÁNY

NÉPFÜRDŐ UTCA

Margaret
Island

KÁRPÁT UTCA

BESSENYEI UTCA

GARAM UTCA

GOGOL UTCA

POZSONYI ÚT

IPOLY UTCA

SARKI
FŰSZERES   THURZÓ UTCA

VICTOR HUGO UTCA

CSANÁDY UTCA

BALZAC   UTCA

CARL LUTZ RAKPART

POZSONYI ÚT

HOLLÁN ERNŐ UTCA

TÁTRA UTCA

PANNÓNIA UTCA

HEGEDŰS GYULA UTCA

VISEGRÁDI UTCA

POZSONYI
KISVENDÉGLŐ

KATONA JÓZSEF UTCA

RADNÓTI   MIKLÓS   UTCA

BUDAPEST
PINBALL
MUSEUM

BUDAPEST
JAZZ CLUB

VELI BEJ
BATH

MOLNÁR
JÁNOS CAVE

LUKÁCS
THERMAL BATH

GÜL BABA'S
TOMB

MARGIT HÍD

MARGARET
BRIDGE

MARGIT HÍD

SCHULEK FRIGYES SÉTÁNY

ÁRPÁD FEJEDELEM ÚTJA

LUKÁCS UTCA

SAJKA
UTCA

BÉCSI ÚT

LAJOS UTCA

ÁRPÁD FEJEDELEM ÚTJA

SLACHTA MARGIT RAKPART

LAJOS UTCA

© MOON.COM

Ottomans in Budapest

The Turks ruled over the city of Buda for 150 years (1541-1686), and you'll find plenty of Ottoman relics in Budapest today. The Turkish baths are the most famous Ottoman contribution to the city—but look closely and you'll find turban-topped tombstones around **Buda Castle** (page 344) or Islamic elements left behind in Christian churches, like the mihrab (a niche in the mosque wall indicating the direction to Mecca) in the **Inner City Church** next to the Danube in Pest. On the hill overlooking the Danube in north Buda, there is also the octagonal tomb of the dervish **Gül Baba** (page 369), who legend has it bought roses to Hungary.

Turkish influences still linger in the language, with words like dohány (smoke) and kávé (coffee) in the Hungarian lexicon. **Paprika,** an ingredient synonymous with Hungarian cooking, arrived in the country during the Ottoman era and became part of peasant cooking after the Turks were seen spicing their stews with the red powder.

Only traces of the occupation can be found in Budapest, like the baths, or the tomb of the dervish Gül Baba.

take tram 4 or 6 to the middle of the bridge and stroll down to the island.

Gül Baba's Tomb

Mecset utca 14; tel. 06/1-618-3842; www. gulbabaalapitvany.hu/en/gul-babas-tomb; daily 10am-6pm; free; tram 4, 6: Margit híd, Budai hídfő

Despite some 150 years of occupation, few intact Ottoman buildings are left in Budapest. Beyond the Turkish baths, one of the most interesting sites from this period is the tomb of the 16th-century dervish Gül Baba. It is the northernmost site of pilgrimage for Muslims. Legend has it this Islamic saint brought roses to Hungary (the local neighborhood's name means "Rose Hill" in Hungarian). When Gül Baba died in 1541, Sultan Suleiman the Magnificent commissioned this tomb, which was completed in 1548, and named the dervish the saint of Buda.

It's worth the climb up to the tomb, via Gül Baba utca, for its rose gardens and views over the Danube. Take the 4 or 6 tram to the Margit híd, Budai hídfő stop, and walk one block in the direction away from the river. As you face the hill, take the street to the right

into Török utca (Turk street). As you walk along the street, you'll want to turn up Gül Baba utca, a sharply inclined cobbled lane lined with Mediterrean-style stone houses and rusty colored facades resembling a setting you'd find in rural Turkey rather than downtown Budapest. It's definitely scenic route, but is discouraged if you struggle with steep hills or you're wearing heels. You can take the gentler way up from Margit körút, by walking up Margit utca and turning right on Mecset utca—which appropriately translates as "Mosque street"—then just follow the signs to the complex.

The mausoleum is a classic octagonal Ottoman structure with the sarcophagus inside covered in silk cloth, surrounded with plush carpets. If the mausoleum is closed, you can peek through the window to see the coffin. The complex has a lovely garden with a colonnade and a few lookout towers.

Make sure you go to the museum, which has the same hours as the tomb and is also free to visit. Just take the stairs down inside the building surrounding the mausoleum, left of the gate or the elevator. You'll get some historic context into life in Ottoman Buda, with artifacts like ceramics, engraved silver cups, and waxworks of Turkish figures in traditional dress. An exhibition room in the back often features contemporary Turkish artists.

SOUTH BUDA
★ Gellért Hill

metro 4, trams 19, 41, 47, 48, 49, 56: Szent Gellért tér
Gellért Hill, a green, rocky outcrop on the banks of the Danube, is named for martyred Venetian bishop St. Gellért, who, according to legend, was thrown down the hill in a barrel full of nails during the Great Pagan Rebellion of the 11th century. His statue still towers above a human-made waterfall, surrounded by columns (with stone pagan Magyars by his feet) opposite Elizabeth Bridge.

You can take the stairs going past the waterfall and the statue of the saint, and then follow a labyrinth of paths to the top of the hill and the Citadel, or you can hike up alternative routes, like the path up by the Danubius Hotel Gellért and the Thermal Baths. Winding trails thread through the woodland covering the hillside, with incredible views through the trees over the river and the castle. Both routes take 15-20 minutes to walk.

If you want the view without the hike, take the number 27 bus from Móricz Zsigmond körtér (metro 4, trams 6, 17, 19, 41, 47, 48, 49, 56, 56A, 61) to the Búsuló Juhász (Citadella) stop for a gentle stroll to the Citadel. Stop at the lookout point on the left for amazing views of the city.

THE CITADEL

Bus 27: Búsuló Juhász (Citadella)
The Citadel fortress crowns the top of the hill. This dramatic structure was built by the Habsburgs after the 1848-1849 War of Independence and became obsolete by the time it was built. Although the museum in the Citadel has closed indefinitely, it's worth the hike up for the views over the Inner City. This is the highest point in downtown Budapest, and you're rewarded with panoramas over the Danube, Buda Castle, and the bridges.

Then wander over to the **Liberty Monument,** which dominates the skyline with its bronze female figure clasping a palm leaf above her head. The monument, a tribute to the Soviet soldiers who died liberating the city, is one of the few Soviet relics in the city center.

Cave Church

Szent Gellért rakpart 1/a; tel. 06/20-775-2472;
Mon-Sat 9:30am-7:30pm; HUF 600; metro 4,
tram 19, 41, 47, 48, 49, 56: Szent Gellért tér
Facing the entrance to the Gellért Baths on a rocky outcrop is the cavernous entrance to the Cave Church. There's evidence that the cave was inhabited as far back as 4,000 years ago, but the earliest known inhabitant was a hermit named Iván, who resided in the Middle Ages and helped cure the sick with the bubbling thermal waters that now fill the pools of the Gellért Baths. The church's rocky interior became a home to Paulite Monks, Hungary's only homegrown monastic order, in 1926. The monks expanded the cave to make way for further chapels and attached a neo-Gothic monastery to the side of the hill looking over the Danube in 1934. The Cave Church led an active life in the 20th century: it sheltered Polish refugees in World War II, and in the 1950s it was seized by the Communists, who briefly walled up the entrance with concrete.

Today the church is functioning again. Outside Mass hours (Mon-Sat 8:30am, 5pm, and 8pm, Sun 11am), the church is open to visitors. You can explore the caverns, which lead into the turreted monastery on the outside.

INNER CITY AND SOUTH PEST
Central Market Hall (Nagyvásárcsarnok)

Vámház körút 1-4; tel. 06/1-366-3300; Mon
6am-5pm, Tue-Fri 6am-6pm, Sat 6am-3pm;
metro 4, tram 2, 47, 48, 49: Fővám tér
As the biggest market in the city, Central Market Hall may attract its fair share of tourists snapping shots of dried paprika and cured

South Buda

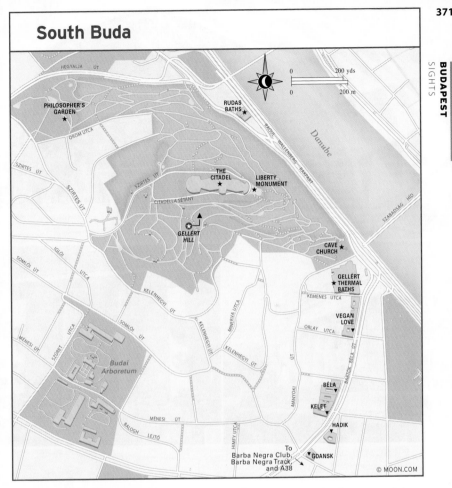

© MOON.COM

sausages, but it's still one of the best markets for locals. This vast, cathedral-like hall with steel beams, iron girders, exposed red brick, and large windows opened in 1897. Goods were once delivered by barges that sailed into the market thanks to special docks. Though coming here by boat is no longer possible, you can still stroll past the baked goods, meat, cheeses, vegetables, and stalls specializing in Hungarian delicacies. Head up to the top floor to find stands selling folk art, such as embroidery and painted woodwork, and to sample Hungarian dishes like lángos. Even if you have no intention to buy, you should visit

the market for its grand architecture and the energy you'll experience there.

The Bálna

Fővám tér 11-12; 06/30-619-2052;
www.balnabudapest.hu; Sun-Thu 10am-8pm,
Fri-Sat 10am-10pm; tram 2: Zsil utca

From the other side of the river, it's impossible to ignore the Bálna ("whale" in Hungarian), a glass structure that's become the poster child of regeneration of the once-dilapidated IX District. Back in the 19th century, this part of the city buzzed with trade, as barges traveled up and down the Danube to the capital and

public warehouses in the area stored wheat and other produce. Many of these red-bricked buildings fell into disrepair by the beginning of the 21st century but soon saw innovative regeneration. The Bálna found new life when Dutch architect Kas Oosterhuis embarked on creating a new complex from the four buildings standing in proximity to the Danube. Oosterhuis added the glass roof, keeping the old buildings' original brickwork.

Today, this unique cultural and shopping center has become a main landmark on the southern part of the river. In the summer, the restaurants, bars, and cafés open up their terraces, and the design and art galleries inside are open all year round. Antique shops and flea markets stand in the base of the "Whale." On the top floor, you'll find exhibitions in the New Budapest Gallery as well as great views over the river through the glass rooftop. The futuristic structure once stood in for NASA Headquarters in Ridley Scott's *The Martian*.

★ Hungarian National Museum
(Magyar Nemzeti Múzeum)
Múzeum körút 14-16; tel. 06/1-338-2122;
www.mnm.hu; Tue-Sun 10am-6pm; HUF 2,600;
metro 3, tram 47, 49: Kalvin tér, metro 2: Astoria

The Hungarian National Museum rises up like a Greek temple. It is Hungary's largest museum, dedicated to the history of the Carpathian Basin from prehistory until the fall of Communism in the country. This museum once played a part in Budapest's history: revolutionaries gathered on its steps on the first day of the 1848 Revolution against the Habsburgs.

An extensive archaeology exhibition can be found on the ground floor; it features excavated artifacts that chart Hungarian history before the Magyar tribes arrived, including relics from the Celts and Romans—like a Scythian gold stag and a statue of Heracles cast in bronze. This exhibit also features

1: the Bálna 2: Hungarian National Museum
3: The site of Aquincum is where the largest Roman settlement was in Budapest. 4: Central Market Hall

artifacts left behind by the first Huns and the Magyar tribes that came later.

In the basement, explore Hungary's Roman history in the incredible lapidarium, filled with mosaics, sculptures, carved headstones, and medieval stonework. The first floor of the museum is a work of art in itself, with colorful frescoes with flecks of gold leaf under a dome. Here, the exhibition splits into two parts—Hungary from the Middle Ages up to the Ottoman occupation, and from the 18th century to the Communist era.

Holocaust Memorial Center
Páva utca 39; tel. 06/1-455-3333;
www.hdke.hu; Tue-Sun 10am-6pm; 1,400 HUF;
metro 3: Corvin-negyed

The powerful Holocaust Memorial Center charts the history of the Holocaust in Hungary, from the dehumanization of the Jews to their extermination at Auschwitz and other concentration camps. It's an interactive multimedia museum where you'll find personal artifacts such as children's dolls, pens, clothing, and eyeglasses left behind. You can watch and listen to personal and family stories on interactive screens. The exhibition ends inside a beautifully renovated synagogue that was originally built in the 1920s.

Zwack Unicum Museum
Dandár utca 1; tel. 06/1-476-2383;
www.zwackunicum.hu/en/zwack-muzeumok/
zwack-muzeum-es-latogatokozpont/bemutato;
Mon-Sat 10am-5pm; HUF 2,400;
tram 2: Haller utca/Soroksári út

You need to go off the beaten track to find this fascinating factory museum in the heart of the IX District, just one street off the Danube. You'll need a guide to visit the distillery, but once you reach the museum, you can explore on your own. The order of the tour can vary, but the first part is usually around the distillery, where you'll learn a few of the secret ingredients in Hungary's iconic drink. You'll begin in a room filled with vats of cardamom pods, chamomile, ginger root, licorice, and peppercorns you can touch and smell. Then,

Inner City and South Pest

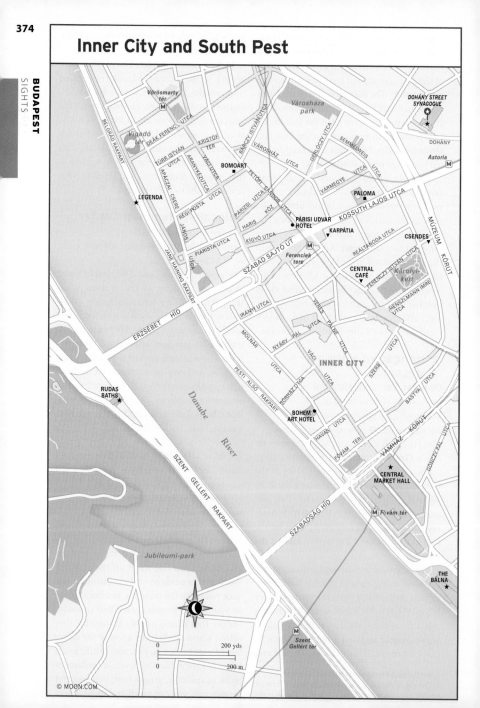

Vörösmarty tér Ⓜ

DOHÁNY STREET SYNAGOGUE ⛧

Városháza park

DOHÁNY

Astoria Ⓜ

BELGRÁD RAKPART

Vigadó tér

DEÁK FERENC UTCA

KRISTÓF TÉR

BÁRCZY ISTVÁN UTCA

VÁROSHÁZ UTCA

GERLÓCZY UTCA

SEMMELWEIS UTCA

TÜRR ISTVÁN UTCA

ARANYKÉZ UTCA

VÁCI UTCA

BOMOART ■

PETŐFI SÁNDOR UTCA

VÁRMEGYE UTCA

APÁCZAI CSERE JÁNOS UTCA

RÉGI POSTA UTCA

PÁRIZSI UTCA

PALOMA ■

LEGENDA ★

HARIS KÖZ

PÁRISI UDVAR HOTEL ●

KOSSUTH LAJOS UTCA

MÚZEUM KÖRÚT

KÍGYÓ UTCA

PIARISTA UTCA

KARPÁTIA ●

REÁLTANODA UTCA

CSENDES ★

JANE HAINING RAKPART

SZABAD SAJTÓ ÚT

Ferenciek tere Ⓜ

CENTRAL CAFÉ ▼

FERENCZY ISTVÁN UTCA

Károlyi-kert

HENSZLMANN IMRE UTCA

ERZSÉBET HÍD

IRÁNYI UTCA

VERES PÁLNÉ UTCA

MOLNÁR UTCA

NYÁRY PÁL UTCA

VÁCI UTCA

INNER CITY

SZERB UTCA

BÁSTYA UTCA

RUDAS BATHS ★

Danube River

PESTI ALSÓ RAKPART

SORHÁZ UTCA

BOHEM ART HOTEL ●

HAVAS UTCA

FŐVÁM TÉR

VÁMHÁZ KÖRÚT

GÖNCZY PÁL UTCA

SZENT GELLÉRT RAKPART

CENTRAL MARKET HALL ★

Jubileumi-park

SZABADSÁG HÍD

Ⓜ Fővám tér

THE BÁLNA ★

N

0   200 yds

0   200 m

Ⓜ Szent Gellért tér

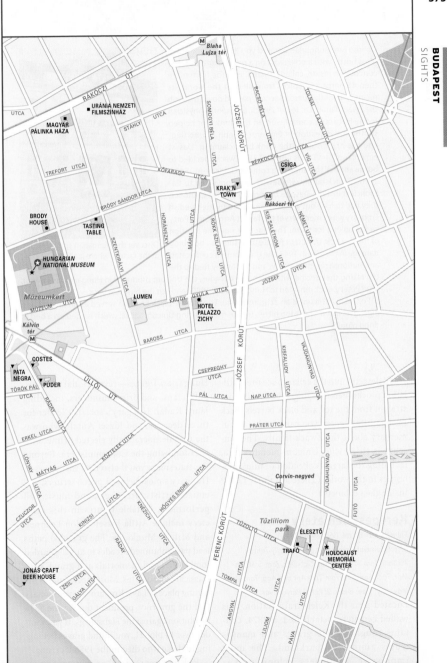

All About Unicum

Go into any Hungarian bar and you'll see a dark-green glass bottle with a gold cross on a red background. The concoction inside, called Unicum, is made from more than 40 herbs and spices from all over the world. Its recipe is a tightly guarded secret, passed down through the Zwack family. Dr. József Zwack, an imperial physician to the Habsburg court, invented the drink that helped soothe the digestion of Emperor Joseph II, who (legend has it) christened the drink by exclaiming "Das ist ein unikum!"—"This is unique!" The Zwacks decided to bottle and sell the drink on a commercial scale in 1840.

The Zwack family was Jewish but converted to Catholicism in 1917. Despite becoming devout Catholics, they had to hide out in cellars protected by the Swedish Embassy when members of the fascist Arrow Cross Party came looking for them. Their factory, now the location of the Zwack Unicum Museum, suffered bombing damage in the war; in 1948, the government confiscated and nationalized the factory, and the family fled to the US, taking their recipe with them. For decades, the Unicum produced in Hungary was inferior, until Peter Zwack returned to Hungary in the 1980s and got the business back.

Discover the Hungarian spirit Unicum at the factory where it all started.

For many, Unicum is an acquired taste. The almost-black liquor is served as an aperitif and digestive. If you find it too bitter, try the fruity-tasting Unicum Szilva, which is aged on a bed of dried plums.

you'll descend into the cellar to see the distillation process before trying a shot of Unicum straight from the red and black barrels. Back in the visitor center, you can watch a documentary about the Zwack family. The museum is filled with Unicum memorabilia, including the largest collection of miniature bottles in the world. (There are about 17,000 inside glass cabinets.)

Kerepesi Cemetery

Fiúmei út 16-18; tel. 06/1-896-3889; http://fiumeiutisirkert.nori.gov.hu; daily 7am or 7:30am-5pm Jan, Feb, and Oct-Dec, 7am-5:30pm Mar, 7am-6pm Sep, 7am-7pm Apr and Aug, 7am-8pm May-July; free; metro 2: Keleti Pályaudvar

Located near the Keleti train station, this walled cemetery, established in 1874, contains roughly 3,000 graves and mausoleums amid lush parkland. The most impressive sepulchers belong to key Hungarian figures—revolutionary heroes, politicians, and prime ministers, including János Kadár, Hungary's socialist leader for three decades, and József Antall, who was the first democratically elected prime minister following the Communist era. Beyond the statesmen, you'll also find the graves of Hungary's most beloved poets, writers, scientists, artists, architects, and music hall performers. Notable figures in this cemetery include Attila József, Ödön Lechner, and Mihály Munkácsy. The graveled paths lead past columned arcades to angel-guarded tombstones and memorials and grand, neoclassical mausoleums. Most spectacular is the resting place of Lajos Kossuth, a revolutionary and the governor-president during the 1848 revolution against the Habsburgs. If you wander over to plot 21, you'll find graves belonging to those who died in the 1956 Uprising.

Pick up a free map at the cemetery entrance

to locate the noteworthy graves. There is also a small museum offering insight into the Hungarian approach to death and burials. If you want to see tradition in action, come on November 1 when the graves are lit up with tea lights and candles.

The Millennium Quarter

Take tram line 2 to the penultimate stop, Müpa-Nemzeti Színház, on the southern part of the Danube banks in Pest, and you'll come to a cultural corner built between 2001 and 2006 as part of an urban regeneration project. The Millennium Quarter is not only a cultural power hub—where you'll find the National Theatre, the Palace of Arts, and the Ludwig Museum in one spot—it's probably Budapest's most adventurous location for experimental modern architecture. You'll find a statue of a submerged "Greek" temple in the lake and a ziggurat overlooking the river.

PALACE OF ARTS
(Müpa)
Komor Marcell utca 1; tel. 06/1-555-3000;
www.mupa.hu; tram 2: Müpa – Nemzeti Színház
The Palace of Arts complex is the most important building in the Millennium cultural complex, award-winning for its cutting-edge design and simplicity. It kind of looks like a windswept box on the outside, and the interior blends a Herculean sense of space with lots of glass. It's like a cultural shopping mall, home to some of the city's most important cultural venues, including the cavernous Béla Bartók National Concert Hall, the Festival Theater, and the Ludwig Museum. The Palace of Arts has some of the best acoustics and sound technology in Europe, and its consistently impressive musical lineup is booked far in advance.

LUDWIG MUSEUM
Komor Marcell utca 1; tel. 06/1-555-3444;
www.ludwigmuseum.hu; Tue-Sun 8am-10pm;
HUF 1,600; tram 2: Müpa – Nemzeti Színház
The Ludwig Museum is inside the Palace of Arts. This contemporary art museum showcases Hungarian and international works.

You'll find an impressive Pop Art collection here, including pieces by Andy Warhol and Roy Liechtenstein, but most of the focus is on Central and Eastern European art. If you're passionate about modern art, it's worth the tram ride to this museum.

NATIONAL THEATRE
(Nemzeti Színház)
Bajor Gizi Park 1; tel. 06/1-476-6800; www.
nemzetiszinhaz.hu; tram 2: Müpa – Nemzeti Színház
The National Theatre exudes architectural drama before you even step inside. There is a small ziggurat between the main building and the Palace of Arts; you can wander up its spirals for views over the river. When viewed outside from the front, you'll notice the theater sits on the bow of a ship, which rises above a human-made moat—look for the submerged Grecian temple. You'll also see statues of Hungarian actors on the park grounds. Inside, the setting is a bit more humble compared to the dramatic exterior (but it's probably better not to get distracted while you're watching a play).

ÓBUDA
Aquincum
Szentendrei út 133-135; tel. 06/1-250-1650;
www.aquincum.hu; Tue-Sun 9am-6pm Apr-Oct,
open otherwise in dry conditions; HUF 1,900;
HÉV 5: Aquincum, bus 34, 106, 134: Záhony utca
Although Roman ruins are scattered around Óbuda, the main ruins are enclosed in the archaeological site of Aquincum, a Roman city built around AD 100, whose citizens numbered between 30,000 and 40,000 by the end of the 2nd century. Allegedly, Roman Emperor Marcus Aurelius penned part of his famous philosophical "Meditations" here in this Roman settlement.

You can follow in the footsteps of Roman society, winding through the excavated ruins, including a reconstruction of a painter's house, the hypocaust systems that once warmed bathhouses, and the worn-down stones once paving the marketplace and the forum. Stroll into the lapidary (with walls

Roman Budapest

The name Óbuda means "Old Buda," which is fitting, since this part of the city has its roots in antiquity. The Roman settlement of **Aquincum** is the most famous reminder of pre-Magyar Budapest, and you'll find Roman ruins scattered around Óbuda.

- Close to Flórián tér, hidden under unsightly overpasses, are the monumental ruins of the **Roman baths** (Flórián téri aluljáró; Tue-Sun 9am-6pm Apr-Oct, open otherwise in dry conditions; free) once belonging to the Roman military camp, accessible from the underpass.

- Travelers can also head over to the **Hercules Villa** (Meggyfa utca 21; Wed-Sun 11am-6pm Aug-Oct; HUF 500), named for the imported mosaic featuring the villa's namesake hero. The villa was discovered in the 1950s when workmen were digging foundations to build a school. There are seven rooms in the villa, accessible via a raised platform so you can get a good look at the mosaics, and there is also a museum and a garden where you'll find ancient ruins.

Other ruins in Budapest include the **amphitheater** close to Kolosy tér that once had the capacity for an audience of 15,000. There are also a few stones of **Contra-Aquincum,** the former Roman military camp in Pest, just below Elizabeth Bridge. Roman Hungary came to an end with Attila the Hun in the 5th century, five centuries before the Magyar tribes led by Árpád conquered the Carpathian Basin.

lined with stone carvings and tablets). Close to the entrance is a modern museum hall set in a former electrical transformer house, which contains excavated mosaic flooring, frescoes, statues, and dolphin-adorned fountains. The museum's most famous piece is the Aquincum organ, dating back to the 3rd century, on display 75 years after its excavation.

Kiscelli Museum

Kiscelli utca 108; tel. 06/1-250-0304; www.kiscellimuzeum.hu; Tue-Sun 10am-6pm Apr-Oct, Tue-Sun 10am-4pm Nov-Mar; HUF 1,600; tram 17, 19, 41: Selmeci utca

It's a significant hike to get to the Kiscelli Museum, which is located in a former 18th-century monastery. This canary-yellow building functioned as a barracks and a military hospital before being bought up by an antiques dealer whose final wishes were for the property to become a museum. The eclectic collection includes 19th-century trade signs and the contents of an entire apothecary once located in Pest. Life in 18th- to early-20th-century Budapest is depicted through antique furniture, sketches of the city, and art nouveau stained glass. Attached to the building is the

shell of an old church, used for contemporary exhibitions.

BUDA HILLS
Children's Railway

Gyermekvasút; tel. 06/1-397-5394; www.gyermekvasut.hu; Tue-Fri 9am-4pm in winter, daily 8:45am-5:45pm in summer; HUF 800; tram 56, 61: Hűvösvölgy, tram 60: Széchenyi-hegy, Gyermekvasút

This small railway line chugs along for just under 12 kilometers (7 mi) from Széchenyi-Hegy to Hűvösvölgy with stops in between. With the exception of the drivers and engineers, all the jobs on the railway line are staffed by school children aged 10-14, who sell and check tickets, signal, and salute passengers as the train pulls in and out of the station. The railway is a relic from the Communist era, built in 1951 to encourage a good work ethic. Today, the tradition continues but without the propaganda. The schools work together with the railway, permitting students with a good academic record to miss the odd day of school to work here. Riding from one end to the other takes 45-50 minutes; the trip goes through the woods and around the Buda Hills. Buy a ticket and go from one end to the other, enjoying the view, or get off along the way and hike a bit.

To reach each end of the railway, either take the 56 or 61 tram to the end of the line at Hűvösvölgy and take the steps up to the station, or opt for the scenic route by taking the cogwheel railway (tram 60, which runs on the public transportation line) up into the hills to Széchenyi-Hegy from Városmajor.

Elizabeth Lookout

daily 8am-8pm; free; bus 291: Zugliget, Libegő

Hike up the highest point in Budapest, János Hill (János-hegy), which rises about 520 meters (1,700 ft) above sea level. At the top of the hill you'll reach the Elizabeth Lookout point, a neo-Romanesque tower with 134 steps leading to incredible views across Budapest and surroundings. If it's a clear day, you might even spot the Tatra Mountains in Slovakia in the distance. Should the tower look familiar, that's because it was designed by the same architect who constructed Fisherman's Bastion in the Castle District.

To get here, get off from the Children's Railway at the János-Hegy stop, or if you're feeling adventurous, take the 291 bus from Nyugati train station to the final stop, Zugliget-Libegő, and take the chairlift (HUF 1,200 one-way, HUF 1,600 round-trip) to the base of the tower (expect to queue on sunny weekends). The climb takes around 15 minutes, and you can use the chairlift year-round from 10am-dusk (3:30pm in the winter to 7pm in the high summer).

Note that on Mondays on even-numbered weeks, it's closed for maintenance (with the exception of public holidays).

GREATER BUDAPEST
★ Memento Park

Balatoni út-Szabadkai utca sarok; tel. 06/1-424-7500; www.mementopark.hu; daily 10am-dusk; HUF 1,500; bus 150: Memento Park

Memento Park is a cross between an open-air museum and a graveyard for Communist statues and street propaganda. Following the fall of the regime, all the statues and propaganda were removed from the city and relocated to this plot of land, which was transformed into a public outdoor museum in the early 1990s. It's a trek to reach, but the excursion up into the XII District's Buda Hills is worth it. Take the **shuttle bus** (daily 11am Apr-Oct, Mon and Sat Nov-Mar; HUF 4,900 round-trip including entry, HUF 3,900 if you book online) from Deák Ferenc Square, a central transport hub on the border of the Inner City and the Jewish Quarter, which returns at 1pm. Or take the 150 bus from Újbuda or the Kelenföld train station.

The Children's Railway is one of the top sites up in the Buda Hills.

It's impossible to miss the imposing gate marking the entrance—a monumental red-brick structure that looks like a socialist caricature of a Greek temple. As you approach the ticket office, socialist songs and communist hymns blast out from the small kiosk. Beyond the kiosk, the walled park contains bronze statues and placards of propaganda. Statues of Hungarian Communist leaders stand side by side with the likes of Lenin and Soviet soldiers. István Kiss's "Republic of Councils Monument" is a behemoth of a sculpture inspired by an avant-garde propaganda poster meant to encourage military recruitment. (The figure looks as if he is sprinting.) On your way out of the park, stop by the time-traveling phone booth, where you can dial in the year and listen to the voices of Communist leaders like Stalin and Béla Kun.

Opposite the park, a replica of the gigantic boots once belonging to a statue of Stalin hold a place on a giant grandstand. Inside, there is a bunker with a few statues and busts of Lenin. Between the statue park and Stalin's boots, there is a barracks-style building with a museum inside, dedicated to the history and the fall of Communism in Hungary. To the right of the entrance, you can sit down to watch a subtitled movie screening of secret police training films from Hungary's Communist era, with interesting insights like how to equip a handbag with a hidden camera.

Thermal Baths

TOP EXPERIENCE

Budapest's thermal baths are a perfect antidote for its wild nightlife. They are a must-do on any visit to Budapest.

At least one section of a bath complex must be filled with natural thermal water to qualify as a thermal bath. Each bath has thermal pools at different temperatures, ranging from cool plunge pools to hot pools (placards recommend staying in for less than 10 minutes), and then a main pool that's usually around body temperature (the recommended bathing time is usually 30-40 minutes). Some thermal baths will also have a swimming pool, saunas, and a wellness area. Massages are offered for an extra charge.

You'll find two categories of baths in Budapest—the baths built by Turks when Hungary was occupied by the Ottoman Empire, and the grand baths built in the late 19th and early 20th centuries. The **Turkish baths** (also called Ottoman Baths) are similar to those you'd find in Turkey, with pin-pricked cupola domes and octagonal pools; but unlike the hammams in Istanbul, the Budapest baths have a plunge pool rather than a marble slab where you're scrubbed down, soaped, and massaged. These baths date back as far as the 16th century. The later **19th-20th-century baths** followed hot on the heels of Central Europe's bathing cure craze; consider Baden-Baden in Germany, or Karlovy Vary in the Czech Republic. Their grandiose baths have complexes indoors and outdoors, often ornamented with neoclassical statues or art nouveau tiling, and you'll find large swimming pools, sauna complexes, and bathing terraces.

THE BATH EXPERIENCE
What to Bring

A few things are smart to bring with you to the baths:

- Bring your own **swimsuit** to Budapest. If you forget your swimsuit, some complexes allow you to rent them, along with towels and bathrobes.

- It's a good idea to pack a pair of **shower slippers** for hygienic reasons, but if you forget them, most baths rent them out as well.

- If you plan to use the swimming pools attached to the baths, make sure you wear a

Choosing a Bath

It's no accident Budapest has earned the nickname "City of Spas." Below the city are over 100 geothermal springs, each with its own mineral profile. There is a bath in Budapest for everyone's taste, whether you want to bathe in a historic monument or go where the locals go.

MOST FAMOUS

The **Széchenyi Baths** is Budapest's largest and most famous thermal bath complex. Go for the stunning columned outdoor pools. Stay because you find out there are even more pools indoors (page 382). This bath is well known for its wild Sparties on Saturday nights.

LOCAL FAVORITE

Laid-back **Lukács** is popular with locals for its understated turn-of-the-century elegance, pump room, and the healing properties of the water (page 384). In the winter, Lukács takes over as host for the Saturday night Sparties.

BEST FOR FAMILIES

Open-air and seasonal, the **Római Open-Air Baths** are popular with kids thanks to the jungle of waterslides there (page 386).

MOST OPULENT

The **Gellért Baths** are an art nouveau architectural treasure (page 385).

BEST BATHING IN THE BUFF

If you go to the **Rudas** on weekdays, the bath is single-sex, and although you won't need a swimsuit, you will be given a loin cloth you need to wear. (The bath is now trying to cut down on full nudity.) Women's days are Tuesdays and men's are Mondays, Wednesdays, Thursdays all day, and Friday mornings (page 384).

QUIETEST TURKISH BATH

You can easily miss the entrance to the **Veli Bej** because you have to enter a hospital to get to this hidden Turkish bath, newly renovated for the 21st century (page 384).

BEST BUDGET OPTION

For a simple thermal bath experience, the **Dandár** is a great choice if you're pinching pennies (page 385).

swimming cap, which you can usually buy at reception, or bring your own (even a shower cap will do).

Buying Tickets

When you buy your ticket, you'll get a wristband that lets you into the bath complex and is used to open and close your locker or cabin (so you can change and lock up your things in the same place). Some baths may offer different ticket packages, like a basic ticket that's only for the thermal section or the swimming pool, while others may charge a surplus for the

sauna. Massages, on the other hand, require an appointment, so if you want one, ask when you're buying your ticket.

Bath Etiquette

Make sure you shower before dipping into the pools and relaxing in the steam, whether you're indoors or outdoors.

Apart from the Rudas baths on weekdays (which is women-only on Tuesdays, and men the rest of the week), the baths are open for both men and women. And although there is no hard and fast rule, they are not recommended for anyone under the age of 14. At the time of writing, the thermal baths were closed due to COVID-19. Check the websites before going to check for opening and any safety measures or restrictions that may apply. Unless you're at one of the infamous spa parties, also known as "Sparties" (www.spartybooking.com; from €50; over 18s only) which are usually ticketed and take place Saturday night at the Széchenyi Baths or the Lukács Baths, Budapest's thermal baths are a place of healing, so try not to be too noisy or splash about, unless you're in one of the outdoor swimming pools.

The best time to go is first thing in the morning before breakfast, as the baths are the cleanest at this point, and you'll beat most of the crowds. Some of the quieter baths, like the Veli Bej, are cozy on a winter's evening.

If you have any health concerns, like a heart condition, it's best to consult your healthcare provider about taking the waters in Budapest.

CASTLE DISTRICT
Király Bath

Fő u. 84; tel. 06-1-202-3688; http://en.kiralyfurdo.hu; daily 9am-9pm; HUF 2,400-2,900; tram 41, 19: Bem József tér

Built by the Turks over 450 years ago, Király Bath is Budapest's oldest operational thermal bath. Its cupola covers an octagonal pool surrounded by crumbling plaster and exposed brickwork. While the Király Bath is in desperate need of a renovation (the last one was completed in the 1950s to fix the damage from World War II), it still merits a visit. Steam hovers above its three thermal pools and its icy immersion pool. A coating of mineral deposits covers the rim of the main bath from decades (perhaps centuries) of mineral water, which pours out of a vintage iron tap in the central pool. Rich in calcium, magnesium, hydrogen-carbonate, and sulfate, with a dash of sodium and the odd fluoride ion, the water is said to soothe conditions such as degenerative joint disease and chronic arthritis.

Following the reoccupation of Buda from the Ottomans, the König family acquired the bath at the end of the 18th century. It's smaller and grittier than the other baths, but many love it for its authenticity. It's the cheapest of the historic baths, so it draws in a more local crowd, mixed with a few tourists. The Király Bath is open to both men and women, and it's a good alternative to the Rudas Baths, which are single-sex on weekdays.

At the time of writing, there were plans to close the Király Baths for renovation, so they may not be open during your visit.

CITY PARK AND AROUND
★ Széchenyi Baths

Állatkerti körút 11; tel. 06/1-363-3210; www.szechenyibath.hu; daily 6am-7pm; HUF 6,200 on weekends, HUF 5,900 on weekdays; metro 1: Széchenyi fürdő

Canary-yellow walls accented by Ionian columns and sculptures of bathing nymphs and youths riding dolphins surround the large turquoise pools of the Széchenyi Baths. Built between 1909 and 1913, it's one of the largest bath complexes of its kind. Once you've explored the 13 indoor pools and the labyrinthine changing rooms above and below the three outdoor pools, it's easy to see why this elegant and relaxing place is so popular.

There are three public entrances to the baths. One main entrance faces the zoo and the circus and has a rococo-inspired entrance hall; the second faces the park and shows off even more opulence, with gold-tipped frescoes and Secessionist ceramics. The third entrance is hidden on the side by the metro. All three entrances are part of the same ticket, but the type of cabin varies, as the baths were initially built with the interior side and its entrance for the aristocracy and upper classes, and the exterior part for the masses.

The complex also includes luxury massage facilities. The all-inclusive Palm House spa (HUF 34,500) can be found in the rooftop greenhouse. There is even a beer spa (HUF 15,700 combined ticket for a beer spa

---

1: the Gellért Baths 2: the famous Széchenyi Baths

1

2

and entry to the baths) where you can lie in a wooden tub filled with hops, malt, yeast, and aromas—and pull your own pints from a separate keg as you soak.

MARGARET ISLAND AND AROUND
Lukács Thermal Bath

Frankel Leó út 25-29; tel. 06/1-326-1695; http:// en.lukacsfurdo.hu; daily 6am-10pm; HUF 3,900 on weekends, HUF 3,500 on weekdays, HUF 800 Sauna World supplement; tram 17, 19, 41: Szent Lukács Gyógyfürdő

Although it may lack the grandeur of the Széchenyi and Gellért baths or the history of the Turkish Baths, this tranquil 19th-century thermal bath is the place locals come to relax with a dose of old-world nostalgia.

To enter the complex, take a stroll through the garden that's next door to the Orfi Hospital, past the placards on the walls from grateful patients whose ailments were cured by the mineral rich water.

Once past the turnstiles, a tiled labyrinth links to the changing rooms and down to a courtyard where you can plunge into two frigid swimming pools. In another courtyard, a warm activity pool bubbles from massaging jets and a circular current.

Indoors, the thermal baths are compact, with dark marble columns and neoclassical statues. Each pool is heated to a different temperature. The water is piped in from one of the world's largest thermal water caves, located just across and under the road, and the pools give off a slight sulfurous whiff. For HUF 600 on weekdays and HUF 800 on weekends, you can access "Sauna World," which includes several types of saunas, a salt cabin, a steam room, and cooling pools where fresh ice is dropped in periodically thanks to a handy automated slide.

Veli Bej Bath

Árpád Fejedelem útja 7; tel. 06/1-438-8587; daily 6am-noon, 3pm-9pm; HUF 3,100; tram 17, 19, 41: Komjádi Béla utca

From the street, it's easy to miss this Turkish bath, as it's hidden behind the glass windows of a rheumatological hospital. The entrance to the bath is through the hospital. Once inside, you'll see a sign that looks like a number counter, which is used when the bath is full (usually on weekend afternoons). If you have the patience to wait around 15-20 minutes, pick a number and wait in the café by the ticket counter. The waiting list system ensures that the bath will never be overcrowded.

Once you're through the ticket office and the changing room, the hospital corridors will lead you into the historic bath complex, built in the 16th century by the Turks. What's different about the Veli Bej Bath is that it's been recently renovated; in place of crumbling stone walls, you'll find fresh paint in clean white and salmon tones. The main octagonal pool is flanked by four chambers, each with a single pool at different temperatures. Pop outdoors between the bath and the hospital to the sauna cabins, where you'll see the original Turkish bath structure in its glory, or head to the corridor on the side to view remains of Ottoman excavations.

SOUTH BUDA
Rudas Thermal Baths

Döbrentei tér 9; tel. 06/1-356-1322; http:// en.rudasfurdo.hu; Turkish bath daily 6am-10pm, wellness center daily 8am-10pm; HUF 3,800 Turkish bath on all days, HUF 6,900 combined ticket for Turkish bath, wellness center, and swimming pool on weekends and HUF 5,500 on weekdays; tram 19, 41, 56: Rudas Gyógyfürdő

Out of all the Turkish Baths, the Rudas Thermal Bath is indisputably the most popular. The complex is composed of three parts: the 16th-century bath built by the Ottoman Turks, the 19th-century colonnaded swimming pool, and the 21st-century wellness center. The old Turkish part of the bath is "nudist," but you will get a loin cloth you need to wear to cover your private parts, and it's single-sex bathing only on weekdays (Tuesdays for women, others for men). On the weekend and Fridays after 1 pm when the bath is mixed, swimsuits are compulsory. Expect long queues if you go on the weekends. Bathing under the cupola, with light shining through its stained glass, it's easy to see why this bath has become so popular.

On the other side, a beautiful swimming pool (filled partly with thermal water) looks more like a Roman bath than a place to take a few laps. The wellness center uses the same water as the Turkish part, from the slightly radioactive Juventus spring, which is said to have anti-aging properties. The pools downstairs are clean, modern, and can be less crowded than the Turkish baths. (And they are open to both sexes throughout the week.) The main draw is the rooftop whirlpool tub that overlooks the Danube.

Gellért Thermal Baths

Kelenhegyi út 4; tel. 06/1-466-6166; www.gellertbath. hu; daily 6am-8pm; HUF 6,200 on weekends, HUF 5,900 on weekdays; metro 4, tram 19, 41, 47, 48, 49, 56: Szent Gellért tér

On the southern slopes of Gellért Hill, the Gellért Thermal Baths capture the grandeur of Budapest's golden age at the turn of the 20th century. The bath complex may be smaller than the vast Széchenyi, but there's plenty on offer both inside and outside.

The main pool lies enclosed in an atrium with Roman-style columns and a glass rooftop. Inside the thermal baths, steam drips off the aquamarine Zsolnay tiles that ornament the indoor thermal pools. Of the outdoor pools, the highlight is the main pool, which still uses a wave machine on the hour (it dates back to 1927) and was one of the very first of its kind. In total there are eight thermal pools ranging from 19°C (66°F) to 38°C (100°F), as well as cool plunge pools and swimming pools.

Gellért draws its water from beneath Gellért Hill—there is a hidden tunnel (not open to the public) running under the hotel and the hill going all the way to the Rudas Baths.

Aside from the medicinal waters and art nouveau splendor, the baths also offer a variety of treatments like mud baths and carbon dioxide baths, a range of massages, and more.

OTHER THERMAL BATHS

Sometimes the more popular baths can get a little crowded. If you want to escape the tourist crowds, try these alternatives.

Margaret Island and Around
PALATINUS

Margitsziget, tel; 06/1-340-4500; http://en.palatinusstrand.hu; daily 8am-8pm; HUF 3,600 on weekends, HUF 3,200 on weekdays; bus 26: Palatinus fürdő

The Palatinus, an open-air thermal complex surrounded by trees, was once the go-to spot during the summer on Margaret Island. Since its renovation in 2017, this art deco bath has extended the invitation to visitors year-round. The thermal water here comes from below the island.

South Pest
DANDÁR

Dandár utca 5-7; tel. 06/1-215-7084; http://en.dandarfurdo.hu; Mon-Fri 6am-9pm, Sat-Sun 8am-9pm; HUF 2,100 thermal bath, HUF 2,600 wellness center and thermal bath; tram 2: Haller utca/Soroksári út

Just behind the Unicum factory in South Pest, you'll notice a brick building on the side street. The Dandár is a small, no-frills thermal bath with two thermal pools indoors. It's popular with locals for medicinal purposes. (There are two outdoor heated pools in the garden, but they don't use thermal water.)

Greater Budapest
PASKÁL

Egressy út 178; tel. 06/1-252-6944; http://en.paskalfurdo.hu; daily 6am-8pm; HUF 3,000; bus 77, 82: Egressy út/Vezér utca

The Paskál Thermal and Open-Air Bath lies far out in residential Zugló and is popular with the locals for its blend of indoor spa with thermal water and outdoor swimming pool. The most attractive feature is the bubbling activity pool that spans both the inside and outside, with the exterior part leading right to a swim-up bar.

RÓMAI

Rozgonyi Piroska utca 2; tel. 06/1-388-9740; http://en.romaistrand.hu; daily 9am-8pm Jun-Sep; HUF 2,800 on weekends, HUF 2,500 on weekdays; HÉV 5, bus 34, 134: Rómaifürdő

Római Open-Air Baths get their name from the Romans, who used the thermal water in the area to supply the baths in Aquincum. Today, this modern outdoor swimming pool also uses the lukewarm water rich in minerals, but unlike other thermal baths, this open-air seasonal bath is popular with kids, thanks to its jungle of waterslides.

Recreation and Activities

PARKS

Budapest has a lot of green spaces, from the woods in the Buda Hills to more mainstream spots like Margaret Island and City Park.

CITY PARK
(Városliget)

Metro 1: Széchenyi fürdő

City Park branches out from the end of Andrássy Avenue and Heroes' Square and extends for more than a kilometer (about a mile) to Ajtósi Dürer sor on the other end. The park itself has evolved over history, along with its name, and is still transforming today with the city's plans to install a new museum quarter (scheduled to open in 2022). It's a popular place for recreation, with the Széchenyi Baths, the zoo, a circus, a lake that's open for boating in the summer and ice skating in the winter, and its own castle, **Vajdahunyad Castle**. The surrounding area is residential—you'll find romantic turreted villas and art nouveau wonders around Stefánia út.

MARGARET ISLAND

Tram 4, 6: Margit Sziget

The island, 2.5 kilometers (1.5 mi) long, is mostly made up of parkland. Apart from a couple of hotels, ruins, thermal baths, and swimming pools, the stretch is populated with green lawns, wooded areas, and spots that are perfect for a small tennis or soccer match with friends. There is a small Japanese garden to the north and a rose garden in the middle. If you want to find a good picnic spot, take the 4 or 6 tram to Margit Sziget, walk the bridge to the musical fountain, and set your blanket down there. The great thing about the island is that any spot is wonderful for lounging in the grass with friends.

PHILOSOPHER'S GARDEN

bus 8E, 27, 108E, 110, 112: Sánc utca

Halfway up Gellért Hill—if you turn right at the statue rather than take the path to the Citadel—you'll find the Philosopher's Garden, named for sculptures representing figures like Gandhi, Jesus, and Lao-Tsu, among others. It's a peaceful patch of green with views over Buda Castle and the river. On the weekends, you'll find people on picnicking and maybe practicing yoga here.

HIKING

Get out of the chaos of the city and explore a side of Budapest that's a world away from the ruin bars.

KECSKE HEGY

Distance (round-trip): *4 km (2.5 mi)*
Duration (round-trip): *2-3 hours*
Effort: *moderate*
Trailhead: *Nagybányai út bus stop*

Take the 11 bus to the end of the line (the ride lasts 25 minutes from Batthyány tér) for hikes up around Kecske Hegy (Goat Hill). Get off at the final stop, Nagybányai út, and you should see trails marked on the trees—take the one that looks like a green arrow in a circle, which indicates a round-trip. One of the most popular sites on this trail is the **Lion's Rock** (Oroszlánszikla), which resembles a lion. Nearby is the rock-covered **Goat Hill** (Kecskehegy), which makes for some great active hiking with some boulder climbing thrown in. Make sure you stop and look back, because the panorama is spectacular.

ELIZABETH LOOKOUT

Distance (round-trip): *4 km (3 mi)*
Duration (round-trip): *1 hour*
Effort: *easy*
Trailhead: *Normafa bus stop*

Take the 21 or 21A bus for approximately half an hour from Széll Kálmán to Normafa for hikes up to Elizabeth Lookout Tower, the highest point in the city. You can see most of the city, the Danube, the surrounding Buda Hills, and on clear days, you can sometimes even see the Mátra Mountains (Hungary's highest range) 80km away. It's an easy 2.5-kilometer (1.5-mi) hike and takes about half an hour to reach.

Around the lookout, you'll find another trail that leads an additional 2.5 kilometers down to **Tündér Szikla** (Fairy Rock), a rocky outcrop with magical views over the Buda Hills and the valley below. If you feel tired after climbing up to the lookout tower, go back to town by taking either the chairlift down (HUF 1,200, free with the Budapest Card) or the **Children's Railway.**

HÁRMASHATÁR HEGY

Distance (round-trip): *14 km (8 mi)*
Duration (round-trip): *3.5-4 hours*
Effort: *moderate*
Trailhead: *Fenyőgyöngye Vendéglő (Inn)*

Hármashatár Hegy (Three Border Hill, named after its location between Buda, Óbuda, and the town of Pesthidegkút) lies in the northern suburbs of the Buda Hills and is one of the most popular hiking destinations in the city, especially as it links up with the Country Blue Trail (a hiking trail that crosses the entire country). It's one of Budapest's highest points (495 m/1623 ft above sea level), making it popular with paragliders as well as hikers. Towering above the northern part of city, it affords views over the Danube, the Buda Hills, and the surrounding Pilis Hills.

The trail takes you to the top of the hill, and the meadows and woodland surrounding it. To reach it, take the 65 bus from Kolosy tér to Fenyőgyöngye (the last stop) and take the trail going up past the Fenyőgyöngye Inn. The easiest way to start is to follow the road marked Hármashatárhegyi út to the Gückler Károly lookout tower, where you'll be treated to incredible views over the city. For a more scenic detour, follow the blue markings on the trees on the left-hand side of the road (this is part of the famous Blue Trail that crosses the country) uphill, which will also take you to the **lookout tower** at the top of the hill.

Continue following the blue symbols as you go down the hill, descending steeply before the trail rises again slightly into a meadow. Cross the clearing to reach **Calvary Hill,** one of the most beautiful spots in the Buda Hills, overlooking the Pilis Hills in the distance. From here, the green symbols lead back to the Hármashatár Hegy parking lot, from which you can take the path back to the bus stop where you began.

CYCLING

For the best cycle-side views, head over to the 27-kilometer (17-mi) bike trail running along the Danube to the picturesque town of Szentendre (page 444). Margaret Island is also a good spot to take a bike—cars are banned from most of the island. You can pick up a MOL BuBi bike on the Buda or Pest side and ride to the island. There are numerous paved paths on the island you can use for cycling.

Bike-Sharing and Rentals

MOL BUBI

https://molbubi.bkk.hu

Budapest is popular with cyclists. Anywhere in the center, you may notice lime green MOL BuBi bike stations. You can operate the MOL

BuBi system by simply using your cell phone. At a MOL BuBi station, follow the instructions to buy a ticket. Your credit card will be charged the rental fee, along with a HUF 25,000 deposit (released when you return your bike). Once you've bought your ticket, you will get a PIN code on your phone (see the website for complete instructions). Return the bike at any of the docking stations in the city. You have the option of buying a ticket for 24 hours (HUF 500), 72 hours (HUF 1,000), or one week (HUF 2,000), which gets you 30 minutes free cycling time. Beyond that there are usage fees that go up the longer you use the bike (60 minutes HUF 500, 2 hours HUF 1,500—see the website for full fares).

BRINGOHINTÓ

Hajós Alfréd sétany 1; www.bringohinto.hu

If you're in a group, renting a quadracycle is a fun way to explore Margaret Island. Bringohintó can rent them on a half-hour (HUF 2,880) or hourly basis (HUF 4,280).

BEACHES

Hungary might be a landlocked country, but it makes the most of its water. The Danube is no exception. Although the Danube is dangerous to swim in due to the powerful undercurrents (and it's illegal in most parts as well), you can still relax by the water and spend an afternoon at the beach. If you take a boat up the Danube, further up the Danube Bend, you'll see small, private beaches with one or two people who got there by canoe or bicycle. But you don't need to seek out isolated spots to enjoy Danube beaches; check out the venues listed here.

RÓMAI PART

HÉV 5, boat 11, 12: Rómaifürdő

Head out to the north part of Buda in the summer to Római Part, a stretch of embankment with pebbly beaches leading gently into the river. Locals bring beach towels and have picnics. There are cordoned-off paddling areas to enjoy (the net will stop you from going further into the river). You'll find bars, street food, and riverside cafés along this leafy stretch of the Danube. You can take the 34 or 106 bus over from Lehel tér (you can reach this by metro 3). In the summer, take the BKK boat service from any of the downtown docks, like Battyány tér, Várkert Bazár, or Kossuth Lajos tér (or head to the beginning of the line like Kopaszi gát or the National Theatre) for HUF 750.

KOPASZI DAM

Boat 11, 12: Kopaszi gát, Buda part, tram 1: Infopark

On the other end of Buda, far south from Római Part, Kopaszi Gát (Kopaszi Dam, tram 1) is a small stretch of land that juts out, dotted with parkland and cafés and bistros. There is a sandy beach in the bay area of the dam, and while it's protected from the main flow of the Danube, swimming can still be risky here. It's closer than Római Part to the city center, so it's more convenient if you don't want to head far into the Óbuda suburbs. I personally like this beach area for its unique setting—the walk down the dam is beautiful, with trees, trendy modern bistros with terraces with waterside views, and a view overlooking the enclosed bay where you can see little boats sailing under the shadow of the old power station. Kopaszi Gát looks its best at the golden hour just before sunset.

LUPA TÓ

HÉV 5: Budakalász

Lupa Tó (lake) lies outside Budapest toward the town of Szentendre. In the past couple of years, it's been the go-to beach for Budapest denizens. This lake has crystal-clear water and has been revamped with sandy beaches and palm trees. In the VIP Lupa Beach section you can rent a waterside curtain-draped double sunbed with pillow from HUF 4,000, where you can sit back and sip a cocktail. Another part of the lake, known as Öböl Beach, is

---

1: Margaret Island 2: In the winter, the lake in City Park becomes a popular ice rink. 3: Elizabeth Lookout Tower on János-hegy 4: Kopaszi Dam is a popular summer spot for water sports and Danube beaches.

simpler and better if you're on a budget. On the weekends entrance to Öböl Beach is HUF 1,500 (weekdays HUF 1,000); for the VIP Lupa Beach area, HUF 3,900 (weekdays HUF 2,900).

CAVE TOURS AND SPELUNKING

Because of an abundance of underground water, Budapest has a secret subterranean world, making the Hungarian capital the world's only city with numerous natural caves running beneath it. There are around 200 caves under Budapest. You can pay a visit to the show caves in the Buda Hills, or go underneath Buda Castle to the labyrinth below—but if you want to get down and dirty, you can also slide through honeycomb-like holes and tunnels on a spelunking expedition. If you plan on visiting the caves, it's a good idea to wear layers (it's around 12°C/54°F in the caves) and closed-toed shoes with a grip.

Cave Tours

The Pálvölgyi Caves and Szemlőhegyi Caves are located relatively close to one another and can be visited on a combined ticket (HUF 3,100). **Caving Under Budapest** (www. caving.hu) provides private English-language

walking tours (HUF 6,000) of these two caves as well.

PÁLVÖLGYI CAVES

Szépvölgyi út 162; tel. 06/1-325-9505; www.dunaipoly.hu/hu/helyek/bemutatohelyek/ pal-volgyi-barlang; Tue-Sun 10am-4pm, tours at quarter past the hour; HUF 1,950; bus 65, 65A: Pál-völgyi cseppkőbarlang

Located in the Buda Hills, the Pálvölgyi cave system takes you through a labyrinth of chambers filled with stalactites and stalagmites, going as deep as 30 meters (98 feet) underground. You can only visit the caves on the 45-minute walking tour, which is given in Hungarian, but it's possible to request a sheet with information in English, and guides can answer questions in English. While much of the show cave is paved, there are times when it will be necessary to scale up a ladder. (But you won't need to get on your hands and knees and get dirty.)

SZEMLŐHEGYI CAVES

Pusztaszeri út 35; tel. 06/1-325-6001; www.dunaipoly. hu/hu/helyek/bemutatohelyek/szemlo-hegyi-barlang; Wed-Mon 10am-4pm, tours on the hour; HUF 1,950; bus 29: Szemlő-hegyi-barlang

Floret-like mineral and crystalline deposits

Up in the Buda Hills, you can join a caving tour with a guide and go spelunking.

coat the cave walls here (created by thermal water coming in from below), which has earned this cave system the nickname "Underwater Flower Garden." It is the most accessible of Budapest's caves. The lower level is sometimes used as a respiratory sanitorium because of its pure air. It needs to be visited on a guided 35- to 45-minute walking tour in Hungarian, but most guides speak English and can answer questions. No climbing or tight spots with this one.

Spelunking and Cave Diving

For subterranean diving, head out to the submerged part of the former Kőbánya stone mine and beer factory and go on a 40-minute dive with **Paprika Divers** (www.paprikadivers.com; €50 not including gear rental).

MÁTYÁSHEGY CAVES

162 Szépvölgyi út; www.caving.hu;

bus 65, 65A: Pál-völgyi cseppkőbarlang

Opposite the Pálvölgy Cave system, just on the other side of Szépvögyi út, is the Mátyáshegy cave network. You'll need a guide to explore these caves, and you'll also need to change into a caving suit and wear a hard hat with a built-in lamp. **Caving Under Budapest** will take you on a three-hour subterranean adventure (HUF 10,000 pp), where you can expect tight squeezes and rock climbing, as well as lots of wriggling on the cave floor. Make sure you book in advance. Although tours run daily, they can fill up quickly, and there is an age limit of 10-55.

MOLNÁR JÁNOS CAVE

www.mjcave.hu

Just a few feet away from the Lukács Baths and the Danube is the Molnár János Cave, which is the largest known active thermal water cave, stretching over 6 kilometers (4 mi); it's filled with water that reaches 27°C (80°F) in places. If you want to take it to another level and you're a qualified cave diver or you have an open-water diving certificate, you can dive here from €60 (for the 50-min cave intro dive, not including dive gear

rental). It's only possible to visit these caves on the diving tour.

BOATING
CITY PARK LAKE

Olof Palme sétány 5; tel. 06/1-261-5209; www. mujegpalya.hu; daily 10am-9pm; metro 1: Hősök tere

In the summer, the lake in City Park turns into a pleasure lake where you can rent a rowboat (HUF 1,800 for 30 min), a canoe (HUF 1,800 for 30 minutes), or a water bicycle (HUF 2,600 for 30 min) for up to four people, and you can gaze at the turrets of Vajdahunyad Castle. Bear in mind that opening hours depend on the weather, and if you're coming between seasons, check the website or give them a call. You'll find a mix of families, friends, and couples boating on the lake on hot sunny days. (Note that the water is unfit for swimming and life jackets are not provided.)

ICE SKATING
CITY PARK ICE RINK

Olof Palme sétány 5; tel. 06/1-363-2673; www.mujegpalya.hu; metro 1: Hősök tere

In the winter, the lake in City Park freezes over and becomes one of Europe's largest open-air ice rinks. With the romantic Vajdahunyad Castle as the backdrop, it's probably one of the most beautiful ice rinks, too. If you're visiting Budapest between December-February, it's a fun place to spend an hour or two. You can buy tickets (HUF 1,500 weekdays, HUF 2,000 weekends) online to skip the queue, and you can also rent skates (HUF 1,800) on-site.

HOTEL PRESIDENT ICE RINK

From the ice rink on top of the Hotel President, you can see the Postal Savings Bank and the Hungarian Parliament Building in the distance. Entrance to the terrace costs HUF 900 (free for hotel guests), and you can rent skates (HUF 490) on the rooftop. The 110-square-meter (1,200-sq-ft) ice rink is made of synthetic ice—good if you're a novice skater. You'll find a mix of locals with kids skating alongside hotel guests. Between skating sessions, grab some mulled wine and a beigli (a rolled Hungarian pastry filled with walnuts or poppy seeds) from the wooden hut beside the ice rink and just take in the view from one of the tables at the terrace.

TOURS

BUDAPEST FREE WALKING TOURS

www.triptobudapest.hu

Familiarize yourself with the city with a free walking tour with Budapest Free Walking Tours. The tours have a number of interesting themes, like Communist Budapest, and there's one of the Jewish Quarter.

TASTE HUNGARY

www.tastehungary.com; $79-110 for culinary tours

Tours with Taste Hungary whet the appetite by exploring the culinary side of Budapest through food and culture walks. There's plenty to choose from, whether you want a market tour, dinner walk, or something more niche, like their coffeehouse walk or Jewish culinary tour.

CONTEXT TRAVEL

www.contexttravel.com; $59-66 to join a group tour

Context Travel caters to the intellectual traveler. The company offers tours of Budapest given by historians and academics, providing alternative insight into the city and covering specific topics like architecture, politics, conflict, and culture. They also provide more general orientation tours of the Jewish Quarter and the Castle District.

BUDAPEST FLOW

www.budapestflow.com; €45 pp per tour

If you want to explore an alternative side of the city, Budapest Flow takes you around the ruin bars or through the more interesting, nontouristy parts of the city, like the heart of the gentrifying VIII District.

CLASSES

CHEFPARADE COOKING BUDAPEST

www.cookingbudapest.com

Learn all about Hungarian cooking hands-on with ChefParade Cooking Budapest. First, you'll visit the Central Market Hall to buy the best produce. Then, you'll learn how to cook three Hungarian dishes. Courses (including the market tour) last around 4.5 hours and cost around €100 per person.

Bars and Nightlife

Many tourists come to Budapest for the ruin bars, and it used to be impossible to avoid costumed groups of bachelor and bachelorette parties in the Jewish Quarter. Sadly, ruin bars are a dying breed, especially with the onset of the coronavirus in 2020, which hit the entire nightlife scene hard. In the summer of 2020, nightlife shifted outdoors to terraces and "kerts" ("gardens" in Hungarian). It's hard to say how Budapest's nightlife will bounce back post-COVID, but venues with outdoor spaces do seem most likely to survive.

When planning a night on the town, it's a good idea to bring plenty of cash—many bars won't take cards, though some of the larger ruin bars like Szimpla Kert or Fogas Ház have ATMs. You'll only come across cover fees for club nights, concerts, or special events. But expect to have your bag searched by bouncers at the door on busy nights. (They want to make sure you're not smuggling alcohol in.)

A glass of beer will cost around HUF 500-1,000 depending on the bar, beer, and size (you can get a pohár, a 300 ml/10 oz glass, or a korsó, a large 500 ml/17 oz beer glass). Cocktails tend to range around HUF 2,500-3,500. Some bars serve bar snacks like pogácsa, a savory cheese or herb scone that helps soak up the booze. Aside from beer, wine, and cocktails, popular spirits include pálinka, a fiery fruit brandy served as a shot, and a bitter herbal liquor called Unicum.

NIGHTLIFE DISTRICTS

You'll find most of the nightlife clustered around the **Jewish Quarter,** which also has the nickname the bulinegyed ("party district") for its density of bars. **Kazinczy utca** (metro 2, tram 47, 48, 49: Astoria), the main nightlife hub, is home to Szimpla Kert and other popular bars, along with **Király** (trams 4, 6: Király utca) near Deák Ferenc tér. Also near Deák Ferenc tér, **Gozsdu Court** (Gozsdu udvar), a series of interconnected courtyards filled with restaurants and bars, is another of the neighborhood's hubs.

RUIN BARS

Set inside crumbling, semi-abandoned buildings filled with eclectic furniture and local art, ruin bars are unique to Budapest. Many bear the name "kert" ("garden" in Hungarian), as some ruin bars pop up in empty plots in the city, serving as urban sanctuaries during the day and party hubs at night. Ruin bars also host cultural events, like farmers markets, movie screenings, or charitable cooking drives. You'll find most of these bars concentrated around the heart of the Jewish Quarter but there are a few beyond it, too.

In recent years the expanding gentrification in the Jewish Quarter and beyond has closed many of these bars down—a situation exacerbated by the coronavirus pandemic. Only a handful remain, along with a few new inauthentic "ruin bars" that have been artificially gutted to mimic the aesthetic. Even the original VII District ruin bars have turned into a tourist attraction, and are eschewed by locals as tourist traps. I do recommend you visit Szimpla on your first visit to Budapest as the place is truly spectacular, and captures a unique piece of history in Budapest's cultural scene. The best time to visit is earlier in the evening, before the crowds pour in.

Jewish Quarter
★ SZIMPLA KERT

Kazinczy utca 14; tel. 06/20-261-8669;
www.szimpla.hu; Mon-Sat noon-4am, Sun 9am-5am;
metro 2: Astoria

Szimpla Kert is the original and most famous ruin bar in Budapest, and it probably draws as many visitors annually as Buda Castle. It spans an entire gutted apartment block. It's like a nocturnal wonderland with fairy lights, old computer monitors, and creaking furniture painted in a kaleidoscope of colors. You can even sit in a Trabant car in the courtyard.

Szimpla Kert is one of the most popular ruin bars in Budapest.

Al Fresco Drinks

Even before the coronavirus pandemic, much of Budapest's spirited nightlife existed outdoors, on terraces and "kerts" (gardens) around the city. Some of the city's best spots for an al-fresco drink include:

RIVER-VIEW TERRACES

- **Jonás Craft Beer House** (page 397), located by the Bálna, has great views overlooking the Danube.

HIDDEN TERRACES AND GARDENS

- **Épitesz Pince** (Ötpacsirta utca 2; https://en.epiteszpince.hu; Mon-Thu 11am-9pm, Fri-Sat 11am-11pm), a secret courtyard, is hidden in the Palace District in a former palace that is now home to the Association of Hungarian Architects.

- **Massolit Books and Café** (Nagydiófa utca 30; tel. 06/1-788-5292; daily 10am-7pm), an independent English-language bookshop with a café, has a secret garden out the back you wouldn't expect unless you are in the know.

OTHER VENUES

- **Pagony Kert** (Kemenes utca 10; https://pagonykert.hu; Mon-Fri midday-10pm, Sat-Sun 11am-10pm May-Sep) is located beside the Gellért Thermal Baths, and actually set in former disused children's pools once belonging to the baths.

- **Csendes Társ** (page 396), the summer terrace at Csendes, is located in the V District.

INSTANT

Akácfa utca 49-51; tel. 06/70-638-5040;
www.instant-fogas.com; daily 4pm-6am;
tram 4, 6: Király utca

Instant once resided in the VI District, but the super-ruin pub has moved here, with Fogas Ház taking over much of the indoor space. There are four dance floors and eight bars from the basement to the top, with music catering to different tastes. The main dance hall features pixel cloud hangings and surreal wall art, and the party goes on all night.

FOGAS HÁZ & KERT

Akácfa utca 51; tel. 06/70-638-5040;
www.instant-fogas.com; daily 4pm-6pm;
tram 4, 6: Király utca

Fogas Ház and Kert got its name ("House of Teeth") from its residence in a former dental lab. Trees wrapped with fairy lights brighten the courtyard next to the main bar area, which

is tucked beneath a circus tent. Since Fogas became housemates with Instant, partygoers have flocked to this ruin bar complex for hedonism until dawn.

KŐLEVES KERT

Kazinczy utca 37-39; tel. 06/20-213-5999;
www.koleves.com; Mon-Fri 1pm-midnight,
Sat-Sun 1pm-1am, summer only; metro 1: Opera

In the summer, this garden comes to life with hammocks, fairy lights, and laughter. Kőleves Kert ("Stone Soup") occupies a plot where a house once stood. There is a bar at the front in a small wooden pavilion where you'll have to get your own beer and stroll over the gravel back to your brightly painted bench or table.

BARS AND PUBS

There's more to Budapest bar life than ruin bars, whether set on rooftops or in cozy corners.

Jewish Quarter
TELEP

Madács Imre út 8; tel. 06/30-633-3608;
Mon-Thu noon-midnight, Fri-Sat noon-2am;
metro 1, 2, 3, tram 47, 48, 49: Deák Ferenc tér
You can spot Telep by the stickers plastered all over the windows and the hip crowd spilling into the street outside. Part art gallery, part bar, Telep has become one of Budapest's core urban meeting points. It's your chance to hang out with the cool crowd in Budapest.

LIEBLING

Akácfa utca 51; tel. 06/1-783-8820; Mon-Sat
6pm-4am; tram 4, 6: Király utca
Liebling is a cozy bar in the Instant-Fogas Ház ruin bar complex. Below the huge lips on the rooftop, Liebling is decked out in brick and wood. The spiral staircase takes you up to a hidden terrace that's popular in the summer. This bar is a good alternative for a drink if you're not in the mood for the hedonism of its ruin bar neighbors.

FEKETE KUTYA

Dob utca 31; tel. 06/30-951-6095; Mon-Wed
5pm-1am, Thu-Sat 5pm-2am, Sun 5pm-midnight;
metro 2, tram 47, 48, 49: Astoria
A cozy pub loved by the locals, Fekete Kutya is found under the arches on Dob utca. The bar is a little on the shabby side but has a welcoming atmosphere and great beer on tap. Make sure you try their chive pogácsa!

KISÜZEM

Kis Diófa utca 2; tel. 06/1-781-6705; Sun-Wed
noon-2am, Thu-Sat noon-3am; tram 4, 6: Király utca
Kisüzem is always packed with an eclectic, local crowd of Hungarian and international bohemians. The bar, clad with brick walls, plants, and rotating art exhibits, is worth visiting for its friendly, familial vibe and budget-friendly drinks. They also serve up tasty bites from their small kitchen, from falafel plates to soup of the day.

★ BLACK SWAN

Klauzál utca 32; tel. 06/30-663-5270; Mon-Tue
6pm-midnight, Wed-Sat 6pm-2am; tram 4, 6:
Wesselényi utca/Erzsébet körút
It's easy to miss the entrance to this elusive cocktail bar, which is marked only by a simple black door and awning with a white swan in the shape of an "S." Inside is a refuge clad in low lighting, velvet booths, and exposed brick walls. The menu is the size of a small book, bursting with craft cocktails inspired by Hungarian culture. Its curious concoctions come with evocative names like "Let Off Steam," a cocktail accented with thyme, grapefruit, salt, and vanilla that captures the spirit of the thermal baths, and "Eureka," which pays tribute to the country's famous inventors. The bar also carries an impressive arsenal of liqueurs, so you can ask the bartender for your favorite if you prefer.

Around Andrássy Avenue
★ BOUTIQ'BAR

Paulay Ede utca 5; tel. 06/30-554-2323;
www.boutiqbar.hu; Tue-Thu 6pm-1am, Fri-Sat
6pm-2am; metro 1: Bajcsy-Zsilinszky út
One for the cocktail lovers—Boutiq'bar can mix up any drink you desire. Try one of their creative concoctions like Bombay Nights (gin with mango masala and yogurt), or Hello Tourist, made with aged apple pálinka, wine, and a hint of pastis with cinnamon and apple. You can ask the award-winning bartenders to prepare you something unique with seasonal ingredients.

360 BAR

Andrássy út 39; tel. 06/30-356-3047; www.360bar.
hu; Mon-Wed 2pm-midnight, Thu-Sat 2pm-2am,
Sun noon-midnight; metro 1, tram 4, 6: Oktogon
360 Bar lives up to its name with panoramic views over Budapest's famous landmarks. You can reach the rooftop terrace with the elevator at the side entrance of the Párizsi department store. In the summer, enjoy drinks al fresco; in winter, the bar sets up transparent igloos so you can still enjoy views over

the Hungarian Parliament Building and St. Stephen's Basilica.

PÓTKULCS

Csengery utca 65/b; tel. 06/1-269-1050; daily 5pm-2am, metro 3; tram 4, 6: Nyugati Pályaudvar

Hidden behind an ivy clad wall and a wooden door, Pótkulcs is a secret oasis. This bar embodies the aesthetics of a stripped-down ruin bar, but caters to a local crowd and hosts regular creative programs ranging from jazz concerts and Balkan folk dancing in its vaulted basement. Your best bet to find out about any programs lined up is to check out their Facebook page. In the summer, the BBQ grill is in full swing in the garden under the foliage covered veranda.

South Buda

BÉLA

Bartók Béla út 23; tel. 06/70-590-7974; www. belabudapest.com; Sun-Mon 11am-11pm, Tue-Wed 11am-midnight, Thu 11am-1am, Fri-Sat 11am-2am; tram 19, 41, 47, 48, 49, 56, 56A: Gárdonyi tér

Salmon-colored wallpaper covered with vintage botanical and zoological prints, tropical plants and ferns dripping from ventilation pipes, and an eclectic collection of vintage lamps and curiosities, Béla is worth going for the "gram." But this curious bar comes with a warm, welcoming atmosphere, and an offering of live music in its cellar room on a regular basis.

GDANSK

Bartók Béla út 46; tel. 06/20-988-1873; Mon-Sat 6pm-11pm; metro 4, tram 4, 6, 19, 41, 47, 49: Móricz Zsigmond körtér

Walking down Bartók Béla Boulevard it's easy to miss the entrance to this tiny bar. There are four tables fitted in around the bookshelves stacked with Polish language books, so it's not easiest to grab a seat if you come later, but if you do you'll be rewarded to good Polish beer, vodka, and if you're lucky, you can even order some homemade pierogi. The vibe is cozy, friendly, and it's often packed with local creatives and bohemian characters.

CSENDES

Ferenczy István utca 5; tel. 06/30-727-2100; www.csend.es; Sun-Wed 10am-midnight, Thu-Sat 10am-2am; metro 2, tram 47, 48, 49: Astoria

This quirky bar is worth visiting for the décor alone, which dramatically blends colorful graffiti, eccentric art work, and random vintage items. The atmosphere is generally relaxed, but it does get packed on weekends. When you come in the summer, head round the corner to their terrace right by the gates of the beautiful Károly Kert, which in my opinion is one of the most underrated summer terraces in Budapest.

WINE BARS

Wine is a big part of Hungarian culture, and at Budapest's wine bars you can find a wide range of grape varieties from different regions across the country.

Lipótváros

DIVINO

Szent István tér 3; tel. 06/70-935-3980; www.divinoborbar.hu; Sun-Wed 4pm-midnight, Thu-Sat 4pm-2am; metro 1: Bajcsy-Zsilinszky út

DiVino serves exclusively Hungarian wines at its downtown location right next to the Basilica. If you want to try the best wines from up-and-coming Hungarian winemakers, look no further. Recommended by Michelin, this wine bar is always a hotspot of activity. DiVino has another branch in Gozsdu Udvar (Király utca 13).

Jewish Quarter

★ DOBLÓ

Dob utca 20; tel. 06/20-398-8863; www.budapestwine.com; Sun-Wed 2pm-2am, Thu-Sat 2pm-4am; metro 2, tram 47, 48, 49: Astoria

Dobló specializes in Hungarian wine and pálinka. You can either take a table or sit up at the mahogany bar in the brick-walled, chandeliered tasting room. There are various tasting packages available, such as ones based on terroir or grape type. There is a secret piano bar in the basement below, so if your waiter is being friendly, try to discretely ask for an exclusive invite to the "Rabbit Bar."

Around Andrássy Avenue
KADARKA

Király utca 42; tel. 06/1-266-5094;
www.kadarkawinebar.com; daily 4pm-midnight;
tram 4, 6: Király utca

This sleek wine bar on Király utca embodies a character different from the surrounding ruin bars. Their impressive wine list features wines not only from Hungary but neighboring countries like Romania as well. You'll get a small plate of pogácsa (savory scones) before tasting begins. Kadarka fills up on the weekends and evenings, so you'd be wise to make a reservation.

CRAFT BEER

Hungary's reputation for wine has grown significantly in recent years, and Budapest's beer scene is not far behind. The recent surge in microbreweries and craft beer bars has made it easier than ever for beer lovers to enjoy great Hungarian beer. Try some locally brewed beers like Keserű Méz, a bitter, unstrained lager from the Fóti Brewery, or a really good IPA called Távoli Galaxis. If you like sour beers, try Rafa from the Fehér Nyúl brewery.

Jewish Quarter
CSAK A JÓ SÖR

Kertész utca 42-44; tel. 06/30-251-4737;
www.csakajosor.hu; Mon-Sat 2pm-9pm;
tram 4, 6: Király utca

Csak a Jó Sör (literally meaning "good beer") lives up to its name. Although it looks like a small shop, it carries a wide range of rare and specialty beers, such as smoky stouts or brews accented with coriander. There are four types on tap if you want to drink some good beer while you're out in the Jewish District, but you can also pick up some great bottles to go.

LÉHŰTŐ

Holló utca 12-14; tel. 06/30-731-0430;
Tue-Thu 4pm-2am, Fri-Sat 4pm-4am, Sun-Mon
4pm-midnight; metro 1, 2, 3, tram 47, 48, 49: Deák
Ferenc tér

You'll find Léhűtő in a brick-walled basement. This spot is popular with local beer connoisseurs, as it carries a top selection of craft beers. Six taps change regularly to showcase the best Hungarian craft beers. In addition, they have 30 local and international beers, including IPAs, stouts, and wheat beers from the best Hungarian breweries.

Inner City and South Pest
★ ÉLESZTŐ

Tűzoltó utca 22; tel. 06/70-336-1279;
www.elesztohaz.hu; Mon-Sat 3pm-3am, Sun
3pm-midnight; metro 3, tram 4, 6: Corvin-negyed

Élesztő was one of the first craft beer places to open in Budapest. It occupies a former glassworks factory and sports a ruin bar aesthetic, but it's unique in that it focuses on craft beer. The main bar has 21 Hungarian beers on tap, and across the courtyard you'll find imported beers.

★ JONÁS CRAFT BEER HOUSE

Fővám tér 11-12; tel. 06/70-930-1392; Mon-Thu
11am-midnight, Fri-Sat 11am-2am, Sun 11am-11pm;
tram 2: Zsil utca

Jonás Craft Beer House is aptly named for its location in the Bálna (Whale). It serves not only wonderful beers but also pálinkas and other drinks, and you can't beat the view over the river from its Danube-side terrace. Jonás regularly changes its Hungarian beers on tap, and there is always an interesting range to try.

KRAK'N TOWN

József körút 31a; tel. 06/30-364-5658; www.
krakntown.com; Mon-Fri 4pm-midnight, Sat-Sun
noon-midnight; metro 4, tram 4, 6: Rákoczi tér

With ship portholes, hot-air balloons hanging from the ceiling, and plenty of brass accents, Krak'n Town may make you feel like you've wandered into a steampunk fantasy. The Hungarian beers on tap change regularly.

LIVE MUSIC
Margaret Island and Around
BUDAPEST JAZZ CLUB

*Hollán Ernő utca 7; tel. 06/1-798-7289; www.bjc.hu;
Mon-Thu 10am-midnight, Fri-Sat 10am-2am;
tram 4,6: Jászai Mari tér*

Budapest Jazz Club is in a converted art deco cinema and features a bar in the lobby. The music offered here is a diverse range of local and international jazz acts. This elegant jazz club is known for its high-quality sound and state-of-the-art equipment.

South Buda
BARBA NEGRA

There are two venues here: **Barba Negra Music Club** (Prielle Kornélia utca 4; tel. 06/20-563-2254; www.barbanegra.hu; tram 17, 41, 47, 48, 56A: Csonka János tér) and **Barba Negra Track** (Neumann János utca 2; tram 1: Infopark), which lies around the corner from its sister club. The former is a large indoor club that hosts rock gigs and all-night parties; the outdoor Track is only open in the summer, with loud music, enthusiastic crowds, and plenty of beer on tap.

CLUBS
Lipótváros
ÖTKERT

*Zrínyi utca 4; tel. 06/70-330-8652;
www.otkert.hu; Thu-Sat 11am-5am, Sun-Wed 11am-11pm; tram 2: Széchenyi István tér*

Like many venues in Budapest, Ötkert has many facets: it's a restaurant and cultural space early in the evenings and a party venue with live music and top DJs at night. The building has a capacity of up to 1,000 people. You may even spot the occasional movie star in the crowd.

They have a strict dress code—no metal or punk looks, no neck tattoos.

Jewish Quarter
DOBOZ

*Klauzál utca 10; tel. 06/20-449-4801; www.doboz.co.hu; Wed-Sat 10pm-6am, Sun 10pm-5am;
metro 2: Blaha Lujza tér*

Doboz fits in with the Jewish District ruin bar look. It occupies an old apartment block. A giant metallic gorilla climbs the 300-year-old tree in the courtyard. Here, DJs work by genre in different rooms, with hip-hop in one and house in another.

LÄRM

Akácfa utca 51; tel. 06/1-783-8820; www.larm.hu; Sun-Wed 10pm-4am, Thu 10pm-5am, Fri-Sat 11pm-6am; tram 4, 6: Wesselényi utca/Erzsébet körút

LÄRM is a club that looks like a black box. It's dedicated to techno lovers, hidden inside the Instant-Fogas Ház complex. Despite being surrounded by the city's most popular bars, it keeps its underground feel. It's simple and all in black, with top audio equipment to keep even the most die-hard techno lovers content in these gut-shaking surroundings.

South Buda
★ A38

*Petőfi híd; tel. 06/1-464-3940; www.a38.hu;
Mon-Sat 7:30am-11pm, Sun 12:30pm-11pm;
tram 4, 6: Petőfi híd, Budai hídfő*

A38 is certainly one of Budapest's most unusual venues. This former Ukrainian stone-carrying ship is permanently moored on the banks of the Danube. The bar and restaurant reside upstairs in the boat section. The stairs descend into a subterranean chamber beneath the Danube. A38 usually hosts indie and alternative concerts and club nights. The cover fee depends on the event (some are free), so check the program.

Performing Arts

PERFORMING ARTS AND CONCERT HALLS

Hungary, and Budapest in particular, has a solid foundation in classical music, opera, and musical theater. Famous Hungarian composers and musicians are known the world over, and within Budapest alone you can find top classical music venues and theaters dedicated to the performing arts.

Lipótváros

VIGADÓ

Vigadó tér 2; tel. 06/1-328-3340; www.vigado.hu; tickets HUF 1,000-3,500; tram 1: Vörösmarty tér

Budapest's second-largest concert hall takes up impressive residence on the Danube. It's in a beautiful Romantic-style building with huge arched windows. The Vigadó also houses exhibitions on the upper floors, but it's most popular for classical concerts. It may not have the best acoustics in the city, but it's worth visiting for the architecture alone.

Around Andrássy Avenue

HUNGARIAN STATE OPERA

Andrássy út 22; tel. 06/1-814-7100; www.opera.hu; metro 1: Opera

This is one of the most beautiful opera houses in Europe, and it's budget-friendly, too. If you have the chance, try to make it to an opera. With recent (and ongoing) renovations, you can expect acoustics to match the stunning architecture. Check the current program of shows on the website. Offerings range from well-known operas by Puccini, Verdi, and Mozart to more obscure work by Hungarian or contemporary composers. There are ballet productions as well. You can get cheap tickets for the top tier. (If you do, you'll need to go through the entrance on the left-hand side to go up. Note: there's no elevator.) Some seats have limited visibility. Make sure you dress up for the occasion.

The less impressive **Erkel Theater** (II János Pál pápa tér 30; tel. 06/1-332-6150; www.opera.hu; metro 4: II János Pál Pápa tér) steps in for productions when the Hungarian State Opera House needs to close for renovations.

BUDAPEST OPERETTA THEATER

Nagymező utca 17; tel. 06/1-312-4866; www.operett.hu; tickets HUF 1,100-8,000; metro 1: Opera

Alongside Vienna and Paris, Budapest is famed for its operetta, and the Budapest Operetta Theater is one of the best places to sample this unique aspect of Hungarian culture. From the outside, the Operetta looks like a pink-frosted cake; inside, it's gilded with stained glass, chandeliers, and plenty of gold. Shows are in Hungarian but subtitled in English.

LISZT FERENC MUSIC ACADEMY

Liszt Ferenc tér 8; tel. 06/1-462-4600; www.lfze.hu; tickets free-HUF 12,000; metro 1, tram 4, 6: Oktogon or Király utca

The Liszt Ferenc Music Academy stands in a stunning art nouveau building on a square between Andrássy Avenue and Király utca, and it's worth a visit for the 50-minute guided tour (1:30pm; HUF 3,500), even if you can't make a concert. Some of Hungary's best composers and musicians have played at this ornate concert hall, and today you can still attend regular classical concerts from local and international orchestras.

Inner City and South Pest

TRAFÓ

Liliom utca 41; tel. 06/1-215-1600; www.trafo.hu; tickets range HUF 2000-2500 HUF; metro 3, tram 4, 6: Corvin-negyed

You'd expect a theater housed inside a former electrical transformer building to be different, and Trafó delivers. If you're looking for avant-garde theater and dance, this is the place for you. (Just prepare yourself for nudity and other surprises.)

Budapest's Broadway

Budapest Operetta Theater

Intersecting Andrássy Avenue, Nagymező utca is a lively street lined with cafés with street-side terraces, museums, and, above all, theaters. Footprints belonging to Hungarian stage and screen stars line the sidewalk outside the Budapest Operetta Theater, a candy-pink building with echoes of belle epoque grandeur.

In its heyday in the early 1900s, Budapest, along with Paris and Vienna, was considered one of the most important cities for operetta theater, and even today the Operetta is among the most popular theaters in the city, staging around 500 shows a year, from traditional Hungarian operettas to international musicals. An operetta is a light opera, characterized by fun melodies and comedic storylines, and you'll find shows here from the most famous Hungarian composers like Ferenc Lehár and Imre Kálmán.

Even if the ambience is more lighthearted than the Hungarian State Opera around the corner, people still like to dress up for a show, so it's best not to turn up in sneakers and jeans. Head across the road to the Komediás Kávéház for a pre- or post-show drink or dinner; you'll pass a bronze statue of Imre Kálmán (one of Hungary's most beloved operetta composers), sitting with a cigar in hand. The entire street is densely packed with theatrical history. Even the cafés on Nagymező utca capture the grandeur, and it's easy to picture an era when divas would come to dine or sip coffee between shows.

CONCERT VENUES
Lipótváros
AKVÁRIUM KLUB

Erzsébet tér 12; tel. 06/30-860-3368; www. akvariumklub.hu; Wed-Sat noon-4:30am, Sun-Tue noon-1am; metro 1, 2, 3, tram 47, 48, 49: Deák Ferenc tér

Akvárium Klub lies beneath an artificial lake at the heart of the city. The glass roof reflects water into the venue, so it feels as if you are inside an aquarium. There is one large concert hall (1,300 capacity) and a smaller one (fits 700). In the evenings, you'll find local and international bands here. The music is pretty eclectic, ranging from rock and metal to jazz, pop, and electronica. Although events tend to run in the evenings, the bars—especially the terrace in the summer—are open during the day.

Inner City and South Pest
BUDAPEST PARK
Soroksári út 60; tel. 06/1-434-7800; www.budapestpark.hu; event days 6pm-dawn; tram 2: Közvágó híd

Budapest Park is one of Budapest's largest open-air venues that has a music-festival feel. It stretches over 11,000 square meters (118,000 sq ft), making it ideal for large concerts and parties. It may seem like a bit of a trek to get to (especially as you have to take the number 2 tram to the end of the line beyond Rákóczi Bridge), but it's worth coming out for the buzzing atmosphere. Check the website for up-to-date schedule.

CINEMA

Budapest's best art houses are cultural hubs that occasionally screen films in English. What's more, they come with stunning cafés and opulent surroundings you'd expect more from a historic theater than a cinema. Some even transform into hip night clubs after the last screening.

Lipótváros
TOLDI
Bajcsy-Zsilinszky út 36-38; www.toldimozi.hu/english; tickets HUF 1200; metro 3: Arany János utca

This two-screen cinema is a countercultural hub for hip young Hungarians. Movies are not dubbed, making this a good place to see English-language films. Toldi is also a popular venue for film festivals covering a range of themes from architectural film days and human rights themes to Japanese to Czech film weeks, when subtitles in English and Hungarian are used. By night, the extensive bar area gets turned into a trendy night club with local DJs and a crowd of cool, young 20-30 somethings.

Around Andrássy Avenue
MŰVÉSZ
Teréz körút 30; www.muveszmozi.hu; tickets HUF 1200; metro 1, tram 4, 6: Oktogon

Bedecked in colorful mirrored mosaics in a style that would make even Antoni Gaudí or Gustav Klimt feel at home, Művész is a beautiful art cinema that has been running since 1910. There are five screens, and it mostly screens art house films with Hungarian subtitles, but it's worth coming in for the quirky décor for an English language film or a drink at the bar.

Inner City and South Pest
URÁNIA NEMZETI FILMSZÍNHÁZ
Rákoczi út 12; www.urania-nf.hu; tickets HUF 1600; metro 2, tram 47, 48, 49: Astoria, bus 5E, 7, 8E, 110, 112, 133E, 178: Uránia

Gold leaf, arched mirrors, and red velvet adorn the main screening room in this jewel box of a cinema, which hosts regular screenings of art house films, documentaries, and theater productions from the world over. Everything is subtitled in Hungarian, so English speakers may only want to come for anglophone productions. If you're in the area, it's worth stopping by the neo-orientalist café on the first floor, which is usually empty (unless it's just before a film screening).

Christmas Markets

The Christmas market outside St. Stephen's Basilica is the most picturesque of the Budapest Christmas markets.

Markets pop up across Central Europe as Christmas draws near, usually running from the middle or end of November-January 1. Budapest's entire downtown area, in addition to the squares in smaller neighborhoods, will fill up with stands selling trinkets and mulled wine. Make sure you get a steaming hot cup of mulled wine to keep you warm as you wander around in sub-freezing temperatures.

Since these markets can get crowded, especially on the weekends, it's important you keep an eye on your belongings at all times.

Festivals and Events

Budapest often has something big going on, whether it's food or wine festivals or art fairs. It also plays host to one of the most important music festivals in Europe.

BUDAPEST 100

Various venues; www.budapest100.hu; May; free

Go behind the scenes in May at Budapest 100 when certain buildings, such as private residential buildings (that are usually out of bounds), are opened to the public. The event is free, and it gives you a different way to see Budapest—from hidden courtyards and staircases. This is a must for any architecture lover who's looking for something

different. Download a map on the website (or pick up a booklet from one of the venues) and simply wander to the buildings that are interesting for you. Some tours are offered, but they are in Hungarian, so it's best to create your own itinerary and just get out to explore.

SZIGET FESTIVAL

Május 9 Park, Óbudai-sziget; www.szigetfetival.com;
Aug; 7-day pass €325, day ticket €79;
HÉV 5: Filatorigát

For one week in the middle of August, thousands of festivalgoers (mostly 18- to 40-year-olds) flood the city for the Sziget Festival,

VÖRÖSMARTY TÉR MARKET

http://budapestchristmas.com/christmas-market-on-vorosmarty-square; Sun-Thu 10am-8pm, Fri-Sat 10am-10pm

Budapest's most famous Christmas market is the one down at Vörösmarty tér, which has 28 cottage-style wooden stalls where you'll find over 100 vendors focusing exclusively on local Hungarian designers. You can pick up all kinds of things like hand-bound notebooks, lavender cosmetics, bags, leatherwork, artisanal jams, chocolate, and cheeses. At the heart, there is a large gastro terrace where you can sample some seasonal delights like roast goose thigh with braised red cabbage or roast pork knuckle.

ST. STEPHEN'S BASILICA MARKET

http://budapestchristmas.com/budapest-basilica-christmas-market; Mon-Thu 10am-8pm, Fri-Sun 10am-10pm, end of Nov to Jan 1

Wander over to St. Stephen's Basilica to find another market that's probably the most beautiful spot for a seasonal photo. Clustered at the base of the iconic cathedral are stalls selling gifts from semi-precious stones and jewelry to wooden spoons and paprika. Every 30 minutes from 4:30pm-10pm, you can enjoy the laser projection show on the Basilica (grab 3D glasses from some of the stalls, as the projections are in 3D). On weekends, children between the ages of 4-14 can enjoy the free skating classes in the market's artificial skating rink (Fri 2pm-8pm, Sat-Sun 10am-6pm).

OTHER MARKETS

There are also markets on nearby Erzsébet Tér and Deák Ferenc utca that feel like an offshoot of the famous Vörösmarty tér market, as they turn this part of the city's downtown into one large festive market. Also, if you head up Andrássy Avenue, you'll spot a few smaller markets on the squares just off the boulevard as well. These are worth the visit if you want to escape the mass crowds of the V District but still enjoy the Christmas market feeling.

which takes place all the way out on Óbuda Island. Sziget features an eclectic lineup with international pop and rock acts plus world and classical music, along with nonmusical attractions in the comedy tent and circus tent. Past acts have included Muse, Lana del Rey, and Rihanna. Visitors come to the festival from over 100 countries.

Sometimes called a European Burning Man, Sziget is about more than music. Over the course of the week, Sziget becomes an "Island of Freedom," which can mean getting creative at one of the art camps, doing some yoga by the Danube, or partying late into the night after the concerts are over.

You can buy tickets months in advance (the price is also lower then—a day ticket costs €65 if you buy them before the end of Dec), but

tickets do sell out quickly, so it's best to buy them by June at the latest.

BUDA CASTLE WINE FESTIVAL

Buda Castle; tel. 06/1-203-8507; www.aborfesztival. hu; Sep; day tickets at the door HUF 3,900; bus 16, 105: Clark Ádám tér

Go on a tasting trip around Hungary with the Budapest Wine Festival. This four-day wine fest takes place around the first week of September on the terrace of Buda Castle, which provides perfect views over the city.

Make sure you buy tickets in advance: not only are they cheaper (HUF 2,990 before mid-Aug), but also the weekend dates tend to sell out. With entry, you'll get a glass and free entry to the Budapest History Museum. Entry does not include the wine, which you pay for as you drink—and with around 200 wineries, you have plenty to choose from. Aside from wine, there are concerts and cultural programs, but the best thing is sipping a glass of wine on the Buda Castle terrace with the view over the Danube.

BUDAPEST DESIGN WEEK

Various venues; www.designweek.hu; Oct

Come and see why Budapest has earned UNESCO's Creative Cities "City of Design" title. For a week in the first half of October, the Hungarian capital transforms into an open showroom for Hungarian contemporary fashion, art, and design, with exhibitions, workshops, and events during Budapest Design Week, which takes place all across the city. Check out the program online (or download the booklet) for events to choose from, like parties, fashion shows, brunches, movie screenings, and open studios. You can download a design map, which you may find useful, even if you don't make it to the events. Most events are free, but they may require advance registration as space is limited.

Shopping

UNESCO awarded Budapest the Creative Cities title of City of Design. To get a taste for Budapest's artistic innovation, start by visiting the city's shops and showrooms. Within basements, on side streets, and hidden in tea room mezzanines, you can find vintage stores selling clothes and accessories from bygone days, and often at a bargain.

SHOPPING DISTRICTS

Váci utca (metro 1: Vörösmarty tér, metro 3: Ferenciek ter) or **Andrássy út** (metro 1: Any stop between Bajcsy-Zsilinszky út and Hősök tere as this metro line runs directly under the boulevard) both offer great high-end shopping. In some of the more exciting neighborhoods, like the Jewish Quarter or the VIII, IX, and XI Districts, you'll find independent boutiques and designers around the downtown streets. Antique lovers flock to **Falk Miksa Street** (tram 4, 6: Jászai Mari tér) for its row of galleries and antique stores. There are around 20 shops just on the row, which comes to life in May during the Falk Art Forum (www.falkart.hu). The event turns antique shopping into a street party with exhibitions, culinary bites, and performances.

Any fashion fiend would do well to head to **Deák Ferenc utca** (metro 1, 2, 3: Deák Ferenc tér). Between Váci utca and Deák Ferenc tér, this small street is replete with luxury boutiques from international designers like Hugo Boss, Tommy Hilfiger, Lacoste, and Massimo Dutti. The street is also lined with luxury hotels and bistros.

MARKETS

While Central Market Hall is the most famous out of Budapest's markets, there are plenty of others to explore, whether you're looking for antiques or artisanal cheese.

Jewish Quarter
GOZSDU COURT
(Gozsdu udvar)

Metro 1, 2, 3, tram 47, 48, 49: Deák Ferenc tér

Gozsdu Court is a set of interconnected courtyards lined with restaurants and bars that fill up with a hip, young crowd in the evenings, but on the weekends, it turns into a curious market with antiques, work from local designers, and more. You can find communist badges and soldiers' helmets on one table, prints from local artists on another, jewelry made from cut-out 100-year-old letters, or necklaces made from tiny globes of glass filled with copper wire. It can be hard to deal with the crowds to look at the stalls, but if you do get tired, fortunately there are plenty of cafés offering refuge.

Best Souvenirs

Uniquely Hungarian items are known as Hungaricum and some make great gifts. You can pick up food and drinks to take home, or folk art, porcelain, or antiques.

FOOD AND DRINKS

- **Paprika:** You can find packs of powdered paprika from Szeged (a Hungarian town in the south) in places like the Central Market Hall, in smaller souvenir shops, or open-air markets like the farmers market at Szimpla Kert on Sunday mornings. Hungarian paprika comes in two varieties: sweet (édes) and hot (erős). If you can pick up a pack of paprika in a cute embroidered or patterned cheesecloth bag, these make great gifts. Bags can range between HUF 1,500-3,700 depending on the size and if any extras like wooden serving spoons are included.

- **Pálinka:** This strong fruit brandy can be found in most wine shops, but a good place to pick up a bottle is the **Magyar Pálinka Háza** (page 408). You can get this fruit brandy in a variety of flavors: plum, apple, pear, apricot, cherry, grape, and rarer types like raspberry and elderflower. I personally like the Rézangyal Brand (HUF 4,290-8,970), but you can always ask for recommendations when you go to a specialist shop.

- **Unicum:** This bitter herbal liquor makes a good gift if you want something uniquely Hungarian. You can find Unicum (HUF 4,250-7,750 depending on the size) pretty much everywhere, including supermarkets and cigarette shops. If you want to take home a bottle that is less bitter, try the Unicum Szilva (HUF 3,199-5,000 depending on the size), which has been aged on a bed of dried plums.

- **Wine:** Hungary is gaining recognition for its wine, so why not take home a bottle? You can get wine at all price ranges, from HUF 700 to well beyond HUF 10,000, but you can find something in between that makes the perfect gift. Head to a wine shop like **Tasting Table** (page 408) where the staff can help you find something quality. If you want something special, pick up a bottle of Tokaj; if you're partial to reds then a good bottle of Egri Bikavér is the way to go.

ART AND DESIGN

- **Herend porcelain:** Herend porcelain stands out because of its delicate motifs, whether in a tea set, tableware with birds and flowers, or hand-painted figures of carnival workers or horses. You can get Herend porcelain for anywhere between HUF 20,000-85,000, although rarer pieces can cost hundreds (if not thousands) of dollars. Do note that there are a lot of fakes on the market, so be careful where you buy. To ensure authenticity, head to one of the official Herend stores (József Nádor tér 10-11).

- **Zsolnay ceramics:** This is a unique type of porcelain that originated in the Hungarian town of Pécs. Zsolnay doesn't just produce architectural ceramics—they also create vases and dinnerware. What makes Zsolnay different from Herend are the vibrant colors, and almost metallic hues and unique designs. There are a few Zsolnay stores (Rákoczi út 4-6) in Budapest, with prices ranging from as low as HUF 8,000 for small figurines to thousands for larger, rarer items.

- **Folk art:** Embroidery makes a wonderful gift, whether on a tablecloth or stitched onto a shirt. You can find unique folk art in the **Central Market Hall** (page 370) in the form of embroidery and lacework. Expect to pay around HUF 10,000-15,000 for quality items, and considerably less for smaller items like doilies.

- **Antiques:** Antiques are great gifts if you're looking to take a piece of history home, whether you pick up some Communist memorabilia from **Ecseri Market** (page 406) or something more valuable on **Falk Miksa utca** (page 404) like a painting, an elegant dinner set, or a wall mirror.

KLAUZÁL SQUARE MARKET

Klauzál tér 11; tel. 06/1-785-4770; Sun 10am-5pm; tram 4, 6: Király utca

At the heart of the Jewish Quarter, Klauzál tér market reopened in 2015 following a renovation. On Sundays, this old red-brick building turns into an antique market with a difference—you can find not only classic antiques but also those that have been given a revamp by local designers. You'll find repainted and upholstered furniture, old watches fitted with new straps, or restrung jewelry.

SZIMPLA FARMERS MARKET

Kazinczy utca 14; tel. http://en.szimpla.hu/ farmers-market; Sun 9am-2pm; metro 2, tram 47, 48, 49: Astoria

Szimpla Kert may be best known as a ruin bar, but every Sunday morning till 2pm it turns into an extravagant farmers market with artisanal cheeses, loaves of spelt bread, and seasonal vegetables—and you can listen to live jazz or Hungarian folk music. There is also a charity cookoff in the back of the bar. For a donation, you can get some freshly cooked gulyás (a spicy beef-paprika soup) or stew.

Greater Budapest
ECSERI MARKET

Nagykőrösi út 150; tel. 06/1-348-3200; Mon-Fri 8am-4pm, Sat 5am-3pm, Sun 8am-1pm; bus: 54, 55: Naszód utca (Használtcikk piac)

Getting to Ecseri Market is an adventure that requires a long bus ride out into the suburbs on bus 54 or 55 to Nászod utca (Használtcikk piac). Then you have to cross the bridge over the highway—but once you're here, this fascinating antiques market is a sight. It's a labyrinth of curiosities, from grand serpentine fountains taken from Buda villas to vintage porcelain, old cameras, gramophones, and portraits of communist political leaders. Even if you're not looking to buy, it's worth visiting just for the experience.

DESIGN SHOPS
Lipótváros
RODODENDRON

Semmelweis utca 19; tel. 06/70-419-5329; www.rododendronart.com; Mon-Fri 11am-7pm, Sat 10am-5pm; metro 2, tram 47, 48, 49: Astoria

Rododendron Art and Design showcases work from around 120 local designers in its ground-floor shop split between Semmelweis utca and Röser courtyard. The main focus is on art and jewelry, but you'll find other bits and pieces in its changing collection.

Jewish Quarter
PRINTA

Rumbach Sebestyén utca 10; tel. 06/30-292-0329; www.printa.hu; Mon-Sat 10am-7pm; metro 1, 2, 3, tram 47, 48, 49: Deák Ferenc tér

Printa is a shop that doubles as a gallery and coffee shop. This trendy silkscreen print studio also carries its own eco-friendly clothing made out of upcycled material. Many of their products also feature Budapest in some way. If you want a silkscreen print to take home or a trendy bag, Printa is your place.

SZIMPLA DESIGN

Kazinczy utca 14; Thurs-Sat noon-7pm, Sun 10am-3pm; metro 2, tram 47, 48, 49: Astoria

Szimpla Design is set in the front of its namesake ruin bar. It's an Aladdin's Cave of items, with purses, postcards, and handwoven beanie dolls amongst curious pieces of antiques and upcycled items. It's a chance to bring home a little of the Budapest ruin chic aesthetic.

Inner City and South Pest
BOMOART

Régiposta utca 14; tel. 06/20-594-2223; www.bomoart.hu; Mon-Fri 10am-6:30pm, Sat 10am-6pm; metro 3: Ferenciek tere

BomoArt is a must for anyone who loves stationery. Their hand-bound diaries and

---

1: Ecseri Market in the suburbs of Pest **2:** Printa is one of the most popular design shops in Budapest. **3:** Szimpla Design

notebooks with leather and prints displaying vintage hot-air balloons, aviaries, and old-fashioned pictures of Budapest make unique souvenirs. They have a second location at the Castle Garden Bazaar, and you can find their products in many shops across town.

FOOD AND WINE

Hungarian food and wine can make good souvenirs, so why not take a packet of paprika or a bottle of Hungarian wine home with you? While somewhere like Central Market Hall is the obvious choice, you can pick up some bites to take home in these shops, too. You can also pick up some Hungarian products from local chain stores like Príma or Spar, but the quality and packaging may not make them ideal for gifts.

Lipótváros
SZAMOS
Kossuth Lajos tér 10; tel. 06/30-290-6655; www.szamos.hu; Mon-Fri 7:30am-7pm, Sun 9am-7pm, metro 2: Kossuth Lajos tér

Nothing makes a better souvenir than a box of marzipan chocolates. You'll find Szamos shops and patisseries all over the city, but this one next to the Hungarian Parliament is special, as there is a chocolate museum on the second floor of the building (http://www. csokolademuzeum.hu/, daily 10am-6pm, admission 500 HUF), where you can learn some history and see how chocolate is made. You can also buy decadent cakes (although these probably won't last the flight home), so why not treat yourself to a Dobos cake (a chocolate cake topped with hardened caramel) and a coffee in the café? Then you can peruse the boxes of chocolates with pictures of the city or Hungarian embroidery to take home.

Inner City and South Pest
TASTING TABLE
Bródy Sándor utca 9; tel. 06/30-720-8197; www. tastehungary.com/tasting-table-budapest; daily noon-8pm; metro 2, tram 47, 48, 49: Astoria

For great Hungarian wines, head to Tasting Table. If you want to try before you buy, they

organize a few wine tastings. You can book these for 3pm or 6pm daily via the website ($39-$59 per person). The people in the shop are friendly, speak English, and can help you find the right bottle. There's a great selection of Tokaj wines here. For something special, try a bottle from Oremus (prices range from HUF 14,00 for the sweet, nectar-like Aszú wines wines from 2010 to HUF 180,000 for rare vintages from the 1950s). You'll also find other wines from Hungary and surrounding regions like Egri Bikavér (Bull's Blood), or sparkling wine from Somló near Lake Balaton.

Prior to the pandemic, Tasting Table hosted Thursday afternoon "Happy Hour Tastings" for HUF 1,000 per wine with three wines on offer between 5pm and 9pm (drop in any time). It's worth checking their website or Facebook page to see whether these have resumed at the time of your visit.

MAGYAR PÁLINKA HÁZA
Rákóczi út 17; tel. 06/30-421-5463; www.magyarpalinkahaza.hu; Mon-Sat 9am-7pm; metro 2, tram 47, 48, 49: Astoria

Magyar Pálinka Háza, which translates as the "Hungarian House of Pálinka," offers this Hungarian spirit in a vast selection, not only in the type of fruit available but also its distilleries. This large shop stocks hundreds of bottles, so deciding may be difficult. You can't taste before you buy, but the staff will help you make the right choice. As most locals will pick up a bottle from the supermarket (or make their own), the huge selection appeals to connoisseurs of the fiery fruit brandy and tourists looking for a special souvenir.

CLOTHING AND ACCESSORIES
Lipótváros
NANUSHKA
Bécsi utca 3; tel. 06/70-394-1954; www.nanushka. com; Mon-Sat 10am-6pm; metro 1: Vörösmarty tér, metro 1, 2, 3, tram 47, 48, 49: Deák Ferenc tér

Nanushka is perhaps Hungary's best-known fashion brand, with boutiques in over 30 countries. The headquarters can be found in downtown Budapest. Nanushka's designs are characterized by lush fabrics and playful cuts designed for the urban woman. Prices are on the high side, with most clothes costing a few hundred euros, but still priced less than international designers.

Jewish Quarter
SZPUTNYIK

Dohány utca 20; tel. 06/1-321-3730
www.szputnyikshop.hu; Mon-Sat 11am-8pm, Sun 10am-6pm; metro 2, tram 47, 48, 49: Astoria
Szputnyik mixes a large range of vintage clothing and accessories with newer, quirky bags, shoes, clothing, and jewelry, plus altered and revamped vintage items. It's a popular shop for fashion-forward, trendy Hungarians skewing more to the alternative, boho crowd. Prices won't break a midrange budget.

RETROCK

Anker köz 2-4; https://retrock.com; tel. 06/30-472-3636; Mon-Fri 1pm-6pm, Sat 11am-7pm; metro 1, 2, 3, tram 47, 48, 49: Deák Ferenc tér

Pick out unique creations made by Hungarian and international designers from used and recycled materials, or secondhand items and accessories. Retrock is a treasure trove of bijoux and unusual fashion items, such as mountain man-style bags, Gothic alien-inspired fashion lines, and handmade cycling accessories.

Inner City and South Pest
PALOMA

Kossuth Lajos utca 14-16; tel. 06/20-961-9160; http://palomabudapest.hu; Mon-Fri 11am-7pm, Sat 11am-3pm; metro 3: Ferenciek tere
Paloma is a collective of designers hidden away in a Budapest courtyard in the Inner City. The series of shops on the first floor up from the winged courtyard staircase showcases work from 40 local, young, up-and-coming designers, with jewelry, bags, clothing, and shoes.

Food

Hungarian food is heavy. Portion sizes are large, meals center around meat, and of course, there's plenty of paprika accenting to give everything a slight kick. You won't leave a restaurant hungry, but if you're on a diet or vegetarian, you may want to visit an international or specialty restaurant.

Breakfast is usually a big deal. Hotels will ply you with cold cuts, chopped vegetables, and plenty of bread in the morning. Fried eggs with bacon or sausage is a typical Hungarian breakfast.

CASTLE DISTRICT
Hungarian
21 MAGYAR VENDÉGLŐ

Fortuna utca 21; tel. 06/1-202-2113; www.21restaurant.hu; daily noon-midnight; HUF 860-8,260; bus 16, 16A, 116: Bécsi kapú tér

Magyar Vendéglő literally means "Hungarian restaurant," but this chic bistro up in the Castle District applies an innovative and lighter twist on traditional dishes, like its paprika chicken made with a paprika reduction and served with homemade dumplings. You may want to try one of their special seasonal dishes like farm duck breast with cottage cheese potato dumplings. Beyond the creative cuisine, this restaurant stands out for friendly service. (Plus, they bottle their own wine.)

MANDRAGÓRA

Kacsa utca 22; tel. 06/1-202-2165; www.mandragorakavehaz.hu; Mon-Fri 11am-5pm; HUF 2,500-4,500; tram 4, 6, 17: Mechwart liget
Mandragóra (named after the mandrake, a humanoid-looking root used in witchcraft in

ENTRÉES

- **Gulyásleves (Hungarian goulash):** Hungarian goulash is known the world over, but it's a soup and not a stew as commonly believed. This rich beef soup made with chunks of potato and peppers is accented with quality red paprika powder, which gives the soup its crimson color.

- **Halászlé:** Similar to gulyásleves but made with fish instead of meat, this fisherman's soup comes from the south of the country, around Szeged.

- **Chicken paprikás:** A creamy chicken dish made with oodles of powdered paprika (which gives it a salmon hue), served with thin dumplings called galuska or nokedli and a side of sour cucumber salad.

Hungarian street food lángos

- **Mangalica pork:** Keep an eye out for mangalica on the menu. This unique Hungarian breed of pig is not only rare for its woolly coat (that kind of looks like a sheep's), but it's dubbed to be the "Kobe beef of pork." It's a fatty meat that's loved for its marbled texture and superb taste.

- For flavoring, **paprika** is a staple in the Hungarian kitchen, with locals reaching for bottles of sweet or spicy powdered paprika in place of pepper at times.

STREET FOOD

Lángos is a deep-fried savory dough similar in texture to a donut that usually comes topped with cheese and sour cream. You'll find this calorific street treat sold in kiosks and food trucks, mainly in parks, festivals, street food courts, and around metro stations.

WINE

Wine plays a big part in Hungarian meals, as the country is home to numerous wine regions (including the famous golden Tokaji dessert wines). Hungarians also like to sip spicy reds from the southern part of the country, such as **Szekszárd** and **Villány,** crisp whites from Lake Balaton's Badacsony region or nearby Somló, and the iconic **Bikavér** (Bull's Blood) red cuvée from Eger.

SPIRITS

- **Pálinka:** A famous fruit brandy distilled from local fruits like plum, pear, apple, quince, and apricot, which is often drunk with heavy Hungarian meals. Locals swear pálinka is a cure for digestive problems, colds, stomach aches, and even heart pains.

- **Unicum:** A bitter liqueur made from a secret recipe of 40 herbs and spices, which is said to help digestion.

the past) evokes images of magic and the occult, but this family-run restaurant employs its magic in the kitchen with its contemporary, seasonal takes on Hungarian classics, like paprika pike perch served with cottage cheese noodles and crumbles of bacon, or creative additions like the coffee spicing up their duck breast served with yellow beetroot. However, what makes Mandragóra really stand out are the desserts, especially the homemade chocolate cake, which is so good that they sell the cake to order so you can take it home.

★ CSALOGÁNY 26

Csalogány utca 26; tel. 06/1-201-7892; www.csalogany26.hu; Tue-Wed noon-3pm, Thurs-Sat noon-3pm and 7pm-10pm; entrées HUF 2,400-6,000 or tasting menu HUF 15,000; metro 2, tram 19, 41: Batthány tér

Csalogány 26 offers inspiring dishes made from local, seasonal ingredients—like a spiced peasant consommé with homemade udon noodles or cottage cheese mousse with sea buckthorn. Some say this restaurant run by a passionate father-and-son team is one of the best in Budapest. Go all-out with their lavish degustation menu, or try the budget-friendly three-course lunch menu for just HUF 3,100.

International
ZÓNA

Lánchíd utca 7-9; tel. 06/30-422-5981; www.zonabudapest.com; Mon-Sat noon-midnight; HUF 3,900-7,700; tram 19, 41: Clark Ádám tér

Zóna embraces a modern, urban aesthetic and prepares creatively executed international dishes. The menu offers an eclectic selection from gourmet burgers to an elegant degustation menu that changes seasonally but may feature dishes like guineafowl goulash and lamb rump served with sweet potato, kale, and panna cotta (yes, the Italian dessert). Zóna focuses on international fusion, mixing up Italian-inspired dishes with street food, along with tastes from Israel and Hungary thrown in.

ARANY KAVIÁR

Ostrom utca 19; tel. 06/1-201-6737; www.aranykaviar.hu; Tue-Sun noon-3pm and 6pm-midnight; HUF 4,900-18,900, metro 2, tram 4, 6, 17, 56, 56A, 61: Széll Kálmán tér

This Russian restaurant embodies the principles of fine dining in an intimate setting and with beautiful food presentation. If you're a fan of fish eggs, try their caviar menu (they have more than five types) accompanied by traditional Russian blinis and smetana (sour cream). If you fancy a splurge, go for their caviar tasting menu (HUF 19,000-49,000). Apparently Brad and Angelina came here on a date night once, so you may want to people-watch if you visit.

Fine Dining
FELIX KITCHEN AND BAR

Ybl Miklós tér 9, tel. 06/30-735-5041, https://felixbudapest.com/, Mon-Fri 8am-11pm, Sat-Sun 9:30am-11pm, mains HUF 3,600-15,990, tram 19, 41: Várkert Bazár

The former Várkert Kiosk, built by Miklós Ybl and located at the base of the Castle Garden Bazaar, is now home to Felix Kitchen and Bar, a relatively new and exciting addition to the Budapest gastronomic scene. The menu offers Central European dishes like Schnitzel and Catfish paprikash, along with an impressive caviar selection. However, it's the grill selection that truly stands out with luxurious cuts of Sirloin from Japan's Kagoshima region and Australian Wagyu beef, among other tasty steak and meat options. Although there is a large terrace area looking over the Danube, it is worth getting a table inside the gorgeous neo-Rennaissance building. The building also houses a cultural center whose temporary exhibitions you can visit without sitting down to dine.

Bistro and Brunch
★ PIERROT

Fortuna utca 14; tel. 06/1-375-6971; www.pierrot.hu; daily noon-11:45pm; HUF 4,900-7,500; bus 16, 16A, 116: Bécsi kapú tér

Pierrot is a stylish bistro on the site of a

13th-century bakery. Its kitchen focuses on Austro-Hungarian cuisine, but it's been updated for the more adventurous tastes of the 21st-century diner. Try their veal goulash or confit of duck baked into puff pastry.

BALTAZÁR GRILL AND WINE BAR

Országház utca 3; tel. 06/1-300-7050; www.baltazarbudapest.com; daily noon-11pm; HUF 3,460-10,760; bus 16, 16A, 116: Bécsi kapú tér

The bistro in this boutique hotel attracts locals and visitors. Baltazár Grill and Wine Bar serves up tantalizing brunches (including pastries), but they are best known for their charcoal-grilled meats and burgers. They also have an extensive wine collection from all around the Carpathian Basin. Another nice touch is their interesting gin selection with tailored garnishes that go toward making the perfect gin and tonic.

Cafés and Cakes

BUDAVÁRI RÉTESVÁR

Balta köz 4; tel. 06/70-408-8696; www.budavariretesvar.hu; daily 8am-8pm; HUF 310; bus 16, 16A, 116: Szentháromság tér

It might take a while to find the Budavári Rétesvár, a hole-in-the-wall discoverable under a dark archway in the Castle District, but worth the exploration just for the strudels. You can find variations of the Hungarian strudel, known as *rétes*, with fillings including sweet poppy seed, plum, or apple, plus savory dill and cottage cheese.

RUSZWURM

Szentháromság utca 7; tel. 06/1-375-5284; www. ruszwurm.hu; Mon-Fri 10am-7pm, Sat-Sun 10am-6pm; HUF 450-850; bus 16, 16A, 116: Szentháromság tér

Ruszwurm, Budapest's oldest functioning café and confectionary—dating back to 1827—is in a pistachio-green Baroque-style house. The interior is minimal, and the cakes are displayed in a wooden apothecary-style cabinet. Try the café's signature cake, the Ruszwurm Cream Pastry, a custard- and cream-based dessert topped with layers flaky dough. (In the high season, you may find it hard to find somewhere to sit!)

LIPÓTVÁROS
Hungarian

★ ZELLER BISTRO

Hercegprímás utca 18; tel. 06/30-651-0880; www.zellerbistro.hu; Tue-Sun noon-midnight; HUF 3,600-5,400; metro 3: Arany János utca

Zeller Bistro specializes in contemporary Hungarian cooking using fresh and seasonal ingredients from local farmers, producers, and small Hungarian wineries. The restaurant is in a cozy downtown setting and blends rustic with industrial chic. I recommend the duck liver brûlée with carrot and mango or the daily fish that comes straight from the market with a side of risotto. The carrot cake is also one of the best in town.

International
DA MARIO

Vécsey utca 3; tel. 06/1-301-0967; www.damario.hu; daily 11:30am-midnight; HUF 2,000-7,000; metro 2, tram 2: Kossuth Lajos tér

For authentic Italian cuisine, Da Mario is the place to go. This Italian-owned restaurant offers classic pasta and pizza, as well as seafood and meat dishes made with the best ingredients sourced from Italy, plus Italian wines. The atmosphere is relaxed and friendly, and the setting is stylish.

BARAKA

Dorottya utca 6; tel. 06/1-200-0817; www.barakarestaurant.hu; Mon-Sat 11am-3pm and 6pm-10pm; tasting menus HUF 23,500-27,500; metro 1: Vörösmarty tér

If you love fine dining and Asian and French food, you'll love Baraka. Since Baraka opened its doors and presented Asian-French fusion with a fine-dining, seasonal slant and a Hungarian accent, it's been a hub for foodie lovers. Seafood dominates the menu, with creative dishes such as bouillabaisse made with steamed-fish gyoza, capers, and seaweed. There are options for meat eaters and vegetarian diners alike here. East-meets-West flavors combine in dishes like togarashi with beetroot, or Hungarian wild boar with ume shiso. Note that prices will have an additional 13.5% service charge added.

Fine Dining
BORKONYHA

Sas utca 3; tel. 06/1-266-0835; www.borkonyha.hu; Mon-Sat noon-4pm and 6pm-midnight; HUF 4,150-7,550; metro 1: Bajcsy-Zsilinszsky út

The menu is always changing at this contemporary Hungarian restaurant headed by Chef Ákos Sárközi. Borkonyha earned its Michelin star for its innovative menu, drawing inspiration mostly from the Transylvanian kitchen, while playing with international ingredients and modern cooking techniques. Try the foie gras wrapped in flaky pastry, and anything that is made with mangalica pork. If you go for a tasting menu, invest in the wine pairing—there is a reason why this restaurant is called "Wine Kitchen" in Hungarian.

Bistro and Brunch
★ SZIMPLY

Károly körút 22 Röser Udvarl www.szimply.com; Mon-Fri 8am-4pm, Sat 9am-4pm; HUF 1,800-2,900; metro 2, tram 47, 48, 49: Astoria

It's hard to get a table in this small breakfast bistro (which does not accept reservations), but Szimply is worth it if you can grab a spot. With a choice of savory and sweet seasonal specials, you can be sure to get fresh and beautifully presented breakfast dishes, from favorites like avocado toast to more innovative ones like zucchini pancakes. During the COVID lockdown, Szimply rebranded as a gourmet lunch box delivery service, but hopefully will return to their restaurant once they can reopen.

KISPIAC

Hold utca 13; tel. 06/1-269-4231; Mon-Sat noon-10pm; HUF 2,300-3,950; metro 3: Arany János utca

Kispiac Bisztró can be found in one of the shopfronts of the Belvárosi market hall, and

the staff serves up hearty Hungarian dishes with generous portions. Ingredients come straight from the market so everything is fresh, and even the preserved ingredients like jams, bread, and pickled vegetables are handcrafted by the restaurant. Each day they put up six dishes to choose from, as well as regular Hungarian specials. (Take note: this bistro only seats 20, so you might have stiff competition for a table.)

Cafés and Cakes
GERBEAUD

Vörösmarty tér 7-8; tel. 06/1-429-9001; www.gerbeaud.hu; Mon-Thurs 9am-7pm, Fri-Sat 9am-8pm; HUF 1,150-4,990; metro 1: Vörösmarty tér

Gerbeaud is an institution in Budapest's café and confectionary culture. Founded in 1858, it eventually became the most fashionable spot in the city for the elite. Today, its palatial interior with rococo friezes, silk drapes, and crystal chandeliers invites guests to sit at the marble-topped tables to sip coffee and take bites from decadent cakes.

JEWISH QUARTER
Jewish

Jewish food in Budapest frequently overlaps Hungarian food, but there are some distinguishing markers. You won't find the pork-heavy recipes you'd get elsewhere. Instead, you'll find beef, lamb, or chicken. Hungarian-Jewish dishes like cholent (a bean stew) or goose feature heavily on menus. Not all restaurants are kosher. The only one that gets kosher approval from the Orthodox community is Hanna (in the courtyard of the Kazinczy Street synagogue), but it is not the place to go if you want an outstanding culinary experience. Other Jewish restaurants also draw influences from Israeli dishes, like hummus and tabbouleh.

MAZEL TOV

Akácfa utca 47; www.mazeltov.hu; tel. 06/70-626-4280; Mon-Fri 6pm-2am, Sat-Sun noon-2am; HUF 1,790-6,990; tram 4, 6: Wesselényi utca/Erzsébet körút

What started out as the next generation of

ruin pubs has morphed into a popular restaurant where a reservation is almost mandatory.

Mazel Tov serves up Israeli fusion, such as pulled lamb with eggplant, tabbouleh and tahini, or classic hummus-centered dishes, and sizzling Middle Eastern grilled meat plates with spicy Moroccan sausages and marinated skewers of meat. The setting—with exposed brick, twinkling fairy lights wrapped around the tree in the courtyard, and Mediterranean-tiled bar—pulls in the crowds as much as the food. Reservations are a must.

KŐLEVES

Kazinczy utca 37-41; tel. 06/20-213-5999; www.kolevesvendeglo.hu; Mon-Sun 11:30am-11pm; HUF 2,050-3,350; tram 4, 6: Wesselényi utca/ Erzsébet körút, metro 1,2,3, tram 47, 48, 49: Deák Ferenc tér

Kőleves ("Stone Soup") serves Jewish-inspired dishes, like *cholent*, a traditional Jewish bean stew served up with egg (or goose egg), and goose broth with a matzo ball. There are also plenty of vegetarian options, like vegetarian gratin made with black lentils, gruyere, and walnuts.

FRÖHLICH

Dob utca 22; tel. 06/20-913-2595; www.frohlich.hu; Mon-Thu 9am-6pm, Fri 9am-2pm, Sun 10am-6pm; HUF 140-950; tram 4, 6: Wesselényi utca/Erzsébet körút, metro 1,2,3, tram 47, 48, 49: Deák Ferenc tér

This kosher café and cake shop is a Jewish staple in the heart of the VII District. Fröhlich is famous for its flódni, a layered Jewish cake with apple, walnut, and poppy seed, but it's also worth trying some of their other baked goods and sweets. The interior has a faded old-world charm to it, with deep red walls and wooden lattice tables.

Hungarian
FRICI PAPA

Király utca 55; tel. 06/1-351-0197; www.fricipapa.hu; Mon-Sat 11am-10pm; HUF 1,000-2,000; tram 4, 6: Király utca

For Hungarian food on a budget, Frici Papa is the place to go. Frici Papa serves up classic Hungarian dishes in generous portions at fair prices. Even though it's located in a downtown, touristy area, it's still popular with locals. Just note that all dishes are sold separately, from meat and mains to side dishes.

M RESTAURANT

Kertész utca 48; tel. 06/1-322-3108; www.metterem.hu; Tue-Sun 6pm-10pm; HUF 2,600-4,800; tram 4, 6: Király utca

The menu at M Restaurant changes daily and features Hungarian specials, sometimes with a French twist. It has a cozy feel in a compact setting with sketched brown paper on the walls. Reservations highly recommended.

BARACK & SZILVA

Klauzál utca 13; tel. 06/1-798-8285; www.barackesszilva.hu; Mon-Sat 6pm-midnight; HUF 3,100-6,700; metro 2, tram 4, 6: Blaha Lujza tér

Barack & Szilva ("Peach and Plum") is a small family-run bistro serving up Hungarian provincial food fused with influences from French, Italian, and Jewish cuisines. You can go à la carte or dive into the seasonal chef's offer with a delicious tasting menu with a wine pairing option.

Fine Dining
BOCK BISZTRÓ

Erzsébet körút 43-49; tel. 06/1-321-0340; www.bockbisztropest.hu; Wed-Sat noon-10pm; HUF 3,400-7,800; tram 4, 6: Király utca

Located in the building belonging to the Corinthia Hotel, Bock Bisztró gives you the chance to try Hungarian delicacies inspired by Spanish tapas. One of the main draws is its excellent and extensive wine list—over 200 to choose from. Chef Lajos Bíró is legendary in local culinary circles, drawing Hungarians and visitors alike to this elegant establishment.

1: Baltazár Grill and Wine Bar **2:** Két Szerecsen

Hungarian Bakeries

Hungarians love their cukrászda (confectionaries serving decadent cakes and coffees). Café culture is a big part of local life and a popular tourist attraction in itself. Old Habsburg-era grand cafés serving dessert and cakes still line the boulevards of Budapest. The New York Café is cited as the most beautiful café in Europe—if not the world—with marble columns, gold-gilt mirrors, rococo-style frescoes on the ceiling, and crystal chandeliers. Other cafés, like Gerbeaud, Művész, Central, and Astoria, also carry on the Austro-Hungarian coffee traditions. New-wave cafés are percolating on the scene, too, catering to hip and trendy crowds who love their flat whites and Chemex coffees.

Look for the following desserts behind the glass cabinets of the city's beloved cukrászdas:

Eszterhazy cake

- **Dobostorta:** A chocolate cake topped with a hard caramel topping.

- **Eszterházy:** Cake made with walnuts and rum.

- **Somloi galuska:** A Hungarian-style tiramisu without the coffee.

- **Krémes:** A custard and cream cake set between layers of flaky pastry.

Street Food
★ BORS GASZTRO BÁR

Kazinczy utca 10; tel. 06/70-935-3263; daily 11:30am-9pm; HUF 850-1,900; metro 2, tram 47, 48, 49: Astoria

You'll always see waiting crowds outside this pantry-sized street food bar. Bors Gasztro Bár elevates street food with a menu that changes daily and is based on fresh, seasonal ingredients. Dishes include soups, baguettes, stews, and pasta, with innovative options like coconut-chili pumpkin cream soup or their French Lady baguette that combines emmentaler cheese and spiced chicken breast, accented with rosemary red onion jam.

KARAVAN

Kazinczy utca 18; tel. 06/30-934-8013; Mar-Sept Sun-Wed 11:30am-11pm, Thu-Sat 11:30am-1am; HUF 750-2,500; metro 2, tram 47, 48, 49: Astoria

If you want a bite to eat before grabbing drinks at Szimpla Kert, Karavan is a great choice. This open-air street food court serves up a range of snacks from its numerous food trucks, from Hungarian lángos (deep-fried savory pastries topped with cheese) to sausages and vegan burgers. Head in with friends, and you can each buy from a different truck and sit together.

Cafés and Cakes
MY LITTLE MELBOURNE

Madács Imre út 3; tel. 06/70-394-7002; www.mylittlemelbourne.hu; Mon-Fri 7am-7pm, Sat-Sun 8:30am-7pm; HUF 600-1,200; metro 1,2,3, tram 47, 48, 49: Deák Ferenc tér

My Little Melbourne was one of the first new-wave coffee bars that opened in Budapest. Get quality espressos and flat whites in their tiny mezzanine café, or head next door to My Little Brew Bar where you can treat yourself to a chemical lab's worth of drip coffees, from Chemex to syphon-made coffees.

NEW YORK CAFÉ

Erzsébet körút 9-11; tel. 06/1-8866-167;
www.newyorkcafe.hu; daily 8am-midnight;
HUF 3,000-18,000; tram 4, 6: Wesselényi utca/
Erzsébet körút

Some say the New York Café is the most beautiful café in the world, and with its curved marble columns, rococo-style balconies and friezes, and generous application of gold leaf, it's certainly a candidate for the most opulent. This is not a place you come to for the food (which could be better, to be honest). However, people do come here for the experience. Along with the coffee and tempting cakes, the café also serves up plenty of history, since it was once a popular hangout for artists, nobility, and writers. Some of the most influential newspapers around 1900 were edited up in the café gallery. One local legend has it that writer Ferenc Molnár stole the keys to the café and tossed them in the Danube so the restaurant would be forced to stay open 24/7. Although it also functions as a restaurant, most come here to have a coffee and admire the scenery. But if coffee is not your thing, try the lemonade (which is based on a 19th-century recipe). Mornings are the best time to pop by, and if you're lucky, a cellist might even serenade you. You'll find the café inside the New York Palace Boscolo Budapest Hotel right on Grand Boulevard. In the afternoons, there is usually a line out the door, so it's a good idea to either book a table, or come first thing in the morning when it's still empty.

AROUND ANDRÁSSY AVENUE
Hungarian
MENZA

Liszt Ferenc tér 2; tel. 06/1-413-1382;
www.menzaetterem.hu; daily 10am-midnight;
HUF 1,990-4,390; metro 1, tram 4, 6: Oktogon

Menza combines retro interior design with Hungarian food classics adapted to the modern palate like gulyás soup. They also offer more contemporary dishes like duck burgers. The menu changes weekly. For a great bargain, come at lunchtime during the week for quality food for only HUF 1,590.

Bistro and Brunch
KÉT SZERECSEN

Nagymező utca 14; tel. 06/1-434-1984;
www.ketszerecsen.hu; Mon-Fri 8am-midnight,
Sat-Sun 9am-midnight; HUF 2,890-5,290;
metro 1, tram 4, 6: Oktogon

This cozy bistro serves up an eclectic menu, with brunch classics such as eggs benedict and international dishes like Moroccan lamb shoulder and Thai curries. Két Szerecsen combines the classic coffeehouse vibe with a Parisian bistro environment. In the summer, there is a very nice terrace area just next to the café. Reservations are a must.

Street Food
PIZZICA

Nagymező utca 21; tel. 06/70-554-1227; Mon-Thu
11am-midnight, Fri-Sat 11am-3am; HUF 280-490;
metro 1, tram 4, 6: Oktogon

For great Italian street food pizza, you can't beat Pizzica. The pizza here comes on the perfect thin base, with toppings like buffalo mozzarella or truffle cream. Slices are cut with scissors and served up on wooden boards. In the mezzanine, local art is usually on display.

Cafés and Cakes
MŰVÉSZ

Andrássy út 29; tel. 06/70-333-2116;
www.muveszkavehaz.hu; Mon-Sat 8am-9pm,
Sun 9am-9pm; HUF 1,100-1,300; metro 1: Opera

A classic on the Hungarian cake and café scene since the 19th century, Művész is known for its cakes, with staples like custard cream and chocolate alongside seasonal specials. Try the house special—the Művész kocka—a layered cake with nuts, chocolate mousse, cream, and sheets of dark chocolate. The café interior captures a fading old-world decadence, with silk wallpaper, marble tables, and crystal chandeliers. The Művész's proximity to the opera house and the theaters on Nagymező utca make it a good pre-theater hangout.

Vegetarian, Vegan, and Gluten-Free

DROP

Hajós utca 27; tel. 06/1-235-0468; www.droprestaurant.com; daily noon-11pm; HUF 3,050-7,950; metro 1: Opera

At Drop, there's a range of tasty gluten-free dishes to try, from salads and cheese plates to pasta dishes and Hungarian specialties. It's also worth popping by for breakfast, especially if you want some gluten-free bread and baked goods. Lactose-free and vegetarian dishes are also available. (Great news for those who are gluten-intolerant or allergic—everything on the menu is gluten-free.)

CITY PARK AND AROUND

Hungarian

BAGOLYVÁR

Károly út 4; tel. 06/1-468-3110; www.bagolyvar.com; daily noon-10pm; HUF 2,950-4,900; metro 1: Széchenyi fürdő

This family restaurant located next to the zoo offers good food at a reasonable cost. Bagolyvár ("Owl Castle"), named for its former avian residents, is the sister restaurant of the fancier, fine-dining Gundel restaurant next door. Bagolyvár serves up innovative cuisine inspired by chef Károly Gundel but in a more relaxed atmosphere—and without the Gundel prices. This restaurant announced temporary closure during the coronavirus pandemic, so check ahead before visiting.

International

ROBINSON

Városligeti tó; tel. 06/1-422-0222; www.robinsonrestaurant.hu; daily noon-3pm and 6pm-11pm; HUF 3,500-6,200; metro 1: Széchenyi fürdő

On a small island in the heart of City Park, Robinson is all about the location. Robinson is in a two-story glass-paneled lake house, so when you're inside, it feels like you're dining on the water. Although you'll find Hungarian dishes like Hortobágy pancakes (meat-filled pancakes topped with a creamy paprika sauce) on the menu, the focus is more on international cuisine (mostly French), along with grilled dishes and sizzling steaks.

Fine Dining

★ GUNDEL

Gundel Károly út 4; tel. 06/1-889-8111; www.gundel. hu; daily noon-midnight; HUF 6,700-39,000; metro 1: Széchenyi fürdő

Gundel is an institution whose founder is considered the Escoffier of Hungarian cuisine. Try the piquant goulash soup made from an in-house recipe, and the walnut pancakes accented with rum, raisins, and lemon zest—and drizzled with bitter chocolate. The extremely popular crepe-like Gundel pancake has inspired similar versions in restaurants across the country. If you want to try Gundel but it's out of your budget, head next door to the more affordable Bagolyvár. This restaurant announced temporary closure during the coronavirus pandemic, so check ahead before visiting.

Bistro and Brunch

VÁROSLIGET CAFÉ AND BAR

Olof Palme sétány 6; tel. 06/30-869-1426; www.varosligetcafe.hu; daily noon-10pm; HUF 3,990-9,990; metro 1: Hősök tere

Városliget Cáfe and Bar overlooks Vajdahunyad Castle with views of the lake (or ice rink, depending on the season). It's in a beautiful 19th-century, neo-Baroque pavilion. The food is a mix of international bistro cuisine with a few Hungarian specials like paprika chicken, stuffed cabbage, and roasted goose leg. The restaurant prides itself on its Tányérhús (slow-cooked boiled beef served over three courses, starting with beef broth, then the marrow on toast, and finally the tender meat with sides like fried potatoes, cream of spinach, and horseradish-spiked apple sauce), inspired by the Austrian Tafelspitz. Make sure you close the meal with their signature Liget Coffee, made with their house blend, roasted and ground on premises.

Home Cooking

Eat&Meet (Danubius utca 14; tel. 06/30-517-5180; www.eatmeet-hungary.com; see website for scheduled dinners; €45 three-course meal including drinks; metro 3: Gyöngyösi utca) is no ordinary restaurant. Set in a private apartment in the XIII District (and in a garden house just outside Budapest in the summer), this unique pop-up restaurant runs regular dinners for those wanting to try authentic Hungarian food as you would have it at home.

Zsuzska Goldbach, a young Hungarian woman who speaks both English and Italian, began Eat&Meet with her parents as a passion project to showcase true Hungrian home cooking you won't find in a restaurant. The three-course meal is seasonal, made with fresh, local ingredients, and dishes are paired with Hungarian wines. Zsuzska explains everything in detail, from specific ingredients to the wines and Hungarian culinary traditions. Guests are welcomed with the family's own aged pálinka. Dinners are scheduled on certain dates, so contact Eat&Meet to arrange when you'd like to come.

You won't really find locals at Eat&Meet, but you feel like you're at an international dinner party where everyone is seated together. You may end the evening with a new friend or two. This restaurant is highly recommended if you're a solo traveler and fed up with dining alone. The food is fantastic and worth the price. It's made even more special by the Goldbach family's passion and attention to detail.

MARGARET ISLAND AND AROUND

Hungarian

POZSONYI KISVENDÉGLŐ

Radnóti Miklós utca 38; tel. 06/1-787-4877; Mon-Fri 9am-midnight, Sat-Sun 10am-midnight; HUF 1,100-3,050; tram 2, 4, 6: Jászai Mari tér

Pozsonyi Kisvendéglő is popular with locals for its friendly, welcoming atmosphere. It's always full, and it can be a challenge to get a table, but with generous portions and budget-friendly prices, it's easy to see why. You'll find all the classic Hungarian dishes, and you may feel overwhelmed by the choices. Try the goulash or the roasted duck, or take advantage of the seasonal menu. Reservations highly recommended.

Cafés and Cakes

SARKI FŰSZERES

Pozsonyi út 53-55; tel. 06/1-238-0600; 8am-7pm Mon-Fri, 9am-7pm Sat, 9am-3pm Sun; HUF 1,390-8,300; tram 2, 4, 6: Jászai Mari tér

This retro café is a great spot for a quick brunch or sandwich. Sarki Fűszeres is both a wine shop and a delicatessen selling platters of cheese and artisanal meat cuts. Whether you have a savory or sweet palate, you can be sure to find a snack to tempt you.

SOUTH BUDA

Bistro and Brunch

HADIK

Bartók Béla út 36; tel. 06/1-279-0290; www.hadik.eu; daily 11am-8pm; HUF 1,890-3,290; tram 19, 41, 47, 48, 49, 56, 56A: Gárdonyi tér

Located on up-and-coming Bartók Béla út, Hadik delivers a mix of classic Hungarian and more experimental dishes. Hadik was once a hangout for the Buda literary elite, and it sports a more laid-back industrial chic look. Neighboring **Szatyor** (www.szatyorbar.com) offers the same menu and has an eclectic ruin bar feel. Both places fill up quickly in the evenings, and during the day they make a great stop for coffee.

Cafés and Cakes

KELET

Bartók Béla út 29; tel. 06/20-456-5507; http://keletkavezo.hu; Mon-Fri 7:30am-10:30pm, Sat-Sun 9am-10:30pm; HUF 790-2,250; tram 19, 41, 47, 48, 49, 56, 56A: Gárdonyi tér

This charming café, covered wall-to-wall

with books, is popular with locals for its third-wave artisanal coffees and tempting snacks, like creative toasted sandwiches made with Indonesian-style peanut butter or exotic chutneys. Make sure you try their hot chocolates or drip coffees made from single-origin beans.

Vegetarian, Vegan, and Gluten-Free
VEGAN LOVE

Bartók Béla út 9; www.veganlove.hu; daily 11am-9pm; HUF 1,590-3,000; metro 4, tram 19, 41, 47, 48, 49, 56, 56A: Szent Gellért tér

For Budapest's best vegan burgers, head to Vegan Love. This street food bar offers delicious vegan options like sweet potato or BBQ tofu burgers and vegan chili dogs. The creations here are adventurous and flavorful, and they will also appeal to non-vegans.

INNER CITY AND SOUTH PEST
Hungarian
KARPÁTIA

Ferenciek tere 7-8; tel. 06/1-317-3596; www.karpatia. hu; daily 5pm-11pm; HUF 4,300-8,900; metro 3: Ferenciek tere

Karpátia dates back to the late 19th century and is worth visiting for the frescoed interior that looks like something out of a museum. When it comes to food, Karpátia serves up classic Hungarian dishes with a range of spicy goulash soups and variations of paprika-laced meat stews made with chicken or beef. If you come in the evening, expect to dine while listening to csárdás (traditional Hungarian-Romani folk dance music).

International
PATA NEGRA

Kálvin tér 8; tel. 06/1-215-5616; www.patanegra.hu; daily 11am-midnight; HUF 790-4,190; metro 3, 4, tram 47, 48, 49: Kálvin tér

Share some tapas at Pata Negra, a Spanish tapas bar featuring classics like patatas bravas, croquetas, and jamón iberico. This restaurant is ideal to visit with a group so you can share different dishes and a jar of sangria, or enjoy a glass of Spanish wine or sherry.

Fine Dining
★ COSTES

Ráday utca 4; tel. 06/1-219-0696; www.costes. hu; Wed-Sun 6:30pm-midnight; tasting menus HUF 31,500-38,500; metro 3, 4, tram 47, 48, 49: Kálvin tér

Costes was the first restaurant in Hungary to receive the much-coveted Michelin star. Chef de Cuisine Eszter Palágyi has created a fine-dining experience that marries Hungarian family recipes with international trends. The restaurant features locally sourced fish dishes and more experimental signature recipes, like wild pigeon served with beetroot and Ethiopian coffee crumbs.

Bistro and Brunch
PÚDER

Ráday utca 8; tel. 06/1-210-7168; www.puderbar.hu; daily noon-1am; HUF 2,490-3,950; metro 3, 4, tram 47, 48, 49: Kálvin tér

Púder is an eclectic bistro and bar with a decor that combines the look of ancient Pompeii with quirky local art and dilapidation. The menu mixes up light bites with more substantial bistro food, like pork knuckles with rosemary, or rosé duck breast with arugula mashed potato and cinnamon-plum red wine ragout.

CSIGA

Vásár utca 2; tel. 06/30-613-2046; daily 8am-11:45pm; HUF 1,550-4,000; metro 4, tram 4, 6: Rákoczi tér

It's almost impossible to get a seat at Csiga, which attracts a local bohemian crowd of artists and VIII District creatives due to its relaxed ambience. The menu includes soups, salads, and modern takes on Hungarian dishes. It's a great choice for vegetarians, and if you want to eat lunch on a budget, take advantage of their lunch menu that changes weekly. (Call to make a reservation.)

Around Bartók Béla Avenue

Running from the Liberty Bridge well into the XI District's Kelenföld Station, Bartók Béla Avenue is a lifeline on the Buda side of the river. The far end takes you past the concrete apartment blocks off the tourist route, and the first stretch until Móricz Zsigmond körtér and Feneketlen tó (the "Bottomless Lake") is an exciting mixture of fin de siécle architecture, contemporary art galleries, alternative cultural centers, vegan street food, and vibrant café culture. The influx of visitors has turned the trendy Inner City areas into a tourist hub. Hip Hungarians now hang out on the other side of the river in cafés like book-lined **Kelet** (page 419) or historic **Hadik** (once the hangout for the Hungarian literary elite, page 419), which has recently undergone a makeover to embrace the trending industrial chic look. Bartók Béla Avenue is the new up-and-coming district, with new cafés and galleries popping up in art nouveau buildings each week.

the area around Bartók Béla Avenue, one of the most happening neighborhoods in Buda

Cafés and Cakes
LUMEN

Horánszky utca 5; tel. 06/20-402-2393; Mon-Fri 8am-midnight, Sat-Sun 10am-midnight; HUF 850-3,250; metro 4, tram 4, 6: Rákoczi tér

Lumen is a café within the heart of the Palace District that draws in the local arts crowd with its laid-back atmosphere and exhibitions held on-site (focusing mostly on photography). This café has its own roastery. You can get some light bites if you're hungry, like soup and hummus, or daily specials on the lunch menu, like curried vegetable soup and lasagna. At the time of writing, this location was closed even for take out due to COVID-19. You can go to their sister café on Mikszáth Kalmán tér for coffee and take out food, and hopefully the original café will reopen soon.

CENTRÁL KÁVÉHÁZ ÉS ÉTTEREM 1887

Károlyi utca 9; tel. 06/1-266-2110; www.centralkavehaz.hu; daily 8am-11pm; HUF 1,900-6,900; metro 3: Ferenciek tere

This historic coffeehouse opened in 1887 and was the hub of Hungarian literary life in the 19th and 20th centuries. Writers once gathered up on the mezzanines to scribble away or edit literary journals, but they also mingled with scientists, artists, and composers during their coffee drinking hours. Today this old world café with marble tables, frescoes, and low hanging chandeliers is an elegant spot for breakfast, coffee, or cake. Try the Central 1887 breakfast plate with a substantial selection of roast beef, duck liver paté, smoked salmon, cheese, egg, and more, or keep things simple with a freshly baked croissant. Or just pick one of the delicious cakes from behind the glass—you really can't go wrong. They also have a restaurant serving Hungarian classics like goulash.

Like many classic institutions, at the time of writing this café had been closed for an indefinite period since March 2020, but there are plans to reopen in the future.

BUDA HILLS
Hungarian
★ NÁNCSI NÉNI

Ördögárok út 80; tel. 06/1-397-2742; www.nancsineni.hu; daily noon-11pm;

HUF 3,150-6,250; bus 157, 157A: Nagyrét utca, bus 63, 257: Széchenyi utca

Náncsi Néni is worth the journey into the leafy Hűvösvölgy area, especially in the summer. It's noted for its exceptional traditional classics (like your Hungarian grandmother would cook), but there are also more creative concoctions, like duck liver marinated in sherry and served with steamed grapes, as well as a number of freshwater fish dishes and steaks. Reservations highly recommended. There is a large, charming garden area where you can sit when the weather is good if you are looking to dine al fresco.

Bistro and Brunch
VILLA BAGATELLE

Németvölgyi út 17; tel. 06/30-359-6295; www.villa-bagatelle.com; Mon-Fri 8am-7pm, Sat-Sun 9am-6pm; HUF 990-3,990; bus 105, 212: Királyhágó tér

In a beautiful bright villa in the Buda Hills, Villa Bagatelle is a special place to have brunch, well worth the excursion out of town. Make sure you try their coffee, which is made with special care using beans from a local roaster. And try their salmon breakfast, where slices of whole-grain toast are topped with avocado, smoked salmon, and a poached egg. Or go all out and indulge in the champagne breakfast.

Accommodations

Picking the right location really depends on what you are looking for. If you want to be in the heart of the action and just crawl into bed straight from the ruin bars, then stay in the Jewish Quarter. If you want a good night's sleep, avoid anything with "Party Hostel" in the name. If seclusion, nature, and peace and quiet are what you desire, you might check into the Grand Hotel on Margaret Island. Hotels in the Inner City lean toward luxury. Budget options lie further afield in neighborhoods such as the residential area around City Park or out in Óbuda, but they give you the chance to immerse yourself more fully in local life.

It's not unusual to find accommodation in formerly residential buildings (or occupying a floor in a still-residential building), which can provide a less-touristy atmosphere while you're in the city. Most hotels do offer breakfast, but some might charge for it, so double-check before booking.

CASTLE DISTRICT
€150-250
PEST-BUDA DESIGN BOUTIQUE HOTEL

Fortuna utca 3; tel. 06/1-800-9213; www.pest-buda.com; €130-250 d; bus 16, 16A, 116: Bécsi kapu tér

One of the oldest hotels in Budapest, the Pest-Buda Design Boutique Hotel opened in 1696. The hotel was renovated in 2016, and it now blends worn wood with a touch of industrial chic and vintage sketches in its 10 individually designed rooms and suites in a three-story house. (Note: there is no elevator, only stairs.) Continental breakfast is available in the popular ground-floor bistro.

BALTAZÁR

Országház utca 31; tel. 06/1-300-7051; www.baltazarbudapest.com; €135-250 d; bus 16, 16A, 116: Bécsi kapu tér

This family-owned boutique hotel, with just 11 rooms and suites, is located at the northern end of Castle Hill. This hotel has a bohemian feel with quirky and colorful rooms and vintage furniture. It's noted for its bistro and grill and its wine bar downstairs.

ART'OTEL

Bem rakpart 16-19; tel. 06/1-487-9487; www. artotels.com/budapest-hotel-hu-h-1011/hunbuart; €135-200 d; tram 19, 41: Halász utca

This four-star hotel overlooking the Danube banks exhibits 600 works by American artist Donald Sultan, and guests can join a free tour to learn more about the artist and his work. Art'otel occupies a modern seven-story building with a small Baroque wing inside. The main draw of the hotel is its views, some overlooking the Castle District up the hill, or overlooking the river. There are 75 rooms here, and the hotel offers access and facilities for people with disabilities.

Over €250

MAISON BISTRO AND HOTEL

Országház utca 17; tel. 06/1-405-4980; www.maisonbudapest.hu; €199-310 d; bus 16, 16A, 116: Bécsi kapu tér

In a Baroque house built upon 15th-century foundations, Maison Bistro and Hotel captures the historical essence of the Castle District. The 17 rooms and suites feature king-size beds, with twins available upon request. Some rooms come with a private garden terrace. Guests are treated to a welcome drink upon arrival.

HILTON

Hess András tér 3; tel. 06/1-889-6600; www.danubiushotels.com/en/our-hotels-budapest/ hilton-budapest; €260-450 d; bus 16, 16A, 116: Szentháromság tér

The Hilton Budapest incorporates the ruins of a 13th-century Dominican monastery into its design. This Hilton is located by Fisherman's Bastion, and it has 298 rooms and 24 luxury suites, some with views over the Danube. The hotel has its own restaurant (ICON) serving Hungarian and international food, and there's a fitness center on-site. It is also accessible for travelers with disabilities.

LIPÓTVÁROS

€150-250

HOTEL PRESIDENT

Hold utca 3; tel. 06/1-510-3400; www.hotelpresident. hu; €110-199 d; metro 3: Arany János utca

With a rooftop terrace overlooking the Royal Postal Savings Bank and the Hungarian Parliament, Hotel President has some of the best views in the city. This four-star hotel has 152 rooms and two suites, as well as a wellness center with a jet stream pool. The highlight is its rooftop, which serves as a café and a restaurant in the summer and becomes an ice rink in the winter (which is free for guests).

Over €250

★ FOUR SEASONS

Széchenyi István tér 5; tel. 06/1-268-6000; www.fourseasons.com/budapest; €380-640 d; tram 2: Eötvös tér

The Four Seasons Hotel Gresham Palace not only ticks the box for one of the best views in town (facing the Chain Bridge and Buda Castle head-on), but it's also one of the most beautiful art nouveau buildings on the Danube. This five-star hotel has 160 rooms (51 of which overlook the Danube) and 19 suites in a palette of cream and ivory. In addition, there's **Kollázs Brasserie & Bar**, its own fine-dining restaurant, and a rooftop spa.

KEMPINSKI HOTEL CORVINUS

Erzsébet tér 7-8; tel. 06/1-429-3777; www.kempinski. com/en/budapest/hotel-corvinus/welcome; €260-450 d; metro 1, 2, 3, tram 47, 48, 49: Deák Ferenc tér

The Kempinski Hotel Corvinus is next door to the Ritz-Carlton, but it sports a different aesthetic. This modern hotel with an in-house Zen spa and gastronomic quarter puts it on the map. There are 351 rooms, including 35 suites. On-site restaurants include Nobu, an avant-garde fusion of Japanese-Peruvian cuisine, and És Bisztró, serving contemporary Austro-Hungarian cuisine, as well as the Living Room and the Blue Fox Bar.

★ ARIA

Hercegprímás utca 5; tel. 06/1-445-4055;
www.ariahotelbudapest.com; €270-495 d;
metro 1: Bajcsy-Zsilinszky út

There is a reason that the Aria Hotel tops numerous lists as one of the world's best hotels. This design hotel was built around an old Inner City townhouse, and it has a musical theme throughout, from its piano key-decorated lobby to its 49 rooms, each of which is named after a musician or composer. Every room comes with its own balcony, and there's a wellness center in the basement. But the real pièce de résistance is the rooftop bar overlooking St. Stephen's Basilica. Guests can also relax to live piano music in the lobby while sampling complimentary wine and cheese between 4pm-6pm.

JEWISH QUARTER
Under €150
WOMBATS CITY HOSTEL BUDAPEST

Király utca 20; tel. 06/1-883-5005;
www.wombats-hostels.com; €20 dorm bed, €65 d;
metro 1, 2, 3, tram 47, 48, 49: Deák Ferenc tér

Wombats City Hostel Budapest is located in the heart of the action in the Jewish Quarter. You can either sleep in a dorm or take a private room in this modern, clean hostel. There is a 24-hour common kitchen and a laundry room, plus social areas. There is also a buffet breakfast on offer.

ROOMBACH HOTEL

Rumbach Sebestyén utca 17; tel. 06/1-413-0253;
https://roombach.accenthotels.com; €68-170 d;
metro 1, 2, 3, tram 47, 48, 49: Deák Ferenc tér

Roombach Hotel stands right next to bustling Király utca and Gozsdu Court, but on a peaceful side street opposite the Rumbach Synagogue. This colorful, youthful hotel with en-suite rooms and geometric décor offers a lovely view of a quiet courtyard. This is a great budget option in the city center.

Over €250
★ CORINTHIA HOTEL BUDAPEST

Erzsébet körút 43-49; tel. 06/1-479-4000;
www.corinthia.com/en/hotels/budapest; €155-380 d;
tram 4, 6: Király utca

Located on the Grand Boulevard, the Corinthia Hotel Budapest possesses a fascinating history. The original mirrored ballroom (as well as a spa) were forgotten for decades, until plans arose to build an underground parking lot. Stories abound in this grand hotel. Behind its original 19th-century façade, you'll find modern luxury, with over 400 rooms in addition to four restaurants, one bar, and a music club. In the marble lobby check out the placard that lists the names of actors, musicians, and other well-known figures who have stayed in the hotel.

NEW YORK PALACE

Erzsébet körút 9-11; tel. 06/1-886-6118;
www.nh-hotels.com/hotel/anantara-new-york-
palace-budapest-hotel; €204-280 d; tram 4, 6:
Wesselényi utca/Erzsébet körút

The New York Palace (formerly the Boscolo Budapest) is in an elegant 19th-century building on the Grand Boulevard—and famous for its extravagant **New York Café.** The hotel's 185 rooms are decorated in an Italian style, with soft, warm tones and lush fabrics. There is a wellness center on-site, with a steam bath and relaxation pool. There's also a fitness center.

AROUND ANDRÁSSY AVENUE
€150-250
HOTEL MOMENTS

Andrássy út 8; tel. 06/1-611-7000;
www.hotelmomentsbudapest.hu; €125-265 d;
metro 1: Bajcsy-Zsilinszky út

Just a few steps from the Hungarian State Opera House, Hotel Moments is centrally located within walking distance of main sights.

This four-star hotel has 99 elegant rooms, as well as an on-site Hungarian bistro where a buffet breakfast is served (which also includes gluten-free baked products).

★ MYSTERY HOTEL

Podmaniczky utca 45; tel. 06/1-616-6000; www.mysteryhotelbudapest.com; €150-250 d; metro 3, tram 4, 6: Nyugati Pályaudvar

Tucked away in an unassuming residential area just behind Andrássy Avenue and the Nyugati railway station, this newcomer on the Budapest hotel scene is simply spectacular. Set in a former Masonic Lodge, this well-priced five-star luxury hotel looks like something out of a surrealist movie set, with marble chessboard floors, Greek columns, Egyptian style frescoes (including some originals from the building's masonic past), and optical illusions like a carpet that leads up to the ceiling. The 82 rooms are decked out in bright colors and reproduction prints of classic paintings. Another highlight is the Secret Garden Spa in the courtyard bedecked with palm trees and statues, where you'll find a jacuzzi, sauna, and gym.

CITY PARK AND AROUND
Under €150
BUDAPEST VILLE BED AND BREAKFAST

Damjanich utca 32; tel. 06/1-791-9962; www.budapestville.com; €45-80 d; bus 70: Nefelejcs utca/Damjanich utca

Budapest Ville Bed and Breakfast occupies a floor in a 19th-century apartment block. It features an arched double courtyard in a quiet neighborhood next to City Park. The design follows a vintage chic look, combining modern comforts with nostalgia in its four rooms.

MIRAGE MEDIC HOTEL

Dózsa György út 88; tel. 06/1-400-6158; www.miragemedichotel.hu; €115-160 d; metro 1: Hősök tere

The Mirage Medic Hotel is in a historic villa on the fringes of City Park. This hotel, owned by a Chinese doctor, offers in-house medical services and holistic remedies ranging from herbalism to acupuncture. The 37 rooms come with mattresses designed to work on pressure points and regulate body temperature. Rooms accessible for people with disabilities are also available. This is not the usual wellness break

the Tinei Room at bohemian boutique hotel Brody House

(there are no saunas on-site), but if you book for more than two nights, you get a holistic diagnosis from the hotel's Chinese doctors. Even if you're not looking for anything to do with alternative medicine, the value and the location merits a stay.

€150-250
MAMAISON HOTEL ANDRASSY BUDAPEST
Andrássy út 111; tel. 06/1-462-2100; www.mamaisonandrassy.com; €150-205 d; metro 1: Bajza utca

Mamaison Hotel Andrassy Budapest is on the illustrious boulevard close to City Park. The hotel has 61 rooms and seven suites decorated in warm colors and a modern design to give it the feel of a boutique hotel. A buffet breakfast is served at the on-site La Perle Noire Restaurant for a surplus of €16.

INNER CITY AND SOUTH PEST
Under €150
★ BRODY HOUSE
Bródy Sándor utca 10; tel. 06/1-266-1211; www.brody. house; €80-130 d; metro 2, tram 47, 48, 49: Astoria

This illustrious townhouse in the Palace District started as an artists' studio and bohemian clubhouse before its owners converted it into a boutique hotel. There are 11 shabby-chic rooms featuring work by the artists who once painted there. Breakfast is available (€10), along with an honesty bar and other concierge services.

HOTEL PALAZZO ZICHY
Lőrincz Pap tér; tel. 06/1-235-4000; www.hotel-palazzo-zichy.hu; €88-150 d; tram 4, 6: Harminckettesek tere

Once the residence of Count Nándor Zichy, this 19th-century mansion blends rococo stuccos and wrought-iron balustrades with contemporary design—plus a glass pyramid roof. Guests can enjoy a complimentary lavish breakfast or beverages in the lobby bar. There are 80 rooms and a sauna and gym on-site.

€150-250
BOHEM ART HOTEL
Molnár utca 35; tel. 06/1-327-9020; www.bohemarthotel.hu; €99-290 d; metro 4, tram 2, 47, 48, 49: Fővám tér

The Bohem Art Hotel uses the concept of a local art gallery (featuring work by young Hungarian artists). Its 60 hotel rooms are each decorated by a different artist, and guests can choose a room based on the art they like in the building's public gallery. You can enjoy a full American breakfast here, served with sparkling wine.

Over €250
PÁRISI UDVAR HOTEL
Petőfi Sándor utca 2-4; tel. 1-576-1600; www.hyatt.com/en-US/hotel/hungary/parisi-udvar-hotel/budub; €320-450 d; metro 3: Ferenciek tere

This luxury hotel by Hyatt resides in a former art nouveau shopping arcade, whose jewel-like stained-glass cupolas and golden neo-Gothic arches capture an old-world feeling. The 110 rooms and suites, meanwhile, embody a clean, luxurious minimalism decked out in pure whites and cream. There is a spa and a fitness center for guests. The brasserie and café are set in the iconic arcade, and it's worth popping in here for a coffee even if you're not staying here just for the stunning architecture.

Information and Services

TOURIST INFORMATION

You can find **Budapestinfo** (Sütő utca 2; tel. 06/1-486-3300; www.budapestinfo.hu; daily 8am-8pm) Tourist Information Points in various locations in the city: in the Inner City, up at the airport terminal, and in the ice rink building at City Park. Pick up free publications and maps, buy tickets for sights, theater, or opera productions, and get some help on navigating the city from the multilingual staff. These Budapestinfo tourism bureaus are also a good place to buy a **Budapest Card**.

BUSINESS HOURS

Most shops in Budapest open at 10am and close at 6pm. At one point, shops were required to close on Sundays, but due to popular demand, they reopened. (Note that opening hours may be shorter, and smaller shops and boutiques may not open on Sunday.) Budapest is not a city with seasonal opening hours, unless what you want to visit is an outdoor attraction, where you may find closing time correlates with the hours of sundown.

EMERGENCY NUMBERS

Hungary's emergency number is **112**. The average time to answer the phone is five seconds, and the operators speak English. However, it's not the only emergency number available. If you need an ambulance, call **104;** fire brigade **105;** police **107.** There is also a 24-hour English-speaking medical hotline called Falck's SOS: 06/1-2000-100.

CRIME

The main crime risks for tourists are **pickpockets** and **restaurant scams.** Take care with your belongings in busy, public spaces and on public transportation. Ask for a menu with a price list when dining out or getting drinks in a bar (especially if you're going for drinks with random girls you've met in the street—this is a classic scam). If you

have any problems, you can call the **Tourist Police** (06/1-438-8080), a 24-hour hotline with English-speaking operators.

HOSPITALS AND PHARMACIES

There are dozens of hospitals in Budapest, usually one for each district. If you're looking for a private option, the **Medicover Health Center** (Teréz körút 55-57; tel. 06/1-435-3100; www.medicover.hu) has English-speaking doctors and a 24-hour receptionist. **FirstMed Centers** (Hattyú utca 14; tel. 06/1-224-9090; www.firstmedcenters.com) accepts some US insurance, and has an entirely English-speaking staff.

You can find pharmacies all over Budapest, denoted by a green cross and the word "gyógyszertár." Most of them are open for regular shopping hours and close in the evenings and on Sundays, but a few are open 24 hours, like Térez körút 41 and Fővám tér 4 in the central areas in Pest.

FOREIGN CONSULATES

If you have an emergency (like losing your passport or you need consular help), the **United States Embassy** (Szabadság tér 12; tel. 06/1-475-4400) is located in the city center, close to the Hungarian Parliament. The **Canadian Embassy** (Ganz utca 12-14; tel.06/1-392-3360) can be found in Buda, along with the **British Embassy** (Füge utca 5-7; tel. 06/1-266-2888) and the South African Embassy (Gárdonyi Géza út 17; tel. 06/1-392-0999). There is no **Australian** (Mattiellistraße 2-4, Vienna; tel. +43-1-506-740) or **New Zealand Embassy** (Mattiellistraße 2-4, Vienna; tel. +43-1-505-3021) in Budapest, so you will have to go to Vienna.

LAUNDRY

Hungary doesn't have as many laundromats as you'd find in big cities in the USA or UK, especially since most households have their own washing machines. However, there are more and more laundromats popping up in the city center you can use literally any time of day. Most centrally located laundromats are very modern, and will include the cost of the detergent and fabric softener in the price. Most laundromats in Budapest require you to pay at the cash register (either notes or coins) and some even take cards.

BUBBLES

Paulay Ede utca 3; www.bubbles.hu; open 24 hours; washing HUF 1,600-2,000, drying HUF 1500-1900; metro 1, 2, 3, tram 47, 48, 49: Deák Ferenc tér

SELF SERVICE LAUNDRY BUDAPEST

Dohány utca 37; www.laundrybudapest.hu; open daily 9am-midnight; washing HUF 800-1000, drying HUF 800; metro 2, tram 4, 6: Blaha Lujza tér

Transportation

GETTING THERE
Air

Budapest has one international airport, the **Ferenc Liszt International Airport** (BUD; tel. 06/1-296-7000; www.bud.hu), sometimes known by its former name of Ferihegy Airport, located in the southeastern suburbs. There are two terminals, but terminal 1 has been closed since 2012, so all flights go in and out of 2A and 2B.

Flights between Budapest and Vienna take 45 minutes and 1 hour 10 minutes for Prague (but once you factor in the time to check-in, getting to the airport, and so on, you're better off taking the train).

AIRPORT TRANSPORTATION

Getting to and from the airport is easy. For door-to-door service, the **miniBUD** (tel. 06/1-550-0000; www.minibud.hu; HUF 4,900 one-way to the city center) minibus service offers easy access to your hotel around the clock. miniBUD customer service counters can be found as soon as you exit arrivals. You may have to wait up to 30 minutes for a mini-bus; they will either call your name or your Budapest address. The journey time depends on your destination in the city, the traffic, or the number of passengers with you (the bus stops door-to-door in the neighborhood), so account for around 30-60 minutes for the journey into town. You can get return tickets when

you buy your ticket at arrivals, or you can book online (latest: five hours before departure).

Another option is to take the **100E bus** (HUF 900), which will take you directly into the city center. The buses usually run on a half-hourly basis (from 4am-11:30pm) and take 30 minutes to get downtown.

A **taxi** from the airport can cost HUF 5,500-7,000 and takes around 30 minutes to reach the city center.

Train

Budapest has four main train stations. **Keleti** (Eastern) Train Station (metro lines 2 and 4) is the main one. The others are the **Nyugati** (Western, metro 3), **Déli** (Southern, metro 2), and **Kelenföld** (metro 4). Except for Kelenföld, all are located in the city center with good transport connections by metro, trams, and buses.

There are a number of trains that go to and from Budapest and other destinations in Hungary and abroad. You can buy tickets and check timetables from **MÁV** (www.mav.hu) for both international and domestic connections. There are regular trains going a few times a day to Vienna and Prague. If you buy an international train ticket from Budapest online, you will get a code, and you'll need to print it from the ticket machine. You can go to the international desks at the Nyugati and Keleti Train Stations.

From Prague: Trains to Budapest run by **Ceske Drahy** (www.cd.cz), **Regiojet** (www.regiojet.com) or **Leo Express** (www.leoexpress.com) depart from Hlavní nádraží every 1-2 hours from about 6am-4pm with a few late night options until midnight. The journey takes about 6.5 hours during the day and about 9-12 hours for an overnight train. Prices ranges roughly 600-1,500 CZK on different carriers and direct trains or transfers.

From Vienna: Trains run from Wien Hauptbahnhof every one to two hours to Budapest Keleti (2.5-3 hours, €13-30) either running with Austria's **ÖBB Railjet** (www.oebb.at) or EuroCity trains that are run by various European train operators, like the Hungarian MÁV. However, do note that if you're leaving Vienna you cannot buy a ticket from the MÁV website, as tickets need to be printed from the ticket machines in the Hungarian train stations—so unless you're starting in Budapest before you go onto Vienna you will need to buy tickets from ÖBB Railjet website or from the ticket offices at Wien Hauptbahnhof.

Bus

The main bus station for international journeys is Népliget Bus Station, which connects to metro line 3. **Flixbus,** in collaboration with the domestic **Volánbusz** company (http://nemzetkozi.volanbusz.hu), is the most reliable international bus service to other European destinations, including Vienna and Prague.

From Prague: Buses from Florenc to Budapest run almost every hour from around 5am-5pm, and then once every 2-3 hours until midnight. The journey takes anywhere from 7-10 hours and ranges from 400-800 CZK with different carriers, including **Regiojet, Leo Express,** and **FlixBus** (www.flixbus.com).

From Vienna: FlixBus (www.flixbus.com) run regular bus services from Vienna Edberg to Budapest several times per day, operating hourly or even more frequently. The journey is around 3 hours and costs €9-14.

Car

There are five motorways and four main roads in Hungary, with eight starting from Budapest. If you're planning to drive on the motorway, you must buy a **motorway sticker** (HUF 3,000 for a 10-day sticker), available at the border crossing or gas stations. The **M1** motorway connects Budapest to Vienna and Prague. The **M3** will take you out of the city toward Eger or Gödöllő and all the way to the Ukrainian border. The **M7** heads toward Lake Balaton, and the **M5** heads down toward the Serbian border. The Hungarian Highway Code (KRESZ) is similar to the rest of the EU, with speed limits within the cities at 50 kilometers/hour (30 mph) and on the motorways at 130 kilometers/hour (80 mph). Front and rear seat belts are compulsory, and mobile phones must be used with a hands-free kit.

From Prague: The 520-kilometer (325-mi) drive can take 5-8 hours depending on traffic. Head south and east on the D1/E65 and D2/E65 highways and cross Slovakia to get to Hungary on the M1. There are tolls on parts of the route (CZK 350 in the Czech Republic, €10 in Slovakia for 10-day stickers).

From Vienna: Drive 240 kilometers (150 mi) southeast on the A4 and M1 highways to reach Budapest (tolls apply, in addition for the Hungarian motorway vignette, the Austrian one costs €9 for a 10-day sticker). The drive takes around 2.5 hours.

GETTING AROUND

Budapest is a relatively compact city that's easy to get around on foot or with public transport operated by Budapest's public transit network, the **Budapesti Közlekedési Központ** (BKK; www.bkk.hu). You have plenty of modes to choose from, incluindg metro, bus, and tram. Just note that single-use tickets are not valid for transfers—except on the metro. Generally speaking, trams are the easiest and quickest way of getting around the city, though buses are the only public transit option for reaching the Castle District.

Don't Forget to Validate!

Unless you have a Budapest Card or a 24-hour or longer pass, you will need to **validate your bus, metro, or tram ticket** by punching it in a slotted box. Find these boxes at metro entrances and onboard the tram and bus. Some older trams require you to put the ticket in vertically and pull it down hard so the ticket punches. **Double-check for the time stamp or punch marks,** as some machines may run out of ink and ticket validation won't be visible.

Ticket inspectors (sometimes in uniform, sometimes plain-clothed with a purple armband) check transport at random for tickets. **Keep your validated tickets with you at all times** as you can be inspected at any point—even when exiting the metro. If you are caught without a ticket, ticket inspectors can get unpleasant and charge a fine of HUF 8,000, which you can pay on the spot or at designated BKK Customer Service Centers (such as Rumbach Sebestyén utca 19-21 or Akácfa utca 22) within two days. You can also pay by bank transfer if you exceed the two-day threshold, but this will cost more (HUF 16,000).

There are a few "fake" ticket inspectors who may insist on a cash fine. If you are suspicious, insist on paying at the BKK Customer Service Centers. (Paying by transfer after two days is more expensive, but at least you'll know that you're not just giving money to someone taking advantage of the system.) If you can get to a customer service center as soon as possible, the fine should be the same as paying immediately.

If you have a pass and left it at the hotel, you can request a form and pay a reduced fine of HUF 2,000 at the BKK Customer Service Center when you prove you had a pass. Typically, inspectors will ask you for identification, and you may be asked to get off the tram/bus/metro if you don't have a validated ticket.

Transit Passes

You can buy transit passes at the kiosk in the metro or from purple machines next to the bus, tram, or metro. Passes can be valid for **24 hours** (HUF 1,650), **72 hours** (HUF 4,150), or **7 days** (HUF 4,950) and can be used on all forms of transport, except the BKK boat on weekends. Single tickets cost HUF 350 or HUF 3,000 for a block of 10.

Metro

Budapest has four metro lines denoted by numbers and colors. The **yellow metro line 1** runs from Vörösmarty tér, traversing the entire stretch of Andrássy Avenue to City Park. The **red metro line 2** passes under the Danube and the city center. The **blue line metro 3** runs from the suburbs in northern Pest into the city center and up toward the airport. **Green metro 4** goes between the Keleti and Kelenföld Train Stations, crossing from Pest into South Buda. You can change between metro lines at Deák Ferenc tér (lines 1, 2, 3), Kálvin tér (lines 3 and 4), and Keleti pályaudvar (lines 2 and 4). At the time of writing there were plans to construct a fifth metro line running from Szentendre to Csepel, Ráckeve. The current **HÉV H5** suburban train line is being called "Metro 5" as of September 2019 (although locals still refer to it by its old name), but this won't affect development. Construction for this extention began in April 2021, but on the southern end of the line.

Metros operate between 4:30am-11:30pm daily.

Tram and Bus

The tram is the easiest and quickest way to get around Budapest. Lines **4** and **6** running along the Grand Boulevard are the most efficient for getting from Buda to Pest and take you all the way around the center—and line 6 runs all night long (most trams run at the same time as the metro, 4:30am-11:30pm). Other tram lines, like **2** or **41,** are a scenic way of seeing the city.

Buses are less attractive for travelers, but they are efficient and will take you further out of the city than the tram. Bus lines **16, 16A,** and **116** will take you up to the Castle District. Bus **150** will get you to Memento Park. If you want to head up to the Buda Hills, then make a note of lines **21, 21A,** and **212.**

Boat

In the summer, you can take BKK's public boat along the Danube, which is free on weekdays with a travel pass, or HUF 750 for a single ticket or on the weekends. There are docks all along the Danube, with some going as far as Rómaifürdő.

Taxi

Avoid hailing a taxi, as there are some rogue operators who take advantage of tourists. Instead, call a reputable taxi company, like **City Taxi** (tel. 06/1-211-1111), **Fő Taxi** (tel. 06/1-222-2222), **Taxi Plus** (tel. 06/1-888-8888), **Taxi 6x6** (tel. 06/1-666-6666), or use an app like **Taxify.**

Day Trips from Budapest

You can spend days, if not weeks, exploring

Budapest, but there is more to Hungary than its capital. The good news is Hungary is a small country, which makes it easy to jaunt off for the day, whether you catch the train down to Lake Balaton—Central Europe's largest lake—ride a boat up the dramatic valleys of the Danube Bend, explore the colorful art colony of Szentendre, or taste the famed "Bull's Blood" wine in the Valley of the Beautiful Woman outside Eger.

PLANNING YOUR TIME

Popular day trips from Budapest include the village of **Szentendre**, which brings in the crowds all year round, accessible on the suburban train in just 40 minutes, or the **Danube Bend,** whose main towns

Highlights

Look for ★ to find recommended sights, activities, dining, and lodging.

© MOON.COM

★ **Hungarian Open Air Museum:** For a taste of life in rural Hungary, visit this open-air museum divided into areas that represent different regions of the country (page 438).

★ **Shopping in Szentendre:** Szentendre, an artists' colony since the 1920s, is a wonderful place to shop for folk crafts and contemporary design alike (page 439).

★ **Visegrád Citadel:** The views from the top of this 13th-century citadel are among the best in Hungary (page 446).

★ **Esztergom Basilica:** Walk around the dome of the largest church in Hungary for sweeping views across the Danube to Slovakia on the other side of the river (page 451).

★ **Boating the Danube Bend from Esztergom to Budapest:** The slow boat back to Budapest is a leisurely float past Esztergom's basilica, the surrounding hills, and local wildlife. Plus, there's a bar on board (page 451).

★ **Tagore Promenade:** This tree-lined promenade in Balatonfüred makes for a beautiful walk along Lake Balaton (page 453).

★ **Tihanyi Levendula Galéria:** Tihany, one of the loveliest spots on Lake Balaton, is known for its fields of lavender. Shop for local lavender products in this quaint shop in the heart of town (page 460).

★ **Siófok Beaches:** Join the Budapest locals who escape the city to sunbathe on these golden beaches on the banks of Lake Balaton in summer (page 464).

★ **Eger Castle:** Explore the interior of this fortress-like castle along with the complex labyrinth of tunnels that snakes beneath it (page 466).

★ **Wine Tasting in the Valley of the Beautiful Woman:** This atmospheric valley outside Eger holds wine cellars ranging from simple to stunning, some of which are carved into the hillside. The cellars are conveniently close to one another (page 470).

Day Trips from Budapest

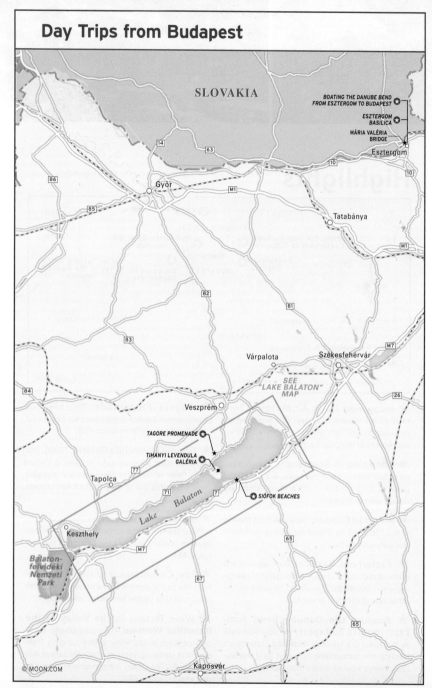

SLOVAKIA

BOATING THE DANUBE BEND
FROM ESZTERGOM TO BUDAPEST

ESZTERGOM
BASILICA

MÁRIA VALÉRIA
BRIDGE

Esztergom

14   63

10

86

10

Győr   M1

85   Tatabánya

M1

82

81

83

M7

Várpalota   Székesfehérvár

SEE
"LAKE BALATON"
MAP

84   26

Veszprém

TAGORE PROMENADE

TIHANYI LEVENDULA
GALÉRIA

Tapolca   77

71   Lake   Balaton   7

SIÓFOK BEACHES

Keszthely

M7   65

Balaton-
felvidéki
Nemzeti
Park   67

65

Kaposvár

© MOON.COM

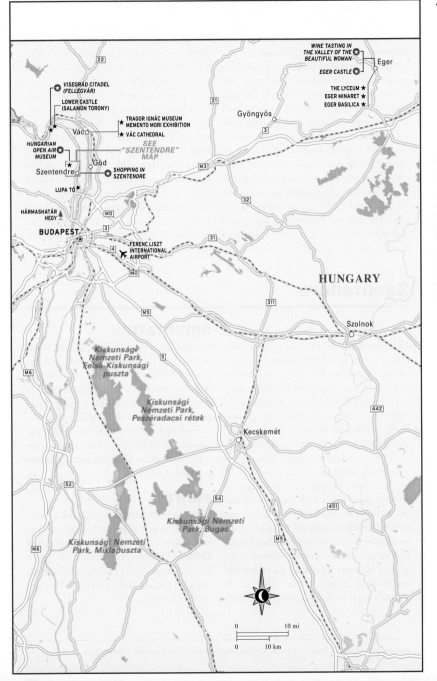

are between 30 minutes to just over an hour away by train or bus. Others also opt to go further afield. Some destinations, such as **Lake Balaton** (1.5-3 hours from Budapest by train) or **Eger** (2 hours from Budapest by train), can be rewarding when done as an overnight trip.

You can also combine day-trip destinations that are geographically close to each other: Szentendre can be combined with other destinations on the Danube Bend, such as Visegrád. One thing to keep in mind if you're planning to visit more than one place in a day is that most destinations, including Szentendre and all of the Danube Bend, lack luggage storage facilities. (The Eger bus station and Siófok train station on Lake Balaton are two exceptions.) If you'll eventually loop back to Budapest, you might want to leave most of your luggage at a **luggage storage** facility (www. budapestluggagestorage.com; €10 for 24 hours per piece; available in the V, VI, VII, VIII Districts) there, bringing only what you need in a light backpack.

Each destination has its seasonal appeal. Lake Balaton is most popular in the summer months, but is still charming in spring and fall if the weather is good. The Danube Bend is beautiful to visit year-round, but if you're planning to take the boat, do note that connections are seasonal, so to experience it fully it's best to visit from late spring to early fall. Szentendre and Eger, on the other hand, buzz all year round, and can make good alternatives if you want to add a day trip during the winter.

Szentendre

For a low-maintenance day trip from Budapest, hop a train or boat to Szentendre (pop. 25,000). In the 18th century, the town had a thriving Serbian community, but it's also known for being an artists' colony since the 1920s and still sports the bohemian atmosphere, with hidden art and ceramic workshops tucked away in the town's courtyards and galleries. Shortly after getting off the train, or even off the boat, you'll find yourself wandering cobbled streets lined with stalls selling antiques and artists painting canvases set up on the sidewalk. Colorful houses undulate under white church towers in warm tones from honeydew to claret red. It can get a little crowded in the summer months when visitors look for an easy way to escape the heat in the city, but in the spring and fall it's a lovely day trip. Since it's so close, you can also just visit for half a day if you fancy a change in scenery.

ORIENTATION

Szentendre is easy to navigate **on foot,** but most of the public transport will put you on the edge of the town. From there it takes 15 minutes to walk to the center, to Blagoveštenska Church and Fő tér, the main public square. Most of the sites are located around Fő tér or within 10 minutes' walk; however, the Hungarian Open Air Museum is a little out of town, and you will need a **bus** or a **taxi** to get there.

SIGHTS

Although Szentendre is a city you can appreciate simply by getting lost in the narrow, steep, back streets around **St. John the Baptist Catholic Church** (Templom tér, Vár Domb; Tue-Sun 10am-5pm) or by taking a stroll along the Danube, there is plenty to keep you busy for the day.

Previous: the town of Szentendre; shopping in Tihany; Valley of the Beautiful Woman, Eger.

Szentendre

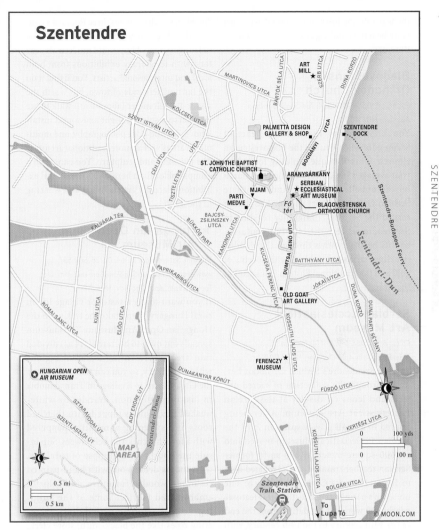

Ferenczy Museum

Kossuth Lajos utca 5; tel. 06/26-779-6657; www. muzeumicentrum.hu; Wed-Sun 10am-6pm; HUF 1,400 (for one exhibition), HUF 1,700 (all exhibitions)

When arriving by the local suburban train or by bus, the Ferenczy Museum is the first museum you'll reach on your way into town. This 18th-century mansion with canary-yellow walls once belonged to the Hungarian Impressionist artist Károly Ferenczy and his family. The museum spreads over three floors and hones in on the local art history, with works from Ferenczy and other Szentendre-based artists. Head to the second floor to see work by the founders of the 1920s artists' settlement known as "The Eight," along with interesting temporary exhibitions.

This museum is part of the Ferenczy Museum Center, a network of 10 museums scattered around Szentendre, but being on the way into the town, it's a good place to get your bearings and figure out your own art itinerary.

Blagoveštenska Orthodox Church

Fő tér; tel. 06/26-310-554; Tue-Sun 10am-5pm Apr-Sep; HUF 400

You know you've reached the heart of Szentendre when you see the Blagoveštenska Church. This Baroque building looks like your average 18th-century Hungarian church on the outside, but you'll find an ornate Serbian Orthodox heart within. The church served the Serbian community residing in Szentendre between the 14th-19th centuries, and its heritage shows through the wooden paneling varnished in black with accents of gold and the traditional Eastern icons around the altar.

Serbian Ecclesiastical Art Museum

Fő tér 6; tel. 06/26-952-474; Tue-Sun 10am-6pm May-Sep; 10am-4pm Oct-Apr; HUF 1,000

Explore Szentendre's Serbian Orthodox heritage through the collection of sacred objects and icons on display at the Serbian Ecclesiastical Art Museum. After being housed in a small private space, in 2019, the Serbian Ecclesiastical Museum moved into a 1,600-square-meter (17,000-sq-ft) former Serbian teacher training school located next to Blagoveštenska Orthodox Church. The museum's permanent collection now features nearly 400 works of art dating from the end of the 13th century to the 19th century, with an interesting display of iconography, books, applied art, chalices, and other ecclesiastical art. There is also a multimedia center and exhibition space in this new and expanding museum.

Art Mill

Bogdányi utca 32; tel. 06/20-779-6657; www. muzeumicentrum.hu; Tue-Sun 10am-6pm; HUF 1,400

Don't let its remote location deceive you: the Art Mill, which occupies three floors of a converted 19th-century red-brick sawmill, is one of Hungary's most important modern art centers, with temporary exhibitions from both local and international artists. You'll find it on the far northern side of town, but worth the scenic 1.4-kilometer (about 1 mi) walk to see its diverse displays of light and sound installations, cutting-edge photography, and multimedia art as well as more traditional art forms like painting and sculpture. You can catch a glimpse of local art here, as it's the central exhibition place for artists living and working in the town.

★ Hungarian Open Air Museum

Skanzen, Sztaravodai út; tel. 06/26-502-537; www.skanzen.hu; Tue-Sun 9am-5pm mid-Mar-Oct, Tue-Sun 9am-4pm Oct-Nov; HUF 2,000

If you want to get a taste for village life in rural Hungary, then make the trek up to the Hungarian Open Air Museum. The museum spreads out over 46 hectares (114 ac) divided into areas representing different regions within Hungary, so you can take a trip from the Great Plains to a village in Transdanubia in just one afternoon. Wander by whitewashed farmhouses topped with thatched roofs and sweeping windmills, peppered with a few churches and bell towers. Slip inside the houses for a glimpse of rural life, with rooms decked out with hand-painted ceramics, wooden furniture, and colorful embroidered fabrics. Some of the buildings feature actors in period dress, recreating roles like the blacksmith, store clerk, or schoolteacher to give you an immersive experience in old Hungarian life. You can also take a train ride through "Hungary"— and through time—on the **Skanzen Train** (www.skanzen.hu/en/plan-your-visit/good-to-know/skanzen-train; departures from the Railway Station Building 10am-4pm on the hour; HUF 500), which dates back to 1927 (but is fully renovated). If you're lucky to make it for one of the days when a fair takes place, usually on the weekends and around festivals, you may catch local artisans and craftspeople around selling unique souvenirs such as embroidered fabrics or decorated gingerbread hearts.

To get to the Hungarian Open Air Museum, grab the bus operated by Volánbusz 878 (on weekdays) and 879 (on weekends) next to the local train station, usually going from bay 7. The bus takes around 20 minutes and costs HUF 230. A taxi will set you back around HUF 3,000. The museum is only open from spring to fall.

★ SHOPPING

Shopping Districts
BOGDÁNYI STREET AND DUMTSA JENŐ ROAD

Szentendre's arts and crafts shopping scene buzzes through the streets clustered around Fő tér and the Orthodox Church, particularly on **Bogdányi Street** and **Dumtsa Jenő Road.** Shops selling folk crafts, contemporary design, and fine art gather along these cobbled streets, and painters usually sit on the sidewalk putting their brush to the easel with stacks of their paintings propped against the yellow- or ochre-colored walls, ready for you to buy one.

Galleries
PALMETTA DESIGN GALLERY & SHOP

Bogdányi út 14; tel. 06/26-313-649; www.palmettadesign.hu; daily 10am-6pm

Couple István and Anna Regős established the Palmetta Design Gallery back in 1998 in a 200-year-old wine cellar under their house at the heart of Szentendre. Twenty years later their mission to create a space dedicated to Hungarian and international design lives on—locals and tourists flock through the doorway of their Baroque house and down the stone steps to visit their showroom. Pick up one of Anna Regős's hand-woven handbags or peruse curiosities from other designers, such as FruFru's matchboxes that double as fridge magnets featuring Hungarian landscapes, or notepads with updated motifs of Hungarian folk art.

PARTI MEDVE

Városház tér 4; tel. 06/20-254-3729; Mon-Fri 7:45am-6:45pm, Sat 9am-6pm, Sun 9am-3pm

Parti Medve is the multitasking sanctuary in the Szentendre shopping scene, occupying a two-story Baroque townhouse opposite the City Hall, where you'll find a café, gallery, and bookshop on site. A great place to take

Hungarian Open Air Museum

the kids, it has toys and books for adults and kids—in English, too—as well as art for sale. Grab a table on the terrace or wander up the spiral staircase to the indoor café for a cup of tea or coffee, before taking home a book, mug, bag, plushy toy, or a local piece of art.

OLD GOAT ART GALLERY

Dumtsa Jenő utca 15; tel. 06/30-523-9184; daily 11am-6pm

This charming gallery run by an artist husband-and-wife pair, Hungarian Eszter Győry and American Osiris O'Connor, has a new-age vibe with colorful surreal paintings and "Soul Angels," angel-shaped statuettes made from alabaster sometimes decorated with paint, Swarovski stones, Bohemian crystals, and Murano glass. Each angel comes with a birth certificate and a number—their "adopter" gets to name them. You can also pick up handcrafted metal pendants and rings. Most of the art work and sculptures are created by the couple, who are happy to chat about their art when you visit the shop.

FOOD
Hungarian
ARANYSÁRKÁNY

Alkotmány utca 1/a; tel. 06/26-301-479; www.aranysarkany.hu; Tue-Sun noon-10pm; HUF 2,500-5,900

The name Aranysárkány, meaning Golden Dragon, may evoke Chinese food but actually carries usual Hungarian favorites from goulash soup to wild boar ragout, plus a few non-Hungarian wildcards such as Serbian dishes. They have a fun variation of a personal Hungarian favorite, fried cheese, that uses breaded port salut, smoked and non-smoked brie, cranberry jam, and tartar sauce. Forgot your reading glasses and struggling with the menu? No worries—they have a selection of prescription glasses in an old tea box you can borrow! The atmosphere here is intimate and

cozy, with rusty carpet weaves and vintage brass pots and pans decorating the walls.

International
MJAM

Városház tér 2; tel. 06/70-440-3700; daily 11am-10pm; entrées HUF 2,500-4,750

You will find an abundance of paprika-laden restaurants scattered around Szentendre, but if you want something a little different that gets away from the violin music and goulash, then try Mjam. From the outside, it looks like your typical Baroque townhouse, but inside this breezy, minimalist restaurant you can tuck into a bold Caribbean fusion menu, with items such as duck breast smoked with tea leaves.

GETTING THERE

Szentendre is a popular **day trip** from Budapest since it's so easy to get to from the city center. The journey by train is the most comfortable. The boat is the slowest way to get there but allows you to take in the scenery along the Danube, including Budapest's landmarks and the tree-covered Danube islands. Also, you can cut out all the walking from the train and bus station as the boat will put you down in the center.

Train

From Budapest, you can grab the **H5** local suburban train (at the time of writing there were plans to turn this into a metro line) operated by BKK (www.bkk.hu) from either Batthyány tér or under Margaret Bridge—just make sure you catch the one going all the way to Szentendre and buy a Suburban Railway Extension ticket that covers the region outside Budapest. (Note that this is sold by how many kilometers you go outside the city boundary—from the city to Szetendendre is a 15 km ticket.) You can buy these from the ticket office in the metro station or from the purple ticket machines across town. If you only have a local ticket, the inspector who gets on at Békásmegyer can sell you an extension, usually for around HUF 370 extra.

1: souvenir shop in Szentendre **2:** Blagoveštenska Orthodox Church **3:** Fő tér is the colorful heart of this former artist's colony.

The train journey takes around 40 minutes. Tickets cost HUF 760, and trains run every 20 minutes (every 10 min in peak times) from 4am-11:30pm. When you arrive in Szentendre, take the underpass just north of the station and then continue north along Kossuth Lajos utca. It will take 10-15 minutes to reach the town center on foot.

Bus

You can take a bus 880, 889, 890 with **Volánbusz** (www.volanbusz.hu) from Újpest-Városkapu in Budapest, which is accessible with metro line 3. The bus ride is only 25 minutes and costs HUF 310, but considering you need to take a metro all the way out of the city, it's not the most convenient way to get to Szentendre; it's a good alternative if you have issues getting the H5. Or if you miss the H5 coming back, the **bus station** is right next to the train station, so you have an alternative. Buses run every 20 minutes during the day (fewer services after 8pm) from 5:30am-10:55pm.

Boat

In the summer, **Mahart Passnave** (www.mahartpassnave.hu) runs boat services to Szentendre from downtown Budapest, at either the Vigadó tér dock or the Batthyány tér. It departs Budapest at 10am, getting to Szentendre around noon. The journey back (leaving at 5pm) is much quicker, only 50 minutes, as you're going downstream. One-way tickets cost HUF 2,540, round-trips HUF 3,820.

Car

Szentendre is only a 30-minute drive from Budapest city center. Take the road along the embankment on the Buda side (the west side of the river) and drive north on **Route 11.** The town is signposted, and you won't need a motorway vignette (a toll pass you need on all the country's highways) on this route. **Parking** is strictly regulated in Szentendre and costs between HUF 280-360 per hour, depending on where you park. The highest parking rates are usually around the Danube promenade.

GETTING AROUND

The best way to get around Szentendre is to **walk,** and apart from the Hungarian Open Air Museum, you won't need to get public transport around town. While the walk to the center follows a straight line, it will take around 15 minutes to get there from the bus

boat docked on the Danube in Szentendre

and the train station (which are located in the same place), so budget some extra time to walk back and forth.

If you want to get a taxi, you can call a couple of local companies: **Szentendre Taxi** (tel. 06/20-266-6662) or **Szentendre Taxi 8 Nagy István** (tel. 06/26-314-314).

LEAVING SZENTENDRE

The last **suburban railway train** back to Budapest leaves around 11:30pm. The last **boat** back to Budapest departs at 5pm. There is also a direct bus from the bus station to **Visegrád** (45 minutes) and Esztergom (1.5 hours) departing at 10:55pm.

Danube Bend

North of Budapest, the Danube River threads through hills and valleys passing medieval castles, Baroque towns, and wild hillsides. If you're into history and dramatic views, then the Danube Bend is the day trip for you. In the summer you can also grab a boat or a hydrofoil from Budapest or from one of the towns on the Danube Bend to really appreciate the scenery hugging the river.

The Danube Bend covers a vast area. You can either explore parts with the rental car, sail down the river and enjoy the scenery from the boat going to or from Budapest, or simply pick one or two of the destinations to visit. I recommend investing in a **Danube Bend Daily Ticket** (HUF 1,999) at any train station ticket office, which gives you unlimited travel on the day on the Danube Bend train and bus services, the HÉV to Szentendre, and the Danube Bend Circle Line (the boat running from Visegrád to the town of Zebegény and back) if you are planning to visit more than one destination and want to throw in a boat excursion.

VÁC

Vác (pop. 33,000) lies just 30 kilometers (19 mi) north of Budapest on the east bank of the Danube. It's the perfect alternative to the more crowded Szentendre, as you can explore its historic cobbled streets with churches and Baroque townhouses, or stroll along the Danube side promenade, away from the crowds that flock to the other side of the river. If you love history, you'll find plenty of it in Vác, one Hungary's oldest towns and once the local seat for the Catholic church.

It takes 10 minutes to walk from the train or bus stations (which are next to each other) in Vác to the town center and the Danube, so the best way to explore this Baroque town is on foot. Just head south in the direction of the river. If you arrive by boat, this will put you down near the town center, only minutes away on foot.

Sights
TRAGOR IGNÁC MUSEUM, MEMENTO MORI EXHIBITION
Marcius 15 tér 19; tel. 06/30-555-3349;
www.muzeumvac.hu; Tue-Sun 10am-6pm Apr-Oct,
10am-5pm Nov-Mar; HUF 1,400

For something truly offbeat, head to the cellar under Március 15 tér 19 to discover the 18th-century mummies and painted coffins found in a secret crypt that was walled up for 200 years. You can see some of the coffins as well as rosaries, crucifixes, icons, and coins excavated in the crypt at the permanent Memento Mori Exhibition in this cool cellar under the Tragor Ignác Museum. The museum also has other exhibitions, including the Ars Memorandi exhibition (included in the price), focusing on the history of the town from the liberation of Ottoman rule to the "Golden Age of Vác" at the end of the 18th century.

Cycling up the Danube

along the Danube in Szentendre

Cycling along the Danube is a great way to take in the city and surrounding area from a different perspective. There are designated cycle paths running along the river in both Buda (very popular, especially in summer) and in Pest (less crowded, but also less scenic, with more development and less greenery).

BUDAPEST TO SZENTENDRE (27 KM/17 MI)

Budapest's most popular cycling trail is the route on the Buda side of the river to Szentendre. This route is part of the of the 4,000-km (2,500-mi) **EuroVelo 6** route, one of Europe's most famous and longest cycling routes, which follows many of Europe's famous rivers, including the Danube. This dedicated paved bike path skirts the banks of the Danube with amazing views and plenty of stopover opportunities on the way. It's mostly flat, so you can relax and focus on the tree-clad riverside landscape all the way to Szentendre.

Once the route gets you out of the center, you'll pass a few of the city's lesser-known curiosities, like the **Óbuda Gasworks,** a disused gas factory that looks like something out of a fairy tale with its turreted water towers. The trail then turns down to **Római Part,** popular for its Danube beaches. You can stop off here for a few fröccs (a white or rosé wine spritzer) at one of the many

VÁC CATHEDRAL

Schuszter Konstantin tér 11; tel. 06/27-814-184; www.vaciegyhazmegye.hu; Mon-Sat 10am-noon and 2pm-5pm, Sun 7:30am-7pm Mar-Nov; free

The impressive Vác Cathedral is just a five-minute walk southeast from the Tragor Ignác Museum. This neoclassical cathedral—in an awkwardly epic scale compared to its humble surroundings—was built in the 18th century. Its grand entrance is marked by a gate of Corinthian columns leading into

a surprisingly breezy interior with cream-colored walls and a vibrant fresco painted by Franz Anton Maulbertsch on the vaulted dome.

Food
MIHÁLYI PATISSERIE

Köztársaság út 21; tel. 06/20-390-3367; www.mihalyipatisserie.com; Tue-Sun 10am-6pm; cakes HUF 990-1,600

Mihályi Patisserie may have only three tables,

riverside bars, like the bike-friendly and stripy-deck-chair-clad **Fellini Római Kultúrbisztró** (Kossuth Lajos üdülőpart 5; www.felliniromai.hu; Mon-Thu 2pm-11pm, Fri noon-midnight, Sun-Sat 10am-midnight May-Oct). If you start around Batthyány tér, it'll take you 30-45 minutes to reach Romai Part; longer if you plan to stop to take in the sights on the way. You can either end your route here and cycle back to the city, or continue onward toward Szentendre.

Once you get beyond the city limits, 1 kilometer (about half a mi) north of Budapest, keep an eye out for **Lupa Island** to your right, a small island only accessible by bike, and **Lupa Tó (Lupa Lake)** to your left. The lake has a popular local beach (HUF 1,000-3,500 entrance fee) complete with sand and palm trees. **Ebihal Büfe** (Budakalász, Lupa-szigeti révátkelő; daily 8am-11pm summer), a bar and café set on a moored boat on the river opposite the island, is a good place to stop for lunch before continuing the remaining 10 kilometers (6 mi) on to Szentendre.

Once you reach Szentendre, you can take the bikes on the HÉV, the local suburban rail network, back to Budapest.

BUDAPEST TO VÁC (40 KIM/25 MI)

An alternate route on the Pest side of the river leads to the Danube Bend town of Vác. This route is a mix of regular roads and a paved bike path. It is relatively flat all the way, and less crowded than the route to Szentendre.

For something different, take a detour to off-beat **Népsziget** (which is still in Budapest, just in the northern suburbs, approximately 8 km/5 mi from the center), an islet that's home to old ship-building factories and quirky fried-fish stands and art collectives. If you decide to bike over here, check out **Kabin** (Népsziget út 727; daily noon-midnight summer), a colorful bar on the north end of Népsziget that backs up to the river and looks across to Római Beach on the Buda side.

Just like from Szentendre, you can usually take your bike back with you on the train after reaching Vác (most have a compartment for bikes).

BIKE RENTAL IN BUDAPEST
Yellow Zebra
Lázár utca 16; www.yellowzebratours.com/yellow-zebra-szentendre-bike-tour.php; rates begin at HUF 1,000 per hour
Rent a bike from a company like Yellow Zebra, which also does private bike tours to Szentendre, if you prefer to have someone guide you.

Bike Base Budapest
Podmaniczky utca 19; www.bikebase.hu; Apr-Sep; rates begin at HUF 2,500 for 5 hours
Bike Base Budapest is another option that's centrally located for rentals.

but its cakes are a work of art. Whether you want to sit with a coffee and a cake or get a few macarons to go to savor by the riverside, you'll be glad you popped in for something sweet.

HEKK TERASZ
Sánc dűlő; tel. 06/70-252-7295; Sun-Thu 11am-9pm, Fri-Sat 11am-7pm; entrées HUF 1,490-3,500
Enjoy some freshly caught and cooked fish at Hekk Terasz. This restaurant on the Danube is a little out of town on the bicycle route but worth the 50-minute walk along the river for its fish dishes and riverside views. Book in advance if you plan to go, as it's very popular with locals and day-trippers from Budapest. The fish is priced by weight, so prices will vary depending on the size and type of fish. If you're not sure what to order, go for the namesake hekk (freshwater hake) that comes deep-fried, and have some fries with their homemade herb- or mayonnaise-based dips.

Getting There

From Budapest, the easiest way to get to Vác is by train from Nyugati train station (25-40 minutes; HUF 650). Trains run every half an hour from 4:52am to 11:52pm.

In the summer, there is a hydrofoil with **Mahart Passnave** (www.mahartpassnave. hu) from the Vigadó dock in Budapest at 9:30am (40 minutes; HUF 3,300).

If you're athletic, you can cycle the path up the Danube (page 444) from Budapest to Vác.

You can also reach Vác by car by driving up Váci út in Pest until you reach Route 2 (1 hour). Parking in Vác costs HUF 300-400 per hour.

Leaving Vác

The last train departing Vác for Budapest Nyugati train station leaves at 11:30pm.

VISEGRÁD

To really appreciate the beauty of the Danube Bend, head to Visegrád (pop. 1,800), a small town on the west bank of the river at the tightest point of the bend, and the only point where the Danube flows north. Most people pick Visegrád for its medieval castle perched on the top of the hill, which you can reach either by car or by hiking the trodden paths through the woodland past the Calvary, an open-air representation of the crucifixion of Christ.

Sights

★ VISEGRÁD CITADEL
(Fellegvár)

Várhegy; tel. 06/26-598-080; daily 9am-5pm Mar and Oct, 9am-6pm Apr-Sep, 9am-4pm Nov-Dec, 9am-4pm Jan-Feb; HUF 1,700

Towering over the valley, the Visegrád Citadel can be seen from miles away, whether you arrive by train or boat. It dates back to the 13th century and its ruined ramparts give it a romantic edge. From the top, get ready for some of the best views in Hungary, overlooking the most dramatic curve of the Danube Bend. The citadel itself is also a fascinating slice of history, and although it looks ruined from afar,

part of it is still intact. You can still patrol the old walls, visit the armory, and even see a mini-waxwork museum inside the citadel.

You can drive or take a taxi, which takes around 10 minutes from the center of town and costs around HUF 1,000. Or hike the somewhat steep trail to the top, which takes about an hour.

LOWER CASTLE
(Salamon Torony)

Salamontorony utca; www.visegradmuzeum.hu; Wed-Sun 9am-5pm Apr-Sep; HUF 700

The Lower Castle, located halfway up the hill to the south of town, is accessible by taking the stairs leading up from the boat jetty for the Budapest boat line. It was a fortification system built in the 13th century that used to connect the Citadel with the Danube and once protected the vulnerable southern entrance. The highlight here is the Solomon Tower, a hexagonal tower that now houses a museum about the town. It gets its name from a local legend that Solomon (an 11th-century Hungarian king) was guarded in the tower after losing against King László and Géza in battle.

THE ROYAL PALACE

Fő utca 29; tel. 06/26-597-010; www. visegradmuzeum.hu; Tue-Sun 9am-5pm; HUF 1,300

Before you leave, make sure you head over to the partly reconstructed Renaissance palace used by King Matthias set on the riverbank. This beautiful palace is easy to reach—no climbing required, just a 10-minute walk from the Nagymaros ferry—and is also accessible for people with disabilities, with ramps and elevators installed in the complex. The palace ruins are very beautiful, with the reconstructed buildings bringing the ruins to life, like the arched-lion Matthias Fountain made out of pink marble and the colonnaded 15th-century courtyard surrounding the fountain.

1: Sail down the Danube Bend from Esztergom. **2:** the Esztergom Basilica **3:** The best way to see the Danube Bend is to hike up to Visegrád Citadel.

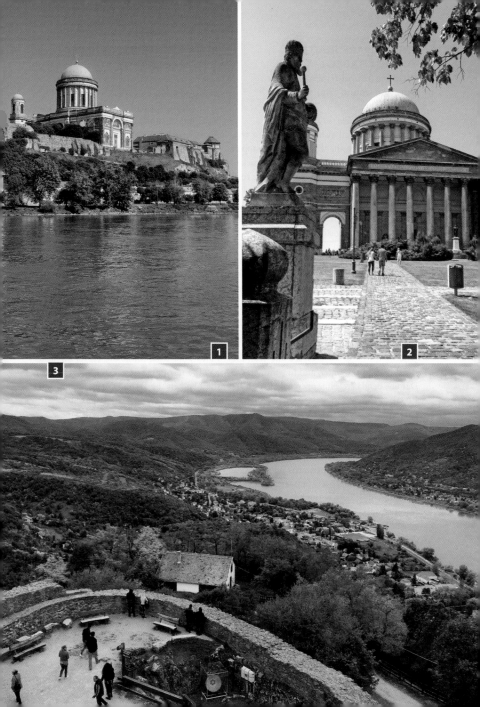

Hiking
THE CALVARY ROUTE TO THE CITADEL

Distance (round-trip): *1.6 km (1 mi)*
Duration (round-trip): *1 hour*
Effort: *moderate*
Trailhead: *Visegrád ferry dock*

If you want to add a short hike to your trip, the trail through the woods up to the top of the Citadel is a good option. From the dock of the Nagymaros-Visegrád ferry, take the road going west up the hill, turn left up Magasköz utca, and then take the path through the woods up to the Calvary. Just follow the trail up the hill (it's very steep and rocky, so wear good shoes) and you will reach the Citadel in another 20-40 minutes. Most of this route goes uphill on woodland paths, so while the trail is quite short compared to most hikes, it's pretty intense.

Boating
DANUBE BEND CIRCLE LINE

One of the best ways to see the Danube Bend is from the water, and in summer, the Danube Bend Circle line operated by **Mahart Passnave** (www.mahartpassnave.hu) is a particularly good way to sit back and appreciate the beautiful scenery of this region. The two-hour route (HUF 500) runs from Visegrád to Zebegény and back. You can disembark at any of the towns on the route if you like, or simply stay onboard and enjoy the riverside views as the boat circles back to Visegrád.

The boat departs Visegrád at 10am and at 2pm daily. Hop on board at the Visegrád dock, located at the base of Salamon Tower (just in front of the Renaissance Restaurant). (Note that this is not the same location as the ferry dock.) Alternatively, if you prefer to hop on the boat straight from the train, you can also get on at the dock in Nagymaros, the town opposite Visegrád.

Food
RENAISSANCE RESTAURANT
Fő utca 11; tel. 06/26-398-081; www.renvisegrad.hu; Sun-Fri noon-10pm, Sat noon-11pm; entrées HUF 2,900-5,500

This family-owned restaurant taps into Visegrád's historical spirit with a medieval feast served up in homemade crockery and locally supplied dishes. It's theatrical, but the food (Hungarian Renaissance meals given a modern upgrade) is actually good—try the venison goulash or freshly grilled trout, all washed down with some Hungarian wine, of course. In the summer you can sit out on their terrace with full views of the river. You can even dress up for the part if you want, or just take a look at the period costumes hanging by the entrance, waiting to be tried on.

PANORÁMA ÉTTEREM
Fekete-hegy Hotel Silvanus; tel. 06/26-398-311; www.hotelsilvanus.hu/en/hotel/gastronomy/panorama-restaurant; daily 7am-10pm; HUF 2,390-5,790

Panoráma Étterem at the Hotel Silvanus has the most amazing terrace overlooking the bend in the Danube. The menu oscillates between Hungarian dishes mostly focused on game, like their goulash served in a mini cauldron, and more international flavors, like their gourmet venison burger. It's 3.5 kilometers (2 mi) outside the town, very close to the citadel, so you may want to either take a taxi or visit after your hike to the castle.

Accommodations
SILVANUS HOTEL
Feketehegy; tel. 06/26-398-311; www.hotelsilvanus.hu; €112-260 d

It's worth staying at the Silvanus just for the view. From the top of the hill, just 300 meters (330 yds) from the Visegrád Citadel, the view over the Danube Bend is spectacular. The Silvanus also boasts a spa and wellness facility, with an outdoor pool with a view over the valley, plus an indoor pool, saunas, and an aroma and salt chamber. Treatments on offer include

Ayurvedic treatments. The hotel has a retro hunting lodge feel with dark wood-paneled walls and autumnal colors. Most price packages include breakfast and dinner.

Getting There

Bus is the most direct way to get to Visegrád, but that doesn't mean it's the best way to get here. I highly recommend the train-and-ferry option over the bus, as it's far more comfortable and actually quicker, despite not being a direct route. In summer, boat is of course the best option.

BUS

The most direct way to get to Visegrád is to take the 880 bus from Újpest-Városkapu in Budapest (accessible on the line 3 metro), which takes one hour 15 minutes (around HUF 750). Buses run once to twice an hour depending on the time of day (more frequent around 1pm-4pm) beginning at 5:35am and running till 10:55pm.

You can also take local bus 880 or 882 from the Szentendre's train station, costing around HUF 465.

TRAIN AND FERRY

You can grab a train run by MÁV (www.mavcsoport.hu) to the Nagymaros-Visegrád station from Nyugati train station in Budapest (40 min; HUF 1,120). This will take you to Nagymaros, a small town on the opposite side of the river and you can take the hourly ferry across the river. Trains go twice an hour from 4:52am-9:52pm. Once you get to Nagymaros, you need to walk 5 minutes westward down Magyar utca to the ferry.

From Nagymaros, the first ferry leaves at 6:30am, then goes on the hour from 8am-8pm. The journey across the river takes around 15 minutes and costs HUF 500. You can also bring a car across for HUF 1,650.

BOAT

When it's running, the best way to get there is by hydrofoil run by Mahart Passnave (www.

mahartpassnave.hu) from Vigadó at 9:30am daily in the summer (returning from Visegrád at 3:30pm), which takes an hour to get to Visegrád (HUF 4,300 one-way, HUF 6,500 round-trip).

There is also a slower boat route run by the same company that takes three and a half hours from Budapest, leaving Vigadó at 9am. Tickets cost HUF 3,180 one-way, HUF 4,760 round-trip. The dock for the Budapest boat is not in the same place as the ferry coming over from Nagymaros, but is toward the north next to the Lower Castle, however in 2020 this service was not running due to COVID-19, so check the Mahart Passnave website to double check this route is running.

CAR

It takes around 30 minutes to drive to Visegrád from Szentendre. There is one route that will take you through the Pilis Hills but this is complicated, so it's easier to follow Route 11 along the Danube banks to the town. This will also offer striking views along the river. From Vác things get a little more complicated as there are no bridges across the Danube in the area, so you will need to take a ferry in Vác to Tahitófalú (going once an hour; HUF 1,500 per car and HUF 430 pp) and then continue on Route 11. This journey will take around an hour. Alternately, you can drive back to Budapest and take the Megyeri Bridge across the Danube and join Route 11. Another variation is to drive northward 20 minutes to Nagymaros and take the ferry across, which also runs on the hour at the same rates. In Visegrád, parking costs around HUF 300 per hour.

Getting Around

The town itself is compact and takes minutes to get around on foot; however, getting up to the castle is a strenuous uphill hike. There's not too much in terms of public transportation. If you need a taxi while you're in town, call Visegrád Taxi (tel. 06/20-266-6662). You can also ask for a taxi at the

Walking to Slovakia

The state border between Slovakia and Hungary is on the Mária Valéria bridge.

If you want to get amazing views of Esztergom and sneak another country in, walk across the **Mária Valéria bridge** (a 10-15-min walk) over to Štúrovo, Slovakia, for wonderful vistas of the basilica and the city. In truth, there's not much to see in Štúrovo, but for some it's worth the journey for the views alone (not to mention the novelty of walking across a national border). Although there are no passport checks (Slovakia and Hungary are in the Schengen Zone), it's a good idea to bring it with you just in case. There are a couple of cafés and restaurants on the riverside, like **BAT** (Námestie slobody 17/17, Štúrovo), which has a nice view but is rather average. Bring euros if you plan to spend on this side of the river.

Nagymaros-Visegrád ferry ticket office when you arrive in Visegrád, as they also manage the taxi service.

Leaving Visegrád

Ferries leave Visegrád for Nagymaros, where you can get the train back to Budapest, 45 minutes past each hour from 7:45am-7:45pm. The last train to Budapest Nyugati train station departs Nagymaros-Visegrád at 11:15pm. Alternatively, you can also get the bus back, which departs Visegrád at 9:50pm.

The last hydrofoil back to Budapest departs Visegrád at 5:30pm. The slower boat back to Budapest normally leaves Visegrád at 5:40pm.

ESZTERGOM

The Danube Bend ends, or rather begins, at the Hungarian-Slovak border by the town of Esztergom (pop. 28,000). Many come to Esztergom for the photogenic view from Hungary's largest basilica, which looms over the river. Vác may have been once the center of Catholicism in Hungary, but that torch has been passed upstream to Esztergom, the hometown of Hungary's first king St. Stephen. In fact, Esztergom was the royal seat of the country from the 10th century to the mid-13th century, so you'll find plenty of history around the old castle walls and historic city streets to keep you busy once you've visited the main site.

Sights
★ ESZTERGOM BASILICA

Szent István tér 1; tel. 06/33-402-354; www.bazilika-
esztergom.hu; Mon-Sat 9am-7pm, Sun 9am-6pm
May-Sep, daily 9am-6pm Sep-Oct and Apr, daily
9am-5pm Mar, daily 9am-4pm Nov-Jan; free entry
for the church, HUF 700 dome, HUF 1,500 combined
ticket to the crypt, dome, and treasury

If you thought St. Stephen's Basilica in
Budapest was impressive, wait till you visit
the Esztergom Basilica, which is the largest
church in Hungary, rising 72 meters (236 ft)
high to its dome! Entry is free for this impressive cathedral, and it's open to visitors
all year round, but if the weather is good (and
you're not scared of heights) it's worth the
climb up the numerous stairs to the dome.
This will take you up to the panorama terrace first—a large hall with a window overlooking the river and a café halfway up the
church—then even more stairs up to the colonnaded corridor on the outside under the
dome. You'll already be treated to wonderful
views over the town, but wait in line to get
right up to the top of the dome (numbers are
restricted). You can walk all the way around
for 360 degrees of the whole region overlooking the Danube, Slovakia (just on the other
side of the river), and the hills leading further
south down the Danube Bend. You can also
see the treasury and the crypt on your visit
to this classical-style cathedral.

Food
PADLIZSÁN

Pázmány Péter utca 21; tel. 06/33-311-212;
daily noon-10pm; entrées HUF 2,200-3,500

Padlizsán ("eggplant" in English) lies at the
base of the castle walls, looking up toward
the Basilica in a small Baroque townhouse.
The food lives up to the view, with modern,
seasonal Hungarian dishes from grilled pike
perch from the Danube to autumnal chicken
in wild mushroom sauce to vegetarian fried
cheese served with cranberry sauce and
apple compote.

PRÍMÁS PINCE

Szent István tér 4; tel. 06/33-541-965; www.
primaspince.hu; Mon-Thu 10am-9pm, Fri 10am-10pm,
Sun 10am-5pm; HUF 2,750-6,990

Prímás Pince in the cellars below the basilica
feels more like a museum than a restaurant,
with high-vaulted ceilings and stone blocks.
But if you're looking for great wine and food,
Prímás delivers, as it carries 100 Hungarian
wines—including rare varieties—and you'll
find plenty of creative takes on Hungarian
dishes on the menu. Try the aged wild boar ten-
derloin served with a sauce made from the famous Eger "Bull's Blood" red wine and plums.
You can also pay a visit to the exhibition about
wine, showing the history of the Hungarian
church and winemaking in Hungary.

★ Boating from Esztergom to Budapest

The best way to spend a day in Esztergom is
to take the train up from Budapest and spend
a couple of hours exploring the Basilica and
the area surrounding it before having lunch.
Then take the 4pm slow boat back to Budapest
for a leisurely four-hour Danube cruise—you
will also get the best views of the Basilica from
the water. Just sit back, relax, and watch the
landscape slip by as you pass the hills around
Visegrád and then the marshy island around
Szentendre dotted with storks and other wildlife at the golden hour—in the late spring the
water here is filled with fallen acacia petals
and smells divine! Unlike the faster hydrofoil,
there is also a bar on this boat.

In 2020 boat service was suspended due
to the coronavirus pandemic. If it's not running during your visit, the hydrofoil offers
an alternative. You can check the timetable and services of all boat services operating between Budapest and Esztergom on the
Mahart Passnave website (www.mahart-
passnave.hu).

Getting There

The train is arguably the fastest and most flexible way to travel from Budapest to Esztergom.

Bus is your best option if you are coming from Visegrád.

TRAIN

There are regular trains from Nyugati train station in Budapest that take a little over an hour (HUF 1,120) to get to Esztergom, but these will still leave you about a 40-minute walk from the center. Trains run every half an hour from 4am-11:15pm. You can either take a **taxi** to town (around HUF 1,000), or hop on local **bus 1** or **11** (HUF 150) and get off at **Bazilika**.

BOAT

In the summer, the best way to reach Esztergom is by hydrofoil, operated by **Mahart Passnave** (www.mahartpassnave.hu), which departs at 10am from Vígadó, and takes one hour 30 minutes (HUF 5,300 one-way, HUF 8,000 round-trip). The return ferry leaves at 5:30pm, getting back to Budapest at 7pm.

The slow ferry by the same company leaves Budapest at 9am (taking 5 hours 20 minutes) and leaves Esztergom at 4pm (taking 4 hours). A one-way ticket is HUF 3,820, a round-trip HUF 5,720. I highly recommend taking the slow boat back in the summer for a scenic leisurely cruise.

Both the boat and the hydrofoil also stop at Visegrád, if you want to break your journey there.

BUS

Volánbusz (www.volanbusz.hu) buses run between Esztergom and Visegrád (45 minutes; HUF 465), leaving Esztergom hourly at 40 minutes past. If you're coming from Visegrád, services go at 50 past the hour from the bus stop next to the jetty.

CAR

It takes an hour to drive to Esztergom from Budapest. Take **Route 10** on the Buda side of the river from Florián tér in northern Buda and follow the signs till Esztergom. **Parking** costs around HUF 300 per hour.

GETTING AROUND

If you need a taxi in Esztergom, try **Esztergom Taxi** (tel. 06/30-634-0403) or **Taxi 1000** (tel. 06/20-622-1000).

Leaving Esztergom

The last train back to Budapest departs Esztergom at 11:35pm. The last bus departs at 10:25pm and also stops in Visegrád and Szentendre.

Lake Balaton

Lake Balaton, with its stretches of turquoise water dotted with yachts and sailboats, is perhaps the most memorable escape from Budapest. The largest lake in Central Europe, it's just a couple of hours from the capital. When the temperatures rise, it seems most of Budapest flees the city to find refuge along the beaches of the "Hungarian Sea."

You can think of Balaton as being split into north and south. The northern shore is more beautiful, with volcanic hills lined with vineyards and elegant resorts, while the south gets the golden beaches and lakeside

party spots like Siófok. There is something for everyone, whether you want to hike up into the hills, take a plunge in the lake, just relax along the water on a summer's day sipping a glass of Kéknyelű, a white wine made from a local grape from Badacsony, or hit the bars in Siófok.

The area around Lake Balaton is vast, and realistically you won't be able to hit all the listed towns in a day. Choose which town or area that interests you the most and focus your trip there. Badacsony could be combined with Balatonfüred, as there are direct train connections between the two (easier if you do this with a rental car), but unless you're spending the night, it's best to choose either Balatonfüred or Badacsony as you won't fit everything into one day. Balaton is a place where locals come to escape the heat of the summer, so expect a relaxed, holiday vibe—the last thing you'll want to do is rush around from town to town. Take the train down and spend a relaxed day by the lake like a local.

BALATONFÜRED

Balatonfüred (pop. 13,000) is a historic resort on the northern shore of Balaton, where you'll find palatial hotels and villas once frequented by the artistic elite from Budapest overlooking the water. It's a couple of hours by train from Budapest, making it the perfect gateway.

Balatonfüred has an old-world appeal as a historic resort and is a great choice for a quiet, yet elegant, day by the lake. It's more than just lakeside town; artists and writers were drawn to the scenic northern shore of Lake Balaton for their health as well as the views. (The town sits on carbonated mineral springs, which you can drink straight from the Kossuth Lajos spring tucked under the colonnaded pavilion.) The town is populated with 18th- and 19th-century villas, a wooded park, and a scenic promenade with a marina and riverside cafés and restaurants.

Sights
BALATON PANTHEON
Gyógy tér; free
Tucked under the arches of the building on the northeastern side of Gyógy tér is an interesting pantheon featuring placards to the famous figures who came to Balatonfüred to take their cures, a kind of who's who of the town, that then stretches out into a woody parkland gently crawling up the hill.

VASZARY VILLA
Honvéd utca 2-4; tel. 06/87-950-876; http://kultura. balatonfured.hu; Tue-Sun 10am-6pm; HUF 1,800
Step inside this beautiful late-19th-century villa, the former home of the once prominent

Vaszary family. The most famous of the family is Hungarian Impressionist painter János Vaszary, whose paintings are exhibited in the villa. The museum also has a delightful collection of art and artifacts from the 18th century.

STATE HOSPITAL OF CARDIOLOGY AND THE KOSSUTH LAJOS SPRING
Gyógy tér 2; free
I personally love Gyógy tér, a square overlooked by the whitewashed walls of the State Hospital of Cardiology—the largest in Hungary—which has drawn in a list of artistic celebrities, including Nobel Prize-winning Indian poet Rabindranath Tagore. Next to the famous hospital, you can get some shade under the trees or under the colonnade surrounding the 19th-century Kossuth Lajos mineral spring, which as far as mineral springs go actually tastes good. The spring spouts out of a four-sided stone fountain lying under a neoclassical pavilion. Bring your own cup or bottle, and just press the button next to the tap on the spring to fill it. The water is said to be high in iron and has been used to treat cardiovascular, digestive, and diabetes-related diseases, but it is also a good, free thirst quencher in the hot summer months.

Beaches and Recreation
★ TAGORE PROMENADE
This tree-lined promenade running along the northern shore makes for wonderful strolls along Lake Balaton. It runs from the marina to the lakeside Eszterházy Beach and Waterpark. The promenade is split into a pedestrian path and a bicycle path, with prominent views over the lake.

ESZTERHÁZY BEACH
Aranyhíd sétány; tel. 06/87-343-817; www. balatonfuredistrandok.hu/eszterhazy.html; daily 8:30am-7pm Jun-Aug; HUF 1,700 for beach entrance
This 450-meter (1,476-ft) beach just off the Tagore promenade offers the perfect place for a family day out. A grassy beach park has plenty of trees for shade, and best of all, you are treated to stunning views over the lake

Lake Balaton

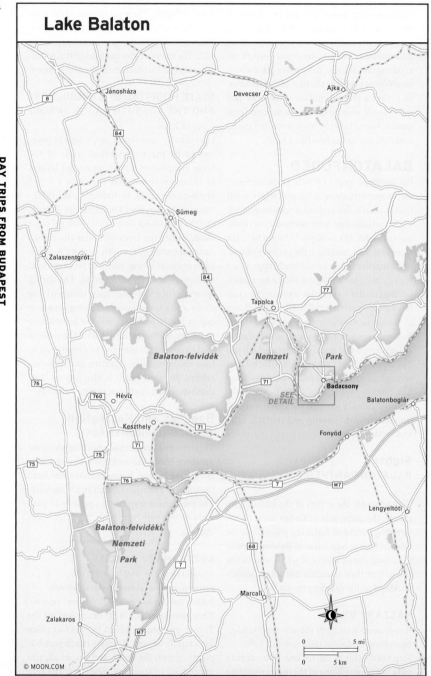

8

Jánosháza   Devecser   Ajka

84

Sümeg

Zalaszentgrót

84

77

Tapolca

Balaton-felvidék   **Nemzeti**   **Park**

76   71   **Badacsony**

760   Hévíz   SEE   Balatonboglár
                                               DETAIL

Keszthely   71   Fonyód

71

75

76   7   M7

75   Lengyeltóti

**Balaton-felvidéki
Nemzeti
Park**   68

7

Marcali

Zalakaros

M7

© MOON.COM

0   5 mi
0   5 km

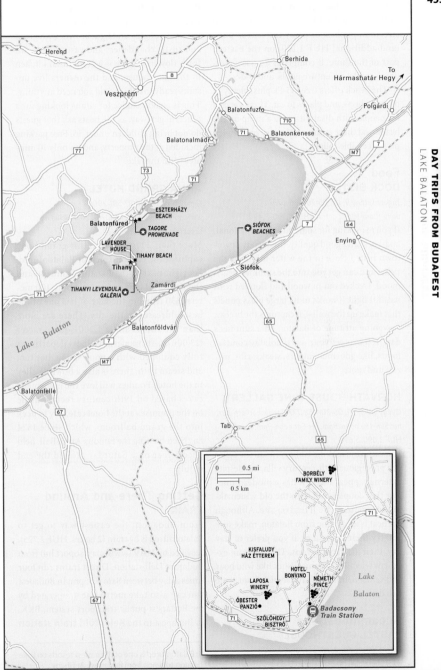

toward the Tihany peninsula. Go for a dip in the lake, get active on the volleyball and streetball pitches, or enjoy the **water park** (and additional HUF 1,100) on the eastern part of the shore: it comprises a mix of children's pools, adventure pools, and slides.

The beach offers free Wi-Fi, plus, plenty of buffets, shops, and places to eat. There's access for people with disabilities via a ramp on the beach and there is also an elevator on the pier, plus accessible toilets.

Food
DOCK BISTRO
Tagore sétány 9; tel. 06/70-636-6707;
daily 10am-10pm; entrées HUF 1,990-3,490

If you're looking for something international, laid-back, and good quality, this trendy downtown bistro close to the water might be the ticket and can get you into the summer-beach mood. Decked out in wood and flooded with natural light (thanks to its large glass panels that make up the walls), it captures the breezy, easygoing attitude of Balaton on a summer's day. You can get your usual holiday comfort foods, like gourmet burgers, steaks, ribs, pizzas, and more.

HORVÁTH HOUSE WINE GALLERY
Gyógy tér 3; tel. 06/30-458-7778; www.horvath-haz.
hu; Sun-Thu noon-8pm, Fri-Sat noon-9pm; entrées
HUF 3,690-5,690

Horváth House Wine Gallery lies in the cellar of a prestigious 19th-century villa, but despite external appearances, it has a modern interior that couples well with the old winemaking apparatuses you'll find on-site. Although the beat is local wine from Balaton, make sure you try their pálinka or, if you prefer to stay dry, their artisanal syrups. They have an excellent selection of game dishes like wild boar and venison, but you can also pick from some fish dishes.

Accommodations
PASTEL GUESTHOUSE
Eötvös Károly Köz 2; tel. 06/70-209-7521;
www.pastelguesthouse.com; €45-55 d

Pastel is an elegant guesthouse decked out with a chic, vintage aesthetic in natural pastel shades of gray and light brown, with green and rustic chandeliers and vases filled with fresh flowers. There is a communal kitchen in the guesthouse, and the owners live upstairs ready to help should you need anything. This is a good choice for adults looking for a peaceful getaway, as the hosts ask that guests do not bring children under 16. Free parking included at the property, and it's only 10 minutes from the lake.

ANNA GRAND HOTEL
Gyógy tér 1; tel. 06/87-581-200;
www.annagrandhotel.hu; €126-220 d including
breakfast and dinner

More than 200 years old, this grand hotel captures the elegant spirit of Balatonfüred. Set right next to the Balaton Pantheon and the Kossuth Lajos spring, and only 100 meters (330 ft) from the lake, it has one of the best addresses in the city. There are more than 100 rooms and a 1,200-square-meter (13,000-sq-ft) modern wellness department fully equipped with a pool, sauna, hot tub, and steam bath; there is also a bowling alley in the hotel. Foodies will love the homemade cakes based on 19th-century recipes made on the premises at the hotel café. Try to peek into the grand ballroom, which since 1824 has been hosting the famous Anna Ball, held once a year on a Saturday around the end of July.

Getting There and Around
TRAIN
From Budapest, the easiest way to get to Balatonfüred is by train (2 hours, HUF 2,725), serviced by **MÁV** (www.mavcsoport.hu) from Budapest Déli station. Direct trains run four times a day between 8am-3:55pm. In Budapest you can also take metro line 4, operated by the Budapest public transport system, BKK, in Budapest to the **Kelenföld train station**

1: Balatonfüred is one of the easiest resorts on Lake Balaton to reach from Budapest. **2:** Tihany

in the western suburbs and take the train to Balatonfüred from there. Make sure you book a ticket (with seat reservation) during high season as trains get very full.

The center of Balatonfüred is a good 15-20-minute walk southeast from the train station. Call Taxi Balatonfüred (tel. 06/30-751-7518) if you prefer not to walk, or take the local bus lines 1 (every two hours, even-numbered hours), 1B (10 past the hour, every one to two hours), or 2 (every two hours, 30 past the hour for odd-numbered hours); buy a ticket (HUF 310) from the driver.

CAR

The drive from Budapest to Balatonfüred takes around an hour and a half. Take the **M7** southwest of the city. Parking in Balatonfüred ranges from HUF 140-500 per hour depending on the zone and the season.

Leaving Balatonfüred

The last train from Balatonfüred to Budapest departs at around 9pm in high season (late Jun-Aug) and as early as 6pm in the off season. Do confirm the timetable on https://jegy.mav.hu to be sure you don't miss the last train back, as the times for this trainline can be fickle, especially off-season.

TIHANY

Tihany (pop. 1,400) is a peninsula that sticks out into the middle of Lake Balaton. In my opinion, it is one of the most beautiful spots on the lake. The town rises high above the water, crowned with the Baroque bell towers of Benedictine Abbey. Although the main town lies perched on the hillside, you can hike to the shore down winding steps and paths slinking in and out of the woods past flaking villas to the jetty—or you can even follow marked trails that guide you to secret beaches you can't reach by car. If you come in June, the lavender fields are in full bloom, and you can pick your own bunches of lavender, but even off-season you can still buy all kind of lavender products at the vintage-style shops scattered around Tihany.

Sights

THE BENEDICTINE ABBEY OF TIHANY

András tér 1; tel. 06/87-538-200; www.tihanyiapatsag.hu; daily 10am-6pm May-Sep, 10am-5pm Apr and Oct, 10am-4pm Nov-Mar; HUF 1,800

The ochre-colored Benedictine Abbey of Tihany with its twin bell towers rises above the town and the lake from the top of the volcanic hill. Entrance to the abbey includes the museum, which is accessed from the crypt of the church. The museum displays artifacts from the old abbey, manuscripts, and even contemporary art. Make sure you stop in the abbey shop on the way out and buy some of the craft beers brewed by the abbey monks. After the abbey shop, head to the viewing platform on the rampart next to the abbey to look out across the turquoise lake dotted with little sailboats.

LAVENDER HOUSE

Major utca 67; tel. 06/87-538-033; daily 9am-6pm Jun-Aug, 10am-5pm Sep, 10am-4pm Oct-Nov; HUF 1,200

This fun visitor's center covers local geology, nature, and culture, from the peninsula's dramatic volcanic past to its current lavender production. Spend an hour here getting oriented to the peninsula, then check out the gift shop for local products made from lavender and other regional herbs.

Hiking

The **tourist information center** on Tihany can provide detailed information on hiking trails.

ROUND TRIP ON THE TIHANY PENINSULA

Distance (round-trip): *11.4 km (7 mi)*
Duration (round-trip): *4.5 hours*
Effort: *easy*
Trailhead: *Lavender House (Levendula Ház)*
There are two lakes on the Tihany Peninsula: the Inner Lake (Belső tó) and Outer Lake (Külső tó), both of which formed from the

craters of two volcanoes that make up the peninsula. This loop trail includes part of the shores of each lake, giving you spectacular views.

From **Lavender House,** follow the path along the shore of the Inner Lake to the edge of the sports field to your left til you reach a fenced cattle pasture next to the lake, about 400 meters (1,300 ft) from your starting place. Turn left at the yellow cross on the corner of this fence, taking the path going to the left side of the pasture, away from the lake. Two minutes later, you'll come to another crossroads. Take the road left into the woods. The route will rise up toward the **Geyser Fields**—with some 50 geyser cones—where you can join the famous **Lóczy study trail** (marked by a green T) until **Apáti hegy** (Apáti Mountain, a spot with beautiful views over to the Balaton Uplands), then follow the yellow triangle and then the green, which will skirt you by the edge of the Outer Lake and back to the other side of the Inner Lake before bringing you back into the town.

Make sure you bring plenty of water with you on this hike—there won't be an opportunity to fill up your bottle once you leave the town.

ÓVÁR AND THE HERMITAGE ROUTE
Distance (round-trip): *4.6 km (2.9 mi)*
Duration (round-trip): *1-1.5 hours*
Effort: *easy*
Trailhead: *The Benedictine Abbey of Tihany*
Another popular route is the wood-dense trail up to the Calvary, an open-air representation of the crucifixion of Jesus, with statues and crosses marking the trail up the hill. The trail winds through a forested valley to a medieval hermitage carved into the rocks by Greek Orthodox hermits in the 11th century.

Begin the hike at the **Benedictine Abbey of Tihany.** Follow the trail marked with the green line, which will take you along **Pisky sétány** promenade, with amazing views over the lake. This will eventually lead to the base of the hill where the Calvary is located; walk up to the top of the Calvary from here. Make

sure you turn around for amazing views of the abbey and Lake Balaton from the top of the hill.

From here, look for signs marked to the hermitage (**Barátlakások**) and follow the woodland trail marked with the green line. It'll take you up Óvár hill, where you'll get great views of the Inner Lake. Then it's onto the historic hermitage. The hermitage is free to visit, and you can enter the caves to get an idea of how the monks lived in the 11th century.

From the hermitage, the route will take you down to the lakeside. To get back to the starting point, follow the green triangle markings back up to the Abbey.

Beaches and Recreation
TIHANY BEACH
Váralja utca 23; tel. 06/30-500-0256; www. tihanybeach.hu; daily 9am-6pm May-Sep; HUF 800
Tihany Beach (the peninsula's largest paid beach) is located next to the harbor on the eastern side of the peninsula. When the weather is clear, you'll be treated to beautiful views over to Balatonfüred here. There's a special area for kids, free Wi-Fi, changing rooms, sunbed and sunshade rental, and also the chance to do some watersports like **stand-up paddling** (HUF 3,000 per hour) or **paddle boat** (HUF 3,000). Parking by the harbor and the beach is free.

SAJKODI BEACH
Sajkodi Sor 22; tel. 06/70-380-0328; www. sajkodistrand.hu; daily 8am-8pm May-Sep; HUF 400
The Sajkodi Beach lies on the western end of the peninsula, far away from the more popular and busier Tihany. It's a 50-minute walk or a 10-minute ride in a car (or a taxi). Compared to other beaches in Balaton, this one is quiet and hidden—perfect if you want to escape the crowds. The grassy banks leading down to the lake, with steps leading into the water, give this beach a green and romantic look. The views from here are incredible—overlooking the western side of the lake, you can see the volcanic mountains of the northern shore in

the distance. You can rent a sunbed for HUF 500, and parking costs HUF 1,200 for the day. You can also rent **water bicycles** (HUF 2,000 per hour, from the ticket office) or **kayaks** (HUF 600-2,000 per hour).

Shopping
★ TIHANYI LEVENDULA GALÉRIA
Kossuth utca 41; tel. 07/366-3367;
www.levendulamanufaktura.hu;
Mon-Fri 10am-4pm, Sat-Sun 10am-6pm
This little boutique in the heart of Tihany specializes in all things lavender. Whether you want to buy bundles of dried flowers artfully wrapped up, artisanal soaps, lavender-based cosmetics, or even cute pastel floral pouches filled with the aromatic flower, you can find a charming gift here. The shop feels inspired by rustic, vintage Provence, with faded white furniture, vintage ceramics, and stone walls. There is another shop in the village on Batthyány út.

Food
★ REGE CÚKRÁSZDA
Kossuth Lajos utca 22; tel. 06/30-289-3647;
www.apatsagicukraszda.hu; Mon-Thu 9am-8pm,
Fri 9am-9pm, Sat 8am-9pm, Sun 8am-8pm May-Oct;
cakes HUF 850-1,200
Rege Cúkrászda is a magical little café and confectionary set just beside the abbey. It merits a visit for its incredible terrace with perfect views and extensive panoramas from 150 meters (500 ft) above Lake Balaton. They serve all kinds of local delicacies such as craft beer made in the abbey next door and lavender lemonade, but a must-try is their lavendula krémes, a layered custard cake with lavender-infused cream.

RÉGI IDŐK UDVARA ÉS SKANZEN
Batthyányi út 3; tel. 06/70-284-6705;
Tue-Sun noon-9pm mid-Apr-mid-Sep;
entrées HUF 3,150-5,200
This unique restaurant does more than just serve up local specials like Hungarian-style fattened goose liver with a ratatouille of local

vegetables and egg barley or cold smoked trout served simply with bread and gherkins. The establishment doubles as an amateur ethnographic museum with old farm equipment hanging in the bar-terrace. It's worth walking around this peaceful garden and inside the whitewashed interior of this traditional Tihany farmhouse. Try the beer—which is brewed on-site.

Accommodations
KÉK LILLIOM HÁZ
Visszhang 1; tel. 06/30-243-9369;
www.booking-tihany.com; €74-102 d apartment
including breakfast
Kék Lilliom Ház is a magical farmhouse complex at the heart of Tihany. From the street it's hidden, but enter through the wooden gate, climb the stone steps, and rise up into an enchanted garden. Swallows nest under the arches of the whitewashed porch in the summer and kids splash about in the small garden pool. The old thatched-roof farmhouse has been split up into apartments catering to two and also parties of four and five. Breakfast is an elaborate spread of seasonal and local specials, like fresh vegetables and local cheeses, and if the weather is good enough you can take it on the terrace; if not just sit in the beamed dining room by the fire. Minimum stay 4 nights.

Information and Services
Tihany has a helpful **tourist information center** (Kossuth Lajos utca 20; tel. 06/87-448-804; www.tourinform.hu; Mon-Fri 10am-4pm Jan-Apr, Sat 10am-3pm mid-April-end-Apr, Mon-Fri 9am-5pm, Sat-Sun 10am-4pm May-Jun, Mon-Fri 9am-6pm, Sat-Sun 10am-6pm Jun-Aug, Mon-Fri 9am-5pm, Sat-Sun 10am-4pm Sep).

Getting There
TRAIN AND BUS
To get to Tihany from Budapest, first take the train to Balatonfüred. Just next to the train station you'll find a bus depot where you

can get the bus to Tihany (it's written on the front of the bus). It will take about 30 minutes from the train station, and you get a really scenic ride thrown in. Buses are operated by **Volánbusz** (www.volanbusz.hu) and go two to three times an hour, up to 15 times a day, and take 20-30 minutes to reach Tihany (tickets HUF 310).

If you take the bus from Balatonfüred, this will put you down at the heart of the small town at the heart of the peninsula. From here most sites, like the famous abbey, are a 5- to 10-minute walk.

CAR

The drive from Balatonfüred takes around 10 minutes. Just follow **Route 71** and the signs to Tihany. **Parking** prices around the town range from HUF 120-250 per hour, depending on the location.

Leaving Tihany

The last bus from Tihany to Balatonfüred leaves at 8:17pm.

BADACSONY

Badacsony (pop. 2,300), a famous wine region on Balaton's northern shore, is known for its volcanic terroir and scenic vineyards. Badacsony lies around a volcanic hill of the same name that kind of looks like a plug—or more appropriately a cork—and you may need to trek up the hill to reach the best vineyards, but it'll be worth it for the view and the wine. The downtown part of Badacsony is a little touristy, with a jetty, souvenir shops, a beach, and restaurants, kind of like what you'll find in Balatonfüred and not really worth the extra minutes on the train. Your best bet is to hit the wineries—try some wine made from the local Kéknyelű grape—on the slopes of the hill to get the best out of Badacsony.

Wineries

The Badacsony wine region is spread out around Badacsony Hill and is away from the bustle of the port-side town, usually a 20-30-minute walk northward up the hill. To reach the wineries, it's best to walk or take a taxi (or drive if you have someone willing to be a designated driver).

BORBÉLY FAMILY WINERY

Káptalantóti út 19; tel. 06/30-927-1414; www.borbelypince.hu; open on demand, tasting appointments by phone or online

Explore this beautiful winery—and drink wine—in the middle of a vineyard. It's worth coming in the summer to taste their wines on the terrace overlooking the surrounding countryside, but if the weather is off there is a cozy cellar, too. You need to call or reserve on their website in advance to register for tastings—you can choose whether you want to try 6, 8, or 10 wines (HUF 3,000-6,000 per person). Try their Tomaj Badacsonyi Rózsakő–Olaszrizling-Kéknyelű blend for a classic Badacsony white with mineral hints.

To reach this family-run vineyard, get off the train at the Badacsonytomaj train station instead of Badacsony. Take Kert utca and continue north up the hill. The walk is around 20 minutes and the winery is signposted.

NÉMETH PINCE

Római út 127; tel. 06/70-772-1102; www.nemethpince. hu; daily 11am-6pm May-Oct, appointment only Nov-Apr

This is one of Badacsony's smallest wineries, but its central location (a 10-minute walk from the Badacsony train station) and familial atmosphere make it worth a visit. The vineyard has been passed down through the Németh family over the generations, and it specializes in late-harvested grapes, which makes their wines a little sweeter than the others in the region as the grapes retain more sugar. Another delightful detail is that their wines come in hand-painted bottles—and can be painted to order, so make the perfect gift. Try the Kéknyelű (HUF 1,000 for a glass) or the sweet ice wine—a dessert wine made from grapes that have been frozen on the vine (HUF 1,000).

LAPOSA WINERY

Bogyay Lajos utca 1; tel. 06/20-777-7133;
www.laposa.hu; daily 11am-7pm

The Laposa Estate perches itself on the southern banks of Badacsony Hill overlooking Lake Balaton. Sip through a tasting selection of their quality wines on their terrace with amazing views. Wine tastings come with cold savory bites from local producers—but if you call in advance you can request a meal prepared from family recipes with local produce to go with the wines you want to try. You can choose to taste wines by the glass or try a guided wine tasting of six to nine wines (HUF 3,000-4,000 per person). You can reach Laposa on foot, a 15-minute walk northeast from the train station, or take a taxi.

Food

KISFALUDY HÁZ ÉTTEREM

Kisfaludy Sándor utca 28; tel. 06/87-431-016;
www.kisfaludyhaz.hu; daily 11:30am-10pm; entrées
HUF 2,300-4,900

You can't get further up than the Kisfaludy Ház restaurant, which sits at the highest altitude in the town. You'll find hearty Hungarian food on the menu, like paprika spiced fish soup, roast duck leg, catfish stew, and rich pork dishes. It's worth sitting up here with a glass of Ürmös wine—a special local wine infused with spices and often drunk as an aperitif—with a view over the lake.

SZŐLŐHEGY BISZTRÓ

Kisfaludy Sándor utca 5; tel. 06/87-431-382;
www.szolohegybisztro.hu; daily noon-9pm;
entrées HUF 3,250-7,490

Szőlőhegy Bisztró wins when it comes to location, being high up on the hill overlooking Lake Balaton through the vines. Dine on local dishes and sip the wine from the surrounding vineyards under their vine-covered colonnade above the lake. The menu changes on a seasonal basis, but if you can, try the catfish paprikás with homemade pasta served with cottage cheese, lardons, and sour cream, or the grilled zander fish served with a Kéknyelű wine sauce with sautéed vegetables and polenta.

Accommodations

ÓBESTER PANZIÓ

Római út 203; tel. 06/30-213-0225; www.obester.hu;
€60-77 d including breakfast

This family-owned B&B resides in a 200-year-old building on the western side of the hill. It's a quiet sanctuary enveloped with walnut trees and vines, and it has amazing views across to the lake. The center of Badacsony is a short walk away. The B&B has eight rooms and two apartments, and all come with private bathrooms, refrigerator, and air-conditioning. The look of the hotel blends the old with the new—heavy, dark wood beams and pillars add character to the old farmhouse, whereas the décor is white, brightened up with colorful accents from the pillows and rugs, along with modern abstract art hanging on the walls.

HOTEL BONVINO

Park utca 22; tel. 06/87-532-210; www.hotelbonvino.
hu; €230-260 d including breakfast and dinner

Hotel Bonvino brings you the two pleasures and pastimes on Lake Balaton: wine and wellness. Just 300 meters (330 yds) from the shores of the lake, this modern luxurious hotel has 48 uniquely designed rooms drawing inspirations from the surrounding wine region. There is a state-of-the-art wellness area, with a stunning pool with an artificial waterfall, a whirlpool tub, Finnish and infrared saunas, and a steam room. The hotel restaurant serves up local dishes and snacks; try the locally sourced Mangalica ham or goat cheese, and there are more than 100 wines on the wine list.

Getting There

TRAIN

The easiest way to get to Badacsony is by train operated by **MÁV** from Déli train station in Budapest, in the direction of Tapolca. It's farther than Balatonfüred, taking at least 2 hours 40 minutes from Budapest, but can be over 3 hours if you take a slower train. One-way tickets cost HUF 3,395, and there are four trains per day, the first leaving Budapest at 8am, the last at 3:55pm.

CAR

From Balatonfüred the drive takes around 45 minutes on **Route 71,** which is a scenic drive along the lake. Most wineries have their own parking, but public **parking** in the center of the town close to the lakeside costs around HUF 280 an hour.

Getting Around

You can explore the area **on foot** or get a taxi, like **Badacsony Taxi** (06/20-544-4234).

Leaving Badascony

The last direct train for Budapest leaves Badacsony (stopping at Balatonfüred) at 6pm all year round. Other trains, such as the 8:30pm train going to Székesfehérvár, depart later but are indirect, requiring you to switch trains to get back to Budapest.

SIÓFOK

Set on the southern shore of the lake, what Siófok (pop. 25,000) lacks in scenic hills of the north it makes up with atmosphere, earning its title as the "Capital of Lake Balaton." Budapest flocks to its golden lakeside beaches with its shallow water and its vibrant nightlife in the summer. Siófok has that "seaside" feel, with endless neon signs, cocktail happy hours, and a 50-meter-high (165-ft-high) Ferris wheel around the Petőfi Promenade. Scale the water tower built in 1912, where you'll find viewing platforms and chic bars with incredible views over the lake.

Because Siófok lies on the southern shore of the lake, it's difficult to combine with the resorts of the northern shore unless you're planning to spend the night.

Sights
PETŐFI PROMENADE

Running parallel to Siófok Main Beach, the Petőfi Promenade is packed in summer with people in shorts, slapping the sidewalk with flip-flops as they walk along the mile-long stretch. Tall trees, umbrella-covered beach bars, restaurants, street food vendors, and pop-up shops in wooden huts line this road just south of the beach. After 7pm, it becomes a pedestrian-only zone, and by night it becomes a happening spot clad in neon lighting and partygoers staggering to and from the clubs and pubs. Most of the hotels in the area are immediately surrounding it.

swans on Lake Balaton in Siófok

THE FERRIS WHEEL

Petőfi sétány; www.siofokoriaskerek.hu; Sun-Thu 4pm-midnight, Fri-Sat 4pm-1am Jun-Sep; HUF 2,000

Towering more 50 meters (165 ft) tall, the Ferris wheel in Siófok is the very first Hungarian-made wheel. Not only that, during the 10-minute ride you can enjoy views over Central Europe's most famous lake from open-air pods that can fit five to six people. You can see all the way over to Tihany and even spot the twin towers of its famous abbey, as well as the volcanic hills on the northern shore of the lake.

Note that you can only access the Ferris wheel inside the Siófok Main Beach, so you will need to get a ticket for this, too, but if you go between 4pm-6pm, the beach entrance is included (get this ticket at the Kinizsi Pál utca entrance).

SIÓFOK WATER TOWER

Fő tér 11; tel. 06/30-244-8888; www.viztorony. com; daily 9am-midnight Jun-Sep, Tue-Thu and Sun 10am-5pm, Fri 10am-9pm, Sat 10am-10pm Oct-May; HUF 850

Since it was built in 1912, the Siófok Water Tower has become a symbol of the town. It rises up 45 meters (150 ft), made out of reinforced concrete. This historic tower is now a huge tourist draw following its renovation in 2012. Now it has an open-air viewing platform with 360-degree views; the Water Tower Café & Oxygen Bar (same opening hours as above) and the Samsung Experience Center (same opening hours as above) are set inside the old tower. The Samsung Experience Center occupies the top floor on a rotating platform, with panoramic views and interactive touchscreen games.

★ Beaches
SIÓFOK MAIN BEACH

Petőfi sétány 3; tel. 06/84-310-327; https://balaton-parti.hu; daily 8am-6pm May-Sep; HUF 1,000

Siófok's Main Beach is Balaton's largest beach, covering an area that's over 8 hectares (20 ac), with a capacity for 13,500 people. This is not the beach for you if you want peace and quiet, but with its Bluewave Flag (indicating the water quality here is excellent) and its high services, you can still get that resort feel in Hungary, even though it's a landlocked country. Although most of the beach area is covered with grass, the eastern part is sandy, popular for families with kids. Trendy young people head over to Plázs (www.plazssiofok. hu; entrance fee HUF 1,500), a beach club with a huge sundeck, pool, terrace, and sun loungers.

SIÓFOK GOLDEN COAST PUBLIC BEACH

Szent István sétány; tel. 06/84-696-236; daily 8am-9pm; HUF 200 8am-4pm, HUF 100 4pm-6pm, free after 6pm

If you want an alternative to the Main Beach, head east to Siófok's Golden Coast Public Beach, which offers bathing on a budget. Tickets are cheap, and free after 6pm, and you have plenty of places to set a towel down on the 4-kilometer-long (2.5-mi-long) grassy stretch. The views are wonderful at sunset, so it's worth staying here till the sun goes down, after which you can saunter back to the Petőfi Prominade for the evening.

Nightlife

Siófok, Hungary's "summer capital", is quite the party hub. The area surrounding the Main Beach pumps out techno music all day long, and crowds spill in an out of the bars surrounding **Petőfi sétány** promenade, even while the sun beats down. Stick around the Petőfi sétány area for its bars and clubs that will go on late into the night. Some bars have well-known Hungarian or international DJs when the season is swinging, although some redevelopment projects have affected the nightlife. (One of the hottest clubs, Palace Dance Club, was demolished in 2020 to make way for a new hotel.)

RENEGADE PUB

Petőfi sétány 3; tel. 06/20-317-3304;
www.renegadepub.hu; Mon-Sat 7pm-7am, Sun
7pm-midnight Jun-Sep; no cover charge

The party goes on till late in this wooden-beamed pub on the busy Petőfi sétány. Things can get a little out of hand when the live music or the DJ kicks off the party and the dance floor gets so cramped that party-going hedonists will get on top of the tables to dance.

Food

CALVADOS

Erkel Ferenc utca 11; tel. 06/84-314-579;
www.calvados.hu; daily noon-10pm;
HUF 2,500-5,000 entrées

Calvados serves up a selection of Hungarian dishes with international inspirations. It's perched right next to the marina, about a 10-minute walk from the main beach area. Ask the server for recommendations, but you can fall back on the goose liver cooked in Tokaj wine sauce or any of their fish dishes from the local catch. Sit out on the terrace if you can get a table, but since there is a large indoor section, the restaurant is also open off-season.

MALA GARDEN RESTAURANT

Petőfi sétány 15/a; tel. 06/84-506-688;
http://en.malagarden.hu/restaurant; daily
11am-10:30pm off-season, 11am-midnight
peak season; HUF 2,790-6,990 entrées

Grab a table on the terrace at Mala Garden Restaurant overlooking the beach along the lake. The menu is eclectic, with modern takes on Hungarian favorites like paprika chicken and roasted pork cutlets, as well as some Mediterranean specials and Southeast Asian noodle dishes. You can try a range of Hungarian wines from their extensive wine menu, but if you're feeling adventurous, make sure you have a shot of the celery pálinka!

Accommodations

MALA GARDEN HOTEL SUPERIOR

Petőfi sétány 15/a; tel. 06/84-506-688; http://
en.malagarden.hu; €82-125 d including breakfast

Balaton may buzz with crowds on the beach by day and with its hedonistic nightlife by night, but Mala Garden offers an oasis of tranquility when you want some rest. The hotel backs onto the grassy banks of the Danube shore, with the deluxe rooms overlooking the lake (although all rooms have their own balcony). The rooms are a globetrotter's fantasy decorated with warm red walls, vintage kilims (hand-knotted Persian carpets), and hand-crafted items from Bali. A luxurious champagne breakfast is included in the price, as is the use of the wellness center.

Luggage Storage

In Siófok train station, you'll find luggage storage lockers (HUF 500-700 for 24 hours). Prices vary depending on the luggage size.

Getting There

TRAIN

Siófok takes 1 hour 20 minutes from Déli station in the direction of Nagykanizsa or Keszthely. Tickets cost HUF 2,200-2,500, and trains run up to nine times a day, 6:30am-7:30pm. Siófok's main **train station** puts you right in the heart of the town, just a five-minute walk from the lake and the main sites like the water tower.

CAR

The drive from Budapest takes just over an hour; take the **M7** southwest and follow the signs to Siófok. **Parking** costs between HUF 160-320 per hour depending on the location and the season.

Leaving Siófok

The last train back to Budapest departs Siófok at 10pm year-round.

Eger (pop. 53,000) has gone down in Hungarian legend as a bastion that resisted the Ottoman occupation in the 16th century. The city paints a vibrant picture, with Baroque houses adorned with intricate ironwork, in addition to the northernmost Ottoman minaret; its impressive medieval castle famed for its siege is still a draw today. All of this makes a perfect day trip for anyone who loves history. You can also come just for the wine. Eger is known for its spicy Bikavér (Bull's Blood) wine—named partly for its deep red color, but also believed by the Turks to have given the Hungarians superhuman power during battle. Taste it in the wineries around the city, or head to the cellars embedded in the caves at the Valley of the Beautiful Woman.

Eger is a compact city that's easy to get around on foot, as most of the sites are clustered around Eszterházy tér and Dobó István tér. The only part that is a little further afield is the Valley of the Beautiful Woman, which you can reach via a 20-minute walk or a 5-minute taxi ride from the center. You can also take in the sights around the town on the little trackless train (**Eger Városnéző Kisvonat;** begins on Egészségház utca; www.kisvonatok.hu/eger; daily 10am-6pm; HUF 1,200) that will take you out to the Valley of the Beautiful Woman.

SIGHTS
★ Eger Castle

Vár 1; tel. 06/36-312-744; www.egrivar.hu; castle gate open 8am-6pm Nov-Mar, 8am-10pm Apr-Oct, exhibitions 10pm-4pm Nov-Mar, 10am-6pm Apr-Oct; HUF 2,000 for the museums, HUF 1,000 grounds

Eger Castle resides on 500 square meters (5,400 square feet) of land at the top of a hill and is built more like a fortress than a fairy-tale castle. It was built up over several centuries—you'll even find foundations of a 12th-century cathedral on site—but most of what you see dates to the 15th and 16th centuries, including the Gothic Bishop's Palace (mostly a 20th-century reconstruction but still contains elements from the original 15th-century palace) and the wood-turret-topped stone walls of the Bornemissza Bastion (1554) at the main gate.

It's worth walking along the path running parallel to the battlements just for views over the terracotta-hued rooftops, the minaret, and the towers of Baroque churches. High stone walls enclose the grounds housing a cluster of buildings, like the aforementioned the Bishop's Palace (including a museum of the castle on the second floor) and modern buildings containing the Eger Art Gallery.

There is a complex labyrinth of tunnels and casemates carved into solid rock running underneath the castle, some going as far as 24 kilometers (15 mi) from the town. You can only visit about 300 meters (330 yds) in the casemates exhibition, but it offers a fascinating glimpse into Eger's intricate castle engineering—part of the secret why Eger held out against the Turks for such a long time. The price for the museums includes admission to the casemates and the interactive exhibition chronicling the history of the castle. You can access the casemates through the entrance at the Dark Gate in the eastern part of the castle complex.

The best way to reach Eger Castle is to walk up the path from Tinódi Sebestyén tér at the foot of the castle, which will bring you up to the castle gate. The gentle 300-meter (330-yd) stroll up to the castle walls is worth it for the view alone. You'll see a panorama over the terracotta rooftops, church spires, and even the minaret.

1: Tihany is famous for lavender. **2:** Eger is famous for its wine production. **3:** historic town of Eger

The Lyceum

Eszterházy tér 1; tel. 06/36-520-400; www.
uni-eszterhazy.hu, tower and astronomical museum
www.varazstorony.hu; Tue-Sun 9:30am-5:30pm
May-Aug, 9:30am-3:30pm Mar-Apr and Sep-Oct,
9:30am-1pm Fri-Sun Nov-Dec and Feb-Mar, library
Tue-Sun 9:30am-1:30pm Mar-Apr, 9:30am-3:30pm
May-Sep; HUF 1,700, library HUF 1,000

If you like beautiful old libraries, vintage observatories, and historic university buildings, then pay a visit to Eger's Lyceum, an 18th-century college building that is a particularly fascinating landmark. The Lyceum towers above the city center, even taller than the church and basilica. Climb to the top of the tower to see one of the three camera obscuras in the world that's still operational today. On the way up, you can break your journey with an astronomical museum set in an old observatory with 18th-century telescopes and curiosities, and there is also the "Magic Tower," an interactive physics laboratory that's fun for kids as well as adults. The highlight of the Lyceum, which began as a theological college in the 1700s, is the Baroque, wood-clad library with beautiful frescoes on the first floor.

Eger Minaret

Knézich Károly utca; tel. 06/70-202-43-53;
www.minareteger.hu; daily 10am-6pm Jun-Sep,
10am-5pm Oct-Mar; HUF 400

Eger may symbolize the Hungarian resistance against the Turks, but you'll find plenty of traces of the Ottomans embedded into the cityscape. Eger's minaret—the northernmost building from the Ottoman era in Europe—is quite the sight, rising 40 meters (130 ft) with 97 spiral steps to the top. The Turks built the minaret in 1596 following their victory. When the Habsburg army recaptured the town 91 years later, they tried to pull it down with 400 oxen, but the tower held out. The balcony at the top of the tower is worth it for the view, but it is rather narrow and the climb is intense. Don't be surprised if you find you feel dizzy or claustrophobic, since the stairway up is also pretty tight. If you are uncomfortable

with heights or enclosed spaces, then I advise you appreciate this site from outside.

Eger Basilica

Pyrker János tér 1; tel. 06/36-420-970; www.
eger-bazilika.plebania.hu; Mon-Sat 8:30am-6pm,
Sun 1pm-6pm; HUF 300 suggested donation

Eger Basilica is the third largest in Hungary, after Esztergom and Budapest. You'll find this neoclassical basilica facing the Lyceum, looking like an overwrought Roman temple with imposing Corinthian columns. It merits a look inside (especially if you appreciate frescoes), and the murals that adorn the three huge domes in bright bold colors will impress any art lover.

WINE CELLARS

Wine has got its tendrils into Eger like the vines climbing the terraces surrounding the town. Thanks to Eger's mild microclimate, you can find both excellent whites and reds in the region. Although you can get single-varietal wines, particularly from the quality cellars, Eger is most famous for its cuvées. The spicy, blood-red Egri Bikavér—the Bull's Blood of Eger—blends three to five grape types. If you're partial to whites, try the Egri Csillag—the Star of Eger—a dry, crisp white blend made from local grape types with floral and fruity notes.

There are good wine producers in Eger. Keep an eye out for St. Andrea, Bolyki, or Orsolya. However, these wineries are located far out of town and require a car to get you there. If you want to taste local wine, sample some Eger specials at the following cellar.

GÁL TIBOR FÚZIÓ

Csiki Sándor utca 10; tel. 06/20-852-5002;
www.galtibor.hu; Tue-Thu 10am-7pm, Fri-Sat
10am-11pm, Sun 10am-1pm

Winemaker Gál Tibor has 40 hectares (100 ac) of vineyards around Eger, but the good news is you don't need to go far out of town to try these fantastic wines. In downtown Eger, Gál Tibor Fúzió occupies a 1,400-square-meter

(15,000-sq-ft) complex, home to a 500-year-old wine cellar in addition to a bar and a wine tasting room that can seat 120 people. The building is worth the visit for its blend of modern design, with features like wireframe lampshades and chalkboard art, and its history. There is also a free museum dedicated to the history of Bull's Blood wine on the first floor. Try the zingy and floral Egri Csillag or the pinot noir rosé with hints of strawberry.

FOOD

DEPRESSO KÁVÉHÁZ ÉS ÉTTEREM

Érsek utca 14/Dobó tér; tel. 06/30-886-6742; www.depresso.hu; Mon-Thu 9am-8pm, Fri-Sat 9am-9pm, Sun 9am-6pm; entrées HUF 2,100-3,150

This third-wave café wins the best terrace view in the city with front row seats overlooking Dobó Square and the castle. Pick up light bites like sandwiches and salads, plus excellent breakfast foods like bagels and eggs till 11:30am. There also are more substantial meals on offer, like pulled water buffalo burgers and seasonal dishes, along with local wine, Hungarian craft beer, and mixed drinks. Make sure you end your meal with one of their excellent specialty coffees. I am partial to their Depresso Tonic (a shot of espresso served with iced tonic and lemon) in the summer.

1552

Eger Castle; tel. 06/30-869-6219; www.1552.hu; daily 11am-10pm; entrées HUF 2,790-6,890

1552 is the only restaurant in Eger Castle, but it has done something quite original, combining Hungarian cuisine, Turkish dishes (a nod to its Ottoman past), and cutting-edge culinary techniques. Daunted by the menu? Go for the game, as chef Mátyás Hegyi's specialty is wild boar. The décor inside is bold, with claret leatherette seating, exposed brick set against patterned peach wallpaper, Turkish-style tiles, and bulbs hanging inside birdcages. This is not a place to come when you're in a hurry, though, as the service can be a bit slow.

MACOK BISTRO AND WINE BAR

Tinódi Sebestyén tér 4; tel. 06/36-516-180; www. imolaudvarhaz.hu/en/the-macok-bisztro-wine-bar. html; Sun-Thu noon-10pm, Fri-Sat noon-11pm; entrées HUF 2,950-7,900

Just because Macok Bistro and Wine Bar lies by the entrance of the castle doesn't make it a tourist trap. You'll find Hungarians and an international crowd at this eccentric restaurant that blends industrial chic with its own quirky style. But what's even better is its modern, adventurous kitchen, offering gourmet degustation menus at excellent prices. Creative dishes, such as duck liver brûlée served with homemade milk loaf and plum jam, or coconut and pumpkin soup with pumpkin seed mousse, are beautifully presented and use locally sourced ingredients. The wine list features Eger's best local wineries—try some spicy reds from St. Andrea, Gál Tibor, or Attila Pince.

ACCOMMODATIONS

SENATOR HOUSE HOTEL

Dobó tér 11; tel. 06/36-320-466; www.senatorhaz.hu; €64-81 d including breakfast

Senator House Hotel lies right at the heart of Eger in an 18th-century inn. There are 11 cozy rooms on the upper floors decorated all in white with accents coming from brightly colored oil paintings, pillows, and flowers. The reception area, filled with curiosities and antiques, shares the ground floor with a restaurant. The best thing is really the location, as rooms look out to either Dobó square or one of the narrow side streets.

HOTEL EGER & PARK

Szálloda utca 3; tel. 06/36-522-200; www. hotelegerpark.hu; €90-170 d including breakfast

The Hotel Eger & Park is actually two hotels: the Park Hotel was Eger's first hotel, which opened in the 1929, and is built in a neo-Baroque style, whereas the Hotel Eger was built at the end of the 20th century. Today the two hotels are joined by a connecting corridor, and guests from both hotels can use

☆ Wine Tasting in the Valley of the Beautiful Woman

the Valley of the Beautiful Woman

For quality wine, you may be better off going to a wine bar in Eger or a winery in the surrounding countryside, but if it's atmosphere you're looking for, the Valley of the Beautiful Woman (Szépasszony-völgy) has it in spades.

There are close to 200 cellars embedded in a crescent-shaped valley in the suburbs of Eger. Some of the cellars are stunning: completely carved into the hillside and looking more like a church than a wine cellar. Others are more modest with just a few plastic chairs propped up against the bare cave walls. I love going from musty cellar to cellar, tasting wine straight from the barrel. The experience is best shared with friends and with a slice of zsíros kenyér—bread spread with goose or pork fat, raw onions, and paprika (and, yes, it is more delicious than it sounds)—or a pince lepény, a kind of baked savory pancake with cheese and ham (these are usually extra and will set you back around HUF 500).

There are dozens of legends behind the region's seductive name, by the way. One recounts the story about a beautiful Hungarian girl who escaped marriage to a Turk by giving him some Bull's Blood wine (he wasn't used to drinking wine), and another says the beautiful woman was a prehistoric goddess who received sacrifices in the valley.

WINES

The wines vary depending on the harvest and the winery, but you can find the famous red cuvée, **Bull's Blood,** and other wines like those from indigenous grapes including **Egri leányka**

the state-of-the-art wellness facility and spa, with thermal water pools, swimming pools, infrared sauna, aroma cabin, and salt chamber. The Park Hotel is much smaller, with only 35 rooms, whereas the Hotel Eger has over 170 rooms. You can find the filling buffet breakfast in the elegant dining rooms in the Park Hotel.

INFORMATION AND SERVICES

If you need a little help getting oriented, head to the **Eger Tourinform** (Bajcsy-Zsilinszky utca 9; tel. 06/36-517-715; Mon-Fri 8am-6pm, Sat 10am-4pm). For **luggage storage,** Eger bus station has facilities where you can store any baggage (6am-noon and 1pm-6pm

(a dry white wine), olaszrizling (a white wine that can be sweet or dry), and hárslevelű (an aromatic sweet white). Should you like any of the wine, you can take some back in a plastic bottle—directly from the barrel, one liter will cost around HUF 1,000—which is only a good idea if you plan to drink it before your flight home.

WINE CELLARS

Wine cellars in this area are informal, and most people come for the experience rather than to visit a specific cellar. However, the following three are worth seeking out:

Hagymási Pincészet

Szépasszony-völgy 19; tel. 06/20-326-4364; www.bormester.hu; daily 9am-11pm

Stepping inside this cellar feels more like you've entered a temple dedicated to wine. Set on two levels, this wine cellar fortified with bricks can fit up to 100 guests. Old winemaking equipment hangs on the stone walls, and a stone statue resides in the niche in the brick arch above the bar. You can try 18 wines here, as well as two types of pálinka. If you're hungry you must try their pince lepény!

Petrény Superior Pince & Terasz

Szépasszony-völgy 47; tel. 06/70-329-3398; www.petreny.hu; daily 10am-10pm

Whether you prefer to drink in a musty cellar or sit on a terrace in the sun, this winery has got you covered. This is perhaps one of the better cellars to come to for quality wine. Petrény serves up some robust reds. For a good Bull's Blood wine, I recommend tthe Big Band Egri Bikavér Superior.

Sike Tamás

Disznófősor 43; tel. 06/742-9024; www.sikeboraszat.hu; Mon-Thu 10:30am-9pm, Fri-Sat 10:30am-11pm, Sun 9am-7pm

This 100-meter-long (330-ft-long) cellar carved into the rock in the hillside fits 120 people inside and 60 on the terrace. Wines are matured in oak barrels and bottles in the inner part of the cellar, and the great thing about this traditional cellar is the staff who are happy to teach you about the wines you're drinking. Individuals and small groups can drop in for tastings, but do contact the cellar in advance if you're coming in a big group. Taste their merlot or syrah, or their blend of Egri Csillag if you prefer a white.

GETTING THERE

The cellars are a 20-minute walk from Eger's city center. You can also take the little trackless train to Szépasszony-völgy or take a taxi (you can ask for "Valley of the Beautiful Woman" or even "Pretty Lady Valley" if you can't pronounce the Hungarian, as most will know the English names). The valley is compact and all the cellars lie right next to each other, so just explore the area on foot.

weekdays, 8am-noon and 1pm-4pm weekends; HUF 200 for the first hour, HUF 50 any additional hours).

GETTING THERE

You can catch the train operated by MÁV to Eger from Keleti train station in Budapest (2 hours; HUF 2,725). You can also get a direct bus with Volánbusz from the Stadion bus station in Budapest (2 hours; HUF 2,725). There are nine trains a day from 5am-7pm, and buses run every half hour 8:15am-10:45pm. When you get arrive in Eger by bus, you will be in the city center (the bus station is a 3-minute walk from Eger Basilica). The train, on the other hand, puts you a 20-minute walk away in the south of the town. Local bus services are sporadic, so you may be better off taking a taxi (which will set you back around HUF 1,000). Try **City Taxi Eger** (tel. 06/36-555-555) if you need a cab.

The drive by **car** takes around 1 hour 40 minutes from Budapest. Take the **M3**

northeast and keep an eye out for signposts to Eger. **Parking** costs in Eger range between HUF 200 and 360 per hour.

LEAVING EGER

The last bus back to Budapest leaves Eger at 8:15pm. The last train to Budapest leaves at 7pm.

Background

The Landscape

GEOGRAPHY

The landscapes throughout the Central European region are quite similar. Prague, Vienna, and Budapest are all marked by their proximity to a major river, with one side with hills and the other flat. In Prague and Budapest, the rivers (the Vltava and Danube, respectively) divide the cities into two distinct halves. In Vienna, the Danube lies a little outside the city center, with the Danube Island stretching down the river for 13 miles.

   In Budapest, a fault line running along the bed of the Danube

has caused some 80 geothermal springs to bubble up under the city, inspiring the construction of its famed thermal baths. Some 200 caves (some of which visitors can explore) lie underneath the hills of Buda on Budapest's west bank.

CLIMATE

As with the landscape, the climate is fairly consistent across Central Europe. Winters are usually cold, sometimes freezing.

Budapest can be brutally cold—so much so the Danube sometimes freezes over—with heavy snow or sleet. Prague and Vienna both also experience some snow, with average winter temperatures around or below freezing. Summers are hot—temperatures can approach or even exceed 100°F (38°C)—and balmy with a breeze.

Weather in all three cities can be unpredictable. Pack an umbrella and raincoat for almost every season to be on the safe side.

Architecture

Each Central European country has its own architectural DNA with a few crossovers. You will notice similarities as you stroll the streets of Prague, Vienna, and Budapest, but also the nuances that make them different. Prague adds drama to the skies with its Gothic spires, Budapest carries a taste of the exotic with its Ottoman bathhouses and Asian inspired art nouveau, whereas Vienna mixes up Baroque opulence with Secessionist styles and avant-garde, modern architecture.

GOTHIC

Piercing spires, dramatic buttresses, and soaring towers capture the spirit of Central European Gothic architecture. In the 14th century, Prague rose to become one of the greatest cities in Europe, setting the foundations for the town with the stunning St. Vitus Cathedral, the Old Town Hall and its Astronomical Clock and the foundations of Charles Bridge. Vienna also has its share of Austrian Gothic style, most notably St. Stephen's Cathedral with its jagged spires and vaulted arches. Budapest, on the other hand, has very little left behind from the period—much of the Medieval architecture was destroyed over various occupations—although you can catch a glimpse of Gothic art in the

Budapest History Museum with its collections of Gothic sculptures or the Hungarian National Gallery with its triptychs.

BAROQUE

Forget less-means-more when it comes to Baroque architecture, which you'll find in abundance throughout Central Europe dating back to the 17th and 18th centuries. Vienna has some of the most opulent examples, with winged palaces, lashings of marble and enough ornate gold leaf and fiddly friezes to tire your eyes out. Baroque architecture embodies grand cupolas, marble columns, and over the top frescoes, which you'll find in abundance in the Habsburg palaces and at Vienna's Karlskirche. Curved forms and elaborate details embody the Baroque style, which you'll see in Budapest and Prague, too. Architecture is a little more modest in the cities that were satellites to Vienna as the Habsburg Empire capital. Churches with copper-green domed bell towers dot the Central European cities and countryside, whereas pastel-colored townhouses with floral frieze details or statues also capture the style. And if you thought that Baroque was over the top—pay a visit to Maria Theresa's rooms in Schönbrunn Palace for its even fussier and more ornate successor: rococo.

HISTORICISM AND ECLECTIC STYLE

In the 19th century, historical revival came into vogue in cities like Vienna and Budapest. All the "neos"—neo-classicism, neo-Gothic, neo-orientalism, and neo-Renaissance styles peppered the wide boulevards of Budapest and along Vienna's newly built Ringstraße. This eclectic style adds a richness to the cities of Central Europe and a new form of opulence that's more individual than the formulaic Baroque. If you ride on a tram along the Ringstraße, you'll spot buildings that resemble Greek Temples, Renaissance Palaces and even Flemish style Gothic builds. Budapest, too, embraced this aesthetic in the prosperous years it joined hands as a dual capital with Vienna in the Austro-Hungarian Empire. Prague also took its architectural cues from Vienna's historicism, copying all the "neo" styles, particularly neo-Gothic.

ART NOUVEAU

Although art nouveau is a label you can slap on the three cities, each country has its own national interpretation of the style. Vienna's Secessionist style, led by artists like Gustav Klimt and architects such as Otto Wagner, focused more on floral motifs, sensual feminine forms, and lashings of gold, or stark modernism by Adolf Loos. Prague, as a contrast, blended a more ornate Parisian style with Vienna's subdued art nouveau. Of course, much of what we think of as art nouveau in art has a heavy Czech influence thanks to Alphons Mucha. Budapest drew art nouveau inspiration from Hungarian folk art and orientalism loved by Ödön Lechner, whose colorful buildings resemble Gaudí more than Wagner's brand of architecture.

EARLY-MID 20TH CENTURY

The 20th century is perhaps the most diverse in style between each city. In the 1930s

and 40s, Hungarian architects embraced the Bauhaus movement, which blended functionality with style. As Budapest expanded with new apartment blocks, many in the area outside the Grand Boulevard drew inspiration from Bauhaus with its elegant, simple curves and art deco accents. Vienna also saw urban expansion in the interwar period, with the Werkbund Estates, social housing built in the period known as "Red Vienna," when the Social Democrats were in power between 1918-1934. The Nazi era in Vienna left little concerning architecture, except for the imposing Flak Towers you can still see in recreational parks like the Augarten. Architecture in Prague moved away from the curves of Bauhaus and the simple lines of Red Vienna to cubism in architectural form. It never caught on outside the Czech Republic as a style of architecture, but you can find a few examples of this unique style in Prague, like the cubist street lamp or the House of the Black Madonna.

COMMUNIST FUNCTIONALITY AND SOCIALIST REALISM

Once Hungary and the Czech Republic fell under the communist regime, a new architectural style defined these two capitals. Budapest's "panel" houses (sizeable concrete apartment blocks) and Prague's functionalist and brutalist buildings may not be the most beautiful sites in the respective cities, but they are still a part of its history. For a taste of Socialist Realism, head out to Budapest's Memento Park, which has become a graveyard to communist statues, or Prague's former Hotel International.

MODERN

Many think of Prague, Vienna, and Budapest as historic cities, but scattered between the grand old buildings modern pieces of architecture pop. In Vienna, the Hundertwasserhaus by Friedensreich Hundertwasser brightens the streets close to the Danube Canal with bright colors and irregular forms, and the same can be said about the Dancing House in Prague by Vlado Milunic and Frank Gehry, where glass and steel melt into each other along the Vltava River. Budapest blends the old and the new with the "Whale," an undulating glass structure built on the foundations of the red brick warehouses set along the Danube. Vienna also combines history with modernity in the MuseumsQuartier, the former stables once belonging to the Habsburg rulers now transformed into a modern art hub. Modern art playfully invades the three cities. The twisted towers of the Dancing House embrace along the Vltava Riverbanks, whereas tiny micro statues that appear out of nowhere have become Easter eggs for observant pedestrians along the banks of the Danube in Budapest.

Government and Economy

PRAGUE
Politics and Government

The Czech Republic is a parliamentary democracy with both a Prime Minister, who holds more political power, and a president who often resides in the Prague Castle. The president acts as more of a ceremonial state figurehead but also holds some important political responsibilities, such as appointing the Prime Minister. The Czech Republic is a multi-party system often built on coalitions between multiple parties.

Current President Miloš Zeman was re-elected in 2018 and is often compared to Donald Trump for his nationalist, anti-immigrant beliefs and blunt statements. Prime Minister (at the time of writing) Andrej Babiš is a media magnate and one of the country's wealthiest men. He is known for tabloid scandals and EU investigations into alleged financial fraud, which have resulted in ongoing public protests calling for his resignation.

The current Czech Parliament is divided between ANO 2011, a populist party founded by Andrej Babiš in 2011; the anti-EU, conservative ODS party; the new pro-transparency Czech Pirate party; the anti-immigrant, anti-EU SPD party (ironically, founded by a Japanese-Czech immigrant); and a handful of smaller groups including the Communist and Green parties. Prague's Mayor Zdeněk Hřib (Pirate party) made international headlines in recent years for two things: recognizing Taiwanese independence, thus creating conflicts between the Czech and Chinese governments, and using his medical background to volunteer in Czech hospitals during the COVID-19 crisis.

Mentioning politics to many Czechs will be met with eye rolls and complaints of corruption, but many citizens remain politically active. Wenceslas Square still fills with crowds for both political protests as well as patriotic celebrations of historical anniversaries.

Economy

The Czech Republic may not have the highest salaries in the EU (quite the opposite, in fact, ranking 20th out of 28 countries) but it can claim one of the lowest rates of income inequality in Europe. The local economy has traditionally centered on manufacturing industries like automotive parts and diesel engines, with Prague's tourism and service sectors growing rapidly before the onset of the coronavirus pandemic in 2020. EU Commission reports show that GDP has continued to rise in recent years, and an innovative startup scene has produced success stories like booking agent Kiwi.com (formerly Skypicker) and local rideshare app Liftago.

VIENNA
Politics and Government

Austria is a federal republic with a parliamentary democracy made up of nine independent federal states. Each state has its own provincial government, but on the whole, the federal legislation comes from the Nationalrat, the national council, together with the Bundesrat, the Upper House of Parliament. Austria is a member of the European Union, and has been a republic since the fall of the Habsburgs in 1918, and then again following World War II. Since the war, the power has been shared between the Social Democratic Party (SPÖ) and the conservative People's Party (ÖVP). Other parties, like the nationalist Freedom Party (FPÖ) and the Green Party, have risen in popularity over the past few years. Austria has a president, which is a mostly ceremonial position, with Alexander van der Bellen—a Green Party politician who ran independently— elected in December 2016. The head of the Austrian government is the federal chancellor, Sebastian Kurz, who became the youngest head of government in December 2017. Kurz heads up the People's Party, and formed a coalition with the Freedom Party, making it the only country in Western Europe with a far-right presence in government.

Economy

Vienna is one of the wealthiest cities in the European Union, and ranks highly as one of the most livable cities in the world. Vienna's most important economic division is the service sector, followed by industry and commerce. Trade, scientific and technological services, and real estate are also a core part of Vienna's economy. Research and development play a significant role in the local sector, along with tourism, too.

BUDAPEST
Politics and Government

Hungarian politics reside in a framework of a parliamentary democratic republic, with Budapest as the seat of the Hungarian government. Like Austria, Hungary has a President (currently János Áder) who acts in a mostly ceremonial position as head of state, and a Prime Minister who is the head of government in a multi-party system. Multiple parties can run for office, but the main parties in Hungary are the ruling conservative Fidesz party, headed up by Prime Minister Viktor Orbán, and two considerable oppositions, the Hungarian Socialist Party (MSZP) and far-right Jobbik. There are a few other smaller parties who have gained more traction in the 2018 elections, such as Politics Can Be Different (LMP), Democratic Coalition (DK), Dialogue for Hungary (PM) and Together (Együtt), among others. Budapest elected Gergely Karácsony from the Dialogue for Hungary Party in 2019 as the mayor of Budapest. Hungary is criticized by some as being a "flawed democracy."

Economy

Budapest is the epicenter of Hungary's economic world, being home to major corporations and banks. Beyond Hungarian companies, the capital is an international hub with international offices from big-name companies who hold branches in the city. Most of Budapest's income comes from retail, construction materials, schools, and food processing. It's also become a hub for the start-up and tech scene in recent years, with businesses like Prezi and LogMeln springing up from the capital. Until the coronavirus pandemic, tourism had been another booming area of Budapest's economy, but the city suffered considerably due to lockdowns and border closures. Whether the sector will bounce back in the future remains to be seen.

People and Culture

The first rule of Central Europe is you do not confuse it with Eastern Europe. Vienna seems to avoid the "East" label, but if you say either Prague, Budapest, or Bratislava are in Eastern Europe you will lose any new friends you've made on your travels pretty quickly. Central Europe lies at Europe's geographic heart whose countries both share a common past—having mostly been part of the Austro-Hungarian Empire under the rule of the Habsburgs—and yet are divided by their political and economic history—where one part lay behind the Iron Curtain as communist satellite states to the Soviet Union, such as Hungary, Czech Republic, Slovakia, Poland, Slovenia, and East Germany, while the other side resided in the affluent West, like Austria, West Germany, Switzerland and Liechtenstein. This economic divide is still apparent today, as the countries in the eastern part of Central Europe are trying to catch up with their wealthy neighbors after shaking off their communist past and are also quite "new" countries, geopolitically speaking.

PRAGUE
Demographics

The population of Prague hovers around 1.3 million people, which is more than triple the size of the second-largest city of Brno. If the city center feels like a blend of languages and cultures, you're likely feeling the effect of around 10 million tourists who visit yearly, while the resident population remains largely homogenous, with around 85-90 percent of the population sticking close to their Czech roots. The 10-15 percent of transplants to the Czech capital come largely from Ukraine (around 50,000), Slovakia (around 30,000), Russia (around 22,000), with roughly 6,000 Americans coming in fifth.

Around 250,000 Romani (also called Roma) people call the Czech Republic home.

Roma communities have historically faced discrimination and social exclusion within Czech society. Brno's Museum of Romani Culture (www.rommuz.cz) is a good resource to learn more about the Czech Republic's largest national minority. The annual Khamoro festival in Prague, usually held in May or June, also celebrates the music and culture of Roma communities.

A significant Vietnamese minority—roughly 80,000 in the Czech Republic and around 12,000 in Prague—has lived alongside Czechs since the 1960s, largely due to a guest worker and study program under the Communist government that also allowed for an escape from the Vietnam War. This influence is most visible to visitors in the number of Vietnamese restaurants as well as the local habit of referring to convenience stores and small grocer's often run by this community as "Vietnamese shops."

Religion

The Czech Republic is a largely atheist or agnostic country—a 2017 Pew Research study found that 72 percent of Czechs do not identify with a specific religious group—but the country overall remains fairly tolerant toward many religions. (There is, however, definitely some strong anti-Islamic sentiment among segments of the population.) Spiritual beliefs are largely seen as a private matter in Prague. Holidays like Christmas and Easter are treated as cultural celebrations with religious and pagan rituals mixed together rather than sacred holy days for devoted churchgoers.

There are practicing communities of Catholic, Protestant, and Jewish faiths in the Czech capital. The local sense of humor is also known to arise when asked about religion. Over 15,000 residents embraced the Force

1: the art nouveau Museum of Applied Arts in Budapest 2: Gothic cathedral in Prague 3: Vienna's Belvedere Palace 4: Gellért Baths in Budapest

and wrote "Jedi" under religious affiliation in the last census.

Language

Czech is the official language of the Czech Republic. There is less English signage in Prague than in many European capitals, especially outside the city center. Learning a few basic phrases or numbers in Czech can help, but the locals are also not used to foreigners speaking their language and may have trouble with anything less than native pronunciation. With that said, the language landscape is rapidly changing. English is much more prevalent among younger generations.

On the bright side, Czech is a phonetic language, so you can pronounce words the way they are written (just watch for letters like š, č, ř, ž, j, or c that are pronounced differently than English). You may also be pleasantly surprised by how much communication is actually possible when approached with politeness, patience, and a willingness to use body language to get your point across.

VIENNA
Demographics

As of January 2018, Vienna's population clocked in at 1.9 million. Half the city's population has migration in its background, either having been born abroad or has at least one parent who has. Most of Vienna's international population come from the surrounding countries like the Czech Republic, Hungary, and Slovakia, with significant populations from the Balkans and Germany. There is also a significant Asian and Turkish population within Vienna.

Religion

Austria is a majority Catholic country, but its capital Vienna has seen a significant decrease in practicing Catholics. Since 2001, the number of Roman Catholics in the capital has declined from around 50 percent to 35 percent in 2016. Those with no religion increased from 26 to 30 percent in 15 years, and other religions like Orthodox Christianity and Islam have risen in correlation with the growing migrant populations. Vienna used to be a city with one of the largest Jewish communities in Europe, but ever since the Holocaust, the city's Jews fell into a marginal minority. The 2001 census listed only 6,988 Jews living in Vienna.

Language

Vienna may be a city of immigrants, but German is still the primary language you'll encounter in the Austrian capital. Austrian German differs from German spoken in Germany the same way that British English differs from American English, with minor differences in word usage, grammar, spelling, and pronunciation.

Although German is the official language, you'll find plenty of people who speak English as a second language.

BUDAPEST
Demographics

In 2017 Budapest's population reached 1.8 million, with over 3 million in the metropolitan area. Over 30 percent of the Hungarian population lives in the vicinity of the capital in commuting distance. Budapest is less diverse than nearby Vienna, though there is a growing Chinese community, and even a "Chinatown" area in the suburbs.

Within Budapest, the main minority groups are the Jews and the Romani. Budapest is home to one of the largest Jewish communities in Europe, which, unlike Vienna, bounced back the decades following the Holocaust and World War II. The Romani population, whose origins are believed to stem from North India and first appeared in Hungary in the 14th-15th centuries, is the most substantial minority in the country, and there is a sizable population—around 1 percent—living in Budapest. There are still issues with discrimination against the Romani, many of whom fall below the poverty line in Hungary.

Religion

Hungary and its government like to cite that it's a Christian country. In Budapest, the religious composition is mostly Roman Catholic, numbering at 32 percent in 2015, with the Hungarian Reformed Church clocking up the numbers at 26.5 percent and the Evangelicals at 15.5 percent. There is also a minority Eastern Orthodox number at 1 percent. Budapest has a 2 percent Jewish population, with those citing no religion or atheist at 23 percent.

Language

Hungary has one of the most curious languages in Europe, as it's not part of the Indo-European group and has little to nothing in common with those spoken in neighboring countries. Hungarian is part of the Finno-Ugric language family, which also includes Finnish and Estonian, and is supposed to originate from the Uralic regions in Russia with a few Siberian languages having similarities with Hungarian. Hungarian has a few words it's picked up over the centuries from Turkish, Slavic, and German, but the chances are even if you speak German or any Slavic language there would be very little you would recognize. Fortunately, Hungarian uses a Latin script so you can read the signs and metro station names easily enough. In Budapest, there are a lot of people who speak English, some who speak German, and some of the older generations speak Russian.

Some languages, like Romanian and Slovakian area, are also spoken among migrants from the neighboring countries, and the Romani population, although they speak Hungarian, have their own language, too. If you're strolling around the Jewish Quarter, don't be surprised if you spot Hebrew script on some of the doors or signs around the synagogues.

Essentials

Getting There

Travelers arriving via air have the option to fly into Prague's **Vaclav Havel International Airport** (Aviatická; www.prg.aero), **Vienna International Airport** (VIE; tel. 01/700-722-233; www.viennaairport.com), or Budapest's **Ferenc Liszt International Airport** (BUD; tel. 06/1-296-7000; www.bud.hu).

FROM THE UNITED STATES
Prague

Finding a direct flight into Prague from anywhere in the US is

tough, and flights are often seasonal. You may find non-stop service from Newark on **United Airlines** (www.united.com), from Philadelphia or Chicago on **American Airlines** (www.aa.com), or from New York (JFK) on **Delta Airlines** (www.delta.com), with flight times around 8.5 hours, but transferring in a major hub like London, Amsterdam, or Frankfurt is more common.

Vienna

Reaching Vienna from the US is easy. **Austrian Airlines** (www.austrian.com) runs direct flights to Vienna International Airport from Chicago and New York (Newark). Direct flights take around 8.5 hours. Before the coronavirus pandemic, there were also direct flights to Los Angeles and Miami, which may return in the future.

Budapest

Budapest has no direct flight connections from the US. If you fly in from any of the major US cities, you will need to change planes in somewhere like London, Frankfurt, Munich, or even Reykjavik. In 2018, **LOT Airlines** (www.lot.com) launched new routes from Budapest Liszt Ferenc Airport with direct flights between New York and Chicago with flight times lasting around 10-11 hours, but this route has ceased during the coronavirus pandemic.

FROM EUROPE

The great thing about traveling in Central Europe is you have an abundant selection when it comes to which mode of transport to pick. You can go by bus, train, car, plane, or in some instances by ferry.

Air

Low-cost airlines like **EasyJet** (www.easyjet.com), **WizzAir** (www.wizzair.com), and **Ryanair** (www.ryanair.com) offer inexpensive flights to the main airports of Prague,

Vienna, and Budapest from many European destinations. Ryanair also flies into Bratislava. It takes between 2-2.5 hours to reach Central Europe from London by plane.

Train

Traveling by train through Europe is a pleasure. You get to see the landscape change as you ride. If you're heading to Hungary or Austria from Western Europe, chances are you're in for a ride through the Alps. You can plan your train itinerary on the website **Bahn.de,** which shows plenty of train timetables and connections to destinations like Prague, Vienna, and Budapest so you can prepare more efficiently.

If you're feeling adventurous—or simply hate flying—you also have the option of traveling to Central Europe by train. You can take the **Eurostar** (www.eurostar.com) to Brussels (train tickets for this leg only are usually around €100-200), which go every two hours from London St. Pancras Station. However, from Brussels you will need to go to either Frankfurt or Cologne and change trains again to journey onto Vienna and Prague (Budapest will require another change at Vienna) with the total journey time (with the fewest connections) lasting between 15-19 hours. Tickets for onward journeys from Brussels could also cost an extra €150-250. This is not the most budget nor the most time friendly way to travel, but definitely an adventure!

Bus

Buses can be relatively cheap, and although they may not be as comfortable as a train, buses like **Eurolines** (www.eurolines.com) and **FlixBus** (www.flixbus.com) are quite comfortable, usually having toilets on board and operating across Europe. Taking the bus across Europe is quite the odyssey, and I would recommend doing it only if you really want to save money traveling overland—and with low-cost airlines offering frequent flights to Europe, you're not really saving that much.

You have the option to take a bus from London. Eurolines runs buses on this route more or less daily, and this trip will take around 25 hours (€100-125). Flixbus used to run a weekly route from London to Vienna, but in November 2020, the company temporarily discontinued all their bus services within Austria. **RegioJet** (www.regiojet.com) operates daily bus services to Prague, taking around 18.5 hours costing €60-110. There are no direct buses from London to Budapest.

Ferry

If you want to move between countries in Central Europe, your best bet is to go on a river cruise—some even go as far as coming from Norway all the way down to Budapest connection to the Danube via canals. **AMA Waterways** (www.amawaterways.com) and **Viking River Cruises** (www.vikingrivercruises.co.uk) run river cruises from Amsterdam to Budapest (and vice-versa), which take around 15 days. Sadly, the cruise industry took a big hit during the pandemic, but cruises were being rescheduled at the time of writing in spring of 2021.

Car

Europe has a well-connected highway network, so depending on how far you're planning to drive, it's relatively easy to reach Central Europe. Highways are smooth and well maintained throughout the region, but you may find some roads in the countryside, in Hungary especially, in poorer condition. Most roads are well lit and well maintained but do note that you must use winter tires during the winter if you're planning to drive across Central Europe as the roads—especially in the mountains in Austria—can get icy and slippery.

ROAD RULES

Driving laws vary throughout the region. In Hungary the minimum driving age is 17, whereas the Czech Republic and Austria both have minimum ages of 18. Blood alcohol levels permitted while driving in Austria are 50mg in 100 milliliters of blood, whereas in Hungary there is zero tolerance for any alcohol detected in the blood. There is one road rule the countries of continental Europe do have in common: You must drive on the right side of the road.

All the countries covered in this guide require a vignette for the country you're in where most main roads have tolls. You can usually buy these from gas stations, at the border, or online (www.asfinag.at/toll/vignette for Austria; www.hungary-vignette.eu for Hungary; eznamka.sk/selfcare/purchase for Slovakia; you cannot buy vignettes online for the Czech Republic) for some countries. These will need to be displayed in the window of your car unless it's an electronic one tied to your number plate.

While traveling, you'll need your passport and driver's license. If you're from the US, UK, or Canada, it may be a good idea also to get an **International Driving Permit** (IDP). This is an official translation of your license from back home, and although you won't need it in all countries, it's a good idea if you're planning on driving in Austria, Hungary, Poland, Croatia, Greece, Slovenia or Slovakia. You can get a permit from the American Automobile Association (AAA.com) or the Canadian Automobile Association Office (CCA.ca) for $20.

BORDER CROSSINGS

Ever since the Schengen Agreement removed border controls between the members of the EU states, traveling by car throughout Europe has gotten easier. Some countries may check at the border at random, however, so always have your papers—like your passport or ID, license (International Drivers Permit, if applicable), registration, insurance papers—to hand over. Peak seasons may lead to queues at the border.

SAFETY

In the winter, mountain passes may be slow, or even closed off if the weather is bad. If you're driving through the Alps, it's best to keep an eye on the news and drive through smaller roads at low speeds. You must also fit your car with winter tires or all-season tires between the months of November-April. Also carry snow chains with you this season. Winter conditions tend to be the worst from December-February, but it's not impossible to have snow in early November, late March or even early April. Winter controls are enforced at control points, especially in Austria. And—all year round—if you're planning on driving through Germany note that some highways won't have speed limits so expect some crazy road runners.

CAR RENTALS

If you want to head out on an epic road trip from one European country to another with a rental car, you'll want to pick a company like **Europcar** (www.europcar.com), **Sixt** (www. sixt.com), or **Hertz** (www.hertz.com), who have offices in other countries that allow you just to drop the car off, but these will include a "drop fee" which is an extra added charge to return the car to another office. Talk to your rental company about your itinerary. You can find the best rental deal with price comparison sites like **Skyscanner** (www. skyscanner.com) or **Kayak** (www.kayak.com). The minimum age to rent a car in the Czech Republic and Hungary is 21; it's 19 in Austria. Some companies require you to be at least 25

years of age, so confirm with your rental car company.

Should you prefer to cross Europe by car, but prefer not to drive yourself, you can also try the car-sharing service **Bla Bla Car** (www. blablacar.com) a carpooling service that matches up drivers and passengers at reasonable prices.

FROM AUSTRALIA AND NEW ZEALAND

There are no direct flights from Australia and New Zealand to Central Europe. The quickest and most direct route is to connect through Bangkok, Doha, Dubai, or Shanghai. **Emirates** (www.emirates.com) and **Qatar** (www.qatarairways.com) serve most of the flights from Australia and New Zealand, which take around 22 hours or more, including transfers. **Air China** (www.airchina.com) and **Thai Airways** (www.thaiairways.com) also have services connecting the region to Oceania.

FROM SOUTH AFRICA

There are no direct flights from South Africa to Prague, Vienna, or Budapest. The easiest way is to fly with **Emirates** or **Qatar Airways** and change in Dubai or Doha. Flights take around 15 to 18 hours or more. Some routes also go through Paris Charles de Gaulle with Air France or Zurich with Swiss Airlines on route from Johannesburg.

Getting Around

CITY TRANSPORT

One thing Central European cities have in common is excellent **public transport.** Each city has a well-connected subway service, a vast network of tram lines, and of course, buses. Each of the three cities' public transit systems are operated by one managing entity, so you use the same passes on multiple forms of transit, such as bus and metro. All three cities have passes that are sold in chunks of time,

so you can get a pass for 24 hours, 48 hours, etc. (In Budapest and Vienna, it's also possible to purchase single-ride tickets.)

You can also get around each city by **bike,** as all three have bike-sharing systems. Budapest and Vienna are bike friendly cities, with designated bicycle lanes and paths all across the city. Prague is not quite as bike-friendly inside the city, and drivers are not always known for giving way or stopping for crosswalks, but there are numerous cycling paths once you get into the countryside (see www.czechtrails.com for details).

Validating Transit Tickets

Another thing each municipality shares is the honesty system when it comes to enforcing public transit tickets. It works like this: you buy a ticket or a pass, and you validate it and keep it with you. Most of the time, there are no ticket inspectors, but if there are and you don't have a valid ticket prepare for trouble. Ticket inspectors are usually in civilian dress, so until the armband comes on or the ID gets put out from under the shirt you won't know, and they take no prisoners nor excuses. If your ticket is not validated or valid, you will get fined—and the experience can ruin your trip. You can usually buy tickets from automated machines, tobacconists, or ticket offices. You typically need to validate them when you enter the metro or get on the tram or bus. Look out for the validation boxes and double check the validation mark shows. Sometimes, passes won't need validating—in Budapest passes are issued from the date you request—but in Vienna, for example, you will need to validate the pass the first time you use it. Sometimes you can also buy tickets via an app: PIC Lítačka for Prague, WienMobil for Vienna, or Mobiljegy for Public Transport in Budapest.

GETTING AROUND CENTRAL EUROPE

Getting between Prague, Vienna, and Budapest, the easiest way is to go by train or by bus. Each city has direct connections. The main rail companies running in Central Europe are **ÖBB Railjet** (www.oebb.at), **MÁV** (www.mavcsoport.hu), **České Dráhy** (www.cd.cz), **RegioJet** (www.regiojet.com) and **Deutsche Bahn** (www.bahn.de). You can check timetables for all continental European connections on Deutsche Bahn's website (www.bahn.de). There are also regular buses operated by companies like **Flixbus** (www.flixbus.com) and **Eurolines** (www.eurolines.eu).

You also have the option to fly between the cities, but unless you're flying between Budapest and Prague with **Czech Airlines** (www.csa.cz), which operates flights three times a day for €75-300 one way taking an hour and a half, you won't actually save much time once you've checked in and gone through security. Trains and buses are fast, efficient, and much cheaper than flying. If you really must fly, **Austrian Airlines** (www.austrian.com) does connect Vienna with both cities.

In the past, you could take the ferry between Vienna and Budapest, but unfortunately, the route has been canceled. You can travel between Vienna and Bratislava by boat if you wish.

Visas and Officialdom

Austria, Czech Republic, Hungary, and Slovakia all reside within the EU and the Schengen Zone. Non-EU travelers who used to enter the Schengen Area freely on visa-waiver agreements, including US and UK travelers, will eventually be required to apply for ETIAS authorization (www.etiasvisa.com) before traveling. ETIAS was originally due to start in 2021, but at the time of writing was expected to be implemented in late 2022. Check the website for the latest guidelines.

US TRAVELERS

As a US citizen, you currently do not need an entry permit (visa) to enter any of the countries. You can come to Austria, Czech Republic, and Hungary as a tourist for up to 90 days in any 180-day period. However, you do require a passport that is valid for at least three months after your departure from the European Union.

UK TRAVELERS

UK travelers should check for new regulations post-Brexit. At the time of writing, UK citizens will have similar entry rights to US citizens and can enter the EU visa free for up to 90 days in any 180-day period. You will require a passport that is valid for at least 6 months after the date of travel and must be less than 10 years old.

EU/SCHENGEN TRAVELERS

If you're from another EU state, you do not need a visa to enter any of the Schengen countries, like Austria, Czech Republic, or Hungary. When you travel from one Schengen country to another, chances are you won't even have your passport or ID checked, although it's a good idea to keep it on you as some borders still check IDs, such as the train from Budapest to Vienna.

TRAVELERS FROM AUSTRALIA AND NEW ZEALAND

Australians and New Zealanders can come to Austria, Czech Republic, and Hungary visa-free for a maximum period of 90 days in any 180-day period without taking up employment. Your passport must be valid for three months beyond the planned date of departure from the Schengen area.

TRAVELERS FROM SOUTH AFRICA

South Africans require a visa to enter the Schengen Area. You can obtain a Schengen visa from any of the Schengen Area member countries, which will allow for free movement between the whole Schengen zone. It's best to apply for the country you're planning to visit first, for example, if you're flying into Austria, apply for a tourist visa from the Austrian Embassy, but make sure it's a Uniform Schengen Visa (USV) if you're planning on traveling onto Budapest, Prague, or even Bratislava. This visa will grant entry for 90 days in a 180-day period.

For Austria, visa applications should be submitted at the Austria Visa Application Center in Johannesburg, Cape Town, or Durban. These will be assessed by the Embassy of Austria in Pretoria.

If your first country is Hungary, then you can apply for your Schengen Visa from the Embassy of Hungary in Pretoria, or apply at the consulates in Durban or Cape Town.

Travelers beginning their journey in Prague should apply for the Schengen Visa at the Embassy of the Czech Republic in Pretoria.

Festivals and Events

Many seasonal events were rescheduled in 2020 and 2021 due to coronavirus pandemic. Check ahead before planning a trip around any events listed below.

JANUARY

New Year's Day Concerts (Vienna and Budapest) are a local tradition, especially in Vienna. The Musikverein hosts the most famous New Year's Day concert, which is broadcast globally. Although Vienna takes the spotlight, Budapest also has its fair share of classical concerts to ring in the New Year.

FEBRUARY

Opera Ball (Vienna) is the most important event on the Viennese social calendar. Out of some 300 balls held in January and February, Vienna's Opera Ball is the most lavish and anticipated.

MARCH

March 15 (Budapest) is a huge national holiday in Hungary to remember the revolution of 1848 against the Habsburg rule.

APRIL

Easter Markets (Prague and Vienna) take place at Schönbrunn Palace and across Prague squares, exhibiting Easter decorations, local crafts, and refreshments.

Čarodejnice ("Witches Day") (Prague) on April 30 marks the end of winter. Families gather in parks to prepare bonfires topped with wooden figures dressed in witch's clothes.

MAY

Prague Spring Festival (Prague) brings music to the city's concert halls, with everyone from symphony orchestras to young musicians competing for prizes.

Budapest 100 (Budapest) gets you a behind-the-scenes look inside private residential buildings which are normally closed to the public.

Falk Art Forum (Budapest) opens up the streets around 50 Budapest galleries for festivities, performances, music, theater, and food.

Prague Fringe Festival (Prague) brings nine days of comedy, cabaret, music, dance, and theater to the city.

JUNE

Donauinselfest (Vienna) is a free music festival held on the Danube Island. It lasts for three days and is the largest festival of its kind.

Regenbogenparade (Vienna) is a massive LGBTQ+ festival attracting over 150,000 people to the Ringstraße.

Karlovy Vary International Film Festival (Czech Republic) runs for eight days in early June or late July, and screens films all over town.

JULY

Jazz Fest Wien (Vienna) bring jazz, blues, and soul to Vienna's large and small venues, from the Staatsoper to small clubs.

Formula 1 Grand Prix (Budapest) is one the most important events in motorsports, bringing thousands to Budapest each year for the races.

Identities (Vienna) is an International Queer Film Festival that takes place every other year in June.

AUGUST

Sziget Festival (Budapest) is one of Europe's largest music festivals, taking place on Óbuda Island. The week-long festival pulls thousands in from around Europe.

Prague Pride parade

Prague Pride (Prague) includes a week of concerts, events, and a lively parade through town, held in early August and organized by members of the local LGBTQ+ community.

SEPTEMBER
Budapest Wine Festival (Budapest) gets the best Hungarian winemakers up to Buda Castle. Sip and taste wines from the region with fantastic views over the river.

OCTOBER
Budapest Design Week (Budapest) takes over the city during the first half of October. Exhibits of Hungarian contemporary fashion, art, and design are scattered throughout Budapest, and most events are free.

Prague Signal Festival (Prague) is a celebration of light installations and video shows, often projected onto Prague's architecturally attractive buildings.

Czechoslovak Independence Day (Prague) is usually celebrated with concerts and crowds in Wenceslas Square, marking the foundation of an independent Czechoslovakia on October 28, 1918.

Art Market Budapest (Budapest) takes place every October and is the leading art fair of Central and Eastern Europe. All manner of art is showcased here, to view and to buy, and there is a different guest country participant every year.

NOVEMBER
Saint Martin's Day (Prague) celebrates Saint Martin bringing the first snow of the season. The first taste of Svatomartinské young wine is poured on November 11th.

Struggle for Freedom and Democracy Day (Prague) commemorates political demonstrations that happened on November 17 in both 1939 and 1989, often with a mix of concerts or political protests covering Wenceslas Square.

DECEMBER
Christmas Markets in all three cities set up shop from the end of November till the end of December, and are a considerable draw to the region.

New Year (Vienna and Budapest) is an epic party in any city, and in the center of Vienna and Budapest, it becomes quite the street party. In Vienna, the Grand Ball takes place at the Hofburg and gives you the chance to see in the New Year in style.

Food and Nightlife

Food in Central Europe is dominated by meat, particularly pork. Starchy ingredients like potatoes and dumplings also make up the base for food in this part of the world, and vegetables—especially in Hungary and the Czech Republic—tend to come in pickled form.

MEALTIMES
Prague
Breakfast in Prague is often small—a quick pastry on the go—and the lunch hour starts early around 11am, with daily lunch specials usually served until 2pm. You can usually expect dinner service to last until at least 10pm.

Vienna
Breakfast is eaten between 7am-10am and is usually a lavish affair with a roll, a boiled egg, jam and butter, and some juice, at the minimum—and a coffee, naturally. Meal times in Austria are similar to the rest of Central Europe, with lunch taking place between midday and 2pm, dinner 7pm-9pm.

Budapest
Hungary shares similar meal times with Austria. Most people will have breakfast between 7am-10pm, with lunch usually taking place at 12-1:30pm, dinner around 7pm, but can be as early as 6pm or late as 8:30pm.

TIPPING

Tipping is not required, but is customary for good service. The general rule is to round up for small amounts (e.g. 50 CZK for a 42 CZK beer) or around 10 percent for a nice meal. You should tell your server how much you want to pay on the spot, when handing them cash or your card (e.g. Server: "That's 565 crowns." You: "600, please.") Don't leave cash on the table and your credit card slip will not come with a line to add the tip. In Hungary especially, if you give a note over and say "thank you," the waiter will assume that includes tip and you won't get change.

DIETARY RESTRICTIONS

Central Europe's vegetarian scene is slowly improving, with lots of raw and vegan restaurants opening in recent years in all three cities—and there is even a vegetarian Michelin star restaurant in Vienna. However, in many Czech, Austrian, and Hungarian restaurants, the meat-free menu is still limited to fried cheese (smažený sýr in Czech, rántott sajt in Hungarian, and Gebackener Käse in German) and vegans may struggle to find anything suitable outside of restaurants that specifically cater to their diet. Seafood, ham, bacon, lard, and even rabbit have been known to pop up on vegetarian sections in village pubs, so double-check with your server to be 100% sure.

Some restaurants are better than others when it comes to dairy or gluten sensitivity. Requests to leave out certain ingredients are usually honored when possible, but substitutions or asking for ingredients on the side is not common practice and will likely be met with confusion or annoyance—especially in rural areas. Restaurants are required to list certain allergens on their menus. For severe allergies, printing a list of the specific words in Czech, German, or Hungarian may help communicate your needs.

Accommodations

HOTELS

Hotels in Central Europe get graded on a star system running from one to five stars. Just how many stars a hotel will have depends on factors like the services and facilities available in the hotel, the infrastructure, and quality. Five-star hotels will offer luxury, like the Four Seasons Gresham Palace or the Hotel Sacher. There will usually be a spa and fine dining options. Three-star hotels are generally comfortable for most travelers. The term boutique hotel will pop up while traveling. This usually refers to a smaller hotel with 10 to 100 rooms, and may even have a design twist, that gives it a unique selling point for visitors. Most hotels will have en suite bathrooms—especially for hotels three stars and above—but it's best to check before booking if you're uncertain.

Basic toiletries will always be provided, like soap and shampoo, for hotels over 3 stars.

Hotels will ask for your ID or passport upon arrival and may also want to photocopy your documents. Sometimes a city tax will be added to your bill on top of your hotel fee, and check to make sure breakfast is included in the price of the room. Many hotels include a complimentary breakfast in the price in Hungary but in Austria and the Czech Republic it's pretty common to charge extra for breakfast, especially in four- or five-star hotels. When it comes to tipping hotel staff, it's enough to give a bellhop or porter a couple of euros or 500 HUF per bag. If you're happy with the cleaning service, then you can leave a similar gratuity on the bed each night for the housekeeper. Tipping hotel staff in the Czech Republic is not expected, but 20 CZK per bag or 100-200 CZK per stay for the cleaning staff is still a nice way to express gratitude.

1: traditional Hungarian fried bread lángos
2: European dessert in Salzburg 3: Czech cuisine often centers around meat and potatoes.

BED AND BREAKFASTS

Bed and Breakfasts are usually smaller than a hotel and independently owned. Breakfast is often included in the price, and often cooked by the owner. If you're looking for a place with a familial feel, then a B&B is a good choice. Rates are usually much lower than in a larger hotel, and you will get a more authentic feel in the area.

Do note though that some B&Bs occupy old residential apartments and houses, so bathrooms and toilets may not be located in the room but down the hall. You can usually request en suite when booking the B&B.

HOSTELS

Young travelers, backpackers, and those on a budget will love hostels. Most hostels offer rooms in 6- to 8-bed dorms, but some may have single or double rooms at budget prices too, however bathrooms and toilets will usually be shared and located outside the room. Some travelers also love hostels for the community spirit, as they usually come with a common room or a shared kitchen which provides an excellent opportunity for travelers to meet and mingle. Breakfast is usually extra, if offered by the hostel. However, if peace, quiet, and a good night's sleep is what you're after, steer clear of the Party Hostels, with their regular happy hours, in-house bars or clubs—which can also be great if you want to get to see the city's nightlife or make friends with other travelers.

APARTMENT RENTALS

If you prefer to self-cater or have the experience of living like a local in the city you're visiting, then an apartment rental may be the option for you. The most popular way of doing this is Airbnb, but this has caused significant controversy for pushing up the rents of locals, especially in cities like Budapest and Prague. Booking.com also rents out apartments. Just note in some apartment rentals, the toilet may be shared and located out in the hall—even in Vienna—so do your research before you book one. Also, note that with the independence an apartment will give you, you won't have the support concerning tourist information and orientation that you would have with a hotel.

Conduct and Customs

LOCAL HABITS

Hungary, Austria, and the Czech Republic share some habits, but they also have their differences. Austrians tend to be more formal than their Bohemian and Hungarian neighbors, and you'll find there is more formality than in Anglo-Saxon countries in all the Central European countries. You may even notice that people won't smile at you all the time like back home. Don't expect service with a smile in Central Europe. Some places have friendly staff, but as a rule, most waitstaff, especially classic cafés, will be on the surly side. Although smiles are not mandatory, politeness is. Always say hello or good day in the local language if you can whenever you go into a shop or a café, stand on the right of the escalator in the metro and give up your seat to the elderly on the bus. When it comes to tipping, it's best to say how much you'd like to pay in total when paying rather than leaving change on the table.

GREETINGS

Greetings are especially important in Central Europe. It's expected you say good day when you enter a shop. Even if you've brushed up on your German, don't use the classic German "Guten Tag," but instead go with the local greeting of "Grüß Gott"—pronounced "gruess got." In Hungary, you can say "Jó napot kívanok," pronounced "your nap-ot kee-van-ok," and in the Czech Republic you would say "dobrý den" pronounced "dough-bree-den"

It's also considered polite to say goodbye when leaving.

Greeting one another with a couple of kisses on the cheek is also common in Central Europe, but this usually happens between men and women, and women and women. In some cases, such as close family or older men, you may see the men do it, too. Kisses are generally exchanged at the beginning and the end of most social encounters. In business settings or between two men, a handshake is often the norm. This intimate tradition was hindered by COVID-19, and whether it'll return as a tradition in a post-pandemic Central Europe remains to be seen.

ALCOHOL

Alcohol rules in Central Europe are more relaxed than in the States, with the legal drinking age being 18 in the Czech Republic and Hungary. Austria is more relaxed in parts of the country, with the drinking age in Vienna (it varies based on the province between 16-18) being 16. However, despite the more liberal attitude to alcohol, getting very drunk in public in Vienna is more frowned upon than in countries like the UK, and there are fines for anti-social behavior while drunk. In Hungary, particularly in the countryside, don't be surprised to see locals doing a shot first thing in the morning, and in the Czech Republic, you may be surprised to find that the beer can be cheaper than water much of the time. Note that public alcohol consumption is illegal in many areas of Prague, particularly in historical areas with cobblestoned streets. Recent years have seen a rise in police issuing fines for loud, drunken tourists, while well-behaved guests are usually left alone.

There are restrictions on the sale of alcohol at certain times. In Budapest, for example, certain districts put a cap on late night shops selling alcohol after 11pm. And don't think of driving even if you've had one beer—drinking and driving is taken very seriously and can incur punishment if any shows up in a test.

SMOKING

Smoking is legal from the age of 18, and the laws will vary between the countries. In Hungary, you can only buy cigarettes from National Tobacco Shops (Nemzeti Dohány Bolt), which have brown signs and an 18 logo inside a red circle and the colors of the Hungarian flag—red, white, green. A lot of Hungarians smoke, but it's not allowed inside and only in designated areas outside in restaurants and cafés, and the Czech Republic is the same. (Up until May 2017, ashtrays were an essential part of most pubs in Prague, but the recent smoking ban has restricted cigarettes to only outdoor dining areas.) Austria is very relaxed when it comes to smoking. Don't be surprised to find restaurants and cafés with smoking sections indoors. Keep an eye out for the smoking and no smoking signs on the doors when you go out to eat or drink.

DRUGS

The Central European region has never had a reputation as being a drug hotbed, but dealing still happens around train stations and transport hubs. Hungary, where cannabis is entirely illegal, has stricter drug laws than the Czech Republic, where personal possession of marijuana has been decriminalized and medical marijuana is also legal. Austria has also relaxed its cannabis laws, allowing for it to be used for medicinal purposes, and decriminalized small quantities, but it's still discouraged to smoke marijuana in public places. Other drugs are illegal in all three countries, and possession can lead to up to two years imprisonment in Hungary and up to six months in Austria. It's best to play it safe while traveling and avoid consuming or possessing drugs—even in small quantities.

PROSTITUTION

Prostitution in Austria is legal and regulated. Sex workers must be registered and work from licensed brothels. Legal prostitution operates around the northern Gürtel, Naschmarkt, and in Leopoldstadt.

Although prostitution has been legalized in Hungary and sex workers pay tax, there is no official red light district in Budapest, and in the Czech Republic the line is even more blurred. Despite being legal, Czech laws prohibit organized prostitution and sex work is not regulated. There are some 200 brothels in Prague alone but their operations are not quite legal thanks to ambiguously written laws.

DRESS

Hungary and the Czech Republic have a more relaxed dress code. You'll see people walking around in jeans and T-shirts in Prague and Budapest, where most restaurants—unless we're talking somewhere elite—won't enforce a strict dress code. On the other hand, in Vienna, especially in the I District, you'll notice the locals tend to be elegantly dressed in smart casual attire. For high-class restaurants or a night at the opera, formal wear is preferred, which also applies to Prague. Although with the opera, you may notice some people in jeans and casual attire in the last-minute standing seats. In most churches, women will be expected to cover shoulders and wear skirts below the knee.

Health and Safety

EMERGENCY NUMBERS

The number to dial in an emergency is the same throughout continental Europe: **112.**

CRIME AND THEFT

Crime and theft in Central Europe are moderate. When it comes to violent crime, Vienna, Prague, and Budapest are generally safe cities. Pickpockets perhaps present the primary risk in crowded places like public transportation or festivals, so keep an eye out for your belongings when out and about. Scams are another thing to be aware of, like the classic Budapest scam when young, attractive women approach you (if you are male) on Váci utca asking for directions and then invite you to a drink—and take you to bar with no menus that will fleece you for as much money as you have. In Prague, avoid changing money on the street or you'll likely end up with a currency that isn't Czech Koruna. The Honest Guide channel on YouTube also highlights some Prague scams to look out for, from overpriced cabs to deceptive exchange offices and fake charities. It's important not to let your guard down, but with a little common sense and avoiding areas with a bad reputation—such as the areas surrounding train stations—you should be fine.

MEDICAL SERVICES

In the past, vaccines were not required for any of the countries in Central Europe. (At the time of writing in spring 2021, whether proof of a COVID vaccine would be required remained to be seen.) Certainly, a COVID vaccine is recommended prior to travel, and if you're traveling in the window between November-March, you may also want to get a flu shot. Also, if you're planning to head out into nature, you may want to get a Tick-Borne Encephalitis vaccine, as ticks are a growing risk in Central Europe. You can also pick up bug spray in local pharmacies that is good to ward off mosquitos and ticks, so if you haven't been vaccinated, it's a good idea to take precautions when in parks or wooded areas—even within the city.

Medical care in Austria is excellent, but in Hungary, standards will vary depending on the hospital, with some being better than others. Public health services in Hungary are understaffed and overburdened. The Czech Republic falls somewhere in between the two countries.

DRINKING WATER

The water is not only safe to drink in all three cities, but it's actually pretty good—especially in Vienna—so go ahead and feel free to bottle some tap water.

PHARMACIES

Pharmacies in Central Europe can help you pick up any medications, vitamins, or herbal supplements you may need while traveling. Drugs like ibuprofen and paracetamol (acetaminophen) won't require a prescription in European pharmacies, but some drugs will require a local prescription from a doctor of that country, like antibiotics or sedatives. European pharmacies also sell more than just medication, but you can also buy skincare products and toiletries developed by dermatologists (if you've heard about beauty bloggers rave about French pharmacy skin care products, the good news is you can find the same French brands like La Roche-Posay and Nuxe in larger Central European pharmacies). You may also find European pharmacies sell alternative medicines like homeopathy as well.

You can spot a pharmacy in each country by the bright green cross symbol. You can find a pharmacy that's open any time of day or night, either in an assigned all night pharmacy like those in Budapest, or rotating with the schedule printed on the door of each pharmacy as in Vienna.

SECURITY

Prague and Budapest to date have not seen any terrorist attacks; Vienna, however, has had instances of lone wolf knife attacks and in November 2020 a series of shootings by a lone gunman. Austria is the most likely out of the three countries to be at risk from terrorism. Just like any city in Europe, it's best to be vigilant and consult your embassy for travel advice. Also, if offered, register your travel with your embassy before traveling so that you're entitled to consular help.

Practical Details

WHAT TO PACK

When it comes to packing, the best bet is to pack smart-casual attire and plenty of layers. The climate in the region is changeable, so keep a jacket or a cardigan in your bag for those days when the cooler evening chill sets in.

Expect to do a lot of walking in each city so pack a pair of **comfortable shoes.** The old towns in Prague, Vienna, and Budapest have cobbles so bear that in mind when considering footwear. Since the climate is changeable—in the summer you can go from blazing heat to flash storms—pack layers and an umbrella or a raincoat to hand. If you're going in the winter, pack warm clothes as the temperatures can plummet below zero.

It's a good idea to bring **swimwear** if you're traveling to Budapest or Vienna since Budapest has its famous thermal baths and Vienna also has some stunning pools worth taking a dip in.

If you're coming from the UK or the States, make sure you pack an **adapter** so you can use your electronics in Continental Europe. Plugs in Central Europe use two round prongs with a voltage of 220V. You will definitely want a camera or at least a good quality phone to snap pics, but bring extra memory cards, because you will need them!

Depending on COVID-19 conditions, **facemasks** or respirators (KN95 or FFP2) may be required in many places, so toss some into your bag for as many days as you'll be abroad. Small bottles of **hand sanitizer** and **disinfecting wipes** can be helpful for navigating public spaces and transport. You should also print and carry hard copies of any **medical information and insurance cards** rather than storing them on a mobile phone. Czech hospitals in particular may need to photocopy your documents.

Finally, **earbuds or headphones** can

Coronavirus in Central Europe

Central Europe was significantly impacted by the effects of the coronavirus pandemic. Most of the region went into lockdown, closing international borders as well as restaurants, museums, thermal baths, bars, hotels, and more. Face masks (and, specifically, KN95 or FFP2 masks in the Czech Republic) were required, with possible fines for those who didn't comply. However, at the time of writing in May 2021, the situation was improving, with the potential for open borders in sight and venues starting to re-open (though some for fully vaccinated travelers only).

Now more than ever, Moon encourages its readers to be courteous and ethical in their travel. We ask travelers to be respectful to residents, and mindful of the evolving situation in their chosen destination when planning their trip.

BEFORE YOU GO

- Check local websites (listed below) for **local restrictions** and the **overall health status** of the destination and your point of origin. If you're traveling to or from an area that is currently a COVID-19 hotspot, you may want to reconsider your trip.

- Get **vaccinated** if your health status allows, and if possible, take a **coronavirus test** with enough time to receive your results before your departure. Some destinations may require proof of vaccination or a negative COVID test result before arrival, along with other tests and potentially a self-quarantine period, once you've arrived. Check local requirements and factor these into your plans.

- If you plan to fly, check with your airline and the destination's health authority for updated **travel requirements.** Some airlines may be taking more steps than others to help you travel safely, such as limited occupancy; check their websites for more information before buying your ticket, and consider a very early or very late flight to limit exposure. Flights may be more infrequent, with increased cancellations.

- Check the website of any museums and other venues you wish to patronize to confirm that they're open, if their hours have been adjusted, and to learn about any specific visitation requirements, such as **mandatory reservations** or **limited occupancy.**

- Pack **hand sanitizer, a thermometer,** and plenty of **face masks** (including KN95 or FFP2 masks for the Czech Republic). Consider packing **snacks, bottled water,** a **cooler,** or anything else you might need to limit the number of stops along your route, and to be prepared for possible closures and reduced services over the course of your travels.

- **Assess the risk** of entering crowded spaces, joining tours, and taking public transit.

- Expect **general disruptions.** Events may be postponed or cancelled, and some tours and venues may require reservations, enforce limits on the number of guests, require KN95 or FFP2 masks, be operating during different hours than the ones listed, or be closed entirely.

be useful for accessing museum audio guides that you can download onto your phone.

BUDGETING

One thing you will notice is that prices between the three cities will vary. Vienna is by far the most expensive city out of the three, and Prague and Budapest are cheaper. A cup of coffee in Vienna can cost between $3.40-6.50, whereas in Prague and Budapest you'd pay $2. A beer in Vienna would set you back $3.60-4.60, and around $2.50 in Budapest and Prague. A 24-hour public transport ticket in Vienna will cost $10, $5.50 in Budapest and $5.30 in Prague. If you're planning a budget for the three cities, allocate a higher threshold for Vienna. You may want to balance things out by going for more budget accommodation or self-catering in Vienna while living it up in Budapest or Prague.

GENERAL RESOURCES

· **World Health Organization:** www.who.int/emergencies/diseases/novel-coronavi-rus-2019/travel-advice

· **International Air Transport Organization:** www.iatatravelcentre.com/world.php

· **CDC:** www.cdc.gov/coronavirus/2019-ncov/travelers

· **U.S. State Department:** https://travel.state.gov/content/travel/en/traveladvisories/ea/covid-19-information.html

RESOURCES FOR PRAGUE AND THE CZECH REPUBLIC

· **Czech Ministry of the Interior:** https://koronavirus.mzcr.cz and https://covid.gov.cz

· **Prague COVID-19 testing info:** https://covid.praha.eu

· **Prague Airport testing info:** www.prg.aero/en/testing-covid-19

· **Czech contact-tracing app eRouška:** https://erouska.cz/en

· **Czech Tourism:** www.visitczechrepublic.com/en-US/Covid-19

· **Prague City Tourism:** www.prague.eu/en/articles/prague-x-coronavirus-update-16703

· **COVID-19 hotline:** Dial 1221; 8am-7pm Mon-Fri and 9am-4:40pm weekends; English-language information available

RESOURCES FOR BUDAPEST AND HUNGARY

· **About Hungary:** https://abouthungary.hu

RESOURCES FOR VIENNA AND AUSTRIA

· **Austrian Tourism Board:** www.austria.info

MONEY

The EU is generally great to travel in since you usually have a single currency, but in the case of Prague, Vienna, and Budapest, we're sorry to say that only Austria is in the Eurozone (if you want to pop over to Slovakia for the day, the good news is they also use the euro). The Czech Republic uses the Czech Koruna (also called the Crown), and Hungary the Hungarian Forint.

You'll find that **ATMs** will take foreign cards and most shops (fewer in Prague) will take Visa, Mastercard, or Maestro. Some won't take American Express, so best to check before ordering. If you prefer, you can also change money at official money changers, either in banks or official changers (they usually have a Western Union sign outside, too). Do be aware that many exchange places in Prague use fairly deceptive tactics and below market

When it comes to finding a quiet moment in tourist hot spots, the common refrain among photographers is to arrive before sunrise. The most famous sights can be pretty crowded from morning to evening during summer and Christmas seasons. Saving these sights for weekdays instead of weekends, arriving first thing in the morning, or waiting until nighttime can give you a different experience with fewer crowds. Otherwise, just be patient and take your time at the sights you choose to visit. Wait for the crowds to rise and disperse around you and watch for the moment to get a good view or picture as you immerse yourself in the moment.

Start early or try off-seasons to beat the crowds.

value rates. Two trusted offices to change money are Visitor Change (Na Můstku 2, 9am-7pm) at the information center or eXchange (Kaprova 14) just off Old Town Square past St. Nicholas Church.

Some restaurants and shops will only take **cash;** most markets are cash only. It's a good idea to carry some smaller bills with you if you're planning on paying in cash. Most large supermarkets and restaurants will break larger notes, but you might get a few irritated servers or sellers if you try to pay with a 20,000 HUF note, 1,000 CZK, or a €100 bill in a smaller venue. It's a good idea to keep some small change on you at all times, especially for public toilets (some in Vienna are automated, for example and will only take 50 cent coins).

OPENING HOURS

Shops usually open around 9am-10am and close around 6pm, perhaps later in large shopping malls, Mondays to Saturdays. On Sundays, the case will vary between cities. In Vienna, most shops close on Sundays, whereas in Budapest shops in the city center will open for shorter hours on Sunday, and in Prague, large stores or supermarkets may stay open on Sundays, but others will close. Sometimes, smaller stores will close for lunch hours.

Museums, in general, tend to close on Mondays, but check the opening times of any place you're interested in visiting—some

popular attractions open every day of the week, others may have a rest day on Tuesday or Sunday.

PUBLIC HOLIDAYS

During high holidays, like Christmas and New Year's Day, most shops and attractions will be closed. Businesses also tend to close for religious holidays, but also national holidays, like October 23, March 15, and August 20 in Hungary; and in Austria October 26; in the Czech Republic May 8 and September 28, to name a few.

COMMUNICATIONS
Phones and Cell Phones

The country codes for Austria is 43, for Hungary 36 and the Czech Republic 420. If you're calling from the US, dial the international access code 011, from a US or Canadian landline, or use the plus sign, and add the country code, then dial the number (drop the 0 before calling). From the UK, just dial 00 and then the country code.

Within each country, just dial the number without dropping the 0, if there is one. For long distance calls within Hungary, dial 06. Don't get nervous if phone numbers seem irregular in number. Standards are a little harder to predict. Mobile phone numbers can come with their own prefixes, and sometimes landline number length will also vary.

To call out of the country, dial 00 or the plus sign and the country code. For US and Canada this is 1 and then add in the phone number with the area code.

Most smartphones will work in Central Europe with a US, UK, or Canadian SIM card, but talk to your provider to make sure you don't rattle up any unwanted roaming charges when you go abroad.

Internet Access

You should find it easy to get online in any of the cities. You should find Wi-Fi access in your hotel, but most cafés, malls, and even hotspots in the city center should get you connected online for free. Some free Wi-Fi services may ask you to register with an email and click on their terms and conditions. You often need to ask a server for a password in Prague cafés and restaurants.

Shipping and Postal

If you're looking only to post a card, then you may want to skip the queues at the post office and buy a stamp at the tobacconist (Austria) or newsagent (Hungary, Czech Republic). Should you go to a post office, some require you press a button and take a number for the queue. Postcards to the US will cost around €1-2 to post.

Traveler Advice

ACCESS FOR TRAVELERS WITH DISABILITIES

With its cobbled streets, stairways leading up from one lane to another, and old metro stations, Central Europe can be a challenge for travelers with disabilities. Out of the three cities, Vienna is the most accessible. Ramps leading into buildings are generally standard, as are elevators in the U-Bahn, and buses and trams have spaces allocated for wheelchairs. You can request an Accessible Vienna pamphlet from the Tourist Info Wien for a list of places catering to visitors with specific needs. Even if you go further afield in Austria, ÖBB, the Austrian rail network has the option for Accessible Booking, but make sure you order 24 hours in advance for domestic services.

Prague and Budapest are a little behind when it comes to catering to travelers with disabilities. Historic buildings and hotels may lack lifts, and some of the older metro stations may be stairs only. For more information, contact the **Hungarian Federation of Disabled Persons' Associations** (www.meosz.hu) for Hungary or the **Prague Wheelchair Users Organisation** (www.presbariery.cz) for the Czech Republic.

TRAVELING WITH CHILDREN

Whether you want to visit Europe's oldest zoo, ride a railway staffed by children, or picnic Petřín Hill overlooking Prague, Central Europe offers something for all the family. Kids get discounts on public transport and museums, and some restaurants even offer a children's menu. There's plenty to keep the little ones busy when traveling Central Europe. Some tourist offices will provide brochures with family-friendly ideas. It's worth researching museums to see if any have play areas for children—for example, in Vienna's MuseumsQuartier, ZOOM is a museum with interactive programs that can keep the kids occupied while you pay a visit to the Leopold or mumok.

FEMALE TRAVELERS

Prague, Vienna, and Budapest are relatively safe cities for solo female travelers, but exercise the same caution as you would in any other European city. Most downtown areas are okay to explore your own, even at night. However, if you feel anxious walking down quiet streets after dark, then try to pick accommodations on a main road, since all three cities will have side streets that may unnerve you after dark. Taxis can be a great option to get back if you don't like taking public transport late night, or there are no services to where you're staying, but make sure you take a licensed operator or use an app like the **Bolt** taxi app which also allows you to share your route with a friend or family. And should you go to a bar, take care never to leave your drink unattended.

SENIOR TRAVELERS

Senior travelers may struggle with the cobbled streets and the less accessible sites in Central Europe, but on the whole, it's a region that's great for older travelers. The thermal baths in Budapest, Prague's historical sites, or Vienna's world-class museums all attract travelers of all ages. Most museums have lifts and benches, and of course, discounts for senior citizens. Public transport is either free—in the case of Budapest, it's free for EU citizens aged 65 and over—or at a discount. Just take care not to book a hotel in the heart of a party district, such as Budapest's Jewish Quarter, if you're looking for a peaceful night's sleep.

LGBT TRAVELERS

Austria, Hungary, and the Czech Republic are quite varied when it comes to welcoming gay and lesbian travelers. Hungary has conservative views that seem to become more entrenched each year, and the current government in Hungary is, unfortunately, hostile to the LGBT community. In 2020, trans people lost legal recognition and gay and lesbian couples no longer have the right to adopt. There have also been some violent demonstrations from the far-right in Budapest. That being said, attitudes are changing in the city, with a growing number gay-friendly spaces in the city center. Vienna is tolerant toward gays and lesbian travelers, and like Budapest more so in the capital than in the rest of Austria. Prague has a vibrant cis gay scene, mostly concentrated in the Vinohrady area, but may not feel as welcoming for transgender travelers.

When traveling outside the cities into rural areas, members of the LGBTQ community may feel a little uncomfortable. Austria is a predominantly Catholic country; however same sex marriage became legal in January 2019. LGBTQ travelers in rural Austria should feel as safe as they would be in Western European countries. In rural Hungary—and even in Budapest—members of the LGBTQ community tend to remain invisible, and public displays of affection are not seen. The Czech Republic on the other hand has a more liberal stance but public displays of affection, especially in smaller villages, may still draw looks. The **Spartacus International Gay Guide** (spartacus.gayguide.travel/gayguide) offers a lot of useful information for LGBTQ travelers for all the countries listed in this book. The **Transparent Organization** (www.transparentprague.cz) may be able to answer questions for transgender travelers to the Czech Republic.

TRAVELERS OF COLOR

It's been said that racism is a bigger problem in Central and Eastern Europe than in Western Europe, and it's true that discrimination seems to be more blatant here. Populations in Hungary and the Czech Republic in particular are quite homogenous, and travelers from some ethnic or religious backgrounds, particularly those with darker skin, may experience xenophobic attitudes and unwanted attention. For example, travelers of color are more likely than white travelers to be stopped on public transport to check tickets and may feel themselves being observed while browsing in shops. (This is less true in cosmopolitan Vienna than it is in Prague and Budapest.) Groups that report negative experiences include people from the Roma community, as well as Black, Muslim, and Jewish people. However, while stares and slurs are not unheard of, outright violence against travelers appears, fortunately, to be rare.

A few resources for voices of color in the Czech Republic include **Romea.cz,** focused on Prague's Roma community, and the podcasts **Foreign Insiders** (https://foreigninsiders.com) and **Aliens of Prague** (www.fb.com/aliensofprague). Travelers may find support or advice through the nonprofit **Center for Immigration and Migration** (www.migrace.com/en) or the **Center for Immigration of Foreigners** (www.cicops.cz). Travelers to Hungary looking for a first-person perspective can check out **Black Girl in Budapest** (www.blackgirlinbudapest.com), written by a Black expat living in Hungary's capital.

Resources

Glossary

CZECH

autobus: bus
cukrárna: sweet shop
divadlo: theater
dům: house or building
heslo: password
hospoda: pub
hrad: castle
jízdenka: public transit ticket
kavárna: café/coffee shop
Kč: Czech crown (also abbreviated CZK)
klimatizace: air conditioning
kostel: church
kreditní karta: credit card
lékárna: pharmacy
město: town
most: bridge
muži: men (or men's room)
nádraží: train station
náměstí: town/public square
nástupiště: platform
obchod: shop
odlety (airport)/odjezdy (train or bus station): departures
ostrov: island
pivo: beer
pokladna: ticket office
potraviny: mini-market
přílety (airport); příjezdy (train or bus station): arrivals
řada: row
rouška: mask
sedadlo: seat
ulice: street
vinárna/vinoteka: wine bar
vlak: train
(vyhlídková) věž: (observation) tower
zámek: chateau
zastávka: bus, tram, or train stop
ženy: women (or women's room)

GERMAN

Abfahrt: departure
Ankunft: arrival
Anschluss: connection (transport)
Apotheke: pharmacy
Ausfahrt: exit
Auto: car
Bäckerei: bakery
Badezimmer: bathroom
Bahnhof: station
Beisl: inn/Austrian bistro
Bett: bed
Briefmarke: stamp
Brücke: bridge
Dom: cathedral
Einbahnstraße: one way street
Eingang: entrance
Eisenbahn: railway
Fahrkarte: rail or bus ticket
Fahrkartenschalter: ticket office (railway)
Flughafen: airport
frei: free
Gasse: alley
Gebäude: building
Gegend: neighborhood
Geld: cash
geschlossen: closed
gut: good
heiß: hot
Herberge: hostel
Hilfe: assistance

Kassa: ticket office (theater)/checkout
Kassierer: cashier
Kellner: waiter
Kirche: church
Kleingeld: small change
klimatisiert: air-conditioned
Konditorei: pastry shop
Konsulat: consulate
Kreditkarte: credit card
Laden: shop
Lebensmittelmarkt: grocery store
Markt: market
nicht alkoholisch: nonalcoholic
Ober: waiter
Öffnen: open
Parkplatz: parking lot
Platz: square
Polizei: police
Reservierung: reservation
Strand: beach
Straße: road/street
Straßenbahnhaltestelle: tram stop
Tabak: tobacco shop
Turm: tower
U-Bahn: subway
U-Bahn Haltestelle: U-bahn stop
Vorspeise: appetizer
Ziel: destination
Zeitplan: timetable
Zimmer: room
Zoll: customs
Zug: train

HUNGARIAN

ágy: bed
alkohol: alcohol
alkoholmentes: nonalcoholic
állomás: station
ár: price
autó: car
bejárat: entrance
borozó: wine bar
busz: bus
célállomás: destination
csatlakozást: connection (transport)
cukrászda: pastry shop
dohánybolt: tobacco shop
élelmiszerbolt: grocery store

előétel: appetizer
emlékmű/műemlék: monument
épület: building
érkezés: arrival
étterem: restaurant
fasor: avenue
foglalás: reservation
forró: hot
gyógyszertár: pharmacy
híd: bridge
hitelkártya: credit card
indulás: departure
ingyenes: free
jegy: ticket
jegypénztár: ticket office
készpénz: cash
kijárat: exit
konzulátus: consulate
légkondicionált: air-conditioned
liget: park
menetrend: timetable
metró: subway
metrómegálló: subway stop
mosdó: bathroom
nagykövetség: embassy
nyitva: open
országút: highway
parkoló: parking lot
pékség: bakery
pénztáros: cashier
pénzdarab: coin
piac: market
pincér: waiter
rendőrség: police
repülőtér: airport
segítség: assistance
strand: beach
szálló/hostel: hostel
szálloda: hotel
székesegyház: cathedral
szoba: room
templom: church
tér: square
torony: tower
újságos: newsstand
út: road
utca: street
üzlet/bolt: shop

vám: customs
vasút: railway
villamos megálló: tram stop

vonat: train
zárva: closed

Czech Phrasebook

Czech is quite a difficult language—four genders (neuter, feminine, masculine animate, and masculine inanimate), seven cases that change word endings, formal and informal phrases—plus it includes one sound, the vicious ř, that many schoolchildren need speech therapy to master! On the bright side, the language is phonetic so you can say what you see. Some quirky letters pronounced differently than English include: au, c, č, ď, j, ř, š, ť, ž, and any vowel with an accent mark. Also, the first syllable is stressed for all Czech words, as opposed to the second syllable typical in English (e.g. the second-largest city is pronounced BRR-no instead of brr-NO).

Some locals are delighted by foreigners speaking their language, while others quickly lose patience and get frustrated if you don't understand their responses in Czech. Asking a question in Czech will likely receive an answer in Czech, and most locals are not used to simplifying their own language for foreigners. Some Czechs in the service sector will switch to English to ensure accuracy and efficiency. In many cases, simplicity (e.g. "Liberec?" while pointing to the bus) is easier to facilitate communication. This also makes it easier for the locals to understand than the unavoidable mispronunciation of their own language or small grammatical errors that can change meanings. However, do feel free to try some Czech phrases when you have the time and a willing native speaker.

a   as in "father"
á   longer as in "ahhhh"
au   like "ow" as in "how"
c   "ts" always a soft c as in "patience" (never hard like "ck")
č   "ch" as in "change"
ch   like an "h" but in the back of your throat like the composer "Bach"

ď   a "dy" sound as in "What d'ya want?"
e   as in "egg"
é   like "ai" as in "fair"
ě   like adding a "y" before the "e" as in "yes"
i   as in "fit"
í   like "ee" as in "free"
j   like "y" in "yes"
ň   like "ny" as in "menu"
o   as in "oh"
ó   longer "oh" as in "oooooh"
ř   no English equivalent; in Czech it combines saying "ž" plus a rolled "r" simultaneously, as in the composer's name Dvořák; English speakers can get by with just saying "ž" like the "s" in "pleasure"
š   "sh" as in "shampoo"
ť   a "ty" sound as in creature
u   as in "soup"
ú or ů   like a long "u" as in "true"; the character ú is used at the beginning of a word while ů is used in the middle
y   like a short "i" as in "bit"
ý   like a long "e" as in "me"
ž   like "s" in "measure"

ESSENTIAL PHRASES

Hello Dobrý den (formal, for strangers and acquaintances; used anytime you enter a shop or restaurant)
Hi / Bye Ahoj or Čau (informal, used somewhat interchangeably but only for close friends and family)
Good morning Dobré ráno
Good evening Dobrý večer
Good night Dobrou noc
Goodbye Na shledanou (used anytime you leave a shop or restaurant)
Where are you from? Odkud jste?
I am from the US / England / ... Jsem z USA / Jsem z Anglie ...

Nice to meet you Těší mě

Please/You're welcome Prosím

Excuse me Pardon or Promiňte

Sorry Promiňte

Thank you Děkuji

Excuse me, do you speak English? Promiňte, nemluvíte* Anglicky? (*In Czech the more polite sentence structure is similar to "Don't you speak English?")

Is there WIFI? Nemáte* WIFI? (* In Czech the more polite sentence structure is similar to "Don't you have WIFI?")

What's the WIFI password? Jaké je heslo na WIFI?

Yes Ano (formal, and often shortened to "'no" so be careful because "'no" in Czech means "Yes!")

No Ne

Where is the restroom? Kde jsou toalety?

TRANSPORTATION

bus station autobusové nádraží

train station vlakové nádraží

Where is...? Kde je...?

How far is it to...? Jak daleko je.... odsud?

Is there a bus to Liberec / Brno / ...? Je autobus do Liberce* / Brna* / ...? (* Almost all Czech words, including place names, change depending on the sentence.)

Is this the bus to...? Je to autobus na ...?

What time does the bus/train leave? V kolik hodin autobus / vlak odjíždí?

Where is the subway station? Kde je stanice metra?

Where's the ticket office? Kde je pokladna?

A round-trip/single ticket to... Zpáteční / jízdenku na...

FOOD

Can I make a reservation, please? Mohu si udělat rezervaci, prosím?

A reservation for one/two... Rezervace za jednu osobu / dvě osoby

Two people at 2pm dva lidé ve dvě odpoledne

Do you have a reservation? Máte rezervaci?

Do you have an English menu? Nemáte anglické menu?

Are you ready to order? Máte vybráno?

Excuse me, may I order, please? Promiňte můžu objednat, prosím?

I'm vegetarian / vegan. jsem vegetarian / vegan (masc.) / jsem vegetarianka / veganka (fem.).

I'll have... please. Dám si....prosím.

Is everything okay? Všechno v pořádku?

I would like to pay / We would like to pay, please. Zaplatím / Zaplatíme, prosím.

Cash or card? Hotově nebo kartou?

breakfast snídaně

beer pivo

lunch oběd

dinner večeře

menu jídelní lístek

wine víno

water voda

coffee káva

tea čaj

(soy / almond / oat) milk (sójové / mandlové / ovesné) mléko

dairy-free bez mléka

gluten / gluten-free lepek / bezlepkový

fruit ovoce

bread chléb

meat maso

fish ryby

SHOPPING

money peníze

How much does it cost? Kolik to stojí?

I'm just looking around. Jen se rozhlížím.

HEALTH

drugstore drogérie

pharmacy lékárna

mask rouška

It hurts here. Bolí mě tady.

I have a fever. Mám horečku.

I have a headache. Bolí mě hlava.

I have a stomachache. Bolí mě břicho.

I have a toothache. Bolí mě zub.

I feel nauseated. Je mi nevolno.
I can't breathe. nemůžu dýchat
to vomit zvracet
medicine lékařství
antibiotic antibiotika
pill/tablet pilulka / tabletka
I need a doctor Potřebuji lékaře
To the hospital, please. Do nemocnice,
   prosím.
I am diabetic / pregnant. Jsem diabetik
   / těhotná
I take birth control pills. Užívám
   antikoncepci.
I am allergic to... penicillin. Jsem
   alergický (masc.) / alergická (fem.) na...
   penicilín.
blood type krevní skupina

NUMBERS

0 nula
1 jeden (m.) / jedna (f.) / jedno (n.)
2 dva / dvě
3 tři
4 čtyři
5 pět
6 šest
7 sedm
8 osm
9 devět
10 deset
11 jedenáct
12 dvanáct
13 třináct
14 čtrnáct
15 patnáct
16 šestnáct
17 sedmnáct
18 osmnáct
19 devatenáct
20 dvacet
21 dvacet jedna
30 třicet
40 čtyřicet
50 padesát
60 šedesát
70 sedmdesát
80 osmdesát

90 devadesát
100 sto
200 dvě stě
300 / 400 tři / čtyři sta
500 / 600 / 700 / 800 / 900 pět / šest /
   sedm / osm / devět set
1,000 tisíc
2,000 dva tisíce

TIME
What time is it? Kolik je hodin?
It's 1am / 3pm (15:00) Je jedna hodina / Je
   patnáct hodin
noon/midday poledne
midnight půlnoc
morning (early, before leaving the
   house) ráno
morning (before noon) dopoledne
afternoon odpoledne
evening večer
yesterday včera
today dnes / dneska
tomorrow zítra
now ted'

DAYS AND MONTHS
week týden
month měsíc
Monday pondělí
Tuesday úterý
Wednesday středa
Thursday čtvrtek
Friday pátek
Saturday sobota
Sunday neděle
January leden
February únor
March březen
April duben
May květen
June červen
July červenec
August srpen
September září
October říjen
November listopad
December prosinec

German Phrasebook

German is the national language in Austria, and although there are some regional differences between Austrian German and the standard German you had learned at school (if you studied German, that is), you can still communicate without any issues. German shares a lot of words with English and much of the pronunciation is similar to English words, making it perhaps the easiest language to decipher in the three countries. A couple of phonetic things to note:

ch is pronounced kh (think the ch in the composer Bach's name)

r comes from the back of the throat

ß is a double s

sch is like our sh

tsch is like our ch

ö kind of sounds like er, but think of it as going to say o but changing to an a

ä is like a sort e, like in bet

ü make your lips form the shape they would take if you would say o but try to say e instead.

ESSENTIAL PHRASES

Hello Grüss Gott/Servus
Good morning Guten morgen
Good evening Grüss Gott/Guten abend
Good night Guten nacht
Good bye Auf Wiedersehen
Nice to meet you Es ist schon, Sie kennen zu lemen
Thank you Danke
You're welcome Bitte
Please Bitte
Excuse me Entschuldigung
Sorry Entschuldigung
Do you speak English? Sprechen Sie Englisch?
I don't understand Ich verstehe nicht.
Yes Ja
No Nein
Where is the restroom? Wo ist die Toilette?

TRANSPORTATION

Where is...? Wo ist...?
How far is...? Wie weit ist...?
Is there a bus to...? Gibt es einen Bus nach...?
Does this bus go to...? Fährt dieser Bus nach...?
Where do I get off? Wo muss ich aussteigen?
What time does the bus/train leave? Wann fährt der Bus/Zug ab?
Where is the nearest subway station? Wo ist die nächste U-Bahn Station?
Where's the ticket office? Wo ist der Ticketschalter?
A round-trip ticket/single ticket to... Eine Rückfahrkarte/einfache Fahrkarte nach...

FOOD

A table for one person/two people... Ein Tisch für eine Person/zwei Personen, bitte.
Do you have a menu in English? Gibt es eine Speisekarte auf Englisch?
What is the dish of the day? Was ist das Tagesgericht?
I'm ready to order. Ich möchte bestellen.
I'm vegetarian. Ich bin Vegetarier/Vegetarierin (m/f).
May I have... Kann ich... haben?
The check, please. Zahlen, bitte.
beer Bier
breakfast Frühstück
cash Bar geld/bar
check Rechnung
coffee Kaffee
dinner Abendessen
glass Glas
hors d'oeuvre Vorspeise
ice Eis
ice cream Eis
lunch Mittagessen

restaurant Restaurant
snack Snack
waiter Ober/Kellner
water Wasser
wine Wein

SHOPPING

money Geld
shop Laden
What time do the shops close? Wann
  schließen die Läden?
How much is this? Was kostet das?
I'm just looking. Ich sehe mich nur um.

HEALTH

drugstore Apotheke
pain Schmerz
fever Fieber
headache Kopfschmerzen
stomach ache Magenschmerzen
toothache Zahnschmerzen
burn Brandwunde
cramp Krampf
nausea Übelkeit
vomiting Erbrechen
medicine Medizin
antibiotic Antibiotikum
pill/tablet Pille/Tablette
aspirin Aspirin
I need a doctor Ich brauche einen Arzt.
Please take me to the hospital Bringen
  Sie mich bitte ins Krankenhaus.
I have a pain here... Es tut hier weh...
I am diabetic/pregnant. Ich bin
  zuckerkrank/schwanger.
I am allergic to penicillin/cortisone. Ich
  bin gegen Penicillin/Kortison allergisch.
My blood group is... positive/
  negative. Ich habe Blutgruppe... positiv/
  negativ.

NUMBER S

0 zero
1 eins
2 zwei
3 drei
4 vier
5 funf

6 sechs
7 sieben
8 acht
9 neun
10 zehn
11 elf
12 zwölf
13 dreizehn
14 vierzehn
15 funfzehn
16 sechszehn
17 seibzehn
18 achtzehn
19 neunzehn
20 zwanzig
21 einundzwanzig
30 dreißig
40 vierzig
50 funfzig
60 sechzig
70 siebzig
80 achtzig
90 neunzig
100 hundert
101 einhundertundeins
200 zweihundert
500 funfhundert
1,000 tausend
10,000 zehntausend
100,000 hunderttausend
1,000,000 million

TIME

What time is it? Wie spät ist es?
It's one/three o'clock. Es ist ein/drei Uhr.
midday Mittag
midnight Midnacht
morning Morgen
afternoon Nachmittag
evening Abend
night Nacht
yesterday Gestern
today Heute
tomorrow Morgen

DAYS AND MONTHS

week Woche
month Monat

Monday Montag
Tuesday Dienstag
Wednesday Mittwoch
Thursday Donnerstag
Friday Freitag
Saturday Samstag
Sunday Sonntag
January Januar
February Februar
March März

April April
May Mai
June Juni
July Juli
August August
September September
October October
November November
December Dezember

RESOURCES
HUNGARIAN PHRASEBOOK

Hungarian Phrasebook

Hungarian is a language that has nothing in common with its Slavic, Germanic, and Latin neighbors around. The good thing is Hungarian is in Latin script, so you should be able to read signs and the basics, but the bad news is apart from borrowed words from English there won't be much you'll understand. Hungarian is quite tricky for English speakers to pronounce, but here are a few basics to help:

s   is pronounced sh
sz is what we think is an s
ny is easiest explained as sounding like the Spanish ñ, but if you don't speak Spanish think of it like the ny in the singer's name Enya.
gy is more like d'ya, the g is very soft
ő   is like a long o and an e put together
ű   resembles a long e and u together
dzs is like our j
j   is like a y
ó   sounds like or, as in Eeyore
é   is a long e
í   is a long i
á   is like a sigh of relief, aah
ú   sounds like oo
ö   is a short and rounded o
ü   is a short and rounded u

ESSENTIAL PHRASES

Hello Szervusz/Szia (informal)
Good morning Jó reggelt
Good afternoon Jó napot
Good evening Jó estét

Good night Jó éjszakát
Good bye Viszontlátásra
Nice to meet you Örvendek
Thank you Köszönöm
You're welcome Szívesen
Please Kérem
Do you speak English? Beszél angolul?
I don't understand. Nem értem.
Yes Igen
No Nem
Where is the restroom? Hol van a WC?

TRANSPORTATION

Where is...? Hol van...?
How far is...? Milyen messze van...?
Is there a bus to...? Van egy busz...?
Does this bus go to...? Ez a busz megy...?
Where do I get off? Hol kell leszállni?
What time does the bus/train leave? Mikor indul a busz/vonat?
Where is the nearest subway station? Hol van a legközelebbi metró?
Where can I buy a ticket? Hol tudok jegyet venni?
A round-trip ticket/single ticket to... Egy menettérti jegyet/jegy...

FOOD

A table for one/two... Egy ember/két ember számára kérek asztalt
Do you have a menu in English? Van angol menü?

What is the dish of the day? Mi a napi
étel?
We're ready to order. Szeretnénk
rendelni.
I'm vegetarian. Vegetáriánus vagyok.
I would like to order a... Szeretnék
rendelni egy...
The check, please. A számlát, kérem.
beer sör
breakfast reggeli
cash készpénz
check számla
coffee kávé
dinner vacsora
glass pohár
hors d'oeuvre előétel
ice jég
ice cream jégkrém
lunch ebéd
restaurant étterem
sandwich szendvics
snack falatozás
waiter pincér
water víz
wine bor

SHOPPING
money pénz
shop bolt/üzlet
What time do the shops close? Mikor
zárnak a boltok?
How much is it? Mennyibe kerül
I'm just looking. Csak nézelődök.
Is there a local specialty? Van egy helyi
specialitás?

HEALTH
drugstore gyógyszertár
pain fájdalom
fever láz
headache fejfájás
stomach ache hasfájás
toothache fogfájás
burn égés
cramp görcs
nausea hányinger
vomiting hányás
medicine gyógyszer

antibiotic antibiotikum
pill/tablet tabletta
aspirin aszpirin
I need a doctor. Szükségem van egy
orvosra.
I need to go to the hospital. Kórházba
kell mennem.
I have a pain here... Fájdalom van itt...
She/he has been stung/
bitten. Elcsípett/megharapott.
I am diabetic/pregnant. Cukorbeteg/
Terhes vagyok
I am allergic to penicillin/
cortisone. Allergiás vagyok a penicillinre
/kortizonra.
My blood group is... positive/
negative. A vércsoportom... pozitív/
negatív.

NUMBERS
0 nulla
1 egy
2 kettő
3 három
4 négy
5 öt
6 hat
7 hét
8 nyolc
9 kilenc
10 tíz
11 tizenegy
12 tizenkettő
13 tizenhárom
14 tizennégy
15 tizenöt
16 tizenhat
17 tizenhét
18 tizennyolc
19 tizenkilenc
20 húsz
21 huszonegy
30 harminc
40 negyven
50 ötven
60 hatvan
70 hetven
80 nyolcvan

90 kilencven
100 száz
101 száz és egy
200 kétszáz
500 ötszáz
1,000 ezer
10,000 tizezer
100,000 százezer
1,000,000 millió

TIME

What time is it? Mennyi az idő?
It's one/three o'clock Egy/Három óra van
midday dél
midnight éjfél
morning reggel
afternoon délután
evening este
night éjszaka
yesterday tegnap
today ma
tomorrow holnap

DAYS AND MONTHS

week hét
month hónap
Monday Hétfő
Tuesday Kedd
Wednesday Szerda
Thursday Csütörtök
Friday Péntek
Saturday Szombat
Sunday Vasárnap
January Január
February Február
March Március
April Április
May Május
June Június
July Július
August Augusztus
September Szeptember
October Oktober
November November
December December

Suggested Reading

PRAGUE
Nonfiction

Prague: A Cultural History. Richard D. Burton. An in-depth, academic look at Czech history, architecture, and culture organized into easy-to-follow sections. The expanded listings on popular monuments and their connections to history add additional context and background for visitors.

The Czechs In a Nutshell. Terje B. Englund. This tongue-in-cheek description of Czech culture by a Norwegian man is a sarcastic encyclopedia-style overview on subjects like beer, beauty pageants, and the Battle of White Mountain. A few observations (from 2004) have changed over time, but the light-hearted tone is a good primer on Czech history, quirks, and cultural differences.

Believe in People: The Essential Karel Čapek. Czech novelist Karel Čapek is best known for inventing the word "robot" in his 1920 sci-fi play *RUR.* This collection of his translated journalistic works and letters to his wife, Olga, paints a picture of early 21st-century Czech life through the interesting observations of a local literary legend.

Prague Winter. Madeline Albright. The former US Secretary of State offers a touching story of discovering her Czech roots later in life. Personal memories from a uniquely political perspective inform her observations of WWII, the rise of Communism, and the Cold War.

Fiction

The Good Soldier Švejk. Jaroslav Hašek. Czech literature is full of anti-heroes and ironic humor and "Svejk" is their most famous archetype. Follow the smartest man in the room (or the luckiest bumbling idiot, depending on your interpretation) as he navigates the Austro-Hungarian army and bureaucracy in general during WWI.

I Served the King of England. Bohumil Hrabal. Another great example of Czech satire, this historical novel is set during WWII and the subsequent Communist occupation. A man named Dítě (meaning "child" in Czech) narrates his life, dreams, and aspirations in the hospitality industry.

HHhH. Laurent Binet & Sam Taylor. Those four Hs stand for Nazi leader Heinrich Himmler and his "brain" ("hirn" in German) Reinhard Heydrich, AKA the "butcher of Prague". A historical tale based on true events, this novel follows Heydrich through his time in the Third Reich to his eventual execution by a young team of Czechs. This story is also available in film form in the movie *Anthropoid* (see below) and provides context for the real-life memorial to the Czech soldiers located in New Town.

The Book of Laughter and Forgetting. Milan Kundera. Kundera's first major international success weaves together politics, philosophy, surrealism, and banality through rumination on the challenges of life in communist Czechoslovakia. In seven different narratives, Kundera explores the theme of forgetting and what that means for relationships both between people and between a government and its subjects.

Me, Myself, & Prague. Rachael Weiss. A single, 40-year-old Australian woman decides to move to Prague, write a novel, and discover her Czech roots. Obviously things don't go as smoothly as planned. Weiss' self-deprecating, semi-biographical recounting offers a relatable read through the eyes of an outsider discovering the Czech capital.

Czech Fairytales. Božena Němcová & Karel Jaromír Erben. Kings, queens, witches, and magic are essential elements of Czech children's literature and ingrained in much of the culture. Want proof? Fairy tales are shown non-stop on television from morning to night on December 24th as part of the Christmas festivities. This collection makes for great bedtime reading in the weeks leading up to your trip.

VIENNA
Nonfiction

Vienna: A Cultural and Literary History. Nicholas T. Parsons. A comprehensive introduction to Vienna's history from prehistory through to the modern day. Great to orientate yourself in the city's history and people and get some background understanding into the city.

Fin de Siècle Vienna. Carl Emil Schorske. The Fin de Siècle marked Vienna in many ways, and this collection of essays offers a comprehensive analysis of the city's politics, art, architecture, and the birth of psychoanalysis.

The World of Yesterday. Stefan Zweig. This beautiful, biographical book chronicles the history of the early 20th century Europe from through the decline of the Habsburg Empire and the World Wars. The evocative prose by Zweig inspired Wes Anderson's *Grand Budapest Hotel.*

Wittgenstein's Vienna. Alan Janik. Follow in the steps of the philosopher Ludwig Wittgenstein across Vienna in a unique portrait of the pre-war city, covering his influences and how this unique city helped formulate his thought.

Only in Vienna. Duncan J.D. Smith. Go off the beaten track in Vienna with this alternative guide to all the quirky and unique places you can only find in the Austrian capital.

The Habsburgs: The History of a Dynasty. Benjamin Curtis. Get some background on the Habsburg family with this in-depth account of Central Europe's most important family.

Hitler's Vienna: A Dictator's Apprenticeship. Brigitte Hamann. Hitler spent his formative years in Vienna, and this book paints a portrait of the terrible dictator who would tear Europe apart.

The Spell of the Vienna Woods: Inspiration and Influence from Beethoven to Kafka. Paul Hofmann. Discover why the Vienna Woods are so iconic for the Viennese with stories and anecdotes about the artists, musicians, and royalty who found inspiration, and sometimes tragedy, in the woods.

Fiction

The Radetzky March. Joseph Roth. This epic tale chronicles four generations of an aristocratic family who lived during the decline and fall of the Habsburg Empire.

The Man Without Qualities. Robert Musil. A modernist door-stopper, this book tells the tale of the morally ambiguous Ulrich, a man with a complicated history as an ex-soldier, mathematician, and seducer. The novel charts the twilight days of the Habsburg Empire at the beginning of World War I.

Dream Story. Arthur Schnitzler. If you've seen Stanley Kubrick's *Eyes Wide Shut*, the plot of this pocket-sized book will seem familiar (it was the original source material). Arthur Schnitzler's novelette is a throwback to a decadent Vienna, wrapped inside a masked psycho-sexual drama that is very Viennese.

The Piano Teacher. Elfriede Jelinek. A high-octane drama set in 1960s Vienna that's not for everyone. Intense, highly sexual, and violent, the story traces the neurotic fantasies of Erika Kohut as she tries to escape her controlling mother's clutches by descending into the dark world of voyeurism, self-harm, and sadomasochism.

BUDAPEST
Nonfiction

Budapest 1900. John Lukacs. This fascinating historical account about Budapest's golden age around the turn of the 20th-century is a fun read that gives you context about the history of the city.

Budapest: A Critical Guide. András Török. Although it's a guidebook with walking tours, Török's voice and anecdotes take you deeper into the city's history and culture, offering excellent local insight into the city.

Hungarian Wine: A Tasting Trip to the New Old World. Robert Smyth. Get acquainted with Hungarian wine, its varieties, and vineyards if you're interested in knowing what to taste on your trip.

Enemies of the People. Kati Marton. If you're curious about life behind the Iron Curtain, this book exposing life under Communism told from the author's point of view, and the story of her family offers insight into life under Soviet eyes.

Journey to a Revolution: A Personal Memoir and History of the Hungarian Revolution of 1956. Michael Korda. Korda's book blends memoir with the history of the 1956 revolution as he returns to his father's homeland.

A Guest in My Own Country: A Hungarian Life. George Konrád. Konrád takes readers back through his life and the turbulent history of mid-20th century Budapest's. After narrowly escaping the Jewish deportations in his hometown in the countryside, Konrád survives the Siege of Budapest and the revolution of 1956; this memoir offers a personal take of the city's history.

Jewish Budapest: Monuments, Rites, History. Kinga Frojimovics, Geza Komoroczy, Viktoria Pusztai, Andrea Strbik. A comprehensive guide to Budapest's Jewish history from the city's grand monuments to the daily life of the city's Jewish community.

Fiction

Fatelessness. Imre Kertész. This semi-autobiographical novel by Nobel Prize-winning author Imre Kertész tells the story of a 14-year-old Hungarian-Jewish boy who is sent to Auschwitz.

Prague. Arthur Phillips. Don't let the title fool you, this is a novel about expat life in postcommunist Budapest, where the whining residents feel they don't have it as good as their fellow Americans in Prague.

The Paul Street Boys. Ferenc Molnár. Despite being a book for young adults, the Paul Street Boys is an exciting piece of classic Hungarian literature capturing the spirit of Budapest's VIII District in the early 20th century.

The Door. Magda Szabó. Visceral, moving, and beautiful, this character-based novel based in Budapest tells the story of a writer and her mysterious cleaning lady.

The Baron's Sons. Mór Jókai. If you want something set during the Hungarian Revolution of 1848 and the War of Independence that followed, this family saga surrounding the Baradlay family and the Hungarian revolution.

Suggested Films and Television

PRAGUE

Anthropoid. This painstakingly researched film tells the story of a small, brave team of Czech soldiers and citizens who pulled off an assassination of a top Nazi general during WWII. It's great for adding context before visiting the New Town memorial to their lives.

Palach. Czech student Jan Palach stood at the top of Wenceslas Square in 1969 and set himself on fire to protest the Russian occupation of Prague. This biography examines the last six months of his life.

Masaryk. Not all of Czech history follows its greatest heroes. *Masaryk* takes a complicated look at Jan Masaryk, the son of the first Czechoslovak president, Tomáš Garrigue Masaryk, and his political role in the events of the mid-20th century.

Carnival Row. The city of Prague with a steampunk makeover is renamed "The Burgue" in this fantasy-thriller series about humans, fairies, centaurs, and other fairy tale creatures.

VIENNA

The Third Man. This iconic film noir starring Orson Welles was filmed on location in 1940s post-war Vienna. If there is one movie you watch before going to Vienna, make it this one - then you can follow in its footsteps.

Before Sunrise. A romantic classic from the 1990s starring Julie Delpy and Ethan Hawke, this delightful movie takes you on a journey through Vienna from the Prater to the Cemetery of the Nameless.

Sissi. This Austrian classic, starring Romy Schneider, is about the life of Empress

Elizabeth and her marriage to Emperor Franz Joseph I.

Amadeus. Although filmed in Prague, *Amadeus* is a delightful romp through Mozart's life and his alleged rivalry against Salieri.

Museum Hours. Get in the mood for a visit to the Kunsthistorisches Museum with this tale of a Canadian tourist and museum steward bonding over the work of art in the museum.

A Dangerous Method. Delve into the friendship and the rift between Sigmund Freud and Carl Jung in this film starring Viggo Mortensen and Michael Fassbender.

BUDAPEST

Kontroll. Filmed entirely on the Budapest subway system, this Hungarian surreal dark comedy about ticket inspectors and a mysteriously hooded murderer makes curious watching.

Son of Saul. This Holocaust drama set in Auschwitz put Hungarian cinema on the map when it won an Oscar in 2015.

The Witness. This 1960s black comedy was banned under the communist regime and went on to become a cult classic. It tells the tale of Pelikán, a simple man who mysteriously moves up the ranks with the communist big guys as they try to bribe him to become a false witness.

Sunshine. Starring Ralph Fiennes, *Sunshine* tells the story of an aristocratic Jewish family in Budapest from the turn of the 20th century through to the Holocaust and under Communism.

White God. *White God* takes place in a world when mixed breeds of dogs are outlawed, and tells the story of 13-year-old Lily and her dog, Hagen. Once Lily is separated from her dog, chaos ensues when 250 dogs follow Hagen on a rampage through the city.

Internet and Digital Resources

PRAGUE
General Information
www.prague.eu/en
Prague City Tourism's website offers tons of basic info and object histories of the most popular tourist sights.

www.czechtourism.com/home
Turn to the country's official website to discover a "Land of Stories" with photos and basic info about both Prague and destinations across the country.

www.youtube.com/c/honestguide
Straightforward, funny advice for tourists on how to avoid scams and tourist traps from a pair of young Czech guys turned YouTube sensations.

www.socialismrealised.eu
An accessible, English-friendly look as the Communist era through a catalog of artifacts, videos, and texts with educational support.

www.expats.cz
Pop culture news, events, and commentary on life as a foreigner in the Czech Republic.

www.tasteofprague.com
Gorgeous food photography and the latest in Prague's gastronomy scene from two passionate Czech foodies.

www.duolingo.com
An easy language-learning app to pick up

some useful Czech vocabulary through five-minute lessons before your visit

Transport
www.dpp.cz/en
The official website for Prague's transport authority offers updated info on construction plus ticket info and maps.

www.cd.cz/en/default.htm
Check train schedules and purchase tickets through the official state-run railway website.

www.regiojet.com
This local coach and train company offers comfortable, affordable service, plus tickets that you can modify or cancel up to 15 or 30 minutes before your departure (check booking details for confirmation) either online or through their smartphone app.

www.liftago.com
Local rideshare app with great customer service and an English interface.

VIENNA
General Information
www.wien.info
This comprehensive website from Vienna's Tourism Board has all the basic information you need.

www.viennawurstelstand.com
An English-language magazine about Viennese life and what's going on about the town.

www.austria.info
Similar to wien.info, but good if you're planning a day trip or anything further afield.

www.wien.gv.at
The city of Vienna's government site.

Transport
www.wienerlinien.at
Vienna's official public transport website

Wiener Linien
Another app from Wiener Linien, where you can buy and download transport tickets onto your smartphone. You can also get public transport information in real time.

www.oebb.at
Purchase tickets and checks the train times for national and international departures.

National Parks
www.donauauen.at
Find all the information you need for the Donau-Auen National Park including the Lobau.

www.bpww.at
Discover all the information about the Vienna Woods Biosphere Reserve surrounding the city.

BUDAPEST
General Information
https://hellohungary.com
The website of the official Hungarian Tourism Agency, with information on Budapest and beyond.

www.welovebudapest.com
Find out all the latest places that have opened, news about events and general information.

https://funzine.hu/en
Keep up to date with all the most recent developments and news in the city with this online English-language magazine.

www.spasbudapest.com
Everything you need to know about Budapest's thermal baths.

Transport
https://bkk.hu

Find out everything you need to know about Budapest's public transport on the official website for the BKK.

BKK App
Download the app to know when the next tram or metro is due in real time.

www.mavcsoport.hu

Buy tickets and check the timetables for national and international trains.

Index

List of Maps

Photo Credits

Trips to Remember

CHILE
with Easter Island
STEPH DYSON

ECUADOR
& THE GALÁPAGOS ISLANDS
BETHANY PITTS

EGYPT
SARAH SMIERCIAK

GREEK ISLANDS & ATHENS
SARAH SOULI

ISLAND ESCAPES WITH TIMELESS VILLAGES,
SCENIC HIKES, AND LOCAL FLAVORS

ICELAND
JENNA GOTTLIEB

WITH A ROAD TRIP ON THE RING ROAD

JAPAN
JONATHAN DEHART

PLAN YOUR TRIP, AVOID THE CROWDS,
AND EXPERIENCE THE REAL JAPAN

TRIP OF A LIFETIME
MACHU PICCHU
with Cusco, Lima & the Inca Trail
RYAN DUBÉ

MOROCCO

PORTUGAL

PRAGUE, VIENNA & BUDAPEST
JENNIFER D. WALKER
& AUBURN SCALLON

ROME, FLORENCE & VENICE

Epic Treks

CAMINO DE SANTIAGO

SACRED SITES,
HISTORIC VILLAGES,
LOCAL FOOD & WINE

BEEBE BAHRAMI

Drive & Hike
APPALACHIAN TRAIL

THE BEST TRAIL TOWNS, DAY HIKES,
AND ROAD TRIPS IN BETWEEN

TIMOTHY MALCOLM

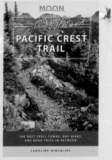

Drive & Hike
PACIFIC CREST TRAIL

THE BEST TRAIL TOWNS, DAY HIKES,
AND ROAD TRIPS IN BETWEEN

CAROLINE HINCHLIFF

Beachy
Getaways

MOON

AMALFI
COAST

ARUBA

BAHAMAS

BAJA

BALI &
LOMBOK

BELIZE

BERMUDA

CARTAGENA
& COLOMBIA'S
CARIBBEAN COAST

COSTA
RICA

DOMINICAN
REPUBLIC

FIJI

FLORIDA
KEYS

JAMAICA

MAUI

PUERTO RICO

Get inspired for your next adventure

Follow @**moonguides** on Instagram or subscribe to our newsletter at **moon.com**

#TravelWithMoon